# Advance praise for *Timely Cash*

"This detailed and engaging account of cash transfer programs over time and space invites the reader to reflect on timeless questions about poverty and whether its causes and solutions lie with individuals or society."

**Oriana Bandiera, Professor of Economics, London School of Economics**

"This global history of cash transfers is a *tour de force*; a brilliant, carefully researched, and well-written must-read for anyone advocating or questioning cash transfers across the globe. It shows how cash transfers are more than money: they reflect the debates, struggles, and challenges across politics and societies throughout history, and as they are mirrored today. This book is more than about cash transfers: it is also a book about insights and worldviews about poverty and the human condition, in the past and today."

**Stefan Dercon, Professor of Economic Policy, University of Oxford**

"This inspiring book is an essential reference to policymakers, professionals, and academia. It is an intellectual piece that transcends history and reflects on the ancient and contemporary social protection from an interdisciplinary perspective. It also challenges the concept of rights and duties between the citizen and the government from a humanitarian, though rational and socio-economic approach to provision of social welfare. This piece of art would not come except from a dedicated human, scholar, and professional person like Ugo Gentilini."

**Nivine El-Kabbag, Former Minister of Social Solidarity, Egypt**

"A fascinating read that traces cash transfers throughout histories, ancient empires, modern nation-building, economic transformations, and the COVID-19 global pandemic . . . As Ugo Gentilini has meticulously researched and convincingly argued, the history of the cash transfer is the history of human progress, and the sacrifice and societal turbulence it entailed. Buried in this history is a road map to address not all, but some, of the poverty generators found in market-oriented systems."

**Ibrahim Elbadawi, Managing Director, Economic Research Forum and former Minister of Finance, Sudan**

"This book is truly a *tour de force*, taking us on a journey across *many* countries and *way* back in time to understand the foundations of transfer programs today. It offers real insights into our current policy debates—it is genuinely a must-read for anyone interested in how to alleviate poverty and improve social protection for all."

**Rema Hanna, Professor of South-East Asia Studies, Harvard University**

"This extraordinary book's long run, historical perspective provides a rich vein of insights, deftly integrated by the author into the results of detailed modern quantitative research on the last half century of cash transfer programs. What we get is a masterful account of the origins and evolution of cash transfers, and the identification of core factors which have been constant despite the variations of time and place. Through it all, the author explodes and exposes myths, and draws lessons which will be helpful to policy analysts and policy makers everywhere."

**Ravi Kanbur, Professor of Economics, Cornell University**

"A masterful exploration ... Gentilini's work stands out for its depth and breadth. *Timely Cash* is an essential read, a crucial resource for understanding the past, present, and future of cash transfers as a cornerstone of social protection and economic policy."

**Cina Lawson, Minister of Digital Economy and Transformation, Togo**

"The Bible tells us that there is nothing new under the sun and, in this book, Gentilini tells us that the same is true about cash transfers. Read it, and you will find out that many of our current debates are not current at all, and you will learn a lot of useful facts and discussions from this 2,500-year history. A wonderful book that will widen your horizons."

**Santiago Levy, Senior Fellow at Brookings and former Deputy Minister of Finance, Mexico**

"This book is among the most awe-inspiring and well-researched pieces of scholarship that I've read in years. It opened my eyes to how sophisticated government social programs have been over many centuries and world regions—from ancient Rome and China to early modern Spain—and how much we can learn from looking back into the past to design effective public programs today."

**Edward Miguel, Professor of Economics, University of California, Berkeley**

"This book is a fascinating account of the history of cash transfers for the poor. We tend to think of cash transfers as a recent invention, but Ugo Gentilini shows us that this kind of social assistance has roots that go back centuries, even as far as classical Athens! The book takes us on a tour of the history of these programs around the world, and shows that many challenges governments confront today have been confronted time and again throughout the history of human civilization."

**Benjamin Olken, Professor of Microeconomics, Massachusetts Institute of Technology**

"*Timely Cash* offers an insightful journey through the history of cash transfers. The book highlights the evolution of social policies and welfare systems over time and reveals that the arguments used in debating the usefulness of cash transfers often are not new. Ugo Gentilini's work allows scholars and policymakers to evaluate the long-term effects of these interventions, and to derive valuable lessons for the development of contemporary social protection programs that are responsive to current societal needs."

**Patrizio Pagano, Head of Secretariat to the Governing Board of the Bank of Italy**

"This fascinating book contains a lot of new and exciting material on the comparative history of cash transfers. Redistribution has a long history, and there's much to learn from it regarding the strength and weaknesses of cash transfers and the need for in-kind transfers and public goods. A must-read!"

**Thomas Piketty, Professor of Economics and Economic History, Paris School of Economics**

"A fascinating breath of fresh air on thinking around social protection that effortlessly crosses boundaries and connects framing, contexts, motivations, and actions. Ugo Gentilini's masterly exploration of a subject bearing relevance to past, present, and future alike will be a treat whether the reader is an expert, a layman, a policymaker, or a political actor. *Timely Cash* avoids the well-known pitfalls of being narrowly prescriptive on a policy choice engaging mind in both the global south and the global north."

**Hossain Zillur Rahman, Executive Chairman, Power and Participation Research Centre, Bangladesh**

"Ugo Gentilini provides a magisterial account of debates over social protection, demonstrating emphatically that contemporary debates have histories dating back not just decades or centuries but even millennia, not just in North-West Europe but globally. This book will change the way we think about social protection."

**Jeremy Seekings, Professor of Political Studies and Sociology, University of Cape Town**

"A fascinating tour of the history of the use of cash transfers across the centuries—providing rich lessons which are highly relevant to this day. Recommended reading for everyone interested in the social, political, and economic impacts of cash transfers—and their transformative potential in addressing poverty and exclusion."

**Rory Stewart, Host of *The Rest Is Politics* podcast and former UK Secretary of State for International Development**

"Ugo Gentilini's book is a demonstration model of the enormous value for public policy practitioners of a thorough understanding of relevant research by historians. This clearly written book is a must-read for policy professionals, and also for historians to inspire them to communicate their important work more widely."

**Simon Szreter, Professor of History and Public Policy, University of Cambridge**

"Cash transfers have existed for 2,500 years and are now present all over the world. No book has ever provided such a comprehensive overview of past and present cash transfer schemes, nor so many insights into the economic, ideological, and political causes of their rise, demise, and stunning variety."

**Philippe Van Parijs, Professor of Economic, Social and Political Sciences, University of Louvain**

"Money matters to those who have it but more to those who don't. Ugo Gentilini's mind-changing book demonstrates that societies across the world have been grappling with the human and policy implications of this truism for millennia. Progress has proved to be neither inevitable nor uniform such that insights from the distant past can have relevance today. One such insight is that society benefits from us sharing our money with those that have less."

**Robert Walker, Professor of Social Policy and Development, Beijing Normal University and University of Oxford**

# Timely Cash

# Timely Cash

## Lessons From 2,500 Years of Giving People Money

Ugo Gentilini

OXFORD
UNIVERSITY PRESS

OXFORD
UNIVERSITY PRESS

Great Clarendon Street, Oxford, OX2 6DP,
United Kingdom

Oxford University Press is a department of the University of Oxford.
It furthers the University's objective of excellence in research, scholarship,
and education by publishing worldwide. Oxford is a registered trade mark of
Oxford University Press in the UK and in certain other countries



Published in the United States of America by Oxford University Press
198 Madison Avenue, New York, NY 10016, United States of America

British Library Cataloguing in Publication Data
Data available

Library of Congress Control Number: 2024940670

ISBN 9780198888116

DOI: 10.1093/9780191994982.001.0001

Printed and bound in the UK by
Clays Ltd, Elcograf S.p.A.

Cover image: painting by Franciszek Smuglewicz, Ostracism over Aristides (around year
1788), oil technique, 155 x 124 cm, inventory no. MNK II-a-1035. Laboratory Stock National
Museum in Krakow.

*To Federica, Margherita, and Giovanni,*

*the three shining stars of my firmament.*

One goal of studying the past is not to be trapped by history but to transcend it.

**Michael Katz (1995, p.8)**[1]

[1] Used with permission of Princeton University Press, from *Improving Poor People: The Welfare State, the "Underclass," and Urban Schools as History*, Michael Katz, 3. print., 1. paperback print, 1995; permission conveyed through Copyright Clearance Center, Inc.

# Contents

# List of Figures

# List of Tables

# List of Boxes

# Preface

The month of September is payday for Alaskans. Since 1982, every resident of Alaska, United States, has been receiving an annual cash transfer from the state government: known as Permanent Fund Dividend, the program redistributes revenues from oil which, alongside other local natural resources, is considered a source of wealth pertaining to the whole population.[1]

The Dividend has elicited extensive debates among Alaskans—is it better to give people money or finance public services instead? As put by an article in the *Juneau Empire*, "[w]e have never resolved just what the Permanent Fund is: an entitlement representing each resident's fair share of the owner-state oil wealth, or a rainy-day savings account to pay for government when it's prudent." To settle the question, the piece called for a vote: " . . . today the political environment is ripe for a public referendum to explicitly express the will of the people."[2]

That's exactly what happened in Athens 2,502 years before the article's publication. Like in Alaska, Athenians received a cash transfer financed by revenues from a natural resource, in their case silver. The Athenian cash transfer program appears to have run regularly—"a passive if not automatic event"[3] —until a major discovery occurred in 483 BC: the mines of Laurium, a nearby coastal town, suddenly yielded a "fountain of silver, a storehouse of treasure buried within the earth."[4]

The newfound riches sparked immediate debate over their use. Two camps emerged: on one side, the statesman Aristides "the Just" championed the continuation of universal cash transfers. He rested his case on tradition and emphasized the notion that bonanzas belonged to people. On the other side, the general Themistocles dared, as chronicled by Plutarch, "to come before the people with a motion that [cash payments] be given up":[5] motivated by the growing military threat posed by Aegina maritime power, his proposal was to shift funds away from cash payments and favor the production of 200 trireme ships for the navy.[6] After much negotiation that ran into the winter of 483 BC, the issue could not be settled in the Assembly and a popular vote was called for the following year.

The referendum took the form of an ostracism. This involved people deciding who to expel or ostracize from the city: all that was needed was to indicate the person's name on a pottery shard, cast the ballot, and count the votes. The choice was clear: by writing down the name of the pro-cash Aristides, Athenians would send him on

[1] The size of the payment is variable, generally ranging between $1,000–$2,000 per capita (in 2023, the amount was $1,312).
[2] Mehrkens (2019).
[3] Samons (2000, p. 62).
[4] Holland 2005 (p. 220).
[5] Seltman (1924, p. 106).
[6] Samons (2000, p. 60), Figueira (1993, p. 406).

(a)

(b)

**Figure P.1** Pottery shards used to vote (a) in favor of cash transfers and (b) against them, 482 BC.

Themistocles's ostracon, image (a) in figure P.1, is a rim of semi-glazed krater and has a diameter of 10 cm (see also Lang (1990, p. 124), where it is catalogued as Plate 3, P 9950, figure 946). Image (b) of figure P.1 shows Aristides's ostracon, in this case a rim of amphora with a diameter of 12.5 cm (see ibid, p. 34, recorded as Plate 1, P 9973, figure 55).
*Source*: Ephorate of Antiquities of Athens–Ancient Agora Excavations/American School of Classical Studies. ©Hellenic Ministry of Culture/Organization of Cultural Resources Development (H.O.C.RE.D.).

exile and boost their naval capabilities instead; by carving out the name of the anti-cash advocate Themistocles, Athens would have continued its cash transfers. In the Spring of 482 BC, votes were cast (Figure P.1). Eventually, Aristides was defeated—a poignant moment captured by Franciszek Smuglewicz's painting reproduced in this book's cover—and the cash dividend was phased out. That one of the first referendums in history was to decide about maintaining cash transfers tells how salient those programs are in our societies.

In prefacing his historical review of unemployment, John Garraty wrote:

> I have called this book *Unemployment in History* instead of *History of Unemployment* because it does not attempt to describe [. . .] why there was unemployment at various times [. . .]. Rather it is a study of how the condition of being without work has been perceived and dealt with in different societies from the beginning of recorded history.[7]

[7] Garraty (1978, p. xi).

In a similar vein, *Timely Cash* discusses cash transfers in history. As such, it does not offer a linear chronology of cash transfers over time; instead, it presents a framework to elucidate varieties and regularities as supported by experiences emerging at different points in time and space. Hopefully, it will help lay the foundations for a renewed conversation on social protection globally, that is, to not only focus on (vitally important) present-day performance, but to also account for the underlying forces that shape longer-term trajectories.

The book builds on my professional experience in researching and implementing cash transfers globally. An initial period of my career involved working in some extreme contexts—from responding to food crises in low-income countries to establishing basic social protection systems in fragile states. This was the time when, in the late 1990s and early 2000s, humanitarian and development organizations started to embrace cash transfer programs more fully. Over those formative years, I witnessed first-hand how mindsets can change, and institutions can evolve. I also started to detect the outsize expectations bestowed on those programs, possibly exposing them to some disillusionment—a theme that recurs in this book. Eventually, my interest in cash transfers, and in social protection more widely, led me to work in an ample range of situations. I learned about the spectacular progress and daunting challenges with social protection in middle-income countries, the sweeping innovations by reform-oriented trailblazers, and the mind-boggling capabilities and whopping blind spots of advanced economies.

While I cherished such overall diversity in contexts, I soon noticed striking similarities between radically different environments. At some fundamental level, ongoing debates across countries may present a degree of uniformity—around why cash transfers should be used, who they should reach, what design features should accompany them, and what alternatives should be considered instead. In fact, concerns about "creating dependency" or "making people lazy" can be widespread. Such reservations are met with a good deal of eye-rolling by social protection practitioners. This is understandable. But instead of frustration, I approach possible concerns with curiosity. This book is animated by a desire to understand rather than judge: to comprehend when reservations emerged, how they spread, and how they influenced approaches in different contexts.

Some dilemmas on cash transfers unfolding centuries ago seem to mirror contemporary quandaries almost verbatim. Why do we keep debating the same issues? Cash transfers stir emotions because they entangle practical and ethical considerations. They are enmeshed in worldviews. As such, they can be perceived by some as "money down the drain", buttressed by reminders that "we need jobs, not welfare." While these concerns are legitimate, evidence has largely disproved them as overstated or misguided. Yet statistics aren't enough: to foster a more constructive dialogue, there is a need to fully comprehend the nature of reservations, trace their origins, and identify their mechanisms of diffusion. Historical perspectives can help illuminating those issues.

History is a refreshing source of practical lessons: " . . . it's important to turn to the past [. . .] to liberate us from preconceptions, and set us on the road to truly new ideas", mused anthropologist David Graeber.[8] Today's core debates do not unfold in isolation, but occur against a backdrop of institutional systems and societal culture which themselves are the cumulative result of narratives, experiences, and practices accumulated over time. It may not be apparent at first, but the type of choices made presently—the strategic directions they lead to, the kind of policy debates they spur, the sort of participation they elicit, and the overall tone of dialogue—ultimately contribute to the stock of institutional legacy that would influence future choices. Current social protection practices are at the same time the tail-end of an interconnected thread, as well as the critical juncture for the thread to come.

There is a wide literature on why we seem not to learn from history.[9] The question appears particularly salient for cash transfers, a field of public policy relying heavily on technocratic framing. Explaining the disconnect between cash transfers and their history is difficult, but I hazard a few hypotheses: for instance, cash transfers are often considered too recent for requiring extensive historical reflection. This is a myth to dispel. By reconstructing the deep, historical roots of cash transfers throughout contexts and over millennia, I hope this book will help reconsider these priors.

Another factor may be that history has no perceived relevance for contemporary practices. Some of my colleagues may be wondering why I pursued this book. What's in it for practitioners? What would some dusty volumes tell us about dealing with urgent, present-day priorities? History can be intellectually entertaining, but what concrete insights does it offer? Many have outlined "why history matters."[10] Nathan Nunn noted that " . . . the economic literature is increasingly coming to understand that where we are (and therefore how we best move forward) has a lot to do with how we got here."[11] I have come to understand history as awakening and thought-provoking: it impels us to ask the big, fundamental questions that lurk in the background of our day-to-day practices. By interrogating the origins and generation of poverty and inequities, and examining how cash transfers were tapped to address them, history doesn't just explain the present—it also *questions* it. And for sure, history makes us humbler in using terms like "for the first time" and "innovations"!

A further reason for the limited uptake of history could be that cash transfers are the product of their time. It might be plausible that little could be learned from radically different societies. This is a serious point. Extrapolations from one context to another are an ever-present risk. The fascinating work of scholars like Peter Turchin, however, has challenged the notion that contexts are too diverse and disconnected to produce common lessons: his "cliodynamics" science, which applies Big Data

[8] Graeber (2017a, p. xviii).
[9] See, for example, Liddell Hart (2012).
[10] Pierson (2004, p. 5). See also Woolcock et al. (2012) and Kanbur (2015, 2020) for brilliant expositions on the theme.
[11] Nunn (2014, p. 395). The point is also elaborated in Nunn (2009, 2020a, 2020b).

techniques to historical records, has shed light on factors that determine recurrent patterns of crises across societies and over time.[12]

A historical perspective reveals that views on cash transfers are ultimately tied to our understanding of human nature. For instance, how to support working age populations in distress? On one hand, it was contended that fear of scarcity and economic insecurity are potent work motivators. Hence, it was in people's best interest that they should receive bare or modest cash assistance, if any.[13] On the other hand, it was posited that basic stability and better living conditions—including as enhanced by cash transfers—were enablers of, and not an impediments to, aspirations and upward mobility.[14] The history of cash transfers is one where the balance between stick (fear and insecurity) and carrot (trust and security) was likely tilted toward the former. Today, such balance is contested.[15]

History makes us recognize the fuller set of causes of the broadly defined "poverty problem." Over time, standard design and recurrent tightening of cash transfer provisions largely conformed to symptomatic and "individualistic" poverty framings. Arguably, people's supposed deficiencies and visible manifestation of poverty (e.g., sporadic income, little savings, limited skills, etc.) received relatively ample attention compared to the underlying forces that embroil and keep people into conditions of perpetual disadvantage (e.g., power imbalances in labor markets, uneven voice and political influence, regressive tax regimes, etc.). History reminds us of the political, economic, and societal responsibilities stemming from a more complete recognition of structural poverty drivers.

History also underscores the value and limits of scientific evidence. Effective storytelling, selective use of data and cogent illustrations can fuse into powerful narratives that "stick." Strategic institutional and communication efforts can convey potent ideological talking points, for example, by projecting cash recipients as preferring leisure over work, being morally reprehensible, and freeriding on efforts by the rest of society. Narratives evoking those images were skillfully articulated centuries ago and their message still reverberates in modern debates. That rhetoric against cash transfers was seldom based on credible and systematic evidence misses the point. Generating high-quality evidence is key, but building a compelling public narrative may matter just as much.

Attempting to trace a global historical lineage of cash transfers is an ambitious, humbling, and inherently imperfect task. As a minimum, it's a lifetime project. Yet it is an exploration worth beginning and the analysis laid out in this volume may

[12] According to Turchin's analysis, societies tend to produce cycles of "elite overproduction" and "population immiseration": these ingredients have invariably coalesced over history, creating explosive consequences that "gradually undermined our civic cohesiveness, the sense of national cooperation without which states quickly rot from within" (Turchin 2023, p. xiv).

[13] As we shall see in Chapter 2, prominent thinkers like Jeremy Bentham, Thomas Malthus and Herbert Spencer, broadly adhered to such school of thought.

[14] Discussed in Chapter 3, this approach was espoused by intellectuals like John Barton, Count Rumford, and Charles Leclerc de Montlinot.

[15] Proponents of basic income, for example, place economic security and stability centerstage (Gentilini et al. 2020).

represent a small step in that direction. Because the book heavily researched a subject that touches many lives directly—about 1.4 billion people received cash transfers worldwide in recent years—writing it was no easy task. I strived to make it accessible enough to the public and sufficiently deep for specialists. If anything, I hope the discussion may spark curiosity on connecting past and present, and the book's relatively extensive bibliography may represent a basecamp for the next climbing phase of research. Reimagining the future starts with questioning the present. And understanding the present begins with history.

# Acknowledgements

Producing a book is an exhilarating, unpredictable, all-absorbing experience. Above all, it is a family stress-test. Put that on top of a demanding daily job and you get a sense of what my wife Federica and children Margherita and Giovanni endured for over five years. Their patience and humor—dinner-table imitations of me staring blankly into space became a family classic—carried me throughout the project's rollercoaster. For several summers, my supportive in-laws, Luisa and Roberto, made their home a perfect writer's cabin. And to Barbro and Cesare, my wonderful parents, I owe, well, everything.

The book benefited from the wisdom, advice, or simply the listening ear of inspiring professionals. Among them, I am particularly indebted to Michal Rutkowski for his unyielding support to pursue this unlikely journey. I am beyond grateful to Harold Alderman, Nicholas Barr, Francesca Bastagli, Paolo Belli, Anush Bezhanyan, Shantayanan Devarajan, Jean Dreze, Marek Gora, Margaret Grosh, Joanna Innes, Peter Lindert, Thomas Piketty, Stephen Pimpare, Jeremy Seekings, Richard Smith, Philippe van Parijs, and Robert Walker for having been so generous with their time, reviews, and encouragement at different stages of the book's production. The late Martin Ravallion was a guiding light in developing the book from an initial seven-page note.

I was lucky to have invaluable, inspiring conversations about the book with Junaid Ahmad, Abhijit Banerjee, Mary Brazelton, Stephen Broadberry, Stefan Dercon, Dawn Greeley, Margaret Somers, Brian Steensland, Simon Szreter, Marco van Leeuwen, and Viviana Zelizer. The information and clarifications provided by Manu V. Devadevan, James Ferguson, Nikolaos Giannakopoulos, William Guanglin Liu, Richard von Glahn, and Dewen Wang helped enormously. And my sincere appreciation goes to Mohamed Almenfi, Sheraz Aziz, Irina Dvorak, Kaleb Froehlich, Tina George, Hrishikesh TMM Iyengar, Josefina Posadas, Tiago Silva Falcao, William Wiseman, Ramy Zeid, and Nahla Zeitoun for their brilliant suggestions and precious help.

The volume benefitted from feedback and comments by seminar participants at the World Bank in Washington, DC, the Cairo's Institute of National Planning (graciously organized by Sherine Al-Shawarby and Hala Abou-Ali), the United Nations World Food Programme (with special thanks to Cheryl Harrison and Arif Husain), Georgetown University (as kindly hosted by Ekin Birol and Shanta Devarajan), and the Massachusetts Institute of Technology. In the latter case, I am particularly grateful to Edward Miguel for his review of a paper drawing from the book, and to Rema Hanna and Benjamin Olken for commissioning it.

I am indebted to the editorial team at Oxford University Press, including Adam Swallow, Kayley Gilbert, Jade Dixon, Abishayareddy Vijaybabu, and Dana Bliss for the care, patience, and thoroughness displayed over the book production process. I am also really thankful to the three anonymous referees that reviewed the initial book proposal.

The book involved locating, and often digitizing, a range of rare historical materials: this wouldn't have been possible without the generous support of Beatrice Tolidjian and Erica Saito at the World Bank, Paul Horsler at the London School of Economics, Linnea Anderson at the Social Welfare History Archives of the University of Minnesota, Raffaella Barbierato and Marina Gentilini at the Biblioteca Statale di Cremona, Sreedevi Satyavolu at Catholic University, Laura Scavarda at Loescher editore, and staff at the Istituto Papirologico di Firenze.

Finally, the process of securing permissions for figures and images benefited from the kind assistance of a variety of professionals, including Agata Ralska, Agnese Pergola, Alicia Niewold, Aspasia Efstathiou, Beatriz Rosso Avila, Ben Kennedy, Bobby Dicks, Cheryl Ingraham, Claire Weatherhead, Cormac Bourke, Ellie King, Georgia Rogers, Greer Ramsey, Hannah Robinson, Karen Peláez, Kerry-Anne Kapp, Kyra Simone, Luca Zizi, Lucia Rinolfi, Michael Plisch, Margaret Wilson, Paula Mea Quilong, Peter Higginbotham, Piera Bertoni, Portia Taylor, Rainer Hugener, Rebecca Laverty, Renata Sawińska, Sohila Badawy, Stephen Weir, Stellina Di Meo, Valentin Groebner, Valeria Intini, Verena Rothenbühler, and staff at the Hellenic Ministry of Culture of Greece.

# Disclaimer

While the author serves as Lead Economist at the World Bank, the book was produced outside his professional duties and only reflects his personal views. The findings, interpretations, and conclusions expressed in this publication are those of the author and should not be attributed in any manner to The World Bank, its Board of Executive Directors, or the governments they represent.

# 1
# The Gist of the Journey

> ... almost any idea that has not been around for a while stands a good chance of being mistaken for an original insight.
>
> **Albert Hirschman (1991, p. 29)**[1]

## 1.1 Now and then

There is a recurring number in cash transfer statistics: "1.4." Almost 1.4 billion *people* recently received cash payments from the state, the largest scale ever reached. An astounding 1.4 million *papers* have been written on the subject in the past few decades. And there is some magic happening: for every dollar provided as cash transfers, nearly 1.4 *dollars* are generated in local economies.[2] In short, cash transfers are popular among, or at least broadly known by practitioners, academics, and the public at large.

Several reasons attest to such interest. For once, they are alluringly simple and intuitive. I haven't defined them yet, but they are not insurance (no "contribution" is need), they are not loans (no repayment), and they are not remittances (they are from the government, not other people)—they are money that states give to people directly.

Now, there are many ways to design them, but their plain nature led some to assert that they are "no rocket science." While they are not *that* simple to implement, it might be fair to acknowledge that, especially when pressured by circumstances, many states have quickly reimagined the frontier of what's possible. During the COVID-19 pandemic, Togo built a national digital platform for cash transfers from scratch in just ten days.[3] In Bangladesh, Colombia, Egypt, and the Philippines, it took less than a week to make the first payment after large-scale programs were announced.[4] Perhaps

[1] *The Rhetoric of Reaction: Perversity, Futility, Jeopardy* by Albert O. Hirschman, Cambridge, Mass.: The Belknap Press of Harvard University Press, 

[2] As is discussed later in the chapter, coverage data is from Gentilini et al. (2022) while the literature is based on a Google scholar search. The figure on multipliers is the average multiplier of 1.32 from 28 data points, 27 of which are reviewed in Gassmann et al. (2023) and the remaining one is from Daidone et al. (2023).

[3] Aiken et al. (2022), Chowdhury et al. (2022), Lawson et al. (2023).

[4] Beazley et al. (2021), Gentilini et al. (2022, p. 62). Yet the global social protection response to the pandemic was often haphazard; see the discussion in Gentilini (2022).

*Timely Cash*. Ugo Gentilini, Oxford University Press. © Ugo Gentilini (2024). DOI: 10.1093/9780191994982.003.0001

the role of history is, as put by Michael Katz, to "... rebut presumptions of inevitability by rejecting the idea that present circumstances result from inexorable, irresistible forces."[5]

Yet there are other aspects of cash transfers that make them seem *more* complex than rocket science. According to NASA, one of the first devices that pioneered rocket flight was a wooden pigeon.[6] Built by the Greek scientist Archytas around 400 BC, the object marveled observers of the time as, suspended on wires, it boosted away by escaping steam. In the same period and place, some of the first cash transfer programs recorded in history were provided by the Athenian state. If rocket science evolved dramatically since, dilemmas on cash transfers are not fundamentally different today than they were at the time of Archytas' pigeon. Maybe cash assistance is not that easy after all.

Cash transfers are considered a relatively recent phenomenon, and their presence in *BC* periods may sound counterintuitive. Among some of us—and certainly me before writing this book—their origins may evoke two historical moments: the formative post-World War II years of the welfare state in many higher-income settings, and the "quiet revolution" unfolding over the past decades in lower-income countries. Before these periods, some dim images of relief given in Oliver Twist times and guilds in the Middle Ages may spring to mind too. While actively engaging in present-day debates, my mental map of cash transfers in history was largely uncharted.

As it turns out, the idea of supporting people with cash has been with us for millennia. Continuities with past practices are striking. For example, ascertaining people's needs is key to tailor programs to recipients' circumstances. To this effect, today's field officials in Brazil "conduct a visit to beneficiaries' homes to assess their family situation [. . .] appraise the type of housing and document its characteristics [and gather] information on employment and income"[7]. Similarly, in 1796 Hamburg's "overseers had printed questionnaires [. . .] to each poor family [. . .] verified by a personal visitation [. . .] to discover the average earning of each member of the family."[8]

Dozens of countries currently register beneficiaries, rank them according to welfare, and assign assistance based such classification. In contemporary Indonesia, "registered households [are] ranked from poorest to richest. Relative eligibility thresholds [are] then applied to that household ranking to select beneficiaries for a range of human development programs."[9] A thousand years earlier, the Chinese Song dynasty had established "empire wide registration systems that graded [. . .] households into a set of ranks [and] relief measures were directed at the fourth and fifth rank households."[10]

[5] Katz (1995, p. 8).
[6] NASA (2021).
[7] GoB (2022, p. 15, 49, 100).
[8] De Schweinitz (1943, p. 92).
[9] Lindert et al. (2020, p. 149).
[10] Von Glahn (2012, p. 52, 55).

Most programs worldwide tie or "condition" the provision of cash to some activity fulfilled by beneficiaries. Such conditional cash transfers (CCTs) revolve around children's education and health: from the mid-1990s, a "CCT wave" swept across the world at a "prodigious rate."[11] Yet the wave may have started gathering in the previous century: in 1811, when Tuscany was under Napoleonic rule, the Arno prefect Jean Antoine Fauchet requested the local relief agency "for lists of all mothers with infant children, and ordered that their [cash] subsidies be stopped unless their children had been vaccinated against smallpox."[12]

A variant of cash conditionalities involves work requirements for adults. According to the 1601 poor laws of England, "[d]irect grants were available for the unemployable and a work policy existed for those who were able-bodied."[13] Fast forward to modern-day Africa, "ablebodiness" is a defining criterion of many contemporary schemes: Ethiopia provides "payments to able-bodied members for participation in labor-intensive public works," and direct transfers are provided to the "labor-constrained ultra-poor" in Malawi.[14]

Another feature stands out in public works programs: nearly half of contemporary schemes are self-targeted,[15] meaning that wages are set below-market levels. This is pursued "with the intention of preventing labour market distortion, reducing demand for [assistance] and targeting the poorest."[16] In a similar vein, in late 1800s Russia "specialists recommended that wages in houses of industry should be lower than the average local wage, lest masses of workers leave their jobs and flood the institution."[17]

Linkages to labor markets also appeared in other ways: in Malta, contemporary claimants for cash assistance "have to document their job-search activities in detail, including not only whether employers were approached but also the employers' names and addresses."[18] In the late 1700s, the "roundsman" system provided daily cash transfers to English rural unemployed people but only after having compelled them to search for work among local employers.[19]

Some early forms of child benefits, also named "family allowances," were introduced during the First World War to compensate for separation of soldiers from their families.[20] There are indications that child benefits were already provided under the Omar Caliphate in the 600s.[21] And when similar programs were introduced around the year 100 in the Italian peninsula, the image of the Roman emperor that presided over their introduction was imprinted on coins.[22] Such element of political signaling

[11] Fiszbein and Schady (2009, p. 3, 29).
[12] Woolf (1986, p.91).
[13] Dolgoff and Feldstein (2009, p.49)
[14] See GoE (2014, p. 1) and GoM (2022, p. ii), respectively.
[15] Subbarao et al. (2013, p. 78) found that such practice was present in about 45% of the cases.
[16] McCord (2012, p. 82).
[17] Lindenmeyr (1996, p. 187).
[18] Immervoll and Knotz (2018, p. 35).
[19] Boyer (1990, p. 16).
[20] Boger et al. (2021, p. 173).
[21] Hasan (1997, p. 149, 241).
[22] O'Brien (2020, p. 41).

may have been present in early 2020, when about 36 million checks carrying the name of the President were sent to US families.[23]

Cash transfers can be used to incentivize people's mobility. In 2008, a program in Bangladesh provided people with a cash transfer to move out from villages at risk of famine. The size of the transfer was equivalent to a roundtrip cost to nearby towns.[24] Stricken by a drought in 1539, authorities of Zamora paid a cash transfer to "foreign beggars" to quit the town in an effort to limit provisions to residents.[25]

Large shares of countries' social protection systems are in-kind, and a growing body of research is exploring their comparative performance relative to cash. In Yemen, a recent experimental evaluation aimed at "estimating the relative impact and cost-effectiveness of cash and food transfers."[26] The trial was akin to a pilot scheme of 1934 in the city of San Francisco: in such context, an "experiment was undertaken as a method of securing more concrete evidence of the practical possibilities of a more extensive cash relief program [in lieu of in-kind food]," also including an analysis of "comparative costs of administering relief in cash and in kind."[27]

In some cases, such selection of cash or food transfers could be determined by recipients themselves. For example, under a recent pilot program in India "beneficiaries are provided a choice as to whether to receive their entitlements in cash or to retain their [food] entitlements."[28] In a similar vein, in 1546 the city officials of Toledo decided to render assistance "in two large lump sums [of cash] or to give the poor a choice between money or bread."[29]

If practices are longstanding, so are debates surrounding them. Questions around the meaning of "needs," who deserves assistance, which institution should house it, or what form should transfers take, have all attracted heated deliberations. For some, the best help is no help at all. These dilemmas apply to virtually any public intervention. Yet the notion of state giving *money* to people has been particularly contentious. Today is no exception. When in April 2023 I met the Minister of Finance of an Asian country, his take on cash transfers was unequivocal: "people have been on the rolls forever and never graduate." His thinking mirrored that of the rector of Shotley, England, who in 1883 admonished that "[cash assistance] tends to make men poor, to keep them poor, to keep them down and to keep them back."[30]

[23] See reproduced checks in Jager and Zamora Vargas (2023, p. 2). The checks were part of the first round of Economic Impact Payments of March 2020, which also included 122 million payments made electronically and 3.5 million via debit cards (see IRS online database: https://www.irs.gov/statistics/soi-tax-stats-coronavirus-aid-relief-and-economic-security-act-cares-act-statistics#EIP1).

[24] Bryan et al. (2014, p. 1678). More recently, the Swedish government offered $34,000 to migrants that agreed to leave the country. See https://www.nytimes.com/2024/09/13/world/europe/sweden-immigration-reform.html.

[25] Flynn (1989, p. 82).

[26] Schwab et al. (2013, p. 2).

[27] Colcord (1936, p. 37, 197).

[28] Muralidharan et al. (2011, p. 16).

[29] Martz (1983, p. 126).

[30] The quote is by Rev. Hervey (GoUK 1884, p. 163).

Now and then, understanding cash transfers means understanding people's worldviews. When I met the Minister, there was little time to identify the roots of his reservations; but he did concede that the "rolls" problem coincided with the economy not producing enough jobs. Perhaps there is a core set of deep-seated beliefs around which there will always be disagreement; but having a fuller, meaningful, and open-minded conversation on the nature of the poverty problem, especially with those that we disagree with, would help weed out a range of misunderstandings on what cash transfers can and cannot achieve.

## 1.2 More than money

I mentioned that both the knowledge base and operational footprint of cash transfers are significant. Let me be more precise: over 1980–2023, the annual publications volume increased by over 26 times, from about 3,600 papers in 1980 to almost a hundred thousand units in 2023 (Figure 1.1). A total of over 1.4 million papers, the number quoted at the beginning of the chapter, have been produced during such period.[31]

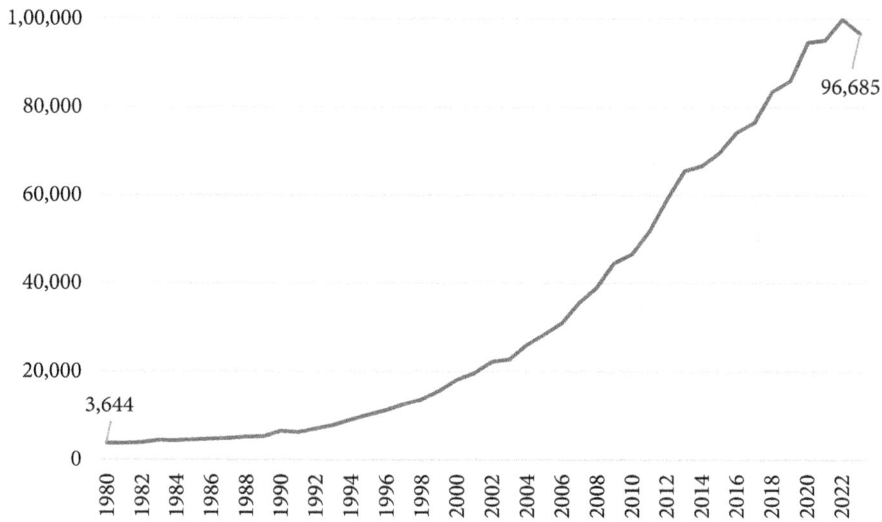


**Figure 1.1** Number of cash transfers publications, 1980–2023.

*Source*: The author, based on Google Scholar (as of June 2024).

Cash transfers are similarly widespread in practice. In 2020–2021, according to a conservative estimate those programs reached almost 1.4 billion people—the other

[31] Keywords used for the Google Scholar search included "conditional cash transfers," "unconditional cash transfers," "cash transfers," "social pensions," "non-contributory pension," "child benefits," "cash grants," "guaranteed minimum income," "basic income," "universal basic income," and "UBI." There could be a degree of double counting, as some papers published, say, as a discussion paper, may also appear in journals. The total number of papers is 1,496,210.

statistic quoted at the outset of the book—as part of pandemic responses.[32] Among those beneficiaries, about 900 million, or one person out of seven, received such payments in low and middle-income countries (Figure 1.2).[33] While temporary, such coverage level was twice that of 2010–2019 and over four times the scale reached in the first decade of the 2000s. When global inflation rose in 2022–2023, countries planned additional cash transfer payments to about a billion people.[34] As of late 2023, coverage was largely back to pre-pandemic levels.[35]

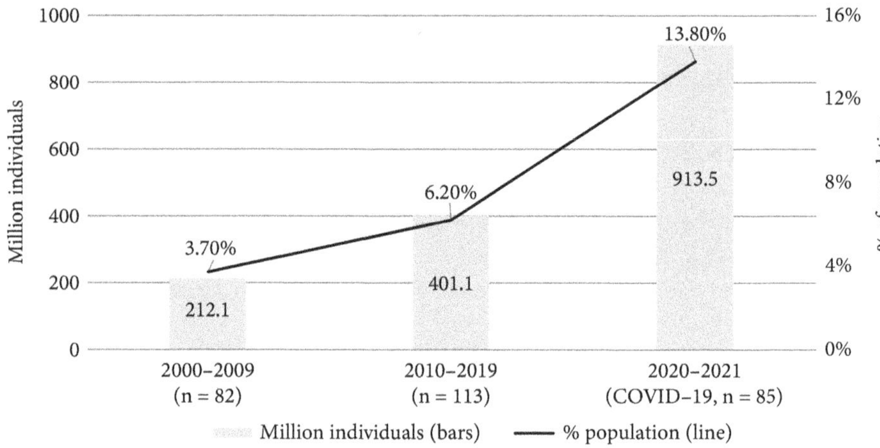


**Figure 1.2** Coverage of cash transfers in low- and middle-income countries, 2000–2022.
*Source*: The author, based on Gentilini et al. (2022), Iyengar et al. (2023), and ASPIRE survey data.

If the literature and operational footprint skyrocketed, so did contentious debates. Cash transfers evoke visions of social protection that are at the same time old and new. If they are celebrated for opening new circuits of redistribution away from traditional welfare regimes,[36] they maintain an aura of grudgingly accorded exception to earning "legitimate" income from the labor market. Even relative to social insurance, cash transfers maintain a sort of subordinate, residual role. A mainstream narrative on cash transfers is that they "... perpetuated their anachronistic existence until they were rendered superfluous by social insurance and social welfare systems in the twentieth century."[37] Far from being anachronistic and superfluous, this volume shows that cash transfers have been an important tool throughout historical contexts and models of economic organization. But this is not an advocacy book, and the reader will hopefully find a balanced interpretation of the contributions and limits of cash transfers in history.

[32] Gentilini et al. (2022).
[33] Rates in Figure 1.2 are population weighted. A description of methodology is included in a technical note by Iyengar et al. (2023).
[34] See Gentilini et al. (2023). While countries intended to cover 795 million people, only 174 million were reached by mid-2023.
[35] See Gentilini (2023a).
[36] Ferguson (2021, 2012).
[37] Sun-Hong (1998, p. 19).

Cash transfers are more than money. They are sites of societal debates on some fundamental issues. It is hard to ignore how conversations on cash programs are underpinned by deeper systemic issues affecting economic models and the generation of inequities. Cash transfers are deeply influenced by philosophical, political, economic, and social doctrines. A common thread underlying those debates has been the notion of "scarcity": if cash transfers provide economic security, then the drive toward industriousness, thrift, and discipline would be hindered. Insecurity is, according to some observers, the ultimate incentive. Such influence should be traced not in lofty declarations; instead, it reveals itself through debates on concrete operational choices—for example, on ways of assessing needs and eligibility, calibrating the level of coverage and generosity, visiting and registering beneficiaries, or the expectation to adhere to a particular social norm or accepted code of conduct. Over the course of the book, I show how these design choices can vary pending on whether poverty is framed as personal deficit or structural feature inherent in societal dynamics.

In a way, this book is akin to solving a puzzle that, to my knowledge, hasn't hitherto been fully tackled—that is, I marshal existing scattered, multi-disciplinary, and sometimes hard-to-trace materials with a view of forming a unified global cash transfers history. Specifically, I pursue three goals: mapping key experiences and practices over time and space; codifying historical diversity and discern possible recurrences or patterns; and leveraging historical antecedent to identify the roots of contentious debates, interpret them, and provide a sense of trajectory to explain current quandaries. Fortunately, this initial exploration builds upon and complements a flourishing literature.

A vast set of contributions has examined cross-country patterns, mostly from a pan-European and United States perspective.[38] Specifically, there is a rich literature on the history of "poor relief" in England,[39] United States,[40] and parts of continental Europe,[41] including at national and city levels.[42] I enlarge such spatial reach by integrating research on historical cash transfers antecedents from different continents and countries.

The book extends the typical time horizon. Most studies tend to focus the analysis on select centuries, especially the consequential period between 1700–1900s,[43] or cover specific historical junctures.[44] Similarly, an emerging literature explains the

[38] The recent voluminous work on Europe by McStay Adams (2023a,b) is a case in point. See also De Schweinitz (1943) and Salter (1926). An incomplete draft by De Schweinitz (undated) offers another example.

[39] The "English poor relief" literature is immense. Among the "classics" are Hammond and Hammond (1913), Nicholls (1854), and Webb and Webb (1927), as well as more recent contributions by Boyer (1990), Marshall (1985) and McIntosh (2012). For earlier work, see for example Fawcett (1871).

[40] Among them, see Axinn and Levin (1982), Katz (1986) and Trattner (1974).

[41] Frohman (2008), Lindenmeyr (1996), Martz (1983) and Pedersen (1993) are some examples.

[42] For cities, see for instance Beckerman Davis (1991), Lindemann (1990), Pullan (1971), and Zemon Davis (1968).

[43] Among them, see Boyer (1990), Himmelfarb (1984a), and Lindert (2004, 2021).

[44] For example, see Pimpare (2004), Skocpol (1992), and Steensland (2008a).

spread of cash transfers in the "global South,"[45] with an intriguing literature covering colonial periods.[46] The analysis in this book resets the clock by several centuries to generate a more complete historical trajectory. Opting for breath comes at the cost of depth, for which footnoted references have a comparative advantage.

There are studies on the long-term evolution of general welfare systems. This branch of literature combines general elements of social assistance, social insurance, health, and education.[47] This volume deliberately zooms into cash transfers as the core focus of analysis, hence providing more nuance to the topic. There is a long-standing literature on poverty history, which examines how ideas, diagnosis, and measurement of the "problem" have evolved over time.[48] I incorporate this precious research into the analysis while placing an emphasis on "policies" against the poverty problem.

Finally, I try to bring together different disciplines, including drawing not only from history and economics, but also borrowing from anthropology, sociology, political sciences, theology, governance, food security, urban development, and crisis management.[49] But let there be no doubt: despite my best efforts, this work will invariably reveal my own biases and incomplete perspective. Ultimately, economics is the dominant discipline on display, and I am telling a story based on my worldview. This book is not presenting *the* history of cash transfers, but a history as I try to understand it.

## 1.3 Navigating the book

In broad strokes, the picture that emerges from the book is one where cash transfers are battlefields of competing aims: they are reasonably successful in providing a basic level of support to vulnerable populations; but they are also caught in—and sometimes get blamed for—authorities' struggles to handle major disruptions.[50] Societies have always been in turmoil, whether due to structural shifts in economic organization; the constant eruption of violence in various forms; the threat posed by ever-present plagues and food inflation; or evolving social norms and demands for social justice. Cash transfers emerged as one of the ways in which governments tried to manage the negative *manifestations* of such constant state of change.

[45] Hanlon et al. (2010), Leisering (2019).

[46] Among others, see Midgley and Piachaud (2011), Schmitt (2020b), and Seekings (2024).

[47] See Day and Schiele (2013), Dolgoff and Feldstein (2009), and Jansson (2009). A fascinating multi-volume, cross-regional work was led by John Dixon in the mid-1980s and early 1990s (Dixon 1987a,b, Dixon and Kim 1985, Dixon and Macarov 1992, Dixon and Scheurell 1990). See also Aspalter (2017) and Palier (2010) summarizing key lessons from their edited volumes mostly dedicated to social insurance, albeit with salient considerations for social assistance.

[48] See Fleischacker (2004) on distributive justice, Piketty (2021) on inequality and Ravallion (2016) on poverty.

[49] Among them, see Barnett, M. (2011), de Sardan and Piccoli (2018), Ferguson (2015), Garnsey (1988), Hickey et al. (2019), Molyneux (2018), Patel and Midgley (2023), and Will and Wong (1991).

[50] See for example Greenbaum (2015), Pimpare (2002) and Ryan (1976).

The practical application of cash transfers led to a wide variety of operational practices, many of which, as discussed, were harbingers of modern assistance. While programs helped recipients with some modest amount of assistance, the force of some disruptions overwhelmed the capacity of institutions to assist populations in need.[51] In attempting to meet demand, in a typical situation provisions were extended, actors proliferated, and costs rose. The process of coexistence between cash transfers and somewhat unaddressed needs may have generated disillusion and frustration. The chain of supposed *causality* now flowed in the other direction: cash transfers produced sloth, and growing needs were attributed to "indiscriminate" assistance (and people receiving it). The canary in the coal mine is the rise of "rolls" and public outlays—purported sentinels of a malaise in the state of society. Thomas Malthus would complain: "notwithstanding the immense sum that is annually collected for the poor . . . that their distresses are not removed is the subject of continual astonishment."[52]

This situation posed an explosive political and social threat. Order had to be reestablished, and this included rationalizing and tightening access to transfers. Migrants and unemployed "beggars" were punished severely. Aiding those reforms were narratives that cast cash transfers as *causes* of the problem itself.[53] The rhetorical argument was powerful, and select reforms were often successful in reducing rolls and spending. As the process of change unfolded, new disruptions were generated, hence recreating pressure for assistance.

Whether curtailing provisions improved living conditions of ex-beneficiaries remains doubtful: instead, what subsequent research proved empirically is that, in the words of Anne Digby, ". . . [cash transfers were] essentially a response to population growth, under-employment, and low wages, rather than their cause."[54] Cash transfers are still caught between these competing forces—the tension arising from pursuing higher standards of living and managing societal costs of the process.

These considerations suggest that societies have been defining and redefining where to draw the lines between two concepts: on one hand, there is legitimate and earned income from the labor market; on the other hand, cash transfers constitute "unearned" income (unless it is for people that can't work).[55] The history of cash transfers is one about where to mark the distinction between earned and unearned income, and determining "the profundity of the divide" between the two.[56]

[51] See Brady (2023) and Calnitsky (2018).

[52] Malthus (1798, p. 74–75)

[53] Desmond (2023b), Katz (1995), Ryan (1971).

[54] Digby (1982, p. 13). Similarly, a recent paper on 1830s England observed that "[to not] work too hard in a long period of a dearth in employment and low wages [. . .] was perceived by the landowning and propertied as due to a loss of morals and directly connected to poor relief policy. [. . .] We might instead read these behaviours as a response to poverty" (Ball et al. 2023, p. 9).

[55] Zelizer (1997). Pensions and other social insurance programs also would gradually become "legitimate" sources of income.

[56] Woolf (1986, p. 141).

Conveying that cash provisions are the exception to the rule is a message reflected in the tightness of design choices.

The volume is organized around seven chapters. Following this introduction, Chapter 2 lays out the groundwork for cash transfers thinking and practice. The ancestors of modern programs are laid out with a view of composing an intergenerational "family tree" of interventions. Their basic features are interpreted in light of poverty narratives that may shape design significantly. The following three chapters argue that cash transfers have been pursuing a variety of broad and complementary objectives, namely facilitating economic transformation, supporting state building efforts, and help attaining social and political stability. These are discussed in Chapters 3, 4, and 5, respectively. Chapter 6 then turns to episodes of reforms: also in this case, three main models are identified. Such reforms pathways illustrate the pattern in action—that of criticism towards "indiscriminate" cash and rekindling assistance along stringent lines. A rapid summary of the chapters is hereafter proposed. Chapter 7 then concludes by reflecting on lessons from the past and their relevance for the future.

## Design archetypes

The tour offered in Chapter 2 shows that cash transfers have been provided for at least two-millennia and a half. For instance, Athens didn't just have the dividend payment mentioned in the book's prologue. Around the year 460 BC, the city-state delivered cash payments to orphaned children, disabled populations and people maimed in war.[57] If we exclude extemporaneous provisions of cash by rulers in Babylonia or temple-based transfers made as part of religious devotion, the Athenian experience is, to my knowledge, among the earliest form of government-run cash transfers "as we know them."

Policymakers have long been grappling with the codification of "deservingness." Desert often involved considerations around being, or not being, "able-bodied." The latter was already enshrined in imperial Roman edict of 382 AD.[58] Cash transfers have also been provided based on social status, like when rendered to industrious populations under financial stress with no fault of their own. Such beneficiaries were known as "shamefaced" poor and were provided transfers discretely and outside public purview for not affecting their pride.[59] Race and indigenousness also played a role in shaping eligibility at specific points in history, such as racially differentiated provisions documented in South Carolina in mid-1700s and Fiji in the late 1800s.[60]

Whether people were truly deserving could be ascertained directly via household visits and indirectly via making programs unpleasant or with limited benefits

[57] Dillon (1995) and Ober (1989).
[58] Parkin (2006).
[59] Jojima (1997), Pullan (1971).
[60] Lockley (2005), Plange (2023).

(work tests). Provisions were largely limited to local residents.[61] If not conditioned by design, there were expectations that beneficiaries behaved in accordance with social norms and moral principles. Those behaviors, including how to spend money, were at times codified in "instructions" from and "contracts" with administrators.

The chapter outlines the basic features of ancient programs. A compilation of a dozen cases of social registry ancestors is laid out, alongside an examination of past interventions like universal basic income, child assistance, guaranteed minimum income, public works, the roundsman system, labor rate, and workhouses. Not all these schemes survived, most notably workhouses; yet their underlying framing may still be present in contemporary conversations. In fact, practices should not be interpreted independently of the prevailing thinking about poverty. As such, the chapter provides a basic overview of different explanations of poverty causes. Within the rich poverty literature, some stylized considerations are distilled, including the basic distinction between poverty stemming from factors beyond people's control (structuralist explanations), those ascribed to circumstances within people's purview (individualist perspectives), and how to reconcile these views. Cash transfers frequently have been "indicted" based on an individualist interpretation of poverty.

Furthermore, cash transfer programs have been a proxy battleground of competing worldviews. Program design may reflect a range of inherently ambivalent values that societies—and elites—may hold. There is an uneasy compromise in the way in which, for example, shared principles of personal responsibility, work ethic, and self-reliance coexist with those of community belonging, solidarity, and mutual support.[62] Such trade-offs can influence choices at design level, e.g., providing meaningful support (solidarity value) versus not discouraging labor supply (self-reliance); cash transfers are meant to address needs of families, hence they are not intended for sharing with others; but not sharing could undermine informal mechanisms of support. Brian Steensland outlined this conundrum eloquently: "[people] value individualism, hard work, and the entrepreneurial spirit, but they also value community, equality, and compassion. ( . . . ) Policy conflicts are often the result of two competing principles coming into tension with one another."[63] These values, some argued, have not be applied in societies uniformly, that is, upper classes may be less subject to value-judgment despite being beneficiaries of potentially large public interventions.[64]

If cash transfers embody a collision between highly held, competing values, this may not facilitate a crisp understanding of those programs by the public: the relatively incoherent way in which the Family Assistance Plan was communicated to the

[61] Woolf (1986).
[62] Ellwood (1988).
[63] Steensland (2008a, p. 220–221).
[64] See discussion on "socialism for the rich, capitalism for the poor" in Desmond (2023). Also of relevance are Mettler (2018), Monbiot (2015), and Somers (2022a, 2022b).

American public in the early 1970s is a case in point. Limited clarity on goals may affect expectations, fuel confusion and harbor hostility towards programs.[65]

## Framing the goals of cash transfers

Looking through the prism of history, cash transfers have been pursuing three broad, big-picture goals. These are intertwined and sub-objectives could fit more than one goal. This set of objectives is laid out in Figure 1.3.

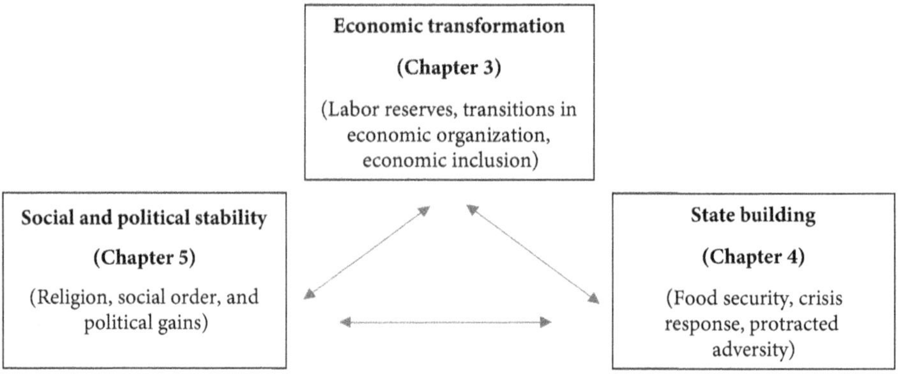


**Figure 1.3** Broad goals pursued by cash transfers over history.

### Economic transformation

Cash transfers can be part of the economic transformation process. Chapter 3 articulates such function into three sub-objectives, namely the use of cash to maintain a pool of labor reserves; enable transitions in models of economic organization; and foster economic inclusion. In terms of the first sub-goal, historical experiences cast new light on the role of cash transfers during the process of industrialization. Structural transformation of economies away from agriculture included an exchange in securities: while land constituted the main source of security for agrarian populations, urban migration required a severance of the person-land relationship. A branch of literature shows that in England, cash transfers played a critical role in providing an alternative source of security for the increasing landless wage employed workers.[66] Nested within a wider institutional architecture, including

[65] In the United States, for instance, the word "welfare," which was until recently associated with cash transfers for low-income single mothers, is politically toxic: the first line in Katz (1986) bluntly asserts that "[n]obody likes welfare" (p. ix); Ellwood (1988, p. ix) argued "[p]eople hated welfare no matter what the evidence,"; the volume by Gilens (1999) fully dedicated, as its title proclaimed, to elucidating "why Americans hate welfare." On the ideology and political economy of welfare provisions, see also Feldman and Zaller (1992), Noble (1997), Pierson (1991), Pierson and Leimgruber (2000). The Family Assistance Plan will be further discussed in Chapter 5.

[66] Solar (1995), Szreter (2020, 2007).

the civil registry and judicial system (Justices of Peace), the much-disputed cash transfers became part of an enforceable, credible, and countercyclical system that helped keep the workforce in proximity of major industrial hubs during turbulent economic cycles.[67] Similar functions were documented, for instance, in Amsterdam and Antwerp.[68] From this perspective, the massive scale-up of cash transfer provisions during COVID-19 may in part conform to a labor reserve rationale.

Another case of accompanying economic transformation is offered by China's experience over the past half-century. China's phased structural transformation process involved a more calibrated role for cash assistance. Initially, cash transfers didn't seem to play a major role: after the heavy lifting of poverty reduction driven by enhanced rural incomes and agricultural productivity, a limited role for transfers bulged, especially in the form of public works.[69] The emphasis on cash transfers seems to have increased over time, including for managing the poverty "residual." This included a combination of multiple instruments, institutional incentives, and high-level political commitment.[70] Experimentation has been a signature feature of Chinese public policy,[71] and three flagship cash programs were established after careful piloting.[72] In the 1990s, those cash programs coexisted with transfers established during the communist era.[73]

In fact, cash transfers assisted countries during broad shifts in economic models. At the time when Russia and China reconfigured their economies along socialist and communist lines, transfers operated in tandem with employment-based social insurance programs.[74] The "birth of the social" itself, or the statistical revolution that paved the way for the introduction of large-scale social insurance, has been of utmost importance for cash transfers. The history of the latter, it has been argued, ". . . cannot be separated from the history of social insurance, and the real question is how their relationship is to be understood."[75]

The advent of social insurance intersects with cash transfers not only in the concrete generation and spread of "categorical" (or not based on income) transfers like social pensions in the early 1900s, but also conceptually: the provision of social insurance is anchored on contingencies, like age, employment, sickness, or life. These can correlate with poverty and thereby anticipate its manifestations (and hence taking some pressure off cash transfers to relieve distress). By being anticipatory, social insurance introduced a mental framework that would affect the reading of poverty-oriented cash transfers as residual and reactive. Insurance and cash are not mutually exclusive as they pursue different goals within a social protection system, namely

[67] Charlesworth (2010a), Solar and Smith (2003).
[68] Lis (1986), Van Leeuwen (1993).
[69] At this historical juncture, public works wages were mostly paid in food or vouchers (Mallory 1926).
[70] Lugo et al. (2021).
[71] Ang (2016).
[72] Gao (2017).
[73] Hammond (2019).
[74] Madison (1980).
[75] Frohman (2008, p. 152).

"[cash transfers are] designed to relieve poverty, social insurance [is] concerned with provision of security and spreading income over the lifecycle, and categorical transfers [are] directed at redistribution between specific groups."[76]

There were deliberate attempts to integrate cash transfers within an economic inclusion framework. While part of the historical literature on public works, workhouses and similar labor measures tends to emphasize their punitive nature, there were cases of sincere attempts to reintegrate beneficiaries into economically viable initiatives. Some approaches also explicitly made the creation of a healthy and comfortable environment a key precondition for harnessing the potential of participants.[77] In general, a generation of economic inclusion interventions envisioned that low-income populations could be fruitfully employed in a way that fused social protection with industrial policy principles. These models included cases like Bristol in the late 1600s, Hamburg and Munich in the late 1700s, Toulouse, Turin, and Florence in the early 1800s, and Elberfeld in the mid-1800s.[78] Some of these experience, especially the German ones, were underpinned by an analytical division of cities into "poverty districts," surveying low-income people and collect data based on home visits (with validation by neighbors), designing personalized coaching and assistance by middle-class volunteer guardians, and providing interventions ranging from public works (e.g., rope yarn, street cleaning) to categorical child benefits (mothers received cash transfers for each child, plus access to daycare) and conditional cash transfers to attend industry schools.[79] The economic sustainability of those experiments ultimately proved limited. With growing cities, program implementers struggled in effectively "knowing the community." In some cases, the demise of economic inclusion schemes also led to a backlash against such provisions, which shifted from economic ventures to corrective measures of character through harsh workhouse conditions.[80]

## State building

The goal of state building could be viewed through three lenses: how cash transfers were part of wider state capabilities and infrastructure for delivering public interventions; the functions that cash played in response to wars and economic shocks; and their institutional role in situations of protracted adversity. These are outlined in Chapter 4.

In terms of the first sub-goal, cash transfers are sometimes closely connected to food security policies. In the case of ancient India in 250–150 BC, paleographic evidence attests to food and cash transfers being prepositioned to help manage food crises.[81] The Chinese elaborate system of granaries was connected to household registration practices. Around the year 1000, these helped rank households to provide

[76] Atkinson and Hills (1991, p. 83).
[77] McStay (2023b).
[78] Butcher (1932), Frohman (2008), Lindemann (1990), Maldini (1982), and McMillan (2019).
[79] De Schwenitz (1943).
[80] Woolf (1986).
[81] Bhandarkar (1932, p. 87).

assistance (and pay taxes) and anticipated some features of contemporary cash programs.[82] The Roman empire offers insights into data-driven state reforms in food subsidies and progressive financing of state provided cash assistance.

Crises could be conduits for enhanced state capacities. The US New Deal flagship public works programs helped to build nascent federal capabilities.[83] Simultaneously, a wave of experimentation swept across major US cities for replacing food commodities with cash transfers. The fact that experienced NGO professionals would join the ranks of public service strengthened cash transfer capabilities of local governments.[84] The Great Depression, however, didn't mark the origins of American cash transfers: these already existed in response to the War of Independence and the Civil War, as well as to support "morally worthy" mothers in the early 1900s.[85]

In some instances, droughts have been an inflection point. In countries like Botswana in the 1970s and Ethiopia in the early 2000s, droughts activated a process of institutional strengthening, including to implement public works.[86] India has extensive, multi-century experience with responses to food crises. In colonial times, responses varied dramatically across states, while a Famine Commission was established to develop the iconic Famines Codes of 1880.[87] The principle of "less eligibility," or that of low-adequacy transfers which characterized the British major reform of cash and other poor relief transfers in 1834, was reflected in those codes (e.g., the guidance envisioned three self-targeting tests as proof of necessity).[88] The Indian post-colonial "Scarcity Manuals" moved the policy focus from the prevention of starvation to the protection of basic entitlements.[89] In Sudan, a similar Famine Code was formally developed in 1920 and helped tame riots and build infrastructure during the 1941–1942 drought.[90]

Such experiences convey a broader point on the legacy of the colonial period.[91] In fact, it was argued that social protection in low- and middle-income countries " . . . cannot be understood without examining the way welfare policies and programmes introduced during the imperial era have continued to influence current policy-making."[92] Approaches adopted by colonizing powers like France, England and Spain diverged markedly. Such differences " . . . still have consequences for today's social policy-making and help to explain why some countries have introduced social assistance schemes and others not."[93]

[82] Von Glahn (2012).
[83] Harvey (2007), Trattner (1974).
[84] Colcord (1936).
[85] Skocpol (1992).
[86] Hickey et al. (2019).
[87] Brennan (1984).
[88] Bhattacharya (2017). The idea of less eligibility principle, a hallmark of the 1834 reform in England, was most notably applied to public works, including the provision of wages below market level. The principle, however, also embraced food transfers, as epitomized by meager "Temple rations" in India. See Chapter 5 for more details.
[89] Dreze (1988).
[90] Barnett (2011), de Waal (1997).
[91] Seekings (2020).
[92] Midgley and Piachaud (2011, p. 10).
[93] Schmitt (2020b, p. 142).

There was significant demand and interest in cash transfers by colonial territories themselves. Often, these experiences featured differentiated provisions along ethnic and racial lines: already in 1682, Jamaica instituted a local version of the poor laws to support European settlers; by 1886, cash transfers could be provided in times of personal financial distress. Similar provisions were established in Mauritius in 1902.[94] South Africa maintained race-differentiated cash-transfer provisions for most of the 1900s.[95]

In other circumstances, protracted economic crises didn't necessarily yield major shifts in action. The contentious period of structural adjustment in 1980s–1990s doesn't appear, based on relatively scant program-level information, to have sparked a broad-based emergence of novel cash transfers. Countries like Brazil and Mexico launched their iconic CCTs in the mid-1990s, but in most countries cash assistance bloomed in the early 2000s and would quadruple its coverage in just two decades.

## Social and political stability

Chapter 5 focuses on the third and final goal of cash transfers, namely attaining social and political stability. Also in this case, the goal subsumes various undercurrents. Within this bucket are experiences with leveraging cash transfers as part of religious and moral precepts; handling the problem of "begging" and mobile populations; and a range of practices in the context of soothing social discontent and engendering political consensus.

Religious precepts would influence how "work" and "giving" were upheld. For instance, the spiritual and ethical interpretation of work has shaped attitudes towards cash transfers among Catholic, Lutheran, and Calvinist approaches.[96] There was diversity even within those doctrines: for example, while Catholic doctrine is often associated with "indiscriminate" giving, the work of the Decretists and their *Summa* at the turn of the first millennium reveals nuances on eligibility and prioritization.[97] Islam is often associated with zakat; yet, there are accounts that Omar bin Al-Khattab, who ruled the Rashidun Caliphate in 634–644, established a department of social security, conducted registrations for social protection purposes, and introduced, as previously mentioned, child allowances.[98]

Cash transfers have been used to cement social hierarchy and class segmentation. Being appointed guardian or overseer may have been a way of combining responsibilities towards communities with private returns in social capital. Accounts from the Dutch Republic or Calvin's Geneva in the 1500s, for example, show that such appointments also generated opportunities for the ruling classes in terms of establishing social status, career advancement, and exerting patronage.[99] Furthermore, cash transfers have been used to demark entitlements and marginalize select populations:

[94] Midgley (1984b, 1994a), Osei (2001), Seekings (2023).
[95] Seekings and Nattrass (2005), Seekings (2007b)
[96] Kahl (2005).
[97] Tierney (1959).
[98] Hasan (1997).
[99] Van Leeuwen (1994).

the use of those benefits to amplifying racial discrimination were already alluded to, with examples stretching from South Carolina to Fiji.

The vast reference to "vagrants," "vagabonds," or "beggars" in history is extensive, raising perpetual dilemmas on how to handle the social, institutional, and fiscal implications of mobile populations. In general, begging (and idleness) among the able-bodied was made illegal and firmly punished. Six "management" measures can be identified: banning and apprehending, corporal punishments (like branding parts of the body with hot metals), forced works, deportations, licensing (with various badges devised for such purpose), and cash payments (e.g., Zamora's case in the 1500s quoted previously).[100]

Politics played a prominent role. A set of brief illustrations could help articulate political dimensions of cash transfer programs. One speaks to the use of cash assistance as a way of taming social turmoil. Historical econometric analysis confirms instances where relief helped attenuate riots.[101] Another scenario includes leveraging cash transfers for political consensus. Recent evidence shows evidence that cash transfers could increase electoral participation and support for incumbents.[102] Furthermore, cash transfers could also be part of the process of deliberate political coalition-building and electoral competition, including in Africa.[103] Finally, the complex politics of cash transfer introduction is explored at a particular historical juncture, including when the United States considered the idea of a guaranteed minimum income program in the 1960–1970s.[104]

## Reform trajectories

Within the diverse set of goals pursued, there are indications of a recurrent pattern. This is set out in Chapter 6. As mentioned, cash transfers were wrapped into societal struggles to manage the sweeping process of change. Cash transfers were accused of "pauperizing" the population, affecting their morality, character, reproduction choices, thrift, and work ethic. By eliminating the "fear of scarcity," transfers purportedly inhibited individuals' drive for betterment, thereby affecting societies at their core. The reforms, which attempted to restore a disciplined labor supply and rebooting the moral compass of those with low income, could be articulated around three main models. These involved a change in main provider, a shift in institutional arrangements within the same provider, and hybrid models (Figure 1.4).

The first set of reforms centered on changing the main provider. The watershed reforms that swept across Europe in the early 1500s embody such transition. The ensuing vibrant set of practices set in motion 500 years ago largely traced the contours

[100] Garraty (1978), Quigley (1996a), Ribton-Turner (1887).
[101] Greif and Iyigun (2013).
[102] Araujo (2023).
[103] Lavers (2022).
[104] Moynihan (1973), Steensland (2008).

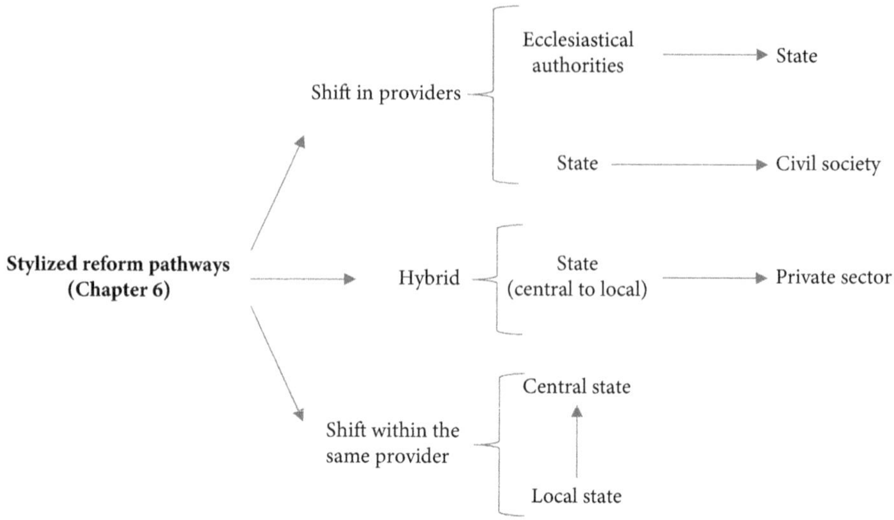


**Figure 1.4** Trajectories of reform.
*Source*: The author.

of contemporary social assistance frameworks. The reforms involved a secularization of transfers (although not a complete one) away from church authorities. The capacity of the latter had been overwhelmed by the demand for assistance stemming from ongoing economic, demographic, and social changes. Intellectual and religious developments considered the state better suited to distinguish deserving from undeserving populations and establish a proper system of organized relief. Public health risks played a role, too: the late 1400s witnessed a rise in the incidence of plagues, and the connection between vagrancy and the spread of contagious diseases like the bubonic plague motivated stricter public controls for cash transfers.[105] States embarked on new responsibilities for cash transfer provisions resulting in a region-wide compilation of city-level experiences.[106]

Shifts in providers also worked the other way around: in the late 1800s, civil society actors like the Charity Organization Society in New York City ramped up "scientific" engagement in cash transfers as opposed to "indiscriminate giving" by public authorities.[107] Charity organizations attempted to re-establish urban social ties; but to do so, it was necessary to *know* the conditions that shape people's lives. To reconcile the twin impulses of "simultaneously investigating and befriending the poor,"[108] scientific relief drew from practices tested in Germany and those

[105] Pullan (1971, p. 222).
[106] De Schweinitz (1943), Geremek (1994), Salter (1926).
[107] Zelizer (1997).
[108] Greeley (2022, p. 20).

piloted by Chalmers in Scotland—and which in turn influenced developments in Canada.[109]

Another stream of reforms reconfigured arrangements within the same institutional provider. Arguably, the most vivid exemplification of the pattern is the way in which cash transfers were reduced in England in 1834—and how that experience offered a rhetorical blueprint for scale-back of provisions in the United States at various points in history.[110] The reform was based on a voluminous official report mostly written "*prior* to the collection of evidence."[111] This report established the primacy of workhouses, the consolidation of parishes into larger administrative units, and the reorganization of eligibility around the twin devices of the work-test and less-eligibility. As noted, these would be reflected, for example, in subsequent approaches to relief in India. Revisionist studies exposed how the process of informing the law and its subsequent implementation was largely driven by ideology instead of evidence.[112]

Hybrid reform models combined elements of internal rearrangements with change in providers. The case of the United States in the 1980–1990s illustrates such a pathway. While the mainstream argument is that public spending was slashed through conservative ideology, data shows that expenditures increased over that period.[113] Larger spending coexisted with tightened eligibility motivated by growing concerns around incentives, work requirements, and dependency. Stricter access reduced benefit uptake, while growing shares of expenditures were directed to private providers, including to monitor and enforce compliance, deliver training, and facilitate work transitions.[114]

What happened to people that stopped being covered or participating in cash programs? For a number of ex-beneficiaries, exclusion didn't mean proof of self-reliance. Left on their own devices, some ex-participants may have re-entered the labor market. For others, retrenchment in public assistance exerted new pressures on civil society provisions. A wider engagement in crime and illegal activities was another implication.[115]

What can explain such pattern overtime and space? Albert Hirschman codified an anti-cash playbook.[116] His work identified a set of mechanisms of influence involving three interconnected theses of "perversity," "futility" and "jeopardy." The perversity thesis maintains that well-intended policies would ultimately

[109] Hareven (1969).
[110] Katz (1986), Pimpare (2004), Ryan (1971), Steenland (2008a).
[111] Shilliam (2018, p. 29), emphasis added.
[112] Baugh (1975), Blaug (1964, 1963), Finer (1972, 1952).
[113] Haveman et al. (2014).
[114] Hybrid reforms have also been pursued in the opposite direction, that is, of actively seeking an expansion of populations covered. This may occur in the context of broader social protection, and not necessarily cash transfers: the mentioned "birth of the social" in the 1800s involved economic, political, and statistical revolutions that ushered the spread of social insurance programs (Ferguson 2015).
[115] Pimpare (2004). Currently, the empirical relationship between reduced cash transfers and increased crime has been clearly demonstrated, among others, in the United States (Garfinkel et al. 2022).
[116] Hirschman (1991).

have the perverse effect of hurting people they are supposed to help; the case of futility states that reform attempts would invariably lead to disappointment; and the jeopardy argument acknowledges that a proposed policy may even be desirable, it involves unacceptable costs wiping out past progress.[117] The interplay of the three theses in general, and the power of the perversity thesis in particular, may have shaped intellectual tactics against cash transfers for centuries.[118]

Chapter 7 brings it all together by reflecting on how the plethora of experiences over millenia can help illuminate, and hopefully inform, modern cash transfer quandaries. It discusses how different historical reforms generally converged in direction and results; it sheds light on whether the past can help us better understand the poverty reproduction process; unpacks the perennial tension between "rolls" and "needs"; and explains why narratives "stick". The chapter then looks ahead by interpreting the meaning of and reasons for continuity in practices; it identifies persistent and new myths to dispel; examines the interface between administrative and human interactions; and ponders the big question on poverty's inherence in economic systems and whether cash transfers can help "shortcutting" it.

[117] Importantly, Hirschmann's playbook is largely, but not exclusively, devoted to uncovering conservative rhetoric. As discussed in Chapter 6, progressive narrative can also rely on a playbook with adopted standard counterpoints.

[118] Block and Somers (2014).

# 2

# Poor Narratives

## The Framing of Poverty and Its Design Implications

> . . . why our laborious poor are so wretched? Does the complaint arise from physical causes, or from the regulations of society?
>
> **Thomas Ruggles (1793), Letter I, p. 5–6**

This chapter's ambitious goal is to draw a general inference between the thinking about poverty and the design of cash transfer interventions. This is pursued by sketching out some key considerations rather than offering a comprehensive analysis. "Poverty," which is here interpreted as encompassing a wide set of deprivations, is the subject of an extensive literature with a deep historical tradition. For instance, Martin Ravallion's "poverty enlightenments" traced fundamental shifts in poverty conception over history;[1] research on the "idea" of poverty is accompanied by extensive quantitative analysis on poverty dynamics;[2] and a vast range of empirical insights have been generated through longstanding, multidisciplinary research on the matter.[3]

Building on such knowledge, the chapter begins by outlining some stylized explanations about poverty's origins. According to a highly simplified framing, the discourse on poverty causes tends to swing between two core narratives: on the one hand, an "individualistic" perspective deems poverty a condition stemming from factors that may be under people's direct purview (e.g., effort, character, morality); on the other hand, a "structuralist" narrative describes poverty as the result of ingrained imbalances in societies' economic organization and power distribution. Those views

[1] Ravallion (2020, 2013). The first enlightenment occurred in the late 1700s and established the moral case for public action against poverty. Such rationale was grounded on the works of Smith, Rousseau, Kant, and Condorcet, among others. While intellectually cogent, the first enlightenment laid the foundations for practical implications that would only emerge in a second stage: "[w]hile the First Poverty Enlightenment brought new thinking relevant to antipoverty policies it did not mark any dramatic change in the lives of the poor, and they were still being blamed for their poverty" (Ravallion 2013, p. 18). The second shift or poverty enlightenment emerged in the 1960s. At that point, poverty was interpreted as an impediment, a bottleneck on personal freedom and capabilities: " . . . once it started to be widely accepted that those born poor could in fact escape poverty through their own efforts, public support congruent with those efforts became more acceptable, and more people joined political coalitions or struggles toward that end" (ibid, p. 80).

[2] See, among others, Allen (2017), Atkinson (2019), Balboni et al. (2020), Barrett et al. (2019), Deaton (2005), Duflo (2017), Pritchett (2006), and Ravallion (2016).

[3] See, for example, Atkinson (2015), Besley (1997), Brady (2023, 2019), Desmond (2023a), Dreze (2017), Kanbur (2011), Kanbur and Squire (1999), Sen (1981), and Townsend (1979).

*Timely Cash*. Ugo Gentilini, Oxford University Press. © Ugo Gentilini (2024). DOI: 10.1093/9780191994982.003.0002

need not to be in competition and could be reconciled under a coherent poverty framework. Over time, the two extreme poles of thought have exerted significant influence on whether, why, and how cash transfers would pan out in practice. The pendulum has swung in both directions, but in the case of cash transfers it generally veered towards individualist explanations.

To shed light on those practical implications, the chapter examines how narratives may imbue the design of cash transfers. After a brief excursus of poverty thinking, cash design choices and current state of the evidence, the chapter interrogates the origins of contemporary programs. It identifies ancestors of cash transfers interventions, with precursors being rooted in centuries-long practices (and in some cases stretching over millennia). The chapter concludes by discussing how, especially over the course of recent centuries, cash transfers were "indicted" by leading intellectuals. While not unanimous and original, their thinking shaped a mindset that would cast cash transfers as "part of the problem." The historical reforms of cash transfers that are discussed later in the book (Chapter 6) are in a way an institutional response to how cash transfers were understood, framed, and perceived in a context of sweeping economic and societal changes.

## 2.1 Running around empty chairs

Structural and individual narratives of poverty are often portrayed as alternative visions: they are presented in stark contrast to each other—sometimes defined in opposition to one another—and framed as irreconcilable approaches. While a range of contributions has attempted to provide a synthesis and establish a coherent middle ground between poverty explanations,[4] the notion that there are opposing "camps" distributed along ideological and political lines may not be that far off from historical records and current deliberations.

Structuralists and individualist explanations are integrated pieces of a wider poverty puzzle: they examine the poverty quandary from diverse perspectives and pose questions of different nature. One way of putting it is that structural explanations ask "how much poverty can exist in a country, and why?" while individual approaches "rank" people within such poverty space and inquire "who is more likely to be poor, and why?"[5]

[4] For example, the "subculture" and "marginality" narratives are sometimes described as variants of individualist theories. The subculture narrative doesn't blame the individual directly—it explains permanent poverty as a matter of surroundings and culture in poverty enclaves. Poverty is purportedly framed as a way of life to which people eventually become accustomed, and which they resist changing (Rainwater 1968, Valentine 1969). Such narrative is interlinked with, for instance, the inner-city explanations of poverty in the United States. The marginality narrative, which was particularly active in Latin America in the 1960s, portrayed people in poverty as a "well-meaning" group unprepared to manage the complex reality of the modern world (Peattie 1974). Yet it soon became clear that the problem often lay not in the poor's inability to take advantage of opportunities, but in the lack of opportunities themselves (Portes and Walton 1976).

[5] As put by Calnitsky (2018), "... [s]tructural accounts tell us whether or not poverty exists in a given society, and if so, how much; if indeed it does exist, individual accounts tell us who ultimately becomes poor" (p. 8–9).

Imagine the game of musical chairs, with participants fast-walking around a limited number of seats and then hastily chasing a spot when the music stops. Inherent in the game is the idea that someone would be left out by design—that there aren't enough chairs for anyone who wants to play. In such metaphor—which I am not alone in evoking[6]—structural factors determine the number of chairs available for the game; and individual narratives may explain the speed at which people move around the chairs, whereas such pace may determine who is likely to be excluded.[7] Let me elaborate more fully.

Structural perspectives on poverty underscore the role played by factors that determine the "availability of poverty." They invoke foundational macro and meso-level determinants that shape the number and distribution of opportunities. These explanations form the institutional and economic backdrop—the "rules of the game"—against which individual agency operates. Such structural factors may encompass variables like economic growth, productivity, technological change, labor market institutions, etc. Structural interpretations are themselves heterogenous. Some "moderate" versions describe poverty as an unnecessary dysfunction in an otherwise viable system, while more "radical" variants interpret poverty as an intrinsic and necessary condition for social and economic order. The mild version doesn't seek revolutionary changes, but reform via redistribution within an accepted system.[8] The New Deal, for example, may have created the dilemma of how to reconcile the recognition of structural causes of unemployment while not overly legitimizing system-wide changes.[9] As for the radical structural interpretation, this can be illustrated by a range of essential functions that poverty may play in sustaining societies.[10]

Individual explanations of poverty refer to the specific traits discernible in a person. These attributes are multiple, including the myriad aspects related to biology, human capital, culture, etc. Each person comes with a stock of these factors at a given point in time. Such amalgamation of features "belongs" to the person—it is enmeshed

[6] See, for example, McChesney (1990) and Rank (2011).

[7] Brady (2023, p. 10) takes the metaphor further: "A scarcity of chairs (e.g., good jobs), not the individuals' quickness at seizing a chair (i.e., behavior), explains why someone is left without a chair (i.e., poor). A political explanation would instead say that there is not so much a scarcity as a distribution problem. Rather than too few chairs, one person is laying across and hoarding three, several chairs are disrepaired and piled nearby in the corner, and someone is then told that they have no place to sit because of what is disingenuously framed as a scarcity."

[8] Portes and Ferguson (1977).

[9] (Rainwater 1967). As put by Portes and Ferguson (1977, p. 89–90), " . . . [p]overty could no longer be attributed to immorality and negligence, but at the same time it could not be defined as a permanent and widespread of consequence capitalism" (p. 89). The latter alternative would have implied " . . . either the need to drastic structural transformation or the requirement that the government subsidize all the poor in an adequate and permanent basis [ . . . ] Poverty with legitimate claim to state aid thus involved a relatively small sector of the population on a permanent basis [i.e., old or disabled populations] and a potentially much broader sector on a temporary basis [i.e., the unemployed because of cyclical downturns]. [ . . . ] The ideology and policy of the New Deal [ . . . ] preserved the work incentive among the labor force by penalizing long-term unemployment."

[10] According to Gans (1971a,b, 1972), the existence of poverty is instrumental for fulfilling a dozen interconnected economic, social, cultural, and political functions. These range from ensuring that low-pay jobs are undertaken to how low-income people subsidize, directly and indirectly, many activities that benefit the affluent; from people in poverty serving as strawmen for uphold the legitimacy of dominant norms to how they help frame political narratives (e.g., that low-income people don't deserve redistribution of "taxpayer's hard-earned money").

in the identity of an individual. However, the fact that these factors are implanted in the person "as we see it" doesn't necessarily entail that their *causes* stem from individual factors or deliberate choices.[11] For example, prolonged spells of unemployment can make people seem "lazy," a condition that reflects both psychological distress (e.g., reduced self-esteem, anxiety, mood disorders, suicidal behavior, and other mental illnesses)[12] and physical hardship (e.g., lethargy and other debilitating effects stemming from inadequate nutrition).[13]

In addition to what we are endowed with at our starting point in life (basic biological traits, perhaps talent, and wealth), there is the "character" factor: this is of more voluntary nature, and it refers to effort, motivation, and choices that are made rationally or (sometimes seemingly) irrationally. Also, we are affected by situational causes. These can be objective natural disasters but may also be "relational" and produced by interactions with other people: examples may include social discrimination, or demand and supply forces that determine market prices. In the musical chairs analogy, people may be induced to move faster because they know they are *competing with others* for a limited number of seats—the "fear of scarcity." Each person conjures a different combination of these three sources: our endowment at birth, our choices, and the surrounding environment. An illustration is the health of an individual: genes can be important, but so are deliberate dietary and physical habits, as well as the affordability of food and healthcare. Or take skills, where talent, effort to harness such talent, and opportunities to deploy it all play a role.[14]

How does this quick and basic tour of concepts relate to cash transfers? The way in which we understand, conceptualize, and diagnose poverty has sizable implications for policy formulation.[15] In our case, this includes whether cash transfers should be considered and how they should be designed in practice. Over history, a straight line has often been drawn from individual attributes (their stock of individual features "as we see them") to character ("attributes are the result of your own choices") to then poverty ("it's your fault")—that is, the sources of poverty lie in the responsibility of individuals. It stems from their lack of motivation, thrift, industriousness, talent. It is a self-inflicted problem of short-sightedness, vice, and overall irresponsibility. Such view stands in stark contrast to research showing that the stressful experience of living in poverty can make people more generous, trusting, and compassionate.[16] In such contexts, the receipt of cash transfers may even engender a sense of responsibility towards the community and help assisting others financially.[17]

Yet over the course of history, a mainstream policy implication is that an intervention like cash transfers can make people worse off. It would only amplify the purported weaknesses. The classic fears of cash transfers generating "dependency"

[11] Nussbaum (2013), Roemer (2000), and Sen (1981).
[12] See, for example, the systematic review of 294 articles by Virgolino et al. (2022).
[13] The seminal works on nutrition poverty traps by Leibenstein (1957) and Mazumdar (1959) are particularly salient.
[14] Calnitsky (2018, p. 3).
[15] Atkinson (2019) and Sen (1999).
[16] See, for example, Piff et al. (2010).
[17] Neves (2023) documents how participants of a cash transfers pilot in Paterson, New Jersey, used money to share with, contribute to, and reciprocate assistance received from households and communities.

are rooted in such logic. When provided, the argument goes, any assistance should be rendered in ways that also treat the root cause of the problem—that is, material help should be an opportunity to rectify character, to impart a moral lesson. Tough love at best, merely punitive at worst. An interrogation of the causes of poverty should not rule out character-based narratives. But these may have likely played an outsized role in poverty narratives over time.

Why have individual narratives been so widely prevalent and "sticky"? In the psychological and sociological literature, a spontaneous adherence to individualistic approaches has been called "fundamental attribution error" and "folk psychology."[18] Various reasons emerge from such body of research.[19] One explanation is that an individualist explanation of poverty is simpler to understand and relate to. Poverty "is what you see," and it avoids engaging in complicated and slippery philosophical questions about what constitutes real "choice," and what is an induced one. It may be tempting to stick with what you see: a person that stopped searching for work is lazy.[20]

Another reason is that it may be *relatively* simpler to tackle individual attributes than addressing systemic sources of inequities and distribution of opportunities. Tackling those sources can raise deep political quandaries. But if poverty is articulated as a "social problem," instead of a political one, it can lead to viewing the solution in mere technocratic terms.[21] And in the context of short political cycles, decision-makers may have more direct control and exert more influence over specific technical interventions: "although seeing [poverty] as conflict issues might provide the right mindset to work for change, restructuring of the system is too much for most of us to undertake."[22]

The "blame game" may play a role in indulging with individual explanations.[23] Addressing structural issues would entail recognizing and accepting a certain degree

[18] Calnitsky (2018).

[19] Alesina and Glaeser (2004), Hacker (2008), and O'Connor (2011).

[20] For example, choices that are taken under limited bandwidth or the high level of stress induced by poverty—the "cognitive tax"—may seem counterintuitive and poverty-generating. They are taken by people, but would the same people had taken the same choices under different circumstances? For instance, the choice of withdrawing from the labor market, that of stopping to search for work, may appear irrational if the goal is to avoid or mitigate poverty; but the situation of a person that had unsuccessfully looked for a job for years in a context of pervasive unemployment might be different from the situation of someone quickly giving up search efforts in a vibrant labor market. The point is that the lines, especially between character and situational factors mentioned previously, might be fuzzy.

[21] Rule was wary of technical solutions because of their overt attempt to frame solutions as politically neutral. Solving a social problem "... is a profoundly political enterprise from beginning to end" (Rule 1978, p. 23). His point is that technical solutions themselves could not be devoid of value judgment around "how a society should look like." In fact, he saw poverty as the result of clashes between competing political interests of the wealthy and those of the poor. From such standpoint, technical solutions tend to concentrate on ways of operating "without really hurting the prosperous [and hence representing] a partisanship, clear cut renunciation of more sweeping steps toward the elimination of poverty" (ibid, p. 25). If those competing interests are ignored, then debates are reduced on how "experts" can use "techniques" to "solve" a social problem.

[22] Day and Schiele (2013, p. 40). The authors also argued that "... if high unemployment among African Americans is defined as racism because of job discrimination, action to end racism is implied [...] However, if high unemployment among African Americans is defined as a social problem, the solution is job training programs, which are much easier to create than racial equality" (ibid).

[23] Piven and Cloward (1971), Ryan (1971).

of collective responsibility for poverty.[24] From this standpoint, societies may blame themselves for the way in which they organized economic and social life; it might be a more politically convenient expediency to shift responsibility on "others," including people who are "visibly" guilty of their own poverty: "... [b]y ignoring the structural nature of poverty, dominant individualistic accounts tend to naturalize it."[25] As put by Matthew Desmond, critics are often "... rehashing an old story [...] that has been handed down from one generation to the next: that our medicine (aid to the poor) is poison."[26]

Finally, individualism may also be the (resilient) product of its times. For example, in Adam Smith's worldview poverty was contemplated as a condition closely connected to the overall state of the economy.[27] But other influential personalities were more adamant about the role of individual traits. In fact, 19th-century social Darwinism lent legitimacy to individualistic interpretations. Herbert Spencer, an English philosopher and coiner of the phrase "survival of the fittest,"[28] asserted that the poor "... were unfit [...] and should be eliminated. The whole effort of nature is to get rid of such, to clear the world of them, and to make room for better."[29] The influence of, among others, Joseph Townsend, Jeremy Bentham, and Thomas Malthus would lay the groundwork for an individualist rhetoric that would persist for centuries.[30] We return to their views after tracing the historical roots of modern cash transfers design.

## 2.2 Design choices as sites of narratives and performance

### Unbundling design choices

The conversation on the origins of poverty has concrete operational ramifications for cash transfers. Before discussing such implications, it might be helpful to briefly define the main parameters of "cash transfers". These are part of social assistance measures that encompass a range of schemes financed on a non-contributory basis. Unlike social insurance programs like pensions, social assistance is provided mostly

[24] Desmond (2023).

[25] Calnitsky (2018, p. 10). A similar point on "poverty normalization" has been made elsewhere: for example, Portes and Ferguson (1977) argue that "... [i]t is the function of dominant ideologies of inequality to transform [...] differences between men from contingencies into historical necessities that become progressively more acceptable to rich and poor alike [...] [P]overty becomes an issue when objective circumstances render previous interpretations increasingly untenable. Such ideological 'breakdown' means that dominant viewpoints become unconvincing to important sectors, including elites and the poor themselves" (p. 72).

[26] Desmond (2023b, p. 85).

[27] Gilbert (2006), Martin (2021).

[28] Spencer (1864, p. 444).

[29] Quoted in Dolgoff and Feldstein (2009, p. 80).

[30] Bentham (1796), Malthus (1798), and Townsend (1786). On their rhetorical legacy, see Hirschman (1991) and Pimpare (2004).

by the state[31] and without beneficiaries having to pay fees or monetary contributions. But besides the common denominator of being non-contributory, the design of social assistance programs can lead to radically different interventions in terms of goals, eligibility, reciprocity (or conditionality), and transfer modality.[32] As such, cash transfers encompass an extended family of programs. Interventions like steady income support for the elderly via social pensions and one-off payments in an emergency are housed under the same cash transfer roof. Such diversity in design affects program outcomes (see Box 2.1). Over the course of the book, the discussion on cash transfers occurs at a higher level (it will mostly refer to "cash transfers" in general), with those practical design nuances being fully recognized as key in shaping performance.

### Box 2.1 Design Matters for Outcomes: A Snapshot of the Evidence around Three Choices

There are at least three contentious design questions affecting outcomes, including on conditionality, transfer selection, and the "layering" of interventions. These compound the polarizing targeting debate mentioned later in the chapter.

The choice of whether to condition transfers on particular human development activities is heavily contested. The debate spans moral, implementation, and empirical issues. In fact, conditionality involves wider issues related to social contracts, societal notions of reciprocity, value attached to "effort," etc., which may affect the ultimate legitimacy and political viability of transfers.[a] A spectrum of conditionality models exists, ranging from "hard" to "soft" conditions, with intermediate and voluntary models (with various degrees of monitoring and enforcing compliance). These not only entail different implementation requirements, but also produce mixed evidence on their effectiveness: a recent review found that in three cases conditional cash transfers (CCTs) outperformed unconditional cash transfers (UCTs); in two cases

[31] Non-contributory programs can also be financed and provided by international and national organizations as part of development and humanitarian assistance. The degree to which states are involved in financing, design and implementation of those programs can greatly vary (Gentilini 2022; Gentilini et al. 2018). This mostly hold for lower-income countries, albeit examples of programs being provided by actors other than the state can also occur in higher-income contexts (e.g., the European Union).

[32] Even a single intervention like public works can, pending on the emphasis placed on aspects of design, like the size of wages, the share of non-wage costs, and the premium put on asset generated, lead to widely different programs (see discussion in Gentilini et al. 2020, p. 81). Other parameters, like payment size, frequency, timing, and gender of recipient, can alter program impacts. For trade-offs in goals and design, see for example Pressman (2005) and Ravallion (2009).

CCTs had the same effect of soft CCTs; in two instances UCTs outpaced CCTs, while in three other cases performance was mixed.[b] Some consistency in empirical findings also emerge: for example, unconditional transfers are found to bolster schooling,[c] although the effectiveness of conditions is slightly stronger.[d] The effectiveness of soft accompanying measures is increasingly documented, especially for nutritional goals.[e] Second-round unintended effects are also captured, including negative as well as positive impacts.[f] Ultimately, the discussion on conditionality is one on paternalism: if UCTs require no reciprocity by the individual, it is likely that her agency will increase. But there might be some actions that might be desirable socially and that the individual may not pursue if not required to do so. An example might be preventable diseases.[g]

Should transfers be provided in cash or in kind? Similarly to the conditionality debate, the "cash versus food" dilemma is one largely revolving around the costs and benefits of paternalism. There is a general microeconomics case that can be made for cash, including based on fungibility and consumer choice. Cost-effectiveness performance also tends to favor cash-based assistance relative to in-kind provisions (e.g., vouchers and food transfers). However, the appropriateness of cash transfers depends on various contextual implementation conditions (e.g., the presence of functioning markets), while the multiplicity of actors and perspectives involved in the debate can make the case for cash more complex than often assumed.[h]

Finally, should transfers be provided "solo" or in tandem with other multi-layered, integrated programs to "graduate" people out of poverty? While comparative evidence is underexplored, recent studies have pointed to the relative efficacy of simple interventions on consumption.[i] Similarly, evidence from Africa found positive effects of cash transfers on income, but it did not detect a statistically significant difference between cash-only, cash-plus, and "graduation" packages.[j] Available evidence from countries like Ethiopia, Uganda, and India show that impacts of multi-layered programs can be sustained for up to a decade after programs ended.[k] Comparative cost-effectiveness of those interventions, however, is limited.

Overall, four main considerations emerge from the previous three questions: "simple" unconditional transfers can be effective across a range of dimensions; it is likely that some benefits increase as transfers become more integrated and/or conditioned, but those benefits also come at a higher implementation cost; both costs and benefits are to be more broadly defined than currently captured (including objective and subjective measures; intended and unintended effects; and over different time horizons); and there might be a difference between individual and societal benefits and costs (e.g., the private cost of fulfilling preventive healthcare conditions should be considered within wider benefits of reducing ex-post hospitalizations; the benefit of giving people cash should be gauged against the risk of increasing inflation affecting wider communities).[l]

[a] For example, in the interest of making a UBI politically viable, Atkinson (1996b) would have sacrificed its unconditionality (but not the other UBI design features). Hence his "participation income" proposal.

[b] See Annex C in Gentilini et al. (2020).

[c] For example, see the 38 evaluations of 22 unconditional cash programs in 18 countries reviewed by Chong and Lau (2023).

[d] While a bit outdated by now, Baird et al. (2013) remains one of the most robust studies on the matter.

[e] See Ahmed et al. (2019) among others.

[f] For examples of behavioral distortions induced by some CCTs, see Bryan et al. (2021, p. 4); on positive effects, see, for example, references on political participation offered in Chapter 5 of this book (e.g., Colombia).

[g] For example, Costa et al. (2022) showed that in Brazil greater CCT coverage was associated with lower oral cancer mortality rates. More generally, estimates show that over 2000–2019 CCTs prevented 738,919 deaths among children under five years of age in Brazil, Ecuador, and Mexico (Cavalcanti et al. 2023).

[h] Gentilini (2023a) uses storytelling techniques for illustrating such different perspectives. For a review of the empirical literature, see Gentilini (2016a,b).

[i] Kondylis and Loeser (2021) found that smaller UCTs have larger impacts on consumption per unit of transfer than larger UCTs; and that the average UCT is 5–43% more effective than multilayered programs in increasing consumption at the average evaluated year (1.5 years for UCTs and 2.6 years for graduation). Legovini (2023) put it forthright: "... the smaller the transfers are, the larger their cost-effectiveness is, suggesting that [unconditional cash] should be thinly and widely distributed across populations in need" (p. 19). However, note that (i) "small" transfers are defined as those less than $1,000 in cost; (ii) only consumption is measured; and (iii) graduation impacts surpass those of UCTs after 3.4 years.

[j] Correa et al. (2023).

[k] See Banerjee et al. (2021a), Loeser et al. (2021), and Ozler (2018).

[l] Dreze and Sen (1991) note that while "... cash transfers can almost always help an individual to acquire food and avoid starvation, it is less obvious that cash support can improve collective security [since cash] may adversely affect other people's entitlements—for example, by exerting an upward pressure on prices" (p. 19).

For illustrative purposes, let us assume that standard approaches take a clear bifurcation: when poverty is believed to have an individualistic root, the design of cash transfer programs would likely be strictly conditioned on particular activities. Yet it is in the "targeting" space that the underlying poverty narratives pan out most vividly. Targeting refers to the tantalizing question of "who deserves assistance" as well as the technical procedure of "how to select beneficiaries." It's a circular dilemma: disagreements on poverty narratives can lead to different poverty definitions; diverse definition can generate diverse poverty measurement; and differences in measurement can generate differing results on who should get assisted.

A contrast with other sectoral approaches may help illustrate the point. In health terms, "needs" can be scientifically tested and replicated. The set of tools at disposal of the health community—blood tests, X-rays, MRIs, etc.—make a needs-based approach objective, verifiable, and one that ultimately establishes a clear relationship between diagnosis and treatment. An "objective" assessment of poverty is more problematic because of the nature of the concept: on one hand, poverty is a conceptual construct, and choices behind setting monetary, nutritional, or asset thresholds may be disputed; put differently, welfare distributions show no discontinuity.[33] On the other hand, as noted by Amartya Sen "... there is no particular reason to suppose that the concept of poverty must itself be clear-cut and sharp."[34] Paraphrasing Sen, the question is not whether poverty is a vague concept, but whether the fuzziness is of the required kind.

These ambiguities form the backdrop for contested debates on who should receive assistance and how to choose beneficiaries.[35] No method performs perfectly across all dimensions, like adequacy of transfers, costs, and coverage.[36] In practice, policymakers may put more weight on some dimensions (e.g., on viability and fiscal costs) than others, hence tilting the preference for certain methods and programs. Those weights and preferences can change, including temporarily in the wake of crises or more permanently because of political and implementation factors.[37] Most importantly, programs with different targeting methods can coexist and be complementary. In fact, they can pursue different functions, like equity, redistribution, and consumption smoothing—all of which have a role to play in social protection systems.[38]

Going beyond these specific debates, as discussed in Chapter 1 the literature on cash transfers is of extraordinary magnitude. Figure 2.1 synthesizes and maps out the *illustrative* strength of the evidence across two dozen themes.[39] The chart positions a theme relative to the availability of robust evidence on that issue (proxied by the

[33] Knox-Vydmanov (2014) and Pritchett and Kenny (2013).

[34] Sen (1981, p. 13).

[35] On the comparative advantages and limitations of alternative methods, see Gentilini et al. (2020, p.90–91), Grosh et al. (2022, p.323–325), and Slater (2023). See also Devereux (2016) and Kidd and Athias (2020).

[36] In general, the pros and cons of each targeting method, particularly those that are based on age versus those centered on welfare metrics, could be interpreted in relation to a dozen dimensions: "precision" (their performance in terms of reaching the intended population); "adequacy" (or the provision of transfers of meaningful size); "progressivity" (extent to which beneficiaries belong to the lower as opposed to the higher income brackets); "viability" (the delivery requirements for implementation); "transparency" (the extent to which eligibility criteria are understood and shared with the public); "arbitrariness" (how artificial eligibility rules can be); "stigma social acceptability" (if people feel ashamed by receipt, and how eligibility aligns with prevailing notions of deservingness); "shock-responsiveness" (how do transfers help dealing with changing circumstances); "labor compatibility" (or whether they disincentivize labor market participation or number of hours works); "political sustainability" (if they supported by most voters); and "costs" (both fiscal and administrative) (Gentilini 2023c).

[37] See Gentilini (2022) for temporary changes, Porisky et al. (2023) for the importance of delivery and institutional infrastructure in Kenya, and Hossain (2022) for political factors Bangladesh.

[38] See Atkinson and Hills (1991, p. 85) for a brilliant discussion on the different functions performed by poverty-targeted and categorical measures.

[39] The evidence mapping is based on my own judgment as informed by the review, curation, and dissemination of about 5,000 cash transfers-related publications conducted on a weekly basis over the last decade (see www.ugogentilini.net). For select comprehensive reviews and meta-analyses of the literature, see Anderson et al. (2017), Banerjee et al. (2024), Bastagli et al. (2019), Grisolia (2024), Handa et al. (2018), Leight et al. (2024), and Pasha et al. (2023); for thematic study compilations, see, among others, Ahmed et al. (2022) on neglected tropical diseases, Baird et al. (2018) and Banerjee et al. (2017) on employment, Behrendt et al. (2022) on child labor, Evans and Popova (2017) on cash usage, Fuller et al. (2022) on child health, Gassmann et al. (2023) on economic multipliers, Guimaraes et al. (2023) on HIV prevention and care, Hunter et al. (2017) on maternity care services, Jacobs et al. (2022) on antenatal care services, Khan et al. (2016) on contraception utilization, Manley et al. (2022) on malnutrition, McGuire (2021) on subjective wellbeing, Richterman et al. (2018) on tuberculosis, Pega et al. (2022) on health, Peterman et al. (2024) on gender, Richterman et al. (2023) on mortality, Semba et al. (2022) on obesity, Wollburg et al. (2023) on mental disorders, Zimmerman et al. (2021) on mental health, and Adhikari and Gentilini (2018) on migration; and for reviews of specific designs, settings or population cohorts, see, for example,

volume of published research) and consistency in the direction of empirical results on that matter (i.e., if results are mostly encouraging, mixed, or presenting limited or no impact).

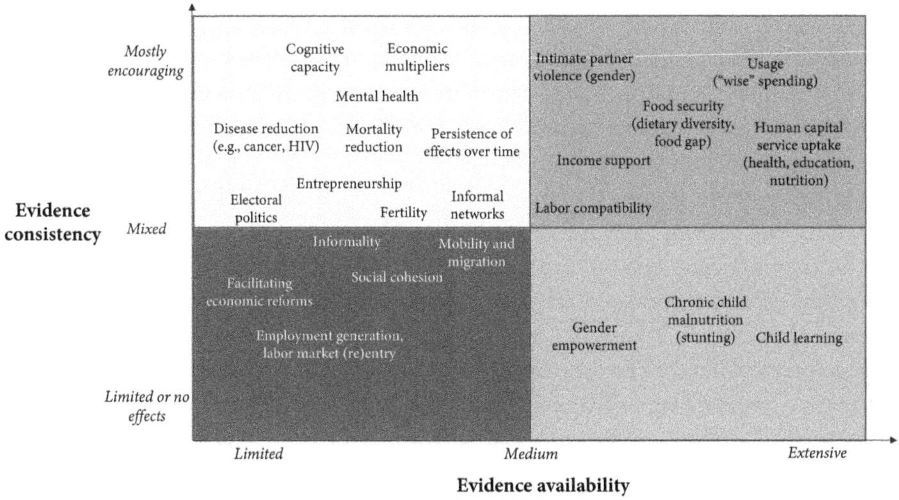


**Figure 2.1** Stylized strength of the evidence.
*Source*: The author.

The indicative mapping of the evidence may suggest that cash transfers have increasingly embraced more ambitious goals (and their evaluations have become more creative). The evidence-base for the variety of objectives pursued is highly uneven. The empirical record is stronger—that is, the upper right quadrant where research is extensive and consistent in the direction of findings—for dimensions like consumption and accessing human capital services. Importantly, "labor compatibility," or not generating perverse incentives, is also located in this quadrant. But not disincentivizing labor supply doesn't mean that cash transfers actively bolster labor supply. Except for programs providing one-off large capital injections or large-scale universal basic income (UBI),[40] the ability of cash transfers to generate employment and labor market entry or reentry is surprisingly limited and underexplored (bottom left quadrant). Cash transfers may have limited effects among human capital outcomes that require more complex set of ingredients. These are more widely documented and include child learning and chronic malnutrition (bottom right quadrant).[41] Other dimensions have high potential and are subject of a growing literature, such as economic

Little et al. (2021), Onwuchekwa et al. (2021), Owusu-Addo et al. (2018), Siddiqi et al. (2018), and Thota et al. (2023).

[40] See Banerjee et al (2024, 2023, 2019) and Gentilini et al. (2020).

[41] This doesn't mean that cash transfers don't impact those dimensions; but it does entail that effect size can be limited in absolute term and in comparison to other measures. For example, see Gentilini and Sabarwal (2022) for a broader discussion (and references) on comparing demand and supply side interventions on learning; for stunting, see the systematic review by Manley et al. (2022) who found positive but small effects (i.e., cash transfers reduced stunting by 1.35%).

multipliers, mental health, and mortality reduction. These are situated in the upper left quadrant.

Some of the studies situated in that quadrant are particularly intriguing. For instance, large swaths of cash transfers evidence have examined their impacts on recipients, with the possible indirect effects on the rest of the population remaining somewhat understudied. As argued by Eric Reinhart, "[w]hat has often been missing from public perception of [cash] programs is recognition of their importance not only for their direct beneficiaries, but also for everyone else. The failure to clarify this importance contributes to their underuse."[42]

A possible implication is that interpreting the effects of cash transfers holistically calls for cross-sectoral and potentially multidisciplinary perspectives. As we discuss in the next chapters, the application of statistical methods to social questions and a harvest of revisionist empirical evidence points the interdependence between, among others, economic, social and health dimensions. For instance, economic insecurity could have a "cascade effect" on various interrelated societal dimensions.[43]

Recent experiences attest to such dynamics: for example, the expanded Child Tax Credit (CTC) in the United States was shown that, at the equivalent cost 7% of the government's defense budget,[44] the program tackled an array of factors determining wellbeing, including decreasing mental health, hospitalizations, and violence—as well as increasing employment.[45] A comprehensive study projected that if institutionalized, the program's benefits would be have been over ten times higher than its cost.[46] Because of these interlocked effects, it was contended that cash transfers should "not be viewed as charity for the poor but should be regarded, codified, and funded as essential public health and safety infrastructure."[47]

Clearly, these broad-based societal impacts may not be generated by any cash transfer program; rather, they may hinge on deliberate design, including in terms of scale, eligibility, and practical implementation choices.[48]

[42] Reinhart (2024, p. 1336).

[43] Historical instances attest to how economic insecurity, as for example driven by mass land dispossession and turbulent business cycles, could produce displaced populations. This, in turn, could ignite upheavals and breed violence; it could fuel haphazard urbanization, disrupt social ties, foster social alienation, and affect mental health; and institutional responses that further exacerbated the poverty problem—such as resorting to corporal punishments, "indoor" workhouses, incarceration, and deportation—were often triggered.

[44] The estimate refers to a yearly cost of about hundred billion, with the equivalence to the defense budget calculated for 2023 (Reinhart 2024).

[45] See for example Bullinger and Boy (2023), Fenton (2023), and Rook et al. (2023). For a dissenting voice, see Lyu et al. (2024).

[46] Garfinkel et al. (2022) estimated that the cost of making child allowances permanent would have been $97 billion per year, while yielding social benefits with net present value of $982 billion per annum.

[47] Reinhart (2024, p. 1336).

[48] For instance, at its core the CTC embraced an approach that prevented hardship rather than assisting people when already in poverty. Such anticipatory nature includes a wider consideration of eligibility criteria based on age or other demographic characteristics; however, it may also involve higher eligibility thresholds among income- or welfare-based programs, or combinations thereof. And human-centered implementation requirements that were leaner administratively, and that didn't establish cumbersome and intrusive practices, may have also helped reducing uncertainty in provisions and increased uptake of benefits.

## Design as manifestation of ideas

Under an individualistic framework, or what were also called residual or "exceptionalist" approaches,[49] the labor market tends to be the main reference framework (as opposed to social justice), with an emphasis placed on limited generosity to ensure incentive-compatibility and favor steady "graduation" out of assistance. Provisions are likely to be more strictly regimented in targeting and eligibility. Instead, a structural explanation of poverty invokes more unconditional and "universal" approaches with eligibility based on criteria other than income—for example, citizenship, disability, age, or children.[50] An individualist frame invites shorter-run provisions with frequent recertification or reassessments of eligibility status. A structural approach favors legislated entitlements that are secured and ring-fenced in the budgeting process. Structuralist perspectives interpret fiscal issues as negotiable political choices: the first step is politics, and that determines fiscal space. Individualists, instead, tend to consider the budget as a given constraint within which make choices. Both propositions ring true: the former displays a "mindset of abundance" and longer-term direction, while the latter is more pragmatic and salient for present-day operations.[51] Figure 2.2 lays out main design parameters and stylized differences.

These features should be interpreted with caution. In fact, reality is more nuanced than such dichotomous model may convey. The shape of the light-gray triangle depicted on top of Figure 2.2 for individualist approaches—and the corresponding black triangle for structuralist narratives—indicate the fluidity of choices.[52] For example, not all universal approaches are necessarily structuralist. Take UBI, which, at face value, may appear a plainly structuralist measure as it shifts the power balance in society.[53] However, the program also enlists a particular line of advocates who place a strong emphasis on individualist causality while maintaining a skeptical view of public services as they "interfere with private freedom."[54] Such a version of UBI might be structural in form, but individualist in spirit.[55] Hence, a single intervention

[49] Day and Schiele (2013) and Ryan (1971).

[50] The term "universal" is debated: this could indicate (i) universality in outcome ("ensuring that all children can read"); universality as approaches independent of needs-based targeting ("universal" social pensions); and universality as everyone in society being covered by social protection. In turn, coverage itself can be defined in terms of "promise" in case a hazard materializes (insurance) or as receipt of transfers (social assistance) (Gentilini et al. 2020).

[51] In reviewing debates on targeting and universality unfolding in the AIDS health community in the 1990s, Mallaby (2004) recognized both the reasonable technical logic behind focusing on the most vulnerable groups as well as the moral imperative of universality. He codified the political message of the latter camp as follows: "... [t]he way to change the world is to proclaim a bold ideal and demand that necessary resources be found. You won't get anywhere with drab debates about trade-offs and cost–benefit analysis" (p. 326).

[52] Out of 180 countries with some form of child cash grants, only 21 display "pure" design provided without any means-related mechanism (ILO and UNICEF 2019). Mixed targeting seems the norm, not the exception.

[53] Calnitski (2018).

[54] Gentilini et al. (2020), Ortiz et al. (2018).

[55] For instance, Friedman (1967) considered a negative income tax, a form of UBI paid through the tax system, a conservative reform in disguise: "... [the negative income tax is] the only practicable route so

| Individualist | | Structuralist |
|---|---|---|
| Accept market-based logic and operate within | *Explicit/implicit logic* | Challenge market logic |
| Facilitate (re)entering the market | *Role of social protection* | Redistribute power ("power to say no") |
| Labor market | *Main framework* | Social justice |
| Means-tested, needs-based | *Eligibility* | Universal |
| In-kind, quasi-cash | *Transfer modality* | Cash |
| Conditional | *Degree of conditionality* | Unconditional |
| Shorter-term, frequent recertification | *Duration* | Longer-term |
| Budget availability | *Level of institutionalization* | Entitlement |
| Difficult, stigmatizing access; emphasis on exit/graduation | *Program entry and exit* | Eased access, limited pressure to exit/graduate |
| Fixed, binding constraint | *Fiscal issues* | Negotiable, financing as political choice |

**Figure 2.2** Illustrative design configuration by poverty narrative.

*Source*: The author.

like UBI could be motivated by fundamentally different philosophies on the role of the state in society. As always, design matters: why the program is considered, how it is introduced (replacing other schemes or as a top-up to existing ones), and financing can shape the identify of an intervention. If funded via progressive taxation, for instance, a UBI could be considered universal in benefits but targeted via taxes.[56]

While debates have mostly focused on the comparative strengths and weakness of targeting methods, relatively little research has been devoted to understanding how those targeting approaches can evolve and complement each other as part of trajectories towards comprehensive social protection systems[57]—and how those approaches align with countries' own systems of values and preferences.[58]

far proposed for dismantling gradually but thoroughly the jerry-built structure of government [. . .] The Left, if it accepts the program, will find that it has bought a Trojan Horse." See Barr (2020) for an elegant analytical review of NIT, UBI and other social assistance designs. Burgess and Stern (1991) also present a structured, logical way of considering design options.

[56] Francese and Prady (2018). There is a broader conversation on which aspect of a UBI could be "sacrificed" in the interest of the idea being considered in practice. As mentioned in a previous footnote (Box 2.1), Atkinson (1996b) compromised on conditionality in his proposed "participation income."

[57] A branch of literature argues that needs-based provisions can be compatible with the progressive realization of human rights, including the right to social security (Grosh et al. 2022). Such journey toward universality involves prioritization and gradualism—thereby targeting—and it is known in the health sector as "progressive universalism" (Cotlear et al 2015, Gentilini 2018). Moreover, needs-based targeting can be functional to a structuralist vision in other two ways: to funnel additional support to particular profiles of beneficiaries (e.g., top-up assistance for low-income people in addition to a basic floor of support); and when used as devices for determining the amount to be provided to everyone instead of serving as mechanisms of eligibility (e.g., like in the case of some food subsidy schemes).

[58] Seekings (2024) warns about the risks of such agendas providing a conduit for "exporting values." For example, McCarthy et al. (2023) document how tight poverty targeting in Indonesia might run counter

What should we expect from cash transfers in terms of tackling the causes of poverty? How should programs be calibrated, and where shall we set our ambition? The evidence may point to an obvious but important insight: addressing structural constraints requires much more than cash transfers. It is possible that particular forms of large-scale cash transfers—like a national jobs guarantee program or UBI—*may* help alter those structural issues in ways that other regular cash transfer programs may not. For example, there is evidence that India's National Rural Employment Guarantee Scheme (NREGS) raised wages in the private sector.[59] Whether those radical interventions will head in the direction desired by structuralists would again hinge on underlying motivations and design details.

Other policies may likely go farther in addressing underlying generators of poverty, like those tackling the tax system, equal pay, or criminal justice reform.[60] For instance, current tax systems in most low- and middle-income countries are regressive and poverty-augmenting: under such circumstances, the net effect of cash transfers could be limited.[61] The downside of such systemic measures is that they may take substantial time, political consensus, and complexity to enact than large-scale cash transfers. Shortcutting structural issues with cash transfers will not solve the underlying problem. It may help to put a lid on those issues before they erupt, but these will keep churning under the surface. Whether to use cash transfers or other policies to address the root causes of societal exclusion is a question of trust—or how much confidence and patience is bestowed upon the political process being committed to tap an ideal arsenal of longer-term tools *versus* opting for something more imperfect but swift.

This point reminds me of a spicy exchange between researchers Lant Pritchett and Christopher Blattman.[62] The spat centered on the balance between supporting people directly (with cash) and addressing countries' systemic constraints. The contrast between investing in longer-term, macro-oriented policies and shorter-run, micro-level interventions was on display vividly. But whereas finding the "secret sauce of growth" remained admittedly elusive, the less-ambitious micro-option of cash transfers was clearer and tangible. As Blattman pointed out, "growth economics needed a little competition and has gotten it"—that is to say, cash transfers are carving out a space in development economics, a field traditionally geared toward country-level issues.

to villages' views of deservingness, while in Ghana it was found "fair" by community members (Ibrahim 2023). In Uganda, Van Ufford et al. (2016) record a disconnect between values of communities and cash transfers categorical criteria.

[59] Muralidharan et al. (2017, p. 3) found that "[m]arket wages rose by 6.1% in treated areas, with a similar 5.7% increase in reported reservation wages, suggesting that an improved NREGS likely improved workers' bargaining power by enhancing outside option."

[60] Following Piketty (2016), "... if we wish to live in a fair and just society, we have to formulate more ambitious objectives which cover the distribution of income and wealth in its entirety and, consequently, the distribution of access to power and opportunities. Our ambition must be that of a society based on a fair return to labour, in other words, a fair wage and not simply a basic income."

[61] Gentilini (2023a).

[62] See Blattman (2017) and Pritchett (2017).

In sum, it can be surprising how the discussion revolving around a seemingly simple tool, the provision of cash to people, can lead to some fundamental philosophical debates, including foundational issues on economic organization. It is not my intention to tackle these big issues any further than here elaborated; however, it is important to keep them in mind, as they will at times resurface in the book (e.g., Chapters 3 and 7).

Technical and operational quandaries can make a significant difference in the performance of cash transfers. Yet the global conversation on those instruments seems increasingly detached from poverty causes and narratives. If history shows that cash transfers can be blamed for problems they didn't generate, a better connection between the problem and the intervention could help to calibrate expectations from and contribution of cash programs realistically. Such connection also means recognizing that cash "can't do it alone." For cash transfers to be effective and operate at their full potential, they need to be part of a broader framework involving a suite of interventions that can tackle the poverty dilemma at different levels.

## 2.3 A family tree: Tracing cash transfers antecedents

This section attempts to trace a rough lineage of cash-based interventions in history. It presents a summary of main traits of past programs and their treatment is expanded over the course of the book with examples drawing from a wide array of settings and historical cases. The discussion offered in this section, therefore, should be intended as laying out the illustrative contours of select programs.

An initial review of past interventions shows that a range of programs were precursors of current schemes: the distribution of cash to families with children were present in Omar's Caliphate in the 600s AD (see Chapter 5). The "Speenhamland model" was essentially a guaranteed minimum income program—and a seminal one to provide inflation-adjusted benefits.[63] The "roundsman system" and the "labor rate" were variants of modern wage subsidies; public employment programs were designed with various degrees of connection to the labor market, from labor-intensive public works to enclaved workhouses. Jobs guarantee programs, a close proxy of which is the contemporary NREGS public works program in India and to some extent the New Deal programs in the United States (Chapter 4), were embodied by Russia's "right to work" principle during the Soviet experience (Chapter 3). Figure 2.3 situates examples of historical cash transfers programs within a cube triangulating design choices around conditionality, targeting, and transfer selection.[64]

[63] Neuman (1969).

[64] Admittedly, some programs lie at the intersection of social assistance and labor market "activation" measures. That's the case for wage subsidies (and to some extent public works). There is a case to be made to incorporate them here as their difference from cash transfers are a matter of degree: public works are a form of conditional transfer based on work. And wage subsidies are similarity to public work: in both cases, the state subsidizes wages, whether for workers engaged in new works for public purposes (public

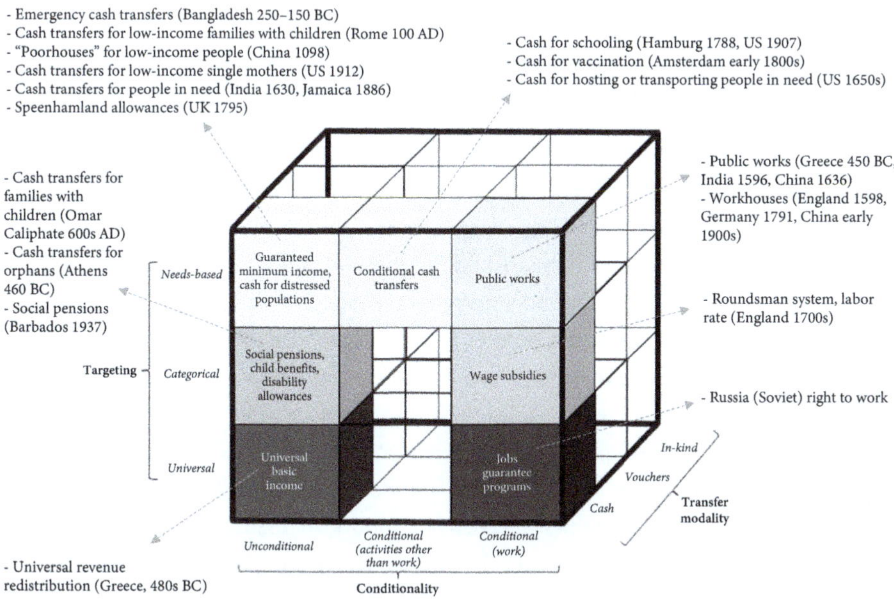


**Figure 2.3** Cash transfers cube.

*Source*: The author, based on Gentilini et al. (2020).

Over history, design choices have tended to favor some features over others. For example, there is a marked preference accorded to work-related requirements for those able to work, with adequacy of transfers being parsimonious. An array of different work-related activities was provided to able-bodied populations ("indoor relief"). Non-work-related services and relief to infirm, seniors, widows, and other vulnerable groups were established ("outdoor relief"). To manage incentives, the size of transfers was modest, ranging from meager payments in Victorian workhouses to Luther's dictum that "the poor should neither freeze nor starve."[65]

In a similar vein, cash transfers were seldom purely "unconditional." Some of these conditions envisioned adherence to expected societal codes of behavior. For example, in 1880s Amsterdam, recipients were required to behave "decently" in society.[66] Detailed records from the village of Great Burstead, Essex, in the 1820s provide insights into possible reasons for curbing assistance.[67] These include keeping pets without overseers' permission and failing to attend church services (personally or not allowing family members to do so). In the latter case, a similar obligation was present in Doncaster (in 1557) and Abingdon (in 1558), where beneficiaries were instructed to attend daily services with seats arranged in a special area of the church.[68]

works) or for workers to be employed or retained in existing, mostly private enterprises (wage subsidies). Those forms of subsidies are considered "categorical" in the cube because they tend to be directed to particular sectors and profile of beneficiaries, like "vulnerable youth" (as such they do present an element of "needs").

[65] Lindemann (1990, p. 14).

[66] Van Leeuwen (1993).

[67] Lindert (2004).

[68] McIntosh (2012).

There were also miscellaneous reasons, like "appearing in unbecoming dress," "being saucy," and excessive alcohol consumption.[69] Relatedly, the idea of moral worth underpinned the provision of cash transfers to the "shamefaced poor" (Box 2.2).

## Box 2.2 A "Silent Gift" to the Shamefaced Poor

The shamefaced poor were impoverished families whose welfare was somewhere between the elite and the poor and subsequently experienced a downturn in living conditions for reasons beyond their control.[a] The struggles of the German "Fallen Artisan" documented in broadsheets around 1535 epitomizes such condition. This class of shamefaced poor was helped with discretion to safeguard respectability (in 1527 Hamburg, a group of *declassé* was protected by a shield of anonymity and wouldn't be listed among "common paupers"). In 1531 France, such category of beneficiaries was the first to receive support; in 1535 Toulouse they were reported as *pauvres honteux*, and in May 1548 Grenoble introduced a list of shamefaced poor people. The Spanish *envergonzantes* were already recognized prior to the 1540 Castilian poor law. Already in 1506, there is reference to "decayed gentlefolks" in Venice whose identity was kept secret when issuing begging licenses. Such group was also known elsewhere in the Italian peninsula as *poverty vergognosi*: this group was one of the 34 types of "vagabonds" who in 1621 was described as "... people ashamed of their needs that would rather die than making their condition known."[b] According to some historians, the *poverty vergognosi* drew from ex-wealthy backgrounds, although the exact boundaries of the concept are contested.[c] In the early 1800s, the charitable organization of *Congregazione di San Martino "detta dei Buonomini"* in Florence was designed to support impoverished nobles. In Turin, the shamefaced poor were, alongside distressed artisans, the largest category claiming assistance. Around the same time, Amsterdam's municipality supported about 800 shamefaced families. Such "silent gifts" involved sparing the recipient from queuing for assistance, which instead could be collected at the home of the poor relief guardians. If the applicant were Catholic, the *schaamsarmen* condition would need to be validated by a confessor confirming the applicant's decent religious conduct, descent, and impoverished conditions. Some of the names of the shamefaced were registered on a separate book, while others were kept in complete secrecy: only one guardian knew their identity, which would be handed over to his successor.

[69] According to a legislation of 1792, a person that spent money in places like alehouses or that didn't apportion a proper amount of earnings to support his family was to be considered "idle and disorderly" (Ribton-Turner 1887).

[a] The box draws from Beckerman Davis (1991), Day and Schiele (2013), Geremek (1994), Jojima (1997), Lindemann (1990), Maldini (1978), McStay Adams (2023a), Pullan (1971), van Leeuwen (1993), and Woolf (1986).
[b] Nobili (1621, p. 49), translated from Italian.
[c] For example, Hughes-Johnson (2017) contested the notion that the poveri vergognosi were exclusively impoverished noblemen or drawing from merchant classes only. Instead of interpreting them as a separate category, she argued that the poveri vergognosi involved certain features—like a refusal to beg, a loss of honor, being pious and "upright" citizens—applicable to a wider share of society.

Sometimes behavioral and moral criteria were formally codified in an agreement between the state and beneficiaries. In 1788, cash transfers beneficiaries in Hamburg received a printed copy of the "Instructions for the Poor." These were "a sort of contract [that] earnestly and emphatically admonished to labor" and send children to school.[70] The instructions laid out the terms of assistance: among the clauses, excessive alcohol consumption or playing the lottery would constitute a breach in the contract.[71] Around the same period, cash beneficiaries in the city of Elberfeld had to keep a "wages book" where the employer would notify instances of idleness and bad behavior.[72]

A true contractual agreement was forged in Chicago between the state legislature and beneficiaries. In the 1930s, a legal hiccup was encountered while planning for a cash distribution: about a century earlier, in 1834, the state's attorney general had declared cash grants illegal on the basis that spending items by beneficiaries are unknown. A creative solution was identified in 1935: monthly checks would be compounded by a beneficiary declaration to be compiled, signed, and returned to the Auditor of Public Accounts. This committed the beneficiary use of cash for "necessities of life" and constituted a legal warrant for the payment (Box 2.3).

## Box 2.3 A Contract between the State and Cash Recipients in Chicago, 1935

The text of the contract was included in an Opinion issued on December 10, 1935. The agreement began with a letter directed to the perspective beneficiary by the Illinois Emergency Relief Commission and read as follows: "Dear Sir, [p]ursuant to your application for relief and an examination thereof, and based on your representation that you are a person who is destitute and in necessitous circumstances, the Illinois Emergency Relief Commission has made an award to you of the amount of $____ for the relief and support of yourself and your family for the period from ____19__

[70] Lindemann (1990, p. 145).
[71] De Schwenitz (1943).
[72] Chance (1897).

to ____ 19__. The Commission, in the discharge of the duty imposed on it by law, hereby undertakes to furnish you with the sum of $____ for the period mentioned above, upon the condition that this sum be used by you for the necessities of life and for the uses and purposes specified on the margin of this letter." A monthly budget was then laid out, with eight key expenditures that needed to be filled in terms of cash allocations to rent, food, gas, light, fuel, clothing, medical care, and other needs.

The recipient would sign a declaration included in the form, stating that "I am the person addressed in the foregoing letter. I am destitute and in necessitous circumstances, without means to provide support for myself and my family. I have relied on the commitment contained in your letter, and certify that the money furnished to me will be used to procure the necessities of life." The form was to be submitted in person to the District Office in Chicago.

*Source*: GoUS (1935, p. 329).

Money itself has a long history as a medium of exchange (Box 2.4). However, it may not always represent a neutral conduit unaffected by society's expectations and interactions. Sociologist Viviana Zelizer unveiled how people treat money differently based on its source, purpose, and surrounding social ecosystem.[73] Her analysis documented the evolving approach that charity societies of the late 1890s and early 1900s adopted towards cash transfer beneficiaries in the United States.[74] Beneficiaries were trained in household economy and accounting practices with the view of transforming a select number of them from purported improvident spenders to competent consumers.[75] This included frequent and lengthy training sessions and agencies personnel accompanying beneficiaries to grocery stores "to point out economies": eligibility to cash transfers largely hinged on conforming to expected efficient consumer behavior.[76] Similarly, ethnographic studies show that a transfer of money can be interpreted as a tool of empowerment or patronage pending on how money is entangled with social, moral, and political narratives.[77] Modern research

[73] Zelizer (1997).
[74] See also Greeley (2022).
[75] In the early 1900s, charities "established separate home-economics departments, thereby formally integrating consumerist expertise into social-work practice [ . . . ] designed to rehabilitate dependent families" (Zelizer 1997, p. 153).
[76] Zelizer (1997, p. 120) recounts the story of "Mrs. C," a widow with six children of Italian descent who in the early 1920s received assistance from the Columbus Family Service Society. She would receive $10/week in "food orders" or vouchers to be used at designated stores. She had to submit written reports of her spending, but when a charity official ("visitor") discovered that she had recorded 25 cents for fresh tomatoes instead of canned ones, she admitted that she acted "extravagant." As a result, she was subject to more training on food buying and discipline (for an entire afternoon twice a week over several months), with the visitor escorting her to groceries to apply the training's concepts in practice.
[77] Greeley (2022).

also attests to the significant psychological effects that expectations can exert on beneficiaries of cash assistance.[78]

## Box 2.4 Rapid Genesis of "Money"

In his detailed essay of the birth of coinage, Robert Mundell compared tracing the genesis of money to " . . . trying to find the origin of a river with many tributaries: we find may possibilities but it is difficult to ascertain which is the main stem."[a] In fact, pending on how money is defined, its history is longstanding and may precede that of letters. As others noted, " . . . the earliest writings known to man invariably allude to money; while the earliest moneys are invariably destitute of letters."[b]

There is a longstanding, contentious debate over money's definition, origins, relationship with debit and credit systems, and temporal sequence with barter mechanisms.[c] Taking an expansive and simplified view, money has taken two main forms over human history, namely money of account (intangible debits and credits on ledgers) and money of exchange (tangible media of exchange made of paper, metal, etc.). The former form of money as an accounting mechanism was present in the Upper Paleolithic era between 43,000 to 26,000 years ago.[d] A close example is the Ishango Bone: discovered in the Democratic Republic of Congo and dated approximately 20,000–25,000 years, it presents an organized series of notches on a tally stick.[e]

Minting of coins seems to have appeared in India, China, and the cities around the Aegean Sea in the 7th century BC. Specifically, coinage was surely present in the year c. 560 BC, although there are references to earlier periods, including the year 687 BC.[f] While Aegean coins in *gold and silver* originated from the kingdom of Lydia[g] in Asia Minor and were heated and hammered with insignia, the Indian coins were punched metal disks. The Chinese coins, first developed in the Great Plain, were made of bronze with holes in the center. The introduction of coins in Italy originated from the Etruscans of Populonia in about 550 BC. Some trace the seminal issuance of banknotes in 7$^{th}$-century China. Their roots were in merchant receipts of deposit during the Tang dynasty (618–907), as merchants and wholesalers desired to avoid the heavy bulk of copper coinage in large commercial transactions. Similar arrangements became prevalent with the expansion of European trade toward the end of the Middle Ages.[h] Goods were supplied to a buyer against a bill of exchange, which constituted the buyer's promise to make payment at some specified future date.[i] Those bills emerged as a mechanism for substantial sums to be transported remotely,

[78] Jaroszewicz et al. (2022), Lassak and Schmidt (2023).

initially (in the 12th century) among merchants, and then becoming of wider use.[j]

[a] Mundell (2002, p. 2).
[b] Del Mar (1885, p. 15). Similarly, Menger (1892) asserted that "... [m]oney has not been generated by law. In its origin it is a social, and not a state-institution ... [and this] has been perfected and adjusted to the manifold and varying needs of an evolving commerce, just as customary rights have been perfected and adjusted by statute law" (p. 255). For a history of money, see also Ridgeway (1892) and Weatherford (1997).
[c] Graeber (2011), Mitchell (1913), and Wray (2012).
[d] Flegg (2002).
[e] Brooks et al. (1995).
[f] Mundell (2002).
[g] While there appears to be no evidence of images on those early silver and gold coins, later coins, apparently, exhibited a bull and lion head on one side, and irregular markings on the other. Based on research by Bolin (1958) using a sample of 61 Lydian coins, Mundell (2002) underscores that the share of gold in those coins varied between 31% and 54.9%; at the same time, their weigh was relatively uniform and varied by less than 2% (average weight was 4.7 grams). The presence of same weight and stamp, as well as different metallic content, led Mundell (2002) to suggest that Lydia was engaged in early practices of "seigniorage": "... if the government bought a pound of electrum containing 70 percent gold and turned it into coin containing 50 percent gold, it would reap the difference as seigniorage profits [...]; it was a benign alternative to increased taxation" (ibid, p. 30). As such, seigniorage can also be thought of as the degree of "overvaluation" of money.
[h] Le Goff (2012).
[i] Naismith (2018).
[j] Spufford (1988).

Historical provisions were largely limited to local residents. The principles underpinning cash assistance were mostly family based and directed to the "known." The use of family as the core focal point for provisions has been a cardinal aspect for anchoring interventions, just like appraising its members' physical ability to work has been a premier criterion for eligibility. One of the most contentious corollaries of such framework is the prohibition of begging, especially by non-residents. This could lead to fines, imprisonment, corporal punishments, deportation, and other penalties (see Chapter 5). To claim that the history of cash transfers cannot be separated from authorities' perennial attempts to curb "vagrancy" and "begging" is only a slight exaggeration. Making begging illegal (unless licensed) attracted longstanding tensions on where to draw the lines between spiritual and secular responsibilities in providing cash transfers. Such tensions would erupt in public debates such as "Alison vs Chalmers" in 1841 Scotland (Chapter 5) and "de Soto vs Robles" in 1545 Spain (Chapter 6).

There is a historical coexistence between cash and in-kind transfers. It was common for "poor relief" to provide a blend of transfer modalities. For example, in France in 1860 only 21% of assistance was provided in cash; similarly, the Dutch Poor Law of 1854 instructed that relief should be provided in kind "as much as possible."[79] As Chapter 3 argues, food and cash transfers are joined at the hip. Over the course of my historical research, it was rare to come across an example of a community, city, region, or country where assistance was entirely provided in cash: the use of cash

[79] Lindert (2004).

transfers clearly grew over time, but they were neither the sole nor the dominant form of assistance. This is echoed in today's social protection systems, where the use of food subsidies, in-kind transfers, or food vouchers may often exceed that of cash assistance.[80]

As mentioned in Chapter 1, the provision of cash transfers was often preceded by assessments and registration activities. These were present in history for a variety of purposes: for example, around 1450 BC Egypt had a comprehensive system of registration for fiscal purposes, inclusive for corvee labor (catalogues of cattle dated back to circa 2400 BC);[81] Chinese population registers of the 6th century BC were used for military conscription;[82] and democratic Athens kept citizens registers in 508 BC.[83]

Connecting the use of registries to the provision of assistance is a relatively more recent phenomenon: China itself would feature them around the year 1000 (see Chapter 4). In 1407, the city of Mantova had a *consorzio* managed by influential families featuring monthly visits to poor families by "honest" citizens.[84] The town of Azpeitia adopted a plan devised by Ignatius Loyola in 1535: under the scheme, two officials, a cleric and a layman, called *majordomos de pobres* were tasked to distribute voluntary-funded assistance to a list of poor people whose needs were assessed by the city council.[85] In 1891, Moscow officials established that " . . . aid could be provided only after investigation of each applicant [and authorities had] to produce a master register of the poor [to prevent them] from availing themselves of aid from more than one charitable agency."[86] These practices are not fundamentally dissimilar from modern "social registries."[87] Table 2.1 sketches out examples of select practices in registration present around or before the 1500s.

Frequently recurring practices also included the appointment of guardians, overseers, and other actors fulfilling similar functions. These would be "spokesmen" for poor populations and "watchdogs" over program design and administration, while providing prestige and social recognition to the upper class.[88] Such administrative foundations are discussed in the context of Chapter 5.

A multiplicity of providers played different role at various stages of cash delivery. For example, analysis conducted on Amsterdam over the period 1800–1850 reveals a plethora of institutions and hierarchy of providers.[89] Support from faith-based organizations, including Protestant, Catholic, and Jewish, were underpinned by a last-resort municipal assistance by the state. Box 2.5 illustrates the process through which municipal relief application, registration, and payment worked in practice. The reminder of the section outlines the contours of select interventions, starting with seminal versions of universal basic income.

[80] This may include, for instance, the United States, India, and Egypt (Alderman et al. 2017).
[81] Flemming (2012, p. 170).
[82] Von Glahn (2012, p. 44).
[83] Flemming (2012, p. 171).
[84] Navarrini and Belfanti (1982) show that the eight visitors were part of a larger pool of 64 elected citizens that would rotate in making visits (and undertaken other administrative functions) every six months (p. 125).
[85] Salas (1958).
[86] Lindenmeyr (1996, p. 150).
[87] See Lindert et al. (2020) for a discussion on contemporary registries.
[88] Lindemann (1990), van Leeuwen (1994).
[89] Van Leeuwen (1993, 2000).

**Table 2.1** Registries of poor relief beneficiaries, select examples up to the 1500s.

| Context (year) | Registry of low-income people/beneficiaries | Source |
|---|---|---|
| Bruges (1526) | "Let those who suffer poverty at home be registered . . . their needs ascertained." | De Schweinitz (1943, p. 31) |
| China (1080) | ". . . the Song enacted an empire-wide registration system that graded property-owning households into a set of ranks." | Von Glahn (2012, p. 52) |
| Como (1485) | ". . . beneficiaries were included in lists [ . . . ] containing key information on their civil status and living conditions." | Dubini (1982, p. 115) |
| Genova (1540) | ". . . lists of the poor had to be updated, but only including the poor residing in the city for over six months." | Grendi (1982, p. 68) |
| Grenoble (1545) | Officials ". . . decided to create registers of the poor [which was conducted] methodically, street-by-street." | Geremek (1994, p. 149–150) |
| Hamburg (1550) | "Each month the deacons were to enter the dwellings of the poor to investigate in minute detail their living conditions, family circumstances, and needs. The they were to meet to discuss their findings and decide on the best allocation of [ . . . ] moneys." | Lindemann (1990, p. 17) |
| London (1579) | "Parish officials were to maintain up to date the registers of their poor." | Geremek (1994, p. 168) |
| Lyon (1534) | ". . . a list was drawn up, based on house-to-house visits by officers of the *Aumone*, of all the poor inhabitants and the state of their need." | Zemon Davis (1968, p. 243) |
| Mantova (1591) | ". . . a census of the poor of the city was conducted, disaggregated by neighborhood." | Navarrini and Belfanti (1982, p. 131) |
| Paris (1544) | ". . . every parish was urged to draw up a list of its poor." | Geremek (1994, p. 130) |
| Ravenna (520s) | ". . . registration lists of the poor [ . . . ] are known to have been kept between 522 and 532." | Mollat (1986, p. 40) |
| Rome (church, 440s) | ". . . *matricula* [referred] to a list naming those paupers who were maintained at church expense." | Mollat (1986, p. 39) |
| Rome (food subsidies, 56 BC–2 AD) | "Pompeus, Caesar and Augustus proceeded with the formulation of lists to limit the number of beneficiaries." | Soraci (2006, p. 352–353) |
| Rheims (470), Laon (520) | ". . . it is known that the poor were registered before 470 in Rheims and around 520 in Laon." | Mollat (1986, p. 40) |

| Context (year) | Registry of low-income people/beneficiaries | Source |
|---|---|---|
| Toledo (1543) | The *Book of the Poor* included a "written record of all needy persons in the twenty-one city parishes." | Martz (1983, p. 121) |
| Valladolid (1561) | "... the 1561 registers didn't include poor people in the city's main hospitals [ ... ] In 1597 a census of the poor was taken [and those] eligible for permanent support [ ... ] were given certificates to that effect." | Geremek (1994, p. 161–162) |

*Source*: The author.

## Box 2.5 Mixed Provisions in Practice: Applying for Cash Transfers in 1800s Amsterdam

In the 1800s, each of Amsterdam's districts had a warden who acted as first point of contact in the relief application process: the claimant would approach the warden, who may subsequently issue a "certificate of poverty" following a visit to the applicant's home—a practice at the intersection of religious and secular administration that has been documented also in Islamic contexts.[a] Such certificate would be submitted by the perspective beneficiary to the Municipal Charity office alongside other documents, such one or more extracts from the baptismal, birth and marriage registers. Additional medical certificates were required regarding sickness, and witnesses were often involved to attest the truthfulness of applications. Additional information from former employers could be sought to validate applicants' willingness to work, and the police could be asked to verify residency.[b] Auditions at the Municipal Charity were held at the beginning of summer and winter. If the regent had the application approved, district officers were then directed to enter beneficiaries' information in the registration book. Such data included name, age, marital status, place of birth, illnesses or disability, plus similar information on spouses and children. These details were then passed on to the "license women" who would carry payments at the home of beneficiaries if their mobility was constrained by disability, age, or large families. Inspectors would subsequently visit beneficiaries at least once a year.

*Source*: Looijesteijn and van Leeuwen (2012).

[a] Ribton-Turner (1887, p. 572) describes the Turkish system of the late 1880s. To receive support from one of the Imaret religious institutions (which are themselves financed by revenues collected by government's Evcaf in charge of administering the Islamic waqfs support), an applicant had to present to Evcaf officials a certificate released by the Imam declaring his poverty conditions. Against such

certificate, a ticket is released by the Evcaf entitling to access Imaret assistance. On the administration of waqfs, see also Kuran (2001).

[b] Migrants from towns like Leiden and Rotterdam would be issued "letters of surety" involving a certified guarantee by an organization or a person to pay for relief of the named individuals within a certain period (two to three years in the case of Leiden).

## Universal basic income

The regular distribution of money to all citizens in a polity is, as discussed in the previous section, referred to as UBI. There are ancient antecedents to the program dating back about 2,500 years. While they may lack the monthly "regularity" in payments and their consistency in transfer amount, UBI programs in antiquity were akin to Alaska's contemporary dividend scheme.[90]

Information on the Greek UBI programs is limited and fragmented, but it may still allow to reconstruct a plausible set to features and practices. According to multiple sources, Athens and Sifnos seemed to have UBI-type programs providing cash to all citizens around the 6th century BC. These were financed by revenues from silver mines.[91] Other cases might have adopted similar schemes.[92] In Athens, payments reached about 30,000 people.[93] The uniform redistribution of cash was rooted in the belief that citizens had a legitimate claim on state revenues from "common" properties. As such, "distributions of cash had to some extent taken the place of land-holding as the symbol of equal share-holding in the *polis*. [ . . . ] [T]here was nothing unusual in the Athenian custom of sharing out the proceeds of the state silver mines among the citizens."[94] Distributions to each citizen (*viritim*) occurred at a rate of ten drachmas per person,[95] with a dedicated decadrachm minted for the occasion (Figure 2.4).[96] Such sum was ten times the daily wage of unskilled labor.[97]

The practice continued until 483 BC when, as anticipated in the book's Preface, a new windfall of silver emerged from the mines of Laurium.[98] Alas, with Aristides's

[90] For Alaska's program, see Gentilini et al. (2020).

[91] Osborne (2006) affirmed that Sifnos used to redistribute revenues among its citizens before "the early fifth century BC" (p. 6). As chronicled by Herodotos, "the people of Siphons [...] used to divide the among themselves the money which came in from the mines every year" (Herodotos 1890, p. 238).

[92] Samons (2000, p. 60) appears to include Thasos among other possible experiences. The case of Lyttos in Crete is also interesting: Latte (1947) refers to "distributions of money that took place on the [festival of] Theodaisia and on May 1" (p. 71). See also Guarducci (1933) and Guizzi (1999).

[93] Samons (2000) refers to distributions to "each man" (p. 60), hence likely making distributions limited by gender.

[94] Humphreys (1978, p. 145). A similar point on sharing was also underscored by Newman et al. (1990): "[r]esources gained, such as a tribute or payments from confederate cities, were distributed among the citizens, as was conquered land" (p. 109). Also, Garnsey (1990) noted that "democratic Athenians believed that all citizens had a stake in the revenues of the state, and in the heyday of empire there was wealth to distribute, but [different from imperial Rome] it was cash rather than food which was made available [...]" (p. 140).

[95] Roselli (2009, p. 8)

[96] Seltman (1924, p. 107). The coin wasn't a "common currency," it was of large size (it weighed 675 g) and included the head of Athena and an owl. It was issued at least in three or four occasions before its interruption.

[97] A drachma, which was equivalent to six obols, corresponded to the daily wage for unskilled labor in 408 BC (the daily cost for food was about two obols or one third of the daily wage) (Jevons 1896, p. 474–475).

[98] Holland (2005, p. 220).

**Figure 2.4** Special decadrachm issued for universal payments.
*Source*: Head (1911, p. 371).

ostracism[99] in 482 BC, Athenians voted for ending cash distributions and to use the newfound proceeds to boost the city's defense capabilities.

## Child assistance

Alongside universal distributions, the city-state of Athens also featured more targeted interventions in the 5th and 4th centuries BC. Cash payments were delivered to war-orphaned children, disabled populations, and people maimed in conflict.[100] Assistance to orphans seems to date about 460 BC, and in 431 BC they would receive an obol/day (or roughly 15% of the unskilled labor wage rate).[101]

There were seminal forms of conditional cash transfers "as we know them," like those in Germany in the late 1700s discussed in Chapter 3 (which also covers how, in early 1800s Amsterdam, children of cash recipients had to attend school and be vaccinated against smallpox[102]—a practice also recorded in contexts like French-annexed Tuscany).[103] By the end of the 19th century, various conditional, "Learnfare" cash transfers emerged in the United States (Box 2.6).

### Box 2.6 "Learnfare" as Early Conditional Cash Transfers

In 1987, waivers were granted for states experimentation with Aid to Families with Dependent Children (AFCD), with Wisconsin implementing the first "learnfare" program. In terms of the program's benefit structure, " . . . compliance with

[99] In January or February of each year, Athenians were asked in the assembly whether they wished to hold an ostracism (if approved, it would be held two months later). At least 6,000 votes had to be cast against the person who was to be banished. Ostracism was only practiced in the 400s BC, with Aristides's possibly being the third (the first one being in 487 BC; see Lang 1990, p. 4–5).
[100] Ober (1989).
[101] Dillon (1995).
[102] Van Leeuwen (1993).
[103] Woolf (1986).

the Learnfare provisions is monitored by the county income maintenance office. Each month, the agency mails a list of students to be monitored to the appropriate school district. The schools send back a record of the number of full days the monitored student is absent. A monitored student may have no more than two unexcused, full-day absences in a month. If the record shows more, the family's AFDC check is reduced in the second month after the noncompliant behavior. To set the amount of the sanction, the noncompliant member of the AFDC family is ignored in calculating the grant amount. Sanctions vary from $58 in large families to $192 in two-person families, the average sanction being about $100. If a sanctioned dependent teen (a nonparent) is the only minor in the AFDC family, a partial grant will be continued for three months, after which the case will be closed."[a]

There were earlier precedents to "Learnfare." In 1888, the 15th Annual Conference of Charities recommended that " . . . [t]he only course we can suggest [for single mothers is] that if she ceases to use proper effort to bring up her children to be decent and respectable, *to send them to school* and to teach them to be industrious when of sufficient age, relief will be withheld, and their children otherwise provided for."[b] Conditional cash transfers were in fact implemented in Buffalo in 1907, including education and health conditions: " . . . [w]here a family has continuing aid, the society demands that the children go regularly to school, and requires a weekly report from the teacher as to their attendance. When the society is supporting a family it also provides and insists upon competent medical examination of the children so that they need not grow up defective and unable to earn."[c]

[a] Corbett et al. (1989, p. 4). The authors also lay out the formidable implementation challenges associated with the program at its early implementation phases.
[b] NCSW (1888, p. 146–147, italics added).
[c] Feder (1936, p. 205).

## Guaranteed minimum income: The Speenhamland model

The Speenhamland program in England was at the center of controversies that emerged on cash transfers in the 1800s. The scheme was introduced in a context of crisis and following the decision taken in the Speenhamland's Pelican Inn, in the county of Berkshire, on May 6, 1795.[104] Chaired by the parliamentarian Charles Dundas, the meeting followed the decision of a local Court the previous month (April 14). In that occasion, Dundas had successfully made the case for the need to raise the wage

[104] Speenhamland is often quoted as an early example of a basic income (Bregman 2017). It is curious to note that a seminal proponent of basic income, Thomas Paine, wrote his pamphlet (*Agrarian Justice Opposed to Agrarian Law, and to Agrarian Monopoly*) making the case for a universal payment in 1795–1796, or exactly the period of Speenhamland's launch (e.g., see discussion in Jager and Zamora Vargas 2023, p. 17–18). See also Rose (1966a,b) for a review of the poor laws around the Speenhamland period.

of laborers to subsistence level. The Speenhamland meeting, attended by 18 people (seven of whom were clergymen), was therefore called for devising the mechanisms to increase salaries.[105]

While there appear to be no official minutes of the event, it contained a resolution that discarded minimum wages[106] and instead adopted a cash transfer pegged on the price of bread, compounded by a soft recommendation for farmers to increase wages.[107] Economists Beatrice and Sidney Webb would recount that instead of "... putting it on employers to accommodate their industries to the minimum conditions required in the public interest," the choice was to "... subsidizing employers out of public funds so as to enable their industries to be carried on *as they were*, and yet permit the workers to live."[108]

The scheme would ensure a minimum standard whereby parishes would fill the gap between wages and a floor based on the price of bread.[109] The benefit size was set at three gallons of loaves/week for working men; their family members, including wife and each child, would need one and a half gallons/week.[110] On that basis, a conversion table would then adjust the floor to bread prices based of specified ratios: for example, if the price of a gallon loaf was 1s, then enough relief should be added by the parish to get the worker's income to 3s; if married, it was raised to 4s 6d; if having one child, to 6s; and so on. Figure 2.5 illustrates the minimum floor of the scheme. Speenhamland was not an unconditional transfer. If employment in the private sector (mostly farmers) wasn't available, workers reported weekly to the parish overseer who would direct them either to the roundsman system or the labor rate (with again the possible difference to the minimum threshold met by the parish). Many parishes would grant unconditional relief only upon receipt of three or more letters from farmers stating that employment was not available. In some cases, parishes would add more local criteria and conditionalities.

It has been argued that the rapid spread of the Speenhamland model can be in part attributed to its handy, pragmatic conversion table.[111] Already in the summer of 1795, the bread scale was documented in Winslow: there, magistrates sent orders

[105] Parker (2023, p. 28–29) reports the meeting's official notes as published in the Reading Mercury on May 11, 1795.

[106] Various national legislations attempted to introduce a minimum wage, although unsuccessfully. However, there are localized experiences that attempted to index-linked wages to prices. For example, Hammond and Hammond (1913) show that on the exact same day the magistrates gathered in Speenhamland in 1795, another meeting at Basingstoke chaired by the mayor directed the fixing of laborer wages in accordance with the price of wheat without any reference to parish relief.

[107] The meeting also recommended overseers to cultivate land, "with little burthen of the occupiers of the land as possible," for potatoes and distribute to workers one quarter of the crop, selling the rest at one were also called to purchase fuel and retail it at subsidized level. According to Hammond and Hammond (1913), "... meshes of the Poor Laws were spread over the entire labor system. The labourers, stripped of their ancient rights and their ancient possessions, refused a minimum wage and allotments, were given instead a universal system of pauperism" (p. 141).

[108] Webb and Webb (1927, p. 423). Farmers feared that an increase in wages during crises would have been challenging to reduce in normal times (see Oxley 1974).

[109] Boyer (1990).

[110] Given the localized level of provision, country-wide data on the generosity (e.g., relative to agricultural wages) of those transfers is scant. As an indicative level for 1795, Blaug (1963) estimated benefit–wage ratios of 0.5–0.67 for "Midlands or Southern counties."

[111] Hammond and Hammond (1913).

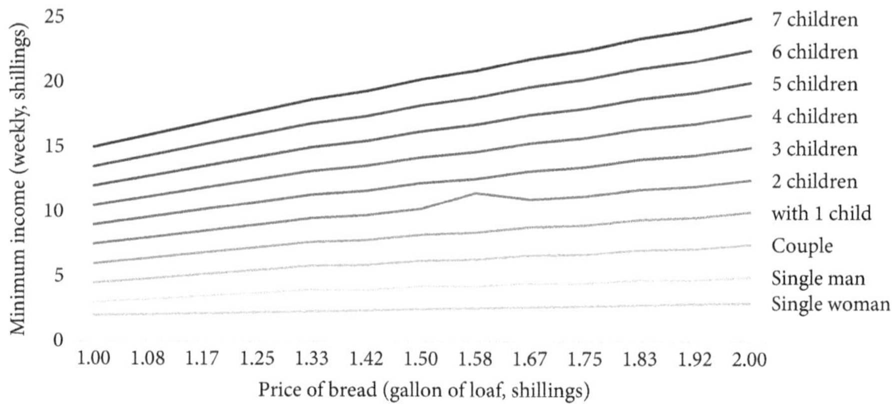


**Figure 2.5** Guaranteed minimum income based on Speenhamland bread scale (1795).
*Source*: The author, based on original Speenhamland table. A Price unit was consolidated: given that 1 shilling (s) = 12 pennies (d), the graph combined shillings (s) and pennies (d) into shillings. For example, if the price of the loaf is 2(s) and 10(d), then the unified price in "s" will be 2.83, where 0.83 is the result of (10 "d"/12= 0.83 "s").

to parishes to raise the income of laborers with weekly sums variable by family size. There are accounts of similar earlier practices: on January 13, 1795, justices in Oxfordshire had directed overseers to ensure a minimum level of income needed by a family. This consisted of 6s/week for a couple; 7s/week if one or two children are present; and for every additional child, no less than a shilling should be added.[112] Why and how the Speenhamland model would become controversial is mentioned later in the chapter and is more extensively covered in Chapter 6.

## Roundsman system and labor rate

The British roundsman program may resemble modern wage subsidies. Under the scheme, seasonally unemployed laborers were offered to farmers at reduced or subsidized wages, with parishes filling the difference relative to a minimum standard. The system was operational before Speenhamland, with cases reported already in 1792 in the parishes of Bottisham and Burwell.[113] There were different models of implementation, with some parishes requiring all labor-hiring farmers to recruit a share of the unemployed, which were then rotated among such farmers; another practice was, as mentioned in Chapter 1, to adopt a voluntary system, with the unemployed being forced to "go the rounds" (knocking on people's doors) in search of work, with farmers having the option to decline such offers. Those that ended up not being hired would receive a daily allowance slightly below that of employed roundsmen. According to examples from 1792, those unconditional allowances were about 16% lower than roundsmen wages.[114] The roundsman wage rate level also varied locally, with its size being set either by farmers themselves or by parishes. In some cases, workers were auctioned out, with the roundsmen going to the lowest bidder.

[112] Hammond and Hammond (1913, p. 139).
[113] Boyer (1990).
[114] Boyer (1990).

A variant of the roundsman system, the labor rate, was adopted starting in the 1820s. Under the scheme, parishes would place workers in private sector employment at wages fixed by the parish and highly subsidized for the employer. As such, the poor rate is a partial wage subsidy scheme used during seasonal unemployment (e.g., winter season). The total wage bill for the season was computed based on age and marital status.[115] The cost was then divided among ratepayers in the parish. A ratepayer could then contribute by either hiring laborers at the wage rate set by the parish or paying the corresponding poor rate amount. Labor rates are distinct from the "poor rates," or the system of British poor relief financing (Box 2.7).

## Box 2.7 The Financing of Transfers via Poor Rates: The Road from Local to Central Financing

The literature on the history of financing social services in general, and social protection in particular, across Europe is rich.[a] Political scientist Mark Dincecco is fusing academic research on fiscal and parliamentary reforms into an integrated analysis of institutional change. Such emerging field helps explain the transition toward effective states as the result of two sequential forces: on one hand, a process of fiscal centralization whereby tax bases were expanded by consolidating the myriads of provinces under a unified national fiscal regimes ruled by authorities (monarchs). Such tax reforms implied that rulers could exert control over greater revenues. On the other hand, an increased authority in revenues sources was counterbalanced by a process of power restrictions in which parliaments established control and oversight over fiscal spending.[b]

In Britain, poor relief was financed via a local tax known as "poor rates." According to historical accounts, the first compulsory poor rate was established in London in 1547. This was earmarked to support residents of its hospitals.[c] The poor rate coexisted alongside other taxes. For example, legislation of 1598 required parishes to establish rates for supporting jails and maimed soldiers, the latter requiring revenues of at least 20s/year.[d] Until 1850, the poor rate was levied not on the owner, but on the *occupier* of properties like land, houses, and buildings. Four considerations emerge: first, in the early days of the law, assessments for poor rates by overseers were calculated in accordance with the occupiers' "ability to pay." Estimating such ability was considered " . . . an imprecise principle which could lead to endless argument and the tendency was to settle for some standard basis of assessment."[e] After some initial experimentation with different options, such standard assessment was anchored in the rental value of property. In this way, tax charges were assessed against a certain share of the declared annual rental of the immovable properties. The measure

[115] See Boyer (1990, Appendix B, p. 49 for a wage scale for labor rate in Wisborough Green parish, 1832.

provided a reasonably accurate proxy of wealth and was able to reflect improvements that may have occurred on a year-to-year basis. Yet demonstrations erupted in high-poverty areas, such as the iconic Poplar protest.[f]

Second, in England and Wales 67% of the poor rates were assessed on land rents, which meant that the fiscal burden fell mostly on farmers (who themselves had to pay rents to landlords as well as tithe).[g] While the occupier ended up making the payment, ultimately the cost was borne by property owners through lower rents.[h]

Third, while the system worked reasonably well, there were loopholes. For example, in cases of ports and mercantile activities property took the form not of land or buildings, but of ships moored at quaysides and stock-in-trade. These led to several disputes in mercantile parishes. It also engendered discontent especially in mountainous, scarcely populated areas where mining activities would frequently fluctuate. In those cases, since it was farmers and shopkeepers as occupiers that had to pay for poor relief in case of unemployment, it " . . . was a clear case of one sector causing poverty for which another had to pay."[i]

Fourth, waivers were granted. Low-income people were in theory liable to pay based on the house they rented; in practice, they were largely exempted by the overseers. An act of 1814 started to requiring waivers to be granted only if the inability to pay is assessed and approved by two justices. The situation changed in 1834. The harsher application of the law de facto resulted in the reduction of the number of poor people exempted from paying the poor rate. For instance, in the extreme case of the Harling division of the Guiltcross Union, magistrates expected poor dwellers to pay the rates and finance their own relief. This led to seizures of the indigents' assets, notably clothing and bedding. In turn, dispossessed populations overwhelmed the capacity of the union workhouse to absorb them. Eventually, poor rate waivers were authorized.[j]

The challenge that local parishes faced in navigating the tension between, on one hand, waiving rates based on needs and, on the other hand, ensuring that financing was available to meet those needs, cannot be understated. In settings where towns included a limited number of parishes, or even a single parish—or where those parishes were socially and economically homogenous—such problem wasn't particularly acute, that is, financing and needs would generally balance out. The problem emerged more starkly in contexts where (i) there were severe economic disruptions, like the closing of mines (in those cases, up to the mid-1600s magistrates had the power to levy a rate on one parish to support another in distress), or (ii) in towns with multiple and diversified parishes, where " . . . responsibility for poor relief [was taken] from the town government and giving it to the parish."[k] It was in the latter cases that the system showed its limits, that is, being one built in a context of simpler needs and that didn't fully adapt to evolving socio-economic conditions. In fact, the landmark 1834 law left the financing model largely intact. Union-level workhouses were still to be funded by parishes. The mechanism was regressive: single parishes had to calculate a three-year average of their spending on relief, and that would be computed to estimate the share of the individual parishes' contribution to the union-level common fund for the workhouse. This implied that parishes with higher poor relief expenditures were paying more than those with lower levels. Such situation led some parishes to look for creative ways to finance the poor rates. For example, in 1839 the Loddon and Clavering parishes financed poor relief by tapping highway funds. Basically, they employed the poor on building and maintaining roads since that model was less expensive than workhouse costs.[l]

A consequential act was approved in 1861 that changed the basis for estimating the parishes' contribution to the common fund: these would be calculated on the average three-year expenditures and hinged on an assessment of parish-level properties. Another breakthrough came in 1896, when legislation established central–local co-financing of poor relief: the rates on agricultural land were to be rated at half their value, while the central government's Exchequer paid the remaining half through a national tax on income.

[a] See for example Webber and Wildawsky (1986).
[b] Dincecco (2011, 2017) and Dincecco and Onorato (2017). See, of course, also the classic work by Tilly (1990).
[c] Slack (1988).
[d] McIntosh (2012).
[e] Oxley (1974, p. 47).
[f] The East London borough of Poplar was renowned not only because its experiment with workhouses (see discussion on workhouses). In the early 20th century, it presented high levels of poverty and unemployment, as well a strong sense of community belonging its inhabitants. While needs were dire, resources for relief were limited due to Poplar's lower ratable value of properties relative to wealthier boroughs—in other words, the council had to set a much higher rate to match the amount produced by low rates in a wealthy boroughs). In addition, its council faced the looming prospect of large increase in taxation from the national government to fund centralized services (e.g., police, water). In 1921, the Poplar council proposed an alternative plan, i.e., to only increase the rates for expenditures for the borough itself while refusing to pay the national rate. Following court litigation, thirty councilors were imprisoned for six weeks, igniting public protests and demonstrations. Eventually, in the winter of 1921 new legislation "... went a significant way towards equalising tax discrepancy between wealthier and poorer boroughs" (Iglikowski-Broad 2021). See also Rose (1990, 1988).
[g] Digby (1978).
[h] Allen (1992), Solar (1995).
[i] Oxley (1974, p. 49).
[j] Digby (1978).
[k] Oxley (1974, p. 50).
[l] Digby (1978).

Some examples of "cash-for-care" initiatives also emerge, including payments, tax credits, and subsidies. For example, in colonial America, towns and parishes employed doctors to treat low-income people.[116] Transaction costs, such as

[116] As an illustration, on October 29, 1656, the Boston Town Meeting agreed that "... Mr. Wales had 6 shillings abated of his tax rate for this year in regard to his poverty" (Trattner 1974, p. 18). In 1664, Boston's selectmen paid a doctor, Mr. Thomas Oliver, five pounds for seven months' attendance upon a

transportation to health facilities, could be subsidized.[117] In other cases, the town would pay for hosting people in need. Low-income people could be auctioned out to the lowest bidder: these occurred at the village tavern on Saturday evenings following the town meeting. The transaction involved a whole family being hosted in the farmer's private house, with towns subsidizing clothing and medical care.[118] Similarly, in the late 1800s communes in Russia would pay one of its families to care for an elderly person or orphan; this complemented assistance "in turn," or households taking turns in feeding and sheltering fellow villagers in need.[119]

## Public works

The use of public works dates back millennia. In part, because of the fluid definition of (and correlation between) "unemployed," "idle," and "vagrant" populations, the practice of "putting people to work" has been an integral part of relief systems and the related management of "begging" (see Chapter 5).[120]

Under the Roman emperor Vespasian (69–79), the use of higher-intensity mechanical technology for stone-moving was rejected in favor of labor-intensive public works that would absorb larger shares of the workforce; similar works to employ the "undisciplined" were undertaken by the Greek general Pericles (495–429 BC).[121] In Spain, idlers and vagabonds could be forcibly employed, including in Toro in 1369, Burgos in 1379, and Briviesca in 1387.[122] The Inca empire used mandatory public works for various goals, including ensuing urban food supplies, military functions, and charity (Box 2.8). In 1538, St. Michael Spurriergate in York paid "for going to Tadcaster to fetch lime"; in 1517–1518, the Holy Trinity parish in Cambridge compensated for "cleaning the gutter beside the church wall and removing dust from the church."[123] There were also more skilled tasks, such as Saffron Walden paying in 1470 for "writing up the churchwardens' annual account"; and the 1520s, St. Mary in London provided cash to "blow the organ at services."[124] In 1860s Sweden, officials considered work activities for the unemployed poor, like labor-intensive roadworks as well as self-employment-oriented handicrafts, "an advantage which cannot be quantified."[125]

needy person; other doctors had their tax remitted or reduced for performing such services, while taxes could be reduced based on need (ibid).

[117] According to Virginia's colonial records of the mid 1650s " . . . towns and parishes even paid for the sick poor to visit health spas. [They would] agree with some person on the best terms they can to carry [the sick to a health center] for the recovery of his health" (Trattner 1974, p. 19).

[118] Trattner (1974, p. 18).

[119] Lindenmeyr (1996, p. 52–53).

[120] Nicholls (1854). He quoted a 1717 legislation ordering persons convicted of various offenses and who are liable to be whipped or burned in the hand, "or have been ordered to any workhouse," may be sent for seven years to American colonies and " . . . be made over to the use of any person who shall contract for such transportation" (p. 4).

[121] Garraty (1978, p. 13).

[122] Flynn (1989, p. 87). A couple of centuries later, in 1597 Valladolid undertook a census of beggars so that "worthy ones were properly cared for" (Garraty 1978, p. 24).

[123] Garraty (1978), Quigley (1996a).

[124] See McIntosh (2012) and Slack (1988).

[125] Forsberg and Bohman (2023, p. 11). However, under certain circumstances Sweden condemned vagabonds to public works for a duration between six months and a year: works were conducted for the

## Box 2.8 "Friends of the Poor"? Public Works and Granaries in the Inca Empire (c. 1400–1532)

During the expansion of the Inca empire from the 1400s to the 1530s, an array of public works was in place to mitigate the effects of natural hazards and enhance food productivity.[a] These activities played a central role in the empire, although with marked differences between the capital Cuzco and other regions. In the former case, a core objective was to assure a steady urban food supply. Rulers intensified agriculture and built food storage complexes, with food directed to Cuzco's population (chiefly soldiers and nobles, as well as being used for official celebrations). During times of distress, food supplies were tapped to buffer the city against food shortfalls. Food transfers were also provided to citizens when sudden shocks materialized (e.g., fires). The labor for increased production and storage capabilities was extracted as tribute from provincial regions: while manpower for building agricultural infrastructure around the capital was fed, provided with land, and equipped with tools of production, the cost of imperial demand for forced labor was likely borne by the periphery in the form of disrupted local social support networks. Outside the capital, the empire featured administrative centers and waystations (*tampu*) of varying size along principal roads to be maintained by local populations. Such stations housed, among others, storage depots to feed laborers in public works projects, and were used during religious festivities (e.g., sun cult), and war-related activities (feeding soldiers).[b] Food supplies that remained unused from those official functions were redistributed to local people in need, like the disabled, widows, and orphans (*waqcha*). Such practice projected an image of the ruler and his wife as benevolent "friends of the poor." Surplus staples could also be used to support communities during crises, although food was not distributed for free (people borrowing food in times of need were expected to repay the debt as hardships soothed).

[a] This box is based on Covey (2020), Covey et al. (2016), LeVine (1992), and Schreiber and Topic (1985).

[b] Storehouses structures involved groups of small circular or rectangular units, with the largest depots hosting about a thousand units.

The point in many cases was not to generate work, but avoiding idleness: in England, parishes "... forced the applicants to give up a certain portion of their time by confining them in a gravel-pit [ ... ] or obliging them to attend a roll-call several times in the day, or by any contrivance which shall prevent their leisure from becoming means either of profit or of amusement."[126] In Massachusetts Bay, a General Court decree

army in a special station or, for a reduction of a third in working time, in prison cells separate from the rest of the inmate population (Ribton-Turner 1887).

[126] GoUK (1834a), quoted in Boyer (1990, p. 21).

of 1633 made "voluntary idleness" illegal and work compulsory. Penalties for those that spent their time "idly or unprofitably" included becoming indentured servants, whipping and deportation from town, or jail.[127]

Public works were not just manual activities. A type of "cash-for-services" took shape with the Greek *misthos* present in at least 403 BC. These were payments for citizens for undertaking jury service conceived to reduce the risk of political patronage and compensate for attendance opportunity costs.[128] In Athens there were about 6,000 jurors serving for 200–300 days a year. One estimate for the payment rate was three obols (half of the daily wage for unskilled labor). There is a debate on the socio-economic status of jurors, but such role seems to have been pursued also by vulnerable populations as an additional income source.[129]

## Moving indoor: Workhouses

Workhouses were a form of public works conducted in designated buildings premises. They were widespread in England, but later emerged in the United States, China, and various other contexts.[130] For example, a report of the Russian government dated 1682 proposed the establishment of workhouses based on "the growing interest in European ideas and practices" on the matter by the Moscow elite.[131]

Workhouses fused prevailing relief principles with regimented factory-type work activities. The level of payment received for the work performed indoor was locally determined.[132] Small performance-based amounts of "reward money" were provided to children and adults as incentives to exceed their production quota established for their age and ability.[133] While workhouses tend to present a range of common features, they also offered some diversity in terms of underlying philosophy and objectives. Chapter 3 further discusses such differentiation, with select pre-1800s approaches being relatively more "industrial" than the later "corrective" approaches of the 19th century. These two competing objectives, however, were often conflated in practice and their conflict contributed to the demise of such institutions.

The system of English workhouses has been subject of a rich literature.[134] Building upon the requirement of the British 1572 law instituting "abiding places," parishes were instructed to assemble " . . . a convenient stock of flax, hemp, wool, thread,

[127] Trattner (1974).

[128] On patronage in Athens, see Millett (1989). For poverty in the city-state, see Rosivach (1991).

[129] Dillon (1995).

[130] For the British case, see the comprehensive workhouse encyclopedia by Higginbotham (2012). A rapid chronology of workhouse introduction may include the following: London Bridewell (1555), Amsterdam (1596), Copenhagen (1605), Bern (1614), Basel (1616), Lyons (1622), Madrid (1622), Brussels (1624) and Stockholm (1624) (De Schwenitz 1943, Garraty 1978, Higginbotham 2012). In Germany, locations that adopted workhouses included "Hansa cites that enjoyed close commercial and social relations with Amsterdam" (Frohman 2008, p. 35): Bremen (1608), Lubeck (1613), Hamburg (1611) and Danzig (1629). These were followed by Nuremberg (1670), Vienna (1671), Frankfurt (1679), Munich (1682), and Berlin (1687). By the end of 1700s, about 110 workhouses were present in Germany (excluding Austria) (Frohman 2008).

[131] Lindenmeyr (1996, p. 29).

[132] For 1905, Fowler (2007) reported an upper bound level of 2s 6d per adult/week and 1s 6d per child.

[133] See discussion in Ottaway (2017, p. 26–27). See also Eden (1797).

[134] See for example Fowler (2007), Higginbotham (2013), and Higgs (2007).

iron and other necessary ware and stuff to set the poor on work." A refusal to work would be punished with prison. These abiding places were described in 1598 as "working houses for the poor" in a measure that encouraged individuals to establish and endow such institutions voluntarily and supplementing parish assistance.[135] In the later 1600s, about 30–40 parishes could form "incorporations" for a common workhouse.[136] Subsequent legislation of the 1720s would encourage churchwardens and overseers—at the time "collectors"[137]—to purchase houses or contract out the "... lodging, keeping, maintaining and employing any or all such poor persons."[138] The law was intended to deter those in need from applying for poor relief by entering workhouses instead. Those refusing to enter—acceptance of refusal was the "test"—could be denied poor relief. Such test supposedly provided the self-evident proof "of the genuineness and desert of the applicant."[139]

Compared to workhouses, "outdoor" or unconditional cash transfers were "more prosaic, more mundane, and involved little that was dramatic or entertaining."[140] High-visibility scandals, like the Andover workhouse, contributed to a reputation of workhouses as degrading, punitive sites.[141] A highly regimented version of workhouses was rolled out in the Poplar parish between 1871 and 1882.[142] The test sanctioned by the 1723 legislation, which would be reframed in 1834 as the "workhouse test," appeared in a ballad that recounted a tragic event at a London workhouse (Box 2.9).[143]

[135] Such contracting could also be jointly undertaken by multiple parishes, hence being a forebearer of subsequent "incorporations" like Bristol's combining indoor activities and external public works. By the 19th century, 3,800 workhouses existed in England with about 83,500 residents (Dolgoff and Feldstein 2009). According to the 1834 Commissioners' survey, 57.3% of the parishes had established these forms of public works (Boyer 1990).

[136] Incorporations gave rise to workhouses typically of two to three storeys that accommodated around 400 people. The Oxford Incorporation built in the 1770s, for example, included a boardroom, chapel, dormitories, dining rooms, kitchen, a wool-carding room, a spinning room, schoolhouse, bakehouse, brewhouse, salt house, deadhouse, correction room, an apothecary, storerooms, and rooms for staff (e.g., supervisors, gardener, housekeepers). An Incorporation in Suffolk had 29 rooms for married couples. After 1834, the Incorporations model was institutionalized through union-level workhouses, a solution opted by about half of the 583 boards of guardians in 1839. When union workhouses were either at capacity or under renovation, payments were made to other unions workhouses to "board out" and accommodate inmates temporarily.

[137] McIntosh (2012) notes that that the change of name from "collectors" or "overseers" may have occurred to keep the distinction with other forms of tax collection, but it "... also implies governance of the poor [which] parallels growing efforts to supervise almshouses and regulate people living in them" (p. 280).

[138] Nicholls (1854, p. 15). In this case, it appears that refusal to work entailed de-registration and banning from future relief.

[139] Almy (1895, p. 174). See also Feder (1936, p. 170).

[140] Crossman (2013, p. 63). Her book also underscores that in the case of Irish workhouses, extensive commentaries were also due to the comparatively high volume of archival material that workhouse administrators were required to keep relative to the management of outdoor relief.

[141] The Andover workhouse was abolished in 1845 soon after it was reported that inmates fought over scraps of rotten meat for fertilizer use (Wheeler 2023). For a compilation of high-profile scandals, see Higginbotham (2012, p. 236–238). See also Horn (2019) and Carter and Thomson (2017).

[142] Under the "Poplar experiment," able-bodied inmates were admitted based on a labor test and were subjected to hard work, strict discipline, and the most basic diet. Based on inmates' performance, they distinguished between "well conducted" and "disorderly," which led to differentiated treatment Higginbotham (2012, p. 214).

[143] Webb and Webb (1927) also recounted that the principle of the workhouse test was already in place in the mid-1600s as a device to compel wandering mendicants to perform a sever task of manual labor as a condition to receive a food transfer.

## Box 2.9 The Workhouse in Popular Culture: A 1731 Ballad in London

The Workhouse Cruelty,

LONDON

In late August and early September 1731, the ballad *The Workhouse Cruelty* rang out on the street of St. Giles in London. The performance popularized a purported "full and true" account of Mrs. Mary Whistle who died in the workhouse of St. Giles in the Fields.[a] The ballad chronicled the cruelty of Matthew Marryott and his sister, Sarah Underhood, master and mistress of the workhouse, respectively. Following the outcry generated by the 'Workhouse Test Act' passed in 1722/3, the ballad and related pamphlets gave " . . . voice to the politics of a wider community than is normally reflected in the print culture of this date."[b] A formal enquire dismissed the purported allegation, although Mr. Marryott was released from his duties within weeks and died shortly after. Aside from the physical violence and hard treatment Ms. Whistle received (to discipline her to work she was confined to starve in a "dark hole" where she eventually passed away), it was the psychological pain and social distress that resonated and made the ballad a popular success:

> ". . . as a dependent parishioner Mary would have had to surrender her meagre possessions on entering the workhouse. Cherished mementos and keepsakes were incompatible with workhouse life. Instead, Mary's suffering lay in her repudiation by the parish, and in the imposition of a new 'improved' system of social relations, made material in the bricks and mortar of a workhouse."[c]

*Source for image*: Hitchcock (2017, p. 154) "The Body in the Workhouse: Death, Burial, and Belonging in Early Eighteenth-Century St Giles in the Fields." In Braddick, M. and Innes, J. (eds.) *Suffering and Happiness in England 1550–1850: Narratives and Representations—A Collection to Honour Paul Slack*. © Reproduced with permission of the Licensor through PLSclear.

[a] Hitchcock (2017).
[b] Hitchcock (2017, p. 155).
[c] Hitchcock (2017, p. 168).

Clothing was sometimes used as a practical deterrent. In addition to the practice of "badging" in use between 1697 and 1810 (see Chapter 5), standard workhouse uniforms were provided after 1834, although the decision to use them was taken at local level.[144] Color-coded and material-based differentiation also occurred within the inmate population: in 1834, at the Bristol Incorporation workhouse prostitutes and single pregnant women wore yellow and red dresses, respectively. Five years later, the Eton union workhouse is reported to make single mothers wear a "felon dress." Similarly, until 1866 unmarried mothers in Norfolk were wearing special jackets.[145] Recently, the use of stigmatizing colors, like safety (prison) orange, was proposed for food stamps cards in Arizona, United States.[146]

Strict living conditions were also the outcome of workhouse contracting. The Webbs argued that the practice of "farming the poor" entailed a "race to the bottom"

[144] In the late 1800s and early 1900s, orders and directives reiterated that uniforms wouldn't be needed. Yet in the nearly half century in which they were in use, uniforms fulfilled a practical function to perform work activities more suitably, as well as representing a mechanism for control and stigmatization. For example, if an inmate left the workhouse without permission while wearing a uniform, it was considered theft of union property punishable with prison sentence and hard labor. Uniforms were provided by the institution, although between 1835–1842, there were unsuccessful attempts to make inmates produce them.

[145] Higginbotham (2012, p. 68–69).

[146] The proposal was made in February 2011, see www.azleg.gov/legtext/50leg/1r/bills/hb2675p.htm.

for outsourcing of workhouse management to private sector contractors,[147] and they asked "what became of those whom it 'deterred'"?[148] There were three possible outcomes: some may have entered the labor market at prevailing market wage; others simply reverted to vagrancy and mendicancy, which the poor laws had intended to address in the first place (for them, they argued that "... the Workhouse Test, in fact, operated in much the same way as an abolition of the Poor Law"). And those that "passed the test" and entered the workhouse found themselves in conditions "... not essentially differing from [ ... ] those of the contemporary prisons." In the St. Martin in the Fields parish, between 1748 and 1818 about 30–40% of elderly women died in the parish workhouse.[149]

A generation of workhouses presented striking architectural similarities with prisons.[150] In the early 1800s, some buildings featured a "supervisory hub" offering a vantage point in the master's quarters providing oversight on inmates' yards. This was in line with Jeremy Bentham's vision for a National Charity Company, where workhouses would be based on the "panopticon" principle involving supervision of a polygonal building undertaken from such a central vantage point.[151] Separation was made not only based on gender (males and females would be located on the opposite sides of the building), but between able-bodied poor and those who were "deserving". Figure 2.6 shows a Y-shaped, hexagonal layout of a workhouse designed by Kempthorne and published by the Poor Law Commission in 1835: "1st-class" inmates were the elderly and infirm, while "2nd-class" inmates were the able bodied. The Thurgarton Incorporation workhouse near Southwell, Nottinghamshire was inaugurated in 1824 and its strict regime (in terms of manual labor, wearing uniforms, and plain diet) also involved a compartmentalized layout based on gender, age, and "guiltless" poor, and the "idle, immoral and improvident able-bodied."

There is some evidence that workhouses performed a rough "shock-responsive" function during times of economic contraction. In those instances, the profile of workhouse participants would include the "casual poor." People living in poverty temporarily were often not residents of the union and would stay overnight in casual wards separate from the rest of the workhouse.[152] In the mid-1800s, three

147 The typical procurement occurred based on lump sums proposals. To win tenders and make activities economically viable, bidders had an incentive to keep costs down. This entailed that "... utmost possible severity was necessary to prevent actual loss to the man who had taken the contract. [ ... ] This, however, was not to deal with the nuisance of destitution, but merely, by failing to deal with it, to reduce the immediate charge on the local Poor Rate" (Webb and Webb 1927, p. 412).

148 Webb and Webb (1927, p. 415).

149 Boulton (2014). See also Smith (1998).

150 The boom of workhouse constructions of 1835–1838 generated a cadre of architects, many of whom proposing signature designs. Among them were Kempthorne, Wilkinson (also active in Ireland), as well as Scott and Moffatt, who designed over 40 workhouses in ten years. See Dickens (1976) for a technical review of workhouses architecture between 1620 and 1922.

151 Bentham (1796).

152 Meals included a supper of 8 ounces of bread and a pint of gruel, preceded by a bath with water and towels shared by three or more inmates. Sleeping occurred on beds, hammocks, or floors in often badly ventilated or heated areas. To support assistance, the costs for relieving the casual poor could, from 1867, be charged to a new Common Poor Fund.

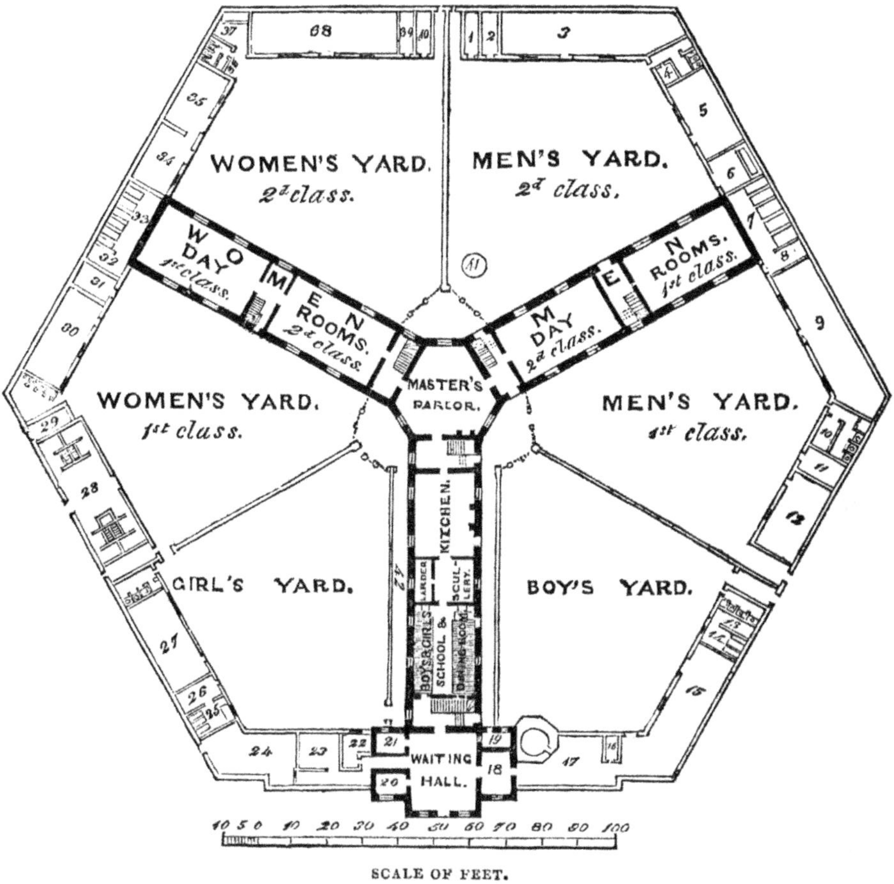


Figure 2.6 Ground floor of hexagonal workhouse, 1835.
*Source*: Higginbotham (2012, p. 26).

legislative measures were enacted to counter temporary demand surges. One of them, which came into effect in 1848, was the so-called Buller Memorandum. This allowed unions to partner with local police forces to issue certificates or "tickets" attesting whether a newly casual pauper was truly so, or was instead a vagrant.[153] Meal tickets were also later issued to be redeemed at specified shops.[154] The other measures, both issued in 1842, allowed for the provision of outdoor public works (usually in a yard adjacent to the workhouse), with half of payments made in kind (e.g., food and clothing); the other law required the casual poor to perform a

[153] See Higginbotham (2012). Through the ticket, the "truly" causal poor seeking employment would be given preferential admission or treatment (like being exempted from work tasks), while the others would be denied access unless at risk of starvation. A range of workhouses took this opportunity to close their casual wards, with a substantial number of casual inmates being curbed in just a year (from 13,714 in 1848 to 5,662 in 1849).

[154] A sample of such ticket issued in Leicestershire in 1915, entitling Mr. Wileman to a half pound of bread and two ounces of cheese, is reproduced at https://www.workhouses.org.uk/vagrants/index.shtml.

four-hour labor task before being released (typically stone breaking and oakum picking).[155] Burials of unknown inmates would occur in unmarked graves. Pauper burials ended in 1997, with the NHS Trusts instructing to ensure dignified and marked graves.[156]

## 2.4 The indictment of cash transfers

The interventions described in the previous section have been matter of extensive, heated debates. This is hardly new: Chapter 4, for instance, offers quotes of eminent state officials in the Roman empire concerned about the dependency and disincentives that gratuitous transfer would have on recipients. However, during the half-century spanning the late 1700s and the early 1800s a particular adversarial rhetoric on cash transfers emerged in England.[157] The negative light in which the provision of cash transfers, and of "poor relief" more widely, were cast has been powerful and enduring.[158]

The fundamental indictment against cash transfers rested on the notion that it *removed the fear of scarcity*, which was the ultimate incentive to work. Without "fear of hunger" there would be no such "natural" effort. Writing in 1786, Joseph Townsend, a medical doctor, maintained that

> . . . hope and fear are the springs of industry. [. . .] In general, it is only hunger which can spur and goad [the poor] on to labour; yet our laws have said they shall never hunger. [. . .] In the progress of society, it will be found, that some must want.

Also, " . . . [w]hereas hunger is not only peaceable, silent, unremitting pressure, but, as the most natural motive to industry and labour, it calls forth the most powerful exertions."[159] By removing such fear, cash relief would cause " . . . more to die from want, than if poverty had been left to finds its proper channel." Hence, fear was to be re-established under a "limited and precarious" system to reduce fertility and enable the population to " . . . regulate itself by the demand for labour."[160]

A decade later, Sir Frederic Eden largely extended Townsend's position. Poor relief would stifle " . . . that emulative spirit of exertion, which the want of necessities, or

[155] Since entry in the causal ward was around 6 p.m. and post-work discharge at 10 a.m., there was little time left for work seeking. Therefore, in 1882 temporary stay were set to two nights, with discharge at 9 a.m. of the second day (from 1871, return to a casual ward of a union couldn't occur before a month, with the entire London metropolitan area counting as a union).

[156] Higginbotham (2012, p. 12).

[157] See the excellent overview in Boyer (1990).

[158] See Chapter 6 for a table compiling those indictments by main protagonists of the time.

[159] Townsend added that " . . . [t]he laws, it must be confessed, have likewise said, they shall be compelled to work. But then legal constraint is attended with much trouble, violence and noise; creates ill will, and never can be productive good and acceptable service" (quoted in Polanyi 1944, p. 118).

[160] Quotes in the paragraph refer to Townsend (1786, p. 23, 27, 43, 62, and 65).

the no less powerful demand for the superfluities, of life, gives birth to."[161] Instead, he suggested that workers be provided a portion of common and wastelands.[162]

Writing in the year of Speenhamland, the clergyman David Davies was aligned with Eden's view that relief "is a great discouragement to the industrious poor" and that the provision of land would reduce "vice and beggary."[163] However, his views differed from Eden's on the origin of escalating poor relief costs: while the latter traced it to relief administration, Davies pointed to rural economic transformations that, since 1750, reduced real incomes among agricultural workers (including enclosures).[164] As such, and here is a second departure from Eden, he favored a system of public works—in winter for males, and year-round for women and children. If no employment could be found, people should be entitled to two-thirds of a day's wage financed by the poor rate.

Some observers were more radical and called for no policy at all. Social Darwinist William Sumner identified the solution in " . . . famine and death, with a social regeneration through decay and the elimination of that part of the society which is not capable of being restored to health and life."[165] These were consistent with Darwin's views on the matter.[166] According to evolutionary theory, "[o]ne's obligation, and society's, to 'the poor' was limited, since Nature herself now sanctioned their misery."[167]

Among the fiercest poor relief critics was Thomas Malthus, who famously quipped that cash and food transfers "create the poor which they maintain."[168] Malthus's hard stance against the poor laws influenced the 1834 commission report in no small measure. Such report was the harbinger of the new Poor Laws, the negative narrative of which proved highly influential in shaping attitudes towards cash transfers internationally. As such, it might be important to extend the discussion on his thinking.

The first of the six editions of his 1798 *Essay*, which he published anonymously, devoted 29 pages of its chapter 5 to poor relief. The second edition, which appeared in 1803 and featured his name, expanded the treatment of the subject to about

161 Eden (1797, p. 448).

162 Eden deemed public works unsuitable as they would compete with workers in similar occupations.

163 Davies (1795, p. 25). He wrote that depriving " . . . laboring people of the expectation of possessing any property in the soil, must be the extinction of every generous principle in their minds" (ibid, p. 102). Young (1801) also proposed a plan to allocate land to every worker with three or more children.

164 On the process of enclosure, which involved the appropriation of common or "waste" land, see among others McCloskey (1972), Wordie (1983), and Fairlie (2009).

165 Sumner (1914, p. 29), although the essay was likely written in 1880.

166 According to Darwin (1871, p. 133–134), " . . . [nature ensures that] the weak in body or mind are soon eliminated; and those that survive commonly exhibit a vigorous state of health. We civilized men, on the other hand, do our utmost to check the process of elimination; we build asylums for the imbecile, the maimed, and the sick; we institute poor-laws [ . . . ] Thus, the weakest members of civilized societies propagate their kind. No one who has attended to the breeding of domestic animals will doubt that this must be highly injurious to the race of man. [ . . . ] We must therefore bear the undoubtedly bad effects of the weak surviving and propagating their kind; but there appears to be at least one check in steady action, namely that the weaker and inferior members of society do no marry so freely."

167 Pimpare (2002, p. 93).

168 Malthus (1798, p. 83).

150 pages.[169] Malthus's critique of the Poor Laws centered on a core principle, that is, helping some people in need would hurt the rest of society (governments " . . . cannot by means of money raise a poor man and enable him to live much better than he did before, without proportionably depressing others in the same class"): if assistance benefitted some in the short term, it inevitably affected society negatively in the long run ("though [the poor laws] may have alleviated a little the intensity of individual misfortune, they have spread the general evil over a much larger surface").[170]

Malthus's idea of wealth (and "happiness") generation was firmly rooted in the Smithsonian cardinal market mechanism of self-interest leading to societal gains via competition.[171] Although the lines between assigning blame on character and responding to incentives can be blurred, some have interpreted Malthus's understanding of poverty as shaped by people's self-interested incentives instead of inherent personal deficiencies.[172] Malthusian concerns on incentives largely revolved around marriage decisions. In the absence of steady income, marriage (and reproduction) choices would be reasoned and prudent; by removing income uncertainty and providing a steady floor, the Poor Laws favored marriage and improvidence ("[a] poor man may marry with little or no prospect of being able to support a family in independence").[173] This, in turn, would spur population growth at a rate outpacing the capacity of food systems to sustain it.

Were Malthus's predictions verified empirically? Like much of the presuppositions informing the 1834 law, they failed to pass most empirical tests (see discussion in Chapter 6).[174] Data from decades preceding the 1834 report point to an opposite narrative, that is, cash transfers were a *response* to demographic and economic processes, not their *causes*.[175] For Samantha Williams " . . . it was 'hard times' rather than marrying young or having a large family alone that tipped the balance for

[169] Smith and Satchell (2018).

[170] Malthus (1798, p. 74, 79).

[171] Friedman (2021). In one passage, he noted that it was " . . . to the apparently narrow principle of self-love, that we are indebted for all the noble exertions of human genius . . . and no sufficient change, has as yet taken place in the nature of civilized man . . . when he may safely throw down the ladder by which he has risen to this eminence" (Malthus 1798, p. 286–287). If individual "self-love" was identified as the engine of broad-based wealth generation, it also helps explain his views on poverty reproduction.

[172] Joanna Innes makes the point vividly: "[Malthus] thought that poverty resulted in large part from ways in which societies and economies were structured, and the implications of that for life chances. [. . .] He saw the poor as, like everyone else, broadly rational (if not always very far-sighted), and likely to respond to changes in incentives. This kind of rational-choice-based model building was what made some of his contemporaries see him as an inspiring social theorist. He should not be confused with those who saw poverty as resulting from individual faults of character, even if he sometimes agreed with such people about some ways in which policy should change" (personal communication, September 5, 2023).

[173] Malthus (1798, p. 85).

[174] I used the word "most" because contributions like the one by Boyer (1990) confirm Malthus's thesis. Yet such analysis was critiqued, e.g., see Wrigley and Smith (2020).

[175] For example, over the 1700s and early 1800s the county of Suffolk experienced high poor relief expenditures because of its deindustrialization associated with declines in the textile industry and related labor surplus (Smith and Satchell 2018, p. 264 and 267).

these families and necessitated a period of parish assistance."[176] Research by Henry French shows that cash support to households with able-bodied men (the most critiqued form of assistance by Malthus) was very limited in time and amount.[177] More to the point, it has been shown that marriage in Speenhamland counties, which were at the epicenter of Malthusian discontent, were similar to other areas: "Malthus was mistaken in supposing that the poor laws led to improvident early marriage."[178]

Malthus's policy prescriptions were radical: they didn't include public works supported by Davies (since they wouldn't allow the wage rate to find its "natural level") or land allotments à la Eden (as they would increase fertility); instead, he insisted that the abolition of poor relief would be beneficial for the poor in the long run. Malthus, however, did outline some specific circumstances under which cash transfers would be beneficial (Box 2.10).

### Box 2.10 Was Malthus Always Critical of Cash Transfers? Insights from His Visit to Famine-Stricken Sweden

As mentioned, Speenhamland, the core object of Malthus's criticism, was implemented in a crisis context. This involved high food prices. Malthus attributed such inflation to Speenhamland's bread scale: such mechanism, in his view, prevented inflation from clearing the market. In the absence of transfers, prices would reflect relative scarcities (i.e., a minority lacking effective demand would be excluded); but the provision of cash transfers allowed prices to rise beyond such level. Hence his conviction that "[the price of corn] could have never reached its present height, but from the system of poor laws and parish allowances."[a]

It was precisely the purported inflationary effect that, ironically, led Malthus to concede that under specific circumstances cash assistance was *beneficial* for society. In a short pamphlet published in 1800, he recounted a visit in the previous year to the drought-affected Värmland region of Sweden.[b] There, grain prices increased more modestly compared to England, but in the absence of a poor law system mortality rose higher.[c] He concluded that the presence of the poor laws contained the death toll in England via inflation: "I am inclined to think that [the poor laws] operation in the present scarcity has been advantageous to the country. The principal benefit which they have produced, is exactly that which is most bitterly complained of—the high price of all the necessaries of life."[d] Why was that the case? Because

[176] Williams (2011, p. 161).
[177] French (2013, 2015a,b).
[178] Wrigley and Smith (2020, p. 51).

by going beyond the market clearing level, transfers-induced inflation engulfed and distressed wider swaths of society, thereby provoking a general discouragement in the use of grains (e.g., farmers were incentivized not to overload the market). In a way, the allowance system was distributing deficits throughout the population instead of (in their absence) locating them only on the most vulnerable. Such analysis was, according to some commentators, reminiscent of Sen's entitlement approach in conditions of dearth.[e]

[a] Malthus (1800, p. 8). Among others, see Wrigley and Smith (2020) for a discussion on Malthus' views on poverty and the poor laws.
[b] For an analysis of the crisis, see Nelson (1988).
[c] This may appear surprising given Sweden's international reputation as torchbearer of social protection. For a short history of the country's experience, see Hort (2011).
[d] Malthus (1800, p. 19).
[e] Wrigley (1999).

Such attitude towards poverty was, in the eyes of Friedrich Engels, " . . . more barbarous than that of laissez-faire, because it interferes actively in cases in which the latter is passive."[179] Yet both Engels and Karl Marx were skeptical of poor relief because it incentivized employers to reduce wages by shifting costs onto the parish.[180] If Townsend considered poverty a condition to be morally corrected, Engels interpreted poverty as the inevitable, structural result of societies transitioning from feudal to capitalist systems (Marx's "early accumulation" stage). The views of Marx and Engels were reflected in range of contributions of historians and economists.[181] Karl Polanyi added a lens to the analysis by arguing that the reduction in wages may have been avoided in the presence of unions and organized mobilizations to defend working class interests.[182] I return to these explanations in the context of assessing historical cash transfers evidence in Chapter 6.

## 2.5 Conclusions

This chapter attempts to weave together two distinct threads of research: on one hand, it lays out some basic features of alternative poverty narratives, including structuralist and individualist perspectives as well as ways to reconcile them. On the other

[179] Engels (1845, p. 188). He summarized Malthus's perspective on poor people as follows: "You are a pest, and if we cannot get rid of you as we do of other pests, you shall feel, at least, that you are a pest, and you shall at least be held in check, kept from bringing into the world other surplus, either directly or through inducing in others laziness and want of employment. Live you shall, but live as an awful warning to all those who might have inducements to become superfluous" (ibid).
[180] Marx (1867, p. 662) argued that " . . . the English farmers and landlords enforced the absolute minimum of wages by paying the agricultural labourers less than the minimum as actual wages and making up the balance in the form of parish relief."
[181] Including, for example, Cunningham (1908), Hammond and Hammond (1911), Hasbach (1894), Polanyi (1944), and Webb and Webb (1927, 1929).
[182] For example, the Anti-Combination Laws prohibited trade union activities.

hand, it presents a paleontology of cash transfers and traces the forebears of contemporary unconditional and conditional programs. Connecting those strands of literature generates three considerations.

First, a comparison between current cash transfers and those present over the past 2,500 years may suggest that there are more commonalities than differences. The strata of history are laden with fossils of schemes from different ages, some appearing to be direct ancestors of modern programs. In reference to the 1700 and 1800s, Peter Lindert had observed that policymakers " . . . kept doing what we do today: they mixed work incentives with at least some outdoor relief for the able-bodied unemployed, while forever tinkering with the details."[183] This chapter confirms his observation and extends to millennia ago. It notes the continuities between the 5th-century revenue-sharing mechanisms in Athens and Sifnos and the current Alaska permanent dividend. Progressively financed child benefits (see Chapter 3) and various forms of conditional transfers of the past requiring children's school attendance or vaccination have a contemporary flavor. Systems of registration of beneficiaries undertaken centuries ago are akin to modern practices. History shows examples of cash transfer programs that maintain purchasing power echoing contemporary strives to index-linking benefits to inflation.

Second, cash transfers are deeply affected by prevailing societal notions of deservingness and morality. Far from a neutral medium of exchange, even the very concept of money can take different meanings pending on narratives and social pressures. Formal design of interventions was accompanied by implicit expectations to conform to standards of belief (e.g., attending church), sobriety, and "decency." In some cases, those criteria were explicitly stipulated in formal contracts between the state and beneficiaries. If modern concerns about cash benefits being used for alcohol consumption are not embedded in contracts, some levels of distrust are still alive and are actively present in contemporary debates. Systems to support the design and implementation of cash transfers—household visits, lists of beneficiaries, etc.—were only mentioned in the chapter and feature in other parts of the book (e.g., Chapter 3). However, the cursory discussion here already points out a thin line separating administrative, surveillance, and moralization goals associated with cash provisions.

Finally, the design of interventions, past and present, is not independent of worldviews and poverty narratives. Around 1380, British poet William Langland wrote "No man knows, I think, who is worthy to receive relief."[184] Four hundred years later, the British indictment of cash transfers confidently implied that very few workers, if any, were worthy to receive relief. The rhetoric that cash transfers are ultimately deleterious for beneficiaries has been a sticky concept not only at that point in time, but as the next chapters show, it influenced mindsets and approaches

[183] Lindert (2004, p. 51).

[184] Langland is the presumed author of the celebrated poem *The Vision of Piers Ploughman*; see translation and commentary in Barr (2014, p. 25).

in several historical instances. This feeds into a growing recognition that "evidence is not enough": while credible empirical work can play an important role in illuminating key aspects of cash transfer provisions, skepticism towards cash transfers may lie in contested technical matters as well as in hard-wired worldviews. Contrasting evidence and rhetoric is one of the themes examined more in depth in Chapter 6.

# 3
# Accompanying Economic Transformation

> In a society with a hypersensitive fear of idleness, work kept paupers within a moral community of citizens.
>
> **Lynn Hollen Lees (1998, p. 64)**[1]

A foundational aspect of economic development relates to structural transformation, or the relative importance of sectors as the economy evolves over time—first agriculture, and gradually industries and services. In this regard, the novel aspect highlighted in this chapter doesn't lie in codifying the economic effects of cash transfers, which have already received significant empirical attention.[2] Instead, the emphasis is placed in highlighting their role within the *process* of economic change. Such process is by no means smooth or linear, and societies that reached higher stages of transformations have experienced dramatic societal disruption. It is in this context that cash transfers emerge as an accompanying ingredient to sustain economic evolution and mitigate its negative effects.

The chapter presents three different pathways for such a role. First, the analysis begins by discussing cash transfers within capitalist modes of economic organization. This includes interpreting cash transfers as maintaining labor reserves, that is, how cash helped facilitate workers' mobility towards industrial areas, support them in those locations during economic downturns, and enhance their readiness to work when labor market conditions improved. The experience of Britain, Belgium, and the Netherlands is featured, alongside a fresh reinterpretation of the recent COVID-19 response through a labor reserves lens. These considerations don't imply that the role of cash transfers is fixed: as the relatively recent Chinese experience shows, the process of economic transformation can present opportunities for "dosing" cash transfers over the process of economic change.

Second, cash transfers have also played an important role in shifts in economic models. The chapter provides a brief discussion of social protection practices in feudal systems. Risk management arrangements of the period, like mutual aid

[1] Lees (1998) *The Solidarities of Strangers. The English Poor Laws and the People 1700–1948.* Cambridge University Press. ©Reproduced with permission of the Licensor through PLSclear.

[2] See, for example, Alderman and Hoddinott (2009), Alderman and Yemtsov (2014), Barrientos and Scott (2008), Correa et al. (2023), Davis et al. (2016), Gassmann et al. (2023), Handa et al. (2018), and Ravallion (2016).

*Timely Cash*. Ugo Gentilini, Oxford University Press. © Ugo Gentilini (2024). DOI: 10.1093/9780191994982.003.0003

societies, were incubators of broader social insurance mechanisms introduced centuries later. The chapter then discusses the advent of social insurance itself and the related implications for cash transfers. Next, the chapter locates those transfers within socialist and communist experiences. Some programs and institutional arrangements introduced during such periods, like the *hukou* system and the cash-based Three-Nos program in China, would be present as countries exited those models and embraced market-oriented reforms.

Finally, the chapter covers historical examples of economic inclusion. These entail cases whereby states leveraged systems of provisions and aligned them with "productivist" principles of industrial policy. If Chapter 2 outlined some core tenets of prison-like workhouses, this chapter shows that they were not always conceived that way. At early stages, "houses of industry" were animated by a genuine ambition to improve living standards in a sustainable way. Also, the chapter showcases interventions, like the Elberfeld model, that married scientific organization with a renewed commitment of the middle class to engage in the economic empowerment of lower-income populations. In large part, these initiatives couldn't adapt to the sweeping forces of urbanization, economic change, and conflict, but their approach and practical insights nevertheless spread in different countries.

## 3.1 Labor reserves and structural shifts

The section sheds light on how "... workers were helped with an allowance so as to keep together a reserve labour force [...] of vital importance to the local economy."[3] Labor reserves constitute a somewhat underrated lens through which we interpret cash transfers' contribution to economic performance. The idea was to use cash to attract workers to and keep them in industrial areas. Cash transfers, however, didn't operate in isolation. The experiences covered in the section showcase how they were situated, at least in England, alongside other institutional pillars (like administrative registries and a judiciary system), which ultimately unleashed the contribution of cash transfers to structural transformation. Without being anchored on such broader institutional architecture, the reliability and credibility of cash transfers as a source of security may have been compromised. Furthermore, the section examines how cash transfers accompanied the Chinese process of reforms unfolding over the past four decades. This includes a relatively minor role at the early stages, with more significant contributions rendered as structural transformation progressed. The recent COVID-19 cash response complements the analysis by elucidating how the historical scale up of 2020–2021 preserved the labor force during the pandemic, including in ways that, largely because of the nature of the crisis, marked a sharp discontinuity with past practices.

[3] Van Leeuwen (1993, p. 332, 337).

## Security exchange and the great decoupling

The process of industrial economic transformation may exert considerable pressure on, and likely overwhelm, "traditional" forms of support. For a steady labor supply to occur, history shows that sometimes workers had to relinquish—often involuntarily and discontentedly—their attachment to assets like land as premier source of security. Within a context of social upheavals and structural transformation, a recalibration in mindset was required for individuals to participate as economic actors in an increasingly commodified society.[4]

Britain is a case in point. As the country gradually pivoted toward industrialization, a new social contract was taking shape.[5] The poor laws seem to have facilitated such shift. In fact, the provision of relief allowed society " . . . to adjust its moral and ethical beliefs so as to accustom itself to the practices and social implications of an increasingly mobile market in land, capital, and labor."[6]

Even if locally provided within parishes (the size of which averaged about 800 people), at the onset of industrialization support was shifting—"detaching"—from the "known" locus of land, family, and kinship entities to a new equilibrium where individuals had a reasonable degree of predictability to receiving public assistance, that is, "solidarity from strangers."[7] Formal provisions of poor relief, for example to the elderly, sick, and disabled, may have created the conditions for higher labor mobility among younger cohorts.[8] The system may have not been optional nor a favored means for security, but it was institutionalized and permanent.

Conferring trust in the system was key to such process. To work effectively and sustain the process of transformation with comparatively low social tensions (at least for continental European standards), the bargain needed to be credible. According to a branch of economic history, poor relief was an ingredient of institutional innovations that in gradual, gestational phases served as *precondition* for economic and social transformation.[9] There were checks and balances: while landlords and farmers could pursue efficiency gains in agricultural productivity via farm consolidation, they had to weigh those economic benefits against their own liability to finance local poor relief for those that were affected in the process.

For the supply of labor to feed industrialization in a relatively undisrupted way, a functioning system of *entitlements* as defined by Amartya Sen needed to be established *first*.[10] The poor relief system was established in its basic form already by the late 1500s, or about two centuries before the peak of industrialization. The

[4] This is not to imply that trajectories of structural transformation from agriculture to industries and services is by any means linear. For example, current transformation pathways observed in some low- and middle-income countries exhibit features that don't necessarily evoke historical antecedents. Fast-paced urbanization may unfold without a process of industrialization and with pervasive informality stifling productivity growth (Gentilini et al. 2021, Rodrik 2022).

[5] See Solar (1995) and Szreter (2020, 2015, 2007).

[6] Szreter (2007, p. 73).

[7] Lees (1998).

[8] Smith (1996, 1986).

[9] Szreter (2007).

[10] Sen (1999, 1981).

compensation component of the "bargain" had not just to be present but also needed to be guaranteed. And this entailed enshrining social assistance as a legally enforceable right.

Examining the poor laws through a legal lens shines a different light on the debate. Ultimately, the (old) poor law was, indeed, a law. Lorie Charlesworth reconstructed the complex, legal apparatus of the poor laws as a system of rights and responsibilities that stretched over a period of nearly 350 years, from the early 1600s to the Beveridgean reforms of 1948. She notes that "... it was not social altruism or 'custom' that motivated the provision of poor relief, rather [...] the legal right of the settled poor to relief when destitute."[11]

Some factors may have contributed in "forgetting" or dismissing the legal nature of the poor laws: among them, "... the persistence of that negative ideology [...] that downplays any positive aspects of the poor law [...] left a message that nothing in welfare's past had value for society and the poor."[12] More to the point, the 1834 reforms discussed in Chapter 6 instilled "... a cultural norm that survives and continues to influence aspects of modern welfare provision"; the net result is the obliteration of "... those positive rights-based aspects whose origins lie much earlier."[13] Yet while the 1834 law didn't reject the legal entitlement to relief, it altered its implementation significantly (Box 3.1).

**Box 3.1 Did the 1834 Reform Abolish the Right to Relief?**

The emergence of the common law was formally codified in the 1601 Act, which instituted the legal obligation to contribute to the poor rate and penalties for non-compliance (seizure of goods and imprisonment until full payment is made). According to some observers, the 1834 reform was equally underpinned by rights, although for a restrictive set of interventions (workhouses) that pathologized poverty among able-bodied populations.[a] The new poor law altered the redressal process (and the type of transfer that people may receive in such process): under the old law, the relief request of a settler to overseers or other officials was based on destitution as subjectively assessed by parish officials. If rejected, the settler had the right to redressal by getting his destitution verified by Justices. If the latter concluded that relief was improperly refused, an Order was issued to compel payment. Under the 1834 law, Justices may only order relief in kind and solely in an emergency.

[a] Charlesworth (2010a,b).

[11] Charlesworth (2010a, p. 17).
[12] Ibid., p. 18.
[13] Ibid., p. 20 and 18, respectively.

Some caution might be required in drawing firm conclusions. Overall, cash transfers provided a reliable source of income during the process of transformation; however, such contribution should be tempered by the notorious flexibility accorded to local implementation. The latter may have generated a degree of uncertainty among beneficiaries and administrators alike.[14] Samuel Finer put it in starker terms: by the early-mid 1800s, assistance was

> . . . administered by 15,000 parishes which were de facto autonomous. There was no 'system'—and indeed the most important single fact about them was their lack of any clear objective. [ . . . ] In 1832, this complex body of law and administration affected everybody, pleased few, and was understood by nobody.[15]

## Institutional trinity: Civil registry, justices of peace, and right to relief

Confidence in the system by ratepayers, administrators and beneficiaries didn't rest solely on poor relief. The latter was part of a broader system with three interlocked institutions: the parish civil registry, Justices of Peace, and the right to poor law. The uncertainty that the joint operation of such trinity of factors removed for the poor relief process is sizable.

Established around 1538, English parish registers, or civil registries, were a " . . . national identity registration system, enabling individuals in a relatively routine, low-cost, and reliable way to verify legally, whenever *they* should need to do so, their identities, kinship relations, marital statuses, inheritance claims, and place of birth."[16] The word "they" is emphasized to underscore that the register was a pragmatic information base accessible and utilized by citizens for daily activities.[17]

Routine disputes were managed by Justices of Peace (or magistrates) who provided a local administrative and legal system for audition, review, and resolution of controversies (including on poor relief). They were pivotal in preventing burden shifting among parishes. It has been argued that insurance systems—and the poor law can be viewed as a form of insurance to pool risk[18]—need to be " . . . robust and accepted rules to ensure a viable balance between the liabilities of those contributing to such a collective, local fund, and the level of demands legitimately made on the

[14] In 1894, Mackay argued that " . . . out-relief is given [ . . . ] with a partiality and uncertainty which, though no doubt unintended, is very apparent to the disappointed applicant." This echoes a comment he made two years earlier: "[t]he unpopularity of the Poor Law is due—not to its stringency, but—to the partiality and uncertainty with which it is administered" (quoted in Lubbock 1895, p. 60–61).

[15] Finer (1952, p. 40, 42).

[16] Szreter (2007, p. 72), emphasis added. See also Szreter and Breckenridge (2012).

[17] While possessing a range of virtues, pre-industrial registries had severe limitations. Ultimately, the registry was a highly localized, parochial system designed for a stage in societal transformation operating under relatively basic and stable conditions. The cracks became visible as the process of industrialization advanced. By the 1830s, " . . . a centralized registry was now needed by individuals and families operating in a truly national, integrated economy" (Szreter 2007, p. 78). On the eve of the poor law reform of 1834, a Real Property Commission had issued a report in 1829 outlining a range of challenges particularly with the transfer of title to land (Howell 1999). The commission's recommendations established a set of interrelated institutions that would accommodate concerns with the system by the propertied middle class.

[18] Solar (1995).

fund."[19] The magistrates were instrumental in managing controversies around parish liabilities.

The emphasis here is that settlement laws were applied flexibly and gradually adapted to the issue of mobility. There is evidence that parishes granted relief to people (especially those with productive potential) even if not resident. Three instruments were used: refunding or subsidies to urban parish from rural parish of origins ("non-resident relief"); "portable certificates" ascertaining coverage by the parish of settlement; and (germane to the theme of this chapter) "casual relief" in industrial areas to keep a reservoir of labor supply to be activated near factories.[20]

The trinity of factors that helped forming a labor reserve—registry, justices, and poor laws—has been shown to broadly align with the three preconditions for economic growth outlined by Douglas North:[21] property rights creating the incentives for economic action in markets; states capable of enforcing the rule of law protecting and policing property rights; and an ideology justifying moral and ethical beliefs in an economy of properties and commodities.[22] Figure 3.1 presents a framework based on the work by historian Simon Szreter that integrates North's growth ingredients with the institutions representing the pre-industrial poor relief ecosystem.

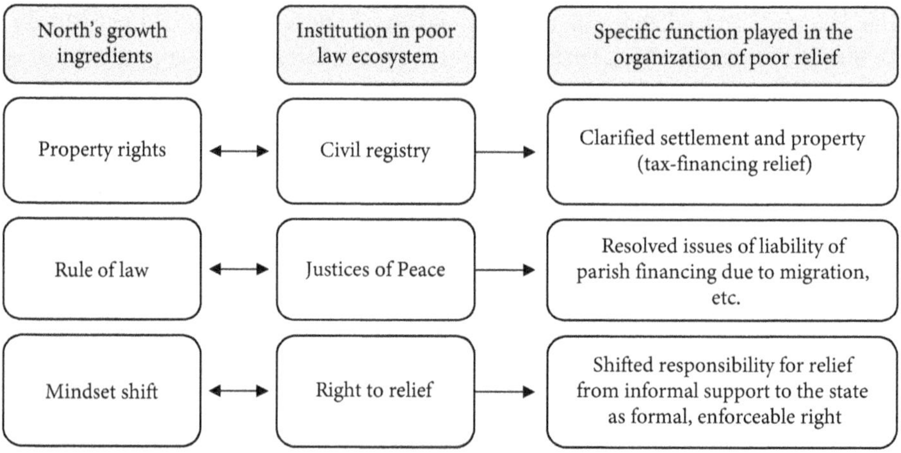


**Figure 3.1** The "Szreter framework".

*Source*: The author.

[19] Szreter (2007, p. 75). Other typical insurance challenges were also tackled, like "moral hazard (e.g., falsely claiming inability work). This was mitigated by the local nature of provisions (potential beneficiaries were well known to local authorities). Similarly, "adverse selection" was limited by the law's coverage of a relatively wide range of lifecycle risks and contingencies.

[20] Solar and Smith (2003).

[21] Szreter (2007, p.71, 76), North and Weingast (1989).

[22] For example, "... [w]e have only to contrast the organization of production in a Third World economy with that in an advanced industrial economy to be impressed by the consequences of poorly defined and/or ineffective property rights" (North 1990, p. 64–65). See also North (1981).

Combined, these considerations may lend credence to the notion that poor relief may have played an important and likely underestimated role in generating conducive conditions for industrialization and structural transformation. As noted by Peter Solar, in pre-industrial times " . . . English relief—a national system that provided credible entitlements backed by local taxation of property—functioned in ways that promoted economic development."[23]

The poor laws may have laid a fertile ground for industrialization also in other ways. For instance, compared to continental Europe (e.g., France), Britain displayed relatively higher social stability and reduced risk of riots induced by enclosures and restricted access to land[24] (such contribution of transfer programs in taming social discontent is further discussed in Chapter 5). Furthermore, poor relief enhanced resilience to crises: analysis by the Cambridge Group for the History of Population analyzed a sample of 4% of parishes and found no evidence of national or regional famine mortality after 1623.[25] The old poor law was one of the key factors eliminating the occurrence of such risk.[26]

More generally, the constellation of features that form the body of poor relief in pre-industrial Britain delineate a model ultimately distinct from developments in the continent.[27] By the 1600s, for instance, the poor laws constituted a "dramatic development of the state . . . which now shaped local social identities and embraced all, or nearly all, of the population as contributors or recipients."[28] Furthermore, issues related to secular–ecclesiastical relationships and the process of reformation also played a distinct role in England.[29] Table 3.1 contrasts core features of British and continental Europe's poor laws from the 1600s to the eve of the English Industrial Revolution.[30]

## Manufacturing and industrial areas

While the literature and historical policy debates have focused extensively on relief in rural areas, assistance played an important role also in manufacturing settings. In England, " . . . industrial cities of the northwest almost uniformly continued to grant outdoor relief to the able-bodied workers until the 1860s."[31] The available evidence points to a counter-cyclical role of relief in urbanizing regions. As opposed to the seasonal nature of rural unemployment, industrial zones faced problems with cyclical

[23] Solar (1995, p. 7).

[24] See, for example, Beier (1983), Clay (1984), Hufton (1983), Stevenson (1979), and Walter (1989).

[25] See Szreter (2021, p.48). Check also Outhwaite (1991) and Szreter (2015) (the latter involves a lecture, with recordings available at https://www.bhru.iph.cam.ac.uk/video-of-bhrus-annual-lecture-2015/).

[26] See Szreter (2007). Solar (1995) suggested that while trade-offs existed, the old poor law spurred growth by encouraging the consolidation of farms, incentivizing agricultural capital formation, and keeping population growth under control (see discussion in ibid., p. 12–16).

[27] Solar (1995).

[28] Braddick (2000, p. 118). See also the comprehensive account by Hindle (2004b).

[29] Smith (2017, 2015).

[30] There is an ample literature explaining and testing the uniqueness of the British experience with poor laws. See for example Innes (2002), Lambrecht and Winter (2018), Lindert (1998), McCloskey (1973), Powell (2020), and Smith (2011).

[31] Boyer (1990, p. 237).

**Table 3.1** British and Continental European poor relief approaches (c. 1600–1750).

| | Britain and Wales | Continental Europe | Select sources |
|---|---|---|---|
| Legislation | Present and enforced via Justices of Peace (local petty matters); possibility of legal appeal/recourse | Present but largely not enforced | Charlesworth (2010a,b), Snell (1991), Mitchison (1989), Sagarra (1977) |
| Organization | Uniform in administration, comprehensive by contingency, national | Diverse, largely driven by local initiatives | Levine (1988), Dorwart (1971) |
| Institutions | Largely rural, decentralized, reliant on volunteer/unpaid managers (overseers), mostly rural and outdoor | Largely urban, centralized management (including professional profiles), more indoor | van Leeuwen (1994, 1993), Lis and Soly (1979), Riis (1981) |
| Financing | Tax-financed, progressive taxation via share of assessed value of property rents (buildings, land) (see Box 2.7 in Chapter 2) | Variety of sources, significant role played by donations | Lindert (2004), Dorwart (1971), Hufton (1983) |
| Labor mobility | Settlement laws but applied flexibly: presence of "casual relief," "non-resident relief," and "portable certificates" | Stricter and less flexible settlement laws, higher degree of local discretion, higher reliance on family, kinship, and neighborhood networks | Solar and Smith (2003), Taylor (1991) |

*Source*: The author, based on Solar (1995).

trade fluctuations. Poor relief, therefore, served as rudimentary unemployment insurance for factory workers being temporarily dismissed or had their work hours reduced during demand slumps.[32]

This "unwritten" urban social contract would ensure that as the economic cycle improved, such dormant labor supply would be readily available. For example, a major downturn occurred 1841–1842, leading to over a doubling of poor relief coverage in textile areas of Lancashire and West Riding; the crisis then sharply subsided in the 1845 "good year" (Figure 3.2, left graph). Similarly, the severe economic contraction of 1847–1848 rose poor relief expenditures in Leeds and Manchester by 90–110%, before rapidly tapering out as conditions improved (Figure 3.2, right graph).[33]

[32] As discussed in Chapter 6, the benefits from locating unemployed populations closer to silk industrial parks was already considered by Lyon officials in the 1590s.

[33] See Ball and Drury (2023, p. 8) for an account of how the collapse in silk prices led to a rise in relief by 70 % in the parish of Sherborne between 1823–1832.

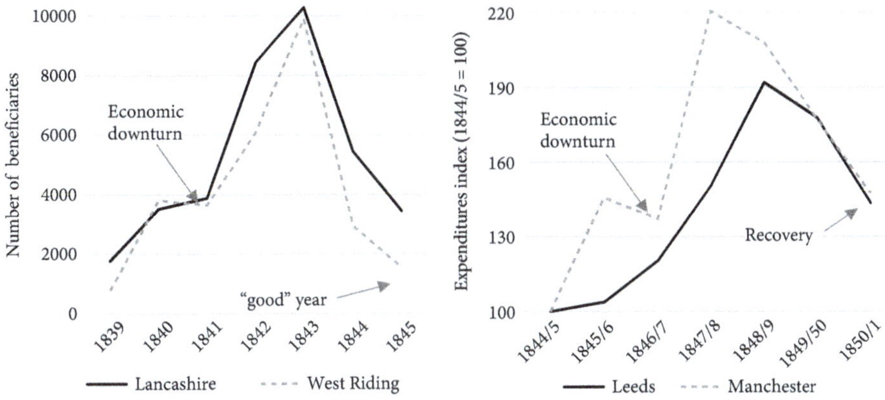


**Figure 3.2** Countercyclical increase in poor relief coverage and expenditures in select periods and industrial zones.
*Source*: The author, based on data from Boyer (1990), table 8.2, p. 236, and table 8.3, p. 238.

A major policy issue with assistance in manufacturing areas was the settlement laws. In cities like 1851 Manchester, for example, migrants constituted 70% of the population.[34] Mobile populations were not eligible since assistance could only be provided in the parish of origin. Moreover, in 1795 an amendment to the Settlement Law made the act of applying to relief a trigger for deportation to the applicant's native location. Accounts show that such policy wasn't fully enacted. Yet it was estimated that non-settlers applying for relief faced a 10–15% average probability of removal.[35]

Poor relief administrators tended to be selective and remove not those with employability potential (like unemployed factor workers), but categories of people that were likely to become a "permanent charge" on urban parish rolls (e.g., the aged, informs, single women with children). The act still played a powerful threat to discourage assistance: "... [m]ost poor people [...] were willing to forgo relief and shift for themselves until the return to better times in order to avoid removal."[36] In turn, this significantly reduced relief expenditures for manufacturers. The legislation was eventually amended in 1846, making those that continuously resided in a parish for five years, recent widows, and those who applied based on sickness or accident "irremovable." This inevitably raised expenditures, which the legislation of 1847–1848 shifted from parishes to the common fund of the parish unions.

## High disruptions in lowlands: Antwerp and Amsterdam in the early 1800s

The experience of poor relief in Antwerp in the first half of the 1800s illustrates another case where cash transfers can help maintaining a labor reserve. A detailed

[34] Boyer (1990).
[35] Ibid.
[36] Ibid., p. 255.

study by Catharina Lis illuminates the economic reallocation and societal dislocation that occurred during an acceleration in structural transformation.[37] In less than a century, Antwerp shifted from being a premier industrial manufacturing center to a commercial hub driven by its international port. Rapid deindustrialization came with disruption and casualization of the labor market.[38] Poor relief played an important role—yet not fully adequate—in complementing incomes of a disrupted working class.[39] Between the early and the mid-1800s, receipt of cash transfers more than doubled (Figure 3.3a), mirroring an upward trend in other Belgian cities (Figure 3.3b).[40]

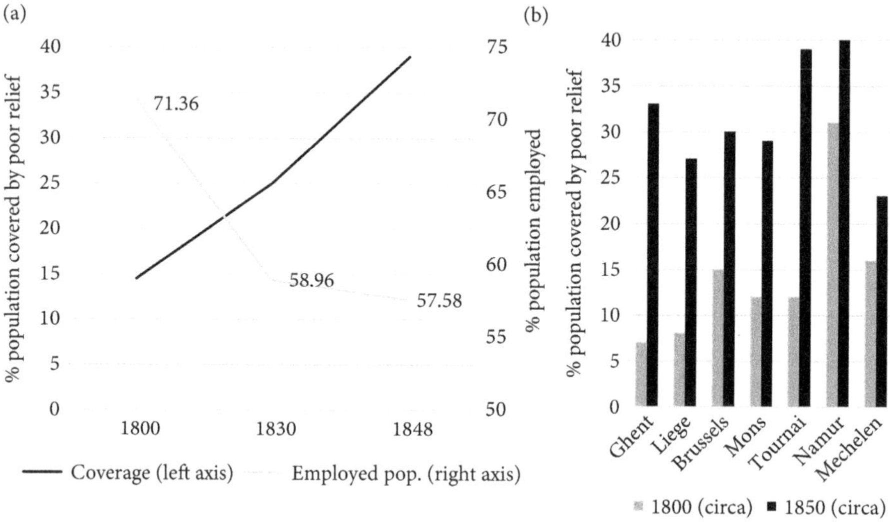


**Figure 3.3** Trends in (a) Antwerp and (b) select Belgian cities, c. 1800–1850.
*Source*: The author, based on data from Lis (1986, p. 32, 111, 113, 114).

While coverage increased, Antwerp's capacity to meet needs was strained. Municipal fiscal allocations didn't seem to match demand—a fact extensively documented by poor relief officials' requests for funds as well as hundreds of letters sent by beneficiaries to the Charity Bureau. This led to episodes of "targeting tightening" and decreases in transfer amounts. In 1799, it was stipulated that eligibility was limited to families with at least two children; subsequently the bar was raised to three children; and in 1823 the "screws were tightened" further: permanent relief was now only accorded to families with at least four children (and whose head of the household

[37] Lis (1986).

[38] The share of the city's "employed population" dropped by 12 percentage points in thirty-five years, while for women the decline was by 34 percentage points in fifty years. The share of men employed in casual labor quintuplicated in a little over three decades (Lis 1986, p. 32, 173).

[39] Poor relief was composed of both cash and food transfers, but the latter only represented about 25% of all expenditures on outdoor relief over the examined period.

[40] In the left graph, the "share of population employed" refers to men and women over 12–13 years of age; coverage includes outdoor relief. In most cases, years are approximate. The specific three years for the "share of population employed" are 1796, 1830, and 1846. For the right figure, the two years are as follows: Ghent 1793–1850; Liege 1808–1850; Brussels 1782–"late 1830"; Mons "end of 18th century"-1850; Numur 1811–"second quarter of 19th century"; and Mechelen 1829–1850.

earned less than 3 guilders/week). The level was eventually raised to a minimum of five children in 1837 (and with a guilder threshold of 1.65/day).

The situation was such that "every time more restrictive standards were applied, the number of families which fulfilled the new conditions soon surpassed the previous level."[41] This led to changes in adequacy, with six revisions in nominal transfer amounts between 1779 and 1850 (three increases and three decreases). But the combination of limited fiscal allocations and inflation tilted purchasing power downward: cash transfers provided to a family of seven members in 1779 would allow to purchase 1.5 kg of bread/day; by around 1850, such amount decreased to 1 kg/day. Limits to entry were established (claimants had to wait for vacant allocations) and lower actual transfers were provided than stipulated. Low incomes led to an erosion of intergenerational support within families.[42] While under strain, however, families maintained informal networks of mutual support within neighborhoods and communities (e.g., temporarily hosting children of an imprisoned person).

Amsterdam is another case in point. Analysis by Marco van Leeuwen reveals the patterns of support to workers in the early 1800s.[43] He shows the effort and hard-working nature of the underemployed for whom poor relief represented a time-bound, supplementary source of income.[44] About 20% of the city's labor force was supported,[45] while benefits were equivalent to 4–11% (pending on provider) of the lowest wage category or 5–14% of the poverty line.[46] Relief wasn't provided unconditionally. Recipients were required to participate to church services while behaving "decently" in society. Their children had to attend school and be vaccinated against smallpox.

Like in other industrial and manufacturing contexts with fluctuations in demand for labor, poor relief in Amsterdam facilitated labor market attachment. As attested by official exchanges between the municipality and the local relief agency, the interruption of poor relief would generate "calamitous" economic consequences. Under that scenario, low-income workers—the labor reserve—would starve, resort to illegal activities, or out-migrate, with a new influx of migrants replacing them. The latter option had the downside of workers "not being known." The Dutch experience shows that it was in the interest of local politicians and employers to keep workers attached to the local economy, and the supplementary nature of relief was instrumental to keep such labor reserve in place.

[41] Soly (1986, p. 106).

[42] For example, in 1827 about 51% of widows 65 years of age and over lived with their children's family; by 1855, such co-residency rate dwindled to 38.5%.

[43] van Leeuwen (1993). As a rule, young and healthy childless adults were not supported.

[44] van Leeuwen (1993) reports the case of casual laborer who, because of the lack of jobs in the docks, streets, and canals of the city, wrote to the municipality in 1837 asking to be placed in a rural labor colony in the North as a form of relief.

[45] Porters were the largest occupation (43%) among municipal relief recipients. This level of assistance was roughly comparable to that of other cities at the time, such as Ghent (10–20% of the workforce was covered pending on trades), Harlem (5–41%), and Nijmegen (6–11%).

[46] The adequacy of assistance (which included both cash and in-kind transfers like bread) was meager and set at modest level just enough to avoid other survival, illegal strategies. The level was consistent with parameters registered in Malines, Antwerp, and other cities. For example, Nijmegen's relief was 6–7% of the lowest wage category and 5% of the poverty line.

## Zeroing in on poverty: Forty years of cash transfers and structural transformation in China

A vast literature offers a detailed analysis of China's transformation process[47] and the dramatic poverty-reduction performance since the early 1980s.[48] What role did cash transfers play over the course of such evolution? The emerging picture point to a calibration of transfers over different stages of economic change.

Between 1980 and the early 1990s, China's poverty performance was mainly driven by enhanced rural incomes and agricultural productivity.[49] Two sub-periods emerge: the first centers on the early 1980s, when poverty declined by about 20 percentage points in five years.[50] Some of the Maoist social protection structures embedded in state-owned enterprises and communes were still intact, and no significant cash transfer program was introduced. The implicit poverty policy seemed to have generally relied on creating favorable price signals for farmers while gradually restructuring urban-oriented food subsidies (Box 3.2).

### Box 3.2 No Fast and Furious: Phasing out Urban Food Subsidies in the Post-Mao Era

In Maoist China, the state fixed prices for both rural producers and urban consumers. Farmers paid an agricultural tax, largely in grain, and sold quotas of production to the state. The state would then resell grain at quota prices to food-deficit localities. These localities were mostly urban areas: between 1952 and 1979, an average of 17% of total output was used to "feed the cities and build up stocks."[a] A smaller share of output, or an average of 7%, was directed for resale to deficit rural areas (a practice that continued after Mao).

A detailed account is provided on how rationing was structured as an urban-oriented system, including being tied to the hukou system introduced in the mid-1950s:

> [w]hile the subsistence of urban residents was guaranteed by the state, rural residents were responsible for feeding themselves [...] All who lived in the countryside and were not state employees were classified as agricultural households and were

[47] Brandt and Rawski (2008), Ma and von Glahn (2022a,b).

[48] Ang (2016), Chen and Ravallion (2021), Ravallion (2021). See Ahmad and Hussain (1991) for a short history of social protection in the country.

[49] Montalvo and Ravallion (2010).

[50] Poverty rates, measured as the share of people living on less than $1.9/day, declined from 87.2% in 1981 to 66.3% in 1985 (Chen and Ravallion 2021).

ineligible for state grain rations [...] Urban residents were entitled to present grain-supply cards to their local grain store to draw local or nation-wide grain tickets as appropriate within the limits of their specified ration. Villages who planned to travel had to bring their own grain to state grain stations where they could exchange it for grain tickets.[b]

Seven categories of cards existed based on residence, occupation, and whether they were for human or animal feed. Some tickets were local, others for nation-wide use. Purchase of food in restaurants required tickets and a cash top-up payment.

With reforms in the early 1980s, a dual-price system was established for the same food commodity: because of different pace of sectoral reforms, procurement prices for producers were raised while subsidized low prices for urban consumers were maintained. An analysis chronicled the gradual and bumpy road towards creating an integrated food market:[c] for urban areas, this meant increasing the grain rationing price in 1991 and abolishing the urban grain coupon system in 1993. It took about 20 years, or until 1998, for government procurement price for rice to be the same as the market price. Such period of "nurturing and tutoring of the market by the state was largely a process of trial and error which inevitably required frequent changes to get food prices right (meaning in the economic jargon that the 'food market clears itself')."[d]

[a] Riskin (1987) provides an example from the Sichuan province showing that a manual laborer received rations of about 22.5–25 kg of grains/month.
[b] Cheng and Selden (1994, p. 658–659).
[c] Du and Deng (2017).
[d] Ibid., p. 322.

Over a second sub-period, or between the mid-1980s to the mid-1990s, deliberate poverty initiatives started to emerge.[51] A role for social protection transfers also bulged (see left bar in Figure 3.4). Such benefits were relatively small-scale and often provided in kind, for example in the form of "food-for-work" schemes as part of agricultural and rural development initiatives.[52] In the *Yigong-Daizhen* ("to offer job opportunities instead of sheer relief") public works programs[53] launched in

[51] For example, the National Poverty Reduction and Development Programs began in the mid-1980s, and the State Council's Leading Group for Poverty Reduction was established in 1986 (World Bank and DRC 2022).

[52] For example, in 1984–1987 over 400,000 beneficiaries were covered by WFP-supported food-for-work programs in Anhui province (WFP 2009). The World Bank and DRC (2022) also report a 1985 Food-for-Work Fund with no coverage data but a spending level of 0.04% of GDP.

[53] As mentioned, these schemes were already documented in 1073 (Yang 1957). More recent antecedents included those supported by the American Red Cross for famine-stricken families in 1920–1921 (Mallory 1926, p. 172).

1984, payments were made based on available resources. These could take various in-kind forms—including grains, cloth, and "low-grade consumer goods"—as well as "industrial vouchers" to be used in local government-run shops.[54]

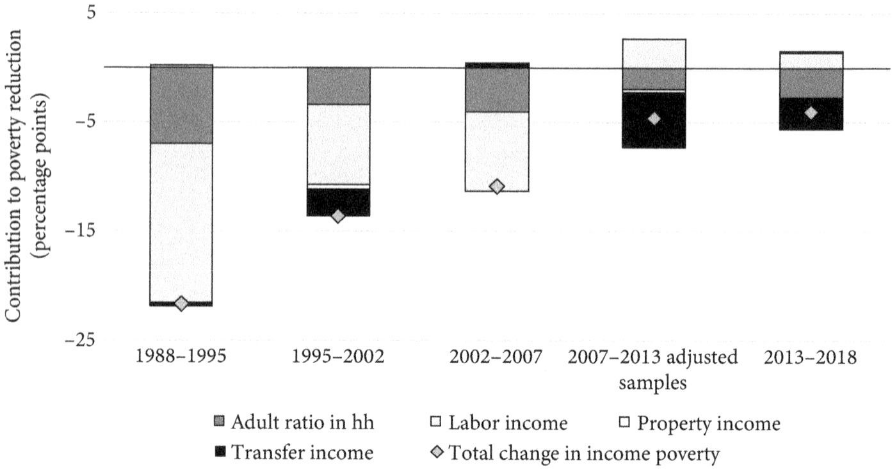


**Figure 3.4** Contribution of income sources to poverty reduction, 1988–2018.
*Source*: Lugo et al. (2021).

Cash transfer programs started to carve out a more significant role in a third, more extended period. This ran from the mid-1990s to the late 2010s. At this stage, sectoral analysis shows that labor productivity in industries was a decisive contributor to poverty reduction.[55] Poverty programs continued to be mostly "area-based" initiatives for lagging regions and low-income counties in rural or urban spaces.[56] Within these geo-spatial frameworks, there was increasing precision and granularity in targeting of places (e.g., shifting from counties to villages) and a gradual evolution "from places to households."[57] While survey data from Figure 3.4 doesn't allow us to identify the contribution of each transfer type—whether they are pensions, social assistance, or remittances—the overall salience of cash transfers increased remarkably.

In fact, three flagship cash programs were established sequentially—a guaranteed minimum-income program in urban areas (*Dibao*) in 1997, its rural version in 2007, and hybrid social pensions shortly after. Efforts to expand assistance in urban areas preceded rural extensions: in urban settings, Mao-era state enterprises and other work units were the core providers of social protection. With their reform

[54] Ling and Zhongyi (1995). The authors also document instances where local governments mobilized compulsory, unpaid work: "... those households with workers who are unwilling to work have to pay an amount to the villagers' group to relieve themselves of work obligations. However, because of the tradition of mutual enforcement of work obligations among members of village communities, especially with regard to projects for the public benefit, failure to work is rare" (ibid., p. 353).

[55] World Bank and DRC (2022).

[56] Examples of development plans include the 1994 "8–7 Poverty Reduction Plan" with a list of 592 poor counties; the 2001–2010 "Outline for Rural Poverty Alleviation and Development Program"; and the 2011 "Outline for Development-Oriented Poverty Reduction for Rural Areas."

[57] World Bank (2009).

and the emergence of private sector employment also came novel forms of unemployment and underemployment. For the same person, work and poverty could now co-exist. Pension payment defaults were also frequent.[58] Combined, these forces required social protection responsibilities to be shifted more fully to the state (Box 3.3).

## Box 3.3 Dibao Experimentation and Scale Up, 1993–1999

Hammond (2019) provides a detailed chronicle of the introduction of Dibao. His comprehensive account shows that urban Dibao was first implemented in Shanghai in 1993 alongside the introduction of a minimum wage (RMB 210/day). This followed intense consultations carried out in 1992: led by the city mayor, Huang Ju, they involved the production of a report laying out options for reform of enterprises. Such consultations encompassed a wide range of government branches, trade unions and various actors. When first executed in July 1993, Shanghai's Dibao reached 7,680 beneficiaries (apparently it wasn't labeled as a "pilot" per se). Funds were provided by the local government and payments received from local enterprises: in the early 1990s, *danwei* "work units" in enterprises were still a helpful platform at a time when other administrative bodies that would govern Dibao in the future were still embryonic. The city of Dalian introduced a guaranteed minimum income program shortly after Shanghai's experience. Differently from Shanghai's blend model of government-enterprise funding and administration, the Dalian Dibao was entirely financed and managed by the local government. The following four years included a range of developments that favored the diffusion of Dibao as spread by meetings and events across localities, especially involving officials at various levels in the Ministry of Civil Affairs. Eventually, Dibao was incorporated in the 9th Five Year Plan (1996–2010), hence elevating it as part of national planning by the central government. An ensuing government Circular (in 1997) and the more binding Regulations (in 1999) mandated all cities to adopt Dibao by October 1999. The final design standards of Dibao were more closely resembling those of the Dalian model rather than Shanghai's.

Similarly, up to the early 2000s, responsibilities for social protection in rural areas were with the communes.[a] Reforms in land, taxation, and the deepening of market-oriented transition weakened the role of communes and called for state action. Rural Dibao became national in 2007, but like its urban counterpart it was

[58] Introduced in the early 1950s, pensions included contributions paid only by the enterprise and funding coming from the government (Gao et al. 2019). With market reforms, state companies were increasingly regarded as legally independent entities responsible for their own profits and losses (Liu and Sun 2016). Employees' pensions were to be paid out of their own funds, which led to payment delays, suspensions, and protests (Feldstein 1999).

the result of years of piloting.[b] Some accounts date a rural minimum income guarantee program in the Shanxi province back to 1992—even before the Shanghai experience.

[a] Gao (2017).
[b] Golan et al. (2015).

The rural Dibao's "longer gestation" occurred in a context where the legacy Five Guarantees program (*Wubao*) was not dismantled, but rather kept rendering in-kind provisions that Dibao's cash complemented. We return to *Wubao* (and Three-Nos *Sanwu*) later in the chapter. Here it should be emphasized that the conceptual difference between *Wubao* and *Dibao* cash transfers was no small matter: according to Daniel Hammond, the latter severed the former's rigid logic of providing cash only to specific profiles or categories of populations:

> . . . being means-tested rather than category based implies a significant change in the Chinese approach to social assistance provision. Poverty was recognized by the state as existing outside of a small number of categories and the traditional association of social assistance and welfare with labor ability has been broken.[59]

By the early 2010s, rural Dibao was reaching over 50 million people, before declining to 34.5 million people in 2021—a level about four times higher than the urban coverage of 8.6 million[60] (Figure 3.5). In the same year, the combined spending for urban and rural Dibao claimed about 0.16% of GDP. As part of Covid-19 responses, Dibao would temporarily reach 83.9 million people, or about 6% of the population.[61]

The implementation of urban and rural Dibao occurs within a broad framework devised centrally, but with ample flexibility accorded at local level. For instance, "Dibao lines" below which people become eligible for assistance vary by province. Access to Dibao activates eligibility to a variety of other services (e.g., medical, housing, and educational benefits), and local officials can exert discretion in managing various "protective" and "promotional" goals.[62]

[59] Hammond (2019, p. 2). The author also pointed out, however, that a more sobering by-product of Dibao's departures from "categories" of eligibility was a higher reliance on quantifiable and "statistically oriented" approach to poverty measurement and treatment that may not entirely match the "lived experience" of deprivation.

[60] The recent decline in Dibao's coverage in both urban and rural areas displayed on Figure 3.5 occurred in a context of growing spending for the scheme. This has to the detection of a "stark hardening" in attitudes towards deservingness and eligibility by the state (Hammond 2019).

[61] Gentilini et al. (2022).

[62] Ravallion and Chen (2015), Zhang et al. (2022). For a review of Dibao evaluations, see Gao (2017) and Walker et al. (2023). Hammond (2019) concluded that whether Dibao was effective depends on how the question is framed: if the goal was to "lessening the effects of [absolute] poverty, while also ensuring that those on the programme do not become trapped in a dependent relationship with the subsidy, then it has made a moderate contribution [ . . . ]. [If the focus was on relative poverty] then Dibao has not been effective" (p. 44).

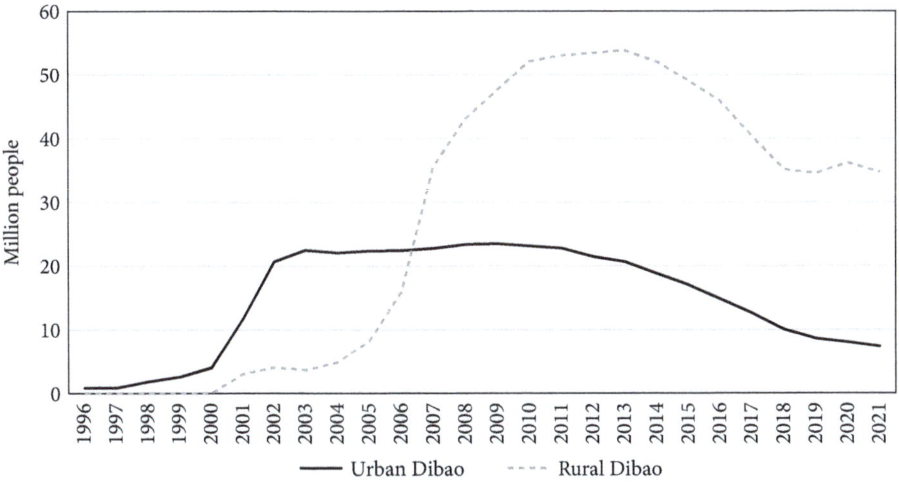


**Figure 3.5** Coverage of urban and rural Dibao, 1996–2021 (million people)
*Source*: World Bank (2022), based on data from Ministry of Civil Affairs.

In addition to Dibao, "quasi" cash transfer programs were established for the elderly. In fact, urban workers not in formal wage employment and rural residents were mostly left out of the pension system. Hence an Urban Employee Basic Pension Insurance was launched in 1997,[63] followed by the New Rural Social Pension Scheme in 2009 and the Urban Resident Basic Pension Insurance two years later.[64] The rural scheme was a hybrid "contributory social pension," including a noncontributory basic pension and a highly subsidized personal savings account.[65] To ensure more spatial equity in provisions, the urban and rural schemes were merged under the Urban and Rural Resident Pension Insurance in 2014.[66] Around 318 million people were recently contributing to the unified model, and 150 million elderly people were receiving payments.[67]

With broad-based structural transformation underway, a new phase was ushered to aggressively unroot residual, entrenched pockets of poverty. Efforts around "Targeted Poverty Alleviation" involved massive campaigns to attack the last mile of poverty—the prevalence of which, after 2013, was single digit (or around

[63] Also in this case, Shanghai and Guangzhou provided early grounds for testing (Dorfman et al. 2013, Wong and Yuan 2020).
[64] Gong and Chen (2023).
[65] The scheme resembled a matching defined-contribution pension in the accumulation phase (small contributions to an individual account with low-returns deposits matched at a rate of 30% by the local government) and presented features of a social pension in the payout stage (basic benefits were financed entirely by the government, with the proportion of central and local funding varying by region) (Packard et al. 2019).
[66] Gao et al. (2018).
[67] World Bank and DRC (2022).

100 million people).[68] High-level exhortation accompanied the pursuit of poverty eradication as a core target of the 13th Five-Year Plan (2016–2020).[69] Cash transfers played a role, but alongside a wide range of other interventions: for instance, governance and administrative arrangements, including fiscal incentives and public servants career promotions, were connected to the achievement of poverty elimination targets.[70]

## Workers' lifeline: the unprecedented global COVID-19 response

"We are moving quickly to deliver cash to all people," announced the late Japanese Prime Minister Shinzo Abe in a televised address in the spring of 2020.[71] The COVID-19 response can be interpreted in various ways; but arguably, one of its premier functions was to maintain a labor reserve until labor markets resumed.[72] In fact, governments around the world have used cash transfers to offset drops in labor earnings resulting from reduced economic activity, stay-at-home orders, and other containment policies. As such, the massive injection of cash transfers responded to an implicit contract by which the government, in pursuit of public health priorities, created the conditions for heightened needs (by constraining the economy) and compensated for it (largely via cash transfers).

The magnitude of the response was unprecedented. Over 2020–2021, a total of 1,023 cash transfer measures were implemented in 203 countries. As mentioned in Chapter 1, those programs reached nearly 1.4 billion individuals globally, that is, one out of six people in the world received at least one cash transfer payment. Coverage ranged from over 40% of the population in high-income countries to nearly 10% in low-income settings (Figure 3.6).[73] In some countries, such massive

[68] The effort "... spanned the whole process from poverty identification to poverty exit, determining whom to help, who should help, how to help, how to exit and how to avoid poverty reoccurrence" (World Bank and DRC 2022, p. 35). The cost of the strategy ranged from 0.35% to about 1% of GDP.

[69] President Xi declared the elimination of poverty one of his "three decisive battles" (Kim 2018). In February 2021, President Xi announced a "complete victory that would go down in history" and "handed out medals to key figures in the poverty fight" (BBC 2021).

[70] About 800,000 officials carrying out "Precise Poverty Identification," with up to 2.9 million government and state enterprises cadres across provinces being deployed to designated villages in 2020. For example, a partnership between the poverty-hit district of Yuanzhou in Ningxia province and the more affluent Mawei district in Fujian province was forged. Under the collaboration, the latter provided both resources and skills to the former, including transferring funds (about $9 million in 2020); facilitating worker exchanges, internships, and trainings; and assigning human resources for a time-bound period (e.g., public servants, doctors, and teachers) (World Bank and DRC 2022).

[71] The announcement was made on April 17, 2020 (https://www.thehindu.com/news/international/coronavirus-japan-offers-930-virus-stimulus-payment-to-all-residents/article31366345.ece).

[72] This section draws heavily from Gentilini (2022). See Marinescu et al. (2020) for a social insurance perspective from the United States.

[73] Gentilini et al. (2022).

redistribution had dramatic (albeit temporary) poverty effects: responses in the United States halved the child poverty rate "to an all-time low,"[74] while in Brazil the rise in poverty was not only contained, but even reduced compared to pre-COVID levels.[75]

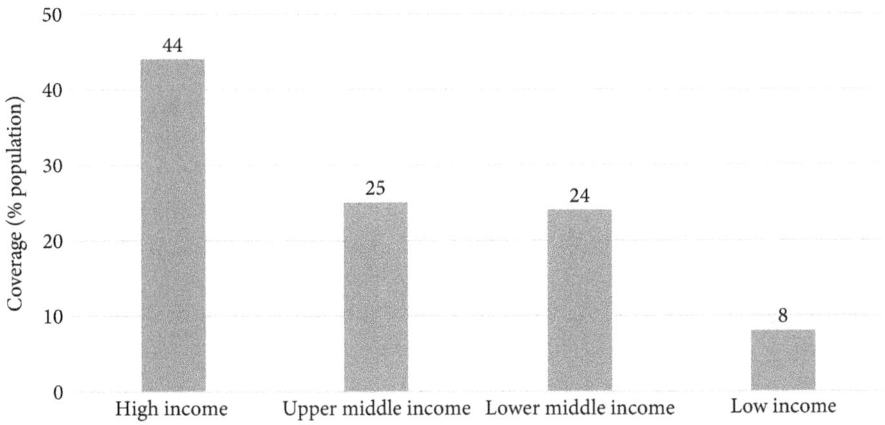


**Figure 3.6** Coverage of pandemic cash transfers, 2020–2021 (% of population).
*Source*: The author, based on Gentilini et al. (2022).

The exceptional nature of the crisis, and the associated labor reserves rationale for preserving workers' welfare, opened the doors for breaking with past practices in several ways.[76] For instance, the profile of a large share of beneficiaries is historically noteworthy. In fact, about 204 million workers received unconditional cash transfers, including 184 million in the informal sector. As discussed in Chapter 2—and as it will be clear in the upcoming ones—assisting the "able-bodied" with "unconditional" cash has been a sort of taboo. For example, South Africa's R350 COVID-19 cash grant was the first in the country's " . . . post-Apartheid era to target unemployed adults—a group who had previously been largely unreached by the system."[77] The R350 program, which, combined with other grants, increased the overall coverage of cash transfers to 41% of the population, will be in place at

[74] Trisi (2023, p. 1). See also Collyer, Hardy, and Wimer (2023).
[75] Lustig et al. (2023, p. 9). Brollo et al. (2024, p. 20) estimate that extreme poverty, defined using the Bolsa Familia eligibility thresholds, fell to a mere 2.3% in 2020.
[76] A compilation over about forty impact evaluations showed that cash transfers helped in mitigating the negative economic and welfare effects of the pandemic significantly; but they couldn't offset the full impact of the crisis. In fact, the performance of cash transfers was stifled by a modest number of payments, short duration of programs, uncertain extensions of benefits, and uneven delivery capabilities (Gentilini 2022).
[77] Kohler and Bhorat (2021, p. 2).

least until March 2025—or five years after inception.[78] The pandemic Child Tax Credit program in the US, a quasi-universal cash transfer scheme, was expected to " . . . fundamentally change the relationship between the state and its citizens."[79] Albeit short-lived, the program reignited debates on large-scale cash transfers coverage that animated the national policy discourse in the late 1960s and early 1970s (see Chapter 5).

To be sure, such design generated no shortage of criticism: like concerns vented in the early 1800s—and echoing the post-Black Death period in the late 1300s discussed in Chapter 5—the large-scale response led to mounting frustration about "people not getting back to work." Once again, state support in the form of cash transfers was framed as part of the problem.[80]

In some cases, a further novel aspect of the pandemic was the use of transfers for the *entire* population. Japan's Abe wasn't alone in his call for universal cash transfers—another ten instances were recorded, including cash transfers provided as a form of unconventional monetary policy or "helicopter money" to spur the economy. East Asia was the epicenter of such interventions, with high-income Japan, South Korea, Singapore, Taiwan, and Hong-Kong pouring a total of $240 billion in universal cash transfer injections.[81]

The pandemic also shed light on the salience of social protection in large cities and sprawling informal settlements or slums. Those areas are traditionally less covered by cash transfers compared to rural settings.[82] This is particularly compelling given how this chapter emphasized the urban dimension of cash provisions. If cash transfers are to facilitate transformation in modern low- and middle-income countries, history suggests that cash assistance can support a dynamic workforce by providing a source of stability in volatile times.

## 3.2 Transitions within and between economic models

This section examines cash transfers in light of major economic shifts that occurred within prevailing models of economic organization, including capitalism, and transitions to different dominant frameworks: the former includes the birth of social insurance (preceded by a brief review of antecedent risk management providers), while the latter involves the Soviet socialist experience and a rapid reference provided to the Maoist era.

[78] See Bhorat and Kohler (2021) for coverage; for extension of expiry date, see https://www.iej.org.za/draft-amendment-to-regulations-indicates-srd-grant-to-end-in-march-2024-whilst-value-and-beneficiary-numbers-eroded-significantly/.

[79] Weisman (2021).

[80] For examples of critical press articles released in the early phases of the pandemic, see Levin (2020), McArdle (2020), and Somers (2020).

[81] Choi et al. (2023). Universal transfers were also recorded in Israel, Mongolia, Serbia, East Timor, Tuvalu, and Jersey (Gentilini 2022).

[82] Gentilini et al. (2021).

## Temples, lords, guilds, and fraternities

Techniques of risk management have longstanding roots.[83] Prehistoric hunter-gatherers developed forms of credit systems and other mechanisms leading to functioning economies *relative* to needs.[84] Contemporary hunting and gathering societies, such as the *Ju/'hoansi* in Namibia, preserve practices like "demand sharing"—a system that gave everyone the right to tax anyone else of their surpluses.[85]

Historically, temples offered important platforms for managing adversity and served "... as social welfare agencies, anticipating major religious institutional functions to follow in later centuries."[86] Temples seem also connected to the management of money over five millennia ago. According to David Graeber, around 3500 BC Mesopotamian civilizations "... temple administrators already appear to have developed a single, uniform system of accountancy [...]. It's easy to see that 'money' [...] was created by bureaucrats in order to keep track of resources and move things back and forth between departments."[87] In fact, temple officials would also provide credit to farmers, such as documented in the city-state of Uruk.[88]

Around 2,000 BC, the Sumerians, who took over parts of modern Turkey, Iraq, and Syria, devoted one eighth of the land for holy shrines: in those sites, "... widows, orphans and the poor were protected by the goddess Nanshe."[89] Those practices would coexist with provisions made by rulers like Hammurabi and Cyrus the Great.[90] In India, "temple help" was part of famine responses in the Thanjavur District of Tamil Nadu in 1054 and 1201 ("state help" was mentioned in the Deccan plateau famine of 1387–1395).[91] And in early African societies, temples were financed through a central treasury to provide, among other services, "public relief for any clan member in need."[92] Poverty and spirituality were connected: in ancient Egypt, the

[83] Widlok (2017) explored the importance of sharing for social relations and subsistence since the dawn of time. On the specific issue of food storage among hunter-gatherers, the journal *Current Anthropology* had in the early 1980s a collection of comments on the article by Testart (1982) by seven authors. See also Ingold (1983).

[84] The work by Marshall Sahlins reveals how prehistoric societies managed their economies: "[h]unters and gatherers have by force of circumstances on objectively low standard of living. But taken as their objective, and given their adequate means of production, all the people's material wants usually can be easily satisfied. [...] It is not that hunters and gatherers have curbed their materialistic 'impulses'; they simply never made an institution of them. [...] The market-industrial system institutes scarcity [...]. Scarcity is the judgement decreed by our economy [yet it] is not an intrinsic property of technical means. It is a relation between means and ends" (Sahlins 1972, p. 4, 5, 13, 35). For a critique of the "original affluent society" concept, see Kaplan (2000).

[85] Suzman (2020a).

[86] Day and Schiele (2013, p. 62), quoting Dolgoff and Feldstein (1984) *Understanding Social Welfare*, 2nd ed.; in this book I used the 8th ed., published in 2009.

[87] Graeber (2011, p. 39).

[88] Suzman (2020b, p. 247). Suzman also considers Mesopotamia "... the first place for which there is solid evidence for money in the form of inscribed clay ledgers" (ibid., p. 246).

[89] Day and Schiele (2013, p. 62).

[90] At the time (1792–1750 BC), Hammurabi, the ruler of Babylonia, made the protection of vulnerable populations an essential part of his Stele code (Polanyi 1944). In the 6th century BC, the Persian monarch Cyrus the Great provided rations to families when a child was born (Heidemarie 1996).

[91] Murton (1984).

[92] Day and Schiele (2013, p. 61).

poor were believed to possibly "curse their oppressors throughout eternity, and those in power feared the curse," hence motivating assistance based on "economic need for workers and the religious need for life after death."[93] This form of material–religious "transaction" between giver and receiver would also recur in Christian almsgiving discussed in Chapter 5.

In the Middle Ages, communities, merchants, and guild networks played a pivotal role in managing risk. Under feudalism, most people lived on feudal manors as serfs protected by their lords against life contingencies like sickness and old age.[94] Those that received no such protection, especially in early urban towns, were supported by membership-based craft and merchant guilds. The latter provided for masters' and journeymen's burial, sickness, old age, and widowhood.[95]

In 1300s France, small manufacturers and artisans wandering from town to town established mutual-aid societies (*un compagnon*) inclusive of a membership card (*un viatique*) entitling to food, shelter, and support to find work.[96] In 15th-century Italy, farmers set up cooperatives to insure each other against bad harvests. An intermediary, the Monte dei Paschi bank, was established in 1473 to facilitate those arrangements.[97] Centuries later, in 1795 Netherlands there were 62 guild-based insurance schemes and nine craftsmen programs.[98] In 1811, the share of male labor force covered by guilds mutual insurance schemes was over 40% in Utrecht and about 20% in Amsterdam.[99] In Russia, mutual-aid societies were relatively widespread and by 1900 there were about 300 such organizations.[100]

Assistance to members was in some cases extended to others, including via "works of charity" for the town's poor. These would take the form of yearly distributions of corn and barley, feeding the needy on feast days, and other types of occasional support.[101] The proliferation of engagement in charity work by merchants has been referred to as the "monetization of alms."[102] Other community arrangements were present, such the "customary poor support."[103]

[93] Ibid.

[94] Among manorial tenants, the serfs who lived on the land of the lord nearest his mansion (or Latin *villa*) were called villeins. They provided services for the lord from in-house help to farming to trades. The highest ranking of these serfs was given tracts of land designated for their own support (Quigley 1996a). For a wider discussion on poverty in the middle-ages, see Riis (1979).

[95] Richardson (2005).

[96] Garraty (1978).

[97] Bernstein (1996). See Kinball (1988) for a discussion on risk aversion, land, and agricultural cooperatives in medieval times.

[98] Van Leeuwen (2012).

[99] Van Leeuwen (2016, p. 30).

[100] Workers joined them to insure against some basic risks (illness, disability, unemployment, and death), although societies gradually took on a broader array of functions, including those typically performed by labor unions (e.g., petitioning the government regarding working conditions, setting up strike funds) (Madison 1980).

[101] Trattner (1974).

[102] Mollat (1986, p. 156).

[103] Such legislated practice permitted peasants in need to pick peas from any field in their village (at daylight and from the edge of the patch) and to collect grain spilled during the harvest (Richardson 2005). A similar arrangement was present in early Judaic traditions: under the Talmud laws, "[f]armers were forbidden to lean the corners of their fields or to pick up fallen fruit, so that those in need might have them" (Day and Schiele 2013, p. 67).

Fraternities also mushroomed. Among their functions, they rendered assistance in cash or in kind to members in need.[104] Most fraternities collected periodic dues, while many imposed entry fees. A few required members to bequeath cash, corn, animals, or land. In 1388 England, there were 234 fraternities active in rural areas: out of these, 18 provided weekly stipends of 3–12d.[105] As risk-sharing institutions, fraternities faced collective action problems of free-riding, moral hazard, and adverse selection. Foreshadowing future state practices, their charitable obligations emphasized the "deserving" poor, or those " . . . pious and industrious peasants who suffered runs of bad luck [ . . . ] who fell into poverty not of his own rashness or negligence."[106]

## Inventing the "social"

The risk management mechanisms mentioned in the previous section were based on "prudence," that is, by voluntarily joining organizations of mutual support. A foundational shift would occur in the early 19th century when mandatory schemes of risk pooling started to spring out. Statistical methods were now applied to the management of *population* risks in terms of crime, labor, health, education, and poverty.[107] Large surveys and data collection efforts allowed to describe, project, and normalize events statistically at aggregate level. Commenting on this period, Michel Foucault noted that " . . . [w]hereas statistics had previously worked within the administrative frame and thus in terms of the functioning of sovereignty, it now gradually reveals that population has its own regularities, its own rate of deaths and diseases, its cycles of scarcity, etc."[108]

The "avalanche of data" produced in the 1800s may have led to fulfill the "law of large numbers" required to make insurance viable.[109] Measurable aggregate regularities in wage employment, like industrial accidents and unemployment, gave rise to technical—and not "moral"—interventions measured in probabilistic terms.[110] The technology of risk pooling based on large populations-wide data marked a

[104] In some cases, fraternities were specific regarding the circumstances activating support, such as losses in housing or cattle due to fire, floods, and theft. An account by Richardson (2005, p. 390) illustrates an example of fraternity established in 1310 by residents of Kyllyngholm, a village in Lincolnshire and which included the following ordinances: "If a brother or sister dies, four brethren shall offer a penny, and each sister shall give a halfpenny loaf. If a brother or sister is unlucky enough to lose a beast worth half a mark, every brother and every sister shall give a halfpenny towards getting another beast. If the house of any brother or sister is burnt by mishap, every brother and every sister shall give a halfpenny towards a new house. Moreover, if the house of any brother or sister is broken into by robbers, and goods carried off worth half a mark, every brother and every sister shall give half a penny to help him."

[105] Bainbridge (1996), Richardson (2005).

[106] Bainbridge (1996, p. 393–394). Such sorting was attained by requiring members to make a formal request for support, which had to be approved by most members; some fraternities applied means tests, while protracted periods of time may occur between admission and benefit receipt.

[107] Adolphe Quetelet's contribution in applying mathematics and probabilistic techniques to social sciences was a key innovation in the early 1800s (Porter 1986).

[108] See Foucault's lecture "Governmentality" delivered in 1978 and included in Burchell et al. (1991, p. 99).

[109] Bernstein (1996), Hacking 1990).

[110] Ferguson (2012).

fundamental shift in considering unemployment not as a moral individual failing, but as an objective structural problem.[111]

Early forms of insurance existed for specific sectors. For example, Belgium introduced a sickness insurance scheme for seafarers in 1844, while Austria covered miners with illness and old age schemes in 1854.[112] In Russia, the earliest proposal for social insurance had been made in 1833, but a law on the subject didn't emerge until half a century later years later, or in 1893.[113] Legislated with an Imperial Decree in 1881, Germany's Bismarckian provisions laid the foundations for a trio of insurance schemes, that is, for sickness (1883), work-related accident (1884), and old age and invalidity insurance (1889).[114]

What factors led to a global "new beginning"? Under the social insurance revolution, the state would extend its realm of action significantly. While highly debated, there are at least three broad and interconnected cultural, economic, and institutional factors that can help explain such broader public reach. The avalanche of data did not only produce "knowledge" of social problems, but also increased social "awareness": the historical review by Samuel Fleischacker argued that the rise of distributive justice can be explained by a

> . . . change in people's sensitivities [ . . . ] It was not new arguments or factual discoveries that led people to have a more sympathetic attitude toward the difficulties of the poor, but new ways of presenting the circumstances of poverty [ . . . ] in the nineteenth century.[115]

[111] As a student of Foucault, Ewald (1986) showed how the statistical process of normalization and distribution of risk underpinned the birth of French social insurance. During the industrial process, routine problems of workplace accidents grew significantly. However, a legislation of 1804 required that compensation claims by injured workers had to be approved by the court, hence raising a range of uncertain, complex and costly steps making the process unfavorable to the injured. Ewald's research shows how a landmark legislation of 1896 (the "Taffeine case") reformed the juridical system of adjudicating responsibility and proving fault. This would automatically compensate workers for "professional risks" through a mandated insurance funds set up by employers and with the state handling compensations.

[112] Also, by 1900, Denmark's public subsidies for old age insurance were four times those of Germany, that is, 0.38% and 0.09% of GDP, respectively, which prompted some observers to "dethrone" Germany of its pioneering aura: it was only after the Second World War era that Germany would be at the forefront of public spending in social protection—which in 1930 topped 5% of GDP—largely driven by poor-relief type measures (4.15%) (Lindert 1994).

[113] The 1893 legislation provided protection against work-related illnesses, injuries, and death of workers in mining, railroads, and the navy. A new law of 1912 extended social insurance with coverage for accidents financed by employers, while contingencies for illness, maternity and death were covered by contributions by both employers and workers. Yet only 23% of the 13 million people in the workforce was covered (Madison 1980).

[114] In 1889, the German Emperor William I declared that " . . . those who are disabled from work by age and invalidity have a well-grounded claim to care from the state" (see https://www.ssa.gov/history/ottob.html). Originally meant to be financed by a tobacco tax, pensions were eventually legislated as a contributory scheme. The Bismarckian approach spread rapidly, and by the end of the 1940s a total of 139 countries had some form of social insurance in place. See Egger et al. (2017) for a discussion on the pace of introduction, modalities, and types of risks covered over time.

[115] Fleischacker (2004, p. 126). The latter part of the century also featured the famous "London poverty maps" of Charles Booth. Produced over the period 1886–1903, the maps involved three editions of his *Life and Labour of the People in London* comprising 17 volumes (see https://booth.lse.ac.uk/ for visuals and a history of Booth's survey work). For poverty analysis and images in London, see also Mayhew (1969) and Sims (1902).

Another factor may relate to economic efficiency. Empirical work on insurance adoption has underscored the role played by economic connectedness.[116] Also, permanent vulnerabilities that the industrial process had generated, such as structural involuntary unemployment and business cycles, may have sparked a new-found spirit of economic organization.[117] Yet the redistributive performance of early Bismarckian reforms may have been mixed.[118]

Another explanation involves institutions and social contracts. The origins and determinants of Germany's insurance were the subject of an extensive literature, including featuring political expediency, manufacturing competitiveness, judiciary burden, comparative efficiency, and other explanations.[119] In general, social insurance not only responded to a nation-building logic,[120] but also constituted a political move to counter the growth of radical movements.[121]

Cash transfers for the elderly would complement social insurance. Contributory pensions were soon followed by non-contributory (mostly means tested) social pensions, the emergence of which first appeared in Iceland (which was part Denmark until 1944) in 1890 and New Zealand in 1898.[122] Australia passed non-contributory legislation in 1908 building on earlier schemes in New South Wales (1900), Victoria (1901), and Queensland (1908).[123] England introduced a means-tested, general taxation-financed, non-contributory social pension in 1908; three years later, in 1911, the country would institute a seminal compulsory unemployment insurance scheme.[124] Overseas, the diversity in approaches of colonial powers was also reflected in the diffusion of social insurance in colonial territories (Box 3.4).

[116] Egger et al. (2017) suggested a significant domino effect whereby countries adopting social insurance would then lead other countries to do the same. Such effects were largely facilitated by an acceleration in global integration of trade and investments. On social insurance diffusion, see also Attanasio and Brugiavini (2003); Becker and Mulligan (1998); Collier and Messick (1975); Gilardi (2016), Kim (2001), Mulligan, Gill, and Sala-i-Martin (2002); and Mulligan and Sala-i-Martin (1999).

[117] Briggs (1961).

[118] In Germany, the costs of insurance were largely borne by workers themselves and their employers: for accidents employers covered the full cost; for sickness, they paid one third of the bill and subsidies were near-zero; for old-age, employers paid half of the cost while the state contributed with just 6% of insurance revenues as of 1891 and only 18% in 1908 (Lindert 2014). The political economy behind those allocations is interesting: according to Ullman (1981), large industries which had already set up company-level insurance viewed the legislation positively as those obligations would be extended to competitors. Smaller-scale firms, which were more spread and labor-intensive, proved less able to organize and oppose the law. Kuhnle and Sander (2010) argued that "social lead" taken by Germany—and not England, for instance—was because the mandate to contribute may have run counter to more liberal principles in parliamentarian regimes.

[119] See Eghigian (2000) and Hennock (2007).

[120] Manow (2005).

[121] Rimlinger (1971), Van Kersbergen and Manow (2009). According to Kuhnle and Sander (2010), "... the idea of social protection to secure the loyalty of workers to the state was supposedly one Bismarck picked up from Napoleon III when he was Prussian ambassador to Paris in the early 1860s" (p. 65).

[122] Briggs (1961).

[123] Jones (2002) reports that "... Robert Johnson, the Tasmanian Registrar General and Statistician, told the federal 1906 Royal Commission on the Old Age Pension that the Victorian Pension was so austere, and the conditions and checks on applicants so detailed and degrading, that the benefit was really a 'pauper dole'. By the end of 1901 Victoria had reduced the pension by 20% and re-examined all existing cases to ensure that all children of pensioners were contributing to their parents' income" (p. 7–8). See also Murphy (2008).

[124] Kuhnle and Sander (2010).

## Box 3.4 Colonial Approaches and Social Insurance Adoption

The French colonial approach meant that specific forms of social insurance would be introduced uniformly across colonies and in a relatively short, compressed period. For instance, 15 French colonies out of 22 launched sickness programs within four years. The British approach was more heterogeneous, for example, as illustrated by retirement schemes like provident funds.[a] This was the case because they constituted a "scaled-back version of social insurance"[b]—a configuration that fitted British preferences for simple, domestically financed, and fiscally conservative interventions in low-capacity contexts.[c] Empirical work shows that legislative introductions of work injury schemes had been in line with general economic circumstances in British colonies, that is, measures were introduced as income rose. This includes adoptions after independence. As discussed in chapter 4, such a relationship is not visible in the case of French colonies, which were subject to more proactive and uniform treatment (introductions often occurred often before independence).[d]

[a] Provident funds were spread mostly in British territories. These were first adopted in Asia (Indonesia and Malaysia in 1951, India in 1952, Singapore in 1953, Sri Lanka in 1958); the Middle East (Egypt in 1955, Iraq in 1956), and later Africa (Nigeria in 1961, Tanzania in 1964, Zambia, Ghana, and Kenya in 1965, Uganda in 1967) (Barrientos 2020a). In Tanganyika, lower ranks of government service were covered by the provident fund of 1942, but the colonial administration was not supportive of a compulsory provident fund for non-governmental formal sector workers (Kunzler 2020). Jamaica opted for flat-rate pensions and Yemen for earning-related schemes.
[b] Barrientos (2020a).
[c] McKinnon et al. (1997), Parrott (1968).
[d] Schmitt (2015, p. 339).

In the century following Iceland's pivotal scheme, 45 countries introduced a social pension (Figure 3.7).[125] In Uruguay, social pensions for the indigent aged and infirmed was introduced in 1911 financed by a levy on property sales and a tax on imported playing cards.[126] During the 1940s, "... in Palestine, Ceylon and Northern Rhodesia, also, investigations were continuing [on introducing a social pension. In] St Helena there had been a demand for non-contributory old-age pensions, although the Governor preferred a compulsory contributory system"[127]. In other cases, introductions occurred in the 1950s: in Cyprus, a social assistance scheme was launched in 1953, while in India the first state to include a non-contributory social pension for those over the age of 70 was Uttar Pradesh (followed by Haryana, Punjab

[125] Out of the 45 schemes, only nine were "universal," or neither non-means- nor pensions-tested. Some started universal (e.g., Netherlands, Cook Islands, and Seychelles), while others became so over time (e.g., New Zealand, Mauritius, and Guyana).
[126] Mesa-Lago (1978).
[127] Seekings (2013, p. 17).

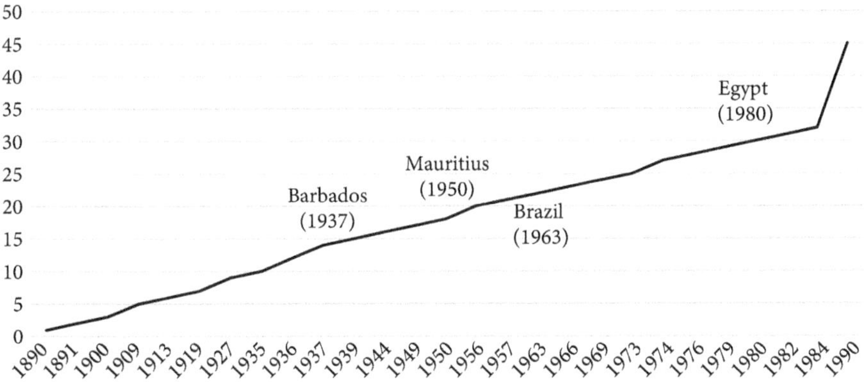


**Figure 3.7** A century of social pensions introduction, 1890–1990.

*Source*: Data from HelpAge social pensions database. Accessed December 2023 (http://www.pension-watch.net/social-pensions-database/social-pensions-database-/).

and Tamil Nadu). Chapter 5 discusses how some schemes were racially differentiated, like social pensions in South Africa and Namibia being initially provided to white populations only.

Following the devastation of the First World War, several nations created insurance programs for survivors (Germany introduced it in 1911), and most countries legislated the extension of social insurance benefits to family members. Chapter 4 shows that similar mechanisms were already introduced in the United States following the Wars of Independence and the Civil War. Around the post-1918 period time, a fifth form of risk was covered, that is, family allowances. For example, New Zealand introduced such scheme in 1926. The fact that such allowances are sometimes considered a form of insurance signals the blurred lines between those instruments and social assistance.

Individualist and structural approaches to poverty did not cease to animate debates; but a body of literature helped casting them less as a dichotomy.[128] Social assistance continued to play an important role dovetailing social insurance. As Larry Frohman suggests:

> Bismarckian social insurance programs have long been regarded as the [origin] of the German welfare state, and this historiographical tradition [. . .] has consistently marginalized all forms of social assistance that cannot be neatly fitted into the narrative [. . .]. This perspective is, at best, one sided (Frohman 2008, p. 141).[129]

[128] The work by Munsterberg (1904), for example, helped elucidate a gradual fusion of individual and societal responsibilities, the integration of character and circumstance, and their explanatory power that helped calibrate social assistance and insurance in a more balanced way. Other notable contributions include Christian Klumker's *Elements of Social Welfare* published in 1918.

[129] Frohman argues that social insurance led not to a reduction in relief expenditures in absolute terms, but to a restructuring of its cost configuration, that is, spending declined in the short term for able-bodied

## Cash transfers, Soviet style

Russia's early experience with cash transfers appears to be generally in line with, and at times predate, developments on poor relief in Europe. Box 3.5 provides a snapshot of such an experience between the 900s and 1800s. The socialist project of the early 1900s was supposed to be a way station toward fully fledged communism.[130] Starting in 1918, the passage to socialism entailed

> ... discarding the deeply embedded notion that economic insecurity is essential for efficiency and material advance. Instead, Soviet welfare planners proclaimed that a high level of economic security [was] essential for maximum production. While aware of the necessity for precautions against [possible disincentives, those concerns would] disappear with the advent of the 'new Communist man' who supposedly places the interest of the collectivity above his own.[131]

**Box 3.5 A Millennium of Relief in Russia (c. 900s–1800s)**

According to comprehensive studies,[a] in 996 the Grand Duke Vladimir issued a Church Statue that made the church responsible for the care and supervision of the poor, sick, aged, and disabled. Resources for programs would come from the "tenth rule," or one tenth of revenues from fines, profits from every tenth week of trading in cities, and a tenth from annual production in grain and cattle. The clergy's engagement in poor relief was significant until the 1500s. Assistance was administered at local level by parish officials. As cities grew, the heterogeneity of people requiring assistance expanded. The state eventually stepped in with more centralized approaches. For instance, at his coronation in 1598 tsar Boris Godunov pledged that "there would be no poor in his empire." During his reign, public works were provided for the able-bodied poor, including the construction of stone buildings in Moscow and other cities.

Tsar Alekseevich's edict in the late 1600s established the state's obligation to care for the poor, specific criteria for categorizing them, and outlined organizational structures for administration. The legislation also envisioned punishments for sturdy beggars, who would be sent to workhouses or, if they refused, exiled to Siberia.

Those measures would be upheld by Peter the Great. His approach centered on relief for the "honest poor," rooting out of "professional begging," and providing

workers (because of sickness and accident insurance) but increased for long-term support for the elderly and infirm.

[130] For a fascinating account on the place of communism in history, see appendix A in Milanovic (2019).

[131] Madison (1980, p. 192).

for veterans in 1720: as such, it was noted that "ex-soldiers were the first group of Russian citizens who were supported by the state."[b] Control of most welfare establishments was assigned to the police, including because of its purported comparative advantage to provide work for the able-bodied and administer "corrective" measures. Again, "idle" beggars were to be caught and punished. Almsgiving was forbidden under severe fines.

Catherine the Great (1762–1796) secularized welfare administration. Specifically, in 1775 she instituted a Committee on Public Assistance ("prikazy") in each province. The Committee was responsible for the local administration of workhouses and poor relief. The prikazy received funds from the central treasury as well as from disparate sources like donations, fines, unused municipal taxes, revenues from licensed pharmacies, church collections, and interests on loans. Under Alexander I, in the early 1800s the establishment of voluntary charitable societies was encouraged to manage fiscal constraints. Such societies were also hoped to exert greater "rehabilitative influence" than government policies. In the meanwhile, the prikazy was replaced by local rural self-governing bodies (zemstvos) in the second half of the 1800s.

[a] The box draws heavily from the work by Lindenmeyr (1996) and Madison (1980).
[b] Danilova (2010, p. 897).

The "road toward communism" was marked by attempts to reconciling individual incentives and societal goals—and grappling with tensions between needs-based and productivity-oriented principles (Box 3.6).[132] If the precept of socialism was "to each according to the quantity and quality of work," that of communism was "to each according to needs." In his labor theory, Marx himself had distinguished between payments according to work and productivity and those according to needs. Reflecting on his *Critique of the Gotha Programme* released in 1875, Amartya Sen posited that Marx preferred the needs principle as a long-run goal, while endorsing a work-based approach as a temporary device until a fuller cultural transition came to fruition.[133] The latter would have involved a shift in the moral compass toward a higher degree of cooperation and selflessness.

[132] Madison (1980) and Minkoff and Turgeon (1977) point out other challenges such as the gulf between ideals and financial, institutional and administrative structures to fulfill them; an evolving interface between state-provided and self-financed social protection arrangements (and how to assist those that benefitted from neither); and the intellectual struggle around the role of marriage and family.

[133] According to Sen (2021, p. 214–215), "Marx considered the needs principle to be fundamentally superior [...] since people do have important needs that can vary [...] [But] he also noted that it may be difficult to combine this principle with an adequate system of incentives for work [and] had accepted that in the near future it would not be possible to have a system based on [needs] [...] The tussle between the demands of need and those of incentives (and work-related entitlements) remains as alive today as it was when Marx was writing."

### Box 3.6 Needs, Work, and Identity

The desire to work is inherent in human beings as they strive for self-reliance, sense of duty, meaning, self-expression, and contribution to and participation in the wider human community. But these attributes can coexist with an impulse for idleness and freedom. These conflicting forces can vary within individuals, cultures, and times, and the oscillation between such competing values has shaped ambivalent attitudes towards employment. Work is often the core frame through which human identity is narrated and understood in social protection, and ambiguity on views toward work is also mirrored in approaches to the specific instrument of cash transfers. John Garraty observed that " . . . [because of] human ambivalence toward labor, policymakers have for centuries debated the relative merits of the carrot and stick approaches to the unemployed."[a]

A concern for broad human needs as opposed to narrow individual economic incentives reflect a recognition, present in the work of both Karl Marx and Amartya Sen, of people's multiple identities.[b] A work-based logic may tend to consider a person only in its unitary identity as "worker," not the suite of identities of human beings as shaped by cultural, community, family, spiritual, geographic, linguistic, and other dimensions. Sen underscores the dangers from an insistence on an exclusive, labor market-focused narrative that doesn't fully recognize such multiplicity: "being a worker cannot be the sole identity of any person [ . . . ] The social analysts who tend to think of identity as a unique—and sharply divisive—classificatory device miss the richness of the multiple identities we all have."[c]

[a] Garraty (1978, p. 6).
[b] Marx (1867), Sen (2006).
[c] Sen (2021, p. 216, 372).

Social protection provisions in Russia adhered to four core principles: variation in provisions by occupation; tying of benefits to earnings; guaranteed employment; and state responsibility for funding programs for the non-agricultural sector. Coverage grew over time[134] and included four main types of programs: social insurance for salaried workers and the wage employed; "universal" child benefits; mutual aid and self-provided arrangements for farm workers (later modified in the mid-1960s); and social assistance for the poorest.[135]

Initially, "independent" workers in farms weren't considered suitable for insurance coverage since they "weren't hired and weren't givers of work."[136] Farmers'

[134] Madison (1980) estimated that between 1920 and 1963, the coverage of social protection programs quadrupled from nearly 10 million people to 39 million, or 17% of the population.
[135] Minkoff and Turgeon (1977).
[136] Madison (1964, p. 195).

source of income in times of distress, for example in cases of illnesses and work accidents, was their own collective farms' mutual aid support fund.[137] The same principle of differentiation that operated in the social insurance system was applied to the collective farms, where the greater a person's earning, the higher the eligible benefits. In 1964, the government established a specific public scheme for collective farmers, but it didn't absorb them into the national social insurance arrangement.[138]

There was some modest social assistance from the state to those not covered by either insurance or mutual aid. This included, on one hand, war invalids and the dependents of military staff; on the other hand, there was a catch-all category defined as "others." The latter was based on evaluations of social welfare personnel and included "... handouts to the most desperately needy, the amount depending upon the funds at the disposal of local welfare departments."[139] Eligibility involved applicants to prove destitution by a statement certified by the management of the building where the person lived, the local militia, or the resident soviet. One-off grants were provided in emergencies.[140]

Universal child benefits would cover both wage and self-employed workers.[141] A legislation of 1936 introduced such payments for all families with seven or more children, while in 1944 the benefit structure was expanded from the third child. In both cases, the program was financed by general revenues. For comparison purposes, the monthly benefit level in 1944 for a family with three children (or 80 rubles) was about one third of the minimum salary of an industrial worker (or 250 rubles). In 1963, spending on child allowances accounted for 0.28% of GDP.[142]

The management of unemployment fell under state's economic planning activities rather than social protection institutions. This included the implementation of "jobs guarantee programs" since employment was a constitutional right.[143] According to such logic:

> ... unemployment represents institutional failure [and] income security for those capable of working is answered through the guarantee of work opportunities rather than through the availability of unemployment benefits [...] which testifies

[137] The funds' finances were to be derived from contributions not more than 2% of annual earnings; a 2% of the value of the farm's output; sums received from social welfare authorities; and fines levied by state courts.

[138] In comparison, since the mid-1970s collective farmers in Bulgaria, Poland, and to some extent Czechoslovakia enjoyed the same rights and provisions as other state employees. Yet not all farms were of collective nature, and independent ones were left largely uncovered (Minkoff and Turgeon 1977).

[139] Madison (1980, p. 56).

[140] Madison (1980).

[141] Madison (1962,1963a,b).

[142] For unmarried women, benefits were paid from the first child and until all children reached 12 years of age (yet there were specific conditions, e.g., grants didn't apply in the case of co-residency of unmarried couples or to adopted children). Small allowances were available also for the first two children of married couples, but these were restricted to low-income families. Benefits were meant to cover the costs of a one-off grant to purchase a layette and monthly transfers to cover for infant food during the first nine months. Both such benefits were cut in half in 1947.

[143] Unemployment benefits were abolished in 1930.

> to their steadfast pursuit of maximum production [...] and high rate of labor force participation.[144]

The emphasis on work also included investments in social and psychological measures to reintegrate the mentally and physically disabled into society. This involved framing work not just as a necessity, but as a therapeutic experience[145] " . . . that reward[s] industriousness and punish[es] sloth."[146]

## Made in China: Mao, the three-no's and five guarantees

There is much debate about poverty during Mao's regime: highly critical accounts arise, for example, on the relationship between the Great Leap Forward's accelerated industrialization (1958–1962) and the concomitant, devastating famine of historical proportions.[147] Similarly, the vexed conditions of state capabilities that reformists inherited in the immediate post-Mao era have been underscored.[148] Other policies seem more favorably assessed. For instance, investments in basic human capital and equal distribution of land may have put China on a conducive course for Deng Xiaoping-era growth.[149] Moreover, the debated *hukou* system, which was formally established in 1958 to curtail rural–urban migration, still plays a central role in current Chinese social assistance architecture, including variants being locally piloted.[150]

The idea that provisions were to be connected to work permeated approaches in the post-1949 Maoist era. Like in the Soviet Union, social protection was organized around enterprises and collectives, that is, social insurance and other services were tied to the place of work.[151] Over this period a set of cash and in-kind transfers were introduced.[152] These included interventions for those excluded from labor-related provisions, namely the "Three-Nos" (*Sanwu*) and the "Five Guarantees" (*Wubao*) mentioned earlier in the chapter.

The Three-Nos and Five-Guarantees presented differences in recipient units (individuals and households), location, eligibility, and institutional arrangements. *Sanwu* was a cash transfer in urban areas. It was geared to individuals that had "no work," "no income," and "no caregiver" and provided limited amounts of cash through local

[144] Minkoff and Turgeon (1977, p. 182, 184, 204).
[145] For an in-depth discussion of work therapy, see Chapter 8 in Madison (1980).
[146] Madison (1964, p. 198).
[147] Estimates on mortality vary, with some reporting the figure of 30 million deaths (Ashton et al. 1984, Li and Yang 2005, Smil 1999).
[148] Ang (2016).
[149] Ravallion and Chen (2007), World Bank and DRC (2022).
[150] The hukou system, which roughly translates as "residence system," assigns the population into rural and urban residency to determine the location of public service provision. Cheng and Selden (1994) trace how, over the course of a decade, *hukou* emerged in the 1950s as an instrument for rural transformation and limiting mobility to urban areas. For a detailed historical review see also Wallace (2014), while World Bank and DRC (2013) discuss more recent provincial *hukou* experimentations.
[151] Hu (2016).
[152] Liu and Sun (2016), Walker and Yang (2024).

governments.[153] *Wubao*, instead, was an in-kind scheme offering food and fuel, housing, clothes, medical care, and burial assistance. It was intended for rural populations via collective organizations.

Yet the programs had a shared identity. Grounded on the principles that family, kinship, and communities are responsible for taking care of those that cannot do so themselves, the profile of last-resort *Sanwu* and *Wubao* participants tended to be elderly people, widows, and children with physical and mental disabilities.

Nearly 60 years after their introduction, and despite a fundamental change in economic organization, both *Sanwu* and *Wubao* were still part of the Chinese social protection system: in 2014, the former reached half-million people (or 3% of the urban *Dibao* program), while the latter covered 5.2 million beneficiaries (or about 10% of the rural *Dibao* scheme).[154] In fact, both the Mao-era Three-Nos and Five Guarantees serve particularly deprived segments of the *Dibao* caseload that conform to the two programs' eligibility criteria.

## 3.3 Economic inclusion

This section presents two sets of cases: one of them refers to instances when workhouses were organized in line with market or "industrial" principles. These include Bristol's 200-year experience with its Incorporation and the shorter-lived case of Tuscany, where French workhouse institutions were implanted by imperial Napoleonic powers. In both instances, policymakers made genuine attempts to organize assistance for low-income populations away from "charity" models. They strived to impart skills and organize the production of marketable goods, mirroring an extension of state industrial policy. Eventually, the models succumbed by attempting to balance core trade-offs, such as upholding the competing principles of not interfering with private markets while seeking sustainability and cost recovery. The pursuit of such equilibrium was hampered by issues of relatively low-quality products and diversified profiles of workhouse populations that proved incompatible with market standards.

The inmate workforce had varying levels of productivity due to the multiplicity, and at times contradictory, goals of workhouses. This tension reflected an international pattern: in Germany's workhouses of the late 1700s, the blend of participants' profiles made those institutions "human dumping grounds."[155] The production in Genova's workhouses or *depots* was compromised by the profile of its residents, such as sick people and young children.[156] In Russia, a law of 1775 established workhouses for two different profiles of beneficiaries: while one was devoted to the "honest,

[153] An (2021), Davis-Friedmann (1983), Hammond (2019).
[154] Gao (2017, p. 4).
[155] Frohman (2008, p. 44).
[156] Assereto (1982).

unemployed poor," the other meant to correct "social deviants"; yet such distinction "never took hold in practice."[157]

In the case of Tuscany, the demise of "industrial" workhouses paved the way for their rapid transition towards instruments of deterrence, including prison-like conditions generating public health hazards. In Bristol, the prevailing administrative and organizing model would inform and be in line with "corrective" principles embraced by the 1834 legislation.

The other compilation of economic inclusion experiences can be framed in terms of economic and social integration. Such instances appear animated less by market principles (which nevertheless were present and defined a number of activities), and more by the goal of establishing a relationship between low-income populations and the upper classes of society. This includes a trio of German cities—Hamburg, Munich, and Elberfeld. By insisting on "knowing," "assessing," and "visiting" beneficiaries, the German models displayed meticulous local-level administrative organization. The emphasis on "locality" would mirror Glasgow's model (Chapter 5), while a committed cadre of middle-class volunteers was forming a movement that found passionate echo in other contexts like the United States (Chapter 4). Policymakers had to confront a difficult trade-off, that is, balancing localized versus centralized management of assistance. The mantra of "knowing" people assumes stable societies, a condition that rapid change spurred by industrialization and mobility would soon upend. The advantages of local-level organization (including the donor–beneficiary personal connection) had to be pondered against the demands for central management of an expanding problem (which would sever the direct donor–recipient contact). The organizational benefits of centralized organization would come at the cost of anonymized provisions.

While the industrial and integration models were hindered by different challenges they shared a common destiny. If the industrial case couldn't attain the desired level of sustainability, the German experience was broken by the forces of structural transformation. Both cases brewed growing mistrust towards cash programs, increased the anonymity of assistance, and grew the risk of misreading poverty causes. These are the very forces that, as discussed in Chapter 1, fuel the pattern of diminished and tighter cash transfer reforms discussed in Chapter 6.

## Workhouses as industries

Workhouses tend to evoke the specter of punishment and harsh living conditions. In his historical review, Alexander Loveday observed that "[t]he hatred of the poorhouse has in many instances proved more strong than the fear of death."[158] Workhouses were widely (and rightly) regarded as ineffective in reducing poverty.[159] If workhouses were able to attain reductions in the number of applicants or "welfare

[157] Lindenmeyr (1996, p. 37).
[158] Loveday (1914, p. 88).
[159] See, for example, Boyer (1990) and Webb and Webb (1927).

rolls," their performance in terms of administrative costs, adequacy of support and facilitating labor market insertion is sobering. Chapter 6 offers data elucidating this point further.

In England and parts of Europe, workhouses in the 18th century seemed to differ from harsher versions emerging in the 19th century in some notable ways. For instance, they were seen as public enterprises for making poor people self-sufficient.[160] As noted by John Garraty:

> [i]n older [workhouses] the objective [ . . . ] was to train, inspire, or force those presumed to be capable to labor to work; in the new the objective was to make the environment so unpleasant that anyone who could possibly do so would shun them like the plague.[161]

Similarly, George Nicholls underscored that workhouses were initially established " . . . with a view to deriving profit from the labor of the inmates, and not as a means of testing the reality of their destitution. [They were] a kind of manufactory, carried out at the risk and cost of the poor-rate."[162]

The long "shadow of the of the poorhouse" of the 1830s, to use the title of Michael Katz's classic book, may obscure the original relationship of some workhouses with labor markets in the broadest sense, that is, not only in terms of organization and regimentation of labor, but also as sites embedded in market-oriented production and labor force formation. For a spell of time, workhouses were at the intersection of relief and industrial policy, before cost-recovery challenges and conflicting goals swung them back in the relief space—and with pugnacious punitive features.[163] For example, historical analysis has been tracing the evolving experience of the Suffolk workhouse incorporation—from the devotion of its founders in 1760s to the gradual disillusionment of local elites in the early 1800s and its eventual demise in 1826.[164]

A recent paper by Susannah Ottaway cast a different light on workhouse operations.[165] Her work confirms unfavorable performance in standard efficiency terms: in the early 1800s, earnings from inmates' labor were limited, including being equivalent to about 7% of workhouses cost (a rate that increased, in some localized cases, up to about 30%). Ottaway's analysis offers some interesting explanations for the persistence of workhouses by illuminating their deeper connections to the surrounding economy and supply chains.

[160] Taylor (1972).
[161] Garraty (1978, p. 84).
[162] Nicholls (1854, p. 18).
[163] De Schweinitz (1943, p. 54) pointed out the " . . . typical confusion and attitude that has always characterized the concept of the employment of the poor. [People want] the enterprise to be economic, but [they justify] it partly on moral grounds; [they advocate] it as an effort toward making the poor self-supporting, but [they] hope for charitable contributions."
[164] Shaw (2019).
[165] Ottaway (2017) shows that the number of English parishes with workhouses nearly doubled in a quarter century, i.e., from about 1,800 in 1776 to nearly 3,300 in 1803. Her analysis embraced a broad perspective on work and workhouses as laid out in Reinarz and Schwarz (2013) and Schwarz (2007).

If 18th-century workhouses were deemed economically unviable, it was also because of an underappreciation of several limiting factors and active contributions. For instance, workhouse activities would include not only basic tasks, but also skilled-intensive works (e.g., spinning). Manufacturers often relied on labor from large, centralized workhouses as part of scattered cloth production ecosystems. Work activities were at times conducted by inmates outside workhouse premises, which contributed to nearby economies (e.g., domestic service rendered by women hosted in urban workhouses). Workhouse inmates performed "hidden" activities to maintain buildings and the inmate population itself, and for which it is difficult to assign monetary value.[166] Furthermore, only about half of typical English workhouse participants were "ablebodied"[167] and a high share were children under 16 years of age.[168] Yet in the case of the latter, there was " . . . tremendous attention to the employment and apprenticeship of children whose exit from the workhouse was often carefully conducted by the 'guardians of the poor' who oversaw the handoff from workhouse master to apprentice master when children turned 10 or so."[169]

## Bristol's dream

The Bristol Incorporation of 1697 was an example of parishes pooling resources to address the dual issue of unemployment and settlement simultaneously.[170] The scheme was conceived by John Cary, a son of a vicar and West India merchant. Its governing body included the mayor and alderman *ex officio*, and 48 locally elected guardians chosen by rate payers. Until 1823, the parish was the basis for assessing and collecting rates: the mayor would receive a certificate from the corporation about the sum required for the year, and then allocated shares of the cost to each parish. Parish officers would break down their quota into individual assessments and collect them.[171]

The corporation was able to produce products of average quality, but encountered stiff challenges in interfacing with the market. Buyers wouldn't pay more than a relatively low price for the product. The corporation attempted to differentiate between higher- and lower-quality production (e.g., fine and coarse yarn). While not profitable, the corporation was also facing pressures from taxpayers to reduce costs, that

[166] For example, blankets or shoes produced for inmates, which would not be reflected in formal accounting (about one quarter of able-bodied inmates would engage in such internal production).

[167] There were practices designed for the non-ablebodied: for example, the Brabazon scheme of 1880 involved training for infirm and crippled inmates in activities like knitting or lacemaking, with products sold in the board room of a workhouse (Marr 1899).

[168] Until 7 years of age, children were allowed to live in the women's wards. After that age, they resided in the boys' or girls' sections, with a daily "interview" allowed if requested by either parent. By the 1880s, some improvements occurred in terms of provisions of toys, books, games, and outdoor excursions.

[169] Ottaway (2017, p. 34–35). For a review of the roles of apprenticeships in the British industrial revolution, see Humphries (2003).

[170] The comprehensive analysis of the Bristol experience by Butcher (1932) provides the bedrock for this section.

[171] There are indications that such arrangement found institutional resistance in the early years of implementation, including by the mayor and parish officers. Subsequent acts gave power to the corporation to both levying and collecting taxes if magistrates and overseers didn't act within 20 days from the request.

is, the function of the workhouse was, in their view, that of reducing the need for relief.

Management redirected activities toward unskilled work and tasks. Typical activities included pin making, oakum picking, and stone breaking. These tasks weren't particularly profitable, and some scandal emerged (e.g., difficulty in monitoring led to stones disappearing from sites; and some inmates were reselling the workhouse food, which was provided relatively abundantly). Apparently only during specific periods (e.g., in 1750–1760, 1789–1792, and 1800) when a contractor was employed and adult able-bodies workers were put on outside tasks (e.g., by the Society for Employing the Labouring Poor), it was possible to avoid a loss. Activities involved street cleaning and other manual activities, including being implemented in some of the poorest parts of the city. A riot occurred in 1832, when the payment for such activities shifted from "piece rates" for the work to "time unit" (48 h/week plus child allowances).

The profile of participants changed rapidly, and the corporation would soon become a hospital. For instance, between 1820 and 1825 the share of "impotent" populations out of total inmates grew from 29% to 69%. In 1832, the high concentration of inmates (a structure that could host 300 people was inhabited by about 600 inmates, with four to eight children sharing a single bed) made the corporation a vector for the rapid spread of cholera: out of the first 105 city cases detected in July–August, 71 were from the corporation.

The corporation was dissolved in 1898, with its operating procedures and personnel ensuring continuity in operationalizing the 1834 legislation. In fact, the new poor law adopted and scaled up nationally some of the corporation's arrangements. Bristol spearheaded signature features such as amalgamating parishes into larger units and having locally elected guardians: " . . . it fell to Bristol [ . . . ] to blaze the trail which over a century later was created a national highway by the Poor Law Reform of 1834."[172]

## From Paris to Florence: Depots and ateliers in Napoleonic times

A detailed account by Stuart Woolf chronicles the transmission and implant of French poor relief institutions in the early 1800s Napoleonic times in Tuscany.[173] The rational, statistics-oriented, and ruled-based nature of Napoleonic administration may have found intellectual resonance with Enlightenment principles in parts of Italy. For instance, in 1787 the Duchy of Modena laid out a comprehensive plan to streamline, consolidate, and centralize institutions involved in poor relief: premised on the notion that "excessive assistance, not crises, generates poverty," the "Ricci plan" identified institutions be eliminated, downsized, maintained, scaled up or reconfigured.[174]

[172] Butcher (1932, p. 1).
[173] Woolf (1986).
[174] Ricci (1787, p. 26). He lamented that a key reason for excessive assistance is compassion and religious impulses (p. 28). Ricci claimed that the number of poor people is proportionate to generosity (p. 35); he observed that when "subsidies" are introduced after a crisis, like the one in 1783, they don't unwind as

French rule in Tuscany introduced three institutions, namely the *bureau de bienfaisance* (coordinating body) in every commune, *dépôt de mendicité* (workhouses) in every department, and *ateliers* (public works) in every *arrondissement* of the cities. The history of those institutions in France is somewhat turbulent. Before Napoleonic times, in 1770 Jacques Turgot, the French minister of finance, reformed the country's *depots* by sending criminals to ordinary jails and using the *ateliers* for other profiles of able-bodied beneficiaries. Enormous pressure would soon be exerted on the *ateliers*' capacity to meet demand for assistance: on July 14, 1789, the day that the Bastille fell, they could only reach 8,600 Parisians out of 120,000, or nearly one fifth of the city's population, that "were reduced to beggary."[175] *Ateliers* would be abolished two years later, before being introduced again in 1793 on a seasonal basis.

In Florence, the number of pre-existing confraternities providing relief were reduced from 21 to 8, the latter being coordinated by the *bureau*. Financing of the relief system shifted more heavily on local administrations (64% in the case of Florence), while overall spending was cut by almost half. Assistance involved the provision of cash and bread, although a complete shift to in-kind modalities could occur during crises.[176]

The creation of *depots* responded to the 1808 ordinance that made begging illegal and regulated under the penal code. Directed to the *depots* were local beggars, while non-residents were dispatched to their place of origin. There were practical hiccups: to identify the appropriate buildings for the *depots*, the number of beggars needed to be estimated. A census was carried out, although the ambiguous definitions of who was "poor" and who was to be considered a "beggar" led to a range of different local definitions and estimates by mayors. Such activity was also time consuming: for example, in the Arno department it took over three years from receiving the initial request for listing the poor (December 19, 1808) to submitting the final list to Paris (March 4, 1812). Hence the assignment of people to *depots* was based not only on relatively inconsistent definitions, but also on outdated information. The result was that local capacities were often overwhelmed: in the case of Arno, its *depot* could host an estimated 535 people, but beggars were about 6,400. Because of ambivalence in definitions, many that were sent to the *depot* couldn't perform physical work.[177]

An initial phase of the *depot* involved activities reflecting the spirit of the *Congregazione di San Giovanni Battista*. The institution provided support to people

conditions improve (p. 69); and he bemoaned that beneficiaries should be required to demonstrate their needs (p. 70).

[175] Garraty (1978, p. 60).

[176] This was the case of during rising grain prices in 1812. All forms of assistance were replaced with bi-daily soup distributions. In Florence, in 1812 about 22,000 soups were distributed to a population of about 72,000 inhabitants. The soup system was extended beyond the high food price-induced crisis, including being implemented the following year as well as in the winter of 1813–1814 (Woolf 1986).

[177] In the Arno example, apparently out of the first 72 beggars that were sent to the local *depot*, 60 had some form of physical or mental impairment. At that point, the prefect ordered that only those able to work were to be directed to such institution, while the others were to be maintained by hospitals or the *bureau*.

whose labor income was insufficient to meet subsistence needs.[178] Inmates could produce textiles, shoes, and other products to supply both the private sector and the *ateliers*. Houses of industries were also launched in Russia (Box 3.7). Importantly, as other similar initiatives in Bristol and Germany revealed, this form of productive employment was not supposed to be in competition with the private sector, but it was still expected to becoming financially sustainable. For instance, wages in the *depots* of Napoleonic Turin of the early 1800s were one third lower than market wages.[179] In general, the enterprise would soon prove to be of unsatisfactory quality, expensive, and unable to meet cost-recovery principles.

### Box 3.7 The Kronstadt House of Industry

In 1872, a charismatic priest, Father Ioann Sergiev, established houses of industry in a parish of Kronstadt.[a] His rationale was straightforward: most poor people are poor because they lacked work and the means to pursue it (nutrition, tools, etc.). While seasonal and unstable labor markets played a major role, he didn't exclude moral causes (the city was an exile location for St. Petersburg's criminals). He established three institutions: housing for beggars, a workhouse for the unemployed adults, and a trade school for children. His work attracted significant public donations, including from the Imperial Family, and the institutions expanded rapidly. Hemp workshops, for example, included 25,000 participants per year. Houses of industries would scale up in the empire, such as in St. Petersburg's slums in 1886, and reached about 150 units by the early 1900s. Eventually, the institution "succumbed to pressure to expand their services. [ . . . ] Temporary relief sometimes turned into long-term care, and some institutions that housed elderly people or children for years become houses of industry in name only."

[a] The box is based on Lindenmeyr (1996, p. 170–172, 178, 181–182).

With productive goals proving elusive, *depots* were repurposed in favor of deterrence functions. The *ateliers*, which (differently from the *depots*) were voluntary, were de facto absorbed in the latter compulsory institution. If capacity constraints denied entry to the *depots* to some, once accepted people were kept for at least a year in the institution. Military guards secured the premises, and prison-like conditions were laid bare by desperate letters sent by inmates. These missives were invoking a relative to act as guarantor and led to a flurry of appeals with municipal authorities—a pattern

[178] Differently from the *Buonomini* congregation, the *Congregazione di San Giovanni Battista* was established to support those of "menial status" who didn't qualify as "shamefaced noble poor" (see Chapter 2, Box 2.2).

[179] Maldini (1982, p. 343).

that later emerged in China in the early 1900s (Chapter 6). Release of inmates with proper family guarantees was rejected even when requested by mayors.

The finale was sobering:

> . . . poverty went deeper and those unable to take advantage of any of the institutions set up for their assistance had to improve ways of resisting hunger and cold. Some tried to solve their problems by theft and assault. The prisons represented the last link in the long thin chain of institutional reactions to the world of poverty.[180]

## German(e) intensions for economic and social integration

### Hamburg

Already in 1527 Hamburg had an established system of poor relief organized around Protestant principles.[181] As narrated eloquently by Mary Lindemann, the plague of the early 1700s marked a temporary expansion in the competencies of the state in providing assistance. And like other cities, from 1622 Hamburg's poor relief was flanked by the *Zuchthaus* (workhouse) fulfilling multiple roles and attracting a variety of beneficiary profiles—a diversity that in part stemmed from the institution's function at the intersection of penal justice and poor relief.[182]

By the 1720s it was clear that *Zuchthaus* confinement was not only stigmatizing, but also detached workers from the labor market and hampered their re-integration. As the manufacturing economy of the city faced steep downturns, cracks started to form on Hamburg's ecclesiastically managed poor relief. The system was ill-suited to cope with the challenge of *die arbeitende Arme*, or the working poor subject to both economic volatility and physical mobility.[183] As such, city leaders commenced reconsidering cash transfers in ways that would be better suited for managing entrenched uncertainty entailed by industrialization and structural transformation.

Against this background, Hamburg's poor relief system of 1788 was hailed as one of the most comprehensive of the time.[184] It remained operational up to the Napoleonic era when, similarly to poor relief in other cities, the program collapsed under the pressure of war.[185] The architects of the Hamburg model, Caspar Voght

[180] Woolf (1986, p. 109).

[181] Under the scheme, parishes would create a *Gotteskasten*, or a chest recommended by Martin Luther and Johannes Bugenhagen, for the collection of alms. The program, however, would taper out by the late 1500s, as finding work for the able-bodied proved ineffective and even home visits withered: "all that survived of a once ambitious program was a scattering of alms and occasional handouts of bread, clothing and fuel" (Lindemann 1990, p. 18). See also Breuilly (1992).

[182] Lindemann (1990) notes that the *Zuchthaus* represented an early attempt to reform penal justice away from capital sentences and corporal punishment and toward imprisonment.

[183] Beck (1995), Lindemann (1990).

[184] De Schweinitz (1943). A detailed account of the scheme was published by von Voght first in 1796 and again in 1817 (von Voght 1817).

[185] When the opportunity to re-introduce the program arose in 1815, city officials opted against it deliberately (Frohman 2008; Lindemann 1990).

and Johann Büsch, had the working poor at the core of their vision, and the approach was underpinned by three key principles. The first was an individualized assistance with volunteer guardians (*Armenpfleger*) in each city district. This would ensure both supervision as well as direct personal contact with and knowledge of the claimant. The second was the notion of civic engagement of guardians who, drawing mostly from the middle class, would need to proactively dedicate time and knowledge to the cause. According to such philosophy, only " . . . [w]hen individuals were personally invested into the system's daily performance and overall outcome they could not sit back and criticize local government or find fault somewhere else, but rather know the challenges personally and seek practical solutions."[186] The third and final principle rested on public accountability. This included annually issued reports on the program, hence increasing access to information and instilling a sense of civic participation (and prompting notoriety of the scheme).

Operationally, the scheme first involved the estimate of the total number of poor people in the city. This was followed by their roughly equal division across five districts, each subdivided in 12 subdistricts. Such subdistricts would be supervised by two directors and included three overseers nominated for three years. Every 12 districts, a total of five physicians and five midwives were appointed for on-demand home assistance.

Equipped with questionnaires, the overseers would survey poor people in their districts and collect data based on home visits (also conducted by doctors) and validate the information with neighbors. The estimated income would serve as reference for determining the type of services offered. Men were employed in various public works activities (e.g., rope yarn, street cleaning). Old and sick people were brought to hospitals or given cash to pay for their board.

There were child benefits programs, both conditional and unconditional. The overall support rendered to children under 6 years of age hinged on family circumstances: where these involved "misery and drunkenness" children were housed by families of "better sorts of poor"; where instead the family was stable, mothers received cash transfers for each child (6–12d/week) and daycare centers were set up for facilitating parents' work. Children 6–16 years of age were obliged to attend school, but they also received two forms of transfers: one was a flat allowance ("payment for his work"), complemented by a performance-based payment resulting from "the compound ratio of his attendance at school, his behavior, and his application to work."[187] Importantly, those were "industry schools,"[188] and the amount of payments was devised based on the difference between what they earned at school and what they may have earned in the labor market.[189] A weekly allowance (24d) for lodging was also included.

Registered people received a printed copy of the "Instructions for the Poor," a contract laying out the terms of assistance. Refusing to work, failure to send children

[186] McMillan (2019, p. 62).
[187] De Schweinitz (1943, p. 92–93).
[188] See Mayer (2011) for an overview of pedagogy in those schools.
[189] Frohman (2008).

to school, excessive alcohol consumption, or playing the lottery would constitute a breach in the contract. To ease management in a large urban area, assistance restricted mobility, with people not being allowed to settle in other districts. Furthermore, single paupers couldn't reside alone and were compelled to lodge with groups of others. In addition to public funds, contributions were personally collected on a rotation basis by people in their neighborhoods.

## Munich

In 1790 Munich started a similar scheme under the leadership of US-born and minister of police Benjamin Thomson (also known as Count Rumford). Here, too, the approach involved dividing the city in subdistricts (16 instead of 60). A committee would register each household and assign it a number. On January 1, all beggars were rounded up, with the able-bodied being directed to the workhouse and the others to the committees for alms giving.[190] Payments for both grants and works would be made in cash. The program generally revolved around the establishment of a workhouse producing military clothing.

The underlying philosophy of Count Rumford was that "happiness" was key for virtuousness, and that "cleanliness," as opposed to "punishment," was key for making "poor and unfortunate people . . . really comfortable."[191] The workhouse building was, according to Thomson's account, hospitable, warm, and light-filled. Treating participants with respect was key, "and, if nothing were done to disgust the Poor, either by treating them harshly, or using *force* to oblige them to frequent the establishments, they would soon avail themselves of the advantages held out to them . . . ."[192] Work was paid by the piece, with top-up incentives for the most productive. Munich's workhouses adopted efficiency standards, including optimizing on food provisions and being non-residential—a more flexible model resembling Vienna's hybrid workhouses.[193] Financing was based, like in Hamburg, on a combination of public and private contributions.

Interestingly, the principles underpinning the Munich philosophy of relief, including the relationship between motivation and the quality of the surrounding environment, seemed in line with the ideas that Charles Leclerc de Montlinot was promulgating while serving as inspector of the *dépôt de mendicité* at Soisson, France, in the late 1770s. Montlinot would stress the importance of adequate hygiene and shelters to overcome "the idle dejection that beggars exhibited when housed in squalid conditions"; and he motivated inmates by instilling hope though labor, showing them that "work gave them the capacity to choose objects of consumption

[190] Garraty (1978).
[191] Quoted in de Schweinitz (1943, p. 91, 95).
[192] Thomson (1796, p. 101–102).
[193] In 1879, Vienna's workhouses had an inmate population of about 45,000, more than a tenfold increase from nearly 3,500 recorded in 1877. Admitted inmates could chose to work in the institution, which granted night shelter, meals and a modest weekly allowance, or work outside the workhouse and only spend the night there. In the latter case, a payment of 10 kreuzers (about 2d) was charged for night lodging (Ribton-Turner 1887, p. 548).

beyond necessities."[194] Similar accounts emerged from the early phases of the Bristol experience.[195]

Monlinot's worldview presents some similarity with those of John Barton in England in the early 1800s.[196] Barton set out an alternative vision on the relationship between cash transfers and poverty rooted in a fundamentally different view of human behavior compared to those of some classical economists.[197] He identified in hope, and not fear, the cardinal vehicle for improved welfare. Specifically, his understanding of human nature posited that "pressure of want" and "the harsh and stormy aspect of severe penury" led not to calculation and rational behavior, but to a deepening of instincts. Restoring prudence, foresight and entrepreneurship requires solidarity and hope, hence a role for more, and not less, social assistance as part of building the industriousness of low-income populations.

Back to the German experience, there are indications of cross-context influence. It was contended that Voght was involved in the restructuring of poor relief in Vienna.[198] In the 1790s, Voght spent 18 months in England, and the enthusiasm for the Hamburg system led him to publish, in that case in Edinburgh, the mentioned 1796 account of the program. Those exchanges were part of a broader flow of learning facilitated by "Enlightenment channels" like the Dublin Society and the Society of Arts.[199]

## Elberfeld

The Elberfeld system of 1853 was an adaptation of Hamburg's model and constitutes a celebrated case of cash and in-kind transfers. Elberfeld fused Enlightenment elements of individual responsibility with societal civic engagement under a coherent operational device.[200] The significance of the Elberfeld system for Germany's history of poor relief has been compared to the salience of the English 1834 new poor law.[201] After its founding by Daniel von der Heydt, the model had, by 1871, spread to other ten German towns; by 1911, it was adopted by 54 cities (Figure 3.8, left side).[202]

[194] McStay Adams (2023b, p. 16). In Montlinot's view, the causes of mendicity stemmed from exploitation of agricultural workers physically strained "over a lifetime of poorly requited toil" for the wealthy, a prelude to the "conception of social security for the aged that would be articulated during the Revolution" (McStay Adams 2023b, p. 17). Their unhealthy and low living standards deprived them "of incentive for productive activity" (ibid).

[195] Butcher (1932, p. 6) chronicled that girls employed in the workhouse "... so 'incouraged' by being new clothed [ ... ] and given food and beds, that they would soon settle down cheerfully [ ... ] which means [the initiative] won them into Civility, and love to their Labour."

[196] Barton (1817, 1820). McCulloch (1828) laid out a similar view.

[197] Grzybek (2024) offers a brilliant discussion on the classical economists "prejudice in scholarly clothes." See also Boyer (2021).

[198] Frohman (2008).

[199] Innes (1999).

[200] Grisewood and Hanewinkel (1898), McMillan (2019), Willis (2016).

[201] See Frohman (2008). According to the author, the Elberfeld system differed from Hamburg's in its broad-based mobilization of the urban middle class, which found in the scheme "... a mechanism through which ... participate in the public life of the city" (p. 91).

[202] The Elberfeld model was introduced at a time when the prevailing framework for poor relief was the Prussian General Code of 1794 which remained in place for over a century.

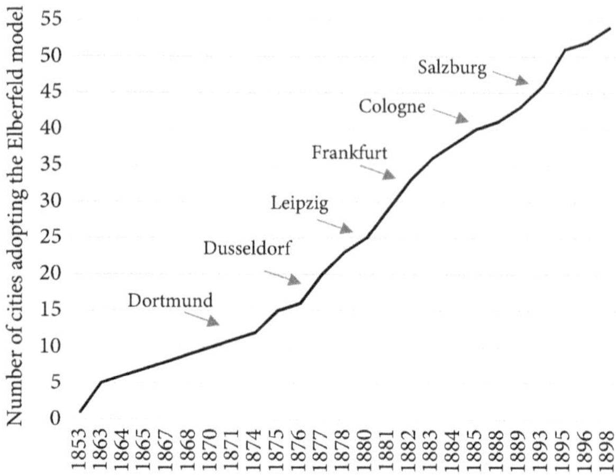

**Figure 3.8** Elberfeld diffusion (1853–1898) and Poor Care Memorial (1922).
*Source*: Data on left-hand graph is from Frohman (2008, p. 97) and refers to modern Germany and Austria; image on right side is from https://en.wikipedia.org/wiki/Elberfeld_system.

The city's practices attracted considerable international attention at a time when other countries, notably England and the United States, were equally grappling with the "Social Problem" of poverty in the age of industrialization.[203] Internationally, Elberfeld found itself at the center of an early process of transnational learning and knowledge transfer: the model " . . . was so successful that relief officials and social reformers came to see it as the embodiment of the very idea of rational, yet compassionate, assistance, and reformers would often debate whether the reorganization of relief in a specific city truly embodied the principles of the Elberfeld System."[204] For instance, as discussed in Chapter 6, there is ample documentation of the influence that "the German model" exerted on the Civil Society Organization in the United States.[205] In England, official visits to and assessments of the model were included in governmental reports discussed before Parliament.[206] And in a report of 1898, Russia proposed localized interventions that were regarded by ecclesiastical authorities as "mere copies of the German Elberfeld system."[207]

Following the Hamburg template, Elberfeld introduced a new relief administration within the municipal government that involved 23 council members. The city was initially split into eight large districts with an overseer in each. Each district was

[203] Himmelfarb (1991).
[204] Frohman (2008, p. 96).
[205] For example, see Pimpare (2004, 2002).
[206] Davy et al. (1888).
[207] Lindermeyr (1996, p. 92). Lindermeyr's study also highlights that the Elberfeld system was by criticized by the church as being "created by rich German merchants and manufacturers to defend themselves against the poot, not to provide them with Christian compassion and charity" (ibid., p. 93). Russia had already gained experience with similar "scientific charity" practices. In fact, a Society for Visiting the Poor was founded in St. Petersburg in 1846, and "files on the poor people investigated by its members [could be consulted] by outside philanthropists [ . . . ] to ensure that their benevolence found worthy recipients" (ibid., p. 117). These matters were also represented in contemporary art: Vladimir Makovsky, a realist, authored in 1874 a painting titled *Visiting the Poor.*

then divided into smaller districts, each with a *pro bono* and compulsory (similarly to today's jury duty) *Armenpfleger* guardian from middle and working-class citizens.[208] Initially, there were 112 guardians in Elberfeld, but their number and that of districts would be reassessed annually (e.g., in 1898 there were 37 districts and 518 guardians). Each guardian would be assigned to no more than four families: this low ratio was meant to favor a personalized service as well as to allow guardians to care for their own families and professions. While there were civic and pecuniary penalties for non-compliance with the obligatory nature of the scheme,[209] its compulsory feature "... was both unique and a responsibility of citizenship, and therefore a great honor."[210] Such honor was also commemorated with arts representing the system (e.g., see the right-hand side of Figure 3.8).

Eligibility to the program was open to people with an income insufficient to meet "the absolute necessities of life." Requests were directed to guardians who would then inquire into the application. Next steps in the process included the following:

> . . . the petitioner's case was brought to the next district meeting where the guardian would share his findings. These meetings occurred every two weeks and it would be here where the amount and type of relief would be determined. Cases were decided on a majority vote by the district guardians and the overseer. Meetings were typically held in communal locations throughout the district, such as a schoolroom.[211]

To avoid resentment and disenfranchisement,[212] the city didn't impose a direct poor relief tax on citizens (a concern shared in Hamburg). Instead, financing came from the taxation of

> . . . interest derived from money invested in the reserve fund of the Saving Bank in Elberfeld, taxing the profits from the local newspaper *Täglicher Anzeiger*, from police fines, the licenses of theaters and concerts, and payments made to the hospital. Another portion of funds came from general taxes of the municipality to supplement what was not covered from the other taxes.[213]

The model wasn't without critics, especially in the early phases of implementation.[214] While participating beneficiaries would receive cash or in-kind transfers on a weekly basis, the latter couldn't be resold, while the use of former wasn't entirely

[208] Edwards (1878).
[209] Refusal to serve involved penalties like being barred from voting for municipal affairs for up to six years and pay up to 25% higher taxes.
[210] McMillan (2019, p. 68). By 1903, there were 110 visitors having served at least 25 years in such capacity.
[211] McMillan (2019, p. 72).
[212] The perceived risk was that with dedicated taxes payers would just "pay away" their contribution, hence undermining the crucial element of proactive participation and direct engagement in the poverty problem.
[213] McMillan (2019, p. 77).
[214] Hennock (2007).

discretionary.[215] Idleness or drunkenness were met with penalties ranging from the termination of relief to up to one month of imprisonment. Based on field reports, the system has been defined as "absolutely inquisitorial," with a "harsh and oppressively rigorous" approach to assessment and cash transfer management.[216] Perspective beneficiaries had to provide information on at least 25 specific issues spanning detailed description of family members' morality, dwellings, and weekly earnings; this would be followed by visitors' duty to "ascertain" the information supplied and conduct "a strict investigation into the circumstances of the man's life and present conditions." The approach amounted to being "constantly 'looked up' by the visitor," with beneficiaries having to report any minimal change in status and keep a "wages book" (*Verdienst buch*): the latter was to be entered by the employer, who would notify earnings and instances of idleness and bad behavior. In other words, " . . . [t]he pauper is, in fact, kept under constant *surveillance*."[217]

Eventually, the model's efficacy was strained by the forces of structural transformation. Just like previous church-based provisions, Elberfeld rested on static social relations whereby a poor guardian could effectively "know the community": this assumed a "manageable" city size and the coexistence of different social classes concentrated spatially. While in the early 1970s half of the population in the region was employed in agriculture, such rate almost halved by early 1900s. Hence, the Elberfeld "natural" socio-economic ecosystem was steadily eroded by rural–urban migration and the emergence of large slum-type settlements hosting the growing cities' "proletariat": " . . . [t]his urban landscape was not a place that would facilitate the close relationship between poor guardian and the impoverished. Rich and poor no longer lived in the same neighborhood, the poor themselves were constantly on the move so the attempt to build relationships with them was almost impossible."[218]

The system tried to adapt to the new landscape in three ways: guardians were dispatched to districts not on the basis of living in proximity to the applicants ("their neighbors"), but on technical abilities to assess needs; local decisions on benefit types and generosity were assigned not to local guardians but to central administrators; and the nature of the guardian function morphed into a blend of *pro bono* and paid service.

Recasting the model, however, came with trade-offs:

> . . . [t]he more centralized the decision making the less inclined individuals felt towards understanding their service as a role of citizenship. The greater reliance on paid guardians meant individuals did not have to feel responsible for the conditions of the poor and in turn caused them to misunderstand poverty's root causes

[215] There were limits to what cash could be used for. For example, " . . . if a member of petitioner's family was [deceased in a workhouse] and the family follows the poor-house hearse in a coach" it was then inferred that such use of money (i.e., for a coach) indicated that the family wasn't truly in need of assistance (Doyle reporting on the Elberfeld system in 1871, quoted by Chance 1897, p. 333).

[216] Chance (1897, p. 332).

[217] Ibid., p. 333.

[218] McMillan (2019, p. 86).

[ . . . ] [This posed a risk of] scapegoating communal responsibilities when the middle- and upper-classes become uninvested and cutoff from the processes of poor relief.[219]

## 3.4 Conclusions

This chapter provides a set of framing devices—labor reserves, various forms of transitions, industrial policy—that may help inject a dose of dynamism in interpreting the role of cash transfers in the process of economic transformation. Five main points stand out from the chapter's analysis.

First is the issue of "sequence." It is sometimes contended that countries would need a critical mass of economic performance *before* investing in cash-based redistribution. There are legitimate considerations in such proposition, and trade-offs between investment priorities should not be easily dismissed. However, the chapter shows that in practice, cash transfers were present *during* successful processes of transformation, including cases in England, the Netherlands, Germany, and China. In the case of England, they have been even framed as enablers of economic change. In general, their relative role and form varied, but they were consistently part of the process. The conversation should not be whether cash transfers are salient at low levels of economic performance, but rather how can they complement some key drivers of the economic development process. In fact, as a part of attending economic transformation, cash transfers were never isolated; they were one aspect of a wider set of ingredients—political commitment, institutional reforms, community mobilization, administrative innovations—that provided the ecosystem facilitating economic evolution.

Second, the challenge of introducing static responses to dynamic problems is in full display. The chapter's description of historical experiences points to deliberate attempts to make the process of economic development inclusive. Cities and countries invested considerable effort in identifying models that would help integrate lower-income populations into the mainstream growth process. The operational tools deployed in Germany for their design and implementation were analytically grounded. Whether such methods translated into economic self-sufficiency of the recipient remains an open question. If their degree of success was probably feeble, it was also because approaches were often better suited for static populations. The forces of urbanization and migration were constantly reconfiguring the operational landscape.

Third, interventions often pursued competing objectives. The visionary characters that spearheaded economic inclusion initiatives would soon have to face the dilemma of prioritizing productivity and equity goals. A single institution like the house of industries would start absorbing a wide range of participants with different profiles that stifled their performance. Today's debates around "graduating" people out of

[219] Ibid., p. 92.

cash transfer programs face similar quandaries in reconciling the twin impulses of serving those most in need and integrating them in labor markets.

Fourth comes the trade-off between "knowing" and "managing." The spirit of commitment that the middle-class visitors displayed in engaging in those interventions was remarkable: such participation may have engendered a sense of common purpose across societal classes and forged a personalized, local donor–recipient relationship. "Knowing" the person would become more challenging, and the centralization of administration was becoming more efficient to manage expanding cities. The administrative gain came at the cost of more alienating, impersonal assistance. The implication was, as put by Dawn Greeley, that cash assistance could be "... angrily demanded by the anonymous poor and grudgingly given by an equally anonymous group of taxpayers, it [ ... ] fostered class feeling."[220]

Finally, economic transformation goes hand in hand with social disruption. As countries improved living standards, the price has been significant dislocation for large swaths of the population. Later in the book (Chapter 5) we discuss the role of cash transfers in taming social discontent, which was often the direct result of sweeping change in economic structures. And Chapter 6 covers reforms occurring precisely because of the change process being too overwhelming. But this chapter suggests that the magnitude of needs generated in the development process is an important entry point for cash transfers. As countries face new set of structural changes—including manufacturing, green, digital, or potential artificial intelligence-related transitions—the experiences of centuries ago may offer some clues on the need for containing the likely social cost of economic advancement.

[220] Greeley (2022, p.18).

# 4
# Building State Capabilities

> . . . the registration of those in need of poor relief was of great concern to all magistrates [ . . . ] to minimize the number of people dependent on poor relief in their jurisdictions.
>
> **Henk Looijesteijn and Marco van Leeuwen (2012, p. 220)**

After having reviewed the role of cash transfers in attending the process of economic transformation, this chapter discusses an equally ambitious, complementary role in building state capabilities. Such function can be subject to multiple definitions and interpretations. The chapter adopts a pragmatic, vignette-based approach to illustrate three such scenarios. First, it examines the place for cash transfers within larger efforts of state (or empire) administrations to attain food security. An initial section provides a brief exploration of experiences from ancient India, China, and Rome. For example, the infrastructure that underpins food assistance programs, such as the Chinese ancient systems of rainfall data collection and household registration, enabled officials to make decisions affecting the level of coverage, duration, and targeting of transfers (including cash benefits) in ways that echo modern provisions. Second, the chapter investigates how crises may offer an opportunity to introduce state-provided cash transfers on a pilot or permanent basis. In doing so, it traces cases where schemes evolved from crisis response interventions to more comprehensive programs. The United States is the main focal point for such illustrations, complemented by a brief reference to more recent instances of crises-born cash transfers globally. Finally, the third section discusses cash transfers in the context of protracted adversity in select low- and middle-income countries, especially in India and Africa. This includes a review of experiences across pre-colonial, colonial, and post-independence periods.

## 4.1 The elephant, dragon, and she-wolf: Food and cash transfers in imperial times

Food security has been a major concern over history. A key way to address it was via "public distribution systems" of commodities currently operational in several countries.[1] Their implementation required logistical capabilities for food procurement,

[1] Alderman et al. (2017).

*Timely Cash*. Ugo Gentilini, Oxford University Press. © Ugo Gentilini (2024). DOI: 10.1093/9780191994982.003.0004

stock management, and accounting, among others. During the Egyptian Dynasties, and especially around the New Kingdom (16th–11th century BC), extensive in-kind collections were centrally, minutely registered and stored in granaries and palaces.[2] Their subsequent distribution may have included an element of income support, although it seemed largely for purposes other than poverty relief, like distribution to bureaucrats.[3] As various forms of food subsidies emerged, these coexisted with small-scale cash assistance. Paleographic evidence suggests that cash transfers were used as food crisis response in ancient India; those transfers were part of wider granary reforms in imperial China; and cash assistance was a more permanent, progressively financed feature of cities across the Italian peninsula in Roman times.[4] In those cases, transfers in cash seem more limited in scale than the corresponding volume of in-kind provisions, but were nonetheless part of evolving systems of social protection.[5]

## India's food and emergency cash transfers of Sohgaura and Mahasthan

As states were gradually formed across India,[6] the ancient text *Arthashastra*, which seems to be written by Kautilya around the 3rd–4th century BC, laid out a series of desirable actions to be undertaken by rulers.[7] The text noted that " . . . general impoverishment relating to money and grain destroys everything and is difficult to redress, while impoverishment related to draught animals and men can be overcome with money and grain."[8] The provision of food and public works programs seems to be present in most of India's history: " . . . [v]arious Indian rulers (such as Mohammad bin Tughlak in the fourteenth century) made extensive use of work projects and income creation for rebuilding lost entitlements."[9] In-kind food was also

[2] Egypt's large-scale bureaucratic system was orchestrated by a grand vizier and included extensive labor-intensive public works for activities like flood prevention. For their implementation, the corvee system established that every adult man had to dedicate one year of work out of seven. For a brief description, see Day and Schiele (2013), Dolgoff and Feldstein (2009), and Jansson (2009). The corvee system was also present in the Inca empire (see Box 2.8 in Chapter 2), where the state's economic output hinged on such labor tax applied to each household on a rotation basis (D'Altroy et al. 1985).

[3] Ezzamel (2002).

[4] The she-wolf is Rome's symbol. The mythology of the city's origins includes a she-wolf nursing the twins Romulus and Remus who are associated with its founding. While the analysis of food subsidies is mostly limited to Rome, the discussion on cash transfers covers the Italian peninsula.

[5] See Gentilini (2016a) for an overview of comparative theory, evidence, and practices of cash and in-kind transfers.

[6] The first states may have been established in the valley of the river Ganga in the 6th century BC. The process of state formation in locations like Maharashtra and Odisha would appear nearly 500 years later—and only within an additional 500 years would the state appear in Karnataka and Tamil Nadu. For state formation in India, see, for example, Roy (1994), Sharma (2007, 1989), and Thapar (1991).
Devadevan (2020).

[7] Prasad (1995). It was pointed out that "... [t]he concept of welfare state is brought closer to political thinking by the dharmaśāstras and the arthaśāstras. They introduce us to the programme of universal protection and state relief of the poor destitute and kindliness" (Kalita 2016, p. 132).

[8] See the text's topic 109, verse 7.5.33 (Kautilya 2013, p. 291).

[9] Dreze and Sen (1989, p. 123). See also Dreze (1988).

a medium for tax payments: the Chola emperor Rajaraja I, who reigned around at the turn of the first millennium AD, collected nearly 87,000 metric tons of paddy per year.[10]

Paleographic evidence attests to the importance of assistance in times of crises. Some of the most ancient records are enshrined in a couple of inscriptions dated around 250–150 BC. One such engraving refers to a bronze plate found in the village of Sohgaura, Uttar Pradesh, and appears to only refer to in-kind transfers.[11] The other inscription appears to include reference to cash assistance: the table was discovered in Mahasthan, Bangladesh, in 1931 (Figure 4.1).[12] The plaque's lines indicate that "when there is an excess of plenty, this granary and the treasury may be replenished with paddy and *gamdnka*," where *gamdnka* refers to gandakas, "a coin of the value of four cowries."[13] There is debate on whether those coins were transfers or loans: some refer to King Kharavela's act of " . . . distributing cash grants,"[14] while others interpret the reference to gandakas as an order to advance loans.[15] According to the latter interpretation, both coins and paddy were distributed, but they were to be paid back to the treasury as the crisis subsided.[16]

**Figure 4.1** Inscription of Mahasthan, 250–150 BC.

*Source*: National Encyclopedia of Bangladesh.[a]

[a] See https://en.banglapedia.org/index.php/Mahasthan_Brahmi_Inscription, where the image is licensed under the Creative Commons 4.0 license. The inscription, which is also reproduced in Bhandarkar (1931) as an intermezzo between pages 84 and 85, is currently exhibited at the Indian Museum in Kolkata.

More accounts of cash transfers emerge in India's (relatively) more recent history.[17] For example, in 1630, Shah Jehan, the Muslim Emperor of the Mughal Empire,

[10] Devadevan (2020).

[11] Unearthed in 1893, the small plaque (6.4 cm × 2.9 cm) involved four lines with seven symbols. The inscription refers to two storehouses meant for storing food commodities like fodder and wheat as well as objects such as canopies and ropes to be used in times of "urgent need" (Barua 1930, Fleet 1907, Singh 2008).

[12] Majumdar (2023).

[13] Bhandarkar (1931, p. 87).

[14] Altekar (1955, p. 40).

[15] Singh (2008).

[16] This implies that in times of abundance authorities were to restock both finances and food storage, that is, "they were to return coins to the treasury and the corn to the granary, in other words, to pay the State back in kind and cash" (Bhandarkar 1931, p. 87).

[17] The review by Loveday (1914, p. 135–138) identifies about 80 episodes of famines and food "scarcities" between 297 and 1907.

ordered weekly distributions, occurring every Monday, of 5,000 rupees to the "deserving poor" of Burhanpur; and 50,000 rupees were delivered to famine-stricken populations in Ahmadabad.[18] We return to India's long-standing famine responses later in chapter.

## The state infrastructure for future delivery of cash transfers: Food subsidies and household registration in Imperial China

### Granaries as harbingers of cash transfers

In antiquity, the legitimacy of Chinese rulers was often shaped by their ability to "nourish the people," or at least averting famines.[19] The establishment and management of a comprehensive grain reserve system responded at least in part to such logic. Fulfilling these political and operational responsibilities would require strong state capabilities.[20]

A mosaic of three granary models emerged gradually:[21] "ever-normal granaries" were geared to smooth out fluctuations in food prices. These were urban oriented, centrally managed, and involved the collection of taxes in the form of commodities and their distribution to cities. They were also provided to the military for financing defense efforts. To fill the gap in rural areas, "community granaries" were established locally and managed outside state structures.[22] This configuration was

[18] See Loveday (1914, p. 22) and chapter 14 in Elliot (1907). Sen (1910, p. 840) reports another distribution of 60,000 rupees to the deserving poor in 1650. For a history of famines, see De Waal (2018).

[19] Moral precepts were intertwined with governance strategies: the relationship between ensuring material security (or basic subsistence), people's morality and social order was emphasized in ancient philosophical texts of Mencius in the 4th century BC as well as the Guanzi, see Edgerton-Tarpley (2014, 2008), Li (2007), and Wong (1997). For a discussion on famines over China's history, see Fuller (2019), Mallory (1926), and Smil (1999). The need for state policy to stabilize prices and manage the "food price dilemma" (Timmer 1986) is longstanding. Analysis of the *Han-Shu* treatise—an eminent record of Chinese civilization over seven centuries—reveals that food subsidies were called upon as early as 650 BC (Ban and Lee Swann 1950, p. 223). Yet military demands on warring Chinese states in preimperial times entailed that proposals on food reserves would remain conceptual and only implemented in the subsequent Imperial era.

[20] To this effect, it has been noted that "... [f]or much of its history, Imperial China had the world's most advanced administrative bureaucracy" (Bikales 2021, p. 9). Some accounts of a robust state bureaucracy date back even further: Von Glahn (2022) argues that already around the year 1045 BC, "... [a] fledging bureaucracy was created, with the [Zhou] kings appointing ministers for revenue collection, public works, and military affairs and hunting. A large staff of scribes and secretaries [ . . . ] preserved government records" (p. 93).

[21] Tabulations for the second half of the 1700s show that, under a range of assumptions, granaries may have covered about 5% of provincial populations with support for two months/year. State supplies equaled about 7% of marketed grains, which implies that beneficiaries received about 15% of their food from granaries. In terms of costs, the system claimed an average about 0.5–2% of annual revenues over 1700–1850 (Will and Wong 1991). From the 1790s, the usage of granaries started to dwindle. Official commitments withered, accompanied by signs of decline in accountability. Later imperial restoration wasn't matched by a re-establishment of the granary system, and the droughts that struck the war-ridden Republic in the first half of the 1900s claimed an estimated 15.7 million lives (Edgerton-Tarpley 2014).

[22] Championed by philosopher Zhu Xi, "community granaries" attempted to curb granary leakages by shifting their management from officials to people locally. Such granaries were mostly funded by private

**Table 4.1** Three models of imperial granaries.

| | Ever-normal granaries | Charity granaries | Community granaries |
|---|---|---|---|
| *Introduction (dynasty)* | Jin (265–420 AD) | Sui (589–618 AD) | Song (960–1279 AD) |
| *Objective* | Price stabilization | Dedicated granaries for famine relief | Serve those not reached by ever-normal |
| *Management* | Central state officials | Local initiatives | Local community (NGO) |
| *Operation* | Purchase (autumn) and sales of grains (spring) at reduced price | Reduced-price sales and loans | Loans (10% interest, used to cover operating costs) |
| *Funding* | State budget | Special taxes and private contributions | Private contributions by wealthy landowners |
| *Location* | Large urban areas | Towns | Rural areas |

*Source*: The author based on Will and Wong (1991).

complemented by an intermediate model of "charity granaries" designated for famine response. Table 4.1 lays out main features of the models.[23]

How does this connect to cash transfer experiences? The administration of food subsidies was part of a broader process of state management that also encompassed features relevant for contemporary programs. In fact, a deeper understanding of the granary system may help illuminate the origins of cash transfer practices and links to broader social protection systems.

For instance, ancient household registration practices informed the targeting of food assistance via welfare-based rankings. Historian Richard von Glahn notes that "... [t]he use of household ranking to determine welfare entitlements [in the Song era] anticipated some features of the modern hukou system."[24] The latter, as discussed in Chapter 3, is a key registration system that classified the population in terms of rural and urban status, a distinction that entailed a sharp differentiation in accessing social protection and other services: "[w]ithout registration, one cannot establish

contributions. Community granaries were largely managed outside official channels and lacked systematic monitoring. From the 1740s the government participated in the stocking of community granaries, including with transfers from ever-normal granaries and the use of provincial funds. Clusters of community granaries were merged—for example, in Hunan the consolidation occurred for every five to ten granaries.

[23] The discussion on granaries offered in this section draws extensively from the encyclopedic work of Will and Wong (1991). Their volume provides a monumental review of operational and analytical issues affecting the Chinese granary system.

[24] von Glahn (2012, p. 55).

eligibility for food, clothing or shelter, obtain employment, go to school, marry or enlist in the army."[25]

While key for food granaries, this state infrastructure also underpinned cash transfers in antiquity: as we shall see, around the turn of the first millennium there are accounts of local cash schemes for families of "certifiably poor status," hence suggesting a link to registration systems.[26] While there is some dispute on whether such support was rendered in cash or as tax rebates, there is less debate that other ancient programs provided money: for example, sales of granary food helped finance poorhouses, where cash and food transfers were dispensed daily.

There are other continuities. During the Maoist regime (Chapter 3), food policy was geared to primarily support urban-oriented industrialization through the management of grain procurement and subsidies (see Box 3.2). A similar primacy of urban objectives was not alien to imperial rulers. And just like imperial community and charity granaries supported rural areas, the structure of food procurement and subsidy systems in both Mao and the immediate post-Mao periods did direct food to disadvantaged rural areas as well.

Another connection with the past relates to experimentation and diffusion of practices. According to Yuen Yuen Ang, one of the main lessons from China's historical experience with poverty reduction is not necessarily *what* to do, but *how* to create the conditions to adapt and learn.[27] For instance, as shown in Chapter 3, the way in which the *Dibao* cash transfer is governed includes the delineation of broad, centrally directed contours as informed by piloting, learning, and cross-fertilization of practices (see Box 3.3). In a similar vein, in the mid-1700s "officials diligently searched for methods to increase the amount of grain stored in rural areas of Zhili"; their success "quickly inspired comparable efforts in other provinces," and the emperor "ordered the governors of [other areas] to consider copying the [Zhili] idea."[28]

As the challenge of stock management became more manifest,[29] the practice of storing silver instead of commodities took root. In the 1730s, Fujian stored 60–70% of its grains as money for local purchases: in line with modern decision-making tools, policymakers expected anticipated efficiency gains from managing cash in terms of fewer logistics and less spoilage.[30] Yet, those modalities implied a heavier reliance on markets and were subject to administrative hurdles.[31]

A further link between past and present relates to governance. A hallmark of the recent zero-poverty strategy is, as discussed in Chapter 3, a high degree of

[25] Cheng and Selden (1994, p. 644), who also write that "[t]he origins of the hukou system lie embedded in the baojia system of population registration and mutual surveillance perfected over millennia" (p. 645).
[26] Apter (2013, p. 9).
[27] Ang (2016).
[28] Will and Wong (1991, p. 70, 71, 72).
[29] In general, provinces were directed to distribute 30% of granaries' reserves annually.
[30] See, for example, Barrett et al. (2007) and Lentz et al. (2013).
[31] Once food was sold for money at county level, it had to be exchanged (likely at a cost) into silver and then transported to provincial treasurers. When it was time for restocking, local officials reclaiming silver from the coffers could be subject to pressures and extortion within the administration. Delays in releasing silver were frequent, leading to possible missed opportunities in seizing low price purchases (Will and Wong 1991).

administrative mobilization. This involved marshalling " . . . several hundred thousand government staff to visit poor rural areas,"[32] establishing targets and rewarding bureaucratic success. In a similar vein, in 1748 targets for grain contributions were set at provincial level and county levels. In 1681, the Yongzheng emperor instituted a policy of rewarding officials who successfully solicited contributions for ever-normal granary reserves in exchange for degrees.[33] And the emperor himself was personally fomenting institutional and administrative action.[34]

In some cases, granaries were connected to public works. For example, in the 1700s the replenishment of community granaries was limited by a threshold (e.g., in 1772 Anhui the limit was 400,000 shi). This offered a link to other programs: the exceeding reserve would be sold, and proceeds were directed to provincial coffers to fund public works for canals and dikes.[35]

Public works could also be used for famine relief (e.g., for city walls repair): a government regulation of 1073 laid out guidance for public works planning, including detailed costing and labor requirements. These should be undertaken for water conservation purposes using grains and funds from ever-normal granaries—in other words, food-for-work programs.[36] As discussed in Chapter 3, these programs would later play a role in the 1980s–1990s: when the schemes enlisted unpaid workers, the mutual reinforcement of work obligations among community members played an important role, somewhat evoking the *wu* system in the Qing era mentioned in Box 4.1.

There were other important innovations for famine response. In the late 1680s, granary efforts were complemented by the collection of rainfall data to produce reports on grain prices, weather, and harvest conditions with a view of informing famine relief.[37] Moreover, grains could be used to meet the needs of other provinces in times of need.[38]

Finally, there were broader connections to economic inclusion. For example, a radical change in approach was proposed during the Song period in the 1060s. During that time, economist and reformer Wang Anshi had established a public microcredit program in lieu of granary commodities:[39] reserves were costly to the state, and market loans were expensive for peasants. Yet Anshi's low-interest loan scheme, known as "green sprout loans," was severely criticized on the basis of state interference

[32] Bikales (2021, p. 3).

[33] The edict rewarded the provision of grain with the "student of the imperial academy" degree (Will and Wong 1991, p. 28).

[34] Will and Wong (1991).

[35] Will and Wong (1991, p. 68).

[36] Will (1990). Yang (1957) points to a collection of "guidebooks for famine relief," inclusive of public works practices, compiled by Yu Sen in 1690.

[37] In the 1660s, a provision allowed for the free distribution of grains when harvests were particularly unfavorable.

[38] This shows that granaries evolved from localized provisions to a system of interprovincial flows to cover shortfalls over a large territory. This was the case, for example, in 1725 when Guangxi supported Guangdong and Jiangxi transferred grains to Fujian.

[39] The scheme was launched at a time of wider Song "New Policy" monetary innovations and expansionary money supply, including the introduction of bills of exchange, new forms of credit and paper money (von Glahn 1996). Some have defined Wang Anshi's reforms as "proto-Keynesian" (Zhao and Drechsler 2018).

with markets.[40] Some have argued that the green sprouts policy influenced the US New Deal approach in the 1930s.[41]

## Registration and targeting

Between 994 and 1033, the Song dynasty issued legislation for registration requirements and practices. Building on previous practices (see Box 4.1), an empire-wide system of household ranking was devised for civil registration, taxation, and providing a degree of progressive redistribution via taxes and transfers.

### Box 4.1 The Origins of Household Registries in Imperial China

One the earliest Chinese population registers can be traced to military purposes in the 6th century BC.[a] This involved conscripting those taller than 161 cm in urban areas and 138 cm in rural settings. The Qin system, which was in place until around 200 BC, included a surveillance-type system of registration based on the principle of "register household to make them equal" (*bianhu qimin*): the whole population had equal status, and this required registered fixed residency and groups of five families (*wu*) in residential proximity sharing legal liability for each other's actions.

Under the Han dynasty up to the early 200s AD, the state conducted two household assessments—a yearly "minor" one during the lean season to update demographic changes, related labor obligations and poll taxes; and such information was consolidated every three years into a "major" assessment compiled for the central government by higher-level officials.

The Song state (960–1279) would use registries for taxation and redistribution purposes. Officials also created the *baojia*, a system for policing purposes à la *wu*. The allocation of *baojia* duties was based on a new "fish-scale" register sorting households by location,[b] with *baojia* units gradually absorbing tax collection functions (the most affluent first and second-ranked households had the responsibility to cover for shortfalls in tax payments within their jurisdiction).

From the 1300s, the Ming state introduced massive household surveys recorded in "yellow registers" by collecting data on all household members every ten years,[c] they again served the purpose of labor service and tax collection as well as determining the heads of the newly established *lijia* system. Rural societies were now organized in *li* groups of 110—that is, 100 households headed by ten wealthy landowners which

[40] Smith (1993).
[41] Li (2019) recounted that "[w]hen the then-U.S. Secretary of Agriculture Henry A. Wallace read a doctoral thesis by Chen Huanzhang, a student at Columbia University, titled *The Economic Principles of Confucius and His School*, he took note of Wang's Green Sprouts Act and later decided to incorporate some of Wang's ideas into new national policies" (p. 52).

would basically govern the *li* for ten years, including tax collection, policing, assigning duties for communal public works for flood control, etc. In the early 1600s, there were about two million volumes of yellow registers from about 20 surveys. The rigid *lijia* system would soon prove inadequate to capture increasing changes in wealth and mobility. Under the Qing dynasty, yellow registers were suspended and replaced with a lighter quinquennial survey, the *biansehn*, while a revamped *baojia* took over the *lijia* system.

[a] The box is largely based on Von Glahn (2012).
[b] Hook and Twitchett (1991, p. 200). In addition to fish-scale registries, the later period of the dynasty would also include an alphabetical register (sorted by surname and associated property list) and "rat-tail" register (with tax assessments ordered from large to small).
[c] County officers were required to check for the individual affidavit submitted by each household (on indeed a decennial basis) and make four certified copies for various government levels.

In the Song era, households were first grouped into "host" (or "native") and "guests": the former were landowners and constituted most of the population,[42] while the latter were propertyless and accounted for about one third of rural households. Host households in rural areas were then ranked into five levels. The head of the household provided self-reported information on a range of demographic and economic variables. Such information was compiled in a detailed statement (*shou-shih*), which was subsequently verified by village officers and entered in a household register ("Five-Rank Registers").[43] Household rankings were based on their size, the number of able-bodied adult males, the amount and quality of land, assets like livestock, seeds and tools, and taxes in arrears. These were converted into monetary value to determine tax and labor due to the state.[44] Statutorily, Song registers were to be updated every three years.[45] While less sophisticated, there are accounts of rankings based on food poverty in Europe in the mid-1800s (Box 4.2).

## Box 4.2 The 1847 Food Survey and Poor Relief in Bern

Christian Pfister provides an interesting account of lists of vulnerable populations in mid-1800s Bern and their connection to poor relief. Following a food riot in October 1846, in March 1847 Mr. Johann Rudolf Schneider, a physician and government

[42] In the year 1099, there were about 13.2 million registered host/native households in the Song empire (Golas 1980, p. 302)
[43] Von Glahn (2012).
[44] Ranks also determined obligations like the *hemai* mandating sales of grains at fixed prices to the state. Indirect taxation was increasingly important: by 1077, indirect taxation accounted for two thirds of annual revenues (Liu 2015, p. 53–54). As such, the Song state has been hailed as "the first sustainable tax state in global history, because it was the earliest financial system established on the basis of indirect taxation" (ibid, p. 72).
[45] According to some accounts, household statements were produced annually and sent to the Public Revenue Department, while the information there contained was included in the register every three years. See discussion in Twitchett (1963, p. 217–218).

official of the Bern Swiss cantonal government, conducted a survey providing an inventory of foods stored in every community. This included the production of a detailed lists of 60,000 households including the profession of their head and available food resources. Complemented by a census of 1850, this information was used to classify households in four categories based on food poverty: two thirds of the population belonged into either "group 0" (landless with no food) or group 1 (wage dependent with a small plot of land, with food sufficient for less than 60 days). Groups 2 and 3 had food for 60–120 days and more than 120 days, respectively. While Bern seemed to lack the Chinese direct relationship between poverty and transfers, it was noted that the bottom Group 0 "would entirely depend on poor relief and soup kitchen during dearth".

*Source:* Pfister (1990, p.299).

The ranking determined the type of labor obligations: the first two categories in rural areas served as village officers, while lower ranks rendered labor for positions like jailers or couriers; the fifth-ranked households were exempted.[46] The fourth and fifth group, which accounted for an estimated 80–90% of the host rural population, were smallholders who had to diversify and supplement farming their own land with work on others' fields and additional activities.[47] Figure 4.2 sketches out household rankings in rural settings.

In urban areas, households were ranked into more finely graded ten categories, including based on rents, business income, and other economic assets. Household classifications were instrumental for granaries eligibility: in general, grains were provided to the bottom 40% of the ranks, that is, to the fourth and fifth categories in rural areas and to ranks six to ten in cities. A further injection of progressivity occurred via tax exemptions in years of bad harvests, which were also calculated based on household ranks.[48]

After a reform of 1070, the presence of able-bodied adults in the household ceased to be considered in the ranking calculation: in fact, the reform also allowed lower-ranked households to replace the payment of taxes in grain and labor with cash. This signaled an early pivotal change towards grading households based on wealth.[49]

Targeting practices varied by granary models. In general, ever-normal granaries were broad-based in eligibility. For example, in 1751 rice shopkeepers in Fujian were allowed to purchase ever-normal granary reserves for resale. While targeting rules could shift based on harvest performance,[50] the overall market and urban-oriented

[46] Families of active or retired officials were also exempted from labor services.
[47] Golas (1980, p. 300 and 302).
[48] Von Glahn (2012, p. 55).
[49] Von Glahn (2012).
[50] For instance, a report by Governor Nasutu of 1738 sets out targeting guidance based on harvest performance and leading to generic, seasonal, and narrow provisions. According to Will and Wong (1991, p. 479), three scenarios were envisaged: (i) when harvests were inadequate and prices high, distribution centers were set up to serve a broad group in both urban and rural areas (the 30% distribution rate could be waived); (ii) in years of favorable harvest, a group of urban dwellers relying on markets would still be served in the spring's lean season; and (iii) when harvest were successful for several consecutive years,

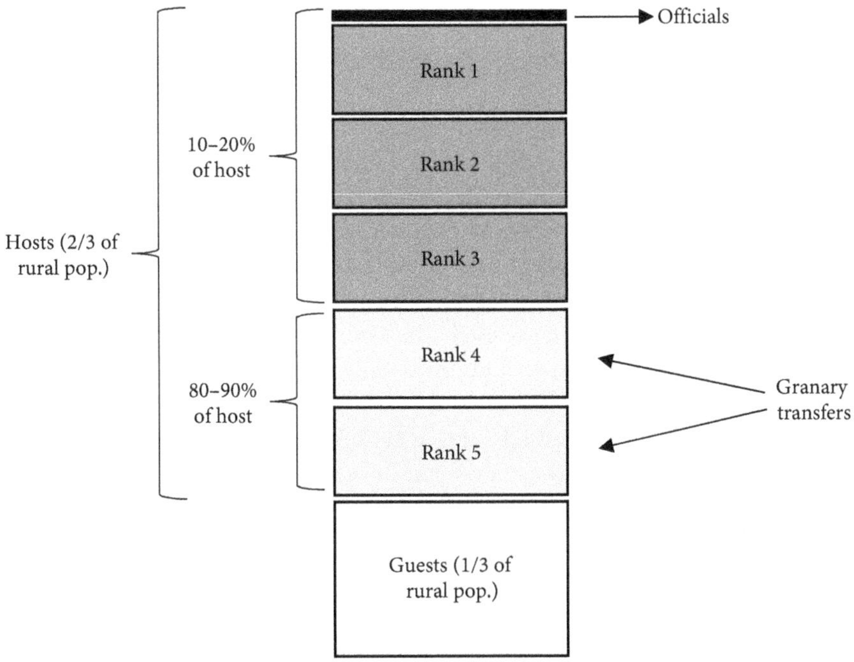


**Figure 4.2** Five-scale rural rankings.
*Source*: The author, adapted from Golas (1980, p. 301).

approach of ever-normal granaries contrasts with the local, rural identity of community granaries (*shecang*). The latter found a champion in an eminent official, Chen Hongmou, due to their participative management and responsiveness to local needs.[51] He set out targeting guidelines: in Jiangsu, neither large landholders nor "prospective borrowers" were deemed eligible, while the Hunan province excluded merchants, soldiers, and officials.[52] Such exclusion criteria are reminiscent of contemporary large-scale cash transfer programs.[53]

In earlier centuries, granaries also pursued family-oriented policies. An example is the "granary for raising children" program managed by the *juzi cang* institution. The initiative involved a one-off transfer to destitute families with newborns. First introduced in Fujian in 1135 (and three years later implemented empire wide), the scheme exhibited stricter targeting criteria: these involved rural families below the fifth grade and urban households below the seventh level of the registry.[54] According to one account, the transfer " . . . usually consisted of between 1 and 1.3 shi of rice

with little price fluctuation occurring between seasons, officials had discretion on how much to sell. In the latter case, only a hard-core group of low-income households was eligible for sales, the amount of which was limited to 0.2 shi/household (which would feed a family of four for a week).

[51] Rowe (1993, p. 29).

[52] Will and Wong (1991, p. 480).

[53] For example, when launched in 2020, the Ehsaas Kafaalat program in Pakistan excluded, among others, "[g]overnment servants and their spouses, taxpayers, car owners, [and] people with history of multiple foreign travels" (GoP 2021, p. 303).

[54] Fan and Long (2022).

or a combined allotment of one shi of rice and one thousand cash (*qian*)."[55] Others attested instead that the latter was to be interpreted as a tax exemption of 4,000 *qian*.[56]

The *juzi cang* was not the only system that possibly combined food and cash provisions: a few decades earlier, in 1098 the Song government established permanent "poorhouses." Building on previous "relief homes," such institution provided shelter and served as a platform for distributing medicines, clothing, firewood, and food to people in need.[57] Adult participants received one *sheng* of rice or beans and ten "cash" per day (children received half of the amount), with a top up for 5 cash/day in the winter season.[58] Other age-based adjustments were also established: people over 90 years of age were given an additional daily ration of vegetables and 20 cash; those above 100 years of age also received meat, silk clothing, and 30 cash.[59] Poorhouses were financed by confiscated assets of the heirless dead and, importantly, from revenues stemming from the sale of ever-normal granaries.

## Permanent cash transfers in the Roman empire

### Subsidies and transfers

There are at least four reasons that make a rapid discussion of Roman food subsidies salient for cash transfers: first, they are too longstanding for not having influenced subsequent thinking and practices on transfer provisions. By being in place for over seven centuries, the provision of food in the Roman era—initially at subsidized prices and later gratuitously—is one of the most enduring programs in history. Second, and similarly to China, Rome's experience is anchored on detailed systems of household registration that would inform eligibility and targeting—practices that are both central to cash transfers. Third, the experience of subsidies elicited early concerns around disincentives and dependency (e.g., by Cicero and Augustus), a key theme for future cash debates. In fact, food subsidies led to seminal legislation on the notion of deservingness. Finally, food subsidies coexisted with cash distributions: these were occasionally provided in Rome and regularly delivered in parts of Italy. This section discusses both forms of cash payments.[60]

Various factors may have contributed to the introduction and perpetuity of food subsidies. These include, among others, considerations around maintaining social

[55] Apter (2013, p. 9).
[56] Fan and Long (2022).
[57] Temporary state officials were also dispatched to collect the homeless and bring them to the poorhouse.
[58] Apter (2013, p. 6–7), Scogin (1978, p. 34). Both sources refer to "cash," which is likely the *qian*.
[59] Scogin (1978, p. 33).
[60] For studies on income, poverty and inequality in Roman times, see Morley (2006), Schiedel and Friesen (2009) and Milanovic (2019). See Cipolla for a review of money used at the time in the Mediterranean region.

stability[61] and feeding the military.[62] Social distinctiveness mattered, and food subsidies symbolized a privileged condition of *civis Romanus domo Roma*—a Roman citizen living in Rome.[63] Images of food distributions were often embedded in Roman coins,[64] and the city's inhabitants were split between those entitled to distributions (*pleb frumentaria*) and those that weren't so (*pleb sordida*, e.g., slaves or migrants).[65]

As Rome's population expanded, the supply of corn became a complex, challenging undertaking: "the 'invisible hand' did not suffice,"[66] and public action was increasingly called upon to ensure predictable supplies and reduce price fluctuations due to weather, transportation, and speculation.[67]

It was in this context that Tiberius Gracchus penned the *lex Sempronia frumentaria* in 123 BC. The law recognized that "corn was not a commodity like others"[68] and it systematized previous measures into a permanent, stable component of the Roman social contract.[69] Gracchus's food subsidy system provided monthly food rations at about half the market price.[70] Figure 4.3 lays out trends in beneficiaries over the course of the program's lifespan.

The program was self-targeted in the sense that it was open to any citizen willing to wait and stand in line.[71] In addition to Roman citizenship, eligibility criteria included residence in Rome and a minimum age of fourteen years, with distributions being restricted to males. Senators and other government employees were excluded.[72] The

[61] Turbulent riots emerged when food supplies were disrupted: for example, hungry crowds assaulted emperor Claudius at the Forum in 51 (Yavetz 1969). Distributions became "intensely political," and "feeding the population became a political necessity, which not even the emperor could escape" (Finley 1973, p. 40). Similarly, the *annona* institution that presided over the management of food subsidies "... wasn't a charitable institution but a political one" (Waltzing 1896, p. 19).

[62] The drafting of soldiers was traditionally linked to property and land. The demands of an expanding empire led to a decoupling of drafting from land in the 2nd century BC. This implied legionary service by larger swaths of the population and for longer periods of time. Upon their return to Rome—the inhabitants of which had reached over a million people—masses of landless soldiers were in permanent need and may have exerted political pressure for support.

[63] Rowland (1976).

[64] Pennestri (1989).

[65] According to Yavetz (1969), a case of *frumentaria* benefitting non-citizens occurred, indirectly, under Nero. The emperor stopped the *frumentaria* distribution after the great fire of 64 and instead flooded the market with supplies accumulated in granaries. This reduced corn prices, hence benefiting also non-citizens. Galba, who succeeded Nero, reintroduced the traditional system.

[66] Veyne (1990, p. 238).

[67] Public measures generally involved pressuring merchants, flooding markets with grains purchased or extracted as taxation, emergency sales at subsidized prices and rationing (fixing price and quantities of food that could be acquired), and the extension of credit to brokers for food procurement. The implementation of such policies was ad hoc and encountered practical and political challenges. See Garnsey (1988), Jones (1986), Rickman (1980), Rostovtzeff (1957), and Veyne (1990).

[68] Veyne (1990, p. 237). The lex established that the state would cover procurement and transportation costs of grains. The construction of warehouses to store grains was also envisioned.

[69] Cristofori (2003), Erdkamp (2016).

[70] Grains were sold at about 1.5 sesterces/bushel "which was, apparently, less than half the normal price" (Veyne 1990, p. 280). Virlouvet (2014) estimated individual consumption needs between 21 and 28kg of cereals per month (the subsidy gave access to a maximum of 35 kg of grains per month).

[71] Haskel (2009). For an analysis of such practice in the context of Egypt in the late 1900s, see Alderman (1987).

[72] Bartlett (1994), Osborne (2006).

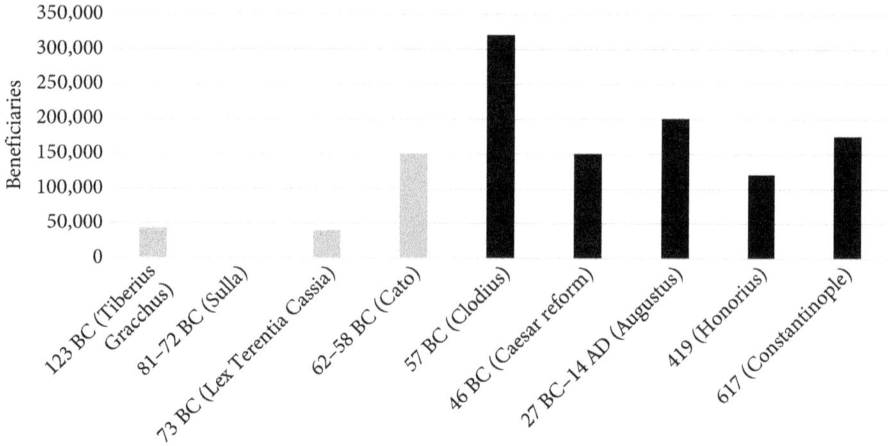


**Figure 4.3** Coverage of food subsidies in Rome, 123 BC–617 AD.

*Source*: Compiled by the author, based on data from Cristofori (2003), Erdkamp (2016), Garnsey (1988), Lo Cascio (1998), and Virlouvet (2014). Gray bars refer to reduced price model; black bars indicate gratuitous distributions. For Cato, the graph includes the average value of the range provided by Garnsey (1988, p. 212).

food subsidy program was de facto financed by other territories in the Empire via taxes, forced sales, or direct shipment of commodities.[73] Funding of the system relied on tribute paid by the provinces or other "empire profits."[74]

The scheme "guaranteed subsistence." As such, it fueled concerns on incentives and fiscal costs. Cicero laid bare these reservations: food subsidies are " . . . appreciated by the plebs, who received food in abundance without work; whereas good citizens were against it, because they thought it was a call to the masses to desert industry for idleness, and saw it was a drain upon the Treasury."[75] While data doesn't allow for exact estimates, it might be plausible that the subsidy initially covered around 43,000 people.[76]

After a period of intense debate on the future of subsidies,[77] Clodius was elected tribune by running on a free-wheat platform, which led to the Lex Clodia in

[73] Virlouvet (2014). The *Lex Sempronia de provincia Asia* regulated tax collection in the Eastern parts of the empire. Complementary policies such as the Gracchus's founding of the Carthage colony appear to have relaxed demographic (via emigration) pressure and increased food production for Rome. For example, Egypt alone would provide Rome with nearly 20 million *modii* of grain, while the requirements for the *frumentaria* was between 9 and 12 million. The remaining grains would be used for restocking, feeding the army, and use for emergency responses (Veyne 1990). See also Hands (1968).

[74] Hands (1968).

[75] The quote appears in both Cristofori (2003, p. 142) and Veyne (1990, p. 237): here I report the sentences that appear more clearly translated in each source. The substance of the Cicero's statement is contested: according to Veyne (1990, p. 237), "that is the cliché [since it] seems unlikely that [the plebs] were not obliged to buy extra grain on the private market."

[76] Cristofori (2003), Virlouvet (1985).

[77] In the decades following Tiberius, various versions of the scheme emerged—some more conservative (by Octavius) and others closer to the original (by Saturninus)—before coming to a halt under Sulla in 81–73 BC. Distributions were reinstated under popular pressure and unrest with the Lex Terentia Cassia.

57 BC. Different from previous provisions, food would now be distributed gratuitously. This unleashed a massive surge in coverage at a cost of about 20% of the state's revenues. By 46 BC, an estimated 320,000 people benefited from free grain distributions.[78]

The *Lex Clodia frumentaria* established a particular institutional body, the *curator annonae*, to manage the list of beneficiaries (*frumentationes*). The increase in beneficiaries was achieved by a relaxation of eligibility criteria: while non-citizens remained ineligible, freedmen, who were the responsibility of wealthier individuals, were now supported; also, the eligibility age was reduced from 14 to ten years of age; finally, by making them free of charge, the Lex Clodia made it easier for the poorest to access food.[79] Under the previous subsidized model, those most in need may have relied on patrons for cash (the scheme subsidized about half the price, not all of it) and milling in return for personal services or part of the milled grains.[80]

Caesar made food subsidies more targeted by halving coverage to 150,000 recipients (he kept a "shock-responsive" component by allowing subsidized prices for all citizens in times of famine). While there is some debate on the criteria established for such reform,[81] Caesar's scheme was predicated on a recertification process informed by a census. The latter included a question on *professions*.[82] Used to gather information on house ownership for fiscal purposes, the question was also used as a criterion for deselection from the food subsidy program: only those that were renting a house, and not their owners, were allowed to participate.[83]

The *tessera frumentaria*, or the coupon that granted access to free food, seems to have been "reserved for a few privileged persons."[84] Eligibility involved four main criteria: new beneficiaries would be included only when existing ones would decease or leave the city (in such cases, participation would become based on inheritance benefiting close family members); a lottery-based system also allowed participation of new recipients;[85] engaging in certain public employment was another entry into

Proposed in 73 BC by the consuls Terentius Varro and Cassius Longinus, the program provided more limited amounts of subsidized corn with coverage of around 40,000 people. It then rose again under Cato.

[78] Cristofori (2003).

[79] Cristofori (2003) reports that the general Pompey, when in charge of law's implementation in 57 BC, attempted to exclude or "reorder" recently freed slaves from the *frumentationes* in the *recensio*, probably a special kind of census for the program. Such exclusion was likely pursued for fiscal purposes. In response, it appears that Clodius had the Temple of the Nymphs, which contained the *recensio*, burned down between September of 57 BC and March of 56 BC.

[80] Garnsey (1988).

[81] Hands (1968). Some maintained that such reduction was likely achieved by better checking proof of citizenship rather than by restricting traditional eligibility (Bartlett 1994).

[82] Lo Cascio (1998).

[83] Lampe (2016) suggests that the reform may have been intended to discourage landless citizens to drift from rural areas to Rome. Later in the empire, or at least by 369, Rome and Constantinople reinstated the entitlement to a food subsidy scheme named *panis aedis* attached to house ownership (as opposed to the *free panis gradilis* per person). Beneficiaries participating in the *panis aedis* and *panis gradilis* were recorded in two distinct lists.

[84] Veyne (1990, p. 242).

[85] Soraci (2006, p. 353) refers to it as the practice of *subsortitio*.

the program (senators weren't eligible); and there appears to be some cases where the *tessera* was purchased. The reform seems to have been relatively successful.[86]

After Cesar, the rolls climbed up again. His successor, Augustus (27 BC-14 AD), was unconvinced about the *frumentationes*. He contemplated their elimination, but the decision could have favored political opponents: "I was strongly inclined to do away forever with distribution of grain, because through dependence on them agriculture was neglected; but I did not carry out my purpose, feeling here that they would one day be renewed through the desire for popular favor."[87]

Augustus not only retained food distributions, but even increased their coverage from 150,000 to around 200,000 beneficiaries.[88] Also, he instituted an office for their management (*cura frumenti populo dividendi*).[89] Furthermore, the emperor issued wooden ration cards indicating the beneficiary's eligibility, the day of collection, and the specific location or *porticus* door for food collection.[90]

Following Augustus, the overall number of people receiving grains remained roughly stable. Yet there were important developments. Citizens received monthly distributions at assigned days and in designated locations (*porticus minucia*). The number of such locations would expand from 45 to around 1320 *gradus* in the city.[91] Provisions were diversified: baked bread (nearly 0.65 kg) replaced corn in the 3rd century, and this was distributed daily in a range of retail-level locations.[92] Free oil distributions emerged under Septimius Severus (193–211AD),[93] while subsequent emperors added other items like wine and pork meat.[94] Eventually, multiple cities of the Empire also began providing similar benefits, including Constantinople, Alexandria, and Antioch.[95]

Emperors would occasionally extend eligibility for grain to particular groups as well as improving distribution and broadening the set of commodities provided. For example, Nero included the Praetorian guard in 65 AD. And around 150–200AD, part of the army would get access to subsidies after a three-year service. More fundamentally, a premier eligibility criterion for food subsidies, as noted, was citizenship. But with Caracalla's extension of citizenship to the empire in 212, the

[86] It was noted that the lack of evidence of starvation following the scale-down of provisions may have indicated that food distributions weren't really needed (Haskel 2009). Yet such outcome may have been facilitated by the outflow of about 80,000 ex-beneficiaries to overseas territories, while large numbers of soldiers had fallen in war (Van Berchem 1939, Yavetz 1969).

[87] Quoted in Yavetz (1969, p. 95).

[88] If the *plebs frumentaria* was limited to those living in the city of Rome itself, and not those in the immediate hinterland, distributions may have reached about 40% of Rome's population (Erdkamp 2016).

[89] Yavetz (1969).

[90] Hands (1968).

[91] Lo Cascio (1998). For a discussion on the distinction between the *pistrina publica*, or entities that produced bread, and the actual distribution sites see Sirks (1991).

[92] Cardinali (1922), Tengström (1974).

[93] Lo Cascio (1998) argued that daily distributions would likely occur in the same gradus used for bread distributions. These included high-ceiling buildings with names of beneficiaries displayed on a bronze table (van Berchem 1939).

[94] For instance, 140,000 people received pork distributions in 452 AD. These were provided daily for five months, and entailed a total quantity of about 1.6 kg/month (Lo Cascio 1998).

[95] Jones (1986).

need for social distinctiveness may have shifted from legal-political to economic differentiation: "[t]he death of the city state inevitably brought about the birth of the poor."[96] An extensive body of literature has debated various factors shaping the purported emergence of poverty in the 4th–6th centuries as a distinct problem.[97]

Importantly, this period marks an early codification of the "deserving" poor into legislation. Because the perennial issue of begging could be motivated by a range of reasons, these required the examination of individual circumstances. Such investigation was not unbiased: historical analysis shows a longstanding mistrust by the elite of the "idle unemployed".[98] Healthy, working-age foreign men who found themselves in distress, and who may have resorted to begging as a desperation strategy, were relatively unlikely to elicit sympathy and help.[99] They evoked laziness and crime—a consistent attitude traced to Hesiod's times (750–650 BC).[100] The act of sorting through deserving and underserving beggars—separating the healthy working-age claimants from the old, the children, and the infirm—was formally legislated with an edict of 382. Issued by emperors Gratian, Valentinian II, and Theodosius I, the edict ordered the urban prefect of Rome (Severus) to examine beggars based on their health and age—that is, ascertaining if they were able-bodied. According to Anneliese Parkin, "... [t]he division of the indigent according to labour potential in the imperial edict of AD 382 is the oldest surviving official acknowledgement of this distinction."[101]

Despite the loss of Egyptian grain, in the 5th century distributions in Rome were still sizable. In the year 419 under Honorius, recipients of pork meat and bread may have amounted to about 120,000 people. After the Vandals conquered northern Africa, Rome lost control of its pipeline for free distributions and the program was discontinued in the city. Yet *frumentationes* persisted in Constantinople under Justinian, and in the mid-6th century they seemed to reach a minimum of 175,000

96 Osborne (2006, p. 10). Finley (1973) argues that attitudes towards poverty in Roman times would be best epitomized by interpreting the law of debt instead of "occasional philanthropy." Such law was applied in a "uniformly harsh and unyielding" way where the defaulting debtor provided compulsory labor by him and his family members.

97 Some attributed the emergence of poverty not to changing systems of belief, but to rapid population growth (Patlagean 1977). Others underscored the "revolution in social imagination" that accompanied the rise of the Christian Church: here being "lovers of the poor," and the corresponding act of public almsgiving, was an assertion of the ultimate cohesion of the human community and the need to reach the "outermost margins of society" (Brown 2002). Furthermore, Osborne (2006) and Rathbone (2006) suggest that the shift was the continuation of earlier attitudes already present in pre-Christian antiquity as shaped by Greek and eastern influences. For example, Parkin (2006) discusses Aristotle's reflections on "pity," an idea that was "picked up by Roman writers" (p. 71), and which stemmed from two conditions: that the observed misfortune is deemed *undeserved*, and that it cursed people in ways that others can relate to (because the poor person is known, or by imagining oneself in such situation).

98 Parkin (2006).

99 There were some "voluntary poor," like the itinerant priests of Cybele and the Cynics mendicant philosophers, who were more keenly supported by popular almsgiving (Parkin 2006).

100 Parkin (2006).

101 Ibid, p. 81. Under the edict, able-bodied beggars, if free born, had to serve the denouncer in perpetuity.

people. The final blow to the 740-year Roman food distribution system came when Egypt, Constantinople's largest supplier, fell to the Persians in 617.[102]

## Alimenta child benefits

The provision of *frumentaria* were at times concomitant with *congiaria* cash distributions.[103] Such largesse was documented under Caesar and Augustus. These involved universal cash payments to citizens on special occasions, for example the first one by Caesar occurred to celebrate his accession in 46 BC.[104] Funding sources ranged from spoils of war to private wealth. Such distributions fitted the larger narrative to "remind the recipient of the real source of his ration."[105] The practices are akin to the Greek concept of euergetism of private donations eliciting public recognition (Box 4.3).

### Box 4.3 Euergetism as Exchange

The concept of euergetism is slightly different from that of "philanthropy," "munificence," or "charity": the latter three only encompass the act of giving by the donor or benefactor. Euergetism, instead, involves not a unilateral, but a reciprocal relationship between giver and receiver. In ancient Greece, for instance, euergetism implied an exchange whereby benefactions would receive honors in return. In a similar way, later in Christianity the provision of assistance to people in need generated expectations of spiritual salvation by the donor (see Chapter 5). In the case of Greece, euergetism would engender public recognition by the community. For example, the local council of Samos issued a degree in honor of a benefactor, Boulagoras, with the inscription acknowledging his repeated provision of food supplies during shortages in the 3rd century BC.[a] Such acknowledgement also materialized into the state offering honorific titles and various recompenses (e.g., seating at public spectacles, inscriptions in a prominent place in the city, citizenship, exemption from certain taxes).[b] Elite public generosity was enmeshed in moral elements: in fact, it has been argued that the practice represented " . . . a crucial instrument in the hands

[102] Erdkamp (2016).

[103] The word stems from the measure *congii* applied to oil, which was the commodity originally distributed as largesse (Lucullus distributed wine to citizens). Augustus extended the congiaria to children below 11 years of age, possibly anticipating subsequent developments on *alimenta* child benefits. There is some evidence on possible distribution-induced migration to the city (this mostly related to regular free in-kind provisions), as well as manipulation attempted by slave owners to administratively free slaves for garnering access to additional in-kind and cash distributions (Hands 1968).

[104] Yavetz (1969) reports at least four *congiaria* distributions of 300–600 sesterces, one of which was carried out in accordance with Caesar's testament while the others were made in 29, 24, and 12 BC. Interestingly, Soraci (2006, p. 371) refers to special food distributions carried out for women, since they were excluded from the regular or ceremonial provisions of food and cash.

[105] Hands (1968, p. 107).

of Greek political leaders to display their innate virtuousness and hence justify their position of power."[c] There are accounts in other contexts and times: for example, in China " . . . private actors played a leading role in charitable programs [for children] grounded in a moral imperative to help the needy from the early Qing to the Republic"; such partnership between the state elites was sanctioned in imperial edicts of 1724, 1741, and 1866, when rulers "pledged financial support and honorary recognition to local organizations that sheltered foundlings and the poor."[d]

[a] Garnsey (1990, p. 128). He also argued that in a context where "treasuries were always virtually empty; wealth was private," the rich preferred an irregular system of contributions to the state that enhanced their status and reputation than the " . . . obligatory transfers that brought no credit to the giver. In this way they effectively preempted the possibility of regular state-funded supply and distribution schemes" (p. 140–141). We will return to the politics of transfers in Chapter 5.

[b] Gygax (2016).

[c] Zuiderhoek (2009, p. 13).

[d] Apter (2013, p. 62).

There were other forms of largesse: for example, the tradition of *donativa* involved the distribution of state money by the general to his troops as military reward, such as practiced by Scipio; and during elections in the Republican period, cash payments were made by *divisores* to specific people for supporting candidates.[106] Such "ceremonial" cash distributions by rulers would also occur later in history on a more targeted basis—a practice that in some cases is still active today.[107]

Cash transfers in Roman times weren't limited to occasional ceremonial distributions. In the year 6 AD, Augustus himself instituted the *aerarium militare*, a permanent revenue (chiefly financed via inheritance and sales taxes) to fund social pensions for army veterans. More localized formal arrangements involved the establishment of Greek-type foundations. For instance, senator Helvius Basila from Atina had left the citizens of that city with 400,000 sesterces: the revenues from such sum were used to provide food to children until their coming of age, at which point they received a one off-transfer of 1,000 sesterces.[108] Such a model is similar to recent universal basic income proposals.[109]

[106] It was illegal to offer money to other tribes, and several laws against canvassing were passed. With the absence of elections in imperial times, Augustus approved the payment at election day of 1,000 sesterces per elector to members of his constituency nostalgic of election largesse (Veyne 1990, p. 228).

[107] Ribton-Turner (1887, p. 52) shows that cash distribution were made by monarchs in England in occasion of Maundy Thursday: introduced by the king in 1363 alongside food and clothing, the practice is still observed nowadays for supporting seniors (see https://www.royal.uk/maundy-thursday). See also Courtenay (1972, p. 284) for Maundy distributions in mid-1200s France, where a charity token of the royal almonry was produced for the *Mandé*.

[108] Jones (1989).

[109] Ackerman and Alstott (2000) suggested that every American should receive a one-off grant of S$80,000 on their 21st birthday, or at 18 years of age for those in college.

The concept of child benefits was established on a larger scale under the *alimenta* scheme. Introduced by emperor Trajan[110] (98–117), *alimenta* provided cash transfers to families with children and it operated in the Italian peninsula. Figure 4.4(a) shows those programs being operational in at least 46 towns. There is some debate on the core objectives of the scheme, for example whether it was an income support program or, because of its financing structure, it was meant to enhance agriculture. Others point to the program's goal to reduce malnutrition[111] and increase fertility.[112] The latter may find credence in numismatic evidence: this includes gold coins depicting Trajan distributing *alimenta* cash transfers to two children (Figure 4.4b).[113]

Historian Richard Duncan-Jones provided a detailed review of the program,[114] and suggests that its funding relied on state-sponsored, low-interest rate loans provided to local landowners possibly in perpetuity. Whether the loans were compulsory is unclear.[115] Specifically, landowners received public funds for an amount equivalent to 8% of their land value at an interest rate of 5% per year.[116] Only lands for a value higher than 20,000 sesterces were accepted as security. A sum twenty times higher than the annual cost of the program was allocated by the treasury and distributed among various local landowners (valuation of land was self-declared by its owner).

Proceeds from interest payments funded the *alimenta*, while the emperor didn't reclaim the capital, nor the land provided as security, as long as the borrower paid the interest.[117] Information on the program's financing is reported by inscriptions on bronze tables (*tabula alimentaria*). Figures 4.5a and 4.5b show such tables for the towns of Ligures Baebiani (101 AD) and Veleia (about 113 AD), respectively.[118] In the latter, it is estimated that 10% of the town's children received *alimenta* at a cost of a

[110] Some trace the scheme to his father emperor Nerva (96–98) (Duncan-Jones 1964).

[111] Evans (1981) comments that "the incidence of malnutrition-related exposure and infanticide [was countered by] the celebrated and much discussed *alimenta*" (p. 429).

[112] However, as we shall see there might have been caps to the number of children supported.

[113] The coin image was also reported by, among others, O'Brien (2020, p. 41).

[114] Duncan-Jones (1964).

[115] Garnsey (1968) expressed skepticism regarding Duncan-Jones' characterization of loans as compulsory. Also Veyne (1990) doesn't regard them as obligatory (p.368). Others noted that Trajan wasn't entirely supportive of loans as a modality, but such arrangement would have ensured a steady stream of funding for a scheme of public interest (Hands 1968).

[116] Such rate was one sixth of normal land dividends, and one twelfth of the "most heavily burdened land"; security against borrowing was roughly a 12.5-fold collateral (Duncan-Jones 1964, Veyne 1990). For a discussion on the arithmetic behind the formula linking loans and properties, see Stewart (2019), who argued that the program in Veleia might have involved fractional computations.

[117] See discussion in Veyne (1990, p. 367–377) and Ferguson (2019).

[118] The tabula of Ligures Beabiani, which is currently located in Rome's Baths of Diocletian complex, recorded the name of the landowner, the name of the land, its location through the description of nearby lands, the value of the land, the amount of the loan, and the interest rate to be paid. In addition, the tabula of Veleia (1.38 m × 2.86 m), which is exhibited at Parma's National Archeological Museum, seems to include the name of the "intermediary person tasked with the description of the land" (see https://complessopilotta.it/museo-archeologico/veleia/).

(a)

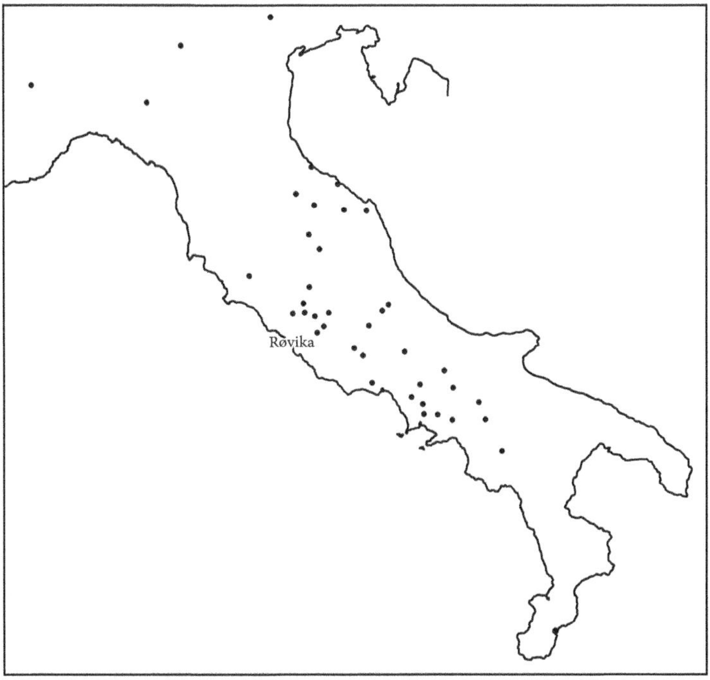


(b)

**Figure 4.4** Location of towns with *alimenta* (a) and coin symbolizing the program (b).

*Source*: (a) Duncan-Jones (1964, p. 125) "The Purpose and Organisation of the Alimenta." *Papers of the British School at Rome* 32: 123–146. ©Reproduced with permission of the Licensor through PLSclear"; (b) ©The Trustees of the British Museum. The coin was produced between the years 103–111.

million sesterces.[119] The use of fund proceedings to finance transfers was replicated centuries later for famine relief in northern Sweden (Box 4.4).

### Box 4.4 Fusing Indian, Chinese, and Roman Experiences: Famine Relief in Northern Sweden during the 1860s

The Vasterbotten county in Northern Sweden suffered a famine in 1867–1868.[a] Induced by unusually cold weather, the shock was part of a wider regional famine also affecting Finland and Estonia. A number of interesting similarities to the Indian, Chinese, and Roman experiences discussed in this chapter emerged. Like in India, Sweden had a granary system of in-kind and cash transfers delivered in times of need as either grants or loans. Similarly to select Chinese provinces, in 1863 the Southern provinces of the country converted granaries into cash funds managed by municipal councils; yet a range of Northern counties (e.g., Vasterbotten and Norrbotten) kept the in-kind system. In 1865, leftover funds from previous granary distributions formed Vasterbotten's emergency relief fund: like in the case of *alimenta*, grants were funded by the fund's annual earned interest.

[a] See Forsberg and Bohman (2023) and Nelson (1988).

While there is some debate on implementation practices,[120] local commissioners invited applications from families of the town. Once the total number of eligible children was identified, a sum required for their annual support was estimated.[121] *Alimenta* cash benefits were gender-differentiated, with boys receiving monthly transfers of HS16 until 18 years of age, while payment for girls amounted to HS12 per month until 16 years of age.[122]

The scheme was administered by local magistrates and supervised by higher-level officials. Although it was considered a distinctively Trajanic initiative, some subsequent emperors embraced the program. For example, Hadrian raised the upper age limit of beneficiaries. Perhaps because of growing fiscal challenges and capital-intensive financing, *alimenta* gradually subsided. After being operational for nearly two centuries, the program might have been discontinued by around the year 275 AD.

[119] Veyne (1990, p. 371).
[120] Woolf (1990).
[121] Duncan-Jones (1964).
[122] It is likely that caps were set on the number of eligible children per family, possibly one or two per household. Orphans didn't seem to be included in the program, while payment rates for illegitimate children were lower (HS12 for boys and HS10 for girls). For a broader discussion on orphanhood in the empire, see Fitzgerald (2016).

(a)

(b)

**Figure 4.5** *Tabula alimentaria* of (a) Ligures Baebiani and (b) Veleia.

*Source*: (a) Licensed by Ministero della Cultura—Museo Nazionale Romano (photo by Giorgio Cargnel and Luciano Mandato); (b) licensed by Ministero della Cultura—Complesso Monumental della Pilotta-Galleria Nazionale di Parma.

## 4.2 Laying the foundations for cash transfers: Crises as catalysts

This section offers a series of illustrations on how cash transfers moved, in their various forms, from local provisions to national schemes. Using three examples from the United States, the first three sub-sections chronicle developments of lesser-known, pre-New Deal experiences with cash assistance. Before the Depression, the country underwent a fascinating evolution with social pensions for veterans of the War of Independence and the Civil War; states provided cash transfers to "morally worthy" mothers as a form of "making unpaid work pay"; and as the Depression unfolded, an innovative wave of experimentation was launched in major cities over the 1930s to replace food commodities with cash transfers. Such trials would fuse civil society experience on cash transfers with local-level public provisions. While not becoming permanent, the fact that experienced non-governmental organization (NGO) professionals would join the ranks of public service strengthened cash transfer capabilities of local governments. The New Deal period would feature cash transfers in the form of flagship public works programs. What is intriguing in such experience is the building on federal capabilities to execute such interventions; the diversity in public works approaches; and the vibrant intellectual milieu that would elevate the thorny problem of unemployment as a framework for connecting macroeconomic and social protection agendas. A final discussion on the recent uptick of cash transfers following macro-crises complements the section.

### Cash transfers to veterans and widows in the 1800s and early 1900s

War-related social pensions are sometimes overlooked as a pioneering form of cash transfers. The United States would rapidly adopt and adapt English poor law provisions.[123] But transfers rendered for service in the battlefield were of different nature. At the turn of the 1900s, such initial spread had a distinct path: sociologist Theda Skocpol noted that "[b]etween the 1870s and 1920s [ . . . ] the United States sought to help not workers but soldiers and mothers."[124]

Provisions pertained to both the War of Independence and the Civil War. In the former case, disability pensions existed for wounded soldiers; in 1818, these were extended to all veterans on a poverty basis. In 1832, they benefitted 33,425 veterans, and in 1836, they were expanded to soldiers' widows. Such growth seems to run counter to trends in other contexts, like France, where veteran pension provisions were made tighter.[125]

[123] Trattner (1974).

[124] Skocpol (1992, p. 525). Her comprehensive work informed this section to a significant extent.

[125] "In contrast to postrevolutionary France, therefore, the postrevolutionary United States can be said to have further liberalized the terms of its military pensions" (Skocpol 1992, p. 105).

A similar pattern could be discerned for Civil War pensions: in 1861, volunteers were first granted regular army benefits, and the following year legislation was enacted to meet the needs of union soldiers and their dependents. Subsequent laws increased the generosity of such benefits as well as devised more specific provisions based on rank (between \$8–\$30/month) and severity of disability. By 1866, pension rolls included 126,722 beneficiaries.

Historical records show that only a small fraction of eligible veterans claimed benefits: in 1875, for example, a mere 6.5% of eligible veterans had signed up for disability pensions. Over time, several acts made the system evolve from one based only on combat injuries and life loss to a more comprehensive system of disability and old age.[126] This resulted in an increased uptake of pensions to 90% of veterans and unleashed significant coverage expansion (Figure 4.6). By the early 1900s, the link between pensions and service-related injuries was severed to the point that "old age alone soon because a sufficient disability, and in 1906 the law was amended to state this explicitly."[127]

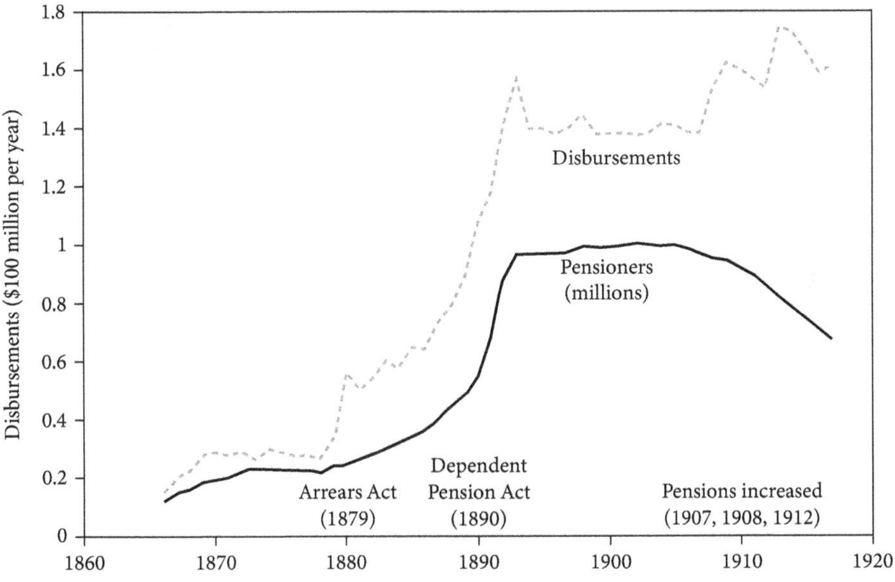


**Figure 4.6** Expansion of US Civil War pensions, 1866–1917.

*Source*: Skocpol (1992, p. 110).[a]

[a] Theda Skocpol, *Protecting Soldiers and Mothers: The Political Origins of Social Policy in the United States*, Cambridge, Mass.: The Belknap Press of Harvard University Press, Copyright ©1992 by the President and Fellows of Harvard College. Used by permission. All rights reserved.

[126] For example, the Arrears Act of 1879 allowed soldiers with newly discovered Civil War disabilities to receive past pension payments in a lump sum.

[127] Skocpol (1992, p. 111).

## Mothers' pensions

The Mothers' Pensions program was the precursor to the 1935 US Federal Aid to Dependent Children program (which in turn preceded AFDC and TANF programs discussed in Chapter 6). Mothers' Pensions were initially launched in Jackson County, Kansas City, during the winter of 1910–1911. Those allowances were provided to mothers who were judged by the Juvenile Court courts as " . . . a proper person, morally, physically, and mentally for the bringing up of her children."[128]

In the decade 1921–1931, the coverage of mother's pensions grew from 45,800 to 93,600 mothers (with 253,300 children). The average cash transfer was relatively generous, or about 30% of family income, and targeted women with children under 14 or 16 years of age. Mothers' pensions weren't legislated nationally but remained operational at state level.[129]

The key goal of the scheme was to provide income supplements to mothers and enhance the likelihood of home-based care of children, hence preventing them from being placed into orphanages or foster homes. As such, allowances weren't meant to be "poor relief" but to provide a type of public service wage. They were a form of "honorable maternal income" like that paid to soldiers and others operating in the public interest.[130] This could be considered an early articulation of the "making unpaid work pay" that underpins modern discussions on cash transfers.[131]

A core engine for mobilizing public opinion was the *Delineator* magazine, an outlet that advocated for and raised awareness on women's rights (Figure 4.7). Recent evidence tested whether the program generated perverse, Malthusian effects: examining data on about 16,000 women who applied for the program between 1911 and 1930, the study found " . . . no differences in the remarriage rates of women who received transfers [ . . . ] [Beneficiaries] were not more likely to have children after the transfer, and they were not less likely to work."[132]

## NGOs as innovation incubators: Experimenting with cash in lieu of in-kind transfers in the 1930s

Mothers' Pensions coexisted with large in-kind provisions.[133] Around the 1930s, four main modalities of in-kind distribution were present in the United States:

[128] Skocpol (1992, p. 428).

[129] Mother's pensions would soon be adopted in Illinois with the "fund for parents" act of 1911, and then rapidly spread and be adapted across states: by 1935, only South Carolina and Georgia didn't legislate the program.

[130] Zelizer (1997, p. 155). As articulated by the Illinois Congress of Mothers, the program was intended to " . . . remove the mother and her children from the disgrace of charity relief and places her in the class of public servants similar to army officers and school teachers," quoted in Skocpol (1992, p. 465).

[131] Gentilini et al. (2020).

[132] Aizer et al. (2020, p. 4).

[133] In that period, "[u]nwillingness of public agencies to entrust clients with cash was probably a survival from the English poor-law of the eighteenth century ( . . . ). [The US] public welfare laws remained, like flies embalmed in amber, a memorial to a vanished social-economic pattern" (Colcord 1936, p. 11).

"With all my worldly goods I thee endow"

FOUR COUNTIES THAT PREFER MOTHERS TO ORPHAN ASYLUMS

BY MARY O'CONNOR NEWELL

To Join
THE HOME LEAGUE
write to William Hard
care of The Delineator
Butterick Building, New York

**Figure 4.7** Printout of article in *The Delineator*, 1912.

*Source*: O'Connor Newell (1912, p. 85).[a]

[a] The article told the story of Mary Ellen McKay, mother of seven children and widow of an ironworker victim of a construction accident. The image was also reproduced in Skocpol (1992, p. 436).

these included typical soup kitchens;[134] "commissaries," where public agencies would purchase large quantities of supplies in bulk that beneficiaries could collect at charity stores;[135] "dealer agreements," also known as "Syracuse plan," where

[134] In Cincinnati, meals were provided to homeless population only, and families with children were prevented from participating. A variant of such option was a "cafeteria" system present among others in Detroit: operational in the spring and summer of 1932, it served about 6,000 families (including children). The scheme was introduced because of limited funds, and the provision of food in such a way ("being fed in public") was conceived as a deterrent in the hope of reducing caseloads (Colcord 1936).

[135] Variety and number of supplies were specified by a social worker who issued on order or voucher. Commissaries were akin to a "domestic food aid" scheme as they were part of the management of internal surplus disposal (Colcord 1936).

private retailers would agree to provide commodities normally distributed through commissaries;[136] and "disbursing orders," which were vouchers (for a given quantity of food or in monetary value) usable at retailers of choice.[137] Other variants were also recorded.[138]

Such modalities were often contested and debated. The arguments made in favor of and against food transfers are familiar to today's social protection practitioners. These generally revolved around people's preferences, spending patterns, and cost-effectiveness.[139] A watershed moment for reform occurred in July 1933, when the newly formed Federal Emergency Relief Administration allowed states and local administrations to experiment with cash grants as alternatives to in-kind relief. As documented in detail by Joanna Colcord, a wave of city-level pilots was launched.[140]

Over the course of 1934, some cities had embraced cash almost completely: in Philadelphia, 99.2% of its relief was in the form of unconditional cash transfers. But in some cases, like Ohio, cities returned to in kind despite overall positive performance of cash transfers.[141] In other instances, like Los Angeles, cities underwent a chaotic, accelerated process of transition from in kind to cash, which yielded mixed results. Between 1933 and 1935, about 478,000 families, or over 1.6 million

[136] Officials of Syracuse (and other cities) used commissary costs as benchmarks, and if retail grocers would be willing to participate at a cost lower than that of the commissaries, such dealer agreements would be forged. Some cities had an innovative variant, namely that staple foods were delivered to recipients' home by the grocery every two weeks.

[137] The agency would also provide information to beneficiaries about the proper spending of resources on food "simply phrased and attractively printed" (Colcord 1936).

[138] In Boston a volunteer committee established three "5-cent" restaurants at the largest of which 103,530 meals were sold in little more than four months. In Detroit, a program of "subsistence gardens" was introduced: known as Pingree Garden Plan, or the Detroit Experiment, it involved an Agricultural Commission selecting 430 acres of land within the city or adjacent to it. These would be cultivated by 945 people selected out of the 3,000 applicants. Participants were provided with various farm inputs and land preparation. After the first year's experiment, one third of an acre was judged sufficient for summer green vegetables and the winter supply of potatoes for a family (Colcord 1936).

[139] For example, defendants of in-kind assistance argued that children were better nourished when the diet was controlled; clients felt no objection to receiving food publicly; employment could be generated in operating the commissary; and in kind was cheaper. Opponents, instead, contended that provisions didn't provide culturally acceptable diversity (e.g., oatmeal was often refused by beneficiaries); food may be diverted, resold, and traded; the full range of administration and logistics costs were not fully considered; and the system was often humiliating and entailing high transaction costs for recipients. See Gentilini (2023b) for a contemporary review.

[140] Design and implementation of cash transfers varied. Some cities like Denver, Philadelphia, and Pittsburgh converted the entire transfer into cash, while the others retain a certain amount of in-kind provisions (e.g., Baltimore only converted cash, while New York, Cleveland, and Detroit continued the furnishment of milk, fuel or rent); four cities started with pilot experiments (i.e., Baltimore, Cleveland, Detroit, and San Francisco), while others built on such experience and skipped the testing phase; and six cities, like Philadelphia, transferred the entire caseload to cash at one time, while in the other cases, the process was more gradual, e.g., in Cleveland due to lower trust on some people's ability to handle cash (Colcord 1936).

[141] For instance, a case study on Cleveland's experience concluded that "[spending on] vegetables and cereal foods was found to be in accordance with accepted standards of diet ( . . . ) No increase had been noted in the unwillingness to accept assignment to work ( . . . ) In the study of 145 families ( . . . .) [And] the advantages of the cash system in the minds of the visitors far outweigh the advantages of relief in kind [i.e., 33 interviewed visitors listed 16 advantages versus 7 drawbacks]" (Colcord 1936, p.70–74).

people, were supported with cash transfers as emergency responses in ten US cities (Table 4.2).[142]

Results from the piloting process are generally positive in terms of impact, while fears of labor market disincentives didn't materialize. A finding from Philadelphia epitomized a broader trend: "[r]efusal to accept [work] had been rare and did not measurably increase after the adoption of cash."[143] A Detroit official of social services proudly declared that

> . . . [w]e feel that the acid test has come, and that cash relief has withstood the test [. . . ] [I]t does seem that the elected officials of the city of Detroit are sold on the idea of cash relief, and that it stood the test of public opinion.[144]

Findings on comparative cost-efficiency, however, were inconclusive.[145] Interestingly, the pilots highlighted some institutional and administrative issues. For instance, in select city governments, like in Baltimore and Cleveland, the piloting was facilitated by staff that had gathered experience with cash transfers with NGOs (see Chapter 6). Charismatic administrators in Detroit and Philadelphia would convince skeptical city relief boards about the value of piloting. And broader institutional innovations were catalyzed: in Los Angeles, the "employable" recipients of direct relief in the department of charities were transferred to the city body handling public works; others, such as Detroit, consolidated functions from district to central-level offices; and in Pittsburgh, the management of checks for different in-kind items was merged in a single financial department for cash transfers.[146]

A range of pressure groups had initially obstructed the introduction of cash relief. Some of them changed perspective after implementation: landlords, for instance, had insisted upon receiving rental checks directly from public agencies; but many recognized how people regularly paid their rents in full or in part via cash transfers; utility companies were similarly "agreeably surprised."[147] In part this was by design: beneficiaries didn't have full discretion in spending money. The amount of cash provided to each family was calculated and segmented based on particular

[142] The conversion from family to individual includes a median family size of 3.4 as estimated by the US census bureau for 1930 (table 2, p.2: https://www2.census.gov/library/publications/decennial/1930/families/families-type-size.pdf). In addition, the state of Delaware experimented with cash in August 1934, although that experience is less documented.

[143] Colcord (1936, p.141).

[144] Colcord (1936, p. 97–98).

[145] Evidence on comparative cost efficiency was lacking due to the complexities of undertaking robust comparisons. Yet some attempts were made leading to conflicting findings. For example, an early 1933 study by the University of California ("Report on the Probable Costs of Administering Food Relief in Alameda County by the Grocery Order, Commissary, and Cash Systems") found that cash was 16.5% more expensive than a commissary system; another 1935 study on Cleveland by the Ohio State Relief Commission ("A Study of Cash Relief in Ohio") found that if 80% of beneficiaries would receive cash, costs for clerical staff would drop by one third (Colcord 1936).

[146] In San Francisco, public works and direct cash relief were merged under a single body, the San Francisco Emergency Relief Administration: however, the unification only lasted seven months, before difficulties and complexities led to a reseparation of functions.

[147] Only milk dealers remained opposed to cash, as bulky home deliveries via drivers were largely replaced by grocery-level purchases by beneficiaries. Medical relief wasn't cashed out.

**Table 4.2** Experimentation and scale-up of public unconditional cash transfers as relief response in the US, 1933–1935.

| City | Initial phase | Scale-up |
|---|---|---|
| San Francisco (November 1933) | Experimentation of cash for 20% of direct relief caseload for two months in two districts. | Citywide experiment in March 1934 for six months; statewide in California in November 1934. No work disincentives detected. |
| New York City (May 1934) | No pilot, with immediate rollout of cash, in kind, and vouchers for rent. | May–June 1934 cash reached 170,000 families. In June 1935, less than 0.5% out of 245,000 families returned to in kind due to inability to manage cash. No increase in beneficiary work refusals. |
| Cleveland (May 1934) | Sequential test in districts between May 1834 and January 1935. | By March 1935, 20% of city relief beneficiaries got cash. In August, fiscal deficit led to return to orders that cost 7% less. |
| Detroit (June 1934) | Small experimentation with ex-public works families that "managed paychecks satisfactorily." | Pilot scale-up by September when a budget reduction of 5% for food relief was due (the reduction would be "more acceptable" by switching to cash). |
| Baltimore (June 1934) | Pilot in three districts, interrupted after a few weeks due to limited funds. | Citywide in August 1934 (coverage of 28,000 families); by October 1934, 88.3% of city relief was in cash; only milk continued to be in kind. |
| Los Angeles (May and December 1934) | Experiment in Pomona in May 1934. | In December 1934 scale-up of cash to 56,000 people. Out of 14,000 inspected cases, half secured employment (seven staff cross-checked beneficiaries and firm payrolls). |
| Chicago (October 1934) | Illinois Attorney General rejects cash grants (see Chapter 2, Figure 2.4). | Decision overturn in December 1935; after four months' pilot in Chicago, cash as statewide policy in March 1936. |
| Philadelphia (November 1934) | Efficient system: cash checks received two days after the visitor put in the request. Cash checks were gender-sensitive (they were in the name of housewives). | In December 1934, 99.2% of the city's direct relief was in cash. In February 1935, 86,000 households received direct cash relief. No labor disincentives observed. |
| Pittsburgh (Jan 1935) | Close collaboration with Philadelphia (joint conferences, monitoring of implementation). Checks issued in the name of both husband and wife. Six days required form visitors' authorization and mailing out of checks. | About 70,000 families reached in Jan 1935. High attention to evaluations: a study of March 1935 among 13,820 families found that less than 1% misspent cash; families moved less frequently and there were fewer evictions. |
| Denver (March 1935) | Consultations with beneficiaries on transfer size (sick and elderly received full transfer; others received 80%). | First citywide cash allowance made in April. The switch involved a reduction of 38 clerical staff in the city's Bureau of Public Welfare. A study on job refusals by cash recipients shows that out of 66 cases, only four were "unjustified refusals." |

*Source*: Compiled by author based on Colcord (1936).

expense items to which beneficiaries were expected to adhere, for example devoting a specific share of the transfers to rent expenditures. Deviance from such allocations could be sanctioned with reinstatement of in-kind provisions (see Chapter 2 for the state-beneficiary "contract" issued in Chicago).

## How New Deal public works built federal capabilities

When the Great Depression hit, the United States had a relief system lacking national scope.[148] While innovations occurred, such as discussed in the previous section, assistance was often based on local work tests and formal declarations of incapacity, that is, a "pauper's oath."[149] Such local arrangements were collapsing under the pressure of the crisis. If the depression temporarily shifted the perception of poverty from an individual responsibility to an involuntary condition,[150] it also presented an opportunity to transition from local poor laws to a federal system: "... [w]ith local finances at a breaking point [the crisis] offered the national government the chance to forge a fundamentally expanded and new role for itself [but] without explicitly planning *permanently* to expand federal spending, let alone budget deficits."[151]

In fact, in addition to the Social Security Act (1933–1935)[152] the New Deal featured large scale, deficit-financed public works.[153] These were included in an "emergency budget," with the "regular" one kept in fiscal balance, and featured a set of institutions and schemes.[154] Responses presented different features in terms of design and coverage (Figure 4.8). Over 1933–1940, the programs reached between 5.1 and 7.1 million households (or 15–25 million people).[155] Among the interventions, the Civil Works Administration (CWA) was defined as "... [t]he greatest public works experiment in American history."[156] Costs ranged from 0.08% to 2.6% of GDP.

[148] See Harvey (1999), Moffitt (2015), O'Connor (2001), Mencher (1968), Piven and Cloward (1971), and Teles (1996).

[149] The oath was a sworn declaration by a person of being completely destitute (Goldberg 2007, Harvey 2007). In 1950, an affidavit was required for AFDC beneficiaries stating that "I also agree to raise my children to the best of my ability and will not knowingly contribute or be a contributing factor to their being shamed by my conduct. I understand that should I violate this agreement, the children will be taken from me" (quoted in Pimpare 2002, p. 102).

[150] Harvey (2007).

[151] Weir and Skocpol (1985, p. 134 and 137).

[152] The Act was structured around four tiles: the first provided grants to the states for aiding seniors; the second established federal pensions with contributions by employees and employers ("Social Security") available independently of income; the third created a federal payroll tax with which states could provide unemployment compensation (selectively so for particular workers, and excluding agricultural and domestic labor); and finally, the fourth title introduced Aid to Dependent Children program, later becoming Aid to Families with Dependent Children (AFDC) and eventually repealed in 1996 in favor of TANF. See Hoey (1944).

[153] David (1971).

[154] These included the Civilian Conservation Corps (CCC), Civil Works Administration (CWA), Public Works Administration (PWA), the Works Progress Administration (WPA), and National Youth Administration (NYA).

[155] See GoUS (1942), Annex 9 (see column "estimated unduplicated total").

[156] Katz (1995, p. 53).

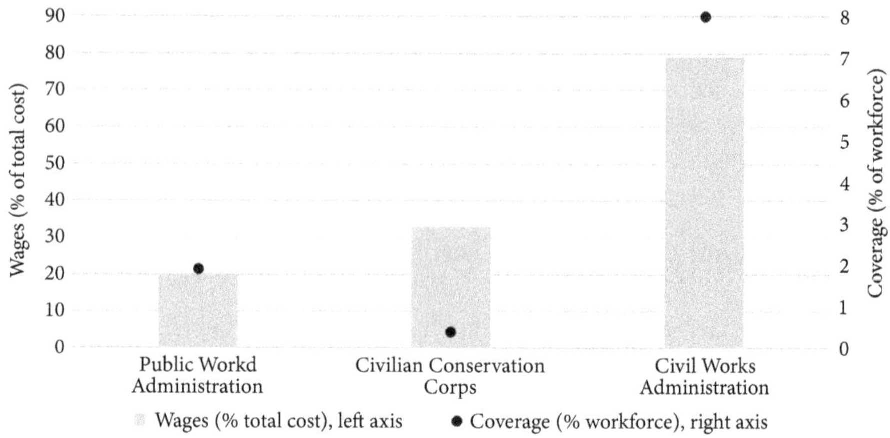


**Figure 4.8** Coverage and structure of select New Deal public works.
*Source*: The author, based on Harvey (2007).

While the public works programs have been reviewed in detail, it might be interesting to flash out some innovative features.[157] The Public Works Administration (PWA) program had large multiplier effects: for every PWA job, between 2.5 and 3.5 indirect jobs were generated from production of materials, capital equipment and other contracts. The CWA works were designed to complement the PWA with a focus on smaller projects that could start and end on short notice: in 10 weeks, they went from covering zero to 4.2 million beneficiaries. The Works Progress Administration, the successor of the CWA, covered unemployed individuals on relief: most public works comprised construction works, while other activities included tasks like serving school lunches. Finally, the National Youth Administration included an "School Work Program" and "Out-Of-School Program": the former was geared to students between 16 and 24 years of age who attended day classes and needed financial assistance (the work comprised activities like clerical assistance); the latter included retail jobs, with eligibility initially income-related and eventually relaxed over time.

The United States public works response occurred within a large set of international public works experiences and debates. For example, governments in Sweden and England hosted committees featuring some key economists of the time.[158] These consultations led to different strategic directions in response: Sweden opted for deficit-financed public works, while England extended social insurance. While the United States didn't establish a committee, there were lively exchanges between government departments and academia,[159] like the Harris Foundation Roundtables in Chicago (Box 4.5). These considerations suggest that a particular form of cash

[157] See Harvey (2007). The features here laid out are based on his paper.

[158] In Sweden, this included an Unemployment Commission that included Myrdal and Ohlin; in England, a committee featured members like Keynes and Pigou (Weir and Skocpol 1985).

[159] For example, an emerging stagnationist school held that private investment would probably not be able to attain full employment, and that permanent injections of public spending would be necessary (Backhouse and Boianovsky 2016, Hansen 1939). See also May (1981) and Tobin (1976).

transfers, in this case public works, has been a key component of macroeconomic deliberations. This is a somewhat refreshing reminder given how much of the debate on cash transfers in history revolved on micro-level incentives.

## Box 4.5 Keynes's Perspective on Public Works in the United States: Insights from a Roundtable Discussion

About 80 leading economists and policymakers met at the Harris Foundation Roundtables in Chicago over June 23–July 2, 1931, and subsequently on January 30, 1932.[a] The events' theme was "unemployment as a world problem" and featured (for the 1931 meeting only) Keynes who, in several occasions, laid out his views on public works. Verbatim notes from the evening of June 29 report Keynes stating that " . . . the argument for public works in [the US] is much weaker than it is in Great Britain [where] I have for a long time past agitated very strongly for a public works program."[b] It was noted that ". . . most if not all of the economists present questioned neither the efficacy nor the advisability of public works," and "Keynes and Hansen were really the only ones to weaken the case for public works."[c] On July 1, Keynes reiterated that

> . . . I should use the public works program to fill the interregnum while I was getting the interest down. The public works program would increase business profits, and therefore relieve people from that exceptional unwillingness to borrow. [ . . . ] I attribute importance to government action in the short run, and to central bank action in the long run. [ . . . ] Unless we are prepared to be much more socialist than we have been hitherto, there is a definite limit to what governments can do.

In other words, Keynes believed that public works should function as a short-term deterrent until the interest rate aligned investment and savings, while American economists supported public works as expansionary fiscal policy to augment spending and enhance return on investment. A similar debate reoccurred in the 1932 meeting.[d]

[a] The box draws from Davis (1971, p.117–129).

[b] He continued: "my argument has been that we are such a center of an international system that we cannot operate on the rate of interest, because if we tried to force the rate of interest down, there is too much lending, and we lose our gold. [ . . . ] [In the US] you can function as though you were a closed system [ . . . ] [and] I would use as my first method operating on the long-term interest rate. [ . . . ] [P]ublic works should be regarded much more as a tonic to change of business conditions, but the means of getting back to the state of equilibrium should be concentrated on the interest rate."

[c] Davis (1971).

[d] Ironically, Alvin Hansen, who was considered the "leader of American Keynesianism" (Lekachman 1966, p.107), was skeptical about public works at the meeting: ". . . I have a feeling that public works have been accepted around the Round Table rather too easily tonight. Isn't true that in the history of Great Britain and Germany they have after all devoted a great deal of attention to the

question of public works, and never found public works any sort of remedy for the situation [ . . . ] You can't put public works suddenly into motion without an enormous waste, and you have to pay for them eventually, and they do react upon the private economy." At that point, Jacob Viner delivered a strong rebuttal arguing that ". . . the history of public works was virtually irrelevant to the present situation, as in the past they have been trivial and not connected to any procedure for increasing the net amount of banking funds in use"; also, he pointed out that public works would have an "altogether favorable" reaction on businesses; and finally charged that ". . . so far as wasting is concerned, [there is a lot] of wastage involved now in the idle capital resources and the idle labor resources that are available and not being used." As observed by Davis (1971, p.129), " . . . what a strange scene—one of the founders of a 'school' [i.e., the Chicago School] which was less enamored with the Keynesian ideas than the rest of the profession trying to persuade one who became the most enamored with Keynesian ideas to adopt what might easily be described in retrospect as a Keynesian idea!"

## The not-so-quiet revolution

Macroeconomic crises have also presented strategic opportunities for cash transfers in more recent times. In Brazil and Mexico, reforms conducted in the mid-1990s led to the launch of flagship conditional cash transfer (CCT) programs like *Bolsa Escola* (1995) and *PROGRESA* (1997), respectively. In Mexico's case, CCTs replaced fifteen subsidy schemes.[160] While there is debate around which of the two countries first piloted CCTs in the region, from a global standpoint Bangladesh had a stipend for girls introduced already in 1982.[161] Such experience comes, as discussed in Chapter 3, nearly two centuries after the case of Germany in the late 1700s. As a result of the East-Asia financial crisis, Indonesia introduced the *Raskin* program in 1998, a seminal national safety net in the country. The program provided 15 kg of rice at subsidized price. It was recently converted into an e-voucher scheme reaching 15 million households.[162]

In a range of low-income contexts, the entry point for social protection was the leveraging of protracted humanitarian assistance (Box 4.6). This was the case for Botswana, discussed later in the chapter. The Ethiopia PSNP launched in 2005 built on decades of previous experience with humanitarian programs and shifted from annual relief planning to a multi-annual framework.[163] Some donors also pegged quantitative targets on similar transitions.[164]

[160] Levy (2007). The program was morphed into a scholarship scheme in 2018 (for a similar scheme in Mexico City, see Dustan 2020).

[161] This includes a female stipend program piloted by USAID which, over the course of the following four decades, would be gradually scaled up nationwide supporting 2 million girls/year (Khandker et al. 2021, p. 40–41).

[162] Alderman et al. (2017), Banerjee et al. (2021a).

[163] Gilligan et al. (2009).

[164] For instance, in 2009 the Department for International Development pledged " . . . to help build social protection systems to [support] 50 million people in over 20 countries over the next three years" (DFID 2009, p. 25).

## Box 4.6 A Brief History of Humanitarian Assistance

International humanitarian assistance has a long tradition. For instance, an early account includes the response to Lisbon's catastrophic earthquake of 1755:[a] Spain sent the equivalent of today's $10.2 million; France offered $4.6 million (which Portugal declined for political reasons); and England provided about $55 million in gold, silver, food, tools, and clothes. The city of Hamburg, a key trading partner, delivered $44 million in cash, food, and goods.

The institutional history of humanitarian assistance, however, is rooted in Dunant's memoire of war atrocities, including injured soldiers abandoned on the battlefield.[b] His work, *Memory of Solferino*, called for an international treaty to guarantee the protection of medical staff and field hospitals. Following favorable opinions of notable figures like Gustave Moynier—the president of the Geneva Society for Public Welfare—an international conference was eventually organized. This took the form of the Geneva Convention of 1864 and paved the way for the establishment of the International Committee of the Red Cross (ICRC). The First World War created further institutions, like the voluntary relief organization such as Save the Children and, after 1918, organizations like UNHCR.

Michael Barnett[c] shows that the principles of the 1834 New Poor Law formed the broad contours of public works-based responses to famines. The year 1834 also marked slaves' emancipation, and according to a range of observers, British abolitionist and missionary movements shared principles and membership.[d] Missionaries began organizing into societies, and in the early 1800s they started receiving funding. Among the precepts preached to colonized populations was "hard work," which was viewed as an essential Christian character.[e] Chapter 5 will discuss this aspect further.

The goals of humanitarian assistance have evolved. Two forms of humanitarianism can be identified: on one hand, there is a "pure" version that strictly adhered to the principles of humanity, impartiality, neutrality, and independence; on the other hand, from the 1990s an "alchemical" version of humanitarianism emerged. Such variant focused on objectives beyond lives-saving and meant to help address the "causes of suffering."[f] Increasingly, humanitarianism started to frame approaches in terms of "linking relief and development" as opposed to adopting a sole humanitarian lens.[g] The links with humanitarian assistance lie at the core of social protection in a vast gamut of contemporary contexts.[h]

[a] On November 1, three disasters hit Portugal's capital inflicting damages equivalent to a hundred Hurricane Katrinas. The first shock was an 8.5-magnitude earthquake, one of the largest to have ever hit a major European city. This was followed by fires and a trio of tsunamis with waves about 20 meters high. The disaster claimed nearly 40,000 lives (16% of the city's population) and affected more than 80% of the city's infrastructure (McCullough 2020a, 2020b).

[b] Dunant (1862).

[c] Barnett (2011).
[d] Grant (2005), Lester and Dussart (2014).
[e] Bashford (2005).
[f] Following Barnett (2011), "... if agencies want to remove the causes of suffering, then they will have to get their hands dirty with politics. They will have to advocate for the redistribution of political power [and] the reallocation of resources [ . . . ] [A]s humanitarians began imagining how to build peace after war, they slipped into building states" (p. 3 and 40–41). The intersection of humanitarian assistance and social protection around state building is currently visible in very concrete ways—from assessments of needs to the management of information systems; from design to implementation of programs (Gentilini et al. 2018).
[g] Buchanan-Smith and Maxwell (1994).
[h] The connections between humanitarian assistance and social protection have been subject to two opposing forces: on the one hand, a wider use of cash transfers in humanitarian assistance is facilitating the potential convergence of between the two spheres. Recent estimates show that about one fifth of humanitarian aid was delivered as cash-based transfers, a steep increase in a realm traditionally dominated by in-kind assistance. On the other hand, less than one percent of humanitarian assistance is channeled via national governments, hence contributing to "parallel systems" and fragmentation. See Development Initiatives (2022), Gentilini et al. (2018), and Kreidler et al. (2022).

The global recession of 2008–2010 led to a further wave in the introduction and institutionalization of national schemes, like Pantawid in the Philippines and BISP in Pakistan. Overall, a dramatic surge in cash transfer programs in low- and middle-income countries occurred since the early 2000s. Figure 4.9 shows that the average coverage rate among 20 select flagship cash programs, which currently reach a combined coverage of nearly 340 million people, quadrupled over the past two decades.[165] Even high-income countries lacking a national guaranteed minimum income scheme would soon introduce it, like Greece and Italy.[166] If the past twenty years have witnessed a vibrant surge in the quantity and quality of coverage, the literature on the topic has been no less voluminous. The story of a "quiet revolution" has been documented and discussed extensively—to the point where it is perhaps no longer so quiet.[167]

If regional and global economic contractions over the past couple of decades unleashed new cash transfer programs, not all situations of economic adversity triggered such outcome. For instance, neither the post-independence nor the adjustment period seems to have produced significant state-provided, cash-based programs in low- and middle-income countries. These are discussed in the next section.

[165] Countries (and programs) include Senegal (PNBSF), Philippines (4Ps), Zambia (SCT), Pakistan (BISP), Egypt (TKP), Brazil (BF), DRC (CVP), Nepal (SSA), Mexico (Pro), Honduras (FA), Dominican Republic (Sol), Turkey (CCT), Romania (CSA), Indonesia (PKH), Tanzania (PSSN), China (DB), Bolivia (JP), Peru (JP), Iraq (SPN), and Ukraine (SA). The reported average coverage rate is not population weighted.
[166] For Greece, see Matsaganis (2018), while Maitino et al. (2022) assess the effects of Italy's guaranteed minimum income program in Tuscany.
[167] See, for example, Banerjee et al. (2023), Barrientos (2013), Barrientos and Hulme (2008), Beegle et al. (2017), Hanlon et al. (2010), Hickey et al. (2019), Lavers (2022), Lindert et al. (2020), Schuring and Loewe (2021), and UNDP (2019).

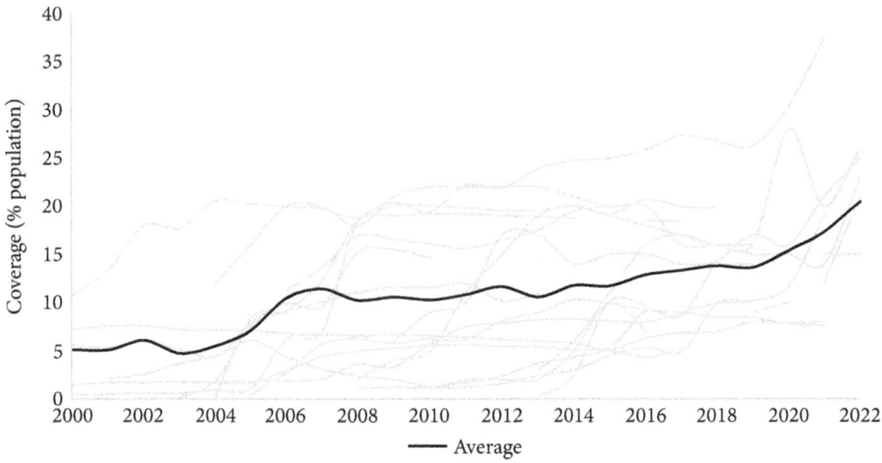


**Figure 4.9** Coverage trends of select flagship cash transfers programs.

*Source*: The author, based on ASPIRE survey data for conditional and unconditional cash transfers (data accessed January 2024).

## 4.3 Building upon protracted adversity

The previous section outlined cases of state-building during and in response to severe crises. This section discusses cases where adversities may have been more protracted and recurrent. It focuses on low- and middle-income countries and their experience on three fronts. First it explains the legacy and adaptations of social assistance programs inherited from colonial periods. It next examines the turbulent post-independence years of structural adjustments through a cash transfers lens. Finally, it identifies repeated drought and famine responses as a juncture for building national social protection capabilities.

### Colonial influence on cash transfers in select low- and middle-income countries

Emerging evidence shows that the legacy of the colonial period is significant.[168] Jeremy Seekings noted that " . . . [t]he boundaries of [the British] empire appear to have had a profound and lasting effect on social protection policy, even into the 2000s."[169] About half of social protection programs in former colonies were introduced before independence.[170]

[168] For literature around the effects of colonialism on local institutions and other development dimensions, see among others Williams (1944), Acemoglu et al. (2001), Banerjee and Iyer (2005), Gennaioli and Rainer (2007), Michalopoulos and Papaioannou (2013), Mkandawire (2010, 2016), Nunn and Wantchekon (2011) and Rodney (2018).

[169] Seekings (2020, p. 109).

[170] Midgley (2011). For reviews around developments occurring over the last century in select middle income countries, see Leisering (2021); for Brazil specifically, see Lavinas (2021).

The influence of colonialism is transmitted not only via social protection approaches, but also through the larger imperial institutional architecture involved in the colonization process.[171] In fact, policymakers sometimes operate within an institutional framework created by former colonial regimes.[172] Moreover, former colonies became proxies for broader geopolitical battles,[173] and social protection was not immune to those dynamics.[174]

A range of factors may help explain the direct or indirect engagement of European powers in social protection in colonial territories. One such ingredient was growing demand and interest by colonial territories themselves. As mentioned in Chapter 1, Jamaica (in 1682 and 1886) and Mauritius (in 1902) instituted a local version of the poor laws to support European settlers: these were criticized by an English Commission of 1909 based on not-too-stringent implementation which, it was claimed, had encouraged indolence among local populations.[175]

Chapter 3 documented the rapid diffusion of social pensions. In 1931, Trinidad and Tobago provided relief for disabled and sick populations, and in 1939 it included a social pension. This occurred two years after Barbados (1937) and five before Guyana (1944). Local labor movements also played a key role. In France, for example, as the debate on social security intensified at home after the Second World War, the country extended the rights of workers to establish unions in colonies: by 1945, there were at least 175 such unions in colonial territories.[176] A range of strikes in British and French colonies centered on workers' income losses due to illnesses and accidents.[177]

Approaches by colonial powers varied. France displayed a relatively uniform, centralized approach.[178] As such, it developed and applied a *Code du Travail* for African colonies in 1952, the production of which entailed six years of debates. A West Africa-wide strike, like by railway workers in Senegal, was instrumental for its final release.[179] The Code placed an emphasis on family allowances as well as insurance for illness and work accidents, although it didn't offer provision on unemployment insurance and pensions: " . . . French officials assumed that African societies provide alternatives to wage employment [and] the problem of old age was left to individual trade unions."[180] In contrast, the British colonial attitude toward social protection fitted a general pattern of preference for social assistance over social insurance. For example, based on data from 92 countries and controlling for a range of global and domestic

[171] Mahoney (2010).
[172] Kangas (2012).
[173] Fukuyama (2014), Obinger and Schmitt (2011).
[174] For example, see Mioni and Petersen (2020) for a discussion on the effects of the Cold War on the development of welfare state approaches in Burma and Malaysia.
[175] Midgley (1984a).
[176] Orr (1966).
[177] Cooper (1996).
[178] Cooper (1996), Iliffe (1987), MacLean (2002).
[179] Cooper (2012, p. 401–402).
[180] Schmitt (2015, p. 334).

factors, the probability of a former British colony having a social pension is 6.7 times higher than in all other countries.[181]

The British approach was predicated on "indirect rule" and leveraging local institutions.[182] Such local institutions and informal provisions, or the mechanisms through which people provide reciprocal support, were—and still are—widespread: currently, one quarter of households in 99 countries report engaging in such forms of support.[183] The term "informal social protection" encompasses an array of different actors and mechanisms. In general, it tends to indicate support rendered by actors other than the "state," for example NGOs, associations, faith-based organizations, clans, kinship, communities, households, and extended family networks. A review of six African countries estimated the presence of nearly 760,000 "non-state social protection actors," largely small and contributory—but also in part rendering cash transfers-type, non-contributory assistance.[184] Boundaries are blurred, as governments can fund a portion of the schemes (e.g., like in the case of Zakat);[185] and many involve finely structured arrangements with rules, benefits, obligations, enforcement mechanisms, and sanctions ironed out over long timeframes.[186] In Africa, some of these arrangements are shaped by "time-tested African traditional values" of solidarity and reciprocity.[187] In other words, " . . . unlike the impersonal nature of formal social protection, informal social protection is based on social relations."[188]

[181] Schmitt (2020b).

[182] Eckert (2004), Midgley (1984a, 1984b), Seekings (2014, 2024).

[183] Evans et al. (2020) estimate that informal mechanisms (excluding remittances) are present among 24.1% of households.

[184] Awortwi (2018, p. 903). Contributions can be sizable as a share of household budgets: for example, surveys show that in Ghana and Ivory Coast, households devote between 10% and 30% of monthly income for helping each other (MacLean 2011, p. 128; her article also provides an insightful review of the literature, see p. 120–121).

[185] Nowak-Garmer (2023). See discussion on Zakat in Chapter 5.

[186] Midgley (1994b) identified four types of culturally institutionalized norms of reciprocity, namely based on (i) narrow family and kinship arrangements; (ii) community support networks (e.g., communal crops storage and cooperative harvesting, or assistance with other agricultural tasks that cannot be effectively undertaken by individual domestic groups alone); (iii) mutual aid associations that pool resources to meet contingencies or promote capital accumulation and savings; and (iv) religiously mandated obligations to provide support. For country examples, see Patel et al. (2015) for a discussion on South African programs like the *isolabantwana* (protection services to children at risk of abuse and neglect), *isibindi* (support to orphans and vulnerable children via safe parks and volunteer programs), the Siyabhabha Trust (which recruits, trains, and uses volunteers to deliver family and community service), and mutual aid associations à la "stokvel" (savings clubs that eventually became rotating savings and credit associations). See also Ntseane and Solo (2007) for other mutual aid mechanisms like burial or funeral associations, cattle loaning (*kuronzera*), and *letsema* (the pooling of human resources for the benefit of an individual or group of people) in South Africa and Botswana.

[187] Mpedi (2018, p. 83). See also Cobbah (1987) and Gumbo (1998). These notions were enshrined in the term ubuntu, an expression of oneness whereby " . . . a person depends on personal relations with others to exercise, develop and fulfil those capacities that make one a person" (Christians 2004, p. 241). However, some authors have warned that "... informal social protection should not be sentimentalised as an answer to all the social protection challenges" (Mpedi 2018, p. 92); as such, there is a need to ". . . guard against romanticising about the role and capacity of informal social security systems" (Kaseke 2008, p. 68).

[188] Devereux and Getu (2013, p. 285).

Furthermore, the notion of "informal" systems tends to be used in reference to a wide-encompassing set of traditional, precolonial arrangements—even if those mechanisms were part of formal, sophisticated kingdoms and empires. The *Zunde RaMambo* (chief's granary) in Zimbabwe provides a contemporary example dating back to the Shona kings of the 1200s.[189] The "age class systems"—where grades correspond to a social position and with grade passages celebrated though rites—are another case in point. Present across precolonial Africa,[190] they provided an institutional vehicle through which skills were imparted and education conferred: for instance, the regimented formation of Zulu adolescents under the authority of the king entailed "absorbing technical instruction and [ . . . ] the glorification of the work ethic."[191]

The diversity and complexity of informal mechanisms shaped a contentious interface with colonial structures. The indirect rule espoused by British colonial policy in Africa presumed a clear understanding of local traditions and customs upon which governance arrangements in the territory were anchored. Studies show that in the case of the Gold Coast, Nigeria, Kenya, and Rhodesia, the codification of local norms and "informal" practices by officials, commissions, and anthropologists was fraught with difficulties and contradictory evidence. This stemmed from limited written bodies of legal and historical knowledge, conflicting oral accounts, blurred tribal lineages, and transactions (e.g., in the case of land) where evolving outcomes would hinge on relations between parties involved.[192] This section later shows how the establishment of institutional roles relevant for contemporary cash transfers implementation (e.g., the "village chief") may or may have not been rooted in local customs.

While there appears to be limited accounts of "informal" cash transfers being used as an instrument of social assistance in colonial times,[193] the economic changes induced by colonial rule—like expanded commercial farming—may have increased the local use of cash as mean of transactions within traditional customs. Historian Sara Berry noted that " . . . payments for land-use rights, bridewealth, titles, etc., were

[189] Machingura (2012). The program established food reserves and provided in-kind food transfers during times of distress, including famines or situations of chronic poverty (Dhemba et al. 2002, Ruparanganda et al. 2017). A common field was designated by the village chief for the production of grain. This involved voluntary work of community members to ploughing, sowing, weeding, and harvesting. On a yearly basis, the produce was stocked up in food reserve (Madembo 1998). Although a sense of belonging motivates villagers to participate in Zunde, community sanctions for not participating in community activities existed, and an attendance register is maintained by a Zunde committee. While colonialism jeopardized the system, it was recently revived in the context of the HIV/AIDS crisis (Mararike 2001).

[190] These included among other Sudan's Nilo-Hamitic populations, the Konso in Ethiopia, Kenya's Gabbra, the Lango in Uganda, Nigeria's Igbo, the Somba in Benin, and Nyakyusa in Tanzania (Bernardi 1985).

[191] Bernardi (1985, p. 117).

[192] See Berry (1993) for a detailed review.

[193] Cash appears in certain ceremonies. For example, Bradbury (1965) describes the mortuary rites of the Edo in Western Nigeria. The first part of the ceremony includes participants offering cloths and small sums of money: such cash is not used in the rite per se but shared among elderly men of the lineage of the deceased (*egbee*) at the end of the ritual.

made in cash and hired labour began to replace [various] forms of domestic servitude. [ . . . ] People continued to invest in marriage, seniority, chieftaincy titles, etc., but their prerogatives were exercised in new ways by new people."[194]

The Spanish colonial process, instead, occurred in the 16th century, the historical period antecedent to the formation of capitalist systems.[195] Spanish colonies became independent in the course of the 19th century, almost a century before British and France colonies.[196] Yet some of the institutions introduced in colonial times " . . . persisted throughout the 19th century and were transformed in the 20th century, becoming the backbone of the modern social security system."[197] For instance, Spanish colonies established the *montepios*, or basic contributory pensions for retirement and survivors similar to Spain's model.[198]

In Spanish colonies, religious and voluntary organizations were encouraged. In Mexico City, charity hospitals run by religious orders and funded by colonial authorities were established as early as 1521; in Peru, the government entrusted the responsibility for poor relief to charities in 1826; and in the Philippines, charitable almshouses date back to 1578.[199] In the latter, in 1941 an executive order of the American administration created a social assistance scheme nationalizing a voluntary organization (the American Charity Organization Society) that had been organizing poor relief in the country.[200] Portuguese brotherhoods providing poor relief also have a rich history.[201]

Colonial social protection also represented a conduit for the transfer of rhetoric and values.[202] For example,

> . . . [t]he influence of the Poor Laws that played a dominant role in shaping Britain's approach to social assistance is still evident in Zimbabwe today. [Social assistance] was seen as a waste of scarce resources, hence the limited focus on assisting only destitute members of society [to not] encourage laziness and dependency.[203]

[194] Berry (1989, p. 43).

[195] The enduring colonial influence on social protection in Latin America seems relatively less studied empirically (Segura-Ubiergo 2007). In examining factors that shape social protection uptake in the region, Diaz-Cayeros and Magaloni (2009) show that variables like inequality, income, state capacity, and the durability of the political regime all contribute to earlier adoption (but economic growth is identified as a potentially delaying factor). See also Cruz-Martinez (2021) for an analysis of broad-based welfare (beyond social protection) trajectories in the region as measured by a multidimensional welfare state development index.

[196] Lange (2004), Mahoney (2010), Schmitt (2020b).

[197] Mesa-Lago (1978, p. 17). See also Mesa-Lago (1991, 2007).

[198] Kunzler (2016).

[199] Midgley (1984a).

[200] Landa Jovcano (1980).

[201] These were tied to the crown's patronage and were established, for example, in Goa (1519), Bahai (1552), Macau (1569), Luanda (1576), Rio de Janeiro (1582), and Mombasa (1593) (Russell-Wood 1969).

[202] Midgley (1994b, 1984c). Social welfare provisions under colonial regimes relied on social workers seconded from Britain (Mupedziswa 1995).

[203] Kaseke (2011, p. 121, 128, 129).

Yet the process of "absorption" of social protection in the colonies wasn't mere replication of approaches developed in Britain. While commonly rooted in the English poor laws, countries under British influence gradually displayed diversity in their approaches to cash transfers, including in terms of design, as well as institutional and financing parameters[204] (Table 4.3). For instance, comparisons between the evolution of cash transfers in Canada and United States have been studies widely (Box 4.7).

**Table 4.3** Variations in English colonial Poor Laws

| | Comparatively limited | Comparatively extensive |
|---|---|---|
| Prevalence of outdoor relief (including unconditional transfers). | Ireland 1860 (3% of total relief).[a] | Scotland (1860) (95% of total relief). |
| Approach to able-bodied claimants. | Scotland Poor Laws of 1845 denied provisions to the able-bodied (limiting them to the "destitute" and "disabled"). | England had various forms of work tests, especially under the new Poor Law of 1834; US New Deal. |
| Role of family. | Relief as a right in England. | British early North American colonies, e.g., Plymouth Colony (1642) (public assistance only if family could not support its members); Australian and New Zealand colonies. |
| Role of religious institutions in provisions. | Ontario in 1830s, with public expansion and regulation of assistance. | Malta (before the Second World War); Quebec (under French rule in 17th century); Cape Town (Dutch rule in 17th century). |
| Eligibility along racial lines to maintain hierarchy. | England and Northern American colonies. | South Africa (early 1900s); West Indies; South Carolina (US); Southern Rhodesia; Barbados (white women forming relationships with black men made them undeserving). |
| Financing via local taxation. | Southern Africa colonies (mostly centrally funded). | England (1601), Scotland (1845). |

*Source*: The author based on Seekings (2024).
[a]Approaches could evolve dramatically: in just 20 years, the coverage of outdoor relief in Ireland would exceed that of workhouses in 1880; see Crossman (2013, p. 48).

[204] Seekings (2023). See Orloff and Skocpol (1984) on contrasting Britain and the United States; for Scotland's poor laws, see Paterson (1976), while Dickey (1992) discussed Australia's relatively limited poverty legislation. For New Zealand, see Tennant (2007).

## Box 4.7 A Rapid Comparison of Canada and United States since the 1800s

While Canada and the Unites States belong to Esping-Andersen's classic "liberal welfare regimes," their experience illustrates the variety of policy design and institutional trajectories possible within a seemingly uniform model.[a] In Canada, French colonies like Quebec replicated French provisions based on Catholic charities with no poor laws involved.[b] Similarly, Ontario had no poor law and relied on Protestant church charity—although public outdoor relief was eventually expanded and regulated by the state, especially around the last quarter of the 1800s.[c] Conversely, when they became subject to British rule the ex-French territory of Nova Scotia, and the ex-Dutch colony of New York, followed the old English poor laws.

During the formative years for the Canadian welfare system from 1880s to 1920s, there were frequent instances of tapping American expertise on "scientific charity" approaches (see discussion in Chapter 6).[d] Such interactions, which involved social reformers like John Joseph Kelso,[e] led to increasingly ambiguous reactions within the Canadian social work community as it sought to balance learning from American practices and adapting them to the Canadian context.[f]

The main point of departure, however, occurred around the Second World War. Financed from general revenues, Canada introduced universal child benefits and social pensions in 1944 and 1951, respectively.[g] These programs provided benefits based on demographic and residency requirements, and without means tests. In the case of child benefits, it has been argued that such direction was taken because of lower cost in administration of universal provisions, their Keynesian rationale in bolstering broad-based consumption, and their political attractiveness among larger swaths of the population.[h] Yet, from the 1990s the political resilience of child benefits proved volatile, and the program was discontinued in favor of US-type social assistance models.[i] Social pensions, instead, deflected political attempts of reform in the 1980s, although their purely universal nature was compromised.[j]

Developments in the United States, as shown in this chapter, took a different route. The United States had veteran pensions introduced well before the New Deal and which were kept separate from poor relief.[k] Then throughout the 1930s–1970s, the country introduced means-tested social assistance schemes which have been referred to as an "unreformed poor law" for the working-age population.[l] Opportunities for universalizing, or almost so, the system were rejected at key junctures, including for example the "Townsend Plan" in the 1930s,[m] the negative income tax debates of the 1960s (see Chapter 6), and, arguably, the COVID-era child tax credit.

[a] See Seekings (2008) for an analytical expansion of the Western typology by Esping-Andersen (1990) to low- and middle-income countries, including "agrarian", "workerist" and "pauperist" regimes. For an extension of Canada-United States comparisons to pensions, see Orloff (1993).
[b] In Upper Canada, the first voluntary agency appeared in 1817, i.e., the Society for the Relief of Strangers modelled on a similar organization in London (Baehre 1981).
[c] See Splane (1965, p.18) and Wallace (1950).
[d] Hareven (1969) chronicles many of those contact points. For example, when in 1898 the American National Conference of Charities and Corrections met in Toronto for the first time, the event was preceded by meetings between thought leaders like Alexander Johnson, former president of the Conference, and Buffalo-based Frederick Almy. This led to the establishment of Canadian Conference on Charities and Corrections. The founding of the United States Children's Bureau in 1912 generated demand for a similar institution in Canada (which eventually took the form of a Health department in 1919). Moreover, American expertise was tapped for professional guidance, such as in 1921 when the city of Toronto invited the Director of the Child Welfare League of America to assess and propose reforms of child-caring agencies of the city.
[e] See Jones and Rutman (1981).
[f] Ibid.
[g] Falvo (2017), Beland and Myles (2005).
[h] Beland and Waddan (2017), Myles (1998).
[i] Through various program mergers and renaming, universal provisions for children were effectively phased out in 1993, reintroduced in 2006, and again eliminated in 2016.
[j] Social pensions include a claw back on top income brackets, see discussion in Beland and Waddan (2017, p.74).
[k] On such separation, Seekings (2023) also points to the experience of Barbados. See also Seekings (2007a).
[l] Ibid.
[m] Tabled by Dr Francis Townsend, a 67-year old physician, the Townsend Plan of 1933 is associated with a social movement that rallied about two million people around the idea of a national social pension. The proposal included a transfer of $200/month (more than twice the median income at Depression times) for every American above the age of 60 and who agreed to spend the monthly transfer within 30 days (Amenta 2006). For photo footage and commemorative items of the movement (e.g., decorative stamps), visit https://www.ssa.gov/history/towns5.html.

In a similar vein, when the iconic Beveridge report appeared in 1942, it sparked considerable attention overseas.[205] In 1943, Mr. Miles, a British officer based in London, wrote a memo in response to queries about the Beveridge Plan from British colonial offices:

> . . . are we to repeat all the fumblings that have been going on [. . .] since the industrial age or are to start with the fruits of the knowledge and experience that has been gained, by laying down, in a clear field, a really co-ordinated system of social services.[206]

[205] See Surender (2013) and Sugita (2014). Beveridge (1942) seemed to consider conditions in the colonies not ripe for the adoption of the report's proposals: "[t]here will, it may be hoped, come a season-when it is profitable to consider the practical relations of social insurance in Britain and of schemes for the same purpose in the Dominions, in the Colonies and in other countries of the world" (p.9). On a different note, some authors pointed out that the report makes reference to intended beneficiaries as those of "British race" (Plange 2023, p.357; Shilliam 2018, p.75). For Beveridge's earlier views on social protection, see for example Beveridge (1927) and his biography by Harris (1977). For a wider discussion on social contracts and social protection in Britain and other high-income contexts in the post-World War II period, see the work by giants like Thomas Humphrey Marshall (Marshall 1963, 1950) and Richard Titmuss (Titmuss 1950).
[206] The memo, dated March 20, is quoted in Seekings (2013, p. 11).

As a detailed historical review shows, the Beveridge Report led the Colonial Office formulating a policy on *Social Security in the Colonial Territories.*[207] The colonization principles of self-financing and reliance on local systems didn't necessarily favor the uptake of Beveridgean recommendations overseas.[208] Instead, local welfare provisions in the colonial period were present, but for European settlers (and in some cases, as we shall see in Chapter 5, at differentiated rates for natives absorbed in the colonial administration).[209]

## Cash transfers (or lack thereof) in post-independence and adjustment periods

The nature and performance of the much-debated period of structural adjustment in the 1980s–1990s are extensively researched, including the intellectual forces animating reforms.[210] A further commentary on such theme goes beyond the scope of this volume. However, it might be helpful to briefly review the cash transfers landscape emerging during those turbulent years. Such a quick tour needs to first consider developments in the post-independence period.

In the early post-colonial years, food subsidies, and the related marketing boards involved in food procurement and distribution, represented an important part of social protection in Africa and beyond.[211] Popular expectations and nationalist ambitions may have fomented the launch of ambitious economic planning programs involving a "big push" by the state. Such ideas "did not take place within an intellectual vacuum," with development economics theories, including those establishing an important role for the state, affecting initial post-colonial policies in contexts like Ghana.[212]

[207] Seekings (2013, p. 15).

[208] Eckert (2004), Porter (1975).

[209] Analysis on Northern Rhodesia in the early 1900s by Gelfand (1961) shows that as the number of European settlers increased, so did the sources of financing and demand for services, including to support the growing number of poor white Afrikaners.

[210] See for example Boyce and Ndikumana (2005), Dollar and Pritchett (1998), Easterly (2001), Homer and Sylla (2005), Mkandawire and Soludo (1998), and Stewart (1995). According to Mkandawire (2006), the adjustment period marked an artificial separation between economic and social policy: "macroeconomics was detached from [eradicating poverty and improving social welfare], becoming increasingly socially blind. Economic policies and the instruments chosen to implement them were no longer constrained by social objectives" (p. 4). Likewise, Harvey (2005) contended that in the late 1970s, "Keynesian fiscal and monetary policies with full employment as the key objective [were] abandoned in favour of a policy designed to quell inflation no matter what the consequences might be for employment" (p. 23). And Chang (2004) offers similar considerations about artificial distinctions between economic and social dimensions in the context of East Asia: in rebuking the notion of the region being a "social policy-free zone," he claims that "there can never be such a thing as an objectively definable economic sphere, neatly separable from other ('social' or whatever) spheres of life" (p. 247–248).

[211] Devereux (2011).

[212] Killick (1978, p. 12).

As a result, the vibrant post-colonial period featured extensive producer price controls for key crops and a proliferation of public or parastatal institutions, such as on domestic marketing in agriculture.[213] In some cases, these policies generated significant challenges, like yielding black markets for basic commodities.[214] Subsidies in agriculture were also present in high-income countries, as manifested by food aid deliveries (Box 4.8). These built on earlier practices, such as in Denmark in 1764–1776[215] and England's "Book of Orders" of 1594.[216] Food and agricultural subsidies are still significant today.[217]

**Box 4.8 Food Aid in the 1960s–1970s**

Newly independent countries introduced parastatal companies to manage food price volatility in ways that guaranteed a basic floor price to famers and accessible food to consumers. These were underpinned by extensive systems of procurement, storage, and distribution. High-income countries pursued similar approaches of public interventions in agriculture, for example via the United States Farm Bills and the European Economic Community Common Agricultural Policy. These policies generated large "surplus disposal" provisions of in-kind food aid to low- and middle-income countries. In the case of the United States, "food aid grew rapidly, accounting for more than half of U.S. food exports and most of the total overseas aid budget by the early 1960s."[a] Both USAID and WFP were formally established in 1961 to help delivering such commodities as part of development and relief support.[b] These were

[213] For example, by the late 1970s, nine out of ten countries in West Africa had established producer price controls for rice; in Southern Africa, seven out of nine countries had them for maize; and all five countries in Central Africa had price controls for maize as well as roots and tubers. In the Sahel, seven out of eight countries had legal monopsony on rice procurement, and other five established it on maize (USDA 1981, p. 127). The same USDA report also noted that government involvement in "marketing of products, that is, procurement, transportation, storage, processing, and packaging [ . . . ] is widespread, particularly for crop procurement" (ibid, p. 129).

[214] See Mhone (2004, p. 329–330) for a discussion of such problems in Zambia over 1975–1990.

[215] In Copenhagen, magistrates exerted control over the price and marketing of food products, which provided a degree of protection against crises (Post 1990, p. 263).

[216] In England, the Orders were issued in response to food crises in the 1590s (Outhwaite 1981). Until 1670, measures centered on the suspension of exports, with an array of operational difficulties related to the timing of bans, their enforcement, as well as forecasting the magnitude of food crises and related deficits. What followed was a ". . . transition from active interventions to a more passive response by the state in the grain market of the seventeenth century" (ibid, p. 405). Outhwaite also notes that ". . . [i]n each potentially deficient year the government had to make decisions and generally make them early, because in years of real deficiency acute problems were presented in the succeeding winter months [ . . . ] Government banning of exports betrays this itchy trigger finger. Such ban was proclaimed in October 1590 because of 'the likelihood of great dearth,' though the wheat harvest was subsequently an 'average' one" (ibid, p. 403–404).

[217] Recent estimates show that global subsidies on food and agriculture amount to about $630 billion/year. Nearly 70% of such support is for producer subsidies. In high-income countries, food and agricultural subsidies for producers account for 12.6% of public expenditures, a level much higher than in middle income countries (4.1–4.9%) and low-income settings (0.6%) (FAO et al. 2022, p. 64).

preceded by an FAO-based Consultative Committee for Surplus Disposal created "... to monitor international shipments of surplus agricultural commodities used as food aid in order to minimize the harmful impact of these shipments on commercial trade and agricultural production."[c] The global food crises of 1973 and country-level famines of 1970s (e.g., Ethiopia in 1973 and Bangladesh 1974) further coalesced countries around the need to uphold food security as a national priority.[d] The provision of food aid was sometimes provided in parallel to existing national structures, while other times they complemented the stocks of established food systems such as India's Public Distribution System (PDS): from this perspective, humanitarian assistance in the late 1950s was a way station toward making food subsidies universal in the early 1970s—a process underpinned by the changing role of the PDS itself from emergency response to a multi-purpose tool spanning across agriculture and income support functions.[e]

[a] Barrett (2002, p. 2147).
[b] Shaw (2001).
[c] See http://www.fao.org/unfao/govbodies/gsb-subject-matter/statutory-bodies-details/en/c/312/?no_cache=1.
[d] The food crises of the 1970s would be at the center of Sen's seminal work on famines as caused by a lack of entitlements (access to food) instead of drops in food availability (Gentilini 2007; Ravallion 1997; Sen 1981).
[e] Alderman et al. (2017).

Across Africa, subsidies tended to be universality-oriented or broad-based in coverage with a view of facilitating industrialization,[218] delivering services in contexts of limited administrative capabilities,[219] and fostering national unity.[220] On the latter point, it was observed that "... the focus of post-colonial nationalists moved towards the pursuit of national unity (nation-building) and equality through socio-economic development anchored in the transformative role of social programmes."[221]

The pursuit and implementation of those policies involved, at least in part, building on state administrative structures introduced in colonial periods: for example, Zambia "continued the colonial policy of 'regrouping' villages into large, stable units to facilitate administrative and political control."[222] In some cases, it might be possible to connect pre-independence institutions and contemporary cash transfers. In the Kenyan context, the sanctioned role of village chiefs—who "do not have roots in customary authority, but were creations of colonial authorities"—was carried over

[218] Nowak-Garmer (2023). For a succinct regional history of subsidies in the Middle East and North Africa, see Vidican Aukto and Loewe (2021, p.10–11).
[219] According to Mkandawire (2006, p. 3), ."... the 'universalism' guiding social policy in many countries was in fact dictated by underdevelopment—targeting was simply too demanding in terms of available sills and administrative capacity."
[220] Chazan et al. (1988).
[221] Kpessa et al. (2011, p. 2123).
[222] Berry (1993, p. 58–59).

and embedded into governance structures in the post-independence period (i.e., as "the lowest level of state administration").[223] Currently, chiefs play an important role in implementing programs like the Cash Transfer for Orphans and Vulnerable Children, including in terms of facilitating targeting processes.[224]

Implemented within a larger package of measures, the adjustment process often entailed the reallocation of expenditures away from generalized energy and food subsidies in favor of more targeted measures. The fact that those reforms yielded a decline in "social expenditures" and "social welfare" has been widely noted.[225] It has also been argued that the period of structural adjustment had amplified the polarization of the contentious targeting debate:[226] "... in the 1980s the issue of targeting [...] underwent a conceptual change [and] the tension between universality and selectiveness in social policy becomes a dilemma: targeting versus universal policies."[227] The "camps" that were formed around that period find echo in contemporary approaches to social protection.[228]

Except for social pensions, disaggregated data on cash transfers spending appears challenging to locate. A review of social funds[229] for the period 1986–1993 found that such instruments were present in 27 countries across Africa and Latin America: the analysis points to select employment generation schemes (e.g., Peru's PAIT, Senegal's AGETIP), food distributions, and trainings. However, reference to cash transfers seems limited.[230]

Another assessment underscored that 78–100% of program costs in Africa were donor-financed (such range was 43–95% in Latin America, excluding Mexico); and only a limited share of the population was reached, such as 0.3% in Ghana and 0.5% in Egypt.[231] For the period 1986–1988, there were at least three cases of "targeted food subsidies" (Tunisia, Morocco, and Nepal) and six public works programs (Tunisia,

[223] Porisky (2022, p. 157). In general, under British colonial policy "chiefs" were often legally constituted as "native authorities," which involved raising and spending revenues on social services under colonial supervision (Mamdani 1996, Nyamweru and Chidongo 2018). Differently from Kenya, in some settings those figures were instead rooted in customary authority: for example, in the case of Ghana they dated back to the Ashanti kingdom of the 1700s, when village chiefs "coordinated social welfare needs" (MacLean 2017, p. 365).

[224] Porisky et al. (2023).

[225] Following Mkandawire and Soludo (1998, p. 44), "... [t]he state's monopsonistic position, usually manifested as marketing boards, has been drastically reduced. Food subsidies and artificial price ceilings have been removed. Credit ceilings in favour of agriculture have been removed, and so have subsidies for inputs." Kaseke (2011) claims "reduced funding for social assistance" (p. 128). Adesina (2011) argued that the period 1981–2005 was, for Sub-Saharan Africa, "grim" as it involved a retrenchment from a wider vision of social policy to a narrower focus on social protection.

[226] Rodriguez Noboa (1992).

[227] Sojo (1990, p. 177, 180).

[228] See Ferguson (2015). For reviews of recent debates, see also Devereux (2016), Devereux et al. (2017), Grosh et al. (2022), and Kidd and Athias (2020).

[229] The funds channeled resources for a variety of projects within infrastructure and social sectors. Relative to typical public sector administrative standards, the funds exhibited a range of exceptions on, for example, remuneration of staff, reporting and adherence to budget cycles. A number of those funds had been transformed into permanent or semi-permanent entities, e.g., see Glaessner et al. (1994) for the early experience of a dozen Latin American countries.

[230] UNCTAD (1993, p. 13, 34). Among the reported examples, the review mentioned that Mexico "combines a basic food basket and cash payments in the education program" (ibid, p. 14).

[231] Vivien (1994).

Chile, Ghana, Mauritania, Sao Tome and Principe, and Guinea).[232] Other public works schemes (Bolivia and Ghana) were designed for former civil servants.[233]

Select episodes of reforms from generalized subsidies to targeted transfers have been recorded.[234] These include Ukraine, were in 1999 approximately 25% of the population was covered at a cost of 0.8% of GDP (down from 5.5% of GDP in generalized subsidies in 1995). And Jamaica implemented a targeted food stamp program in 1984 in lieu of a generalized food-price subsidy: in this case, fiscal costs fell from about 6% of GDP in the late 1970s to around 0.1% since 1993. In various cases, the subsidy reform process increased prices to consumers, with instances of social unrest, which either derailed or diluted reforms.[235]

Overall, evidence on the performance of new or reformed social assistance programs of the period seems anecdotal and lacking systematic evaluations. By the mid-1990s, it was observed that " . . . safety net schemes have, as yet, undertaken very few attempts at social impact evaluation [ . . . ] and there has been no attempt to collect any sort of baseline data."[236] Policy commentaries of the period were generally mixed or underwhelming about the performance of social assistance. Reasons include, among others, limited fiscal resources allocated to compensatory schemes,[237] their low adequacy,[238] and the inherent logic of reform.[239] As a result, the period 1980–2000 in Sub-Saharan has been characterized as "crossing the desert" because of "the absence of significant policies in the field of social protection".[240]

## Drought and famine response in India and Africa over a century, 1870s–1980s

Famine relief can be a strategic juncture for institutionalizing state capabilities. India is probably one of the most widely studied countries on the matter.

[232] Ribe and Carvalho (1990). Tunisia generated substantial budgetary savings from increased targeting of its generalized system of food subsidies, reducing spending from 2.8% of GDP in 1990 to 1% in 1999 (Gupta et al. 2000).

[233] Van der Hoeven (1991).

[234] Gupta et al. (2000).

[235] These included, for example, Jordan in 1989, when an attempt to raise fuel prices sparked riots bringing down the prime minister; Zimbabwe in 1998, when riots erupted in the wake of a currency devaluation; Zambia in 1990, when the government announced an increase in the price of maize; Indonesia in 1998 for energy price increases; Ecuador in 1998 for soaring prices of cooking gas, gasoline, and diesel, a decision that was reversed in 1999; and Nigeria in June 2000 (Gupta et al. 2000). For more recent analysis on reforms and riots, see Ciminelli et al. (2019).

[236] Vivien (1994, p. 14).

[237] For example, Kaseke (1994) estimates that during the adjustment period, in Zimbabwe only one in 20 needy people benefited from social assistance. See also Kaseke (1988, 2000). In Bolivia, however, the emergency social fund, which involved a variety of social interventions like school meals, infrastructure, etc. selected by communities, reached 1.2 million people out of a population of about seven million; and public works in Chile were successfully implemented and supported about half a million people in 1983 (Graham 1994).

[238] Graham (1998).

[239] Mkandawire and Soludo (1998, p. 74) pointed out, for example, that " . . . [p]oor performance is inherent to measures intended to solve problems within a model that denies the emergence of those problems".

[240] Olie et al (2024, p.10).

As recounted in Alexander Loveday's history of Indian famine responses, Emperors would stockpile grain supplies in their capitals as war chests while farmers stored part of their surplus.[241] In some cases, like in the famine of 1687, it seems that people were compelled to release their private stocks. Based on the intensity of food crises, grains in royal storage would be either sold at subsidized prices or distributed directly: on the latter, examples include Muhammad Tughlak's distribution in 1343. This involved the provision of six months' worth of corn supplies to Delhi inhabitants. In 1577, direct distributions of cooked foods were reported in Kutch; and during the famine of 1791–1792 in Gujarat, corn was bought from Nizam and distributed for free.[242] In terms subsidized sales, in 1660 the government procured food from producing provinces and sold them at reduced prices to consumers.[243]

From the 1860s, steps were taken to organize relief more systematically. With enhanced infrastructure and logistics, famines started to become more of a problem of distribution instead of supply. A British colonel's report of the 1860–1861 crisis observed that "[o]ur famines are rather famines of work than of food."[244] The population was generally divided into three groups. In one of them, people able to work would participate in large-scale public works. Such relief works were already established in 1596 in Burhampur and Ahmedabad, while Bombay featured them in 1803—a context that would later be the battlefield of the "Temple ration" debate. This ration consisted of a modest laborer wage sufficient to purchase about a pound of rice/day as imposed by Sir Richard Temple, the Governor of Bombay, in February 1877.[245] Such food transfer provided 1,627 calories per day to those engaged in hard labor at relief camps in Mysore.[246]

Another group of people in need, but for whom rigorous inquiry was required, would perform various forms of light works in the poorhouse "for moral rather

[241] Ibid. The examples provided in the coming paragraphs largely draw from Loveday's review.

[242] In 1396, Sultan Mahmud set up a logistics operation whereby 10,000 bullocks were transporting food from Malwa and Gujarat to supply the crisis-hit kingdom of Bahmini (Loveday 1914, p.23).

[243] India's famine response history features several anecdotes of hording and price controls: during the Kashmir drought of 917–918, the king's ministers and guards sold stored rice at high prices. And in 1291, an attempt to fix grain prices in Delhi in 1291 led to "financial and commercial chaos" (Loveday 1914, p. 11–12)

[244] Smith (1862, p. 24).

[245] See Brewis (2010). Temple's "experiment" was to be applied to public works in Madras and Bombay and aimed at generating fiscal savings. The proposal raised significant criticism, including in the press and among health officials such as Robert Cornish, the Sanitary Commissioner of Madras. It was noted that the one-pound level was about half of prison diets; it wouldn't even "replace the nitrogenous waste of a resting Indian"; and would cause "irreversible muscle wastage" inhibiting workers' return to work post-famine (Hall-Matthews 2008, p. 1194–1195). In fact, public works wages were set below market wages, but the latter were already below subsistence level at times of droughts. The Famine Codes would eventually omit Temple's wages.

[246] In the *Harvard Law Review: Notes* it was pointed out that such calorie level was lower than the 1,750 daily calories provided to prisoners of Buchenwald's Nazi concentration camp in 1944 (and modern standards for hard labor recommend rations of 3,900 calories per day) (HLR Notes 2021).

than economic reasons";[247] those who were unable to leave their homes were provided direct assistance supervised by inspectors. "Village relief" would gradually replace centralized poorhouses, which "people would sooner starve than enter":[248] this decentralized model would include devolving to the village headman responsibility for investigating needs and selecting beneficiaries. Under such system, the poorhouse would not be abolished but play a "second line of defense." Examples include the provision of direct assistance to people that were "too proud to enter the poorhouse," as well as weavers and skilled industrial workers.

While responses began to be more organized, they still struggled to contain famines effectively. India's iconic Famine Codes, a blueprint for response published in 1880 and amended between 1901 and 1907, were the result of a Famine Commission established over the years 1878–1880.[249] The Commission followed haphazard famine responses over 1860–1877. These varied dramatically and resulted in an estimated 8.3 million deaths (Table 4.4).[250] The approach to the Orissa famine of 1865–1866 envisioned little government intervention in grain markets and limited direct relief. Its deaths toll was 1.3 million people. In the Bihar and Bengal famines of 1873–1874, the government intervened with food procurement and distribution, which proved effective in saving lives overall[251] but was deemed expensive (the equivalent of £6.5 million). Interestingly, unconditional transfers were relatively significant: in half of the cases with data, their coverage exceeded that of public works, and in the other half it accounted for 10–40% of the caseload. In 1877, the year when the decision to establish a Commission was made, famines in Madras and Bombay involved heated debates between central and local government over the cost and size of public works. That year's famine in Madras alone claimed 3.5 million lives.

Members of the Famine Commission didn't have a unanimous view on a range of issues and alternative proposals emerged (Box 4.9).[252] Rules laid out by the Codes would only apply to crises, as administrators were opposed to establishing the equivalent of poor laws for "normal times." Famine responses were financed by new taxes levied on merchants and landlords.[253]

[247] Loveday (1914, p. 47).
[248] Ibid (p. 62).
[249] GoUK (1880).
[250] Brennan (1984).
[251] A reported 23 people lost their lives.
[252] An alternative was proposed by Edward Buck, the Agriculture and Revenue Department Secretary. This included agricultural work as opposed to road construction. This was done with the deliberate attempt to reduce mobility within villages, and hence the "hutting" practice (which separated workers from their village). Such practice was also severely criticized by officials of the North-West Provinces, who on the basis of negative health and social effects of the hutting claimed that "[n]o worse blow could be dealt on the constitution of village society" (quoted in Brennan 1984, p. 106).
[253] Williams (1981), Rose (1971).

**Table 4.4** Famine responses in India before the Codes, 1860–1878.

| Province | Year (months) | Government intervention in grain trade | Number of public works beneficiaries (average daily) | Number of unconditional transfer beneficiaries (average daily) | Cost (million Rs) | Deaths (million) |
|---|---|---|---|---|---|---|
| Punjab and NWP | 1860–1861 (10) | No | 34,000 | 84,000 | 4.5 | NA |
| Orissa | 1865–1866 (21) | Not until late | 6,600 | 55,000 | NA | 1.3 |
| Bengal and Bihar | 1866 (21) | No | "Belated" | NA | 0.1 | 0.135 |
| Madras | 1866 (11) | No | "Belated" (max 17,000) | 45,000 | 0.89 | 0.45 |
| NWP | 1868–1869 (12) | Waived taxes and fright lowered | 66,000 | 19,000 | 2.9 | 0.9 |
| Bengal and Bihar | 1873–1874 (10) | Grain imported (Rs 39M) | 662,000 | 452,000 | 22 | ~0 |
| Madras | 1876–1878 (22) | Yes | 460,000 | 327,000 | 68.2 | 3.5 |
| Bombay | 1876–1877 (13) | No | 285,000 | 33,000 | 12.8 | 0.8 |
| NWP | 1877–1878 (12) | No | "Belated" | 14,000 | 2 | 1.25 |

*Source* : The author based on Brennan (1984). NWP = North-West Provinces; Rs = rupees.

**Box 4.9 Inside the Contest of Relief Proposals within the Famine Commission**

The highly debated nature of the Codes is evidenced by the fact that as late as June 1880, divergent perspectives among Commission members still revolved around two key issues: one was the storage of grains by the government in isolated areas. This was based on the Madras model, which in 1876 purchased Rs 300,000 of grains at the early stages of the famine (a policy severely criticized by the India Viceroy). Proposed by one member (James Caird), it was attacked on the basis of costs and disincentivizing private trade ("no merchant would import grains where the government could feed the people"). As such, the Codes would eventually include a tiered approach guided by a principle of no-interference, and provisions of in-kind food only deployed when food wasn't available in local markets. The second issue of divergence related to public works: one camp (mostly Caird) argued that only the able bodied should be involved in those works, and they should be paid at "normal" or "piece rates"; those unable to work should be given unconditional transfers or engage in local light works in the village ("without extracting other labour than such sanitary or other light work as could be advantageously done near their homes"). The village headman's local knowledge would make him ideally positioned, it was argued, to select relief beneficiaries. Restraint in provisions would be ensured by having the village "pay something" for unconditional relief. The rest of the commission members heavily criticized the proposal: they argued the approach would "destroy the use of labor as a test of need," hence attracting masses of claimants and increasing costs exponentially. In 1877, the practice in Mysore, for example, was to provide (semi) unconditional assistance in relief camps, not at home villages, and involving light work activities. Also, it was argued that village authorities were absent in many parts of the country, and local landlords would be reluctant to contributing financially for unconditional relief. Ultimately, Caird's case was successful and unconditional relief would eventually be included in the Codes with the involvement of both village officers and local superintendents.

*Source*: Brennan (1984).

A direct line may be drawn from the Old Poor Laws to Indian famine relief approaches. Economist Sambit Bhattacharya suggested that " . . . Bentham's ideas left a clear impress upon the thought and action of the upper echelons of India's colonial bureaucracy."[254] In fact, the head of the Commission, General Richard Strachey

[254] Bhattacharya (2017, p. 267). For the influence of British political economy approaches on Indian administrators, see also Ambirajan (1978).

" . . . was well known for his Utilitarian sympathies."[255] For instance, the guidance envisioned three self-targeting tests as proof of necessity: a labor test, which established the requirement for a reasonable amount of work (no less than 75% of work performed under normal times) paid at wages "only enough to sustain life"; a distance test, which envisioned people to travel a certain distance up to 15 miles to reach the worksite; and a residency test, with compulsory stay in special areas—known as "relief camps" or "hutting"—away from the home village (an aspect resembling the within-workhouse policy of family separation; see Chapter 2). These features made the Codes essentially " . . . a re-run of what England witnessed in connection with the Poor Law."[256]

The Codes established the duty and responsibility of the government to prevent famine-related starvation:

> . . . the codes were practicable enough, in most provinces, to enable a district officer to manage the complex task of providing either work or gratuitous relief [ . . . ]. And since [ . . . ] personal advancement could be influenced by the administration of famine situations, officers at various levels worked—or adapted—the codes to suit the local situation.[257]

According to Alex de Waal, for the ensuing 35 years since the Codes establishment, " . . . famine relief had the dual effects of dampening political agitation and creating widespread belief that relief had become a civil right."[258] The Bengal famine of 1943 was not declared a famine formally, hence didn't trigger the application of Codes measures and resulted in 1.5 million lives lost.[259] In the same year, it was estimated that a famine in Rwanda possibly generated by wartime Belgian efforts to make the administration self-sufficient (including forced public works and compulsory purchases of food at low price) took the life of about 300,000 people. The relief response mostly rested on an insufficient religious Catholic network of providers.[260]

The Indian post-colonial "Scarcity Manuals" introduced innovations in intervening in the grain market, as well as employment guarantees and the public food distribution system. The Manuals were frequently implemented, such as in 1966–1967, 1971–1973, and 1979–1980: for instance, the drought response in Maharashtra in the early 1970s supported five million people. In general, it was argued that the Manuals

[255] Ibid. Strachey's brother, John, had similar Benthamite views, which he enshrined in his 1888 book, *India*. Frank (2010) reviewed the work of Doyle who, by analyzing the writings of John Strachey, Thomas Macaulay, Henry Maine, Alfred Lyall, and John Seeley". . . encountered a characteristic argument and shared figures of speech indebted to Jeremy Bentham and to James Fitzjames Stephen: the Raj became, especially in Strachey's India (1888) a machine for panoptical surveillance" (p. 323). For example, he commented that". . . Strachey's district officer had become Jeremy Bentham's inspector, exercising the power of surveillance" (p. 340).

[256] Bhattacharya (2017, p. 266).

[257] Brennan (1984, p. 108–109).

[258] De Waal (1997, p. 14).

[259] Sen (1981, p. 52, 79).

[260] De Waal (1997, p. 30).

moved the policy focus from the prevention of starvation among the destitute to the protection of basic entitlements.[261]

In Sudan, a similar Famine Code inspired on the Madras model was formally developed in 1920.[262] These took the form of "Famine Regulations," the implementation of which was hampered by challenges in predicting famines due to limited food market integration. This was compounded by infrastructure deficits and low administrative capacity. Yet, the Regulations helped build military airfields and roads during the 1941–1942 drought.[263]

During colonial times, Kenya launched measures such as famine relief, school feeding, and food-for-work programs centrally coordinated by the colonial government.[264] In Tanganyika, instead, the administration of famine relief occurred at district level rather than being orchestrated by the central government: more than 100,000 people were in receipt of relief in three years over 1953–1963.[265] Those differences in institutional responsibilities persisted in post-independence years.[266] In Rhodesia, public works in response to famine were implemented in 1922, but not in future occasions.[267]

The 1980s would start presenting more conducive grounds for cash-based responses to droughts and famines. The early and mid-1980s witnessed a vibrant academic and operational acceleration in comparing alternative transfer modalities.[268] While the issue was also debated in the United States,[269] the opportunity to use cash as part of drought relief was anchored on increasingly nuanced food policy analysis. At its heart was the distinction between market "pull failures"—or when individuals lost their ability to demand food in the market (e.g., because of unemployment)—and "response failures," including the collapse of command over food because of lack of supply-side response to effective demand (because of traders' capacities or speculative behaviors).[270] A range of humanitarian interventions featured cash-based

[261] Dreze (1988).

[262] Davey et al. (2013), De Waal (1989), Iliffe (1990). See Dreze (1995) for wider lessons on famine prevention in Africa.

[263] De Waal (1997, p. 29).

[264] Maxon (1980).

[265] Bryceson (1990), de Waal (1997).

[266] Kunzler (2020).

[267] De Waal (1997).

[268] See, for example, Alderman and von Braun (1984), Edirisinghe (1998, 1987), Pinstrup-Andersen and Alderman (1988).

[269] A key theme in the literature of the time was the explanation of the "cash out puzzle," that is, the higher food intake yielded by stamps as opposed to an equivalent amount of cash. This was "puzzling" in the sense that economic theory, mostly grounded in Southworth (1945), predicted that "inframarginal" in-kind transfers (or transfers for an amount less than normally consumed by households) would have a similar income effect to cash transfers. See for example, Blackorby and Donaldson (1988), Butler et al. (1985), Devaney and Fraker (1986), Moffitt (1989), Ranney and Kushman (1987), and Senauer and Young (1986). For literature reviews, see Barrett (2002), Breunig et al. (2001), Fraker (1990), Gentilini (2007, 2016a,b, 2023a,b), Lentz et al. (2013), and Reinhart (2013). For food stamps in a historical perspective, see Alderman et al. (2017).

[270] Among others, see discussion in Coate (1989), Devereux (1988), Dreze and Sen (1989, p. 96), and Sen (1988, p. 106).

assistance, such as Ethiopia's "cash for food" program of 1984–1985, which reached almost 95,000 people.[271]

There were examples of clear connections between humanitarian assistance and social protection. For example, in Botswana,[272] when the newly elected government came to power in 1965 (and the country achieved independence the following year), it quickly took control over the response to the looming famine. This included partnering with humanitarian agencies like the World Food Programme (WFP). A clear division of labor emerged between the government and development partners: WFP provided unconditional food transfers and school feeding to between one third and half of the population; the government, instead, managed food-for-work schemes that would be eventually formalized as the Labour-Intensive Public Works Programme.[273]

As droughts recurred in 1978–1979, the combined response by the government and partners reached about 80% of the population.[274] When the country's economic trajectory accelerated in the 1980s, WFP withdrew its presence. During such period, drought relief in the form of labor-intensive public works were introduced and expanded.[275] The government opted to institutionalize relief programs also in "good times" instead of retrenching support. This was pursued in line with local conservative ideology:[276] child grants were dismissed based on perceived risks of undermining family care responsibilities, while social pensions were launched in 1996 following the footsteps of past drought-based programs for "deserving" categories.[277] Schemes were not devised along racial lines, but rather drew from indigenous norms of self-reliance.[278] Such framework still lies at the core of Botswana's approach to social protection.[279]

## 4.4 Conclusions

This chapter attempted to outline a major function played by cash transfers, namely how those programs have been part of state-building efforts. The analysis spanned a wide range of contexts and historical instances, from practices carved out ancient inscriptions to recent expansions in cash transfers. Three stylized observations emerge.

[271] Sponsored by UNICEF, the program included relatively light community-based work schemes (Kumar 1991, 1985, Peppiatt et al. 2001). More nuanced market analysis also entailed new opportunities for locally sourced commodities used for drought in-kind relief (WFP and ADB 1986).

[272] Seekings (2019).

[273] Seekings (2016a,b).

[274] Seekings (2020).

[275] Hay (1988) reported that public works programs were reintroduced in 1982 and three years later had more than tripled in expenditures (p. 1116).

[276] Seleka et al. (2007).

[277] Chinyoka (2019).

[278] Chinyoka and Ulriksen (2020).

[279] Gronbach et al. (2023), Seekings (2016a).

First, the history of cash transfers is intimately connected with the quest for food security. States have been deeply involved in preserving steady food supplies and averting food crises. As part of such endeavors, ensuring access to food in times of dearth was pursued via strategic prepositioning of transfers (e.g., 250 BC India), while the development of household registries and rankings helped deal with chronic deficiencies in access (e.g., China around the turn of the first millennium). Societies with broad coverage of food subsidies faced debates on possible dependency and disincentives by beneficiaries, with early notions of deservingness being legislated nearly 2000 years ago in Imperial Rome. Cash transfers were present in all these circumstances, whether temporarily (India) or permanently to families (Roman *alimenta*) and within poorhouses (China). While they played a relatively minor role compared to the vast state-managed, in-kind granaries systems, the state infrastructure required for emergency response practices, gathering of household information, and legislating eligibility would shape future cash provisions.

Second, some of the most severe crises, including wars and recessions, provided fertile grounds for institutionalizing cash transfers. The United States provides a series of experiences illustrating how cash assistance emerged after the War of Independence and the Civil War, with subsequent refinements moving them from war-related to contingency-based assistance. The Great Depression of the 1930s brought large-scale cash-for-work activities, which helped not only to stem unemployment, but also to build federal institutional capacities that had hitherto relied on a localized poor-relief architecture. It wasn't just public works: this period featured vibrant experimentation with cash transfers, including large scale piloting and research protocols examining the comparative performance of "cash versus in kind" in ways not fundamentally dissimilar from modern trials. Civil society had already matured experience with cash assistance (an aspect that is further discussed in Chapter 6), and their staff and expertise were incorporated into municipal structures: "[p]ressure for the change to cash [came] from the staffs of the agencies themselves involved [in] commodity relief."[280] Local state actors were able to support over 1.6 million people with cash transfers across ten major US cities.

Third, not all adversities immediately present conducive conditions for cash transfers. For instance, the role that cash transfers played in select low- and middle-income countries in the colonial and post-independence period is complex. At one level, dovetailing the established colonial bureaucracy with pre-existing systems of traditional arrangement of mutual support was challenging. In some cases, formal administrative roles were introduced (e.g., village chiefs), which may or may not have been present in local customs. In particular instances, those authorities still play a role in implementing contemporary government cash transfer programs (e.g., Kenya). At another level, colonial structures channeled prevailing approaches of the time: the catastrophic famine responses in 1860–1870s India reveal a haphazard diversity in state-level approaches, some of which reflected a rerun of Benthamites principles (e.g., labor tests). The gradual development of famine response manuals

[280] Colcord (1936, p. 180–181).

built on those soring experiences, with Indian's post-colonial practices introducing a range of innovations. From another perspective, the colonial experience introduced seminal cash transfers but, as we shall see in Chapter 5, they mostly remained race-differentiated in access and quality. Furthermore, the post-independence period was characterized by an abundance of spending in subsidies to bolster, among others, social cohesion. The subsequent dismantling of many of those measures in the 1980s–1990s wasn't necessarily accompanied by the introduction of cash transfers, the development of which would instead start flourishing in the post-adjustment period. However, cases like Botswana show that, even in contexts of protracted adversity, including the repeated occurrence of droughts, there were entry points for institutionalizing transfer measures. These were only in part cash-based, reflecting the coexistence between in-kind food and cash assistance that still largely shapes modern social protection configurations.

# 5
# Social and Political Stability

> [Cash transfers] adoption, design, and implementation are all fundamentally political processes.
>
> **Tom Lavers (2022, p. 30)**[1]

An examination of social and political dimensions of cash transfers could take an infinite number of shapes. The themes are broad and their boundaries fluid, hence posing a challenge in not only treating, but even defining the sphere of analysis. Conscious of such complexity, the chapter addresses three dimensions of a much vaster domain.[2] First, it provides a rapid review of how moral and religious precepts have underpinned cash transfer provisions. The picture that emerges is a nuanced, diverse approach within religious creeds on key questions on deservingness and administration of assistance. Those considerations extend to the second object of the chapter, that is, how cities and countries have addressed the thorny issue of "vagrancy." Societies have been wrestling with debates on if and how to assist local "beggars" and migrant "strangers": the chapter portrays an array of strategies deployed over the past 2000 years, ranging from paying vagrants to leave to forced deportation, and from regulating begging to corporal punishments. The third section of the chapter slices the political dimensions in different parts: these include the use of cash transfers to reduce riots and maintain political stability; to cement racial discriminations and elevate the social status of administrators; and to bolster political consensus. It also offers some reflections on the degree of political ownerships emerging in contexts of recent cash transfers introduction and illustrates the politics behind the failed adoption of a national minimum income guaranteed program.

[1] Lavers, T. (2022) "The Politics of Distributing Social Transfers." In Lavers, T. (ed) *The Politics of Distributing Social Transfers: State Capacity and Political Contestation in Sub-Saharan Africa and South Asia*. Oxford University Press. ©Reproduced with permission of the Licensor through PLSclear.

[2] On the sociology of cash transfers, see for example Leisering (2019) and Patel and Midgley (2023); for an anthropological perspective, see de Sardan and Piccoli (2018) and Ferguson (2015), while the political dimension is treated in Hickey et al. (2019) and Lavers (2022).

*Timely Cash*. Ugo Gentilini, Oxford University Press. © Ugo Gentilini (2024). DOI: 10.1093/9780191994982.003.0005

## 5.1 The moral compass and providers beyond the state

### Christian approaches to deservingness

The examination of social assistance, and cash transfers in particular, through a religious prism tends to be relatively underexplored. Yet, the work of scholars like Sigrun Kahl has illuminated how religious values influenced early cash transfer provisions, their subsequent evolution, and contemporary continuities: ". . . there is hardly another welfare state benefit where religion has been so determining as in social assistance, nor are the benefits with roots as old as those of social assistance."[3]

A set of common issues underpin Christian doctrines, whether of Catholic, Lutheran, Reformed Protestant, or other denominations. Three main dilemmas arise: how to live an earthly life in ways that are attuned with afterlife beliefs; how to reconcile the fundamental quandary between a drive for mutual help (income support) and the nurturing of independence (through labor); and how to determine who can "truly" work.[4] Each tradition has dealt with these questions differently.[5] Table 5.1 summarizes main features of those religious traditions.

#### *Catholicism and the Decretists' debate on eligibility*

The Catholic doctrine included an overall element of sacralization of poverty and glorification of the poor. The relationship between paupers and the "*potens*" ("powerful," "a person who does not have to work") was tied by spiritual transaction: the latter would make generous alms *in person* and, in return, the former prayed for the donor's soul (and accept their unfortunate material circumstances). Alms were a means for the goal of salvation, although poverty alleviation could be a desirable outcome of "good acts."[6] A duty to give wasn't matched by a right to receive. And supporting the poor should stem from compassion, not from a legal duty.

[3] Kahl (2005, p. 93).

[4] The word "work" appears 960 times in the Bible, and the related concept of "labor" permeates many passages. For example, " . . . if a man will not work, he shall not eat" (St. Paul's Second Epistle to the Thessalonians, 3:10); " . . . with labour and toil shalt thou eat thereof all the days of thy life" (Genesis, 3:17); and " . . . the Son of man shall come in the glory of his Father with his angels: and then will he render to every man according to his works" (Matthew, 16:27). The relationship between sin and work, with the latter being an instrument to correct the former, would emerge as a recurrent theme over history. In fact, Porter (2001) argues that " . . . atonement [for past sins] involved not acts of contrition alone, but the performance of good work from which the doer might also benefit. Here lay the possibility of marrying Christian duty with secular self-interest" (p. 209).

[5] Kahl (2014, 2009).

[6] For example, McMillan (2019) provides an account of the "Fuggerei social settlement" established in Augsburg from 1516 to 1523: founded by Jakob Fugger, a member of the wealthy Fugger family, the settlement " . . . comprised fifty-two houses of 106 apartments along with communal squares and a church. [ . . . ] The construction of such a settlement was for the deserving-poor within the community, meaning those who had become poor through no fault perceived of their own. [ . . . ] Rent was extremely low, equivalent to the worth of the widow's mite in the Synoptic Gospels, but residents were also expected to say three prayers (the Lord's Prayer, Hail Mary and the Apostles' Creed) a day for Jakob Fugger and the Fugger family" (p. 20).

**Table 5.1** Summary Catholic, Lutheran and Calvinist Principles for Poor Relief until the 19th Century.

| Attitudes toward... | Catholic | Lutheran | Reformed Protestant, Calvinist |
|---|---|---|---|
| Means for afterlife salvation | "Good works," almsgiving as *direct* "spiritual transaction" between giver and receiver | Faith and scriptures | Predestination, self-discipline |
| Poverty | Compassionate; a holy state, a condition to be accepted; little emphasis on overcoming it; no right to receive support | Compassionate, but with assessments; a state that can change through work; societal responsibility for supporting the poor | Corrective; sign of predetermined damnation; individual failure; poor are responsible for their plight |
| Work | For survival; a burden or pain | Calling; not striving for more than necessary | Restless work; economic success as mark of election |
| Deserving vs. underserving poor | Core role of *caritas*, not much discrimination (or not enforced) | Discrimination | High discrimination |
| Outdoor vs. indoor relief | Indoor via church-operated hospitals (which include different categories of poor people). | Outdoor as core, supplemented by work-related provisions (workhouses and public works) | Primacy of indoor/workhouses, outdoor secondary (provided no incentive to the poor to develop work habits, hence corrupted them further) |

*Source*: Adapted from Kahl (2005 p. 119).

Societal attitudes towards the wandering beggars were more ambiguous. For instance, in order to assure that beggars fulfilled their part of the exchange, municipal edicts for the regulation of almsgiving required a "beggar's exam," that is, beggars had to be able to recite the Lord's Prayer, the Ave Maria, the Apostle's Creed, and the Ten Commandments.[7] The private spiritual returns to the "giver" from almsgiving (as opposed to involving an impersonal intermediary) was advanced as a key reason behind the purported limited states' success in obliging the "able-bodied" poor to work.

[7] Kahl (2005).

In what way did the Catholic clergy determine eligibility for assistance? Brian Tierney offers a fascinating overview of how the *Decretum*, a collection of canonic texts, generated a flurry of opinions on the issue of deservingness and eligibility that stretched about fifty years.[8] His work reviews a dozen "guidance notes," named *summa* or *glossa*, as emerging from the Bolognese, French, and British "schools" on the matter—that is, the Decretists group. These formulated and codified the circumstances under which alms could be provided, that is, they offer a "decision-making framework" on if, why, to whom, and how much assistance could be accorded in line to Catholic precepts.

Underlying the discussions on discriminate or prioritized assistance are, among others, the works of St. Ambrose and St. Augustine.[9] The selectivity laid out by St. Ambrose puts the "just" first (whether the person is "known" or not), then the "known" (within which the order of preference was parents, children, and other household members), and only last the "strangers." St. Augustine was firm in his view that " . . . it is more useful to take bread away from a hungry man if, being sure of his food, he neglected righteousness," as well as in not supporting "infamous professions" (e.g., prostitutes and gladiators).[10]

The Decretists explain their logic under different scenarios: they consider whether provisions are fully funded (to reach all people in need) or if the donor operates under budget constraints; if the alms-seeker was known to the donor or not; the character of the perspective beneficiary ("honesty"); and the amount of assistance. Some denied assistance on ethical grounds (if the person was dishonest), unless the situation of the claimant was very dire; others discriminated only if the budget was limited and provided assistance even to the mentioned "infamous" occupations (alms should only be denied if meant to "exercise their evil arts," not if meant to meet their poverty-related needs).

The Decretists anticipate a range of key themes that would shape the poor laws debates, such as the ability to work, the distinction between indoor and outdoor assistance, and the withholding assistance as a way of correcting character. For instance, the Summa Omnis of 1186, probably written in Oxford, advanced the notion that the work test could be applied also to strangers—a theme that would underpin later British and global debates for centuries. Table 5.2 summarizes the Decretists' views as encapsulated by 11 *summa*.

### *Protestant doctrines*

Luther contested and rejected the notion of the Catholic "salvation transaction." Only faith and scriptures were the means for redemption. The devoid act of direct giving created the space for secular institutions to carry out poor relief. Begging

[8] Tierney (1959a,b). Compiled around the year 1140 by the jurist and bishop Gratian, the *Decretum* discusses governance and approaches of Catholic Church. It was used as the main reference by canonists until the *Decretals*, promulgated by Pope Gregory IX in 1234, obtained legal force.

[9] St. Ambrose served as Bishop of Milan from 374 to 397, while St. Augustine did so in Numidia (roughly today's Algeria) over 395–430.

[10] Tierney (1959a, p. 363).

**Table 5.2** Decretists' Views on Eligibility of Relief.

| Summa (approximate year) | Main view | Class of undeserving poor who would be denied assistance as a matter of principle (even if budget is available) |
|---|---|---|
| Summa by Rufinus (1157–1159) | If budget available: support all "honest" and "known" people; for "strangers," give to all if asking food (refuse if asking too much).<br>Under budget constraints: for honest people, apply St. Ambrose principles. | "Dishonest" people à la St. Augustine to be corrected (idle by choice, preferred to steal instead of working); "infamous professions" not to be supported; both waived if starving. |
| Summa Parisiensis (1160) | Reiterates concepts of indiscriminate and discriminate giving. | Denied only if budget is limited, not as a matter of principle. |
| Summa Stephanus (1165) | Distinction between "hospitality" (similar to indoor relief) to all and "almsgiving" (similar to outdoor relief) to be more strictly regulated. | n/a |
| Summa Elegantius (1169) | If budget available and person is known: provide to all.<br>Under budget constraints and person is known: apply St. Ambrose.<br>No reference to "honesty." | Denied only if budget is limited, not as a matter of principle. |
| Summa by Faventinus (1171) | As Rufinus | As Rufinus |
| Summa Inperatorie (1178) | Only "common" food should be given to the poor, not "delicious." | Denied only if budget is limited, not as a matter of principle. |
| Summa by Sicardus (1180) | As Stephanus. Added that food should be of common quality. | Denied only if budget is limited, not as a matter of principle. |
| Summa Tractaturus (1185) | As Rufinus | As Rufinus |
| Summa Omnis (1186) | Those known: St. Ambrose.<br>Strangers: Give to all, unless "claimed to be a priest" (requires verification) and if able to work (if work could be found). | As Rufinus |

*Continued*

**Table 5.2** *Continued*

| Summa (approximate year) | Main view | Class of undeserving poor who would be denied assistance as a matter of principle (even if budget is available) |
|---|---|---|
| Summa by Huguccio (1190) | If budget available: give to all strangers, unless "claimed to be a priest" (requires verification).<br>Under budget constraints: for known people, priority based on St. Ambrose. | The voluntarily idle to be denied; infamous professions to be supported. |
| Glossa Ordinaria by Teutonicus (1217) | | Endorsed Huguccio |

*Source*: Views tabulated based on Tierney (1959a).

was "blackmail,"[11] and Luther himself penned a foreword of the 1523 volume *Liber Vagatorum* outlining fraudulent begging techniques. In fact, under Lutheranism the importance of work was raised significantly.

With Luther, labor acquired a transformative property. Protestant work ethic generated a drive for personal and religious fulfilment through industry, while poverty became associated with non-work and laziness.[12] As noted by Max Weber, " . . . the moral emphasis on and the religious sanction of organized worldly labor in a calling was mightily increased."[13] Work became an act pleased by God. As such, the term vocation " . . . was transferred by Luther from the cloister to the workshop, [and by working diligently] serving not merely an earthly but also a heavenly master."[14] Luther's principle that "no one should live idle on the work of others" might have sometimes been used to justify workhouses: for example, Hamburg's entrance had the slogan "with labor I feed myself, with labor I am punished."[15]

Chapter 7 discusses how poor relief was secularized and centralized. The state had to ensure all the help possible for the "deserving poor," which gave rise to needs assessments, registries, benefit size according to needs and family composition, and weekly collections of funds ("common chest"). Such secularization however was carried out in cooperation with the church. As shown by the Nuremberg 1522 poor law,

[11] Kahl (2005).
[12] Hill (1952), Tawney (1926).
[13] Weber (1904, p. 42).
[14] Bainton (1964, p. 246).
[15] Frohman (2008).

the common chest was set inside the church. The chest evolved into local poor taxes, and by the late 16th century, poor relief had moved from municipal to the territorial level, and by 1794 it was a responsibility of the Prussian state.[16] The common chest, and the "poor box" discussed in Chapter 6, display a number of commonalities with the *kuppah* institution present in the Jewish tradition (Box 5.1).

## Box 5.1 The Jewish *Kuppah*

Jewish communities historically featured various types of funds. One was the *kuppah* ("box") to support the local poor. This included "weekly grants"[a] paid on Fridays. The kuppah was managed by three trustees "expected to be persons of the highest integrity."[b] They were tasked with ascertaining the deservingness of applicants and determining the amount of cash to be given. It is suggested that eligibility was strict, including for "those at immediate risk of starvation."[c] Members of the community were taxed according to their capacity to pay. Collections from the community were made by two or three people. Another fund was the *tamchui* ("bowl"), which included daily food for locals and strangers alike. Funding included the door-to-door collection of surplus food for redistribution to *tamchui* participants.

[a] Dolgoff and Feldstein (2009, p. 27).
[b] Vorspan and Saperstein (1998, p. 94).
[c] Jacobs (2009, p. 68).

Luther's value of work was not merely amplified under the Calvinist doctrine: it was made a duty. If under Lutheranism the sinner could regain salvation (through faith and humbleness), the Calvinist school of thought was grounded on the notion of predestination: God's "unconditional election" would make human beings either condemned or saved prior to birth. Sinning was of more irreversible nature than under Lutheranism. Then the question was how to recognize predestination. While Lutheranism glorified any type of work, Calvinists praised work leading to economic accomplishments.[17] Work was a divine, sacred act to serve society, while idleness distracted from the pursuit of righteous living. Restless work, and associated economic success, emerged as election hallmarks. Conversely, those not working would be considered damned—and by extension, poverty was a sign of not being chosen by God, a divine punishment for laziness and sinfulness. As the Puritan preacher Cotton Mather said in 1721, " . . . for those who indulge themselves in idleness, the express command of God unto us is, that we should let them starve."[18] Hence the

[16] For example, in 1750, nearly 1.2% of Berlin residents received poor relief, while in 1801 about 7.1% did so (Ole et al. 2002).
[17] Kahl (2015).
[18] Quoted in Eldersveld (2010, p. 69).

notion of "correcting the character" of poor people:[19] "[s]ince God preferred industry to idleness, giving alms to a strange beggar might well be a sin. Relief should be given only after proper investigation: and it should take the form of employment, not of alms, to all except the aged and impotent. Indiscriminate charity was mere self-indulgence."[20]

If poverty was an immoral state, then there was a need for discipline. Christopher Hill frames the problem in terms of transforming "the mental outlook" of low-income populations "to offer their services on the labour market": to do so, a "new pattern of social discipline had to be imposed."[21] The religious dilemma was dual. On the one hand, there was the challenge of managing dispossessed and unemployed populations in the wake of sweeping economic disruption. For them, changing the "mental outlook" may have involved establishing an obligation to work through fear of scarcity, that is, the alternative to work was starvation. This was akin to some of the most extreme positions against cash transfers reviewed in Chapter 2. On the other hand, there was a quandary around how to shield the "vulnerable" working class—the artisans and peasants who constituted most of the population—and not relent the economic process.

There are accounts attesting that while being the object of keen attention of authorities, "paupers" were tolerated in the broader society and may have even elicited empathy.[22] In Germany, well into the 1600s and 1700s the precariousness of living conditions of resident families often compelled them to side with beggars and mobilize against a believed unjust arrest by the bailiffs (see discussion later in the chapter).[23]

Like Germany, Reformed Protestant countries secularized poor relief provisions, but to a lesser extent: for example, German poor relief officials were mainly laymen employed by the state, while in England and the United States they were chiefly representatives of the clergy (although churchwardens and overseers were subordinated to justices of peace). Unlike Germany, England's national legislation left ample room for local flexibility and diversity in implementation,[24] and those implementation variants could be influenced by church and religious doctrines.

The choice of using the religious infrastructure to deliver relief may have presented a twin opportunity. It certainly offered an extensive logistical base ironed out over

[19] "If wealth showed [predestination to salvation and] morality, then surely poverty demonstrated immorality" (Dolgoff and Feldstein 2009, p. 9 and 45).

[20] Hill (1952, p. 43).

[21] Hill (1952, p. 32). Similarly, Larkin (2014) argued that "... aim of 'imposing social discipline,' and reconciling the unemployed with the requirements of the labour market, has been an almost permanent feature of social security law within the common law world" (p. 233). See also Collinson (2001), Slack (1998, 1988), and Todd (1987).

[22] Hill (1952) noted that "... in the 16th century there must have been few peasants who could be confident that eviction and vagrancy might not be their ultimate fate" (p. 43).

[23] Frohman (2008)

[24] As Fraser (2017) puts it, the Poor Laws were "... a tool of social policy of infinite variety and unlimited versatility" (p. 32).

centuries. And it may have also provided a platform for instilling principles and practices of deservingness and ability to work—principles that were also attuned with industrial interests.[25] In general, different Christian denominations had a profound effect in shaping views on state relief and taxation (Box 5.2).[26]

**Box 5.2 Heterogenous Views on Poor Relief among Early North America Colonizers**

Fisher (1989) studied four waves of early migration to North America, including the Puritans, the Anglican Cavaliers, the Quakers, and the Scotch–Irish. The Puritans favored high taxes, sizable governments, and heavy-handed justice. Most towns made a genuine effort to support the poor by abiding to the law, and in some occasion provisions "went beyond the minimum." Fisher quoted Gildrie's 1971 study reporting that in Salem " . . . one man was ordered to be set by the heels in the stocks for being uncharitable to a poor man in distress" (p. 179). The Cavaliers, who populated Virginia, promoted lower taxes, less government spending, and an informal system of justice. "Pauper poverty" was a persistent problem, and where New England towns ". . . spent most of their taxes for the support of churches and schools, southern parishes were compelled to contribute the bulk of their hard-won public funds to poor relief" (Fisher 1989, p. 380). The institutions created by the Quakers in Delaware were an outgrowth of their belief in personal freedoms, with limited government involvement in society and low taxes. Charity was a cornerstone of their creed and a central concern of the Society of Friends. Such ingrained habit of charity was institutionalized through monthly meetings maintaining a "public stock" for the support of indigent Friends. Finally, the institutions of the Scotch–Irish reflected their belief in freedom from the constraints imposed by government. This resulted in light taxes and strong resistance to authority. In a similar fashion, Zerbe and Anderson (2001) analyzed the property rights institutions established during the 1848 California Gold Rush and showed how these reflected the values and beliefs that miners brought with them westward.

## Chalmers's radical experiment in Glasgow

A distinct approach to poor relief emerged on a small scale under the leadership of Thomas Chalmers. While appointed in Glasgow, the Scottish reverend set out an experiment in a particular low-income parish, St. John. There, his relief philosophy was tested for the eighteen years running from 1819 to 1837. Anchored on a firm

[25] Hill (1952).
[26] Galbraith (1958).

belief about people's capabilities and self-reliance, Chalmers laid out a vision whereby organized public poor relief was to be almost entirely abolished.[27] His sermons and writings underscored the value of "locality"—that is, the tangible benefits stemming from operating within a manageable, small, and specific area. As it was put about half a century later in the Report of the Royal Commission on the Poor Laws of 1909,[28] Chalmers' method " . . . was *divide et impera*; break up your problem and parish into parts so small that you can deal with each case as it arises. Even when there are thousands of unemployed [ . . . ] they could easily be dealt with locally."[29]

Chalmers believed that low-income populations possessed sound judgment and qualities ("innumerable fountains and refreshing hills") that made them more self-sufficient than often assumed. People living in poverty had, it was argued, an inherent "own economy," they could rely on robust family ties across the lifecycle and benefitted from strong informal community support in times of distress. These features would be enhanced if a "role model" from higher classes would interact and inspire them through "gracious and purifying attention, advice, civility and goodwill."[30] Such practice was also present in Germany (Chapter 3) and would influence assistance by various civil society organizations in the late 1800s in the United States (Chapter 6).

Based on locality principles, the St. John's experiment reintroduced the office of the deacon—the composition of which drew from affluent segments of society—and assigned it the management of new applications for assistance under precise protocols and guidance. Deacons would be "courteous but firm" in scrutinizing applications against an inquiry into the ability to work, how family could support the person, personal stance on religious matters, residence, and receipt of public assistance from other parishes.

New and existing relief support would be financed by contributions collected during Chalmers' famous services (which drew people from the whole of Glasgow). These revenues would not be channeled to the central treasury of the presbytery, and instead were allowed to be used locally. There would be no transfer of families from private to public funds, so making people gradually responsible for the full financing of assistance.[31]

Four years into the program, its performance appeared successful: out of a population of 8,000, only 20 new applications were accepted, hence bringing down the cost to the public enormously—that is, the parish had been taking over the responsibilities for relief previously been under the Town Hospital.

[27] Cheyne (1985), Furgol (1985).

[28] Produced over 1905–1909, the commissioners were split and two reports were released: a "Majority Report" was backed by 14 commissioners and supported the use of the Poor Law (which was recommended to be renamed "public assistance") (GoUK 1909a); and a "Minority Report," articulated in two volumes, supported by four commissioners including Sydney Webb, called for the abolition of the Poor Laws and the transfer of their functions to other institutions (GoUK 1909b,c). See also Woodroofe (1977).

[29] GoUK (1909a, p. 191).

[30] Chalmers quoted in Schweinitz (1943, p. 108).

[31] The Sunday morning service drew city-wide people and contributions, while evening ones were more locally attended. Deacons would rely on the latter contributions for new applications, while it was expected that Sunday collections would be less and less necessary for relief financing.

The scheme was not without critics. The most notable dissenter was perhaps William Alison, a medical doctor. He and Chalmers debated their opposing poor relief approaches extensively.[32] Such debate was reflected in the mentioned Royal Commission Report of 1909, where Alison's thinking was captured in a 26-page "Memorandum by Professor Smart on the History of the Scots Poor Laws Prior to 1845" annexed to the Report.

Alison supported a uniform assessment of conditions and the provision of an organized, diversified system of poor relief.[33] In his "reply to Chalmers," Alison contended four main points:[34] first, that Chalmer's system relied on voluntary effort, and that such principle could hardly be expected to be systematically acted upon at national level.[35] Second, Alison was of the view that the distinction between deserving and undeserving on the basis of implicit or explicit morality, which was present in Chalmer's scheme, was shown to be ultimately deleterious to both the excluded and society more widely.[36] Morality should only be informing the type of relief to provide, not on whether to provide it. Such diversity in instruments would lend credence to a "legal system of relief." Third, Chalmers had not demonstrated quantitatively that poverty in St. John was reduced by his experiment. Finally, he pointed out that Chalmers was unrealistic in his expectations of what the poor could save and thereby provide for themselves and others in times of distress. The scheme ended, as mentioned, in 1837, mostly because of being a self-contained experiment conducted within a larger system. Taxation for poor relief applied to all Glasgow inhabitants, including St. John's.[37]

## Islam and cash transfers in the Caliphate of Omar Bin Al-Khattab

Commonly translated as "Islamic alms," *zakat* constitutes one of the five pillars of Islamic canonical obligations.[38] In its worship function, zakat is an act of renunciation and devotion. By giving zakat, one purifies oneself and one's possessions. The material gesture of giving wealth away is only valid if it is conducted with purity of intention.[39] The Quran outlines eight categories of beneficiaries. Among these are,

[32] Alison (1841, 1840), Chalmers (1841), Checkland (1985).
[33] Furgol (1987).
[34] Alison (1841).
[35] When participating in a 1830 hearing in England, Chalmer seemed to concede that his system was "precarious" in terms of requiring systematic attention and commitment (de Schweinitz 1943, p. 112; Kerr and Wood 1911).
[36] Alison believed that "... we cannot constitute ourselves judges of the demerits of individuals [...] and the distinction between good and evil lies in the different parts of the character and disposition of every human being" (Alison 1840, p. 136–137).
[37] De Schweinitz (1943).
[38] Bonner (2013).
[39] Hallaq (2009).

for instance, the destitute and the poor. The interpretation of these categories is contentious. One view is that destitute ("fuqara") signifies those who are chronically ill or weak, whereas the poor ("masakin") denotes the soundness of body.[40] There is a general agreement, however, that zakat can either be given directly to the poor or to those who collect and distribute resources for such purposes.

In its material form, zakat is a cash payment. It is due once per Islamic calendar year (usually in the month of Ramadan). Traditionally, it is calculated on five sources of wealth. In practice, zakat corresponds to 2.5% of the owned gold and silver.[41]

Zakat has a long history. Early phases appear to be closely monitored and organized. In recent times the practice adapted to changing conditions, for example, in Palestine. While in the 19th century zakat was closely tied to mosques, in the 20th century it began to be institutionalized under governmental administrative structures.[42] Around the middle of the twentieth century, similar transitions occurred in Saudi Arabia, Malaysia, Libya, Yemen, Pakistan, and Sudan; other states, like Egypt, Jordan, Bahrain, and Kuwait, had government-sponsored agencies to oversee collection and distribution.[43] The Palestinian version also kept an informal shape through local zakat committees. Their deep-rooted connection to local conditions, like the one in Ramallah, allowed assistance to be provided in ways that wouldn't shame beneficiaries (e.g., by not appearing in the public sphere).

Other forms of Islamic transfers exist. A key one is known as *sadaqa* and concerns voluntary donations on top of zakat. Differently from the latter, sadaqa can support close family members (who are ineligible to zakat because there is a fundamental obligation to provide for them).[44] It has been suggested that zakat and sadaqa were institutionalized interpretations of the generosity valued in pre-Islamic Arabian societies. This was grounded on the idea that property embeds a surplus that should be given away. In Islam, the recipient of such gift shifted from a loyalty group to the poor.[45]

A specific form of sadaqa is called *waqf*, which consists of a Muslim legal form of endowment that became increasingly popular from about the 10th century and comprises revenue-yielding properties endowed for a particular purpose. A typical example is a shop provided to a mosque, with the revenues being channeled to sustain

[40] Bonner (2005).

[41] Singer (2008). A minimal amount of wealth is exempted from zakat payment. This threshold is usually set at approximately 85 grams of gold and 593 grams of silver. According to the Islamic Finance Development Report, in 2021 "zakat and charity funds" distributed via Islamic banks accounted for 88% of $1.2 billion disbursed as corporate social responsibility (Islamic Development Bank and Refinitiv 2022, p. 63). In general, the annual volume of Zakat funding is estimated to be between $200 billion and $1 trillion (Stirk 2015). See Hammad (2022) for an excellent global overview of Zakat practices.

[42] Shaeublin (2014).

[43] See Muhammad (2019) for a seven-country comparison of Zakat institutional models, including in relation to overall system governance and transparency, as well as funds collection, distribution, and payment methods.

[44] Another form is the *Zakat al-fitr*. This is also obligatory, but not of the same rank of obligation as zakat, and it is intended to enable needy Muslims to feast and celebrate the Id al-Fitr holiday (previously mostly in kind, it is now mostly in cash).

[45] Singer (2013).

the mosque's activities. These institutions also feed the local indigent through the provision of food transfers.

Public soup kitchens are longstanding institution in the Middle East.[46] Among the oldest is the Table of Abraham, in Hebron. It was attested by the 11th-century Persian traveler Nasir-i Khusraw, who noted that daily, it fed anyone coming to Hebron with a loaf of bread, a bowl of lentils cooked in olive oil, and raisins. In Tabriz, the foundation of Rashid al-Din (1300) included separate kitchens and menus for travelers and for orphans, students, and Sufis. However, it was under the Ottomans that the imarets became multipurpose, serving meals daily to a defined group of beneficiaries. The history of the Hurrem's kitchen in Jerusalem is marked by debates on eligibility: in the 19th century, assistance moved from cooked meals to the distributed flour and oil—a shift that raised demands for participation by higher-income residents.[47]

Caliph Omar bin Al-Khattab, who ruled the Rashidun Caliphate 634–644, oversaw frequent food distributions in Al-Medina in crisis and stable periods. In the former case, there are accounts of distributions twice a day for 40,000–60,000 Bedouins fleeing Al-Majaah droughts.[48] In non-crisis times, Caliph Omar seems to have built warehouses to store flour, dates, and raisins.[49] A department of social security was established to conduct "registrations" of citizens. Such registration appeared to be used for targeting purposes so to "safeguard delivery of primary provisions to impoverished residents."[50]

There were also cash transfer payments from the treasury.[51] These are documented in a voluminous collection of activities by Caliph Omar.[52] Two initiatives stand out: the first consists in the redistribution of cash from spoils of war. After consultations regarding the timing, targeting and amounts to be distributed, a decision was reached for a universal distribution among Muslims. Benefits level would be based on "one's merits with reference to Islam," with the selected metric being the "nearness in relationship to the Holy Prophet."[53] This led to a benefit scale ranging from 12,000 dirhams to the Prophets' widows to 2,000 dirhams to veterans of the Yermuk and Qadissiya battles. In addition, there appeared to be child allowances: these cash transfers were initially based on a criteria of "completed weaning" of newborns, a fulfillment that was later abolished.[54] The system of payments to every newborn was further developed and formalized under Caliph Omar bin Abdul Oziz.[55]

[46] Singer (2008).
[47] Singer (2006, 2005).
[48] Al-Rousan et al. (2020), Ghifari (1989), Hamid (2003), Nadvi (2012).
[49] Al-Rousan et al. (2020).
[50] Nadvi (2022, p. 22).
[51] Hamid (2003).
[52] Hasan (1997).
[53] Hasan (1997, p. 150).
[54] Hasan (1997, p. 241).
[55] Ata (1987, p. 71).

## 5.2 Begging the question of social order

Over history, dealing with begging often meant dealing with unemployment. As mentioned in a historical review of almsgiving, "[b]egging, work and entertainment and extortion are generally a subject of semantic confusion, their division very much in the eye of the beholder."[56] Begging has largely been the manifestation of structural forces whereby the changes in economic organization have outstripped the capacity of societies to manage it. Accounts are filled with local-level administrations struggling to manage a problem—that of people out of work and wandering from town to town—which posed moral, economic, and security challenges. After a brief framing of the "problem," this section lays out five sets of measures to "manage" it, including banning and apprehending, corporate punishments, forced work and deportations, licensing, and cash payments.

### The "problem" of begging

Historical references to begging, vagrancy and mendicancy are longstanding. For instance, Charles Ribton-Turner's voluminous review provides an extraordinary legislative and ethnographic tour of English practices from the 300s to the 1300s.[57] Ribton-Turner suggests that the definition of "able-bodied" vagrants was crystalized legislatively in 1349—a distinction that, as laid out in Chapter 4, was already codified a millennium earlier in Rome.

The mentioned date of 1349 is crucial. Just three years earlier, a virus erupted in the continent: in seven years, *Yersinia pestis*, also known as Black Death, wiped out up to an estimated half of the European population.[58] The pandemic set in motion events that would profoundly influence social protection over the next centuries. One of these was a seminal Statute of Laborers issued, indeed, in 1349 England (Box 5.3). Real wages and incomes for unskilled workers increased (e.g., by one third in France), before returning to pre-plague levels by around 1600.[59] Hence workers' labor market power increased, and the legislation imposed strict sanctions to ensure labor supply.

**Box 5.3 The Black Death and the Duty to Work**

According to Thomas McStay Adams, in medieval times "the distinction between the 'true' and the 'false' poor [...] was not always drawn so sharply," and it was the Black Death that sanctioned such distinction markedly.[a] The 1349 statute stipulated that

[56] Parkin (2006, p. 78).

[57] Ribton-Turner (1887). Part of his review concerned regulating the evolving concept of hosting of "strangers," with the host being liable for the actions of guests and involving the definition of circumstances of voluntary and extorted hosting.

[58] De Witte (2014).

[59] Allen (2003), Clark (1997).

people were *obliged* to work and do so at wages in line with pre-pandemic levels. Specifically, the ordinance of 1349 envisioned the following: first, everyone under 60 *must* work, meaning that anyone able-bodied not already working could be put to work involuntarily. While not exactly slavery, since the person so conscripted was paid, it was akin to forced service or "unfree labor." Second, wages were capped at pre-plague levels, normally "five or six common years before" the ordinance. The 1350 law's update set a fix wage by occupation, for example for mowers and carpenters, and restricted workers' mobility by confining them to the locality where they worked the winter before. Third, workers changing employers or quitting work prior to their term were imprisoned. Fourth, the same penalty was established for supporting able-bodied beggars, including under religious auspices (a copy of the Ordinance was sent to every bishop for alerting people in their communities).[b] There was no prohibition of giving alms to those not able to work. Finally, some general provision was made against abuses, including employers that would hire an excessive number of workers and for food to be priced reasonably.

[a] McStay Adams (2023a, p. 2).
[b] The Ordinance read: "None, none, upon the said pain of imprisonment shall, under the colour of pity or alms, give any thing to such [beggars], which may labour, or presume to favour them towards their desires, so that thereby they may be compelled to labour for their necessary living."

The challenge of the "mobile poor" grew in magnitude in the following centuries. As we discuss in Chapter 6, the long-term economic, institutional, social, and health forces that were unleashed and coalesced around the 1500s generated large swaths of dispossessed, mobile populations. The post-Black Death ordinance may have contributed to conflating, or almost so, laborers, vagrants, and beggars as a homogenous group.[60]

The vast reference to "vagrants," "vagabonds," or "beggars" in history may not always align with population profiles or circumstances that contemporary use of those terms may evoke, for example, homelessness.[61] Instead, the terms indicated a broader class of vulnerable people, which could be more aptly compared to "the unemployed of the Great Depression or the jobless millions in today's inner cities."[62] Figure 5.1a shows a photograph of Mr. William Read, a "vagrant" inmate of London's

[60] As noted by Quigley (1996a, p. 11), "... workers and servants were considered only a step away from being vagrants and beggars, thus they must be compelled to work, compelled to stay at work, compelled to accept lower wages, compelled to stay where they can be put to work, and imprisoned if they disobey. Consequently, vagrants and the beggars were compelled into joining the class of workers."

[61] Around 1545, Barthel Behaim, the Nuremberg artist, produced a popular broadsheet titled "The Twelve Vagrants" featuring a dozen circumstances that shape poverty. His work is reproduced in Jutte (1994, p. 16).

[62] Quigley (1996a, p. 12).

Marylebone workhouse who was examined before a committee of the house of commons in 1846. Alongside Mr. Read are images of work performed at workhouses, including shoemaking (Figure 5.1b) and a local sale of inmate-produced products (Figure 5.1c).[63]

(a) (b) (c)

**Figure 5.1** A (a) Workhouse inmate, (b) shoemaking, and (c) product sale.

*Source*: (a) Ribton-Turner (1887, n.p.); (b) Mitcham shoemaking workshop, 1896 (Higginbotham 2012, p. 295); (c) a sale announcement for produced by the Belper workhouse in 1907 (Higginbotham 2012, p. 45).

How was the challenge addressed internationally? Legislation to contain the demands of workers via Ordinances was enacted in Egypt, Russia, Poland, Hungary, and Prussia, among others.[64] Over time, the reaction to begging was ambivalent and "idleness" was tackled with a multiplicity of approaches.[65] In general, begging was made illegal and firmly punished. But exceptions were granted, and alongside strict anti-vagrancy measures emerged some of the early state-provided cash transfers to prevent the problem among resident populations. Those measure are hereafter reviewed.

## Banning and apprehending

Repeated banning of begging can be found over time. A range of ordinances prohibiting begging occurred in Nuremberg in 1370 and 1478.[66] Based on appeals by the *procuradores* (who represented the towns of Castile at the Crown), in 1521 the city of Cordoba ordered that beggars should be returned to their birthplace—a measure

[63] The first-hand account of Mr. Read's hard plight portrays a vivid painting of the circumstances under which populations migrate in and out of London, their routines at day and night, and the comparative living conditions in workhouses, jails, and houses of refuge (Ribton-Turner 1887, p. 257–258). Specifically, there is a passage in Mr. Read's account where he explains "having lost his character" following a period of multiple jobs and intoxication. In my reading of his life, that seemed to indicate that some form of depression may have affected him hindering his ability to regain control of his life. See also Kennedy (2015) for images of the Marylebone workhouse.

[64] Scheidel (2017).

[65] Block and Somers (2003), Hammond and Hammond (1913), Mollat (1986), Oxley (1974), Ravallion (2016), Webb and Webb (1913).

[66] Clark (2002).

that echoed that of other cities like Moscow, St. Petersburg, and Odessa.[67] Apparently, the Cordoba measure was ineffective, and by 1534 municipal authorities were instructed to appoint "two good persons" to administer assistance and better enforce the new legislation. In 1531, Charles V prohibited begging throughout the Hapsburg empire.[68] In Naples, a legislation of 1559 forbade begging by foreigners with penalties involving five years of prison.[69] In 1561, a papal edict prohibited begging, required the able-bodied poor to perform useful work, and demanded the expulsion of the non-resident poor.[70]

In England, local officials had an obligation to punish beggars. Parishes or townships which failed to apprehend them could be sued and made to forfeit specific amounts of money for each beggar left unattended. In 1589, a commission had authorized the appointment of provost marshals for the apprehension and punishments of sturdy vagabonds. Later in 1662, a system of rewards was established for their apprehension: beginning at 2s, it was raised between 5s–10s in 1744. In colonial United States, a 1661 New Plymouth statute provided that vagabonds should be punished and removed "according to the laws of England"; similarly, a 1672 Virginia act ordered its justices of the peace to "put the lawes of England against vagrant, idle and dissolute persons into strict execution."[71] A royal edict of 1764 ordered the arrest of all beggars in France.[72] As it was put in the context of 1600s–1700s Germany, "the poor law history of many German states [ . . . ] consists of little more than the monotonous repetition of prohibitions on begging [and other practices]."[73]

In the early 1800s, Ireland had constables known as "band beggars" that would expel "strolling and sturdy" claimants from poor relief corporations.[74] In France, a sort of "poor relief police" (*chasse-coquins*) would arrest beggars and put them to forced work or in jail.[75] An account has been presented about the sequential desperation strategies deployed by famine-affected rural populations, and their encounters with the *chasse-coquins*: after failed attempts to borrow, work, and look for charity, rural families would eventually "take to the roads" for begging—at an initial stage by their children (with the older leading the younger ones), then by adults themselves " . . . first as honest beggars, but soon becoming more dangerous."[76] Beggars were pursued by the "evil tempered vergers" *chasse-coquins* in overburdened towns, and

[67] Ribton-Turner (1887).

[68] Under the edict by Charles V, licenses, a measure discussed later in the chapter, authorized begging within a radius of six leagues (or nearly 30 km) from the place of residence. Obtaining a license involved registering with the parish priest and getting authorized by local justices. Licenses, which included information like name, place of residency and notable physical characteristics, were issued on a yearly basis at Easter (Flynn 1989).

[69] Muto (1982).

[70] Gorski (2003).

[71] Quigley (1996b, p. 43–44).

[72] Garraty (1978) reports that about 14,000 of the nearly 70,000 "beggars" perished in jail. Already in 1728, the town of Bayeux in Normandy complained that enforcing the arrest of beggars would have meant incarcerating 1,800 out of its 6,000 inhabitants.

[73] Frohman (2008, p. 41).

[74] Radford (2009), Ribton-Turner (1887).

[75] Garraty (1978).

[76] Goubert (1982, p. 95).

the lack of livelihood options could lead them to theft, attacking carts, or serve as soldiers of the king in return for a bounty. Similarly, in the mid-1500s Germany bailiffs (*bettelnechte* or *vogte*) were hired to enforce laws against street begging, including apprehending, expelling, and punishing such practice.[77]

## Corporal punishments and branding

Some proposals to counter begging envisioned harsh corporal punishments. In England, the 1494 Vagabonds and Beggars Act established a penalty for begging of three days and nights in the stocks on bread and water. The Duke of Somerset's Vagrancy Act of 1547 envisioned two years enslavement and branding. The latter involved marking the chest with a hot metal, including a "V" for vagrant; attempts to escape were punished by lifelong slavery. An "S" for slave was branded on the person's cheek or forehead. A second escape attempt would lead to execution. The law was repealed due to its brutality in 1550.[78] Other letters were also used: an "R" on shoulders for "incorrigible rogues" and an "F" for "falsity" branded on the forehead of runaway "labourers and artificers" (the latter already enacted in 1360). Similarly, in 1754 Switzerland, people caught begging would have their ears cut and the initials of the community branded on foreheads.[79]

## Work and deportation

Chapter 2 discussed how, in several cases, authorities resorted to forced public works as a mechanism to address the plights of vagrancy and begging. Some of the experiences date back to 450 BC in ancient Greece, with a vast gamut of international practices often animated by curbing the scourge of idleness instead of genuinely seeking employment outcomes. In Russia, the type of work to beggars depended on an initial interview and assessment: a Committee on Begging distinguished, for instance, between four categories: among them, those found to be unable to work for age or disability would be placed in charitable institutions; people willing to work and temporarily impoverished received assistance; vagrants were returned to their native towns; while "professional" beggars were sent to workhouses or exiled.[80]

Deportation was indeed another frequent option in antiquity: for instance, Pericles dispatched "idle people" to newfound colonies like Naxos.[81] In Genova, a newly

[77] Frohman (2008).
[78] Dolgoff and Feldstein (2009).
[79] Garraty (1978).
[80] Lindenmeyr (1996, p. 40).
[81] Pericles stated that "... poverty is not disgraceful to anyone, but not to try to escape it by working is disgraceful" (quoted in Balme 1984, p. 148). There are accounts that idleness, as epitomized by the presence of beggars, would compromise civic honor (Carawan 1991, Plastow 2020). In Athens, Dracon

created Magistrate office of 1628 ordered the transfer of vagabonds to Corsica.[82] In Paris, the idle, "bad" or "feeble" workers were forced to participate in public works projects, but refusal resulted in whipping, imprisonment, or being chained to galley oars; and in Venice, begging led to drafting at half pay on merchant ships.[83] A similar approach was embraced in 1600s England: in 1615, a legal basis was established in England for using poor, "idle," and vagrant populations as an additional source of labor to fuel colonization.[84] Workhouse inmates served as a pool for such workforce, and by 1652 justices of the peace were authorized to arrest and transfer beggars to ports for shipment to colonies. For instance, there is evidence that by 1640 able-bodied paupers were transferred from London's workhouses to Thomas Verney's plantation in Barbados.[85] Differently from transportation to a "penal colony," which involved forced labor and the complete loss of rights,[86] "penal transportation" was meant to convert the labor of the "idle" to productive use.[87] Those transported were often the "masterless poor,"[88] "uncontainable poor,"[89] or "the degenerate poor."[90] Yet children and minorities were transported, too.[91]

## Licensing and badging

In Nuremberg, the city's ordinances of 1370 and 1478 allowed begging by residents, effectively licensing it by issuing permits (proven by a metal token or medallion).[92] Permission to begging was to be assessed by "upright citizens" and municipal officers.[93] The English 1531 act, which built on the one of 1494, allowed *certified* "aged poor and impotent" to beg. Cambridge, Southampton, and Louth introduced badging of local beggars in 1536–38, and Nottingham, Lincoln, and King's Lynn did so in 1540–47. Passes were also issued to discharged soldiers and sailors, authorizing them to seek alms during their travel.[94] A measure of 1598 "... situated obscurely within a different statue" authorized certain poor people to solicit relief, but only for food and

has even established the death penalty for idleness, which was repealed by Solon in the 6th century BC (Freeman 1926).

[82] Grendi (1982).

[83] Garraty (1978).

[84] Seal (2021).

[85] Seal (2021).

[86] Anderson (2018) estimated that between 1400-1900s, the overall convict flows in the British, Dutch, French, Portuguese, and Spanish empires amounted to nearly 1.5 million people (ibid, table 1.1, p. 2). The estimate doesn't include flows in the Russian empire, USSR, China, Japan, and other European penal labor camps. According to Jansson (2009), between half and two thirds of white immigrants in the 18th century entered indentured service before or after arriving in America. For deportation of criminals, see Gwenda and Rushton (2013).

[87] Maxwell-Stewart (2018).

[88] Anderson (2018, p. 188).

[89] Rushton and Morgan (2013, p. 19).

[90] Donoghue (2010, p. 958).

[91] Among the cases reported by Seal (2021) are also round-ups of Roma people to be transported to Jamaica and Virginia between 1665 and 1715, as well as an instance in 1698 when about 200 children were crammed aboard of a ship on the Thames waiting for transportation to colonies.

[92] Clark (2002).

[93] Frohman (2008).

[94] Webb and Webb (1927).

within their parish.[95] In Milan, the poor that in the 16th century could afford paying 10 *soldi* to the Scuola of St. Cristoforo were granted licensing of begging in the city.[96] In 1501, the Bern council issued an official certificate allowing a non-resident female widow with two children from Bolzano to beg in the city.[97]

In other cases, certificates would attest that almsgiving to the holder of the document would be earmarked for particular purposes. The University of Oxford issued letters in the 1300s to allow student to collect alms for their studies.[98] Another example is a 1483 Swiss document, currently preserved at Staatsarchiv in Zurich, where the bailiff of Baden confirms that alms to the bearer were meant for rebuilding a church in Schlieren (Figure 5.2).

**Figure 5.2** Almsgiving certificate for church rebuilding in Switzerland, October 1483.
*Source*: State Archives of the Canton of Zurich (StAZH).[a]
[a]The image also appears in Groebner (2007, p. 180).

Licensing involved the provision of badges. Plaques of various size, shape, and ornament were coined. In 1393, Valencia had a regulation requiring beggars to carry a leaden badge on their neck with the name of the town.[99] In 1514, the authorities of York ordered badges to be placed on "overmost garment."[100] Those tokens were provided by wardens and recorded on a book, with begging only allowed on Fridays and Sundays. In London, a 1524 legislation allowed for a special permit to beg outside the parish (but still within specific boundaries) in cases when demand for relief outstripped its parish supply. In such cases, a badge was to be displayed both on the back and chest of the claimant. In 1536, beggars that were sent back to their place of birth with a pass could, after travelling ten miles, receive a meal and hospitality

[95] McIntosh (2012, p. 276).
[96] Ferri Piccaluga (1982).
[97] Groebner (2007).
[98] Ribton-Turner (1887).
[99] Paul (1887).
[100] Seaby (1970).

for a single night.[101] In Bristol in 1571, the cost of producing and applying badging (including cost of sewing and threading), was 9s 3d.[102]

**Figure 5.3** Select beggar badges from Ireland and Scotland.

*Source*: Badges 1–3 are from the National Museums Northern Ireland.[a] Specifically BELUM.O1910.683, Beggar's Badge—No. 23, Shankhill 1774, Courtesy of National Museums NI, Ulster Museum Collection; BELUM.EF6260.1 Beggar's Badge—No.7, Keady, Courtesy of National Museums NI, Ulster Museum Collection; OMAFP.TMP9478 Beggar's Badge—No.8, Kells, Courtesy of National Museums NI, Ulster Museum Collection. Badges 4–6 are from the National Museums Scotland.[b]
[a] See also Seaby (1970, appendix 2, p. 107–110).
[b] See also Kerr and Lockie (1962, p. 300–303).

In Ireland, the practice of badging the local parochial poor dated back at least to 1634.[103] One of the largest badges in the country was used by the city of Kells: dated 1742, the badge was 10.2 cm × 8.3 cm in size and was sewn onto the garment using tiny perforations around the rim (exhibit 1, Figure 5.3).[104] Other badges used in the same Irish province of Ulster were circular or even heart-shaped (exhibits 2 and 3, Figure 5.3). There are detailed descriptions of 87 badges in Scotland: among them were badges from the Scottish towns of Skene (3.9 cm × 2.5 cm) and the tiny ones from Dun (1.45 cm × 1.1 cm) and Rothesay (diameter of 2 cm) (exhibits 4–6, Figure 5.3).[105]

[101] Ribton-Turner (1887, p. 177) mentions alleged cases in the late 1600s of passes being forged or counterfeited.
[102] Seaby (1970).
[103] McCabe (2018, p. 134). Lennon (1999, p. 55) refers to practices dating from 1548.
[104] Seaby (1970).
[105] Kerr and Lockie (1962).

A book by Cardinal Morichini describes a tradition initiated by Pope Leone XII (1823–1829) that granted a begging license to 40 beggars in occasion of the *Quarantore*.[106] The latter was a 40-hour religious fest whereby licensed beggars were allowed to wait, under surveillance by a *caporale dei veterani*, outside a church and receive generous offers. The license was renewed yearly by the clergy based on "good conduct."[107] One third of the chosen beggars were women, while 15 were blind.

Other forms of badging included textures. In England, one such example is a red or blue two-letter badge to be worn on the right shoulder indicating the initial for the parish of residence and a 'P' for pauper (Figure 5.4). The practice was required by the country's 1697 act, although there are earlier examples as well, and was in use until 1810.[108] Not all accounts, however, consider badging a stigmatizing practice.[109]

**Figure 5.4** Pauper badge (Fletching parish, c. 1815).

*Source*: SPK/P/14, East Sussex and Brighton and Hove Record Office at The Keep.[a]
[a]See www.thekeep.info

The use of such badge was also applied in the United States, particularly in Maryland's workhouses as per 1768 state legislation: "... all residents of the almshouse or workhouse to wear 'a large Roman P' made from red or blue cloth on their right sleeve,

[106] Morichini (1842).

[107] The emphasis on conduct stems from instances dating centuries earlier (e.g., Morichini's text refers to Pope Pius V, 1566–1572) when the noise made by the beggars hindered liturgical services.

[108] Higginbotham (2012).

[109] Hindle (2004a) lays out a scenario where badges were testimonials of candid and true deservingness: "... [s]ome paupers may have seen the strategic advantages of wearing the badge, for it publicly advertised the official recognition of their respectability. The badged pauper had satisfied the overseers, and the ratepayers they represented, that they were deserving of the alms of the parish and that they had passed the stringent tests of eligibility on which magistrates and parish officers generally insisted. To be sure, badges symbolised paupers' inability to work, but they also publicised their sobriety, their fear of God, and their past careers of thrift and industry on behalf of themselves and their families" (p. 25).

under pain of suspension of relief, twenty lashes or hard labor."[110] In Rouen in the 1540s, the poor had to wear a yellow cross on their sleeves.[111] Begging licenses are still present nowadays and are rooted in historical experience (Box 5.4).

## Box 5.4 Begging and Licensing, Now and Then

Colonial America instituted "warning-out laws" designed to limit the movement of indigent people from town to town.[a] After the revolution, as towns continued to expand, many states passed Settlement Acts as "... precautionary measures against the moral pestilence of paupers, vagabonds, and possibly convicts."[b] In the late 19th century, anti-begging legislation against "tramps" was pervasive: in 1877, there were more than a million arrests in the United States for vagrancy. In Missouri,

> ... convicted beggars were offered as workers to the highest bidder [while other] locales enacted mandatory sentences as long as three years or fines of up to $50 [...] [T]hose who couldn't pay such fines were put to work [as forced labor in] public prison or private labor camp.[c]

In 1885, Cincinnati introduced woodyards specifically "to relieve citizens from the importunity of vagrants."[d] A similar woodyard arrangement was present in Boston in 1875: almost 500 men were employed on six-day shifts, with a limit of 12 days of work per month.[e] (A survey fielded in 1893 showed that most tramps had some professional skills, were single, and worked intermittently).[f] Fast forward, a report shows that in 2016, out of 187 US cities, 54% prohibited vagrancy and 61% forbade begging in particular public places[g]—and in 2019 those rates increased to 60% and 65%, respectively.[h] In Raleigh, North Carolina, a person must obtain a permit to beg, which is limited to those who can furnish photo identification. Dallas, Texas issued about 2,000 citations for begging in 2015 alone (citations can bar a person from obtaining official photo identification); and three homeless people in Okala, Florida, paid a total of $9,000 in fines and spent 210 days in prison for resting in public spaces.[i]

[a] Benton (2012)
[b] Ortiz et al. (2015, p.4)
[c] Pimpare (2002, p. 164).
[d] Pimpare (2002, p. 170).
[e] Feder (1936).
[f] McCook (1895).
[g] NLCHP (2019).
[h] NLCHP (2019).
[i] NLCHP (2019).

[110] Quigley (1996b, p. 54).
[111] Pimpare (2002).

## Payments

Money payments could be interpreted in three ways: first, in some cases mobility was allowed if the "sending" place would assurance relief coverage. For example, in the mid-1770s, a Pennsylvania legislation introduced a certificate system whereby people seeking to move to a town should prove that prospective poor relief would be reimbursed by the town of origin.[112] Second, there were fines: the 1531 act in England sanctioned people supporting beggars with monetary penalties. A similar measure was taken in Paris, where in 1535 alms given in the street or church were fined.[113]

The other use of money concerned direct payments to beggars conditioned on leaving. The Spanish city of Zamora in the 1500s is a case in point. On April 21, 1539, the city's council ordered that between 7–10am of the following morning, all non-residents had to gather on the bridge of San Julian: there they would get a transfer in cash (2 *maravedíes*), in food (a loaf of bread), and then had to leave the town.[114] The tide was not stemmed, and the council nominated a "constable of paupers" to punish begging in the city. A year after the bridge gathering, the council complemented its local assistance with "progressive mandatory alms," that is, support to individual poor people was provided directly by designated wealthy families.[115]

The city issued a more specific poor law in the 1540s: a committee of eight administrators (drawing from clergy and city council as well as the nobility and lower classes) would examine the poor and collect voluntary contributions. Each person could contribute between 2 maravedíes and 1 blanco/day. The "disenfranchised deserving beggars" were among the beneficiaries of weekly cash transfers (12, 10, and 6 *maravedíes*/day for men, women, and children, respectively). The law stirred debates within the ecclesiastical community as epitomized by the contrasting perspectives of Domingo de Soto and Juan de Robles (Box 5.5).[116]

### Box 5.5 The De Soto vs. Robles Debate of 1545

The 1540 poor relief laws were heavily influenced by cardinal Juan Pardo Tavera. These specified in detail a relatively mild system of begging licensing but were more limited and circumspective on issues beyond begging (the law was printed four years

[112] Quigley (1996b).
[113] Geremek (1994).
[114] Flynn (1989, p. 82–83).
[115] Paupers had not to go "door by door," but rather wear badges on their chest indicating the name of their benefactors.
[116] Garrán Martínez (2004)

after promulgation).[a] The Dominican and professor Domingo de Soto, who taught "almsgiving and poor relief" at the university of Salamanca, had been involved first-hand in Zamora's reform of 1544 prohibiting begging (de Soto accompanied the city *regidores* in visiting the poor in their settlements). Yet after such experience, he became a firm opponent of the laws. In his 1545 book *Deliberacion en la causa de los probres*, de Soto encapsulated a critique of prohibiting begging in a Catholic territory. Instead, he favored an approach based on "mercy" encompassing everyone, and not based on "justice," or judging and discerning the merits of the claimant. He considered the rigorous process of discerning the poor hypocritical: from his standpoint, the examination of need was conducted " . . . not so much out of love and mercy for the deserving poor as of hate and loathing for the whole miserable estate."[b] He also noted that the expulsion of non-resident vagrants would merely shift the problem to the next location they wandered to. Furthermore, de Soto referred to the deliberation of Sorbonne theologians that, in reply to Juan Luis Vives (see Chapter 6), established that alternative ways to support foreign beggars should be secured, but the lack of compulsory financing in the place of origin made such fulfillment challenging. In the same year, the Benedictine Juan de Robles published his book (*De la orden que en algunos pueblos de España se ha puesto en la limosna: para remedio de los verdaderos pobres*) providing an adamant case for differentiated public assistance: such discrimination would help reorient more resources to the deserving poor, while private almsgiving could be provided indiscriminately. In Robles' view, compassion was important, but it should be directed to address the causes of poverty. To this end, mercy and justice could well be exercised in tandem.

[a] See Martz (1983).
[b] Quoted in Martz (1983, p. 24).

Ribton-Turner summed up centuries of attempts to inhibit vagrancy:

> [i]f we look back through the long vista of legislation on vagrancy what do we find? The vagrant has been threatened with every species of punishment known to the law, and he has at different times been stocked, scourged, branded, imprisoned, and hanged, but he still survives [ . . . ]. All history plainly teaches us that [measures] intended to curb him, had only a temporary effect.[117]

[117] In such context, Ribton-Turner recognizes the structuralist origins of the begging problem, but also maintained that such condition was subsequently aggravated by the individual and perpetuated by poor relief. In his words, while the beggar "... was in the first instance largely the offspring of harsh and repressive laws, now he is the noxious parasite fostered by indiscriminate and baneful charity" (Ribton-Turner 1887, p. 331).

## 5.3 The politics of cash transfers

This section provides five succinct, and by no means exhaustive, examples to illustrate political aspects of cash transfer provisions. The first speaks to the use of cash assistance as a way of fostering political stability. This rests on episodes of transfers taming social turmoil. A second example showcases deliberate ways in which transfers are leveraged for cementing differences in social and political status. The third and fourth line of discussion interrogate the use of cash for electoral gains and political consensus, respectively. Finally, the fifth example offers a country-specific vignette: this includes a particular political juncture when the United States pursued the idea of a guaranteed minimum income in the 1960–1970s (and its relatively rapid political demise). As mentioned in Chapter 3, other experiences featured in different parts of the book may still exhibit a sizable political dimension. For example, in China, the impetus sparked by political leadership that infused the country's zero-poverty policy, and the evolving role that cash transfers played within such political vision, illuminates the role of politics as a key driver in cash transfers history.

### Political stability

Over history, there are instances when cash transfers were introduced or expanded in response to events threatening political order. To this effect, a branch of literature explored the relationship between food prices, riots, and relief in 1700–1800s England. For example, the combination of low wages and high cost of food has ignited social unrest: in 1795 alone, the year of Speenhamland, "food disturbances" were recorded in at least twenty-one cities:[118] " . . . amid hay-ricks and corn-barns to which the incendiary torch could easily be set, the labourers could not safely be left to starve."[119]

To some extent, the provision of relief has been shown to attenuate discontent. For instance, in some cases special payments for "failure of silk" were made in English manufacturing parishes, like Sherborne, where falling silk prices led to cuts in wages, layoffs, and riots.[120] And an analysis of six periods over 1650–1815 revealed that an increase by one standard deviation in per capita amount of poor relief in a preceding period reduced food riots in the subsequent period by about 50%.[121] Yet, the deterring effects of poor relief on rioting seem to be limited after the turn of the 19th century.[122] In fact, one of the contributing factors to the 1834 shift toward stricter assistance in England may have been the elite's perceived inability of the old poor

[118] See Booth (1977, p. 90–91).
[119] Webb and Webb (1927, p. 418).
[120] Ball et al. (2023, p. 7).
[121] Greif and Iyigun (2013).
[122] See Brundage (1978), Cody (2000), and Mandler (1987).

law to ensure political stability. As it was recently put, landed interests had " . . . given up on the relatively generous paternalism [ . . . ] in reaction to the to the Captain Swing riots against farmers and landlords in 1830–31 [which undermined the belief that] the Old Poor Law would continue to purchase gratitude and social peace."[123]

The issue of tapping cash transfers to soothe social discontent involves the complex balancing of competing goals in a context of rapid societal transformations—that is, responding to growing needs of industrial workers versus the demands of economic management and ensuring labor reserves (Chapter 3). For example, the depression that hit the United States in 1873–1878 occurred within a critical juncture of local governments pondering how to manage a cardinal quandary:

> . . . [t]he dilemma was that while insecurity rose, so too did the need for a malleable, insecure labor force to support burgeoning industry [ . . . ] [In other words] how to reconcile the demands of workers, who began to look more to government as a countervailing power against capital, with the needs of those producers who were making cities centers of power and wealth.[124]

The 1930s provide further evidence of how economic contraction could ignite violent "relief insurgencies" in the country: ". . . crowds of jobless men and women descended on relief offices, cornered and harassed administrators, and even took the offices until their demands were met—until money or goods were distributed to them."[125] More widely, between 1934 and 1938 the Great Depression sparked unrest in British Honduras, Trinidad, and British Guiana. Such eruptions occurred in a context where ". . . [i]ndigence and poor relief were subject to local variations of the English Poor Law and the vagaries of charity by religious bodies and individual philanthropists."[126] A few decades later, social unrest in 1966–1967 challenged the colonial government in Hong Kong.[127] Eventually, this led to the establishment of cash-based public assistance in 1971, followed by disability assistance and social pensions.[128]

In more recent history, select crisis responses have been similarly interpretated, among other goals, as preserving governments' political legitimacy. For example, it has been argued that the food crisis of 2002–2003 in Ethiopia posed a sizable political risk to the ruling party and paved the way for instituting the Productive Safety Net Program in 2005.[129] According to political economy studies, Ethiopia (and of

[123] Lindert (2021, p. 42). On the Swing uprisings, see Hobsbawm and Rude (1968) and Jones (2007).
[124] Pimpare (2002, p. 27–28).
[125] Piven and Cloward (1977, p. 56). See also discussion on NYC in the late 1800s offered in Chapter 6.
[126] Midgley (2011, p. 60).
[127] Tang (2011).
[128] Tang (1997).
[129] See Lavers (2019a,b).

Rwanda) embody cases where cash transfer programs were clothed with "productivist" visions, which were at least in part functional to legitimize the ruling class and deter threats to centralized political settlements.[130]

## The other side of stability: Maintaining social discrimination

In some historical instances, relief was leveraged to cement racial hierarchies.[131] For example, unlike other colonies in the United States (e.g., Virginia and North Carolina), vestries in mid-18th-century rural South Carolina[132] played a wider role in local government and had exclusive responsibility for management of poor relief.[133] Vestry functions were fulfilled by merchants and plantation elites. And because of the in-person process of relief application by beneficiaries, vestry meetings were " . . . a space where rich and poor intersected, and where class and gender hierarchies were regularly reaffirmed."[134] Available evidence documents that South Carolina's provisions were selectively benevolent: applications had a high likelihood of being accepted, a typical "chronic pauper" colonizer was on the parish rolls for about six years, and the size of cash in rural areas was almost double of that in Northern colonies.[135] In such context with high prevalence of slaves and ex-slaves, "setting public relief at a far more generous rate [ . . . ] showed that there were privileges of race to which all whites were entitled."[136]

The case of Fiji illustrates the architecture of a "colonial welfare regime" articulated along racial lines.[137] Like other countries absorbed in the British empire, social protection provisions were provided in a three-tiered system: European colonial officers and settlers would receive formal pensions, unemployment insurance, and other benefits; selected native officers in the colonial service were

[130] Hayman (2009), Hickey et al. (2019), Lavers (2019a,b), Pruce and Hickey (2019), Whitfield and Fraser (2010).

[131] For example, see Seekings (2023), Fletcher (1992), Forde-Jones (1998), and French (1988) for discriminatory practices in the Caribbean.

[132] See Byrd (1973), Easterby (1941), Fraser (1983), and Klebaner (1954) for an overview of relief practices and their soaring cost in urban Charleston during the late colonial era.

[133] For example, parish vestries in Virginia and North Carolina managed poor relief, but only county courts could indenture poor and orphan children (Lockley 2005).

[134] Lockley (2005, p. 965–966).

[135] Lockley (2005) shows that transfers in rural South Carolina were nearly £7 sterling/beneficiary/year, a higher level than in Charlestown (£5) and Northern colonies like Boston, New York, and Philadelphia (£3–4). However, coverage was comparatively low: county-level estimates show that 0.7–1.2% of the population in the Carolinas received relief over 1820–1860 (Lockley 2005, p. 962, note 28). Low coverage might have been the result of high labor market wages that made work preferable to relief: professions like carpenters, bricklayers, and tailors had earnings about ten times higher than relief (or £60–70 sterling/year).

[136] Lockley (2005, p. 971–972). In comparison, South Carolina planters spent a little over £1/year for food for each slave, or about one fifth of the cash transfers' size.

[137] See Plange (2023) for the structure and evolution of the Fiji system since 1870.

included in pensions and other programs, but only on a basis of being "deserving" and at the discretion of the Governor. The benefit structure was also actuarially differentiated, with the private sector reflecting similar discriminations.[138] The rest of the population was expected to rely on informal arrangements rooted in local traditions.[139] The "rest," however, also included non-local populations, including various forms of indentured labor from India and forced labor from other Pacific islands.[140] Indentured labor would receive food rations at near-starvation level, the "Temple rations" (Chapter 4). Eventually, cash transfers for destitute non-Europeans were first extended to indentured labor and later to Fijians.[141]

South Africa provides another example in that its tax-financed, means-tested social pensions introduced in 1928–1929 resembled the scheme introduced in the England in 1908 (Chapter 4).[142] Social assistance was provided generously to those "deserving," especially the elderly and disabled (and to some extent children and mothers in need), compounded by public works for able-bodied adults. However, programs were segmented along racial lines until 1944: access was granted to African and Indian people, but benefit levels were equalized only in 1992 (Figure 5.5).[143]

Similarly, in Zimbabwe the Old Age Pension Act of 1936 was meant for non-Africans only on the grounds that " . . . the needs of the in indigenous population were perceived to be so simple that they could be met through traditional support systems."[144] A political economy perspective may suggest that social pensions created a constituency, and " . . . the apartheid-style devolution of responsibility to compliant

[138] For example, the Sugar Industry Employees Benefit and Provident Fund provided employees of European descent with medical benefits and life pensions; Fijian and Indian workers would only receive price subsidies for goods purchased at the company's shop. Wage differentials were in the order of one to seven (see Plange 2023, p. 363).

[139] See Eckert (2004), Gardner (2013), Keese (2011), and Shilliam (2018).

[140] The analysis by Plange (2023) reveals not only differentiated social protection provisions, but also illuminates the system that intensified poverty in the country. For instance, officials "outsourced" social protection for indigenous populations to their informal arrangements. Yet working populations become increasingly detached from their villages to seek employment opportunities under the transformed colonial economic system. Also, indigenous populations would share communal land: access to such arrangement encouraged employers to underpay labor, with global volatility in commodity prices further deepening wage reductions. See Hickel (2018) for a radical review of the system of colonial wealth generation and exploitation.

[141] Almost half a century after the onset of indentured labor in Fiji, Indian populations could eventually access an unfunded, racially targeted "Destitute Allowance" in 1936. In addition to indenture condition, the scheme eligibility criteria involved the absence of "any visible means of livelihood" and "no visible means for a return passage to home of Recruitment." The classic distinction of indoor and outdoor modalities was also envisioned. Almost a quarter-century later, in 1960 the Destitute Allowance was de-racialized, and Fijians were granted eligibility. There was no protection for "ordinary workers" that weren't destitute, a situation that led to an imperial secondment of an Industrial Officer to explore options (Plange 2023).

[142] Seekings (2013).

[143] Seekings (2020), Weible and Leisering (2012).

[144] Kaseke (2011, p. 122).

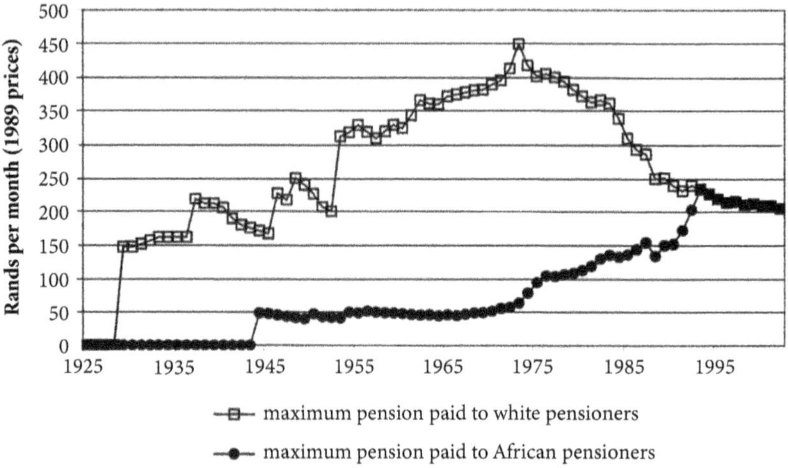


**Figure 5.5** Real value of maximum social pensions in South Africa, 1925–2000.

*Source*: Seekings and Nattrass (2005, p. 131) *Class, Race, and Inequality in South Africa*. Yale University Press. ©Reproduced with permission of the Licensor through PLSclear.

African leaders meant that their legitimacy would vanish if they were complicit in the abolition of the pensions."[145] The net result was that:

> ... [w]hile racial discrimination in eligibility and benefits has been abolished, the basic design of the welfare state in the 2010s remains much the same as it did in the 1930: the state supported the same categories of deserving poor through tax-financed, means-tested grants and able-bodied, working-age adults through workfare programs.[146]

Even when not organized according to racial lines, cash transfers have been deployed to consolidate social hierarchy and class segmentation. Starting about five centuries ago, but even before then in some cases, the provision of cash transfers was subject to close social investigation into deservingness of claimants. Such process was led by various local elites (e.g., nobles, wives of prominent professionals, young businessmen), with better-off classes being actively engaged in visiting, assessing, ranking, and deliberating on whether, what and how assistance to poor households should be provided (see for instance Chapters 2 and 3).

Being appointed as guardian or overseer may have been a way of combining responsibilities towards communities with private returns in social capital. Accounts from the Dutch Republic and Calvin's Geneva, for example, show that such appointments also generated opportunities for the ruling classes in terms of establishing social status, fulfilling career advancement, and exerting patronage.[147]

145 Seekings (2020, p. 119).
146 Ibid, p. 118 and 122.
147 See van Leeuwen (1994).

## Electoral consensus

Political participation, or lack thereof, may shed some light on the ability of perspective beneficiaries to voice preferences for cash assistance. For instance, it is possible that harsh, workhouse-style approaches to poor relief in England until the 1880s may have coincided with the lack of political voice by the lower strata of society.[148] Growing political participation, combined with other factors such as "visual" poverty diagnostics by Charles Booth for London and by Seebohm Rowntree for York,[149] may have paved the way for political demand for higher social protection provisions in the 1900s.

Contemporary experiences offer further insights on political participation. In Mexico, experimental data shows that enrollment in the early phases of the PROGRESA program increased voter turnout and the incumbent's vote share in the 2000 presidential election.[150] Such increase in political participation among beneficiaries have also been recorded in Brazil[151] and Colombia.[152] In the United States, there is intergenerational evidence of cash transfers increasing low-income children's voting propensity in adulthood.[153]

Cash transfers may, relative to tax deductions, provide further opportunities for political labeling. While those instruments may lead to the same microeconomic effects (e.g., deducting a dollar via taxes or paying a dollar via transfers is economically equivalent), they may be perceived and used differently by beneficiaries.[154] Unlike the tax-based recession response in 2009,[155] initial US pandemic programs

[148] Three years before the new poor law reform, or 1831, the share of population having the right to vote was only 8.6%. The poor didn't participate, as voting was restricted to people owning real estate generating at least 40s. Reforms gradually made voting more inclusive and progressive: as such, the median income of voters evolved from being 2.73 times higher than national median income in 1831 to a near equality (1.13 times) in 1911 (Lindert 2021).

[149] See Bales (1999) for a review of Booth's influence and the political and media use of poverty research. See also Morgan (2019) for a vivid collection of maps, and Linsley and Linsley (1993) for technical issues related to survey findings and measurement.

[150] De La O (2013).

[151] Araujo (2023) found that the Renda Basica de Cidadania program in the Marica municipality of Rio increased voter turnout by 4% (or 3 percentage points). At national level, Zucco (2013) documented that the *Bolsa* program boosted incumbent party presidential candidates in three Brazilian elections in 2002–2010.

[152] Conover et al. (2020) show that the conditionalities involved in the flagship conditional cash transfer program *Familias en Acción* involved activities at community level (e.g., growth-monitoring sessions, nutrition workshops), which increased beneficiary women's interaction with multiple stakeholders and their awareness of the importance of political participation.

[153] See Akee et al. (2018) for their analysis of unconditional cash transfers as part of the EBCN scheme.

[154] For example, Cherry et al. (2012) investigated factors behind public opposition to environmental taxes and revealed the role played by non-economic issues like trust, limited understanding about the instrument, and behavioral considerations such as perceptions of unfairness and coerciveness. Indeed, in parts of Africa taxation is connected to historical episodes of violence and coercion (Moore et al. 2018).

[155] Furman (2020) argues that the 2009 tax response was in part dictated by administrative expediency; yet it was recognized that transfers may have encouraged people to spend money faster and with more sizable economic multipliers than tax credits. His assumption was that transfers would be made time-bound, hence bolstering spending. Such rationale was present in COVID-19 responses in Korea and Taiwan (Gentilini 2022, p. 17).

delivered benefits in the form of "tangible" checks.[156] According to an observer, "... the flat cash checks to almost every American were by far the most visible part of the country's policy response to the Covid-19 pandemic."[157] Noteworthily, checks displayed the President's name (Figure 5.6): while the fact that such feature occurred in an election year attracted extensive debate,[158] the point is that tax rebates may have been comparatively less conducive for political branding.

**Figure 5.6** Prototype of the first Economic Impact Payment check in the United States.
*Source*: Jager and Zamora Vargas (2023, p. 2).[a]
[a] See also discussion in Wagner et al. (2020).

Cash transfers can be part of the process of deliberate political coalition-building and electoral competition, especially in Africa.[159] In Uganda, a pilot program originally devised as a donor-funded demonstration to counter skepticism towards cash was expanded before elections to areas influenced by the opposition.[160] In Lesotho, social pensions payment rates became a matter of electoral debate.[161] In Malawi, the President's embracement of cash transfers for vulnerable groups in the 2014 election situated the issue more permanently on the political agenda.[162]

[156] Baudisch and Neuenkirch (2024) compared Germany's VAT rate reduction during the pandemic to cash transfers such as those implemented by a cohort of high-income countries like Canada, Denmark, Japan, and the United States. The paper concluded that cash transfers were more cost-effective at boosting consumer spending because "more comprehensible, salient, and actionable ... in a dynamic environment with high uncertainty induced by unclear future economic prospects" (p. 1).

[157] Matthews (2021).

[158] For media debates on the signature, see for example Gittleson (2021) and Rein (2020).

[159] See the excellent literature review by Lavers (2022).

[160] See Bukenya and Hickey (2019). The Uganda example speaks to another broad debate: while the influence of external actors on social protection has been matter of extensive literature, new evidence is challenging the magnitude of such influence on cash transfers "adoption" processes; instead, an emphasis is placed on domestic-external "alignments." Following Hickey et al. (2019), "... programme adoption and expansion [in Eastern and Southern Africa occurred] when domestic political factors shift or where donors realign their advocacy efforts to fit with dominant ideas and incentives within national-level politics" (p. 15). For related domestic resource mobilization issues in Uganda, see Ulriksen and Katusiimeh (2014).

[161] Saminathen (2019).

[162] However, the President's campaign wasn't successful; see Hamer and Seekings (2019) for a discussion on Malawi's experience.

In Ghana, there are accounts that participation in the flagship cash transfer programs may be linked to political party affiliation.[163] In India, the "poor" were an important political constituency for public works under the National Rural Employment Guarantee Act.[164] It has been argued that India's "new welfarism" involves the provision of tangible transfers as part of an emergent model of political branding "forging a personalized, emotive connect with the voter, with welfare as the means to generate legitimacy" and projecting a direct attribution of cash and in-kind transfer provisions by current leadership.[165] In other cases, campaigns have been framed around differentiated transfer design: for example, in the 1980s Botswana's Democratic party ran on a platform including drought relief, school feeding, and public works—the latter being also endorsed by the successful candidate in the 2009 election.[166]

Specific design features can also be synchronized dynamically with evolving political circumstances. Uruguay illustrates this point: in the mid-2000s, the country established two conditional cash transfer programs. For nearly a decade, neither program enforced its conditions. Then in 2013, education conditionalities were suddenly monitored and sanctioned. With a hardening of public attitudes towards poverty, redistribution, and deservingness, the transition from lenient to stringent conditionality enforcement was likely politically motivated to counter the opposition's critique and avoid alienating a shifting electorate.[167]

## Political ownership

In the first decade of the 2000s, or shortly after the turbulent experience with structural adjustment discussed in Chapter 4, initiatives on social protection flourished. Appraisals at regional and country level blossomed,[168] while assessments were codified into global tools.[169] Diagnostic activities informed a flurry of national social protection strategies and policies,[170] especially in Africa. The latter these increased from none in 2001 to 35 in 2019.[171] This trend was matched by strategic frameworks

[163] Stakeholder interviews reported by Langnel and Tweneboah-Koduah (2024) show that political influence in the LEAP program participation is exerted via partisan composition of the District Level Implementation Committees, which in some cases select eligible beneficiaries based on political affiliation, including requiring to hold party membership cards.
[164] Roy (2023).
[165] Aiyar (2023). See also Anand et al. (2020).
[166] Seekings (2019).
[167] Rossel et al. (2023).
[168] For example, see Ribe et al. (2010), World Bank (2007a,b, 2006).
[169] A premier example is the set of Interagency Social Protection Assessment (ISPA) tools produced under the auspices of the Social Protection Inter-Agency Cooperation Board (SPIAC-B) established in 2011 upon request from the G20 Development Working Group.
[170] For example, see GoA (2008), GoC et al. (2009), GoE (2009), GoM (2007), GoP (2007), and PNA (2010).
[171] Devereux (2020).

and related updates by international organizations,[172] with a large body of work attempting to identify common ground or convergence among approaches.[173] These national and international developments often had cash transfers at their center.

Building on earlier experiences,[174] the promotion of social justice and rights-based agendas were also growing in the early 2000s.[175] Among their functions, these aimed at building political momentum for cash transfers: at a high-level forum, it was declared that ". . . we [members of Parliament of Angola and Mozambique] reiterate that, with the requisite political will, social transfers are affordable and that our governments should explore, prioritise and implement social transfers in their various forms."[176] India's embracement of the right to food security in 2001 led to the establishment of NREGA in 2005 operating alongside initiatives like an improved public distribution system of food.[177] Global initiatives mirrored a number of rights-oriented principles.[178]

Concomitantly, the mid-2000s witnessed a plethora of pilot cash transfer programs in Africa.[179] Bilateral donors would become particularly active in encouraging experimentation, building transnational alliances, and engaging in the domestic political economy.[180] In fact, the political clout and influence of transnational actors on domestic policy process is an area of rapid literature growth—and so is the influence

[172] See among others UNICEF (2019, 2012, 2008), WFP (2004, 2012), and World Bank (2001, 2012).

[173] Conway and Norton (2002), Devereux and Sabates-Wheeler (2007), DFID et al. (2009), IDS et al. (2010), Sabates-Wheeler and Haddad (2005).

[174] In the first half of early 1900s, the ILO became increasingly engaged in facilitating the spread of social protection, including based on the right to social security as promulgated by the 1944 Philadelphia declaration (ILO 1994). The human rights declaration of 1948 cemented such case, and " . . . colonial powers could no longer wholly ignore increasing demands for social security and they began participating in international meetings on labor questions from 1948 onward" (Schmitt 2015, p. 333). See also Maul (2019, 2012).

[175] Green (2008, p. 208) suggests that "... instead of treating poor people as 'beneficiaries,' [...] promoting the combination of active citizens and effective states [is] crucial to development." See also Barrientos and Hulme (2008), Devereux and Sabates-Wheeler (2007), Holmes and Jones (2009), Townsend (2009), and UN (2010).

[176] SADC Parliamentary Forum and RHVP (2009, p. 2). See also the intergovernmental conferences held in Livingstone in 2006, with follow-up consultations in 2008: convened by the African Union, the events called upon African governments to galvanize political and economic commitment to social protection (AU 2008, GoZ and AU 2006).

[177] The literature on the effects of NREGA is extensive (Dreze and Khera 2017). See Ravallion (2018) for a discussion, including finding that almost half of people who want to work don't get a job under the scheme due to administrative hurdles. For a wider overview on job guarantee programs, see Gentilini et al. (2020), the debate between Standing (2012) and Tcherneva (2012), as well as Harvey (2010). For improvements of the PDS, see Puri (2022) and Alderman et al. (2017).

[178] For example, see the UN social protection floor (ILO and WHO 2009) and the ILO recommendation 202 (ILO 2012).

[179] The seminal UNICEF-supported pilots in Zambia and Malawi attracted global attention (Schubert 2005, Schubert and Huijbregts 2006).

[180] DFID was among the most entrepreneurial donors in such space (Davies 2009, DFID 2011, Hickey et al. 2019).

exerted by domestic (often elite) constituencies on national policy dynamics.[181] Considerable attention has also been paid to "policy transfer" initiatives.[182]

In general, donors and external actors made significant headways in promoting the introduction and scale up of cash transfers. For example, regression analysis shows that the involvement of external actors increases the probability of adopting conditional cash transfers (CCT) by 30% and family support programs by 45%.[183](The overall evidence for CCT adoption in other regions like Latin America seems more mixed).[184] Mechanisms of influence included for example evidence generation, study tours and knowledge exchange initiatives.[185] Such technocratic approach to policy diffusion enlisted political "champions" to advance the cash transfers agenda in domestic political circuits. However, scale-up coexisted with intense debates on cash-induced "dependency"[186] and the cultural acceptability of design parameters.[187]

More fundamentally, evidence from Southern African contexts shows that intense transnational efforts were in some cases aligned with short-term electoral incentives of politicians; yet investments had more limited effects in altering the underlying societal values and belief around deservingness and state redistribution.[188] According to recent literature, a key metric to ascertain the political embracement of cash transfers lies in their funding source. As it was put, ". . . [t]he litmus test of the 'Global Rise of Social Cash Transfers' lies in its

[181] See among others Abdulai (2020), Awortwi (2017), Barrientos (2020a), Devereux (2020), Hickey et al. (2019), Lavers and Hickey (2016), and Schmitt (2020a).

[182] For the concept of policy transfers, see Dobbin et al. (2007). For the influence of international organization, see Cemen and Yoruk (2020), Deacon (2013), Devereux and Coll-Black (2007), Foli (2016), Hickey and Seekings (2019), Hulme and Hulme (2008), Kaasch and Martens (2015), Kott and Droux (2013), Maupain (2009), Orenstein (2010), Ouma and Adesina (2019), Schmitt (2020a), and Stubbs (2003).

[183] Dodlova (2020). Her analysis shows that external influence also triggers down to more granular design choices, e.g., the involvement of actors like DFID (now FCDO) and UNICEF increases the probability of using categorical targeting by 30%, while WFP's assistance is associated with the more frequent use of geographical targeting by about 60%.

[184] Borges (2018) finds that left ideology has contributed to the diffusion of CCTs. In investigating the spread of CCTs in the region, Borges and Sugiyama (2011) find no support for variables capturing needs, capacity and governing coalition ideology; instead, the role of international organizations seems significant. This is in line with the analysis by Martínez Franzoni and Voorend (2011), which emphasized the importance of international lessons sharing initiatives in shaping CCTs in Chile, Costa Rica, and El Salvador. Similarly, Brooks (2015) shows that cash transfers were influenced by international knowledge, as well as democracy and macroeconomic conditions. Instead, Fenwick (2013) shows that transnational actors played a secondary role with CCT adoption in Brazil and Argentina. Moreover, a comprehensive analysis by Garay (2016) finds little evidence that transnational actors have played a significant role in social assistance expansion in Mexico, Argentina, Brazil, and Chile.

[185] The discussion on donor-sponsored learning should not understate direct government-to-government initiatives. These were significant, especially in Latin America. For example, see Gonnet and Rodríguez (2023) for how Paraguay learned and adapted its conditional cash transfer from Chile's over 2003–2005.

[186] See Bukenya and Hickey (2019), Pruce and Hickey (2019), and Ulriksen (2019).

[187] For example, Haang'andu and Beland (2020) observe that " . . . [o]ne of the biggest challenges with transnational human rights-oriented policy diffusion in Africa is the overlooking of historically entrenched collective identities which are essentially non-individualistic" (p. 319). See also Chinyoka and Ulriksen (2020), Christians (2004), Grech (2015), and van Ufford et al. (2016).

[188] For Zambia, see Kuss and Gerstenberg (2023); for Lesotho and Malawi, see Hemsteede (2023). See also Leisering (2018), who argued that cash transfers involved a "socialization" of politics.

sustainability, based on government funding rather than external support."[189] African scholars have echoed such point: " . . . [t]axation—not international solidarity—is the foundation of building and consolidating a sustainable welfare system."[190]

## The politics of a guaranteed minimum income "revolution"

In his last book, *Where Do We Go from Here: Chaos or Community?*, Martin Luther King, Jr. declared that "... I am now convinced that the simplest approach will prove to be most effective—the solution to poverty is to abolish it directly by a now widely discussed measure: the guarantee income."[191]

The turbulent social and political events that unfolded in the United States over the 1960s marked an intense debate over guaranteed minimum income (GMI) proposals. Brian Steensland termed this period a "failed revolution."[192] The quest for such scheme is still ongoing today, with "basic income" pilots exhibiting features swinging between Dr. King's GMI and a universal basic income (UBI).[193]

Similarly, the rubric of GMI proposals proliferating in the 1960s were diverse—and even competing—in underlying ideology, definitions, design, and goals (e.g., poverty reduction, fiscal efficiency, leaner bureaucracy).[194] Yet this diversity wasn't fully apparent at the early stages and helped raise the issue in the public discourse. In general, GMI proposals aimed to erase the conceptual and programmatic lines distinguishing categories among the poor, and to provide assistance based on economic need alone—that is, (mostly) independently of family structure and work ethic.[195] While diverse, the proposals posited that poverty was circumstantial or temporary, not behavioral. As such, programs sparked a cultural

[189] Chinyoka and Ulriksen (2020, p. 266). Devereux (2020) notes that in Malawi, donors have been investing in the scale-up of social cash transfers, while the government preferred to allocate funds to supporting farmers with fertilizer and seed subsidies in a politically influential constituency: "... one strategy that governments deploy to balance [...] competing priorities is to use the donors to finance certain programmes favoured by international agencies—such as social cash transfers—and to commit government resources to interventions that are more popular domestically" (ibid, p. 46).

[190] Awortwi (2017, p. 119). Similar points were raised for Zimbabwe, where the downscaling of a cash program illustrated " . . . the dangers of heavy reliance on external funding. No program can be sustained indefinitely by donors, as they are accountable to their own constituencies and their priorities are constantly shifting between programs, sectors and countries" (Devereux and Kapingidza 2020, p. 291).

[191] King (1968, p. 171).

[192] Steensland (2008a) provides one of the most comprehensive accounts about the attempted introduction of a GMI during those years. For a shorter version, see Steensland (2008b).

[193] As of May 2023, an online map produced by the Stanford Basic Income Lab reported 104 basic income "sites" in the United States, 47 of which were "active" (see https://basicincome.stanford.edu/experiments-map/).

[194] Gentilini et al. (2020), Van Parijs and Vanderborght (2019)

[195] While GMI initiatives didn't pan out in practice, they were instrumental in several ways. For instance, they challenged the prevailing, deep-rooted cognitive template of distinguishing between "deserving," "underserving," and "working" poor. The former would receive relatively generous provisions that were politically protected ("social security"). What began with supporting "deserving" widows through the ADC (in 1935) and later AFDC (in 1962) program gradually became a vehicle for assisting "underserving" people—namely unemployed men head of the household—through meager and variable

shift treating the poverty problem as a continuum, and not in terms of compartmentalized categories.[196] Interestingly, the year 1970 also witnessed a Supreme Court opinion that came "dangerously close in identifying a property right in welfare."[197]

While there are some antecedents of the GMI idea (see Chapter 2),[198] the discussion took centerstage following an influential article in the mid-1940s[199] and the subsequent work by Milton Friedman on a negative income tax (NIT)[200]—the form of GMI that would lay the bedrock for a proposal by the Nixon administration. In the spring of 1968, John Kenneth, James Tobin, and about 1,200 other signatories called for adopting "a system of national guarantees and supplements";[201] and in the summer, Paul Samuelson and Henry Wallich penned columns on the NIT in *Newsweek* and *Vogue*, respectively.[202] President Lyndon Johnson, while not endorsing a GMI per se,[203] appointed a commission that would later support a GMI plan during the first year of the Nixon government.[204] Box 5.6 lays out how Speenhamland was still evoked in the early days of the NIT conception—an issue discussed further in Chapter 6.

programs. This was the much contentious and polarizing set of programs pejoratively known as "welfare." The third profile of poor people, the working poor, wasn't supported by particular measures (Gilens 1999).

196 Over the 1960s–1970s, a fascinating body of literature has pointed the evolving disciplinary lens through which antipoverty policy was examined: until the 1960s it was the realm of social workers drawing from sociology, anthropology and psychology; with the War on Poverty (e.g., Brauer 1982), the role of community organizers and economists increased; and the latter tended to dominate the Nixon-era, GMI-oriented debates (O'Connor 2001).

197 The *Goldberg v. Kelly* case (March 23, 1970) dealt with 20 individuals who were denied municipal benefits because they were suspected of welfare fraud by New York City officials. The majority of the Court (5:3) stated that benefits termination would require a due process, including a notice and hearing (Pimpare 2002, p. 96). John Kelly, acting on behalf of New York residents receiving financial assistance either under the federally assisted program for Families with Dependent Children or under New York State's home relief program, challenged the constitutionality of procedures for notice and termination of such aid.

198 Gordon (1964), Jager and Zamora Vargas (2023), Torry (2021).

199 Stigler (1946) argued that "[i]ncomes of the poor cannot be increased without impairing incentives. Skillful policies will, for a given increase in the incomes of the poor, impair incentives less than clumsy policies. But the more completely poverty is eliminated, given the level of intelligence with which this is done, the greater will be the impairment of incentives. This is a price we must pay [and society] must determine, through its legislators, what minimum income (or addition to income) should be guaranteed to each family" (p. 364).

200 Friedman (1967). Jager and Zamora Vargas (2023, p. 35) argue that Friedman's NIT was influenced by literature on "social dividends" of Oskar Lange and Abba Lerner in the mid-1930s (the latter advocated for a social dividend delivered through the tax system) as well as by the tax scheme laid out by Juliet Rhys-Williams in 1943. If the use of tax systems mirrored Friedman's vision (he himself spent time in the US government Division of Tax Research in 1941–1943), these proposals differed from Friedman's in his steadfast rejection of any form of beneficiary control and work conditions attached to the scheme.

201 Moynihan (1973, p. 126).

202 Samuelson (1968), Wallich (1968).

203 In a passage of the hearings on President Johnsons' 1966 economic report to Congress, Congressman Griffiths asked Treasury Secretary Fowler, " . . . have you ever considered this negative tax?," to which he replied, " . . . I have heard of it and have heard it discussed. But I have not seriously come to a point of deciding whether to recommend it or not" (GoUS 1966, p. 204).

204 Interest in NIT wasn't limited to the United States: for example, in 1975 da Silveira penned a first proposal for Brazil—and three years later, another version was tabled by Bacha and Unger (Suplicy 2002).

## Box 5.6 The Long Shadow of Speenhamland

Over the three weeks following Nixon's blessing for a guaranteed minimum income (at the time provisionally named Family Security System), a debate on the effects of the FSS ensued among some of the President's closest advisers. On April 14, 1969, a critical memo was submitted by Martin Anderson. As we discuss in Chapter 6, he raised the prospects of a guaranteed minimum income incurring in the same purported negative incentives of the Speenhamland scheme.[a] His concerns were compounded by a proposal from Arthur Burns to "reduce the welfare rolls" via work requirements focused on single mothers. Burns, a counsel on domestic policy and future Chairman of the Federal Reserve Board, penned a 41-page paper on "Investing in Human Dignity." His plan was basically devoted to "free people from the dependency on welfare" than addressing poverty (which was mentioned only once in the paper).

Upon Nixon's request, Daniel Moynihan (executive secretary of the Urban Affairs Council), Paul McCraken (chairman of the CEA), and George Shultz (Labor Secretary) formulated responses to the Anderson's memo on April 22, April 24, and May 7, respectively.[b] The trio argued that the FSS was more incentives-compatible as it posed a 50% marginal tax rate on earnings, while Speenhamland's was 100%; that part of the 1795 scheme's demise was its coupling of benefits with work requirements; and that those two features combined made Speenhamland similar to the existing AFDC program (see Chapter 7), not the new FSS, hence corroborating the need for reform. The FSS would eventually become the frontrunner choice with revisions made in the direction of enhancing work incentives.[c]

[a] The box is based on Steensland (2008a).

[b] There was also a separate commenting session on Burns's proposal, for which other top members of the administration were mildly favorable due to, for example, half of its costs ($2.5 billion) compared to FSS.

[c] For example, Shultz advised to include "income disregards" to facilitate labor market entry by single mothers (i.e., earnings exempted from taxes and benefit reductions), while Burns favored measures like training and childcare.

Excerpts from the proposal that Nixon's staff prepared for him framed the Family Security System as "... the most significant departure yet made from the Poor Laws of Elizabethan England from which our present practices have descended with all too little change."[205] The proposal, which was eventually named the Family Assistance

[205] Moynihan (1973, p. 161). For an example on the influence exerted by technical advisors on the Presidential agenda, see Cherrier (2019) for an account of Walter Heller, the chairman of the Council of Economic Advisors, and his success in persuading President Kennedy to pass a "tax cut" in the 1960s.

Plan (FAP),[206] wasn't an unconditional scheme: beneficiaries in the "employable" category were required to register for training and job placement, or lose their family benefits.[207] The program would have reached 24 million people (11.5% of the population), with baseline benefits for a family of four set at $1,500/year (later adjusted to $1,600, or 17% of median income) at an annual cost of $2 billion (with $700 million financed by replacing state programs), or about 0.18% of GDP.[208] Food stamps were included in the original proposal (Figure 5.7).

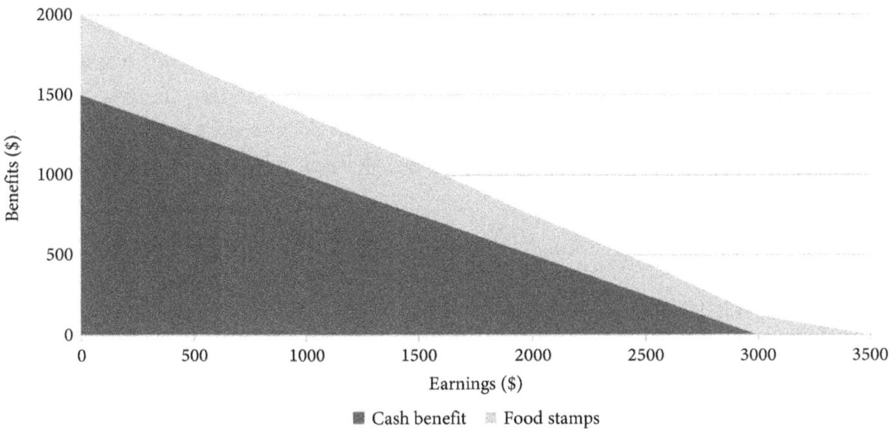


**Figure 5.7** Benefit structure of Family Assistance Plan.
*Source*: The author, based on data from Moynihan (1973, p. 138).

In the meanwhile, a set of proposals was tested through pilots.[209] The experiments were conducted between the late 1960s and early 1970s, and involved over 10,000 households in seven US states plus a trial in Canada's Manitoba.[210] While initial results from the NIT experiments "... were not analyzed until a decade later,"[211] the experiments funneled concerns (and shaped political attitudes) around work incentives, fertility, and other negative effects. How this evidence was misinterpreted is discussed further in Chapter 6.

[206] President Nixon announced the "Family Assistance System" in an address to the nation on August 8, 1969 (watch the speech at around minute 4:15, https://www.youtube.com/watch?v=6vHYFzYvCak), Other names under consideration were Base Pay, Take-Home Supplement, Paylift, Fair Share, Work Incentive Assistance, and Workfare. His address has been referred as an example of ambiguous, incoherent messaging (Asen 2001, Steensland 2008a, 2006).

[207] Moynihan (1973) recalled that "[h]ad the planners of [the negative income tax] been free of any restraint, a straight negative income tax could have been [...] simple. But they were forced to superimpose a new system on an old one and at points did not so much compound complexity as expose it" (p. 503).

[208] Moynihan (1973, p. 162, 535). In his memoir, he shared his frustration with the often-raised question of "how can people survive on $1600/year?" He argued that it would be rare for participants to have "zero earnings," and the FAP was meant to "add further to their income." See discussion on p. 139–140. For Moynihan's wider views on poverty, see Moynihan (1968, 1965).

[209] Moffit (2003b), Widerquist (2005).

[210] The trials involved different urban–rural contexts, beneficiary profiles, benefit structure, and duration (one arm was supposed to last 20 years but was reduced to nine and comprised data only for five years). See Forget (2011, 2018), Gentilini et al. (2020), GoUS (1983), Marinescu (2018), Munnell (1986), and Widerquist (2005).

[211] Haveman et al. (2014, p. 599).

There is much debate on why FAP eventually succumbed in the Senate Finance Committee in December 1970.[212] Among the responses, it was argued that "symbolic pollution" of welfare stigma played an important role: such effect meant that the broadening of the beneficiary base would reduce stigma associated with more specific provisions; instead, the opposite seemed to have occurred, with stigma engulfing the entire potential FAP caseload.[213] It was underscored that " . . . [t]he working poor never lobbied for the program [and] did not consider themselves to be 'welfare' recipients; in fact, they actively distanced themselves from the label"; similarly, instead of welcoming the subsidized costs of low-wage labor, conservative business leaders " . . . feared stigmatizing the working poor with 'welfare' benefits and the associated repercussions this stigma might have on work ethic."[214] Curiously, there was a second attempt to institute the FAP. The administration developed a revised plan, the FAP-II, which included several design compromises but nonetheless faced the same fate as its predecessor.[215]

## 5.4 Conclusions

A comprehensive account of the relationship between cash transfers and moral, social, and political dynamics would each deserve a separate volume. The chapter presented three select themes building on long-standing and relatively recent historical practices. Three main considerations emerge from the analysis.

First, moral precepts deeply affect the conception, form, and implementation of cash transfers. The motivation for providing or denying cash assistance can be rooted in values like the relationship between donor and recipient, effort, and work. These may stem at least in part from religious beliefs. An examination of religious thinking, like enshrined in the Catholic summa and early Islamic practices, reveals a decision-making process involving notions of deservingness and practical prioritization of recipients. In a way, the same practical debates that are part of secular provisions occurred within ecclesiastic communities. Brian Tierney eloquently suggested that:

> [t]he problem [of religious almsgiving] is the perennial one of discrimination in poor relief—whether eligibility for relief should be determined by need alone or by

[212] The Senate Finance Committee voted 10–6 against the FAP.

[213] Douglas (1966).

[214] Steensland (2008a, p. 15).

[215] The differences between FAP and FAP-II have been reviewed in detail (Bowler 1974; Burke and Burke 1974; Handler 1995). Among them, FAP-II replaced food stamps with cash transfers and raised the income floor to $2,400; the marginal tax rate rose to 67%; work requirements were made stricter (mothers were exempted from requirements until a child was 3 instead of 6 years of age); the type of work that could be refused was made tighter; and fiscal relief to states was expanded. FAP-II was rejected by the Senate Finance Committee in the summer of 1972. In October of that year, a legislation called the "Talmadge amendment" required that mothers receiving welfare benefits register to work when children reach school age; for those who couldn't find work, the government would provide public service jobs paid at no more than welfare benefits.

> other considerations, whether there should be any fixed order of preference among eligible applicants, whether the principles of selection should be conditioned by a desire to reform, or alternatively to punish, the paupers seeking relief.[216]

For centuries, societies have been debating where to draw the lines between spiritual obligations and secular responsibilities: should the religious impulse to help others be regimented or be indiscriminate? If regimented, does spiritual empathy inherently obfuscate a credible prioritization of recipients, hence leading to unsustainable provisions? Would the state's ability to assess and rationalize risk be too impersonal and thereby counterproductive for both the giver and receiver of assistance? While Chapter 6 outlines how those considerations triggered sweeping reforms in the management of assistance, the basic questions that animated public debates like Chalmers versus Allison in the 1800s epitomize the complex, modern nature of the quandaries.[217]

Second, cash transfers have been part of the broader, centuries-long challenge on how to manage the flow of dispossessed mobile populations. Religious, economic, social, health, and security issues converged around the debate on if and how to support out-of-work and mobile populations. Debates like Robles versus De Soto in the 1500s maintain a contemporary flavor. The lines between vagrancy and chronic unemployment were blurred, with begging often resulting from structural changes occurring at rapid pace. Local-level authorities have been struggling with the magnitude and persistence of the problem, and policies mostly veered toward various sorts of punishments. Their performance has been sobering, with even some of the most repressive measures not yielding a sustained reduction in begging and vagrancy.[218]

Third, the politics of cash transfers has been a constant tenet in the historical cases reviewed in this chapter. Whether to tame social discontent and riots (because of food insecurity, jobs dislocation, etc.) or pursue electoral gains, cash transfers have been instrumental for political considerations. Cash assistance has been the source of both hope and discrimination: on the one hand, they underpinned the ambition to reimagine a system establishing a basic floor in the American society and overriding previous categorically based approaches. On the other hand, cash transfers may have further cemented racial marginalization through differentiated provisions in contexts like South Africa, Fiji, and others. Moreover, cash provided some important solace to recipients, but also offered a conduit for social capital and upward mobility to administrators. These considerations suggest that cash transfers could generate multiple interpretations—for example, cash could make societies more stable (and

216 Tierney (1959a, p. 361).

217 Some went quite far in ascribing poverty to religion explicitly: in Italy at the end of the 1700s, Ricci (1787) traced the origins of "sloth and vagrancy" to the 4th century, when the first Christian emperor Constantine "moderated the austerity of old laws, and allowed the poor to beg around" (p. 30).

218 Garraty (1978) concludes that "experience had repeatedly demonstrated that neither government projects, nor repressive laws, nor the exhortations of philosophers, clergymen, and magistrates had succeeded in clearing the roads of vagabond or the cities of beggars" (p. 54).

less riotous), but such "stability" could also entail the preservation of discriminations. As such, a historical interpretation of cash transfers should carefully consider the context where transfers were applied, the core motivations behind their use, and the different perspectives that may underpin them.

# 6
# Reform Trajectories

> More often than not, "reform" [ . . . ] is burdened or sustained by the past, and often exhibits recurring cycles.
>
> **Thomas McStay Adams (2023a, p. 5)**[1]

This chapter furthers the practical, institutional, and operational aspects associated with three main reform pathways. These reforms trajectories share the same goal, that is, they are motivated by the notion of rationalizing "indiscriminate" transfers and reorganize them along tighter criteria and stricter provisions. The first section identifies episodes of reforms that entailed a *change* in main provider in full or in part. Such shift involves two scenarios. The first is a change from ecclesiastical to state authorities across the European continent in the early 1500s. This transition could be best interpreted in terms of degree of secularization: the church continued to play a relatively significant role in contexts like Zamora and Toledo, while in cases such as Geneva and Lyon the clergy's involvement was comparatively limited. The second transition features a change in provider in the opposing direction, that is, away from the state and towards civil society. The latter would be analyzed through the experience of the United States in the late 1800s.

The second section shows a reform within the *same* provider: the new poor laws of 1834 England were a critical example of consolidation within the same (state) institutional provider, including a reconfiguration of assistance from local to central administrative units. The third section featured a *blend* model, including a case both embedding a shift within the same provider (although from central to local authorities) and a wider role played by private sector actors. The fourth section covers how reforms were carried out in practice and includes a discussion of their institutional implementation. The section is complemented by a review of empirical evidence on the reforms' effects, and a reflection on the mechanisms of rhetorical diffusion and persistence.

[1] © McStay Adams, T. (2023a) Europe's Welfare Traditions Since 1500: Reform Without End. Volume 1: 1500–1700. Bloomsbury Academic, an imprint of Bloomsbury Publishing Plc.

*Timely Cash*. Ugo Gentilini, Oxford University Press. © Ugo Gentilini (2024). DOI: 10.1093/9780191994982.003.0006

## 6.1 Shift in providers

### From the church to the state: Rationalizing "indiscriminate" transfers

The compilation of reforms that swept across Europe in the early 1500s involved a reconfiguration of institutional responsibilities between state and ecclesiastical authorities. Such transition was tilted towards the former, although the operational involvement of the church remained in most cases significant. The section offers a rapid tour of such experiences unfolding in a dozen cities. In general, the reviewed practices lie at the core of modern-day cash transfer programs. The section then reviews another model of reform operating in the opposite direction: there were historical instances when, for example, in the late 1800s in New York City, the balance between local state assistance and civil society-led initiatives was broadly rekindled in favor of the latter. The experiences of Germany and Scotland discussed in Chapters 3 and 5, respectively, helped inform such initiatives.

### The 1500s wave: Secularizing transfers

The first decades of the 1500s witnessed one of the most spectacular waves of reforms in cash and food assistance in history. It was a defining moment, when a range of future institutional and operational practices would be established. Reforms emerged, among others, in Nuremberg (1522), Kitzgingen (1523), Regensburg (1523), Strasburg (1523), Ypres (1525), Paris (1525), Mons (1525), Bruges (1526), Hamburg (1527), Venice (1528), Lyon (1531), and Rouen (1934); and wider legislation was issued for the Hapsburg Empire (1531), Scotland (1535), England (1536), and Spain (1540). The coverage of poor relief around the reform period is variable, ranging between 5–20% of cities' population (Figure 6.1).

Reforms were connected, and a vibrant literature traces the direction in practice diffusion and learning. For example, some argue that English poor laws had their source in continental reforms.[2] The experience of Ypres may have been sketched out in London, when Juan Luis Vives had encounters with Lauwereyens, a former mayor of the Belgian city.[3] Some contended that reforms in Ypres and Mons were closely resembling those of Strasburg.[4] Approaches in Venice might have been influenced

[2] See Ashley (1906) and Webb and Webb (1927). There is debate on whether the 1536 legislation was influenced by the Ypres experience (Kingdon 1971). The law was based on a draft of 1535 that seemed to have been prepared and formatted in non-traditional ways, hence suggesting the involvement of a possible outsider: a hypothesis was advanced that the draft was written by William Marshall, a printer who translated Vives's work in English and was connected to chief minister Thomas Cromwell (Elton 1953).

[3] Spicker (2020).

[4] Bonenfant (1927).

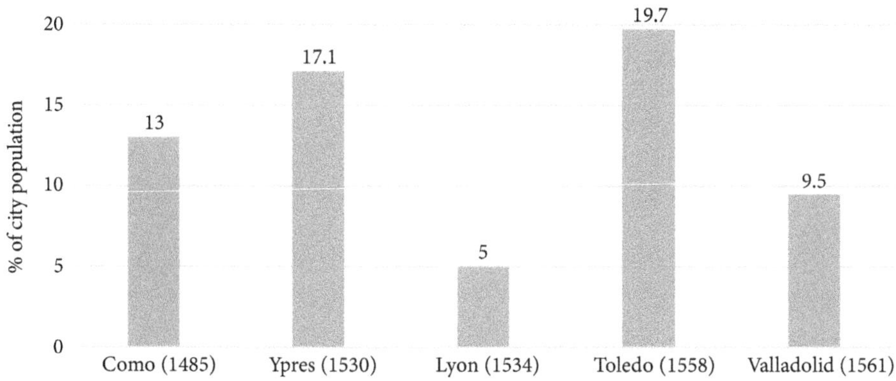


**Figure 6.1** Coverage of poor relief around the reform period, select cities.

*Source*: Como (Dubini 1982, p. 108); Lyon (Zemon Davis 1968, p. 274); Toledo (Martz 1983, p. 134); Valladolid (Geremek 1994, p. 161); for Ypres, absolute number of recipients are the average of the range provided by Geremek (1994, p. 140), while population refers to 1469 as provided by Stabel (1995, p. 210).

by Nuremberg.[5] The Dutch influence over Hamburg's poor relief made the latter a "German Amsterdam."[6] And "... similarities between the *Aumone-Generale* founded in the much-studied Catholic city of Lyons and the General Hospital founded in Protestant Geneva are striking."[7] Furthermore, intense interactions on city poor relief statutes occurred within countries, like in France.[8]

Why did such wave of pan-European reforms happen in the early 1500s? An array of factors was at play.[9] A set of explanations situated the emergence of state-organized poor relief apparatuses within broader ecclesiastical reforms along Lutheran lines.[10] Others focused on institutional change and reconfiguration of sovereignty in nascent territorial states.[11] Another body of research traced the reform of relief as a response to structural shifts in demographics, economic systems, and social stability.[12] And as discussed in Chapter 5, empirical analysis examined how upheavals sparked by high food prices encouraged state-organized relief.[13]

Furthermore, health risks may have played a role: the early 1500s witnessed a rise in the incidence of plagues, and the connection between vagrancy and the spread of contagious diseases like the bubonic plague motivated stricter public controls for

[5] For example, "... in 1505 Nuremberg had copied Venetian wardship laws. It seems at least possible that Venice returned the compliment when economic crisis forced its government to reform her legislation" (Kingdon 1971, p. 68).

[6] The influence, of course, wasn't limited to poor relief. For instance, Hamburg's 1558 stock exchange followed the Antwerp model (Lindemann 1990, p. 34).

[7] Martz (1983, p. 1).

[8] Fosseyeux (1934).

[9] See Innes (2021), Jutte (1996) and Lis and Soly (1979). In England, Slack (1998, p. 5) argued over the period 1500-1560 "... projects, policies and civic activity for welfare purposes all came together for the first time under a single banner—that of the common weal" (where "weal" refers to "wealth").

[10] Jutte (1994).

[11] Frohman (2008).

[12] Geremek (1994), Pullan (2005, 1994).

[13] Mollat (1986).

poor relief.[14] Following an epidemic in 1587, Grenoble officials conducted police raids to apprehend "alien beggars."[15] Measures devised to make surprise home visits and searches to ascertain residents' deservingness were introduced.[16] In Venice, the establishment of permanent public health authorities in 1486 was "... contributing to a more coherent policy [ ... ] for the relief of deserving cases of poverty,"[17] while Hamburg was on the alert for "beggars who carried the plague seed"[18] (Box 6.1).

## Box 6.1 Poor Relief as "Plague Prophylaxis"

The two centuries roughly between 1500 and 1700 witnessed a surge in the plague's spread across European cities, with acute spikes over the 1600s.[a] The pandemic shifted the interpretation of poverty and relief, including being elevated as matters of "public health." For instance, in 1528 Venice, temporary shelters were built to confine the poor.[b] The plague of late 1600s–early 1700s triggered a range of public containment measures in Hamburg. Starting from 1707, travelers were to obtain health passes, and a Board of Health was tasked with the coordination of plague responses. A thriving economy shrank, and by 1712 more than half of the city's population may have been unemployed (40,000 unemployed people out of a population of 70,000). With the plague, poverty stopped being a "personal, parish, or even a Christian matter [and] rapidly became an issue of state and matter of public record."[c] As the government canvassed door-to-door to identify unreported plague cases, a concomitant aggressive campaign was mounted to register the poor. An Improved Poor Relief Ordinance of 1711 temporarily centralized poor relief functions under the Board of Health. In other words, poor relief was a form of "plague prophylaxis."[d] The Board was empowered to "cut through the red tape" and use enhanced methods for surveillance and investigation. The principle of voluntary finance was preserved; but now contributions were pursued not just through the *Gotteskasten* chest, but with home visits by Board representatives recording contributions on special ledgers. As the plague receded, special centralized measures subsided. Board president Garlieb Sillem unsuccessfully proposed to make the

[14] On healthcare and poor relief in Europe, see Ole et al. (1997).

[15] Geremek (1994, p. 151).

[16] See McDonnell (2007) and Slack (1988). Similarly, the enforcement of "man in the house" rules in the 1960s United States, which prevented women receiving relief from living with men who might provide support, involved officials' impromptu visits. There are accounts of such visits occurring at 4am in Colorado (Piven and Cloward 1971, p. 285). By 1962, eight states and 18 cities had established special investigative units for activities like "midnight raids" (Warde 2017). Those searches echo recent practices. For example, in 2021 the City of San Diego terminated "Project 100%": operational since 1997, the initiative included unannounced, invasive home visits by public officers in search for evidence of fraud by welfare applicants. Investigators had broad powers over eligibility decisions (Moran 2021; ACLU 2016).

[17] Pullan (1971, p. 222).

[18] Lindemann (1990, p. 28). Similar concerns emerged in Lyon (Zemon Davis 1968).

centralized system permanent, and the administration of poor relief returned to decentralized and *Gotteskasten*-based arrangements. Yet the guiding pled laid out in 1711 would soon help inform subsequent reforms in 1725–1726 with a renewed emphasis on work, discipline, and workhouses as a "test of worth."[e]

[a] Kaniewski and Marriner (2020).
[b] Taxes amounted to a levy of 2.5% per ducat paid on rent, or the ratable value attributed to homeowners in the latest fiscal survey of the property (Pullan 1971, p. 247).
[c] Lindemann (1990, p. 30).
[d] Ibid (p. 29).
[e] Tomkins (2021).

This compilation of factors played an important role in the emergence of secularized relief. But a common denominator seems to underpin many experiences of reform: the canary in the coal mine was an inexorable growth of "begging" by resident and non-resident populations, including mobile populations referred to as migrants, vagrants, vagabonds, or mendicants. The problem of "begging," the management of which was discussed in Chapter 5, gradually overwhelmed the capacity of ecclesiastical organizations to handle it.[19] The jury was in: charity-based assistance was deemed unfit to meet the challenge of the time, and a new model of poor relief was required.[20]

The cornerstone of "sounder ideas," according to economic historian William Ashley, rested on distinguishing the "shameless beggar" from the "honest hardworking poor," an inquiry that could not be expected by a "charitably disposed person." That process of sorting was the rationale for state intervention, that is, "to put an end to the old pauperizing system of *indiscriminate charity*. This could only be done if the relief of the poor was transferred to public authorities [while private charity was] restricted within narrow bounds."[21]

The secularization and centralization in the organization of poor relief shouldn't be solely interpreted through an institutional lens; rather, it marked a tectonic shift in reorienting the reference system of values guiding the social fabric. The provision of cash and food transfers organized around charitable and faith-based principles formed an ingrained body of precepts, rituals, and beliefs molded over centuries.

[19] As put by Flynn (1989), "... [f]or those of us living in societies in which welfare systems are centrally organized [ . . . ] the traditional foundation of poor relief upon religious prescriptions is apt to appear unreliable" (p. 75).

[20] Tierney (1959) noted that "... perhaps the issue [of providing relief to parishioners versus travelers] did not seem particularly important in the thirteenth century, but it was desperately important in the fifteenth century. [ . . . ] What was really needed by the fourteenth century was a kind of scholastic critique of employability on able bodied vagrants" (p. 119). Instead, traditional canonists or "decretists" examined in Chapter 5 "repeated thirteenth century arguments at three times the length" (Zemon Davis 1968, p. 234).

[21] Ashley (1914, p. 340), emphasis added.

The secularization of poor relief challenged the Catholic customary, cultural, and administrative complex at its core: in fact, such a historical juncture "provoked deep introspection and intense debate. [It] amounted to an 'epistemic' change in thinking, a subversion of the entire symbolic order, for charitable ritual consecrated a particular moral and aesthetic perspective."[22] Juan Luis Vives, a torchbearer of the new poor relief era, was indeed declared heretical by the Franciscan vicar of the Belgian city of Tournai.[23]

## Leisnig, Ypres, and Bruges

In 1520, Martin Luther asked: " . . . [i]s it not unnatural, not to say unchristian, that one member should not help another and prevent its destruction?"[24] Three years later, he devised an integrated relief, religious, and educational plan for the city of Leisnig. The plan called for a "Common Chest" in which " . . . bread, cheese, eggs, meat, and other food and provisions shall be placed and there shall also be a box or two wherein money may be put for the upkeep of the common chest."[25] Such funds would pay for ten overseers, chosen in an open meeting, as well as covering for the salary of clergymen, church officials, schoolmasters, and for other relief costs. Eventually, Leisnig included voluntary contributions compounded by mandatory provisions.[26]

Luther's view of relief was crystallized in a subsequent preface written for an anonymously edited book on vagabonds published around 1510. In such volume, which was defined as the "first modern poor relief manual,"[27] Luther argued that " . . . every town and village should know their own paupers, as written down in the Register, and assist them. But as to outlandish and strange beggars they ought not to be born with, unless they have proper letters and certificates."[28]

After a "qualified approval" from theologians at the Sorbonne,[29] the relief plan of the city of Ypres went into effect on December 3, 1525. The city was undergoing a severe decline in crafts and textiles.[30] The goal was to ensure that " . . . everyone have sufficient to maintain nature; not one in all the city be seen to go a-bagging." It was a highly influential initiative: for instance, it appears that Emperor Charles V received copy of the Ypres relief plan in September 1531, and that this may have helped inform his subsequent ban on begging in October of the same year.[31] Excerpts from the

[22] Flynn (1989, p. 75).
[23] Martz (1983).
[24] Luther (1520, p. 3).
[25] Salter (1926, p. 87).
[26] According to de Schweinitz (1943, p. 36–37), " . . . each inheritor, citizen, and peasant must contribute some money each year to the Chest. Servants and young manual laborers who did not own houses but had parish rights were to contribute a silver groat a year, their employers collecting this money."
[27] Frohman (2008, p. 16).
[28] Quoted in de Schweinitz (1943, p. 37).
[29] The local clergy supported the plan, but later the mendicant orders opposed it and called upon the Sorbonne for an opinion. The ensuing view from that university was that the plan was "hard but wholesome," and its endorsement was "qualified" in sense that legislation against begging should have not led to further impoverishment of the poor, who should be allowed to beg in the absence of other support received (de Schweinitz 1943, p. 36).
[30] See Geremek (1994, p. 137).
[31] Salter (1926, p. 34).

original plan show that young men should be in either school or imparted skills (e.g., handicrafts), with beggars being compelled to work. Strangers that "only for the intent to take alms come with a great flock of children to inhabit our city" would not be supported, except for a limited number (relative to the city's "ability to bear") of populations displaced by war, shipwreck, or similar misfortunes. In-kind provisions (meat, drink, and beds) would be provided to these populations for a period of two to four days. The program's administration and oversight were accorded to four authorities—"men of good name and fame"—of the city.

Funding was raised via a door-to-door collection of alms, the use of chests in churches, bequests, and exhortations by the clergy (an explicit feature that appears in England in 1531). Foreshadowing similar developments in the 1800s in the United States (discussed later in this chapter), Germany (Chapter 3), and Scotland (Chapter 5), the emphasis in Ypres was not just on almsgiving, but also on the moral act of "the good man and good wife . . . in visiting, comforting, helping and in executing the deeds of pity."[32]

On January 6, 1526, Vives laid out his relief plan for the city of Bruges before its Consuls and Senate. Several modern "building blocks" of social assistance diagnostics, design, delivery, and complementary interventions are reflected in his writings.[33] These include poverty assessments[34] ("Let two censors . . . inquire into the life and morals of the poor"[35] ); social registries ("Let those who suffer poverty at home be registered . . . their needs ascertained"); community-based targeting validation (" . . . it will be easy to learn from the neighbors what sort of men they are, how they live and what their habits are"); skills training ("should the native poor be asked whether they have learned a trade? Yes; and those that have not . . . should be taught one"); and apprenticeships and self-employment ("Let a certain number of those who cannot find any work by themselves be assigned to each artisan. If anyone has progressed far enough in his trade let him open a workshop").

Everyone was called into action, and idleness wasn't tolerated, even among disabled populations ("Nor would I allow the blind either to sit idle or to wander around in idleness. There are great many things at which they may employ themselves"). His view was not to discriminate between a structuralist and individualist cause of poverty ("Even those that dissipated their fortunes in riotous living . . . must be relieved, for no one must die from hunger"); however, he did point to differential provisions ("To them more irksome tasks should be assigned and smaller rations, that they may be an example to others"). According to the plan, the program would generate a surplus because of the generation of employment for the poor—an ambition that animated industrial policy-oriented approaches presented in Chapter 3.[36]

[32] De Schweinitz (1943, p. 36).

[33] Vives (2020/1526).

[34] The ensuing excerpts from Vives proposed in the paragraph are quoted in de Schweinitz (1943, p. 31–32).

[35] Interestingly, he also directed the same censors to " . . . inquire about the youth and the sons of the wealthy . . . of the manner in which their time is spent, what pursuits and what employment they follow."

[36] According to de Schweinitz (1943, p. 33), Vives's definition of public works tasks amounted to a " . . . forecast of the activities of the Works Projects Administration and the Public Works Administration in the United States [in the 1930s]" (discussed in Chapter 4).

New revenues would be sought voluntarily (via collection boxes in churches) as well as with public support. The latter would come from efficiency gains and reallocation (e.g., review of bequests administration, redirecting resources from public games).

## Geneva and Zurich

The experience of Geneva offers an opportunity to examine an episode of reform as shaped by Calvinist principles.[37] In making such institutional shift, the city differed in the degree of secular management. Its layman leaders' "uncompromising brand of Protestantism" was carried out without facing strong headwinds encountered in other settings, like in Spain.[38]

Elected *procurers*, mostly drawing from the city's ruling elite, would meet on Sundays at 6 a.m. at the hospital, a key institution for poor relief founded in 1535. They would review individual family applications for bread provisions, with the list of applicants being subject to a pre-review by local-level officials. The endurance of Geneva's secular reforms is significant, as the *Hospice Général* is still functional as a core public assistance institution.[39]

The *Articles Touching Almsgiving* of Zurich, which were influenced by the pastor Ulrich Zwingli, come to light in January 1525. The legislation followed a reform that occurred the previous month, when monastic orders were abolished, and their functions absorbed by public authorities. Under the Articles, voluntary contributions were supplemented with revenues from endowments of suppressed religious assets. Funding was directed to low-income populations as well as supporting wayfarers on their lawful passing though the city.[40]

The legislation didn't envision support for licensed beggars, while recipients had to wear a badge (Chapter 5). In essence, "only a particular kind of poor [ . . . ]—the involuntary dependent and humble—were the 'worthy' poor" as opposed to false beggars."[41] No provisions were made for compulsory payments like in Leisnig, but the Articles retained an inquiry into recipients' character similar to Luther's plan.

While ecclesiastical properties were largely secularized, linkages between religion and poverty relief persisted. For example, Heinrich Bullinger, the chief minister of Zurich, expected revenues from confiscated church properties to be used for

[37] Under the leadership of John Calvin, Geneva became a "Protestant Rome," albeit many of the secular reforms were enacted before Calvin's return to the city in 1541 (Kingdon 1971).

[38] Kingdon (1971).

[39] Milicevic (2002) traces the roots of the words "hospice" and "hospital" to the 4th century, which meant hospitality provided to the poor, sick, pilgrims, and travelers. In 2022, Geneva's *Hospice Général* supported about 35,000 people (see https://rapportsannuels.hospicegeneral.ch/2022/les-chiffres-essentiels/).

[40] As noted by Salter (1926), the support of wayfarers was a "provision carrying on into the modern world a very common feature of the late Middle Ages, except that mediaeval endowments were private rather than municipal, and were not connected to ordinary travel so much as with pilgrimages" (p. 98). Similarly, he documented that in the city of Coblenz, a special fund provided bread, wine, bacon, and peas for Hungarian pilgrims directed to Aachen.

[41] Wandel (1990, p. 171)

communal needs, while he maintained that magistrates would benefit from religious ministers' guidance in poor relief reform.[42]

## Venice, Mantova, and Como

The Venetian Senate issued two legislations of poor relief reforms in March 1528 and April 1529.[43] Devastated by plague, the city's first-order objective was to separate the residents (*terrieri*) and non-residents, with the latter being expelled with "letters of commendations to the governors of the place of origin" to ensure their assistance and non-return.[44] Then there was the typical distinction made between able-bodied and the "impotent": the latter, it was legislated, should be supported by the parish priest if they owned a house (and were forbidden to beg), while they were directed to the hospital if no housing was possessed. Widows were to be employed by the parish in various activities (e.g., domestic service), while guilds were instructed to accept a select number of children as apprentices. Able-bodied "sturdy beggars," as mentioned in Chapter 5, were embarked on ships as sailors at half the wage paid by master merchants.[45] The Senate law didn't establish a centralized state structure for fund management (e.g., a general almonry or common chest), and various providers like monasteries, hospitals, and *scuole* maintained a degree of flexibility and independence. Financing remained voluntary, with a "poor box" placed in every church and equipped with three keys held by the priest, a noble deputy, and a citizen.[46]

Other northern Italian cities present similar reforms.[47] In 1450, the town of Mantova consolidated, with approval from the church, the functions of various ecclesiastical bodies into the Magno hospital. City officials identified seven types of poor people divided into three major classes: the "useful" poor (skilled and other "productive" profiles affected by covariate shocks like droughts); the "unhelpful" poor included young beggars (who could be employed with some works in the hospital before "sloth would drag them into vice"); and the "dangerous" class of poor people, namely "professional" vagabonds, beggars, prostitutes, and carriers of plague which would be punished if caught begging.[48] In 1540 Genova, a distinction of "defective" and "healthy" poor was made. The lists of poor people had to be updated and would only include those residing in the city for at least six months: "the contemplated intervention was the distribution of bread and money."[49]

[42] Chung-Kim (2017, p. 311). Similarly, it was noted that in Strasbourg, the first administrator of poor relief, appointed in 1523, was a former chaplain (Wandel 1990, p. 13).

[43] Pullan (1964).

[44] Ibid.

[45] Pullan (1971, p. 252). See also Garraty (1978, p. 29) and Salter (1926, p. 13).

[46] A similar three-key-box was present in 1547 England, with keys held by the minister of the church and the other two "by churchwardens or men named by the parish" (McIntosh 2012, p. 128)

[47] Southern cities like Rome and Naples seemed less affected by the initial European wave of reforms (Muto 1982, Simoncelli 1982).

[48] Navarrini and Belfanti (1982, p. 133). Apparently Mantova made regular visits to transfer recipients: on September 17, 1414, authorities approved the distribution of flour and bread for the poor "after the validation conducted through periodic visits" (ibid, p. 126).

[49] Grendi (1982, p. 68).

In Como, ecclesiastical charity faced significant challenges in management and coordination.[50] As such, it was replaced in 1485 by a laic organization, the hospital of St. Anna. The institution assisted populations in need with transfers in cash and in kind: provisions were modest, with a cash "Christmas distribution" to low-income populations registered on a dedicated registry.[51] The average amount provided was modest or equivalent to the daily wage of an unskilled worker (8–12 soldi). In-kind transfers mostly included meager annual distributions of bread, cereals, and wine. Both types of transfers were partially financed by the hospital's lands: a share of the surplus derived from the land's production was either distributed as food or sold to finance the hospital's activities. Between 1485 and 1520, about 36% of beneficiaries were textile workers affected by business cycles[52] — a theme that presents an early antecedent to industrial poor relief discussed in Chapter 3. The hospital's list of beneficiaries was transferred to a companying institution, the Casa Pia di Misericordia. Established in 1541, the latter would operate for centuries till the establishment of the *Ente Comunale di Assistenza* of 1937.

## Paris, Lyon, and Toulouse

Paris had gradually started the secularization of its hospitals already in 1505.[53] By the spring of 1525, the problem of poverty was discussed in parliament and tackled in two main ways: limiting the influx of the "alien poor" into the city and establishing a system of public works financed through a special indirect tax. The program struggled to meet the needs of both the shamefaced poor (e.g., unemployed craftsmen, tailors, printers) and the "idlers and vagrants."[54] Importantly, the special tax would be soon followed by the establishment of a special institution, the *Aumone Generale*, managed by city magistrates. And in 1544, "every parish was urged to draw up a list of its poor."[55] Yet the church "remained a great buffer" against poverty.[56]

Lyon is one of the most iconic reforms of the time.[57] The city's *Aumone Generale* was launched in 1534 following three years of famines and riots. It marked a decisive shift from ecclesiastical to secular management, and had among its founders two clerics, namely Jean de Vauzelles and Dominican humanist Santi Pagnini.[58] The *Aumone*

[50] Dubini (1982).
[51] In 1553, the estimated poverty level in Como was 37% of the population (ibid, p. 114).
[52] Dubini (1982, p. 119). The author provides an account from 1491: Mr. Donato Caspani, a textile worker, married with three children and resident of the San Fedele neighborhood of Como, requested and received monthly assistance until being employed, which available documents show happening shortly after (ibid, p. 116).
[53] See Geremek (1994, p. 125–131). For instance, from the end of the fifth century the town council administered the Hotel-Dieu from the chapter of Notre Dame (Zemon Davis (1968, p. 242). See also McStay-Adams (2011) and Ramsey (2002).
[54] The option of a differentiated, lower wage for the latter group was discarded out of risk of social tensions: wages were already "lower than any labourer's wage in the city", and in 1534 able-bodied beggars had to participate to public works "on pain of death" (Geremek 1994, p. 146–147).
[55] Geremek (1944, p. 130).
[56] Garraty (1978, p. 46).
[57] Zemon Davis (1968). For the city of Nimes, see Mentzer (1991) and Pugh (1974); for Lille, see Duplessis (1977).
[58] In his sermons, de Vauzelles attempted to exhort Lyon's elite to keep contributing to poor relief, including making the case based on costs (it would be more efficient than "handing out alms at their

was managed by eight unpaid rectors supervising a cadre of money collectors, bakers, nurses, and police. Financing was provided by private contributions, the clergy, royal subsidies, fines, and local taxation.[59] Eligibility involved a residency requirement of three to seven years. After assessments through door-to-door home visits by *Aumone* officials, those eligible were provided weekly payments in bread (twelve pounds) and cash (one sou or penny). Payments occurred on Sunday mornings at specified distribution points. The name of the beneficiary, the amount of assistance, and its duration were reported on recipient "tickets." These were recorded on paper if support was temporary, and on parchment if assistance was prolonged.[60] Orphans and children of the indigent were provided with trainings in hospital asylums, and partnerships were established with industrial parks (like silk manufacturing) to absorb them.[61] Again, this represents another practice akin to economic inclusion approaches of Chapter 3. In May 1534, up to 4,450 people per day were supported with about 3,000 bread loafs and cash (about 150 *livres tournois*).[62]

Toulouse represented a blend model. Centralization and rationalization of assistance occurred first among some institutions, like the hospital, while other components were left fragmented. Three stages in the city's reform can be identified. The first involved the emergence of an overall hospital structure in the early 1500s. Based on such complex, the creation of apprenticeship programs for orphans started to develop in the mid-1520s.[63] Second, the mid-1520s also included large scale public works. As the city embarked on a vast number of urban development projects, "sturdy beggars" would be deployed for manual tasks like rebuilding of the city hall and enhancing war-related fortifications. Vagabonds would be forcibly employed in collars and chains: " . . . the expression '*pauvres enchaines*' formalized the difference between sturdy beggars and vagabonds, and the latter increasingly risk being placed in irons."[64] Up to this point no permanent institution for the management of relief was established, like in Lyon: in fact, a third phase involved an ordinance promulgated in 1534 which institutionalized practices and introduced some novel aspects. Based on earlier *kalendrier* contributions,[65] the ordinance established taxes and contributions. Following a census of needs in 1536, *capitouls*, or city magistrates, would verify relief rolls and adjust payments according to those needs. Administrative evidence from the city's populous district of Saint-Etienne shows that the system kept

door") and social stability ("the only way to end the threat of riots was to end starvation"). And at the same time, Pagnini brought "vernacular eloquence on behalf of welfare reform." See discussion in Zemon Davis (1968, p. 234).

[59] Garraty (1978, p. 25).

[60] Zemon Davis (1968, p. 243).

[61] In the 1590s, Barthelemy de Laffemas, the Controller General of Commerce, proposed to physically locate the unemployed closer to industrial zones. His plan involved special villages in the cities' outskirts where the unemployed could be put at work in silk manufacturing.

[62] Zemon Davis (1968, p. 275).

[63] Beckerman Davis (1991). At the beginning, the apprenticeship obliged guilds to train orphans at no subsidized cost. Later, it offered artisans tax incentives. The program also intersected with industrial policy, with a new silk manufacturing factory that would employ poor girls and women.

[64] Beckerman Davis (1991, p. 285).

[65] The practice involved a yearly fundraising from the city elite to complement hospital revenues.

targeting typical categories of beneficiaries (e.g., widows with children, the aged) and missed vulnerable, semi-skilled workers.[66]

## Toledo

Toledo offered an interesting variant. The reform of relief commenced in 1543 in response to a harvest failure the year before. Interestingly, and differently from other continental reforms (e.g., Geneva and Lyon), the church played an active role in organizing and financing a structured program—perhaps to counter the growing criticism of its relief activities. While Toledo's scheme was temporary and provided in-kind food transfers, some of its features, like the Book of the Poor, provided a harbinger of future assessment and registration practices.[67] The Book was a written record of populations in need, with the compilation of the list being conducted by ecclesiastical authorities and "honorable parishioners." During house visits, data was collected on the "manner of living," the number of children and dependent family members, and if anyone begged publicly. Based on this information, the amount of bread required per person was estimated, with a "slip of paper" indicating such quantity. Weekly parochial bread distributions involved bakers and were adjusted seasonally. Institutionally, the reform was "organized, implemented and paid for by the church [while city authorities took] responsibility for punishing those persons who broke the law by begging publicly."[68] Examples of providing beneficiaries with choice between cash and in-kind transfers found early evidence in Toledo (Box 6.2).

### Box 6.2 Cash or Food Transfers? A Seminal Choice-Based Approach in 1546

In the 1540s, Toledo had an active Committee for the Relief of the Poor with secular and religious representation. The Committee would soon be called for an unusual decision: on April 10, 1546, a high-level ecclesiastical authority of the city, Cardinal Siliceo, donated a large sum of 5,000 ducats for poor relief. After a meeting on April 20, the Committee decided to allocate 4,000 ducats to the parish poor and 1,000 to beggars.[a] Payments to 10,729 beneficiaries would be made in two installments: the first, on May 1, provided people with a choice between a cash transfer of two *reales* (equal to two days wages for an unskilled worker) and an equivalent amount of bread (ten pounds); the second payment, on June 13, was in-kind only. Unfortunately, there appears to be limited information on the motivations behind the Committee's decision to convert the donation into cash and the principle of providing choice.[b] Yet the

[66] Beckerman Davis (1991, p. 288).
[67] Martz (1983, p. 121).
[68] Martz (1983, p. 122, 123).

initiative provides a nearly five-century precursor of modern approaches favoring a beneficiary-centered, choice-based approach to cash and food transfers, such as tested in India.[c]

[a] Begging was illegal, and the decision by the committee to support beggars may be the result of competing forces in the Committee which included Dominicans (who likely supported unrestricted assistance) and humanists, most notably Dr. Juan de Vergara.
[b] Martz (1983, p. 126).
[c] See Muralidharan et al. (2018, 2011).

## From the state to civil society: The "moral uplift in lieu of cash"

As discussed in Chapter 4, the United States underwent a period of experimentation with cash transfers in 1930s. In that context, it was observed that state authorities, including at city and municipal level, were in some cases equipped with staff with previous experience in cash transfers provided by civil society organizations. This section focuses on the seminal period when the Charity Organization Society (COS) became particularly active in shaping the debate and approaches on cash transfers.[69] The extensive analysis conducted by, among others, Dawn Greeley, Stephen Pimpare, and Viviana Zelizer has shed light on COS practices and the intellectual milieu that underpinned them.[70]

The depression of 1873–1878 followed a period of public relief expansion in the mid-1800s occurring in the context of structural change and social upheavals.[71] In the state of New York, for example, relief coverage soared from about 1% of the population in 1823 to nearly 7% in 1859; assistance was mostly provided in the form of "outdoor" relief (especially for unemployed adults).[72]

The COS was established in 1877 as a reaction to purported "lavish," "indiscriminate" relief (both public and private).[73]Activities under the COS umbrella were managed and funded by wealthy elites, businesses, and upper middle-class professionals, although they also received public financing.[74] While the average COS

[69] Watson (1922).
[70] Greeley (2022), Pimpare (2004, 2002), and Zelizer (1997).
[71] Bernstein (1956), Rezneck (1950). For instance, from 1881 to 1905 about seven million workers were involved in 37,000 strikes nationally (Pimpare 2002). See Kerr (2011, p. 16–17) for a discussion on the emergence of the COS in Cleveland after the 1877 railroad strikes of 1877.
[72] See Katz (1986) and Pimpare (2002). For Ohio, see Gunckel (1897).
[73] This followed other civil society organizations, like the Society for the Prevention of Pauperism and the Associations for Improving the Condition of the Poor (AICP) founded in 1817 and 1843, respectively. The latter was established following extreme winter weather and economic crisis in NYC in 1837–1838 with the view to limit the "false and dangerous methods of relief" pursued by early relief agencies (Pimpare 2002, p. 31). On the "mixed economy" of public-private assistance, see Katz and Sachesse (1996) for a cross-country analysis, MacKay (1893) for England and Murphy (2006) for Australia. Van Bavel and Rijpma (2016) provide a long-run perspective. On the theme, see also Henderson (1897, 1894).
[74] By 1897, in New York State the income of charitable institutions was about $21.2 million, out of which about half ($9.5 million) was contributed by state, city and county governments (Katz 1995).

organization size was small,[75] their presence spread rapidly: by 1915, there were 327 COS agencies nationwide and their presence was recorded in 20 countries.[76]

The COS contended that private relief was superior to government assistance. The argument was that the former would put a wedge between politicians and voters, hence reducing the risk of political patronage. Furthermore, private giving was deemed more effective in sorting through deserving and undeserving populations: " . . . private relief was discretionary, and allowed its distributors to act upon moral judgments about who would and who would not receive their benevolence."[77]

More fundamentally, private assistance would reshape the relationship between giver and receiver in ways that would better address the perceived (individualist) causes of poverty. The COS approach was predicated on correcting character and morality. Therefore, if assistance was rendered privately, the donor (instead of the impersonal state) would provide not only material support, but also time, attention, and inspiration: "the gift without the giver is not only bare, it is an active agent of injury."[78] Private assistance contemplated a "moral uplift in lieu of cash"[79] so to help "discover hidden springs of virtue within themselves from which alone their prosperity might flow."[80] Private "visitors" would provide a role model to address individual deficiencies, that is, to " . . . try to remove the flaw, to bring the labor to the market where it is in demand, and never to treat an able-bodied workman to a dole of bread till he and his children degenerate into paupers."[81] In other words, the underlying approach was geared at reconciling society and avoided engagement in structural causes of poverty. As a COS worker quipped, " . . . [t]hey let us deal with the wrecks, but we can't touch or even show up the conditions that produce them."[82]

Operationally, COS embraced the scientific drive of Elberfeld (Chapter 3) and similar experiences.[83] The emphasis on rigorous organization would materialize in various ways: for example, these include the analytical partition of a city into sections (278 in the case of NYC) and maintaining a centralized city-wide register of relief

[75] For example, in New York a COS handled an average of 2,000 cases/year over 1889–1898.

[76] Pimpare (2002).

[77] Pimpare (2002, p. 95).

[78] Edward Devine (1904), quoted in Pimpare (2002 p. 39). Similar arguments on the superior nature of private relief were made by Lowell (1884), Rector (2000), and Spencer (1843).

[79] Pimpare (2002, p. 38).

[80] Watson (1922, p. 78).

[81] Evans (1889), quoted in Pimpare (2002, p. 48). Visitors were mostly women. According to some observers, the visitors embodied a contradiction: while they meant to encourage independence, beneficiaries had to conform to the recommendations of visitors, some of whom with little labor market experience (Katz 1986). Ziliak (1997) found no statistically significant impact of visitors on finding employment.

[82] Quoted in Pimpare (2002, p. 43).

[83] Katz (1995, p. 38) argues that from England, the COS ". . . inherited a method (friendly visiting); a key operational distinction (the difference between worthy and unworthy); and an enemy (outdoor relief)." Similarly, Watson (1922, p. 399) notes that the COS represented " . . . a protest against the methods of administration of public outdoor relief," which was considered "a tool of unscrupulous politicians, wasteful of the taxpayers' money and pauperizing in its effects," while "the administration of public outdoor relief had from the beginning of the movement been foreign to the spirit and methods of charity organization." Feder (1936) reported that in Buffalo " . . . the Rev. S. H. Gurteen established the Buffalo Charity Organization Society in December, 1877, his former association with the London society of that name led him to copy many of its principles and to insist that relief in the homes should be left to private charity. In Boston the European and English systems had influenced the formation of the Co-operative Society of Volunteer Visitors among the Poor in 1875" (p. 61).

recipients managed by a special agency.[84] Because of the emphasis on "not alms, but a friend,"[85] cash transfers were "dangerous and even cruel [and] would be offered only as a last resort to those who could not find assistance elsewhere."[86] Public works were designed according to strict self-targeting, less-eligibility principles.[87] Between 1893–1897, the East Side Relief Committee in NYC provided home-based work in sewing, knitting, and mat and quilt making to a weekly average of 122 women for 16 weeks at $3/week. Weaving wasn't always reserved for women: in Boston, arrangements were made so that rug weaving was also conducted by men unfit for heavy labor.[88] The Committee also delivered products to cyclone-affected areas of South Carolina. Similarly, the Chicago Relief and Aid Society supported victims of the great Chicago fire of 1871—first with in-kind provisions, and subsequently with cash grants.[89] The pressure that the latter Society faced for providing assistance in 1873 epitomizes the environment of widespread needs in which COS operated (Box 6.3).

**Box 6.3 Repurposing Expenses for Relief amid Public Protests**

In 1873, the Chicago Relief and Aid Society had a financial surplus in a special "Fire Fund," which accrued interest for $700,000.[a] The agency intended to save the amount for future fire victims and had made no plans to use it to relieve unemployment. With the city's adverse employment landscape, the decision generated a protest

[84] Katz (1995).
[85] Watson (1922, p. 15).
[86] Cash transfers "... fostered dependency, took away incentives to work," and "offered false hope for a better future: cash might minimize momentary suffering, but it could never get at the causes of poverty"; as such, COS "... engaged in an effort to ensure both that poor relief [...] would not become a right" (Pimpare 2002, p. 37, 39). According to Devine (1898), fewer than one third of applications was deemed worthy of relief.
[87] An article of 1895 observed that "... [t]he work given must be adequate in amount to prevent families from suffering either hunger or cold; but at the same time it must be really hard work in order to prevent dabbling, and it must be decidedly underpaid in order not to attract those who already have work at half-time, or who have otherwise disagreeable work. The whole must be so unattractive as to guarantee that, when other work can be had, the laborer will seek it" (Philip Ayres, quoted in Feder 1936, p. 179).
[88] In New York, Mayor Fernando Wood, in a message to the Common Council on October 23, 1857, proposed the use of public works for the unemployed to build new streets and a reservoir in Central Park. From 600 to 1,100 men were employed for the task during the winter of 1857–1858 at a wage of $1/day for six days' work (the mayor had initially proposed payments in food). The same wage rate was provided in 1875 for public works in Boston. These included breaking stones, grading streets, and removing rock from ledges, for which "... [t]he low daily wage of $1 during the winter was justified [...] on the ground that in summer the competition of farm work and other lines of active industry was large" (Feder 1936, p. 68).
[89] The shift in transfer modalities was partial (in kind was maintained for providing fuel, blankets and shoes) and occurred because of complaints with the quality of in-kind provisions. The annual report of the Chicago Relief and Aid Society of 1873 argued that compared to in-kind provisions, cash assistance "... certainly takes away all ground of complaint. The applicants can in most cases make as good or better use of the money in providing only that which they most need, and being obliged to receive nothing they do not want. The mass of worthy, honest, and economical poor should not be treated as thieves and paupers, because [...] a few of them may possibly succeed in [frauding]" (quoted in Colcord 1936, p. 10).

with 20,000 people gathering before the Common Council. The government stepped in, and since no municipal money was available, on December 26 the mayor of Chicago asked and obtained (reluctantly) from the Relief and Aid Society to lend the city $700,000 for public works. About 1,000 people applied for assistance in bulk at the office of the Relief and Aid Society. Staff was overwhelmed: to deter applications, proof of vaccination was called for and the situation required police's intervention. Some 50 new visitors[b] were deployed to investigate the caseloads of applicants, 40% of whom were enrolled (mostly unemployed men and their families).

[a] Box based on Pimpare (2002, p. 151).
[b] In 1887, in large cities like New York and Chicago there was one visitor for every 400 cases.

Were COSs successful in achieving their goals? Basically, the COS model posited that, over time, public assistance fostered dependency; instead, COS methods would help "graduate" people out of relief and put them on a path of self-reliance. In terms of facilitating the reduction in "rolls," especially outdoor assistance, COSs were likely effective. Among the top 50 largest US cities in 1900, 78% had COSs: within this cohort, 84% reduced relief.[90] In New York City, between 1860–1864 and 1890–1894 poor relief coverage declined from about 20% to less than 7% of the population.[91]

However, the COS performance in fostering self-reliance is probably more modest. Econometric analysis by Stephen Ziliak examined such performance in Indianapolis.[92] Based on household-level COS caseworker data compiled over a quarter of a century, the study reveals that, after an initial rise in the probability of exiting relief, the hope of increasing self-reliance didn't materialize (Figure 6.2a). The actual pattern followed by COS beneficiaries mirrors the alleged dependency induced by the "public dole" (Figure 6.2b).

In general, "[c]harity organization seems to have been more successful than welfare at moving people rapidly off of relief [but it] fell short of its goal of moving a high percentage of able-bodied poor into economies of self-support."[93] In many cases, beneficiaries simply switched institutional home: the newfound ineligible would be hosted by multiple specialized institutions, for example orphanages, asylums, mental health institutions, and prisons.[94]

[90] Pimpare (2002).
[91] Hannon (1997). However, one should be careful in drawing causality between those reductions and COS assistance. For example, in the District of Columbia relief was reduced without the presence of COS.
[92] Ziliak (2004). As in other cities, public assistance in Indianapolis dwindled while private relief increased and even surpassed public spending in 1882 and 1883.
[93] Ziliak (2004, p. 457).
[94] Katz (1983), Pimpare (2002).

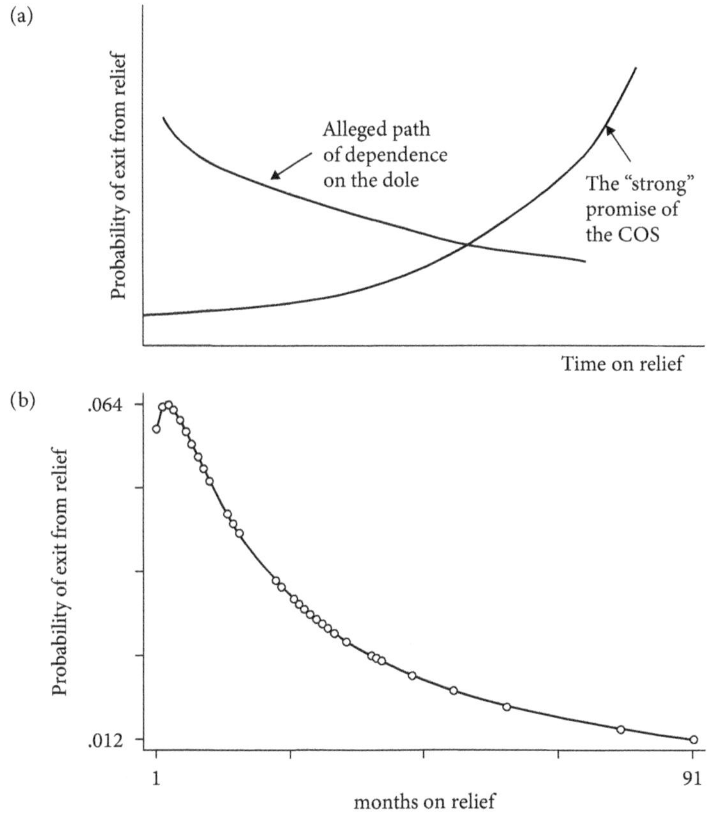


**Figure 6.2** Effects of COS assistance in (a) theory and (b) practice, Indianapolis (1881–1889).

*Source*: Adapted from Ziliak (2004) "Self-Reliance Before the Welfare State: Evidence from the Charity Organization Movement in the United States." *Journal of Economic History* 64(2): 433–461.

[a] See Ziliak (2004, p. 450, 452).

## 6.2 Reform within the same provider: Centralization and moving indoor

The debate among classical economists discussed in Chapter 2 intensified during the crisis that unfolded in England over 1795–1800.[95] This culminated with the landmark 1834 Report of the "Royal Commission to Investigate the Poor Laws," which laid the foundations for the New Poor Law unveiled in the same year. Led by William Nassau Senior, an Oxford lawyer and political economist, and Edwin Chadwick, a Benthamite social reformer, the Commission was appointed in 1832 by the new bourgeoisie-leaning government.

[95] Poynter (1969).

The Report has been considered "... by far the most extensive sociological survey that had at that date ever been undertaken."[96] The overall package featured 26 volumes and 13,000 pages, making it difficult to counter in the immediate short term:[97] "[n]one of the numerous contemporary opponents of the New Poor Law had the stomach for such an undertaking."[98]

In terms of content, " . . . the [1834] Act was and is seen as more or less Benthamite."[99] It has been argued that members of the Report's Commission "... started with an overwhelming intellectual prepossession, and they made only the very smallest effort to free their investigations and reports from bias [against the Speenhamland system]."[100] In brief, the historian Edward Palmer Thompson defined the new poor laws as " . . . perhaps the most sustained attempt to impose an ideological dogma [ . . . ] in English history."[101] Box 6.4 sketches out the main tenets of Bentham's vision.

**Box 6.4 Bentham's Proposal for a National Charity Company**

Bentham proposed the formation of a National Charity Company.[a] This involved a network of 250 "industry houses," each hosting around 2,000 paupers, erected on wastelands and financed by small investors. Bentham was convinced that "the luxuries seen in many instances to be enjoyed by beggars, are a sort of insult to the hard-working child of industry." Conditions should be harsh and unpleasant, so to discourage begging by stigmatizing relief as "an object of wholesome horror." The Company would have powers of apprehending, detaining, and employing all persons "with no visible or assignable property, nor honest and sufficient means of livelihood." There would be monetary rewards for people bringing in beggars (10–20s). The system would be managed based on "mercantile principles," with "undivided authority," and furnished with a "competent stock of land and capital." In particular, beggars would have a "self-liberation account" to be balanced out not by money, but by a corresponding amount of labor. In other words, the person would have to work to repay for the apprehension reward, all expense of conveyance (food, clothing, bedding, medicine, and even a life insurance "... equivalent for the chance of him dying before his account is balanced").[b] The beggar would not be discharged without a bondsman providing a job. When discharged, the person would undergo a period

[96] Webb and Webb (1927, p. 54).
[97] Brundage (1978).
[98] Blaug (1964, p. 230). Himmelfarb (1984a) mentions that "... the official report [was] a readable 200-page volume, of which 10,000 copies were sold and another 10,000 distributed free to parish authorities" (p. 155), with the report being reprinted three times by the Stationary Office before the end of the 19th century.
[99] Stokes (2001, p. 711).
[100] Webb and Webb (1927, p. 88).
[101] Quoted in Hirschman (1991, p. 31).

of probation (a full year), working during the day and return to the industry house at night. Failure to return would be considered an escape, with a reward quadruple to the original one. After probation, the beggar would be released and receive a "certificate of full emancipation." The original reward would be doubled every time of relapse into the begging. Differently from existing workhouses, which involved a duration of stay not connected to the inmate's effort, Bentham argued that his plan would involve "no punishment," a duration depending on the person's efforts (sometimes it could be just weeks), a master selected by a trusted public company, and a list of other 15 "pauper comforts."

[a] The box is based on Bahmueller (1981), Bentham (1796), and Semple (1993).
[b] Bentham (1796, p. 402).

The 1834 Report was fiercely critical of the poor laws in general, and of the Speenhamland allowance system specifically. Its conclusion was that unemployment was a byproduct of relief itself. Labor surplus would be "rapidly reduced and ultimately disappear, if relief were no longer granted, except in return for actual labour, and subject to the restraints of a workhouse."[102] In other words, " . . . the [1834] law in its essence proclaims the poor criminals, the workhouses prisons, their inmates [ . . . ] objects of disgust and repulsion [ . . . ]. In practice, the spirit and not the letter of the law is followed in the treatment of the poor."[103] The Commissioners didn't advise to abolish poor relief *tout court*, as did Malthus (Chapter 2).[104] Specifically, it marshalled an attack against three supposed problems: unfair competition among subsidized and non-subsidized employers, labor supply disincentives, and malpractices in local administration. Three corresponding solutions emerged: the principle of less eligibility, the workhouse test, and a higher degree of administrative centralization.[105] Figure 6.3 illustrates the three problems and proposed solutions.

The less-eligibility principle contended that "most essential of all conditions" was to ensure that the utility low-income people derived from public assistance was less than the utility that lowest-paid workers acquired from the labor market.[106] Specifically, the fulfillment of the less-eligibility condition required the provision of assistance to able-bodied workers and their families only in workhouses:

[102] GoUK (1834a, p. 354). The theory of the Report was that supply of labor would increase, workers would become diligent, productivity would rise, returns to capital augment, resources expand, and higher wages provided.
[103] Engels (1845, p. 189).
[104] Rose (1966b).
[105] After 1834, the administration of relief was consolidated from 13,264 local parishes into 568 Poor Law Unions (20–30 parishes) with locally elected Board of Guardians.
[106] Boyer (1990).

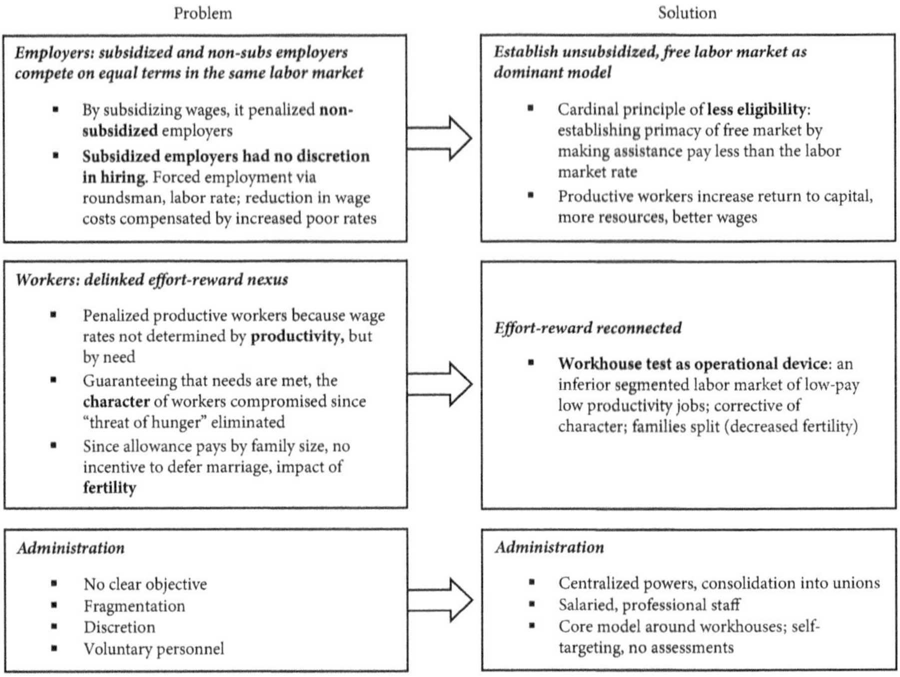


**Figure 6.3** Commissioners' stylized view of three core problems and related interventions.
*Source*: The author.

> . . . [i[t was not necessary to abolish public relief, merely to make it so unattractive that most paupers would decline to accept it. If any did still choose to accept it, they would, by the same token, be separated by so wide margin from the rewards of independent work as no longer to compete with it on equal terms. The tendency of the allowance system to expand itself would not merely be stopped but reversed.[107]

In a relatively short period of time, the new poor law managed to slash spending significantly. If 16th-century approaches were concerned with the "prevention of poverty," subsequent centuries shifted to the "prevention of expenditures."[108] Starting in 1820, in less than a century poor relief spending in England decreased by a factor of four (Table 6.1). Between 1830 and 1840, the cost of poor relief assistance was halved, falling from 2% to 1.1% of GDP.[109]

[107] Finer (1952, p. 45).
[108] Ball et al. (2023, p. 9).
[109] Lindert (2014, 2021). The downturn trend would continue till 1910, when spending would be 0.68% of GDP. France, Belgium, and the Netherlands displayed a similar trajectory. Countries that would start from very low levels of spending, like the United States and Sweden, would instead gradually allocate more resources to poor relief, although they remained low in the case of the United States. Spending in Germany, Denmark, and Spain remained relatively stable.

**Table 6.1** Spending on Poor Relief (% of GDP), 1820–1910.

| | Belgium | Denmark | France | Germany | Netherlands | Spain | Sweden | UK | US |
|---|---|---|---|---|---|---|---|---|---|
| 1820 | 1.03 | | 0.63 | | 1.36 | | | 2.66 | 0.1 |
| 1830 | 0.34 | | 0.63 | | | | 0.02 | 2 | 0.12 |
| 1840 | 0.28 | | 0.46 | | | | | 1.12 | 0.12 |
| 1850 | | | 0.47 | | 1.38 | 0.84 | | 1.07 | 0.13 |
| 1860 | | 0.66 | 0.49 | | 1.24 | 0.98 | 0.6 | 0.86 | 0.2 |
| 1870 | | 0.8 | 0.5 | | 1.18 | 1.17 | | 0.85 | 0.31 |
| 1880 | 0.11 | 0.85 | 0.21 | 0.5 | 0.29 | 0.87 | 0.6 | 0.73 | 0.38 |
| 1890 | 0.11 | 0.81 | 0.25 | 0.5 | 0.3 | 1.02 | 0.69 | 0.67 | 0.3 |
| 1900 | 0.09 | 0.57 | 0.3 | 0.5 | 0.39 | 1.06 | 0.66 | 0.71 | |
| 1910 | 0.16 | 0.67 | 0.29 | 0.5 | 0.39 | 1 | 0.72 | 0.68 | |

*Source*: Adapted based on Lindert (2021 p. 38).

Relatedly, taxes for poor relief, or "poor rates," fell. During the fifty years between the end of the 1700s and early 1800s, or the period when Speenhamland was introduced and spread in parts of England, resources raised via poor rates had quintuplicated. In the four years following the 1834 act, resources raised via the poor rates in 1840 declined by 38%, before rising again (Figure 6.4).[110]

**Figure 6.4** Million pounds levied on poor rates, 1776–1859.

*Source*: Data from Purdy (1860), annex table I, p. 314.

[110] The fact that the new government represented the constituency which funded the programs may have helped to pass the 1834 legislation. Finer (1952) presents slightly different figures: the costs dwindled from £6.75 million in 1830–1834 to £4.56 million in 1835–1839, and £4.88 million in 1840–1844.

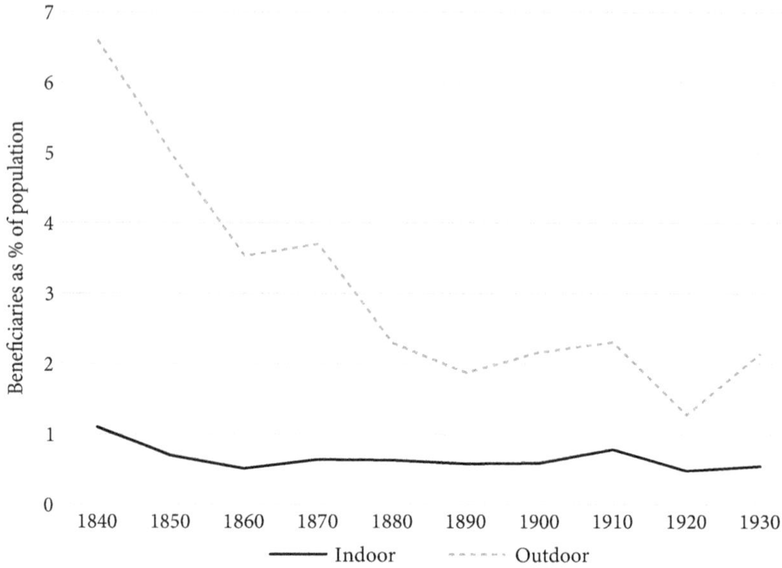


**Figure 6.5** Indoor and outdoor "relieved paupers" in England and Wales, 1840–1930.
*Source*: The author, based on data from Higginbotham (2012, p. 306–309).

The New Poor Law was also effective in reducing coverage: over the 1830s the share of the population receiving poor relief in England and Wales was halved.[111] Simultaneously, the shift of the epicenter of assistance toward workhouses ignited a long-term trend.[112] Yet outdoor assistance continued to be provided: even if steeply falling, outdoor relief consistently exceeded the provision of workhouses (Figure 6.5).[113]

As assistance moved its center of gravity toward indoor relief, administrative costs soared. Over 1860–1911, in England and Wales the share of outdoor beneficiaries (out of total beneficiaries) decreased by over 25 percentage points (from 86.8% to 60.4%); simultaneously, administrative costs for overall relief more than doubled, climbing from 11.4% to 24.7% of total relief costs[114] (Figure 6.6).[115] According to Peter Lindert, " . . . [o]fficials and taxpayers faced the same kind of choice that we face:

[111] Coverage dwindled from 10.2% in 1831 to 5.4% in 1837 (Higginbotham 2012, p. 305).

[112] See the analysis by MacKinnon (1987) on the "crusade" against outdoor relief. In reference to the perspective number of paupers that would accept the workhouse, the symbolic "one in ten" ratio seems to have been used in multiple cases: Lubbock (1895), for example, quotes Fleming, an inspector of the poor laws, stating in a 1889–1890 annual report that " . . . [w]hen the destitution of applicants is tested by workhouse orders, about one in ten accepts in-door relief"; similarly, she reports professor Bryce claiming in 1876 that " . . . the truth is that when applicants are told that they must enter the workhouse, and not be relieved out of it, nice out of every ten of them slip away, and only one remains to accept the workhouse" (ibid, p. 54–55).

[113] Taylor (1972). Similarly, in previous decades costs considerations and the local nature of assistance provided to "known" people may explain why " . . . there is little evidence of unemployed rural workers being forced to enter workhouses from 1780 to 1834" (Boyer 1990, p. 23).

[114] In absolute terms, in 1872 England the weekly cost of supporting a family with indoor relief was 10s, while the cost of outdoor assistance amounted to only 4s (Lindert 2021).

[115] In a similar fashion, as cities and towns in the US were also shifting toward workhouses in the 1800s, it was noted that local authorities " . . . often spent more money ridding themselves of paupers than they would have spent supporting them" (Katz 1986, p. 21).

spend even more to supervise the poor carefully and seek ways of finding work for them or save on administrative costs by guiding them less."[116]

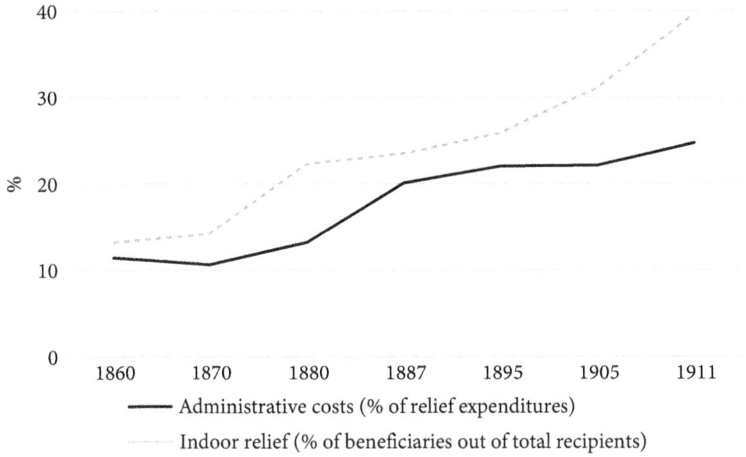


**Figure 6.6** Administrative costs and indoor beneficiaries in England and Wales, 1860–1911.
*Source*: The author, based on data from Lindert (2004, p. 53).

## 6.3 Hybrid reforms

In the United States, the last two decades of the 20th century were characterized by a change in rhetoric and general tightening in provisions. Although widely perceived as a period of fiscal contraction, this wasn't necessarily so in quantitative terms. Overall, it was a period of reconfiguration and rhetorical retrenchment.[117] Welfare spending continued to grow, but programs would be structured in ways that address concerns around incentives, work requirements and dependency: " . . . administration priorities shifted emphasis from social policy spending to other spending programs, including assistance to state governments; [this allowed states] to obtain waivers [. . .] involving reduced cash benefits and strengthened work requirements."[118]

[116] Lindert (2004, p. 55).

[117] In the US and UK, for example, this period " . . . did not lead to a systematic onslaught on the institutions of the welfare state but instead brought about complex, selective process of adaptation" (Klein 2009, p. 199). Similarly, while " . . . political conflicts in the 1980s touched upon the very survival of the welfare state, [ . . . ] that even radical retrenchment does not necessarily hollow out the welfare state as a whole was an insight of the 1990s" (Nullmeier and Kaufmann 2010, p. 88). Taylor-Gooby (2002, p. 598) refers to this phase as the "interregnum of the 1980s and 1990s" to underscore its ambivalent character. See also Pierson (1994, p. 49). Schmidt (2002) argues that in the UK, the government " . . . appealed to Victorian values [and] insisted on distinguishing between the 'deserving' and the 'undeserving' poor" (p. 174). Yet it didn't cut overall social expenditures, but only those social assistance programs that didn't confirm to those values (ibid, p. 175).

[118] Haveman et al. (2014, p. 602). In his latest memoir, President Obama recounted how, in the context of health insurance, there were missed junctures for a fundamental overhaul of the system towards universality as opposed to working within the existing framework. In particular, he recalled how the late 1940s, "[r]ather than challenging private insurance head-on, progressives shifted their energy to help those populations the marketplace had left behind" (Obama 2020, p. 376). Harvey (2005) offers a similar

Specific social assistance programs faced significant budget cuts: for example, in the early 1980s, food stamps and other programs introduced or expanded since the 1960s were reduced by almost one fifth.[119] Waivers were granted for states experimentation with AFCD cash benefits, including tying provisions to Learnfare conditional cash transfers (see Box 2.4, Chapter 2).[120] Other pilots included workfare, time limits, and family.[121] Legislation established work requirements for 15% of AFDC beneficiaries. By the mid-1980s, procedural changes in AFDC eligibility rendered ineligible almost half million families, per capita expenditures declined, and adequacy of benefits was reduced by 90%.[122] Those policies were accompanied by anti-welfare narratives and images.[123]

Similar reforms were enacted in the 1990s.[124] These repealed AFDC and introduced Temporary Assistance for Needy Families (TANF): the former was an entitlement providing cash to all those that would meet eligibility criteria; the latter, instead, included fixed block grants to states.[125] Participants of TANF were required to work after two years of benefits and most beneficiaries couldn't participate for more than five years.

As a result of such reforms, cash coverage was reduced to its lowest level since 1964.[126] Yet between 1994 and 2012, the number of families *eligible* for AFDC/TANF was relatively stable (Figure 6.7a).[127] What declined steeply was the share of eligible beneficiaries who enrolled and received assistance in *practice*: while these were about

reflection and claims that the left "failed to go much beyond traditional social democratic and corporatist solutions and these had by the mid-1970s proven inconsistent with the requirements of capital accumulation" (p. 13).

[119] Danziger and Haveman (1987, p. 14). See also MacDonald (1963) for a case made in favor of guaranteed minimum income programs.

[120] Following the wave of experimentation, the legislation established learnfare; increased benefits for children could be denied if they were born while mothers were beneficiaries ("family cap"); and cash could be reduced by up to 25% if women recipients didn't identify children's biological father (Pimpare 2002, p. 175).

[121] Pimpare (2002).

[122] About 493,000 families were affected by procedural changes. Per capita spending declined from $665 in 1970 to $370 in 1993. Benefits as percentage of personal income, which increased from 6% in 1965 to 10% in 1975, declined to 1% in 1985 (Pimpare 2002). Tax policy also affected low-income earners: between 1980 and 1984, a family earning less than $10,000/year paid $95 more in taxes, while taxation at the top of the distribution was reduced (Katz 1986).

[123] For instance, Reagan's iconic "Welfare Queen" (a terms used by Gilder (1981), "these welfare queens on their leisured thrones") that so vividly captured the essence of his message of welfare recipients being predatory, dependent paupers was not new (Albelda et al. 1996). In 1877, Dugdale prepared a paper on "the Juke family," a licentious multi-generational household that was claimed to cost government over a million dollars in 75 years (Dugdale 1877). About a decade later, McColloch (1888) wrote about the "tribe of Ishmael" displaying similar vicious traits. See also Levin (2019) for a recent account of the story of Linda Taylor, the 1974 welfare queen herself from the South Side of Chicago. For the enduring political divisions that followed those years, see Phillips (1990); also, using Richmond, Virginia, as a case study, Green (2017) offers a fascinating historical analysis connecting reforms of the 1990s to colonial poor laws.

[124] In 1996, the Personal Responsibility and Work Opportunity Reconciliation Act (PRWORA) was launched. The process leading to the reform, its structure and effects are subject to a large literature (e.g., Besharov and Call 2009; Moffitt 2003a; Weaver 2000).

[125] Part of the literature identified the limited constituency for AFDC as a core political vulnerability of the program (Brown 1995, Guadagno 1994, Steensland 2008b). See Teles (1996) for discussion on entitlements.

[126] Grogger et al. (2003). While five million families were reached by cash transfers in 1994, only 2.1 million families received them in 2000.

[127] Falk et al. (2016). For a reflection on the 1996 welfare reform from the standpoint of a policymaker, see Ellwood (2001).

80% in 1996, such rate declined by over 30 percentage points five years later (Figure 6.7b).

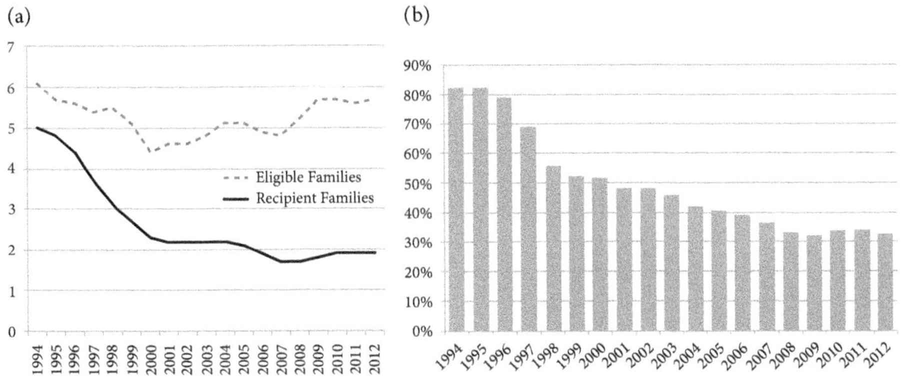


**Figure 6.7** Number of TANF (a) eligible and recipient families (million) and (b) share of recipient out of total eligible.
*Source*: Falk et al. (2016, p. 17–18).

Similar reforms geared at making access to cash transfers stricter were observed in an array of high-income settings. A synthetic indicator of "sanction strictness" in 21 advanced economies points to participation requirements becoming more stringent across countries in the 1980s and 1990s, reaching a peak around 2000.[128] Similarly, over 1980–2010 the share of countries with no requirements for jobseekers to report their job-search activities declined steadily, while the share of countries establishing compulsory job-seeking agreements (where job-seekers and employment services intensively plan search activities) rose sharply since the mid-1990s (Figure 6.8).

In the United States, strictness in benefits clearly reduced welfare rolls.[129] More contentious, however, is determining the fate of ex-beneficiaries. Evidence shows that rolls reduction was due to a combination of higher exit from and lower entry into the program: the former included reasons like possible re-entry in the labor market, time limits and sanctions leading to removal from the program. Lower entries, instead, may again be due to higher employment opportunities as well as design requirements that can deter families from participating (states could condition TANF eligibility on various factors).[130] One study attributed one third of relief-rolls declines to sanctions;[131] others estimated such level to be up to 45%.[132] In fact, spending on TANF was $4 billion higher than it was projected under AFDC:[133] while states typically allocated 80% of budgets for cash transfers in the pre-1996 era, such share was reduced to 50%

[128] See Immervoll and Knotz (2018, p. 16, figure 3, panel A). Their strictness indicator averages the scores for strictness of sanctions for voluntary unemployment, and for initial and subsequent refusals of suitable job offers. See also Knotz (2020a,b) and data published in the Comparative Unemployment Benefit Conditions & Sanctions Dataset: https://cknotz.github.io/benefitconditionalitydata/

[129] Besharov and Germanis (2001), Mead (1998), Seligman (2000).

[130] Grogger et al. (2003).

[131] Oliphant (2000).

[132] Besharov and Germanis (2001), Blank (2001).

[133] Mead (2001).

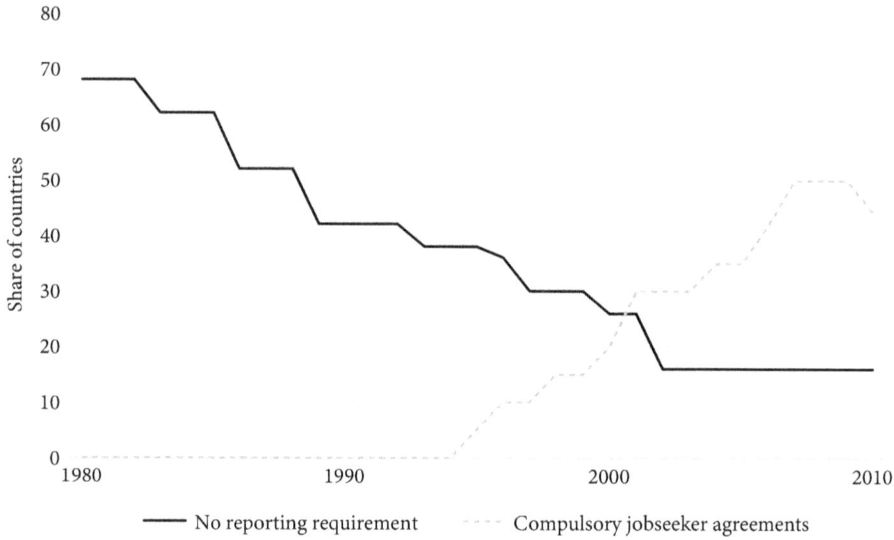


**Figure 6.8** Requirements for jobseeker benefit eligibility, 1980–2010 (share of advanced economies).
*Source*: The author, based on data from Immervoll and Knotz (2018, p. 16).

in 2001. State spending was now directed significantly to service providers, including private companies that, for example, monitor and enforce compliance, provide trainings, and facilitate work transitions.[134] Such trends mirrored the outcomes of the 1834 retrenchment discussed earlier in this chapter.

It was concluded that, at best, 60% of those who left the rolls were working at any time, and among the employed, some 70% earned below-poverty wages.[135] In other words, reforms "reduced the rolls" in large part by making assistance harder to access and through the "less eligibility" principle. Robert Haveman and colleagues suggested that the reform "... appears to have had a greater impact on reducing the caseload rather than on increasing employment rates or reducing poverty."[136]

## 6.4 How reforms happened

This section discusses the institutional process that made possible for the influential 1834 Report to be produced, endorsed and implemented. This also includes illuminating how its diffusion and influence materialized—as well as scrutinizing its main claims empirically. A broader theory is discussed on how narratives inspired by those developments were reproduced over time and space.

[134] Pimpare (2002).
[135] Boushey (2001), Greenberg et al. (2000), Haskins et al. (2001), Pimpare (2004, 2002).
[136] Haveman et al. (2014, p. 605). Moreover, Pimpare (2002) argues that rolls reductions should be interpreted within a wider range of concurrent developments, including rising levels of soup kitchens and food banks usage, homelessness and emergency shelters, and imprisonment.

## From rhetoric to institutional change

The 1834 report that ushered the British "new poor law" era was not just a bureaucratic endeavor.[137] It set the terms of domestic and international debates on cash transfers for nearly two centuries. As discussed in Chapter 2, the indictment of cash assistance was effectively articulated by leading voices, including in reference to purportedly deleterious effects on, among others, labor supply, fertility, and moral character, as well as public coffers. The shadow of the 1834 report still fuels fears of "dependency" and "disincentives" in contemporary debates.[138] To be sure, cash transfers are no silver bullet and certainly not immune from legitimate criticism.[139] Yet the a priori skepticism towards them has been largely fueled by constructed narratives underpinned by ideological forces.

It is important to situate this important historical juncture within the wider cultural milieu in parts of the Western hemisphere. The vibrant set of ideas, proposals and interventions that emerged in the late 1700s and early 1800s were, it was argued, "a direct product of the American and French Revolutions": the Speenhamland system, for instance, "was an intimidatory use of its supposed 'rights' by the poor,"[140] and famine conditions in the year of its introduction "raised fears of domestic insurrection."[141] While the scheme and other measures "were *not* proposals to resolve the 'social problem,' as that problem came to be understood in the nineteenth and twentieth centuries," they may have still challenged existing institutions and religious assumptions about poverty.[142] They were "bound to stir controversy," hence calling for government policy initiatives "in a period of revolutionary discontent and total war."[143]

The post-revolution "anti-utopian cast of mind" reframed the poverty agenda "as a bleakly individual battle against the temptations of the flesh."[144] The 1834 report may have played a major role in funneling part of such rhetoric towards cash transfers. The Report was part of a fervent process that, over 1817–1831, involved several parliamentary initiatives to assess the efficacy of poor relief and explore options for reform. Before the commission was formed in 1932, three governmental reports in 1817, 1818, and 1824 had already set a damning, adversarial tone against cash transfers.[145] John Poynter concluded that " . . . it was in these years that fundamental

[137] Edsall (1971) discusses an anti-Poor Law "movement".

[138] For example, see reviews by Baird et al. (2018), Banerjee et al. (2024, 2017), Bastagli and Lowe (2021), Bastagli et al. (2019), Handa et al. (2018), and Peterman (2021). See also the evidence mapping laid out in Chapter 2.

[139] For recent literature on the unintended effects of cash transfers, see Della Guardia et al. (2022) on social cohesion, Filmer et al. (2023) on malnutrition, Levy and Cruces (2021) on informality, and Mora et al. (2022) on poverty.

[140] Stedman Jones (2004, p. 224).

[141] Waterman (1991, p. 25).

[142] Stedman Jones (2004, p. 224), emphasis added. According to the author, the purpose of the scheme " . . . was not to remove the hostility of the working classes towards private property or to overcome the antagonism between labour and capital, since these were not yet perceived as intractable problems" (ibid).

[143] Hilton (1988, p. 37).

[144] Stedman Jones (2004, p. 226).

[145] Blaug (1963, p.160)

disapproval of a legal provision for the poor (and especially for the able-bodied) became sufficiently widespread to be regarded as orthodox, while defense of the Poor Law became, if not quite heretical, at least old-fashioned."[146]

Turning to the production of the 1834 report, shortly after his appointment as Commissioner Nassau William Senior approached Edwin Chadwick to investigate the operation of the law in London.[147] Their views on the direction of reform were slightly different, with Senior being initially a Malthusian extremist.[148] Just a year before being appointed commissioner, Senior had made a clear case to abolish assistance for the able-bodied poor in the context of the Irish poor laws debate.[149] Senior's views later veered closer to Chadwick's, who acted as " . . . the carrier of the Benthamite lymph in the Poor Law Commission."[150]

But how did Benthamite ideas, the dominant ideology permeating the 1834 report, influence its genesis? In a meticulous account of the mechanisms through which ideas were (partially) translated into practice, political scientist Samuel Finer shows that Benthamite views were absorbed into legislation through three interconnected processes of "irradiation," "suscitation," and "permeation."[151] Through irradiation, the missionary zeal of Bentham's trusted inner circle would spread his notions to a wider audience via editorial boards, clubs, and other influential platforms.[152] The process of suscitation involved managing public inquiries and media communications to forge a favorable opinion among elites and the wider public. To this effect, securing and leveraging strategic governmental bodies, such as controlling Commissions, was essential to translate Benthamite precepts into the state's

146 Poynter (1969, p.224).

147 See Englander (1998) and Finer (1952).

148 When the Commission's works began there were three "camps" of opinions for reforming relief: the popular-Radicals arguing that the Laws were for "keeping them, but they provide too little," and what was needed was more finance (Cobbett), allotments (Gaskell), or better magistrates (Walter at *The Times*); a second group included those that favored "reform of the existing model," especially in the direction of workhouse incorporations; and then those of Malthusian spirit, including Senior, favoring the "abolishment of the laws" altogether (Finer 1972, 1952).

149 He stated: ". . . if testimonies of all ages and all countries have any weight, it is established that idleness and improvidence can be prevented only by leaving them to the punishment inflicted by nature—want and degradation. [Therefore] I anxiously wish to prevent the existence in Ireland, not of a legal provision for charitable purposes, but of a legal provision for the able-bodied poor" (Senior 1831, p. 36, 45). He referred to support to the able-bodied poor as an "evil" undermining "industry, providence, and mutual benevolence": " . . . [the law] says to the idle and heedless, your subsistence shall not depend on your exertions or your contrivance; to the young, marry as soon as you like, your families shall be provided for; the well employed, spend all your earnings, the parish will support you when they fail" (p. 25). Senior warned that such state " . . . if not immediately remedied, threatens the destruction of society, and of which the remedy becomes every day more dangerous, as the disease becomes every day more intolerable" (p. 28).

150 Bhattacharya (2017, p. 265).

151 Finer (1972).

152 This would include aristocrats with ministerial patronage, businessmen who were also members of parliament, and other influential actors who would later turn civil servants. The platforms for irradiation included joining editorial teams of Benthamite periodicals. Another vector were various societies, such as the "Political Economy Club." Established in 1821, it included 28 founding members, like Mill, Ricardo, Malthus, Chadwick, and Senior. Other societies included, for example, the Society for the Diffusion of Useful Knowledge (founded in 1827) and the Society for the Diffusion of Practical Knowledge (1833). Chadwick and Senior were also members of the London Statistical Society, a more catholic and non-propagandist body.

official position.[153] Finally, the stage of permeation entailed securing key official positions and filling strategic vacancies to reproduce and amplify irradiation and suscitation.[154]

The role that Chadwick played in the Report's production sheds light on the biased nature of the process. After ten months from the commission's establishment, members were suddenly asked to provide the Cabinet with their "most representative finding[s]" to be published as "Extracts of Information." Instead of providing a summary, Chadwick submitted a full report inclusive of six key conclusions.[155] His work received support in the commission, and the Extracts eventually consisted of about 400 pages that would lay the basis for the final Report. In the latter, Chadwick would pen, among others, the Report's Annex A on "Evidence." This was published in an incomplete form (it was claimed that " . . . the reminder of Mr Chadwick's evidence will follow shortly"). Also, the Evidence was largely devoted to "repressive measures" to dismantle the allowance system. It was meant to be accompanied by "collateral aids" that would have made the law more popular; but apparently Chadwick had purposely left those measures unpublished so to have a "freer hand" to use them when he would be appointed in the execution of the Law. This didn't occur, and Chadwick was involved in numerous disputes in clarifying the tensions between what was in the report and his own unexpressed vision.[156]

## Scrutinizing the indictment empirically

Almost a century after the Commissioners 1834 report, a large body of literature questioned and largely disproved its claims. Table 6.2 lays out main arguments made against and in support of the Speenhamland model. Three broad bands of literature emerge: the body of materials that the Commissioners mostly relied upon framed cash transfers as the problem (reflected in the upper row of the table). Malthus and Townsend, some of the protagonists of Chapter 2, pertain to this group. A second branch of literature was more ambivalent: it conceded that a problem existed, but the mechanisms were different. Presented in the central rows of the table, those views posited that relief could be problematic not because of its negative workers incentives, but because of behavioral responses by employers (who were incentivized to

[153] According to Finer (1972, p. 18–19), when Benthamites obtain official positions " . . . it often fell to them to recommend persons for filling vacant positions in their offices. They tended to select persons of their own way of thinking [ . . . ] ."

[154] Over the first decade of the Political Economy Club, almost half (46%) of them won political elections, a rate that nearly doubled (82%) by 1843. Among the elected officials in the 1821–1830 cohort was Senior, while it was through Althorp, the sole aristocrat elected at the time, that Chadwick came into government's Poor Law Office (he would be later elected as well).

[155] In brief, these included: (i) that the existing system is destructive of the industry, forethought and honesty of the laborers; (ii) that professionalization of management was required; (iii) settlement law was to be abolished; (iv) relief to able bodied should be provided via workhouses; (v) changes would have desirable effects on marriage; and (vi) centralization of powers was needed.

[156] Finer (1952).

**Table 6.2** Mapping out the Speenhamland Debate

| Conclusion | Proponents | Mechanism | Specific outcome |
|---|---|---|---|
| Relief as **cause** of a structural problem. **Workers' incentives** ("biological" mechanism) leads to negative outcomes. | Townsend (1786), Eden (1797), Malthus (1798), 1817, 1818, 1834 Reports, de Tocqueville (1835), Olasky (1992). | Widespread use of bread scale undermines scarcity and fear necessary for market self-regulation and efficiency. | Poor relief works as perverse incentive to early marriage, increased fertility, and voluntary unemployment. Reduced productivity, lower wages, excessive population growth, and increased poverty. |
| Same negative outcomes, but via **employer incentives.** | Davies (1795), Marx (1867), Engels (1845), Cunningham (1908), Hammond and Hammond (1911), Webb and Webb (1927), Thompson (1963). | Wide use of bread scale facilitates unilateral wage reductions by employers. Farmers shift costs on to the parish to save on their wage bills. | Reduced productivity and lower wages. |
| | Polanyi (1944). | Farmers shift costs on to the parish at a time when rural workers couldn't act collectively.<br>Wide use of bread scale and anti-union legislation (Anti-Combination Acts) facilitate unilateral wage reductions by employers. | Reduced productivity and lower wages. |
| Relief as **response** to a structural problem. Positive (or non-negative) outcomes. | Blaug (1964, 1963), Finer (1972), Baugh (1975), Cowherd (1977), Brundage (1978), Henriques (1979), Snell (1985), Huzel (1989), Sokoll (1993), Lees (1998), King (2000), Block and Somers (2003). | Bread scale not widely used; rural impoverishment caused by shift of industries to North and de-industrialization in the South; ongoing automation, enclosures. Economic contraction after 1815, deflation, limited credit, agricultural unemployment and social unrest. | Poor relief mitigated the effects of unemployment, helped meet basic needs. Agricultural productivity increased. Population grew, but because of reduced infant death rates. |

*Source*: Adapted from Block and Somers (2003 p. 292).

pay lower wages). For example, Barbara and John Hammond as well as Beatrice and Sidney Webb reached the conclusion that the growing cost of the poor laws was the result of tumultuous transformations in the rural economy, principally caused by land enclosure.[157] But they maintained a slightly more ambiguous position relative to the Report and deemed that the Speenhamland system was "a wrong and disastrous answer to certain difficult questions [ . . . ] [but wasn't] the one and original source of all evils."[158] They argued that the endurance of the allowance system was supported by large farmers and landlords who disliked other interventions.[159] Marx, Engels, and Polanyi may also be located in this bucket. A third cluster of empirical contributions points to a different story. Under the revisionist work by Mark Blaug and Daniel Baugh, for example, cash assistance and other relief transfers emerge in a completely different light.

The rebuttal delivered by revisionist literature centered on seven main points. First, Commissioners seemed to have enjoyed a certain flexibility in distilling information and shaping messages: they " . . . could pick and choose among the evidence supplied by them, giving prominence to the views they wished to recommend and suppressing views which contradicted them."[160] The Report's main text reflected the voluminous information included in the annexes minimally. The Commissioners circulated questions in rural districts, but " . . . not all parishes were visited, and it is impossible to tell whether the replies constitute anything like a representative sample."[161] Noteworthily, the production of the report involved an extensive collection of international practices. The extent to which England could learn from other countries' experiences was a question animating policymakers and official proceedings. Innovative reformers such as Chalmers in Scotland (Chapter 5) were invited to testify before Committee hearings in 1830;[162] and there are indications that pamphlets of the Hamburg system (Chapter 3) were provided to a member of parliament.[163] Alas, the wealth of global practices collected in a separate, 756-page annex didn't seem to have any palpable influence on the final Report (Box 6.5). In fact, "by the time that the foreign data had been assembled and published [ . . . ], the Poor Law of 1834 was already a statute of the realm."[164]

[157] Hammond and Hammond (1913) and Webb and Webb (1927),
[158] Hammond and Hammond (1913, p. 232).
[159] These included minimum wages ("once wages were raised to meet the rise in prices it would not be easy to reduce them when the famine was over") and allotments ("the large farmer, who did not like saucy labourers, and the shopkeeper, who knew the more food the labourer raised on his little estate the less he buy at the village store") (Hammond and Hammond 1913, p. 144, 159). In reference to the roundsman system, it allowed a farmer to pay workers "as little as he liked, knowing that the balance would be made up by the parish" (Webb and Webb 1927, p. 191).
[160] Finer (1972, p. 22).
[161] Blaug (1963, p. 157–59).
[162] Kerr and Wood (1911).
[163] De Schweinitz (1943).
[164] De Schweinitz (1943, p. 98).

## Box 6.5 The Seemingly Forgotten "Appendix (F)" on International Experiences

The process of collecting overseas experiences under the 1834 Report unfolded in three phases. At the beginning, members pursued such information " . . . through their personal friends, and in this manner obtained several valuable communications".[a] But as these proved limited, they requested Viscount Palmerston (Principal Secretary of State for the Foreign Department) to send a circular to the diplomatic body soliciting information on country-level legislation, principles, administration, benefit levels, funding, and performance of antipoverty practices. The circular, sent on August 12, 1833, included a select number of guiding questions and was later complemented by a second circular sent on November 30th, 1833 featuring a more structured questionnaire. This involved 64 questions spanning programs by profile of beneficiaries (e.g., vagrants, children), effects on incentives and behaviors, and expenditures and financing. The final materials stemming from these three sources of information (personal communications, the August circular, and the November one) included submissions from a total of 95 localities collected in a 756-page volume catalogued as "Appendix (F)—Foreign Communications."

Eventually, the timeframe accorded for completing and submitting information was compressed. For example, the second circular was sent less than three months ahead of the Report's final submission to His Majesty (Figure B6.1). As such, precious cross-country information couldn't be reflected in the Report nor was it made available to officials in advance of the Report's launch. For instance, my analysis of the appendix shows that, out of the total submission that included an actual date in the signature by the British official in loco (or 43 out of 95), only 35% had a date antecedent to the report's submission (note that the signature date doesn't mean *arrival* date in London). The Report acknowledged that the analysis " . . . did not extend beyond England and Wales," and that personal communications were inserted into the Appendix (" . . . a considerable portion [of the Appendix] is still in the press"). In fact, the materials that arrived before the submission date were sent to the printer on February 21, 1833, or the day following the Report's submission. The bulk of the remainder materials were printed probably over 1834–1835 after English translations were completed (the last material received was from Bahia on October 31, 1834). In fact, p. 7–9 of the Report discusses the somewhat hectic way in which responses to the two Palmerston circulars were received, their diversity in content, choices on how organize them, and whether they should be published in full or selectively.

While there seems to have been no real attempt to systematically distill findings from domestic, parish-level surveys, for international experiences there is at least a cross-country summary by Senior as part of the Appendix F preface. This was penned on May 16, 1835, or over a year after the report's submission.

[a] GoUK (1834a, p. iii).

Second, while the report contended that cash transfers depressed wages, the latter were, between 1795 and 1830, generally below Speenhamland's subsistence minimum. This prevented market-clearing mechanisms to reduce unemployment by further reductions in wages.[165] The response of Speenhamland, therefore, was an integration of wages so to provide the biological minimum to supply labor. The subsidy was modest in amount and increased less than proportionately with each additional child (see Chapter 2). The adequacy of the allowance system was continuously reduced between 1815 and 1834, with a net decline of one third over 1795–1834, making laborers' life "wretched and squalid in the extreme."[166] The amount of a typical Speenhamland subsidy represented " . . . about one-half of what a parsimonious Board of Guardians would [ . . . ] regard as bare subsistence."[167] This may have hardly spurred leisure and fertility, but there is some nuance: in the Speenhamland counties, it was argued, more generous relief may have promoted population growth, but via *reduction of infant mortality* (and increased registered births).[168]

Third, the Report claimed that employers could dismiss workers as they pleased knowing that parishes would provide cash transfers as a buffer. There were checks and balances: on the one hand, the Speenhamland funding system ("poor rates") was devised in a way that farmers-employers paid a major share of the cost.[169] On the other hand, the small size of most rural parishes allowed overseers to exercise local knowledge and judgment to determine the legitimacy of relief requests.[170] This perhaps made abuse of relief less likely.[171] Such built-in accountabilities may suggest that Speenhamland might have been more judiciously administered and fiscally prudent than claimed by the Commissioners.

A fourth set of findings contradicting the report involves the prevalence of the Speenhamland model. There was little difference between per capita food relief expenditures in parishes that adopted the bread scale model and those that used other relief interventions.[172] Furthermore, at the time of data collection for the report

[165] Blaug (1964). On market clearance, see Box 2.10 in Chapter 2.

[166] Hammond and Hammond (1913, p. 186).

[167] Webb and Webb (1927, p. 182).

[168] Blaug (1963).

[169] Blaug (1963) suggests that the Speenhamland model " . . . added to the wages paid by farmers with one hand what it took from them in rates with the other; the link between taxpayer and beneficiary was much closer than it is with modern income-support programs" (p. 176). See also Elder (1964).

[170] Blaug (1963), for instance, reports that " . . . two thirds of poor law authorities were concerned with only a few hundred families and, therefore, might be expected to be familiar with the personal circumstances of relief recipients" (p. 160).

[171] Sharpe (1997).

[172] Block and Somers (2003), Sokoll (1993).

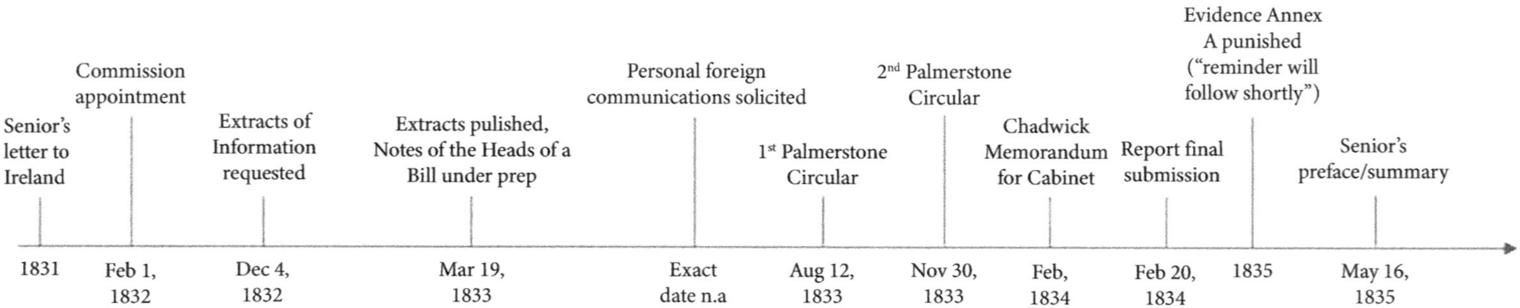


**Figure B6.1** Timeline of Appendix F production

*Source*: The author, based on Finer (1952) and GoUK (1834b).

" . . . the Speenhamland System as such had generally disappeared by 1832, even in the South."[173]

The fifth revisionist issue relates to political economy of support for Speenhamland by the rural elite. The program operated within *evolving* structural shifts and economic crises. The Speenhamland bread scale moved from providing support in an inflationary context to supporting unemployed workers in a deflationary environment. Before 1815, high food prices sparked food riots,[174] prompting local elites to address the threat of famine and disorder.[175] After the 1815–1820 period, relief expenditures dropped as wheat prices plummeted. The ensuing economic contraction reduced credit and sparked rural unemployment. Also in this case, the crisis fueled discontent (e.g., the "Captain Swing" riots) the eruption of which may have undermined elite support for the old poor laws as "riot containment."[176]

Next, in terms of specific operational issues, the cardinal "less eligibility" principle was more conceptual than practical.[177] The operationalization of the principle was difficult to fully comprehend because it was a relative principle, hence with infinite degrees of administrative discretion. Implementers struggled to identify what type of activities was the principle supposed to be compared against, or to define what constitutes a "sudden emergency" that could allow to drop it temporarily.[178]

Finally, while the 1834 did reduce public spending and the prevalence of "outdoor" cash transfers, it may have not enhanced people's welfare: Dr. Brindley, a speaker intervening at the West Midland Poor Laws conference of 1883, emphatically stated that:

> . . . the Poor Law has been so effectually administered as to have had the desired effect of decreasing pauperism, and this has been done by increasing human misery. In other words, [the law] acted in the direction of preventing application from the really deserving and respectable poor, who have preferred to starve and die rather than submit to a fearful humiliation for a doubtful benefit.[179]

[173] Blaug (1964, p. 231).

[174] In three instances—1795, 1802–1803, and 1812—the combination of two harvest failures in a row coincided with wartime limitations on agricultural imports from Europe. As a result, wheat prices were beyond the reach of most worker (Block and Somers 2003).

[175] Harrison (1988), Wells (1988).

[176] Hobsbawm and Rude (1968), Mandler (1990, 1987).

[177] Chadwick's assertiveness about the less eligibility principle transpires from his own words: " . . . I may claim to have been the first to demonstrate by irrefrangible evidence that which had not been seen by Mr Ricardo, Dr Malthus, or any other political economists, and which governs the question of a compulsory system of relief—that the condition of the recipient should not on the whole be more eligible than that of any laborer living on the fruits of his own industry . . . the master principle of 'administering relief'" (quoted in Finer 1952, p. 74).

[178] Chadwick had taken as reference the general level of independent laborers—an already low standard. While empirically grounded, his standard was a family consumption of 118 oz bread/person/week, which itself would yield at best 2,250 calories/day (no fewer than 3,500 calories/day were needed for an active outdoor life). Even the new workhouse dietary guidance could not reduce its scale below 129 oz of solid food/person/week. Chadwick acknowledged that " . . . the diet of a gaol is generally more profuse than that of the workhouse" (Finer 1952, p. 83).

[179] GoUK (1884, p. 20).

In fact, employers weren't *induced* to increase wages as supposed by the Report's theory of change, and these fell.[180] Not only did wages dwindle, but these were now not supplemented by the allowance system. As a result, workers' real income dropped significantly. One reason for the wages' fall was the "gang system": the workhouse led workers to accept very low-paid jobs, and the consequent impoverishment drove the rest of the family on to the labor market. Those new addition in labor supply further drive wages down.[181]

Blaug's counter-indictment of the report was unequivocal: " . . . [n]ot only did [the Commissioners] fail in any way to take account of the special problem of structural unemployment in the countryside, but what evidence they did present consisted of little more than picturesque anecdotes of maladministration."[182] A year later, he added that "... [t]he Report of 1834 would have us believe that the causal chain ran from outdoor relief to low wages. On the weight of the evidence, however, it is more reasonable to think that low wages were the cause and outdoor relief to large families the effect."[183]

## Explaining influence and recurrence

While flawed in hindsight, the 1834 report was nevertheless influential. Establishing empirical causality between an approach at a specific time and subsequent developments elsewhere is challenging. However, literature produced over the past decades can help identify salient tipping points and offer some clues on the mechanisms of influence and transmission of ideas.

The 1834 principles were influential in a range of contexts. As discussed in Chapter 4, for instance, they played a role in shaping crisis responses in India and Sudan. In Russia, members of the 1892 Grot Commission tasked with reforming public assistance in the country "were undoubtedly influenced by the 1834 English Poor Law, which in their interpretation established a model system of poor relief."[184]

In China, the rhetoric on workhouses was like England's. By the mid-1800s, the country had inherited four types of indoor assistance.[185] These institutions didn't

[180] See Blaug (1963, Annex D, p. 182–183).
[181] The spiral appears to come to a halt only when the Corn Laws were repealed (Finer 1952).
[182] Blaug (1963, p. 177).
[183] Blaug (1964, p. 241–242). Similarly, Fred Block and Margaret Somers concluded that "... [i]nstead of bread scales undermining work effort, we get a picture of a rural population facing broad structural forces that undermine their capacities for self-support. In this context it is difficult to see increasing poor relief as anything but a partial remedy to problems outside the control of the rural poor. [ . . . ] In sum, the Speenhamland myth was created in the years of agricultural downturn to divert blame for a deep agricultural crisis away from government policy [like the return to the gold parity in 1819] and toward the rural poor who were the major victims of the economic downturn" (Block and Somers 2003, p. 308, 312).
[184] Lindenmeyr (1996, p. 82). Konstantin Grot was the chairman of the Commission that was approved by Alexander III and which operated between 1892 and 1897.
[185] These included "nurture homes" (*yang-ji yuan*) which were locally managed and funded. These provided transfers in cash, food, and cloths exclusively for residents in local jurisdictions. "Universal relief halls" (*pu-ji tang*) distributed similar transfers, although their management was affected by an unstable fiscal base. This was due to a large role played by local private donations in addition to state subsidies.

involve work requirements and other conditionalities. Fiscal challenges began to harden attitudes toward poverty. By the late 1890s and early 1900s, poverty was increasingly interpreted as a pathology detrimental to the country's aspirations, pride, and national predicament.[186] Work would become increasingly central to poor relief, and regimes of detention and labor redefined provisions.[187]

The Qing embracement of industrial training centers and penal systems reforms led to the establishment of workhouses (*xi-yi suo*) as a key relief device.[188] These changes were informed by international practices. External approaches were already on display in the country, such as local missionaries managing charities in line with Western's wider use of conditionalities. Such methods appealed to local elites, and Japanese penology, Anglo-American sociology, and commercial activities seemed to all have provided some level of international perspective and inspiration to Chinese reformers.[189]

As a result, vagrant shelters started to provide job training to its inmates, such as in Tianjin 1878 and the following year in Shanghai. Universal relief halls required work as a condition for relief. And Japanese-style workhouses mushroomed:[190] Tianjin adopted it in 1904 (for criminals) and 1905 (for vagrants); Beijing's version for both criminals and non-criminals was established in 1906; and Shanghai, Chengdu, and other cities following rapidly.[191] By the early 1900s, Qing China had three indoor institutions: nurture homes for those "unable to work"; workhouses for petty criminals and vagrants; and "nurture-teaching homes" for the "unruly." It was observed that "[t]his shift from the centuries-old state relief system based on Confucian benevolence and Buddhist kindness to Western-style workhouses and poorhouses based on 'compulsory labour in exchange for relief' demonstrates the influence of Western social ideas and institutions."[192] Eventually, in 1935 the government consolidated the various indoor institutions into a single "relief home" (*jiuji yuan*).[193]

From the 1940s, "universalist" perspectives helped reshape the perception of poverty.[194] The view changed from the 1920s interpretation of poverty as a crime resulting from laziness to that of a social condition stemming from war and other

The halls, however, were accessible to non-residents too. The other two indoor modalities included soup kitchens (*zhou chang*) and vagrants' shelters (*qi-liu suo*). See Hu (2021).

[186] Hammond (2019).

[187] Chen (2012).

[188] Lipkin (2005).

[189] Hu (2021), Chen (2012). According to Reynolds (1993), in 1897–1898 the Hunan province initiated the reform of its *baojia* security and surveillance system based on international experiences (reform plans were drawn by a leading diplomat who served in the US and Japan).

[190] A description of a workhouse in Osaka is offered by a *Hiogo News* journalist who visited the premises in 1874. The workhouse, named *Hin-in*, included 180 inmates—85 of whom were adult men, 15 women, and the rest children—who as ex-beggars were forcibly taken to the institution (they were native of the city, but lacked family support). Men worked during the day, women were thought trades, children got basic education, and all were "free to leave whenever he or she could give satisfactory proof that they could earn an honest living outside" (Hiogo News 1874).

[191] Rowe (2017), Dryburgh (2016), Stapleton (2000). Drawing on hundreds of letters directed to municipal officials by workhouses inmates and their families, Chen (2012) documented the emergence of such institutions in Beijing and Shanghai and related changing attitudes toward poverty.

[192] Hu (2021, p. 63).

[193] Hu (2021).

[194] ILO (1942), Ma (2012). Beveridge's report was translated in Chinese in 1943.

factors.[195] The newly established Ministry of Social Affairs, which was staffed with a number of Western-educated social scientists, including its minister, promulgated a Social Relief Law in 1943. The law codified the state's responsibility for relief, emphasized the role of prevention as opposed to ex-post assistance, and extended coverage beyond specific categories of beneficiaries (e.g., seniors).

Early approaches in the United States were rooted in British approaches.[196] Yet the 1834 developments may also have influenced later developments in the country. For example, during the Depression of the 1870s, "... many businessmen tended to lean toward the British system [...] of 1834. States [...] disclosed a remarkable unanimity in the spirit of ferocity and oppression against a class of unfortunates who, without fault of their own, are out of work."[197] In the same year of the 1834 Law, for instance, New York passed the County Poorhouse Act that decreed that no adult able-bodied person (18–50 years of age) was eligible for assistance except in the workhouse or prison.[198] And as discussed earlier, civil society approaches enshrined the less eligibility principle in their operations.[199] Figure 6.9 provides a simplified illustration of the channels through which the 1834 principles have influenced development in the United States.

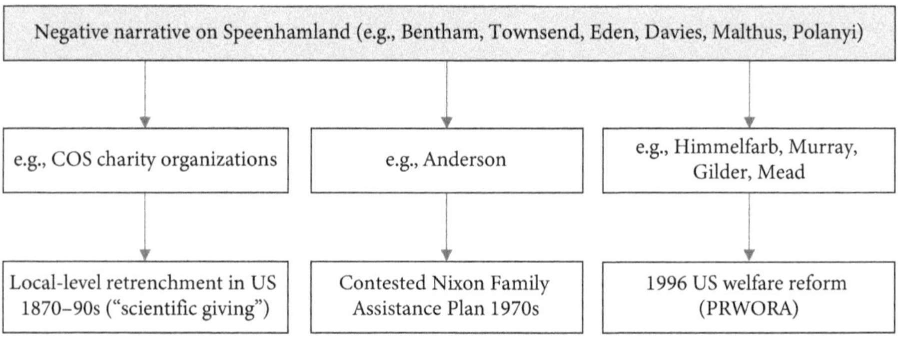


**Figure 6.9** Illustrative conduits spreading the 1834 narratives in the United States.
*Source*: The author.

As Figure 6.9 suggests, the influence occurred not only in two episodes of reform described here, but also in the attempted reforms chronicled in Chapter 5, most notably the process of developing Nixon's Family Assistance Plan (FAP). In that context, one contrarian voice in the administration was Martin Anderson. At a particular moment when Nixon was leaning for a negative income tax (NIT), he wrote a highly critical, cautionary six-pager for the President titled "A Short History of Family Social

[195] Hu (2021).
[196] As highlighted by William Quigley, "... [a]s early as 1647, Rhode Island proclaimed that the core of their poor relief system was to be based on English poor laws" (Quigley 1996b, p.43). Bremer (2020) argued that the first form of (private) assistance given to needy colonists was provided by the Native Americans who assisted Columbus and other Europeans.
[197] Bernstein (1956, p. 76–77).
[198] Hannon (1984).
[199] Pimpare (2002).

Security Systems." This simply consisted of a sequence of excerpts from Polanyi's (1944) chapter 7 on the Speenhamland system.[200]

The intended message was that by establishing economic security as a right through income supplements to the *working* poor, the FAP (at the time named Family Security System) was bound to repeat the purported disastrous outcomes of the Speenhamland experience.[201] There are accounts that Nixon was alarmed about the memo and asked a range of advisers for feedback (see Box 5.6).

The similarities between the 1834 debate and those later unfolding in the United States are particularly evident in the content of pilots designed to inform the FAP over the 1960s–1970s. As experimental results started to emerge, one of the most consequential findings was a purported effect on marriage dissolution. According to an influential study, such rate was about 40–60% higher for participants than the control group.[202] The result led Daniel Moynihan, one of the FAP political supporters, to disavow the program[203] at a Congressional hearing: " . . . I'm shocked to look at these findings and say we scientists were wrong."[204] Such results may have curtailed the Carter administration's prospects to institute a guaranteed income scheme.[205]

However, Steensland points out that such "welfare mess" " . . . was not an objective problem. It was constructed as one."[206] Findings were counterintuitive because " . . . the least generous negative income tax plans, which offered about the same or lower cash payments as did AFDC, induced the largest destabilizing effect, while the most generous plan had essentially no destabilizing effect. This is the opposite of the theoretically expected result."[207] A careful empirical reexamination of the SIME/DIME dataset shows that there was basically no family dissolutions.[208] It turns out that negative effects " . . . dissipated when the separate plans and extra years of the experiment are included."[209] Subsequent studies also found no effects on threatening marital stability.[210] Table 6.3 dissects revisionist findings for five dimensions.

In terms of labor market outcomes, the experiments had a mildly negative impact on labor supply, although effects were of limited size and mostly statistically insignificant.[211] According to economist Robert Solow, " . . . there is a labor supply effect, as

[200] One of the quotes reported by Steensland (2008a) was that " . . . . [o]nly when a grave deterioration of the productive capacities of the masses resulted [ . . . ] did the necessity of abolishing the unconditional right of the poor to relief impose itself upon the consciousness of the community. [ . . . ] The outcome was merely the pauperization of the masses, who almost lost their human shape in the process." As discussed, Polanyi was critical about Speenhamland, but not for the reasons advanced by the 1834 commissioners.

[201] Anderson (1978).

[202] The finding is presented in Groeneveld et al. (1980) and Hannan et al. (1977).

[203] Forget (2011).

[204] Quoted in Bregman (2017, p. 284).

[205] Levine et al. (2005). Before the Carter administration, NIT proposals were unsuccessfully drafted by Weinberger in 1974 and Griffith in 1976.

[206] Steensland (2008, p. 223).

[207] Cain (1986, p. 75)

[208] Cain and Wissoker (1990a).

[209] (Cain 1986, p. 89). See also the reply by Hannan and Tuma (1990) and counter-reply by Cain and Wissoker (1990b).

[210] Marinescu (2018), Widerquist (2005)

[211] Moffitt and Kehrer (2012).

Table 6.3 Revisionist Evidence on Negative Income Tax (NIT) Pilots.

| Effects | Source |
|---|---|
| **Labor supply** | |
| Overall negative effect on employment (extensive margin), but not statistically significant: Only the experiment with most generous transfers and largest sample size (SIME/DIME) showed statistically significant effects (4 percentage point decline in the employment rate).<br>Effects on hours worked (intensive margin):<br>- NIT experiments show a negative impact on hours worked, though the effect is not always statistically significant;<br>- On average, the reduction in labor supply was between two and four weeks of full-time employment over a year;<br>- Mincome* reduction in hours worked by 1% for men, 3% for wives, and 5% for unmarried women (also statistically not significant).<br><br>Parametric models to identify income and substitution effects:<br>- Income effect: $1 increase in cash payments decreased earnings by 6–10 cents.<br>- Substitution effect: $1 increase in hourly wage increased earnings by 8–17 cents;<br>- Canadian Mincome: Both are insignificant, and the estimated income effect is zero;<br>- Wives are more sensitive to the substitution effect, i.e., implicit taxes on their earnings, than to the income effect. The opposite is true for husbands.<br><br>Likely overestimation of labor supply effects and caution for results interpretation:<br>- NIT recipients underreported earnings to get larger benefits (e.g., Seattle/Denver experiments relied on self-reported earnings information, rather than using official government records);<br>- In the Gary experiment, the entire negative effect on hours worked can be explained by misreporting;<br>- Selective attrition: treated families who received no payment (because they had higher outside earnings) and therefore likely had no labor supply response to the NIT were more likely to leave the experiment, affecting the sample;<br>- Diverse econometric models deployed limiting comparability;<br>- Highly technical and complex reports, hard to interpret for non-specialists;<br>- Possible that unemployed participants waited longer to enter the labor market to find better job matching (or quitting jobs in favor of searching for better ones);<br>- Likely changes within the household for unpaid work/care and training. | Bastagli (2020).Marinescu (2018), Widerquist (2005), Matthews (2014), Hum and Simpson (1993), Ashenfelter and Plant (1990), Burtless (1986), Ashenfelter (1986), Robins (1985); Aaron (1975); Hall (1975). |

| Effects | Source |
|---|---|
| **Food security and nutrition**<br>No systematic evidence: Rural NIT in Iowa and North Carolina showed positive impacts on the quality of nutrition. | Salkind and Haskins (1982). |
| **Education**<br>Generally positive effects:<br>- School attendance, grades, and test scores for the children of participants who received the NIT were typically higher;<br>- New Jersey experiment, NIT of mid-range generosity increased odds of completing high school by 25–30%;<br>- Impact on test scores was larger for younger children and for children from poorer families. | Forget (2011), Hanushek (1986), Salkind and Haskins (1982), Maynard and Murnane (1979). |
| **Health**<br>Only available for Canadian Mincome:<br>- NIT reduced hospitalization by 8.5% compared to matched control towns;<br>- Effects were particularly large for mental health, accidents, and injuries. | Forget (2011). |
| **Marriage and fertility**<br>Overall, no impact on marriage and fertility:<br>- Highly disputed effects on divorce;<br>- In the Gary NIT, treatment decreased fertility and increased birth weights;<br>- Mincome had no effect on divorce, fertility, or birth weights. | Cain and Wissoker (1990a), Salkind and Haskins (1982), Groeneveld et al. (1980). |

*Source*: The author.
*= Manitoba Basic Annual Income Experiment.

every economist thought there would be; but it could hardly be described as large enough to jeopardize the work ethic."[212]

With the rise of advanced statistical methods and econometric analysis in the 1960s–1970s, new ways of diagnosing and conceptualizing poverty emerged. For instance, the use of randomized controlled trials in cash transfers were first used in the NIT demonstration pilots.[213] Simultaneously, some observers and government officials of the time noted that such methods tended to alter the way in which poverty

[212] Solow (1986, p. 220). Stronger effects were detected among wives, followed by women-headed (single-parent) households. Effects on husbands were very limited. However, impacts were largely driven by (and only had statistically significant effects for) the Seattle/Denver scheme—the largest among the trials. Also, some methodological issues may have led to under or over-estimation of effects (Burtless 1986). Hall (1975) contested findings with disaggregated effects by ethnicity.

[213] Moffitt (2003c).

was understood. In their view, this trend may have shifted the balance away from structural forces that generate poverty and in favor of individual-level incentives guided by rational choices.[214]

While the rhetoric against cash transfers is varied, it has generally succeeded in a key outcome—that is, in shifting the pendulum toward narratives that embrace, corroborate, and justify the notion of poverty stemming from individuals' behaviors, thereby moving their moralization—in Michael Katz's terms "improving poor people"—centerstage.[215] Such individualistic, incentives-oriented mindset was effectively used by Charles Murray for a powerful rejection of the welfare system. Through the use of illustrative examples of a low-income couple ("Harold and Phyllis"), he argued that " . . . from an economic point of view, getting married is dumb" and contended that economic dependency was induced by the welfare system and emerged as a rational choice among a range of alternatives faced by poor people.[216] His analysis was heavily criticized,[217] but "the damage had been done in the public mind."[218] Others argued that previous attempted GMI reforms focused solely on the rights of poor people—and not on their responsibilities—hence calling for a renewed focus on the obligation to work and toward family.[219] Similarly, commentators reproposed the labor market as the only legitimate source of economic security, associated poverty with the choice of not working, and revamped a drive to discipline the poor.[220] Table 6.4 lays out key arguments against cash transfers in recent centuries.

The recurrence of such influence has been codified. For instance, Albert Hirschman offers a theory involving three interconnected theses of "perversity," "futility," and "jeopardy."[221] The perversity thesis asserts that well-intended policies would ultimately have the perverse effect of backfiring—it is not just that their objectives will not be achieved, but policies will also generate unexpected negative impacts. They will exacerbate the problem intended to be addressed:[222] the notion of a seemingly harsh policy at individual level, but one that would ultimately yield societal benefits, permeated the 1834 Report.[223] The futility thesis establishes that

[214] See Kershaw (1972), Levine (1975), and Rivlin (1971).
[215] Katz (1995).
[216] Murray (1984, p.160). See also Murray (1994) and Manhattan Institute for Policy Research (1985).
[217] Katz (1989). See McLanahan et al. (1985) for a critique of Murray' Losing Ground book.
[218] Steensland (2008, p. 224).
[219] Mead (1986).
[220] For example, see Gilder (1981).
[221] Hirschman (1991).
[222] This mirrors Adam Smith's insight on self-regulating markets; see the discussion in Friedman (2021, p. 4).
[223] " . . . [t]he logic behind the rhetoric is impeccable—if assistance is actually hurting the poor by creating dependence, then denying it is not cruel but compassionate, as it restores their morally necessary autonomy" (Block and Somers 2014, p. 157). Lubbock (1895) quotes the 1834 poor law commission report claiming, in reference to the workhouse, that " . . . even if it be in some rare cases a hardship, it appears from the evidence that it is a hardship to which the good of society requires the applicant to submit. The express or implied ground of his application is that he is in danger of perishing from want. Requesting to be rescued from that danger out of the property of others, he must accept assistance on the terms, whatever they may be, which the common welfare requires" (ibid, p. 41). Similarly, Browell, a member of parliament, argued in 1890 that " . . . [r]efusing out-relief and insisting upon the house-test might in individual cases

**Table 6.4** Matrix of Key Arguments against Cash Transfers over Time.

| | Late 1700s/Early 1800s | Late 1800s/Early 1900s | Late 1900s/Early 2000s |
|---|---|---|---|
| Work incentives | Townsend (1786); Eden (1797); Davies (1795); GoUK (1834a); de Tocqueville (1835); Spencer (1843). | Hyslop (1894); MacKay (1894); Pell (1890). | Kaus (1992). |
| Fertility and marriage | Malthus (1798). | Darwin (1871); Sumner (1880). | Murray (1984, 2006); Gilder (1981); Greenberg (2002). |
| Morality, character, independence, thrift, "culture of poverty." | | Lowell (1890); Dugdale (1877); McColloch (1888); Feder (1936); Holmes (1897, in Patterson 1994); Riis (1890); Nill et al (1891); Gurteen (1882); Aschrott (1902); Bishop (1902). | Moynihan (1965), Lewis (1966); Banfield (1974); Himmelfarb (1995, 1984a, 1984b, 1970); Olasky (1992); Schwartz (2000); Niskanen (1996). |
| Superiority of private relative to public relief. | | Lowell (1884); McGonnigle (1894); Gladden (1892). | Mead (1996, 1994); Gingrich (1996); Rector (2000). |
| Administrative limits, negative effects of taxation, indefinite expansion. | Mill (1848). | Fawcett (1871); Loch (1895, 1893); Garland (1891); Fowle (1881); Spender (1892). | |

*Source*: The author.

attempts at reforms would invariably lead to disappointment and not affect change. Alleged reforms would, in other words, be illusory and superficial, and underlying societal structural drivers would be left unaffected. Finally, the jeopardy thesis holds that while the proposed policy may even be desirable, it involves unacceptable societal costs wiping out previous, hard-won achievements.

appear cruel and hard, but the general good must not be sacrificed to considerations raised by exceptional cases" (ibid, p. 47).

The arguments are most typically used as conservative talking points against progressive ideas, although there are cases where the latter deployed the same logic to assault the former.[224] As Hirschman himself explained in the last chapter of his book, the treatise was meant to highlight a few "danger signals" on the road toward constructive dialogue. Those signals were represented by the polarizing and reflexive theses that (mostly) conservatives and (some) progressives adopt and that ultimately stifle national dialogue. His analysis represents, therefore, not an attempt to dismiss arguments from either sides—that is, the fact that partisan arguments are somewhat repeated and predictable doesn't make them refutable per se. Instead, he calls out "the rhetoric of intransigence," which grossly lacks nuance and balance, and argues for dialogue away from the extremes.

The interplay of the three theses in general, and the power of the perversity thesis in particular, shaped intellectual tactics against cash transfers for centuries.[225] In fact, the perversity thesis is deeply rooted into the British poor relief experience of the 1800s (Box 6.6).

### Box 6.6 Skepticism of Local Poor Relief Administrators in the 1800s

The collection of extracts included in Lubbock (1895) offers a curated, 300-page compilation of quotes on poor relief drawing in large part from British local administrators and officials' statements, conference proceedings, and annual reports produced over the 1800s. Among them, here are ten select examples of cases that epitomize the perversity thesis:

> "*A prodigal system of out-relief will in the long run defeat the object in view and increase the misery which it is intended to alleviate.*" E. Wodehouse, 1872
>
> "*I think we ought gradually, if possible, to do away with out-door relief, not merely to relieve expense, but for the benefit of the poor themselves.*" E. Spencer, 1876
>
> "*The out-door relief system tends to make men poor, to keep them poor, to keep them down and to keep them back; to create the very poverty it subsequently attempts most imperfectly to alleviate.*" Rev. J. Hervey, 1883

[224] A progressive counter-argument, conveyed in no less-ideological terms, to the perversity thesis would typically claim that *not* taking the contemplated action would bring disastrous effects; in reference to the futility thesis, the perspective policy would be backed by "historical forces already on the march" (being "on the right side of history"); and in relation to the conservative jeopardy argument, a progressive rebuttal would argue that old and new reforms would mutually reinforce each other (see chapter 7 in Hirschman 1991).

[225] Block and Somers (2014).

> *"Out-relief instead of being a kindness to the people is deeply injurious to them [. . .] Out-relief is the chief cause of pauperism."* T. Garland, 1888 and 1891
>
> *"An out-relief system manufactures paupers wholesale, and makes any improvementin the condition of the poor impossible."* A. Crowder, 1888
>
> *" . . . nine-tenth of the Poor Law applicants are created by the system, and if it was not for the system, those people would not have existed in their present conditions at all."* W. Vallance, 1889
>
> *"To those who desire improved administration out-relief stands condemned for two chief reasons. Firstly, because it perpetuates the misery it professes to relieve, and secondly because of its cruelty."* B. Fleming, 1890
>
> *"It is the mal-administration of the Poor Law in the past which has made so much misery in our parishes."* C. Willes, 1890
>
> *"An outdoor relief system provokes want, and tends to increase starvation."* C. Loch, 1892
>
> *"Guardians cannot indulge themselves in this easy way of giving relief without causing a great amount of suffering, and doing great injury to the character and condition of people."* Rev. W. Bury, 1895

## 6.5 Conclusions

This chapter outlined reform illustrations stretching over 500 years. Experiences emerging from such long period were organized around three main reform pathways: "scientific" rationalization via change in provider, centralization within the same provider, and blend models. Three main lessons stand out from such historical trajectories.

First, reforms presented diversity and continuities. The protagonists of reforms were diverse, including lay administrators, ecclesiastical authorities, civil society, and private sector. The mechanics of transitions differed, too, ranging from sophisticated assignment of institutional roles to like-minded reformers to grassroot community mobilization. The scale of reforms varied as well, from continent-wide reconfigurations to city-based initiatives. Some of the reforms were short-lived, while the echoes of others still reverberate in modern debates. Reform experiences were not isolated cases: even in the 1500s, authorities were connected through a relatively vibrant web of exchanges and learning whereby examples of other cities' reforms were cross-referenced.

Yet, the overall origin and direction of those diverse experiences were consistent: reforms attempted to restore control over a perceived or real chaotic situation and decline in living standards. The decline was epitomized by forms of purported excessive or indiscriminate cash transfers—a sign of decay that equally ill-suited intellectual reason and religious precepts. Reorganizing assistance meant helping restoring order. A cardinal aspect of the process was that "distinction must be made between the relief offered to the able-bodied and to the sick and infirm. It is the classification of the population which forms the foundation of the existing system."[226] Vulnerable adults with a low income or who were out of work were the main target of reforms. Differentiating "sturdy beggars" from other populations was mostly pursued by hardening eligibility and receipt. Borrowing from the concepts outlined in Chapter 2, a largely "structuralist" problem was treated in "individualist" terms. In brief, the change ongoing in societies generated social, economic, and moral disruptions; these generated a need for assistance, which often outstripped the capacity of states to provide it; the reform of cash transfers was then meant to reduce chaos and bring back order.

Second, a generally consistent pattern emerges in terms of reform outcomes. Making assistance stricter appears to have been successful in reducing people "on the rolls." Among those supported, the share of those served via tighter provisions rose. Effects on public spending would be mixed: while in some cases they declined markedly (they would in England in the 1800s, but not necessarily in the United States in the 1980–1990s), the administrative costs entailed by stricter measures would soar across the board. The effects on "graduation" of beneficiaries didn't materialize as hoped, and soon enough the relentless structural forces of economic and non-economic change would exert new pressures for assistance. The idea that "[o]ld remedies for poverty and social disorder return in new guises" seems broadly confirmed in the examined reform patterns.[227]

Third, reforms of cash transfers were accompanied, especially in the past couple of centuries, by tactical narratives. The rhetoric against cash was generally based on plausible, seemingly benign, and common-sense arguments that gradually infused transition processes. If labor markets were considered the premier source of "legitimate" income, the injection of another source of "unearned" cash was bound to be deleterious for both the recipient and society. Hirschman codifies the cyclical process of generation and use of narratives exhaustively. The rhetorical argument that cash assistance was part of the problem was clearly rebuked by revisionist evidence.[228] A large body of empirical literature reversed the direction of causality: following historian Anne Digby, " . . . [cash transfers were] essentially a response to population growth, under-employment, and low wages, rather than their cause."[229]

[226] Loveday (1914, p. 85).
[227] McStay Adams (2023a, p. 5).
[228] See for example the Science article by Duncan et al. (1988).
[229] Digby (1982, p. 13).

# 7
# Where Do We Go from Here?

> ... we can perhaps learn to free ourselves from a politics of nostalgia, and see new sorts of futures [ . . . ] that only a properly historicized sense of the future might be able to detect.
>
> **James Ferguson (2012, p. 511)**

The chapter offers two sets of reflections. These involve an equal number of observations—four devoted to "looking back" and another four geared at "looking ahead." The former envision an array of issues around how different trajectories of reform shared a common goal; the conflation of causes and effects, and the role of history in providing a sense of direction in causality; the likely competing goals of addressing "needs" and reducing "rolls"; and explaining the stickiness of narratives.

These issues may provide some indication for navigating the future of cash transfers. However, additional considerations are also laid out for prospective experiences. Projecting our collective, 2,500-year-long experience into the future is a challenging task. Yet the relatively rapid historical excursus offered in this volume may hold some insights for inferring likely pathways. I hazard some brief extrapolations with a view of not laying out a prescriptive blueprint, but rather offering a set of interconnected observations around which more consideration and exploration might be required. As such, the "looking ahead" section discusses the implications from continuity in practices; the importance of dispelling four long-standing and recent "myths"; the risks from the growingly technocratic nature of cash transfer provisions; and the "big question" on poverty inherency in economic systems and the role of cash transfers within them.

## 7.1 Looking back

### Different reforms trajectories, shared direction (and similar results)

Even if implemented in a relatively uniform way, the multiplicity of goals that cash transfers pursued is striking. The book reviewed the role of cash transfer in three broad domains, like economic transformation, state building, and social and political stability, which in turn illuminated a dozen sub-goals. Such application

*Timely Cash*. Ugo Gentilini, Oxford University Press. © Ugo Gentilini (2024). DOI: 10.1093/9780191994982.003.0007

across a broad array of purposes reveals the flexibility that cash transfer can offer to policymakers. Cash transfers facilitated economic change in industrializing England; they were part of China's transition to communism as well as the post-Mao era; in ancient Greece, the Roman empire, and post-colonial Unites States, war created the conditions for some seminal provisions of cash for veterans and their families; and responses to droughts (in Botswana) and famines (in India) would build the foundations for subsequent social protection. Not all experiences yielded encouraging outcomes: for example, attempts to reintegrate people in the labor market in Elberfeld and Indianapolis generated modest results. The religious impulse to support people in need followed a prioritization of deservingness in both Catholic and Islamic experiences, and the debates between ecclesiastical and secular authorities (like in Spain in the 1500s and in the 1800s in Scotland) present conflicting implications for design. And if cash transfers were part of a broader communal philosophy in ancient Athens, they also reinforced racial segmentation in South Africa and Fiji.

Such diversity in goals nevertheless tended to follow an overall pattern of reform. The sweeping nature of economic and social transformation generated disruptions and prompted demand to re-establish social order. At times, the state was deemed better suited to reorganize relief; other times, civil society took up the mantle. But the direction of travel was consistent, that is, to tight provisions, contain spending, and provide benefits only to those "truly deserving." The historical record shows that such reforms—whether entailing a change in provider, conducted by the same providers, or hybrid models—reduced coverage consistently; contained spending in many cases; and seldom "graduated" beneficiaries.

## Is cash the villain? A long-term perspective on poverty causes and responses

One reason why cash transfers were (and are) highly contested is because the poverty problem itself is disputed. Some observers have contended that the identification of poverty sources is "hidden in almost impenetrable obscurity."[1] Sorting through structural and individualist causes—or the tantalizing dilemma of whether circumstances are more powerful than the capabilities of the individual to overcome them—has been (and still is) subject of intense debate. Ascertaining where responsibility ends and where solidarity begins is tricky. This poses a limit to whether causal explanations can ever be fully objective and unambiguous—and for that matter, whether they can inform cash transfer debates adequately.

While history contemplates multiple poverty explanations, a long-run perspective can help observe an overall direction in causality. Cash transfers have been "indicted"

[1] Munsterberg (1904, p. 340).

and compared to "weeds in a garden lot,"[2] a "spreading epidemic,"[3] an "infectious temptation,"[4] a "narcotic,"[5] a "poison,"[6] a "disease that mingles in the blood of children,"[7] and a "monster destroying its own parents."[8] And transfer claimants were depicted as "social cannibals with their hands upon the throat of society,"[9] "vultures flocking to the carrion,"[10] "nest of vipers,"[11] "alligators" and "wolves,"[12] and a "swarm of bees ceasing to store honey and basking in the sunshine of constant expectation."[13]

Cash programs have been introduced, expanded, adapted, and downscaled to help manage—or resist—sweeping forces of change. At first sight, it might appear that transfers are about "poverty," "vulnerability," and other forms of absolute or relative deprivation. These problems are real. Yet they are a manifestation of deeper challenges. The value of a historical perspective is that it reveals how embedded transfers are into wider forces playing a premier role in poverty generation.

In the long-run, needs are generated because of shifts in the composition of the economy, of barriers in labor market participation and remuneration, of rampant social discrimination, of glaring imbalances in political voice, etc. While these quandaries are slippery and subject to multiple interpretations, they are often bigger than what most governments can handle in short political cycles. They present dilemmas in perpetual motion affecting societies over centuries: whether it was Imperial China, Northern Italy in the late 1400s, Antwerp in the late 1700s, or New York in the late 1800s, the preceding chapters show that transfers helped countries mitigate, albeit imperfectly, the turbulence of structural economic change. They were a short-term response to a systemic problem.

The pattern outlined in this book posits that if cash transfers help with the manifestation of those problems, they can also be charged with their causes. Cash transfers can become a scapegoat for polities' inability or unwillingness to tackle the core generators of inequities. As needs become entrenched, outcries for people "still on the rolls" and that "never graduate" ensue. Reforms along restrictive lines may attempt to make access to transfers more stringent, but not necessarily address the underlying needs.

The more we extend the time horizon, the more structural explanations of poverty gather salience. And as their explanative power rises, it illuminates the constant oscillation in framing of cash transfers as causes and responses to the poverty problem. Without a historical perspective, this oscillation would be less visible and the cause-effect relationship more blurred.

[2] Riis (1890).
[3] Almy (1900).
[4] Lowell (1894), quoted in Pimpare (2002, p.110).
[5] Niskanen (1996).
[6] Bishop (1902).
[7] Brace (1880).
[8] Barnett (1899).
[9] Glenn (1892).
[10] Nill et al. (1891).
[11] Pimpare (2002).
[12] The claim was made at a session of the US House of Representatives on March 24, 1995 (Pimpare 2002).
[13] Barbour, quoted in Nill et al. (1891).

## Rolls ≠ needs

In principle, the reduction of cash transfer provisions should be the result of corresponding declines in need—a broad-based improvement in well-being that makes transfers unnecessary. Instead, the experiences presented in previous chapters recount instances where reductions in coverage weren't spurred by more conducive social and economic conditions, but by political and institutional forces. Rather than operating on the causes of the problem, those forces intervened on removing the manifestation of it. The yardstick of success in addressing "dependency" was the hardening and restructuring of provisions, not the amelioration of underlying conditions that perpetuated reliance on cash transfers.

Herbert Gans pinned down the issue to a basic choice: the problem, he argued, "... is really in the heart of the [ . . . ] economy, which simply does not need all the unemployed looking for work at a living wage and which cannot provide for all the working poor who require higher wages to support their families." Hence societies have a choice to "either remaking the economy so that it produces full employment at a living wage, or altering public beliefs about welfare so that the Government will provide the [unemployed] and underpaid with a decent income."[14]

Calls for "reducing the rolls" are a constant feature in the history of cash transfers: Caesar's effort to halve the number of food subsidy beneficiaries at the beginning of the first millennium; reforms across Europe in the 1500s; Britain's curbing of relief spending in the 1800s; instances of reducing recipients of cash transfers in 1890s, 1980s and 1990s United States—all speak to a similar core set of issues. They show that the number of beneficiaries—the "rolls"—have grown out of proportion, that such level of coverage and spending is unwarranted, and that "reform" would be required to restore a more sustainable level of provisions.

Results from those reforms have, in many cases, undoubtedly led to cost savings in the short run. Coverage also decreased, although in many cases, it was less participation, not fewer expenditures, that drove the decline. This is because programs were made more stringent in requirements, making it harder to participate despite being eligible in principle. Mainstream shifts to workhouses as a participation deterrent are a case in point.

In the medium term, however, another force entered the equation. This made the extent to which cost savings were achieved more uncertain: in fact, stringency in participation required enhanced investments in monitoring and enforcement relative to unconditional cash transfers. This led to sizable increases in administrative costs in several post-reform programs.

What happened to those who stopped being covered or participating in cash programs? It is possible that some beneficiaries could manage without support. But for the overwhelming majority, exclusion didn't mean proof of self-reliance. It meant that the state shifted the costs of provision onto people themselves. Left on their

[14] Gans (1971b, p. 26).

own devices, ex-beneficiaries may have lowered the bar of living conditions to the point where it could be hardly lowered further. Stephen Pimpare argued that such retrenchment of assistance did play a role in the rise of incarceration, asylums, and orphanages (and related expenses) as well as overwhelming informal and civil society capacities: " . . . by misreading the meaning of declines in relief receipt—by resuming that they constituted evidence that prior relief had been unnecessary or overgenerous—[decision makers] were unwilling or unable to identify the immiseration and growing discontent among the poor and hidden classes as a product of reform."[15]

## Why narratives stick

The analysis points to the enduring power that adversarial narratives can exert. These largely relied on selective evidence, or even anecdotes, and appealed to common sense. They were conceptually coherent—even elegant—and clothed in mild benevolence. In fact, they displayed most of the properties that, according to business literature, "make ideas stick," like simplicity, unexpectedness, concreteness, credibility, generating emotions, and storytelling.[16] The influence of such rhetoric has been hardly neutralized with equally persuasive counter-narratives.

Why have such narratives been so effective? One factor explaining their persistence is that they appeal to perennial tensions inherent in the market system—that is, between self-interest and societal utility, between security and scarcity. These tensions animate the very idea of a self-regulating market. The latter posits that under the right conditions, the pursuit of individual self-interest—which may appear deleterious to society—is eventually the premier generator of societal wealth.[17] In the same spirit, the dominant narrative of the past centuries insisted that the hardening of access to cash transfers—which may seem detrimental to the claimant—is ultimately in the best interest of the person and society. The two narratives share the paradox or the counter-intuitive notion that something apparently negative—like inducing short-term pain or allowing self-interest to flourish—may be positive for longer-term gains for both individuals and the common good.

Societies, however, have accorded protection to those deemed deserving. Over time, deservingness was largely equated with inability to work. Because of the difficulties in establishing whether an "able-bodied" person was in need because of his behavior or due to factors beyond his control, the solution was for working-age adults to *self-reveal* deservingness. Enter the mechanism of less-eligibility, that is, making cash transfers unpleasant enough to attract only the truly desperate who have

[15] Pimpare (2004, p. 144).
[16] See Heath and Heath (2007).
[17] Friedman (2021, p. 97) wrote: " . . . [c]hanneled through competition carried out in markets, and operating through the effect of that competition on prices, the effort of each individual to do more than improve his own condition was [in Adam Smith's words] the principle from which publick and national, as well as private opulence is originally derived."

exhausted all other source of support (family, community networks, labor market) before applying for assistance.

To illustrate such reasoning, Frederic Almy compared the "latent powers of the poor" to those of children "... who swim when thrown into the water, although they were sure they could not."[18] Rooted in an individualistic framework, the assumption is that people can overcome poverty if they really want to—they have latent potential to do so, and that potential needs to be revealed and unleashed through a test. People who claim they can't swim would be thrown into the water: that would activate a screening process, whereby few would emerge immediately and swim away (the non-poor) while most would stay underwater unable to swim (the poor). Some would receive a life-ring after a few seconds (deserving poor), while others would be left underwater for additional time (undeserving poor). Among the latter, some would grasp for air and perhaps stay afloat out of sheer desperation: such act would be regarded as proof of self-sufficiency and they would be put off the rolls (these are poor people who prefer to take their chances in a constrained labor market even with wages below subsistence level than entering workhouses); the remaining "undeserving" poor would, upon true exhaustion, be given help by accepting "the house" or similar arrangements.

These principles still animate contemporary debates. Reservations around cash transfers center on the idea that desperation prompts labor supply and ignites other behavioral responses; and the notion that transfers would stifle such response is alive in policy circles. By not undergoing "necessary" pain (the swimming in the previous analogy), recipients would side-step earning "legitimate" income from the labor market and rely on "unearned" income from the state. They would leapfrog the supposed crucial ingredients of effort, sacrifice, thrift, and restraint. That is probably the very essence of the debate: whether economic *security*—as opposed to *insecurity*—could be a springboard igniting upward mobility instead of activating a downward spiral. Narratives against cash transfers have emphasized the role of insecurity, which resonated with reformers. To the extent that these ideas of insecurity or pain being needed to spur incentives are dominant, the narratives that shaped past reform pathways may find avenues to influence present-day reform trajectories.

## 7.2 Looking ahead

### Déjà vu? Interpreting continuity in practices

An examination of past practices may evoke a sense of déjà vu. The book has shown that practices in cash transfers design and implementation have remained broadly consistent over time. It can be shocking to realize that we may have been approaching cash transfers in roughly similar ways over millennia. This sparks three distinct reflections.

[18] Almy (1899b, p. 69).

First, an overall consistency in operational approach doesn't mean that experiences lacked specific innovation, diversity, or adaptation. Previous chapters have documented different practices, including leading to a variety of configurations in design and providers (e.g., Chapters 2 and 5). Diversity existed, but this could be more aptly described in terms of variance within an overall framework instead of major departures from it. Core cash transfer design was grounded on activities like assessing ability to work, visiting recipients at their homes, producing lists of beneficiaries, devising various forms of conditionalities, and setting transfers at modest levels. Such activities broadly conform to contemporary arrangements. In undertaking the registration of beneficiaries, for instance, societies navigated the delicate balance between acquiring a granular understanding of people's living conditions and an overzeal in ascertaining people's circumstances minutely—between "knowing" and "intruding" into the beneficiary's lives. Today's social protection debates on collecting and managing people's information evoke similar tensions.

Second, recurrence may tell us more about the nature of the problem than the effectiveness of the instrument. Cash transfers walked a narrow path filled with competing pressures. One reading of history is that cash transfers helped, however imperfectly and contradictorily, mitigating the sweeping and evolving challenges faced by societies. As discussed earlier, those forces are well beyond the scope of cash transfers. From this standpoint, cash transfers may have been a relatively static instrument. Precisely because they were not intended to address the causes of poverty, like dislocation induced by industrialization or the spread of plagues, cash transfers have been largely designed for local, relatively sedentary populations. Provisions have been limited to locals because of suspicion, social privilege, and identity, as well as fiscal and public health considerations. Dispossessed and pauperized migrants were largely excluded from cash transfers. Town and country authorities have enacted various forms of measures for deterring "strangers" from claiming assistance. The presence of "vagrants" and casual laborers was relentless. While officials attempted to stem the mobility tide, poverty-induced migration has seldom been disrupted. The volume has chronicled some rudimentary antecedents to portability, like the commitment of certain "sending" localities to cover for assistance of migrants in the "receiving" areas. Modern-era accelerations in migration present similar quandaries in devising portable coverage by mobile populations.

Third, similarities between ancient and modern practices may invite humility. The idea of "able-bodiedness," for example, has been a cardinal criterion for past provisions. Such notion is still a lynchpin for organizing interventions in several low- and middle-income countries. To some extent, the core framework for assistance involves a long-standing programmatic differentiation, that is, public works for the able-bodied adults, and various forms of transfers for "deserving" categories like children, disabled populations, and seniors. In fact, some of the fastest-growing programs in recent decades, like conditional cash transfers and social pensions discussed in Chapter 4, are designed for supporting low-income families with young children and the vulnerable elderly, respectively. In other words, routine cash transfer programs tend not to be designed for working-age adults, which instead were among the key target group of the COVID-19 pandemic response (e.g., R350 grant in South Africa).

History shows that some countries moved away from the sole provision of cash organized along specific categories of people. Those programs were complemented by a guaranteed minimum income scheme establishing a national floor for anyone, independent of age or other contingencies. The establishment of minimum income standards, of which Speenhamland was a seminal example, was unsuccessfully attempted in the United States in the early 1970s.[19] Instead, its introduction succeeded in China in the early 1990s.

Yet also modern guaranteed minimum income schemes, which are the hallmark of cash transfers in most high-income settings, may reveal close continuities with the past. In broad terms, concerns for adverse effects on labor supply have maintained the principle of less-eligibility salient. In designing guaranteed minimum income programs, many countries have been "prioritizing employment incentives over the primary objective of poverty alleviation."[20] This was pursued by providing relatively low benefits[21] in combination with requirements to deter participation of those "who are relatively employable [and that should] look for and find a new job independently."[22] These requirements, which somewhat contrast with principles to ease access to assistance as opposed to make it harder,[23] were made tighter in past decades.[24] Such stricter measures didn't seem to have increased employment among beneficiaries.[25] Those results echo findings from similar approaches in the 1800s England and United States.

## Dispelling two long-standing myths . . . and bursting two bulging ones

Two powerful myths have been holding back cash transfers for a long time. It's time to debunk them. Two other myths, however, risk propelling cash transfers too far in the other direction and they need to be handled with care. If the first two myths are

[19] The US SNAP program provides such floor, albeit in the form of food vouchers. Research has shown the erosion of the floor over the past three decades (Jolliffe et al. 2019).

[20] Coady et al. (2021, p. 17).

[21] In most OECD countries, for many families the maximum benefits from programs are below the income earned from a 40-hour work week at the minimum wage (Coady et al. 2021). To reduce disincentives, countries often allow for smooth tapering out of assistance as participants earn more income as well as disregarding some forms of income in determining eligibility.

[22] Immervoll and Knotz (2018, p. 29). In their analysis they cover unemployment benefits and guaranteed minimum income programs, where "eligibility criteria for [the latter] are neither generally stricter nor generally more lenient than for [the former]" (ibid, p. 12). Examples of requirements include reporting on the outcomes of independent job-search efforts, the obligation to participate in training and other active labor market programs, and various sanctions for non-compliance with such rules.

[23] It terms of easing access to assistance and understanding the lived experience of claiming benefits, see the growing literature on "human-centered design," e.g., see Rosinsky et al. (2022).

[24] As discussed in Chapter 6, over the past four decades, there has been a "notable tightening of jobsearch and reporting requirements" (Immervoll and Knotz 2018, p. 15).

[25] Some requirements pressuring participants, like more active job-search, have been estimated to increase employment, while no similar evidence is found among more "punitive" sanctions (Knotz 2020b).

dispelled convincingly, and the other two myths are handled effectively, then there might be a viable, balanced pathway for cash transfers to play a wider role in societies.

The first recurrent myth comes in different forms, like "jobs, not welfare" or "infrastructure, not social protection." The basic idea is that there is an inherent sequence in which countries are supposed to first invest in "growth," and only later can they devote attention to "redistribution." Some great minds have reconciled such spurious dichotomy from a historical perspective.[26] The analysis offered in this book shows that economic transformation and cash transfers can coexist. There can be endless debates on the effectiveness of specific programs in particular instances and contexts. But in general, the experience of countries like China, England, Germany, and the Netherlands, for example, shows that cash transfers were present *during* the process of economic development. They weren't an afterthought. They helped contain the side effects of transformation—and in some cases, it was argued they were instrumental to facilitate the process itself (via the labor reserve channel). In principle, such historical insight suggests that the relationship between cash transfers and the growth process is one of complementarity, not a dichotomy. Calibrating the right "dose" and form of cash transfers is then a fascinating technical contextual question. It's a matter of "how," not of "if."

This brings me to the second myth. This is a micro-variant of the above macro-reflection. Recent literature reviews and impact evaluations have shown that, on average, cash transfers don't affect labor supply negatively.[27] Combined with the mentioned revisionist evidence presented in Chapter 6, a large body of contemporary and historical evidence points to a key finding: the purported disincentives effects of cash transfers that animated large-scale reforms were vastly exaggerated. The evidence, as discussed, tends to run in the opposite direction, that is, for those who receive them, cash transfers minimize the effects stemming from labor market contractions and other sources of societal turbulence. Furthermore, the historical experiences reviewed in this book attest that if circumstances around them are made conducive, people *want* to work. In the late 1700s, Rumford in Germany and Montlinot in France recognized that people at the margins of labor markets face particular challenges, and that they can flourish when favorable environments are created. Main approaches have invested in administrative efforts to force "able-bodied" people to work instead of creating those enabling conditions (e.g., childcare, meaningful wages).

The bursting of the above two myths implies a renewed and more prominent role for cash transfers. However, the third myth, that "cash does it all," requires a word of caution. Chapter 2 showed how cash transfers are studied through an astonishingly wide gamut of empirical lenses—from reducing mortality among children to affecting the size of their brain; from bolstering reforestation to participating in political elections; from preventing cardiovascular diseases to improving mental health; or from supporting adolescent girls to stay in school to generating economic

[26] See for example Chang (2004, 2003) and Mkandawire (2006, 2001).
[27] Baird et al. (2018), Banerjee et al. (2024), Davis et al. (2016), Handa et al. (2018).

multipliers.[28] Such diversity is an appealing asset for building broad-based coalitions of constituencies—were they the minister of finance, political actors, civil society, the median voter, donors, etc. However, a multisectoral empirical base may convey the misleading impression that those goals are attainable *simultaneously*. Trade-offs among these intended objectives are inevitable, while unintended side effects have been documented.[29] There is a concrete risk of "silver bulleting," overpromising and inflating expectations,[30] and these may potentially backfire in terms of reduced long-run credibility. Excessive advocacy can be the enemy of good policy. This puts a premium on being clear about what those programs can and cannot realistically achieve in a given context.

The fourth myth is that "evidence is enough." Take the case of the United States, where the works of David Ellwood, Michael Katz and Martin Gilens exposed how cash transfers and "welfare" can be unpopular.[31] But why do other income support programs, like school meals, enjoy broad-based political support in the US and elsewhere?[32] The reason is only in part empirical:[33] school meals evoke three images that resonate with societies, namely "food" (where food is something people "deserve," while cash is supposedly to be "earned"); "children" (who lack self-help as opposed to "workers" or other adult groups); and "schools" (as productive sites of hope and investment as opposed to "the dole"). The point is that investments in evidence generation should be married to efforts in understanding worldviews. If anything, it would help producing more evidence of "the right kind." The socio-political salience of cash transfers evidence, like showing that they saved lives or generated jobs, might amplify the resonance of those programs among the broad public. Changing mindsets may require not only credible evidence, but credible evidence that helps building salient societal narratives.

## Administration versus human contact

As the forces of economic and social transformation advanced, the institutional architecture for the provision of cash transfers grew. Gradually, the jurisdiction and administration of cash moved up from local units like parishes to larger institutional bodies. This is broadly in synch with the expanding profile of risks faced by societies, which required a broader base for risk pooling. Systemic crises may have helped accelerate such a shift, like Roosevelt's New Deal. As such transition unfolded, a trade-off emerged between administrative consolidation and localized knowledge

[28] See Richterman et al. (2023), Weissman et al. (2023), Ferraro and Simorangkir (2020), Conover et al. (2020), Pescarini et al. (2022), McGuire (2021), Baird et al. (2019) and Gassmann et al. (2023). respectively.

[29] See for example Filmer et al. (2023).

[30] Dercon (2023).

[31] See Ellwood (1988, p. ix), Katz (1986, p. ix), Gilens (1999), respectively.

[32] Various authorities have recently established a global school meals coalition (https://schoolmealscoalition.org/).

[33] School meals are indeed supported by a vast empirical literature, e.g., see Gentilini and Sabarwal (2022). For the wider cash versus in-kind debate, see Gentilini (2023b).

and engagement. The shift towards centralized relief had organizational benefits in terms of economies of scale and coordination with other social and economic measures.[34] But the process severed a direct connection between "donors and recipients": states tend to mediate the donor–recipient relationship through formal bureaucracies. And as those bureaucracies deepened, the anonymity of the recipient and the impersonal nature of the donor (an unknown "taxpayer") fueled suspicion and distrust among both.[35]

Influenced by Hamburg and similar models, the rise of "scientific giving" in places like New York City in the late 1800s was dubbed by some as "bourgeois' self-interest."[36] Yet such an approach was the result of poverty narratives fusing a strong individual element of responsibility with a proactive role for societal participation beyond taxation. In a way, they meant to provide transfers with higher technical rigor while re-establishing the connection between cash donors and recipients that was lost in the wake of industrialization, mobility, and urbanization.[37] The voluntary contributions of time and effort were gradually institutionalized through the professionalization of social workers under government bodies.[38] This might have augmented the quality of assistance, but may have also reduced civic engagement.

History shows that broad challenges need a commensurate base of risk management. Tackling downturns in the global financial system, climatic risks, and pandemics may increasingly call for institutional architectures of cash transfers that are aligned with the magnitude of the risks.[39] How to devise such arrangements in ways that don't further alienate society is a challenge for us all, that is, to rediscover cash transfers not as ATMs, but as sites for human contact.

## The big question on poverty inherency . . . and shortcutting it

Whether poverty is explained through a structuralist or individualist lens, or some combination thereof, the outcome can be similar: people lack money. This crude observation is here posed provocatively not to underemphasize critical non-monetary dimensions of the problem, but to expose a series of conundrums closely related to cash transfers.

Two schools of thought emerge. On the one hand, a body of literature alluringly frames poverty as indeed simply "lack of cash."[40] For instance, Eduardo Suplicy argues in Confucian terms that the answer to poverty is obvious: "the exit is through

[34] McMillan (2019).
[35] Atkinson (2015), Cottam (2018), Zelizer (1997).
[36] Lindenmeyr (1996).
[37] Greeley (2022), Zelizer (1997).
[38] Ruswick (2012).
[39] For example, there are calls for a global fund for social protection (UN 2021).
[40] See, among others, Blattman and Niehaus (2014), Hanlon et al. (2010), Lowrey (2018), Santens (2021), and Yang (2018).

the door," and cash transfers provide a direct way of addressing the problem.[41] Rutger Bregman is more forthright: " . . . I've come to believe that poverty is not a very difficult subject. Poverty is just a lack of cash."[42] In other words, poverty can be cashed away. As such, cash programs offer a concrete, tangible direct route for action against deep-seated and often elusive causes of poverty.

The drawback of the "just give people money" mantra is that it conceals an underlying problem whose mechanisms weren't fixed but patched temporarily. Over the 1960s, Lawrence Mead insisted that poverty in the United States " . . . didn't disappear; it was overwhelmed by cash."[43] A more nuanced framing may posit that cash can help address *some* causes of poverty. Cash helps rectify a situation that has deeper imbalances. Some constraints can be addressed by cash, while most structural bottlenecks often remain clogged and keep generating inequities.[44]

Hence, equating poverty with lack of cash is not incorrect per se: on the surface, poverty is a lack of cash. However, framing poverty in this way focuses on the outcome, not the process. The question on "shortcutting" is ultimately one on whether the "process" is *bound* to generate poverty, that is, if poverty is somewhat endemic in our societal organization and reproduces itself via labor markets and other sites of power relations.[45]

This is where the analysis hits some fundamental systemic dilemmas. For a long time, labor markets have been considered the premier sources of "legitimate" income. The future of cash transfers would in part depend on the trust bestowed on labor markets as engines of wealth generation and inclusion.[46] To put it simply, to what extent are poverty generators "fixable" and to what degree are they inherent in economic organization and social systems? Is poverty a necessary condition for market-oriented systems to thrive? Did other systems of economic organization solve the problem? These are treacherous waters to navigate, and the book is not meant to venture too far out in their exploration. But they do feature in the analysis, and to gain a "properly historicized sense of the future," as the chapter's epigraph states, we ought to ask and reflect more on these cardinal questions.

Ultimately, the study of the history of cash transfers helps reveal the true cost of progress. Plotted graphically, global per capita economic growth over the past couple of millennia remains a flat line until the 1800s, when it suddenly rises vertically.[47] The story of cash transfers sheds light on real-world hopes, struggles, and tragedies of ordinary people when the line was flat—and it illuminates the sacrifice and societal turbulence those people endured for raising the line. To them we owe the elevation of our collective standards of living.

[41] Suplicy (2002).
[42] Interview on NPR, "Is A Universal Basic Income the Answer to Ending Poverty?" (January 12) (see transcript at https://www.npr.org/transcripts/577436742).
[43] Mead (1986, p. 40).
[44] Piketty (2016).
[45] Desmond (2023b).
[46] Ferguson (2015), Gill (2017), Matthews (2022), Standing (2011), Tcherneva (2012), Van Parijs and Vanderborght (2019).
[47] See https://ourworldindata.org/grapher/global-average-gdp-per-capita-over-the-long-run.

# Bibliography


Aaron, H. (1975) "Cautionary Notes on the Experiment." In Pechman, J., and Timpane, M. (eds) *Work Incentives and Income Guarantees: The New Jersey Negative Income Tax Experiment.* Brookings Institution.

Abdulai, A. (2020) "Competitive Clientelism, Donors and the Politics of Social Protection Uptake in Ghana." *Critical Social Policy* 41(2): 270–293.

Acemoglu, D., Johnson, S., and Robinson, J. (2001) "The Colonial Origins of Comparative Development: An Empirical Investigation." *American Economic Review* 91(5): 1369–1401.

Ackerman, B., and Alstott, A. (2000) *The Stakeholder Society.* Yale University Press.

ACLU (American Civil Liberties Union) (2016) *Project 100%: History, Problems, and Your Rights.* American Civil Liberties Union.

Adesina, J. (2011) "Beyond the Social Protection Paradigm: Social Policy in Africa's Development." *Canadian Journal of Development Studies* 32(4): 454–470.

Adhikari, S., and Gentilini, U. (2018) "Should I Stay or Should I Go: Do Cash Transfers Affect Migration?" Policy Research Working Paper 8525. World Bank.

Ahmad, E., and Hussain, A. (1991) "Social Security in China: A Historical Perspective." In Ahmad, E., Dreze, J., Hills, J., and Sen, A. (eds) *Social Security in Developing Countries*, 246–304. Oxford University Press.

Ahmed, A., Aune, D., Vineis, P., Pescarini, J., Millett, C., and Hone, T. (2022) "The Effect of Conditional Cash Transfers on the Control of Neglected Tropical Disease: A Systematic Review." *The Lancet Global Health* 10(5): E640–E648.

Ahmed, A., Hoddinott, J., and Roy, S. (2019) "Food Transfers, Cash Transfers, Behavior Change Communication and Child Nutrition: Evidence from Bangladesh." Discussion Paper 1868. IFPRI.

Aiken, E., Bellue, S., Karlan, D., Udry, C., and Blumenstock, J. (2022) "Machine Learning and Phone Data Can Improve Targeting of Humanitarian Aid." *Nature* 603(7903): 864–870.

Aiyar, Y. (2023) *Citizen vs. Labharthi? Interrogating the Welfare State.* Centre for Policy Research.

Aizer, A., Eli, S., and Lleras-Muney, A. (2020) *The Incentive Effects of Cash Transfers to the Poor.* NBER Working Paper 27523. National Bureau of Economic Research.

Akee, R., Copeland, W., Costello, E., and Simeonova, E. (2018) "How Does Household Income Affect Child Personality Traits and Behaviors?" *American Economic Review* 108(3): 775–827.

Albelda. R., Folbre, N. and the Center for Popular Economics (1996) *The War on the Poor: A Defense Manual.* New Press.

Alderman, H. (1987) "Allocation of Goods through Non-Price Mechanisms: Evidence on Distribution by Willingness to Wait." *Journal of Development Economics* 25(1): 105–124

Alderman, H., and Hoddinott, J. (2009) "Growth-Promoting Social Safety Nets." In von Braun, J., Vargas Hill, R., and Pandya-Lorch, R. (eds) *The Poorest and Hungry. Assessments, Analyses, and Action*, 279–286. IFPRI.

Alderman, H. and von Braun, J. (1984) "The Effects of the Egyptian Food Rationing and Subsidy System on Income Distribution and Consumption." Research Report 45. IFPRI.

Alderman, H., and Yemtsov, R. (2014) "How Can Safety Nets Contribute to Economic Growth?" *World Bank Economic Review* 28(1): 1–20.

Alderman, H., Gentilini, U., and Yemtsov, R. (eds) (2017) *The 1.5 Billion People Question: Food, Vouchers or Cash Transfers?* World Bank.

Alesina, A., and Glaeser, E. (2004) *Fighting Poverty in the US and Europe: A World of Difference.* Oxford University Press.

Alison, W. (1840) *Observations on the Management of the Poor in Scotland, and its Effects on the Health of the Great Towns.* William Blackwood and Sons.

Alison, W. (1841) *Reply to Dr. Chalmers' Objections to an Improvement of the Legal Provision for the Poor in Scotland.* William Blackwood and Sons.

Allen, R. (1992) *Enclosure and the Yeoman: The Agricultural Development of the South Midlands, 1450–1850.* Oxford University Press.

Allen, R. (2003) "Progress and Poverty in Early Modern Europe." *Economic History Review* 56(3): 403–443.

Allen, R. (2017) "Absolute Poverty: When Necessity Displaces Desire." *American Economic Review* 107(12): 3690–3721.

Almy, F. (1895) "The Problem of Charity from Another Point of View." *Charity Review* 4: 71.

Almy, F. (1899) "The Relation Between Public and Private Outdoor Relief—Part II." *Charities Review* 9(2): 65–71.

Almy, F. (1900) "Public or Private Outdoor Relief." National Conference of Charities and Correction: 134–145.

Al-Rousan, M., Al-Azzam, T., and Al-Rousan, S. (2020) "The Social Welfare in the Succession of Omar Bin Al-Khattab (A Histological Approach)." *International Journal of Humanities and Social Science* 10(1): 97–102.

Altekar, A. (1955) "The Planned State in Ancient India." *Proceedings of the Indian History Congress* 18: 33–40.

Ambirajan, S. (1978) *Classical Political Economy and British Policy in India.* Cambridge University Press.

Amenta, E. (2006) *When Movements Matter: The Townsend Plan and the Rise of Social Security.* Princeton University Press.

An, C. (2021) "Social Citizenship of Chinese Low-Income Families." In Guo, Z. (ed) *The Routledge Handbook of Chinese Citizenship*, 89–102. Routledge.

Anand, A., Dimble, V., and Subramanian, A. (2020, December 22) "New Welfarism of India's Right." The Indian Express.

Anderson, C. (2018) "Introduction: A Global History of Convicts and Penal Colonies." In Anderson, C. (ed) *A Global History of Convicts and Penal Colonies*, 1–35. Bloomsbury Academic.

Anderson, L., Reynolds, T., Biscaye, P., Coomes, D., Ebeling, E., Favreau, A. and Madsen, T. (2017, November 2013) "Review of Evidence on Long-term Impacts of Cash Transfer Programs," EPAR Technical Report 359. [online]. https://epar.evans.uw.edu/research/review-long-term-impacts-cash-transfer-programs

Anderson, M. (1978) *Welfare: The Political Economy of Welfare Reform in the United States.* Hoover Institution Press.

Ang, Y. (2016) *How China Escaped the Poverty Trap.* Cornell University Press.

Apter, N. (2013) "Saving the Young: A History of the Child Relief Movement in Modern China." PhD dissertation, University of California, Los Angeles.

Araujo, V. (2023) "Mobilization versus Mitigation: How Do Cash Transfers Affect Participation in Elections?" Equality of Opportunity Research Series 13. University of Zurich.

Aschrott, P. (1902) *The English Poor Law System, Past and Present.* Knight and Co.

Asen, R. (2001) "Nixon's Welfare Reform: Enacting Historical Contradictions of Poverty Discourses." *Rhetoric and Public Affairs* 4(2): 261–279.

Ashenfelter, O. (1986) "Discussion of 'The Work Response to a Guaranteed Income. A Survey of Experimental Evidence.'" In Munnell, A. (ed) *Lessons from the Income Maintenance Experiments*. Federal Reserve Bank of Boston.

Ashenfelter, O., and Plant, D. (1990) "Nonparametric Estimates of the Labor-Supply Effects of Negative Income Tax Programs." *Journal of Labor Economics* 8(1): S396–S415.

Ashley, W. (1906) *An Introduction on English Economic History and Theory—Part II: The End of the Middle Ages*, 4th edn. Longmans, Green & Co.

Ashton, B., Hill, K., Piazza, A., and Zeitz, R. (1984) "Famine in China, 1958–61." *Population and Development Review* 10(4): 613–645.

Aspalter, C. (2017) "Lessons from Around the World: By Way of Conclusion." In Aspalter, C. (ed) *The Routledge International Handbook of Welfare State Systems*. Routledge.

Assereto, G. (1982) "Aspetti dell'Assistenza Pubblica a Genova nei Primi Anni dell'Ottocento." In Politi, G., Rosa, M. and Della Peruta, F. (eds) *Timore e Carità: I Poveri nell'Italia Moderna*, 347–357. Biblioteca Statale e Libreria Civica di Cremona.

Ata, A. (1987) "Jordan." In Dixon, J. (ed) *Social Welfare in the Middle East*, 71–97. Routledge Revivals.

Atkinson, A. (1996a) *Public Economics in Action: The Basic Income/Flat Tax Proposal*. Oxford University Press.

Atkinson, A. (1996b) "The Case for a Participation Income." *Political Quarterly* 67(1) 67–70.

Atkinson, A. (2015) *Inequality: What Can Be Done?* Harvard University Press.

Atkinson, A. (2019) *Measuring Poverty Around the World*. Princeton University Press.

Atkinson, A., and Hills, J. (1991) "Social Security in Developed Countries: Are There Lessons for Developing Countries?" In Ahmad, E., Dreze, J., Hills, J., and Sen, A. (eds) *Social Security in Developing Countries*, 81–111. Oxford University Press.

Attanasio, O., and Brugiavini, A. (2003) "Social Security and Households' Saving." *Quarterly Journal of Economics* 118(3): 1075–1119.

AU (African Union) (2008) "Social Policy Framework for Africa." CAMSD/EXP/4(I). African Union Commission.

Awortwi, N. (2017) "Conclusion: Reluctant Domestic and Enthusiastic International Actors of Cash Transfer Programmes in Africa." In Awortwi, N., and Aiyede, E. (eds) *Politics, Public Policy and Social Protection in Africa: Evidence from Cash Transfer Programmes*, 116–128. Routledge.

Awortwi, N. (2018) "Social Protection is a Grassroots Reality: Making the Case for Policy Reflections on Community-based Social Protection Actors and Services in Africa." *Development Policy Review* 36(S2): 897–913.

Axinn, J., and Levin. H. (1982). *Social Welfare: A History of the American Response to Need*. Longman.

Backhouse, R., and Boianovsky, M. (2016) "Secular Stagnation: The History of a Macroeconomic Heresy." *European Journal of the History of Economic Thought* 23: 946–970.

Baehre, R. (1981) "Paupers and Poor Relief in Upper Canada." *Historical Papers* 16(1): 57–80.

Bahmueller, C. (1981) *The National Charity Company. Jeremy Bentham's Silent Revolution*. University of California Press.

Bainbridge, V. (1996) *Guilds in the Medieval Countryside: Social and Religious Change in Cambridgeshire, c.1350–1558*. Boydell Press.

Bainton, R. (1964) *The Reformation of the Sixteenth Century*. Beacon Press.

Baird, S., Ferreira, F., Özler, B., and Woolcock, M. (2013) "Relative Effectiveness of Conditional and Unconditional Cash Transfers for Schooling Outcomes in Developing Countries: A Systematic Review." *Campbell Systematic Review* 9(1): 1–124.

Baird, S., McKenzie, D., and Özler, B. (2018) "The Effects of Cash Transfers on Adult Labor Market Outcomes." *Policy Research Working Paper* 8404. World Bank.

Baird, S., Ozler, B., and McIntosh, C. (2019) "When the Money Runs Out: Do Cash Transfers Have Sustained Effects on Human Capital Accumulation?" *Journal of Development Economics* 140: 169–185.

Balboni, C., Bandiera, O., Burgess, R., Ghatak M., and Heil, A. (2020) "Why Do People Stay Poor?" *Economic Organisation and Public Policy Discussion Papers* 67. London School of Economics.

Bales, K. (1999) "Popular Reactions to Sociological Research: The Case of Charles Booth." *Sociology* 33(1): 153–168.

Ball, R., Poole, S., and Drury, J. (2023) "The Sherborne Riots of October 1831." Working Paper. University of the West of England.

Balme, M. (1984) "Attitudes to Work and Leisure in Ancient Greece." *Greece & Rome* 31(2): 140–152.

Ban, G., and Swann, N. (1950) *Food and Money in Ancient China*. Princeton University Press.

Banerjee, A. Faye, M., Krueger, A., Niehaus, P., and Suri, T. (2023, September 15) "Universal Basic Income: Short-Term Results from a Long-Term Experiment in Kenya." NBER Conference Paper. Cambridge University Press.

Banerjee, A., and Iyer, L. (2005) "History, Institutions and Economic Performance: The Legacy of Colonial Land Tenure Systems in India." *American Economic Review* 95(4): 1190–1213.

Banerjee, A., Duflo, E., and Sharma, G. (2021) "Long-Term Effects of the Targeting the Ultra Poor Program." *American Economic Review: Insights* 3(4): 471–486.

Banerjee, A., Hanna, R., Kreindler, G., and Olken, B. (2017) "Debunking the Stereotype of the Lazy Welfare Recipient: Evidence from Cash Transfer Programs." *World Bank Research Observer* 32(2): 155–184.

Banerjee, A., Hanna, R., Olken, B., and Sverdlin Lisker, D. (2024) *Social Protection in the Developing World*. NBER Working Paper 32382. National Bureau of Economic Research.

Banerjee, A., Niehaus, P., and Tavneet, S. (2019) *Universal Basic Income in the Developing World*. NBER Working Paper 25598. National Bureau of Economic Research.

Banfield, E. (1974) *The Unheavenly City Revisited*. Little, Brown & Co.

Barbelet, V., Davies, G., Flint, J., and Davey, E. (2021) Interrogating the Evidence Base on Humanitarian Localisation: A Literature Study. ODI.

Barnett, S. (1899) "Charity Versus Outdoor Relief". The Nineteenth Century 46 (November): 818-826

Barnett, M. (2011) *Empire of Humanity. A History of Humanitarianism*. Cornell University Press.

Barr, H. (2014) "Major Episodes and Moments in *Piers Plowman* B." In Cole, A., and Galloway, A. (eds) *The Cambridge Companion to Piers Plowman*. Cambridge University Press.

Barr, N. (2020) *The Economics of the Welfare State*, 6th edn. Oxford University Press.

Barrett, C. (2002) "Food Security and Food Assistance Programs." In Gardner B., and Rausser, G. (eds) *Handbook of Agricultural Economics—Volume 2B: Agricultural and Food Policy*, 2103–2190. Elsevier.

Barrett, C., Carter, M., and Chavas, J-P. (eds) (2019) *The Economics of Poverty Traps*. University of Chicago Press.

Barrett, C., Lentz, E., and Maxwell, D. (2007) *A Market Analysis and Decision Tree Tool for Response Analysis: Cash, Local Purchase and/or Imported Food Aid? The Decision Tree Tool*. CARE.

Barrientos, A. (2013) *Social Assistance in Developing Countries*. Cambridge University Press.

Barrientos, A. (2020) "Transnational Actors and Institutionalization of Social Protection in the Global South." In Schmitt, C. (ed) *From Colonialism to International Aid: External Actors and Social Protection in the Global South*, 333–356. Palgrave MacMillan.

Barrientos, A., and Hulme, D. (2008) "Social Protection for the Poor and Poorest in Developing Countries: Reflections on a Quiet Revolution." Working Paper 30. Brooks World Poverty Institute.

Barrientos, A., and Scott, J. (2008) "Social Transfers and Growth: A Review." *Working Paper* 52. Brooks World Poverty Institute.

Bartlett, B. (1994) "How Excessive Government Killed Ancient Rome." *Cato Journal* 14(2): 287–303.

Barton, J. (1817) *Observations on the Circumstances Which Influence the Condition of Labouring Classes of Society*. John & Arthur Arch.

Barton, J. (1820) *An Inquiry into the Progressive Depreciation of Agricultural Labour in Modern Times with Suggestion for its Remedy*. John & Arthur Arch.

Barua, B. (1930) "The Sohgaura Copper-Plate Inscription." *Annals of the Bhandarkar Oriental Research Institute* 11(1): 32–48.

Bashford, A. (2005) *Imperial Hygiene. A Critical History of Colonialism, Nationalism and Public Health*. Palgrave Macmillian.

Bastagli, F. (2020) "Universal Basic Income and Work." In Gentilini, U., Grosh, M., Rigolini, J., and Yemtsov, R. (eds) *Exploring Universal Basic Income. A Guide to Navigating Concepts, Evidence, and Practices*. World Bank.

Bastagli, F., and Lowe, C. (2021) "Social Protection Response to Covid-19 and Beyond: Emerging Evidence and Learning for Future Crises." Working Paper 614. ODI.

Bastagli, F., Hagen-Zanker, J., Harman, L., Barca, V., Sturge, G., and Schmidt, T. (2019) "The Impact of Cash Transfers: A Review of Evidence from Low- and Middle-Income Countries." *Journal of Social Policy* 48(3): 569–594.

Baudisch, V., and Neuenkirch, M. (2024) "A Comparative Evaluation of Fiscal Stabilization Strategies during the Covid-19 Pandemic with Germany as a Reference Point." *The Economists' Voice* 21(1) [online]. doi.org/10.1515/ev-2024-0019.

Baugh, D. (1975) "The Cost of Poor Relief in South-East England, 1790–1834." *Economic History Review* 28(1): 50–68.

BBC (2021, February 25) "China's Xi Declares Victory in Ending Extreme Poverty." [online]. https://www.bbc.co.uk/news/world-asia-china-56194622

Beazley, R., Marzi, M., and Steller, R. (2021) "Drivers of Timely and Large-Scale Cash Responses to COVID19: What Does the Data Say?" Social Protection Approaches to COVID-19 Expert Advice Service (SPACE). DAI Global UK Ltd. https://socialprotection.org/sites/default/files/publications_files/SPACE_Drivers%20of%20Timely%20and%20Large%20Scale%20Cash%20Responses%20to%20COVID_19%20%281%29.pdf

Beck, H. (1995) *The Origins of the Authoritarian Welfare State in Prussia: Conservatives, Bureaucracy, and the Social Question, 1815–70*. University of Michigan Press.

Becker, G., and Mulligan, C. (1998) *Deadweight Costs and the Size of Government*. NBER Working Paper 6789. National Bureau of Economic Research.

Beckerman Davis, B. (1991) "Poverty and Poor Relief in Sixteenth-Century Toulouse." *Historical Reflections* 17(3): 267–296.

Beegle, K., Coudouel, A., and Monsalve, E. (eds) (2017) *Realizing the Full Potential of Social Safety Nets in Africa*. World Bank.

Behrendt, C., Blanco, F., Groppo, V., Guilbert, N., Lyon, S., Mahe, C., Orton, I., Richardson, D., Smith, B., Tessier, L., and Tirivayi, N. (2022) *The Role of Social Protection in the Elimination of Child Labour: Evidence Review and Policy Implications*. ILO/UNICEF.

Beier, A. (1983) *The Problem of the Poor in Tudor and Early Stuart England*. Routledge.

Beland, D., and Myles, J. (2005) "Stasis amidst Change: Canadian Pension Reform in an Age of Retrenchment." In Bonoli, G., and Shinkawa, T. (eds) *Ageing and Pension Reform around the World*, 252–273. Edward Elgar.

Beland, D., and Waddan, A. (2017) "Why Are There No Universal Social Programs in the United States?: A Historical Institutionalist Comparison with Canada," *World Affairs* 180(1), 64–92.

Bentham, J. (1796) *Tracts on Poor Laws and Pauper Management: The Works of Jeremy Bentham*, Volume 8. Bowring, J. (ed). William Tait.

Benton, J. (2012) *Warning Out in New England, 1656–1817*. Ulan Press.

Bernardi, B. (1985) *Age Class Systems: Social Institutions and Polities Based on Age*. Cambridge University Press.

Bernstein, P. (1996) *Against the Gods: The Remarkable Story of Risk*. John Wiley and Sons.

Bernstein, S. (1956) "American Labor in the Long Depression, 1873–1878." *Science & Society* 20(1): 59–83.

Berry, S. (1989) "Social Institutions and Access to Resources." *Africa: Journal of the International African Institute* 59(1): 41–55.

Berry, S. (1993) *No Condition Is Permanent: The Social Dynamics of Agrarian Change in Sub-Saharan Africa*. University of Wisconsin Press.

Besharov, D., and Call, D. (2009) *Poverty, Welfare, and Public Policy*. Wiley-Blackwell.

Besharov, D., and Germanis, P. (2001) "Welfare Reform: Four Years Later." In Besharow, D. J., Germanis, P., Hein, J., Jonas, D. K., and Sherman, A. L. (eds) *Ending Dependency: Lessons from Welfare Reform in the USA*, 43–58. Institute for the Study of Civil Society.

Besley, T. (1997) "Political Economy of Alleviating Poverty: Theory and Institutions." In Bruno, M., and Pleskovic, B. (eds) Annual World Bank Conference on Development Economics 1996. World Bank.

Beveridge, W. (1927) "Unemployment Insurance in the War and After." In Shotwell, J. (ed) *War and Insurance*. Carnegie Endowment Series 232. London.

Beveridge, W. (1942) *Social Insurance and Allied Services*. His Majesty's Stationery Office.

Bhandarkar, D. (1932) "Mauryan Brahmi Inscription of Mahasthan." In Sastri, I., Dikshit, K. and Chakravarti, N. (eds) *Epigraphia Indica and Record of the Archeological Survey of India*, 83–91.Government of India.

Bhattacharya, S. (2017) "The Concept of Poverty in Colonial India." In Chakrabarti, S., and Patnaik, U. (eds) *Agrarian and Other Histories: Essays for Binay Bhushan Chaudhuri*, 267–276. Tulika Books.

Bhorat, H., and Kohler, T. (2021) "Casting the Net Wider: How South Africa's COVID-19 Grant Has Reached the Once Forgotten." Working Paper *Econ3x3* [online]. https://www.econ3x3.org/sites/default/files/articles/Bhorat%2C%20H_SA%20COVID%20grant_Aug21%5B1%5D_0.pdf

Bikales, B. (2021) *Reflections on Poverty Reduction in China*. Embassy of Switzerland in China.

Bishop, S. (1902) "The New Movement in Charity." *American Journal of Sociology* 7(5): 595–610.

Blackorby, C., and Donaldson, D. (1988) "Cash Versus Kind, Self-Selection and Efficient Transfers." *American Economic Review* 78(4): 691–700.

Blank, R. (2001) "What Causes Public Assistance Caseloads to Grow?" *Journal of Human Resources* 36(1): 85–118.

Blattman, C. (2017, March 30) "Two Views on Fighting World Poverty." *Center for Global Development* [blog]. https://www.cgdev.org/blog/two-views-fighting-world-poverty

Blattman, C., Cerero, D., Duncan, G., Hernandez, S., Lessing, B., Martinez, J., Mesa-Mejía, J., Montoya, H., and Tobon, S. (2020) "Crime in the Time of Covid-19: How Colombian Gangs Responded to the Pandemic." IPA, University of Chicago, and Universidad EAFIT.

Blattman, C., Dercon, S., and Franklin, S. (2022) "Impacts of Industrial and Entrepreneurial Jobs on Youth: 5-year Experimental Evidence on Factory Job Offers and Cash Grants in Ethiopia." *Journal of Development Economics* 156,102807.

Blattman, C., Fiala, N., and Martinez, S. (2018) *The Long-Term Impacts of Grants on Poverty: 9-year Evidence from Uganda's Youth Opportunities.* NBER Working Paper 24999. National Bureau of Economic Research.

Blattman, C., and Niehaus, P. (2014) "Show Them the Money: Why Giving Cash Helps Alleviate Poverty." *Foreign Affairs* (May/June): 117–126.

Blaug, M. (1963) "The Myth of the Old Poor Law and the Making of the New." *Journal of Economic History* 23(2): 151–184.

Blaug, M. (1964) "The Poor Law Report Reexamined." *Journal of Economic History* 24(2): 229–245.

Block, F., and Somers, M. (2003) "In the Shadow of Speenhamland: Social Policy and the Old Poor Law." *Politics and Society* 31(2): 283–322.

Block, F., and Somers, M. (2014) *The Power of Market Fundamentalism: Karl Polanyi's Critique.* Harvard University Press.

Boger, T., Son, K., and Tonelli, S. (2021) "Origins of Family Policy: Prerequisites or Diffusion." In Windzio, M., Mossig, I., Besche-Truthe, F., and Seitzer, H. (eds) *Networks and Geographies of Global Social Policy Diffusion: Culture, Economy, and Colonial Legacies*, 169–193. Springer.

Bolin, S. (1958) *State and Currency in the Roman Empire to 300 A.D.* Almqvist and Wiksell.

Bonenfant, P. (1927) "Les origines et le caractère de la réforme de la bienfaisance publique aux Pays-Bas sous le règne de Charles-Quint." *Revue belge de Philologie et d'Histoire* 6(1–2): 207–230.

Bonner, M. (2005) "Poverty and Economics in the Qur'an." *Journal of Interdisciplinary History* 35(3): 391–406.

Bonner, M. (2013) "Poverty and Charity in the Rise of Islam." In Bonner, M., Ener, M., and Singer, A. (eds) *Poverty and Charity in the Middle Eastern Context*, 13–30. State University of New York Press.

Booth, A. (1977) "Food Riots in the North-West of England 1790–1801." *Past & Present* 77(1): 84–107.

Borges, F. (2018) "Neoliberalism with a Human Face." *Comparative Politics* 50(2): 147–167.

Borges, F., and Sugiyama, N. (2011) "The Diffusion of Conditional Cash Transfer Programs in the Americas." *Global Social Policy* 11 (2–3): 250–278.

Boulton, J. (2014) "Indoors or Outdoors? Welfare Priorities and Pauper Choices in the Metropolis Under the Old Poor Law, 1718–1824." In Briggs, C., Kitson, P., and Thompson, S. (eds) *Population, Welfare and Economic Change in Britain, 1290–1834.* Boydell Press.

Boushey, H. (2001, September 20) "Testimony before the U.S. House of Representatives Committee on Education and the Workforce." Subcommittee on 21st Century Competitiveness. US Government Printing Office.

Bowler, K. (1974) *The Nixon Guaranteed Income Proposal: Substance and Process in Policy Change.* Ballinger.

Boyce, J., and Ndikumana, L. (2005) "Africa's Debt: Who Owes Whom?" In Epstein, G. (ed) *Capital Flight and Capital Controls in Developing Countries*, 334–340. Edward Elgar.

Boyer, G. (1990) *An Economic History of the English Poor Law, 1750–1850.* Cambridge University Press.

Boyer, G. (2021) *The Winding Road to the Welfare State. Economic Insecurity and Social Welfare Policy in Britain.* Princeton University Press.

Brace, C. (1880) The Dangerous Classes of New York and Twenty Years' Work Among Them. Patterson Smith.

Bradbury, R. (1965) "Father and Senior Son in Edo Mortuary Ritual." International African Institute (ed) *African Systems of Thought*, 111. Oxford University Press.

Braddick, M. (2000) *State Formation in Early Modern England, c. 1550–1700*. Cambridge University Press.

Brady, D. (2023) "Poverty, Not the Poor." *Science Advances* 9(1469): 1–17.

Brady, D. (2019) "Theories of the Causes of Poverty." *Annual Review of Sociology* 45: 155–17.

Brandt, L., and Rawski, T. (2008) *China's Great Economic Transformation*. Cambridge University Press.

Brauer, C. (1982) "Kennedy, Johnson, and the War on Poverty." *Journal of American History* 69(1): 98–119.

Bregman, R. (2017) *Utopia for Realists: How We Can Build the Ideal World*. Little, Brown and Company.

Bremer, F. (2020) *One Small Candle: The Plymouth Puritans and the Beginning of English New England*. Oxford University Press.

Brennan, L. (1984) "The Development of the Indian Famine Codes Personalities, Politics, and Policies." In Currey, B., and Hugo, G. (eds) *Famine as a Geographical Phenomenon*, 91–111. Reidel Publishing.

Breuilly, J. (1992) "Hamburg: The German City of Laissez-Faire." *History Journal* 35(3): 701–712.

Breunig, R., Dasgupta, I., Gundersen, C., and Pattanaik, P. (2001) "Explaining the Food Stamp Cash-Out Puzzle." *Food Assistance and Nutrition Research Report* 12. USDA-ERS.

Brewer, J., and Hellmuth, E. (ed) (1999) *Rethinking Leviathan: The Eighteenth-Century State in Britain and Germany*. Oxford University Press.

Brewis, G. (2010) "Fill Full the Mouth of Famine: Voluntary Action in Famine Relief in India 1896–1901." *Modern Asian Studies* 44(4): 887–918.

Briggs, A. (1961) "The Welfare State in Historical Perspective." *European Journal of Sociology* 2(2): 221–258.

Brollo, F., Ibarra, G., and Campante Vale, R. (2024) "Strengthening Income Stabilization through Social Protection in Emerging and Developing Economies: The Brazilian Experience." Working Paper WP/24/52. IMF.

Brooks, A., Helgren, D., Cramer, J., Franklin, A., Hornyak, W., Keating, J., Klein, R., Rink, W., Schwarcz, H., Smith, L., Stewart, K., Todd, N., Verniers, J., and Yellen, J. (1995) "Dating and Context of Three Middle Stone Age Sites with Bone Points in the Upper Semliki Valley, Zaire." *Science* 268(5210): 548–553.

Brooks, S. (2015) "Social Protection for the Poorest: The Adoption of Antipoverty Cash Transfer Programs in the Global South." *Politics and Society* 43(4): 551–582.

Brown, P. (2002) *Poverty and Leadership in the Later Roman Empire*. Brandeis University Press.

Brown, R. (1995) "Party Cleavages and Welfare Effort in the American States." *American Political Science Review* 89(1): 23–33.

Brundage, A. (1978) *The Making of the New Poor Law: The Politics of Inquiry, Enactment, and Implementation, 1832–1839*. Rutgers University Press.

Bryan G., Chowdhury S., and Mobarak A. (2014) "Underinvestment in a Profitable Technology: The Case of Seasonal Migration in Bangladesh." *Econometrica* 82(5): 1671–1748.

Bryan, G., Chowdhury, S., Mobarak, A, Morten, M., and Smits, J. (2021) "Encouragement and Distortionary Effects of Conditional Cash Transfers." Discussion Paper 14326. IZA.

Bryceson, D. (1990) *Food Insecurity and the Social Division of Labour in Tanzania, 1919–85*. St. Martin's Press.

Buchanan-Smith, M., and Maxwell, S. (1994) "Linking Relief and Development: An Introduction and Overview." *IDS Bulletin* 25(4): 2–16.

Bukenya, B., and Hickey, S. (2019) "The Politics of Promoting Social Protection in Uganda: A Comparative Analysis of Social Cash Transfers and Social Health Insurance." In Hickey,

S., Lavers, T., Niño-Zarazúa, M., and Seekings, J. (eds) *The Politics of Social Protection in Eastern and Southern Africa*, 202–224. Oxford University Press.
Bullinger L., and Boy A. (2023) "Association of Expanded Child Tax Credit Payments with Child Abuse and Neglect Emergency Department Visits." *JAMA Network Open* 6(2): e2255639.
Burchell, G., Gordon, C., and Miller, P. (eds) (1991) *The Foucault Effect*. University of Chicago Press.
Burgess, R., and Stern, N. (1991) "Social Security in Developing Countries: What, Why, Who, and How?" In Ahmad, E., Dreze, J., Hills, J., and Sen, A. (eds) *Social Security in Developing Countries*, 41–80. Oxford University Press.
Burke, V., and Burke, V. (1974) *Nixon's Good Deed: Welfare Reform*. Columbia University Press.
Burtless, G. (1986) "The Work Response to a Guaranteed Income: A Survey of Experimental Evidence." In Munnell, A. H. (ed.) *Lessons from the Income Maintenance Experiments*, 22–52. Federal Reserve Bank of Boston.
Butcher, E. (1932) *Bristol Corporation of the Poor: Selected Record 1696–1898—Volume III*. Bristol Record Society Publications.
Butler, J., Ohls, J., and Posner, B. (1985) "The Effect of the Food Stamp Program on the Nutrient Intake of the Eligible Elderly." *Journal of Human Resources* 20(3): 405–420.
Byrd, M. (1973) *"Ye Have the Poor Always with You": Attitudes Toward Relief of the Poor in Colonial Charles Town*. University of South Carolina.
Cain, G. (1986) "The Income Maintenance Experiments and the Issues of Marital Stability and Family Composition." In Munnell, A. H. (ed.) *Lessons from the Income Maintenance Experiments*. Federal Reserve Bank of Boston.
Cain, G., and Wissoker, D. (1990a) "A Reanalysis of Marital Stability in the Seattle–Denver Income-Maintenance Experiment." *American Journal of Sociology* 95(5): 1235–1269.
Cain, G., and Wissoker, D. (1990b) "A Response to Hannan and Tuma." *American Journal of Sociology* 95(5): 1299–1314.
Calnitsky, D. (2018) "Structural and Individualistic Theories of Poverty." *Sociology Compass* 12(12): 1–14.
Carawan, E. (1991) "ΕΦΕΤΑΙ and Athenian Courts for Homicide in the Age of the Orators." *Classical Philology* 86(1): 1–16.
Cardinali, G. (1922) "Frumentatio." In De Ruggiero, E. (ed) *Dizionario Epigrafico di Antichità Romane*, 225–315. L'Erma di Bretschneider.
Carter, P., and Thomson, K. (eds) (2017) *Pauper Prisons, Pauper Palaces: The Victorian Poor Law in the East and West Midlands 1834–1871*. Troubador Publishing.
Cavalcanti, D., Ordonez, J., Aransiola, T., Almeida, C., Diaz, J., Mayorga, D., Sosa, A., Tasca, R., Campello, T., de Souza, L., Hessel, P., Chivardi, C., Moncayo, A., and Rasella, D. (2023) "Evaluation and Forecasting Analysis of the Association of Conditional Cash Transfer with Child Mortality in Latin America, 2000–2030." *JAMA Network Open* 6(7): e2323489.
Çemen, R., and Yörük, E. (2020) "The World Bank and the Contentious Politics of Global Social Spending." In Schmitt, C. (ed) *From Colonialism to International Aid: External Actors and Social Protection in the Global South*, 221–243. Palgrave MacMillan.
Chalmers, T. (1841) *On the Sufficiency of the Parochial System, Without a Poor Rate, for the Right Management of the Poor*. William Collins.
Chance, W. (1897) "The Elberfeld and English Poor Law Systems: A Comparison." *Economic Journal* 7(27): 332–345.
Chang, H-J. (2003) *Kicking Away the Ladder: Development Strategy in Historical Perspective*. Anthem Press.

Chang, H-J. (2004) "The Role of Social Policy in Economic Development: Some Theoretical Reflections and Lessons from East Asia." In Mkandawire, T. (eds) *Social Policy in a Development Context*, 246–261. UNRISD.
Charlesworth, L. (2010a) "Welfare's Forgotten Past: A Socio-Legal History of the Poor Law." *Amicus Curiae* 81(Spring): 16–20.
Charlesworth, L. (2010b) *Welfare's Forgotten Past: A Socio-Legal History of the Poor Law.* Routledge.
Chazan, N., Mortimer, R., Ravenhill, J., and Rithchild, D. (1988) *Politics and Society in Contemporary Africa*. Rienner Publishers.
Checkland, O. (1985) "Chalmers and William Pulteney Alison: A Conflict of Views on Scottish Social Policy." In Cheyne, A. (ed) *The Practical and the Pious: Essays on Thomas Chalmers (1780–1847)*. The Saint Andrew Press.
Chen, J. (2012) *Guilty of Indigence: The Urban Poor in China, 1900–1953*. Princeton University Press.
Chen, S., and Ravallion, M. (2021) "Reconciling the Conflicting Narratives on Poverty in China." *Journal of Development Economics* 153(5): 102711.
Cheng, T., and Selden, M. (1994) "The Origins and Social Consequences of China's Hukou System." *China Quarterly* 139: 644–668.
Cherrier, B. (2019) "How to Write a Memo to Convince a President: Walter Heller, Policy-Advising, and the Kennedy Tax Cut." *Oeconomia* 9(2): 315–335.
Cherry, T., Kallbekken, S., and Kroll, S. (2012). "The Acceptability of Efficiency-Enhancing Environmental Taxes, Subsidies and Regulation: An Experimental Investigation." *Environmental Science and Policy* 16: 90–96.
Cheyne, A. (1985) "Thomas Chalmers: Then and Now." In Cheyne, A. (ed) *The Practical and the Pious: Essays on Thomas Chalmers (1780–1847)*, 79–106. The Saint Andrew Press.
Chinyoka, I. (2019) "Familial Child Welfare Regimes: The Case of Botswana." CSSR Working Paper 430. University of Cape Town.
Chinyoka, I., and Ulriksen, M. (2020) "The Limits of the Influence of International Donors: Social Protection in Botswana." In Schmitt, C. (ed) *From Colonialism to International Aid: External Actors and Social Protection in the Global South*, 245–271. Palgrave MacMillan.
Choi, Y.J., Noh, H.S., Han, S.H., and Gentilini, U. (2023) "Diversity within Universality: Codifying Universal Cash Transfers During Covid-19 in East Asia." Yonsei University/World Bank.
Chong, Z., and Lau, S. (2023) "A Systematic Review and Meta-Analysis of the Educational Effects of Unconditional Cash Transfers." MPRA Paper 113587. Munich Personal RePEc Archive.
Chowdhury, A., Lawson, C., Kellison, E., Chia, H., Kharas, H., Fuller, J., Faye, M., Rutkowski, M., Salvado, R., and Dercon, S. (2022, February 17) "Accelerating Digital Cash Transfers to the World's Poorest." *Brookings* Commentary [online]. https://www.brookings.edu/articles/accelerating-digital-cash-transfers-to-the-worlds-poorest/
Christians, C. (2004) "Ubuntu and Communitarianism in Media Ethics." *Ecquid Novi: African Journalism Studies* 25(2): 235–256.
Chung-Kim, E. (2017) "Advocating for Poor Relief in Zurich: Heinrich Bullinger's Contributions to Religious Ideals and Policy Reforms." *Church History* 86(2): 311–338.
Ciminelli, G., Furceri, D., Ge, J., Ostry, J., and Papageorgiou, C. (2019, October 18) "The Political Costs of Reforms: Fear or Reality?" *Staff Discussion Notes* [online]. IMF. https://www.imf.org/en/Publications/Staff-Discussion-Notes/Issues/2019/10/17/The-Political-Costs-of-Reforms-Fear-or-Reality-48735
Cipolla, C. (1957) *Moneta e Civiltà Mediterranea*. Neri Pozza Editore.

Clark, E. (2002) "Institutional and Legal Responses to Begging in Medieval England." *Social Science History* 26(3): 447–473.

Clark, G. (1997) "The Long March of History: Farm Wages, Population, and Economic Growth, England 1209–1869." *Economic History Review* 60(1): 97–135.

Clay, C. (1984) *Economic Expansion and Social Change: England, 1500–1700.* Cambridge University Press.

Coady, D., Jahan, S., Matsumoto, R., and Shang, B. (2021) "Guaranteed Minimum Income Schemes in Europe: Landscape and Design." Working Paper 21/179. IMF.

Coate, S. (1989) "Cash versus Direct Food Relief." *Journal of Development Economics* 30(2): 199–224.

Cobbah, J. (1987) "African Values and the Human Rights Debate: An African Perspective" *Human Rights Quarterly* 9(3): 309–331.

Cody, L. (2000) "The Politics of Illegitimacy in an Age of Reform: Women, Reproduction, and Political Economy in England's New Poor Law of 1834." *Journal of Women's History* 11(4): 131–156.

Colcord, J. (1936) *Cash Relief.* Russell Sage.

Collier, D., and Messick, R. (1975) "Prerequisites versus Diffusion: Testing Alternative Explanations of Social Security Adoption." *American Political Science Review* 69(4): 1299–1315.

Collinson, P. (2001) "Puritanism and the Poor." In Horrox, R., and Rees-Jones, S. (eds) *Pragmatic Utopias: Ideals and Communities,* 1200–1630. Cambridge University Press.

Collyer, S., Hardy, B., and Wimer, C. (2023, March 1) "The Antipoverty Effects of the Expanded Child Tax Credit across States: Where Were the Historic Reductions Felt?." *Brookings Commentary* [online]. https://www.brookings.edu/articles/the-antipoverty-effects-of-the-expanded-child-tax-credit-across-states-where-were-the-historic-reductions-felt/

Conover, E., Zarate, R., Camacho, A., and Baez, J. (2020) "Cash and Ballots: Conditional Transfers, Political Participation, and Voting Behavior." *Economic Development and Cultural Change* 68(2): 541–566.

Conway, T., and Norton, A. (2002) "Nets, Ropes, Ladders and Trampolines: The Place of Social Protection within Current Debates on Poverty Reduction." *Development Policy Review* 20(5): 533–540.

Cooper, F. (1996) *Decolonization and African Society. The Labor Question in French and British Africa.* Cambridge University Press.

Cooper, F. (2012) "Decolonization and Citizenship: Africa between Empires and a World of Nations." In Bogaerts, E., and Raben, R. (eds) *Beyond Empire and Nation: The Decolonization of African and Asian societies, 1930s–1970s.* Brill.

Corbett, T., Deloya, J., Manning, W., and Uhr, L. (1989) "Learnfare: The Wisconsin Experience." Institute for Research on Poverty, *Focus* 12(2): 1–10. Madison.

Correa, J., Daidone, S., Davis, B., and Sitko, N. (2023) "Social Protection and Rural Transformation in Africa." *Annual Review of Resource Economics* 15: 305–327.

Costa, E., Rocha, N., Rocha, T., Lima, H., Vissoci, J., Queiroz, R., and Thomaz, E. (2022) "Bolsa Família Program and Deaths from Oral Cancer in Brazil: An Ecological Study." *Pan American Journal of Public Health* 46: e208.

Cotlear, D., Nagpal, S., Smith, O., Tandon, A., and Cortez, R. (2015) *Going Universal: How 24 Developing Countries Are Implementing Universal Health Coverage Reforms from the Bottom Up.* World Bank.

Cottam, H. (2018) *Radical Help: How We Can Remake the Relationship between Us and Revolutionise the Welfare State.* Virago Press.

Courtenay, W. (1972) "Token Coinage and the Administration of Poor Relief during the Late Middle Ages." *Journal of Interdisciplinary History* 3(2): 275–295.

Covey, A. (2020) "Inca Responses to Environmental Hazards in the Capital Region and Provinces." In Dijkman, J., and van Leeuwen, B. (eds) *Economic History of Famine Resilience*, 74–92. Routledge.

Covey, A., Quave, K., and Covey, C. (2016) "Inka Storage Systems in the Imperial Heartland (Cuzco, Peru): Risk Management, Economic Growth, and Political Economy." In Manzanilla, L., and Rothman, M. (eds) *Storage in Ancient Complex Societies: Administration, Organization, and Control*, 167–188. Routledge.

Cowherd, R. (1977) *Political Economists and the English Poor Laws*. Ohio University Press.

Cristofori, A. (2003) "Grain Distribution in Late Republican Rome." In Jensen, H. (ed) *The Welfare State: Past, Present, Future*, 141–153. Plus.

Crossman, V. (2013) *Poverty and the Poor Law in Ireland, 1850–1914*. Liverpool University Press.

Cruz-Martinez, J. (2021) "Mapping Welfare State Development in (Post) Neoliberal Latin America." *Social Indicators Research*, 157(1): 175–201.

Cunningham, W. (1908) *The Industrial Revolution*. Cambridge University Press.

Daidone, S., Kagin, J., and Taylor, J. (2023) "Local Economy-Wide Impact Evaluation of the United Republic of Tanzania's Productive Social Safety Nets." FAO.

Danziger, S., and Haveman, R. (1987) *The Reagan Administration's Budget Cuts: Their Impact on the Poor*. University of Wisconsin, Institute for Research on Poverty.

Darwin, C. (1871) *The Descent of Man, and Selection in Relation to Sex*. Appleton and Company.

Davey, E., Borton, J., and Foley, M. (2013) *A History of the Humanitarian System: Western Origins and Foundations*. ODI.

Davies, D. (1795) *The Case of Labourers in Husbandry Stated and Considered*. Cambridge University Press (2011 edition).

Davies, M. (2009) "DFID Social Transfers Evaluation Summary Report." Research Report 60. IDS.

Davis, B., Handa, S., Hyper, N., Winder Rossi, N., Winters, P., and Yablonski, J. (2016) "The Transfer Project, Cash Transfers, and Impact Evaluation in Sub-Saharan Africa." In Davis, B., Handa, S., Hyper, N., Winder Rossi, N., Winters, P., and Yablonski (eds) *From Evidence to Action: The Story of Cash Transfers and Impact Evaluation in Sub-Saharan Africa*, 1–16. Oxford University Press.

Davis, R. (1971) *The New Economics and the Old Economists*. Iowa State University Press.

Davis-Friedmann, D. (1983) Long Lives: Chinese Elderly and the Communist Revolution. Stanford University Press

Davy, J. Loch, C., and Hanewinkel, A. (1888) "Elberfeld Poor Law System: Reports on the Elberfeld Poor Law System and German Workmen's Colonies." *Government of the UK Report Presented to Both Houses of Parliament by Command of Her Majesty*. HMSO.

Day, P., and Schiele, J. (2013) *A New History of Social Welfare*, 7th edn. Pearson.

de Haan, A. (2014) "The Rise of Social Protection in Development: Progress, Pitfalls and Politics." *European Journal of Development Research* 26(3): 311–321

De La O, A. (2013) "Do Conditional Cash Transfers Affect Electoral Behavior? Evidence from a Randomized Experiment in Mexico." *American Journal of Political Science* 57(1): 1–14.

de Sardan, J. P., and Piccoli, E. (eds) (2018) *Cash Transfers in Context: An Anthropological Perspective*. Berghahn.

De Schweinitz, K. (1943) *England's Road to Social Security*. Barnes and Company.

De Schweinitz, K. (undated) *The Dilemma of Need*. Unfinished manuscript.

de Tocqueville, A. (1835) *Memoir on Pauperism*. Civitas (1997 edition).

de Waal, A. (1989) *The Sudan Famine Code of 1920: Successes and Failures of the Indian Model of Famine Relief in Colonial Sudan*. ActionAid.

de Waal, A. (1997) *Famine Crimes: Politics and the Disaster Relief Industry in Africa.* Indiana University Press.

de Waal, A. (2018) *Mass Starvation. The History and Future of Famine.* Polity Press.

De Witte S. (2014) "Mortality Risk and Survival in the Aftermath of the Medieval Black Death." *PLoS One* 9(5): e96513.

Deacon, B. (2013) *Global Social Policy in the Making: The Foundations of the Social Protection Floor.* Policy Press.

Deaton, A. (2005) "Measuring Poverty in a Growing World (or Measuring Growth in a Poor World)." *Review of Economics and Statistics* 87(1): 1–19.

Del Mar, A. (1885) *A History of Money in Ancient Countries from the Earliest Times to the Present.* George Bell and Sons.

Della Guardia, A., Lake M., and Schnitzer, P. (2022) "Selective Inclusion in Cash Transfer Programs: Unintended Consequences for Social Cohesion." *World Development* 157(3): 105922.

Department for International Development (DFID) (2009) "Eliminating World Poverty: Building Our Common Future." London.

Department for International Development (DFID) (2011) "Cash Transfers Evidence Paper." London.

Dercon, S. (2023) "Scaling Social Protection Systems: What Holds It Back?." Keynote presentation at the *Global Forum on Adaptive Social Protection* (Berlin, June 12–14). (Recording available at https://www.youtube.com/watch?v=n_lOa7rKP2E at 00:27–00:49).

Desmond, M. (2023a, March 9) "Why Poverty Persists in America." New York Times [online]. https://www.nytimes.com/2023/03/09/magazine/poverty-by-america-matthew-desmond.html

Desmond, M. (2023b) *Poverty, by America.* Crown.

Devadevan, M.V. (2020) *The "Early Medieval" Origins of India.* Cambridge University Press.

Devaney, B., and Fraker, T. (1986) "Cashing Out Food Stamps: Impacts on Food Expenditures and Diet Quality." *Journal of Policy Analysis and Management* 5(4): 725–741.

Development Initiatives (2022) "Global Humanitarian Assistance Report 2022." Development Initiatives Poverty Research Ltd.

Devereux, S. (1988) "Entitlements, Availability and Famine." *Food Policy* 13(3): 270–282.

Devereux, S. (2011) "Social Protection in South Africa: Exceptional or Exceptionalism?" *Canadian Journal of Development Studies* 32(4): 414–425

Devereux, S. (2016) "Is Targeting Ethical?" *Global Social Policy* 16(2): 166–181

Devereux, S. (2020) "Policy Pollination: A Brief History of Social Protection's Brief History in Africa." Working Paper 543. IDS.

Devereux, S., and Getu, M. (2013) "Conclusion." In Devereux, S. and Getu, M. (eds) *Informal and Formal Social Protection Systems in Sub-Saharan Africa*, 285–297. Fountain Publishers.

Devereux, S., and Kapingidza, S. (2020) "External Donors and Social Protection in Africa: A Case Study of Zimbabwe." In Schmitt, C. (ed) *From Colonialism to International Aid: External Actors and Social Protection in the Global South*, 273–302. Palgrave MacMillan.

Devereux, S., and Sabates-Wheeler, R. (2007) "Editorial Introduction: Debating Social Protection." *IDS Bulletin* 28(3): 1–7.

Devereux, S., Masset, E., Sabates-Wheeler, S., Samson, M., Rivas. A., and Lintelo, D. (2017) "The Targeting Effectiveness of Social Transfers." *Journal of Development Effectiveness* 9(2): 162–211.

Dhemba, J. Gumbo, P., and Nyamusara, J. (2002) "Social Security in Zimbabwe—Phase II: Zundera Mambo and Burial Societies." *Journal of Social Development in Africa* 17(2): 132–156.

Díaz-Cayeros, A., and Magaloni, B. (2009) "Aiding Latin America's Poor." *Journal of Democracy* 20(4): 36–49.

Dickens, A. (1976, December 1) "The Architect and the Workhouse." *Architectural Review* [online]. https://www.architectural-review.com/archive/the-architect-and-the-workhouse
Dickey, B. (1992) "Why Were There No Poor Laws in Australia?." *Journal of Policy History* 4(2): 111–133.
Digby, A. (1976) "The Rural Poor Law." In Fraser, D. (ed) *The New Poor Law in the Nineteenth Century*, 149–170. Macmillian.
Digby, A. (1978) *Pauper Palaces*. Routledge.
Digby, A. (1982) *The Poor Law in Nineteenth-Century England and Wales*. The Historical Association.
Dillon, M. (1995) "Payments to the Disabled at Athens: Social Justice or Fear of Aristocratic Patronage?" *Ancient Society* 26: 27–57.
Dincecco, M. (2011) *Political Transformations and Public Finances: Europe, 1650–1913*. Cambridge University Press.
Dincecco, M. (2017) *State Capacity and Economic Development: Past and Present*. Cambridge University Press.
Dincecco, M., and Onorato, M. (2017) *From Warfare to Wealth: The Military Origins of Urban Prosperity in Europe*. Cambridge University Press.
Dixon, J. (ed) (1987a) *Social Welfare in the Middle East*. Routledge Revivals.
Dixon, J. (ed) (1987b) *Social Welfare in Africa*. Routledge Revivals.
Dixon, J., and Kim, H. (eds) (1985) *Social Welfare in Asia*. Routledge Revivals.
Dixon, J., and Macarov, D. (eds) (1992) *Social Welfare in Socialist Countries*. Routledge Revivals.
Dixon, J. and Scheurell, R. P. (eds) (1990) *Social Welfare in Latin America*. Routledge Revivals.
Dobbin, F., Simmons, B., and Garrett, G. (2007) "The Global Diffusion of Public Policies: Social Construction, Coercion, Competition, or Learning?" *Annual Review of Sociology* 33(1): 449–472.
Dodlova, M. (2020) "International Donors and Social Policy Diffusion in the Global South." In Schmitt, C. (ed) *From Colonialism to International Aid: External Actors and Social Protection in the Global South*, 189–220. Palgrave MacMillan.
Dolgoff, R., and Feldstein, D. (2009) *Understanding Social Welfare: A Search for Social Justice*, 8th edn. Pearson.
Dollar, D., and Pritchett, L. (1998) *Assessing Aid: What Works, What Doesn't, and Why*. World Bank.
Donoghue, J. (2010) "Out of the Land of Bondage: The English Revolution and the Atlantic Origins of Abolition." *American Historical Review* 115(4): 943–974.
Dorfman, M., Wang, D., O'Keefe, P., and Cheng, J. (2013) "China's Pension Schemes for Rural and Urban Residents." In Hinz, R., Holzmann, R., Tuesta, D., and Takayama, N. (eds) *Matching Contributions for Pensions: A Review of International Experience*, 217. World Bank
Dorwart, R. (1971) *The Prussian Welfare State Before 1740*. Harvard University Press.
Douglas, M. (1966) *Purity and Danger: An Analysis of Concepts of Pollution and Taboo*. Routledge.
Dreze, J. (1988) "Famine Prevention in India." Working Paper 45. UNU/WIDER.
Dreze, J. (1995) "Famine Prevention in Africa: Some Experiences and Lessons." In Dreze, J. Sen, A., and Hussain, A. (eds) *The Political Economy of Hunger—Selected Essays*, 554–604. Oxford University Press.
Dreze, J. (2017) *Sense and Solidarity: Jholawala Economics for Everyone*. Oxford University Press.
Dreze, J., and Khera, R. (2017) "Recent Social Security Initiatives in India." *World Development* 98(C): 555–572.
Dreze, J., and Sen, A. (1989) *Hunger and Public Action*. Oxford University Press.

Dreze, J., and Sen, A. (1991) "Public Action for Social Security: Foundations and Strategy." In Ahmad, E., Dreze, J., Hills, J., and Sen, A. (eds) *Social Security in Developing Countries*, 2–40. Oxford University Press.

Dryburgh, M. (2016) "Living on the Edge: Welfare and the Urban Poor in 1930s Beijing." *Social History* 41(1): 14–33.

Du, J., and Deng, K. (2017) "To Get the Prices Right for Food: The State Versus the Market in Reforming China, 1979–2006." *European Review of Economic History* 21(3): 302–325.

Dubini, M. (1982) "Padroni di Niente." Povertà e Assistanza a Como tra Medioevo ed Età Moderna." In Politi, G., Rosa, M. and Della Peruta, F. (eds) *Timore e Carità: I Poveri nell'Italia Moderna*. Biblioteca Statale e Libreria Civica di Cremona.

Duflo, E. (2017) "The Economist as Plumber." *American Economic Review* 107(5): 1–26.

Dugdale, R. (1877) *The Jukes: A Study of Crime, Pauperism, Disease, and Heredity*. Putnam's Sons.

Dunant, H. (1862) *A Memory of Solferino*. Impremerie Jules-Guillaume Fick.

Duncan, G., Hill, M., and Hoffman, S. (1988) "Welfare Dependence Within and Across Generations." *Science* 239(4839): 467–471.

Duncan-Jones, R. (1964) "The Purpose and Organisation of the Alimenta." *Papers of the British School at Rome* 32: 123–146.

Duplessis, R. (1977) "Charité Municipale et Autorité Publique Autorité Publique Au XIXe Siècle: L'Exemple de Lille." *Revue Du Nord* 59(233): 193–219.

Dustan, A. (2020) "Can Large, Untargeted Conditional Cash Transfers Increase Urban High School Graduation Rates? Evidence from Mexico City's Prepa Sí." *Journal of Development Economics* 143(March): 102392.

Easterby, J. (1941) "Public Poor Relief in Colonial Charleston: A Report to the Commons House of Assembly about the Year 1767." *South Carolina Historical and Genealogical Magazine* 42(2): 83–86.

Easterly, W. (2001) "Debt Relief." *Foreign Policy* 127 (Nov–Dec): 20–26.

Eckert, A. (2004) "Regulating the Social: Social Security, Social Welfare and The State in Late Colonial Tanzania." *Journal of African History* 45(3): 467–489.

Eden, F. (1797) *The State of the Poor*. Frank Class (1966 edition).

Edgerton-Tarpley, K. (2008) *Tears from Iron: Cultural Responses to Famine in Nineteenth Century China*. University of California Press.

Edgerton-Tarpley, K. (2014) "From 'Nourish the People' to 'Sacrifice for the Nation': Changing Responses to Disaster in Late Imperial and Modern China." *Journal of Asian Studies* 73(2): 447–469.

Edirisinghe, N. (1987) "The Food Stamp Scheme in Sri Lanka: Costs, Benefits, and Options for Modification." Research Report 58. IFPRI.

Edirisinghe, N. (1998) "The Food Factor." Background paper for conference *Time for Change: Food Aid and Development Consultation* (October 23–24). WFP.

Edsall, N. (1971) *The Anti-Poor Law Movement, 1834–44*. Manchester University Press.

Edwards, W. (1878) "The Poor-Law Experiment at Elberfeld." *Contemporary Review* 52(July): 675–693.

Egger, P., Radulescu, D., and Strecker, N. (2017) "On the Spread of Social Protection Systems." *International Tax and Public Finance* 24: 550–574.

Eghigian, G. (2000) *Making Security Social: Disability, Insurance, and the Birth of the Social Entitlement State in Germany*. University of Michigan Press.

Elder, W. (1964) "Speenhamland Revisited." *Social Service Review* 38(3): 294–302.

Eldersveld, S. (2010) *Poor America: A Comparative-Historical Study of Poverty in the U.S. and Western Europe*. Lexington Books.

Elliot, H. (1907) *The Mohammedan Period as Described by its Own Historians* Williams Jackson, A. (ed) History of India series, Volume 5. Grolier Society.

Ellwood, D. (1988) *Poor Support: Poverty in the American Family*. Basic.

Ellwood, D. (2001, November 19) "Welfare Reform as I Knew It: When Bad Things Happen to Good Policies." *American Prospect* [online]. https://prospect.org/economy/welfare-reform-knew-it-bad-things-happen-good-policies/

Elton, G. (1953) "An Early Tudor Poor Law." *Economic History Review* 6(1): 55–67.

Engels, F. (1845) *The Condition of the Working Class in England*. Oxford University Press (1993 edition).

Englander, D. (1998) *Poverty and Poor Law Reform in Nineteenth-Century Britain, 1834-1914: From Chadwick to Booth*. Routledge.

Epstein, S. (2000) *Freedom and Growth: Markets and States in Europe, 1300–1750*. Routledge.

Erdkamp, P. (2016) "Annona (grain)." Oxford Classical Dictionary [online]. Oxford University Press. https://doi.org/10.1093/acrefore/9780199381135.013.8000

Ertman, T. (1997) *Birth of the Leviathan: Building States and Regimes in Medieval and Early Modern Europe*. Cambridge University Press.

Esping-Andersen, G. (1990) *The Three Worlds of Welfare Capitalism*. Princeton University Press.

Evans, D., and Popova, A. (2017) "Cash Transfers and Temptation Goods." *Economic Development and Cultural Change* 65(2): 189–221.

Evans, J. (1981) "Wheat Production and its Social Consequences in the Roman World." *Classical Quarterly* 31(2): 428–444.

Evans, M., Harkness, S., and Salomon, H. (2020) "Informal Taxes and Transfers in Sub-Saharan Africa: A Review and Analysis of Incidence in Rwanda." Working Paper 598. ODI.

Ezzamel, M. (2002) "Accounting and Redistribution: The Palace and Mortuary Cult in the Middle Kingdom, Ancient Egypt." *Accounting Historians Journal* 29(1): 61–103.

Fairlie, S. (2009) "A Short History of Enclosure in Britain." *The Land* 7 (Summer): 16–31.

Falk, G., Aussenberg, R., and McCarty, M. (2016) "Work Requirements, Time Limits, and Work Incentives in TANF, SNAP, and Housing Assistance." Report 43400. Congressional Research Service.

Falvo, N. (2017, May 5) "The Introduction and Evolution of Child Benefits in Canada." Tamarack Institute [blog]. https://www.tamarackcommunity.ca/latest/the-introduction-and-evolution-of-child-benefits-in-canada.

Fan, C., and Long, Y. (2022) "The Secularization of Religious Figures: A Study of Mahoraga in the Song Dynasty (960–1279)." *Religions* 13(177): 1–17.

FAO, IFAD, UNICEF, WFP, and WHO (2022) *The State of Food Security and Nutrition in the World 2022: Repurposing Food and Agricultural Policies to Make Healthy Diets More Affordable*. FAO.

Fawcett, H. (1871) *Pauperism: Its Causes and Remedies*. MacMillan and Co.

Feder, L. (1936) *Unemployment Relief in Periods of Depression: A Study of Measures Adopted in Certain American Cities, 1857–1922*. Russell Sage.

Feldman, S., and Zaller, J. (1992) "The Political Culture of Ambivalence: Ideological Responses to the Welfare State." *American Journal of Political Science* 36(1): 268–307.

Feldstein, M. (1999) "Social Security Pension Reform in China." *China Economic Review* 10(2): 99–107.

Fenton, G. (2023) *Gains from Expanded Child Tax Credit Outweigh Overstated Employment Worries*. Center on Budget and Policy Priorities.

Fenwick, T. (2013) "Stuck Between the Past and the Future: Conditional Cash Transfer Programme Development and Policy Feedbacks in Brazil and Argentina." *Global Social Policy* 13(2): 144–167.

Ferguson, J. (2012) "What Comes after the Social? Historicizing the Future of Social Assistance and Identity Registration in Africa." In Breckenridge, K., and Szreter, S. (eds) *Recognition and Registration: Documenting the Person in History*, 495–516. Oxford University Press.

Ferguson, J. (2015) *Give a Man a Fish: Reflections on the New Politics of Distribution*. Duke University Press.
Ferguson, J. (2019) "Proletarian Politics Today: On the Perils and Possibilities of Historical Analogy." *Comparative Studies in Society and History* 61(1): 4–22.
Ferguson, J. (2021) *Presence and Social Obligation: An Essay on the Share*. Prickly Paradigm Press.
Ferraro, P., and Simorangkir, R. (2020) "Conditional Cash Transfers to Alleviate Poverty Also Reduced Deforestation in Indonesia." *Science Advances* 6(24): 1–8.
Ferri Piccaluga, G. (1982) "La Riforma della Pubblica Assistenza Sotto il Governo di Maria Teresa: L'Architetto Francesco Croce e la Costruzione dell'Albergo dei Poveri nella Città di Milano." In Politi, G., Rosa, M., and Della Peruta, F. (eds) *Timore e Carità: I Poveri nell'Italia Moderna*, 225–235. Biblioteca Statale e Libreria Civica di Cremona.
Filmer, D., Friedman, J., Kandpal, E., and Onishi, J. (2023) "Cash Transfers, Food Prices, and Nutrition Impacts on Ineligible Children." *Review of Economics and Statistics* 105(2): 327–343.
Finer, S. (1952) *The Life and Times of Sir Edwin Chadwick*. Routledge.
Finer, S. (1972) "The Transmission of Benthamite Ideas 1820–1850." In Sutherland, G. (ed) *Studies in the Growth of Nineteenth-Century Government*, 11–32. Routledge.
Finley, M. I. (1973) *The Ancient Economy*. University of California Press.
Fiszbein, A., and Schady, N. (2009) *Conditional Cash Transfers: Reducing Present and Future Poverty*. World Bank.
Fitzgerald, J. (2016) "Orphans in Mediterranean Antiquity and Early Christianity." *Acta Theologica* 23: 29–48.
Fleet, J. (1907) "The Inscription on the Sohgaura Plate." *Journal of the Royal Asiatic Society of Great Britain and Ireland* 21: 509–532.
Flegg, G. (2002) *Numbers: Their History and Meaning*. Courier Dover Publications.
Fleischacker, S. (2004) *A Short History of Distributive Justice*. Harvard University Press.
Flemming, R. (2012) "Identity Registration in the Classical Mediterranean World." In Breckenridge, K., and Szreter, S. (eds) *Recognition and Registration: Documenting the Person in History*, 169–190. Oxford University Press.
Fletcher, L. P. (1992) "The Evolution of Poor Relief in Barbados 1900 to 1969." *Caribbean Studies* 25(3/4): 255–276.
Flynn, M. (1989) *Sacred Charity: Confraternities and Social Welfare in Spain, 1400–1700*. MacMillan.
Foli, R. (2016) "Transnational Actors and Policymaking in Ghana: The Case of the Livelihood Empowerment Against Poverty." *Global Social Policy* 16(3): 268–286
Forde-Jones, C. (1998) "Mapping Racial Boundaries: Gender, Race, and Poor Relief in Barbadian Plantation Society." *Journal of Women's History* 10(3): 9–31.
Forget, E. (2011) "The Town with No Poverty: The Health Effects of a Canadian Guaranteed Annual Income Field Experiment." *Canadian Public Policy* 37(3): 283–305.
Forget, E. (2018) *Basic Income for Canadians: The Key to a Healthier, Happier, More Secure Life for All*. Lorimer.
Forsberg, H., and Bohman, M. (2023) "Relieving Famine. Northern Sweden (Västerbotten) Between State, Market, and Civil Society During the 1860s." *Scandinavian Economic History Review* [online]. https://doi.org/10.1080/03585522.2023.2279215
Fosseyeux, M. (1934) "Les premiers budgets municipaux d'assistance. La taxe des pauvres au XVIe siècle." *Revue d'Histoire de l'Église de France* 88: 407–432
Fowle, T. (1881) *The Poor Law*. Macmillan.
Fowler, S. (2007) *The Workhouse: The People, The Places, The Life Behind Doors*. National Archives.

Fraker, T. 1990 "The Effects of Food Stamps on Food Consumption: A Review of the Literature." USDA.
Francese, M., and Prady, D. (2018) "Universal Basic Income: Debate and Impact Assessment." Working Paper WP/18/273. IMF.
Frank, L. (2010) "Panoptical Delusions: British India in *The Sign of Four*." *Dickens Studies Annual* 41: 323–362.
Fraser, D. (2017) *The Evolution of the British Welfare State: A History of Social Policy Since the Industrial Revolution*, 5th ed. MacMillan.
Fraser, W. (1983) "The City Elite, 'Disorder' and the Poor Children of Pre-Revolutionary Charleston." *South Carolina Historical Magazine* 84(3): 167–179.
Freeman, K. (1926) *The Work and Life of Solon. With a Translation of His Poems*. University of Wales Press Board.
French, H. (2013) "Living in Poverty in Eighteenth-Century Terling." In Hindle, S., Shepard, A., and Walter, J. (eds) *Remaking English Society: Social Relations and Social Change in Early Modern England*, 281–316. Woodbridge.
French, H. (2015a) "How Dependent Were the 'Dependent Poor'? Poor Relief and the Life-Course in Terling, Essex, 1760–1834." *Continuity and Change* 30: 192–222.
French, H. (2015b) "An Irrevocable Gift: Detailing the Dynamics of Rural Poverty in Southern England, 1762–1834: A Case Study." *Economic History Review* 68(3): 759–805.
French, P. (1988) "Colonial Policy Towards Women After the 1938 Uprising: The Case of Jamaica." *Caribbean Quarterly* 34(3–4): 38–61.
Friedman, B. (2021) *Religion and the Rise of Capitalism*. Knopfs.
Friedman, M. (1967, March 7) "The Case for the Negative Income Tax." *National Review*: 239–241.
Frohman, L. (2008) *Poor Relief and Welfare in Germany from the Reformation to World War I*. Cambridge University Press.
Fukuyama, F. (2014) *Political Order and Political Decay: From the Industrial Revolution to the Globalization of Democracy*. Farrar, Straus and Giroux.
Fuller, A., Zaffar, N., Cohen, E., Pentland, M., Siddiqi, A., Vandermorris, A., Van Den Heuvel, M., Birken, C., Guttmann, A., and de Oliveira, C. (2022) "Cash Transfer Programs and Child Health and Family Economic Outcomes: A Systematic Review." *Canadian Journal of Public Health* 113: 433–445.
Fuller, P. (2019) *Famine Relief in Warlord China*. Harvard University Asia Center.
Furgol, M. (1985) "Chalmers and Poor Relief: An Incidental Sideline?" In Cheyne, A. (ed) *The Practical and the Pious: Essays on Thomas Chalmers (1780–1847)*. The Saint Andrew Press.
Furgol, M. (1987) "Thomas Chalmers' Poor Relief Theories and Their Implementation in the Early Nineteenth Century." PhD Thesis, University of Edinburgh.
Furman, J. (2020) "The Fiscal Response to the Great Recession: Steps Taken, Paths Rejected, and Lessons for Next Time." In Bernanke, B. S., Geithner, T. F., and Paulson, H. M., Jr., with Liang, J. N. (eds) *First Responders: Inside the U.S. Strategy for Fighting the 2007–2009 Global Financial Crisis*, 451–488. Yale University Press.
Galbraith, J. (1958) *The Affluent Society*. Houghton Mifflin.
Gans, H. (1971a) "The Uses of Poverty: The Poor Pay All." *Social Policy* (July/August): 20–24.
Gans, H. (1971b, March 7) "Three Ways to Solve the Welfare Problem." *New York Times* (Section SM: 26).
Gans, H. (1972) "The Positive Functions of Poverty." *American Journal of Sociology* 78(2): 275–289.
Gao, Q. (2017) *Welfare, Work and Poverty: Social Assistance in China*. Oxford University Press.
Gao, Q., Yang, S., and Zhai, F. (2019) "Social Policy and Income Inequality During the Hu-Wen Era: A Progressive Legacy?" *China Quarterly* 237: 82–107.

Garay, C. (2016) *Social Policy Expansion in Latin America*. Cambridge University Press.

Gardner, L. (2013) *Taxing Colonial Africa: The Political Economy of British Imperialism*. Oxford University Press.

Garfinkel, I., Sariscsany, L., Ananat, E., Collyer, S., Hartley, S., Wang, B., and Wimer, C. (2022) *The Benefits and Costs of a U.S. Child Allowance*. NBER Working Paper 29854. National Bureau of Economic Research.

Garland, T. (1891) "The Annual Meeting." *Charity Organization Review* 7(78): 237–254.

Garnsey, P. (1968) "Trajan's Alimenta: Some Problems." *Historia* 17(3): 367–381.

Garnsey, P. (1988) *Famine and Food Supply in the Graeco-Roman World: Responses to Risk and Crisis*. Cambridge University Press.

Garnsey, P. (1990) "Responses to Food Crisis in the Ancient Mediterranean World." In Newman, L. (ed) *Hunger in History: Food Shortage, Poverty and Deprivation*, 126–146. Blackwell.

Garran Martinez, J. (2004) *La Prohibición de la Mendicidad: La Controversia Entre Domingo de Soto y Juan de Robles en Salamanca (1545)*. Ediciones Universidad Salamanca.

Garraty, J. (1978) *Unemployment in History. Economic Thought and Public Policy*. Harper & Row.

Gassmann, F., Gentilini, U., Morais, J., Nunnenmacher, C., and Okamura, Y. (2023) "Is the Magic Happening? A Systematic Literature Review of the Economic Multiplier of Cash Transfers." Policy Research Working Paper 10529. World Bank.

Gelfand, M. (1961) *Northern Rhodesia in the Days of the Charter: A Medical and Social Study, 1878–1924*. Basil Blackwell.

Gennaioli N., and Rainer, I. (2007) "The Modern Impact of Precolonial Centralization in Africa." *Journal of Economic Growth* 12(3): 185–234.

Gentilini, U. (2007) "Cash and Food Transfers: A Primer." Discussion Paper 18. WFP.

Gentilini, U. (2016a) "Revisiting the "Cash versus Food" Debate: New Evidence for an Old Puzzle?" *World Bank Research Observer* 31(1): 135–167.

Gentilini, U. (2016b) *The Other Side of the Coin: The Comparative Evidence of Cash and In-Kind Transfers in Humanitarian Situations*. World Bank.

Gentilini, U. (2018, August 22) "What Lessons for Social Protection from Universal Health Coverage?" Let's Talk Development [blog]. World Bank. https://blogs.worldbank.org/en/developmenttalk/what-lessons-social-protection-universal-health-coverage

Gentilini, U. (2022) *Cash Transfers in Pandemic Times: Evidence, Practices, and Implications from the Largest Scale Up in History*. World Bank.

Gentilini, U. (2023a, November 14) "Where Has All the Social Protection Gone ... and Where Will It Come From?" *Brookings* Commentary [online]. https://www.brookings.edu/articles/where-has-all-the-social-protection-gone-where-will-it-come-from/

Gentilini, U. (2023b, June 30) "Why Does In-Kind Assistance Persist When Evidence Favors Cash Transfers? Meet the Six People Shaping the Debate." *Brookings Commentary* [online]. https://www.brookings.edu/articles/why-does-in-kind-assistance-persist-when-evidence-favors-cash-transfers/

Gentilini, U. (2023c) *Ten Reflections on Targeting and Universality*. World Bank.

Gentilini, U., and Sabarwal, S. (2022, April 25) "School Meals Bring Social Protection and Education to the Table." *Center for Global Development* Comment [online]. https://www.cgdev.org/blog/are-school-meals-worth-cost-contributions-biniam-bedasso-farzana-afridi-ugo-gentilini-and

Gentilini, U., Almenfi, M., Iyengar, H., Okamura, Y., Downes, J. A., Dale, P., Weber, M., Newhouse, D., Rodriguez Alas, C., Kamran, M., Mujica, I., Fontenez, M., Ezzat, M., Asieduah, S., Martinez, V., Hartley, G., Demarco, G., Abels, M., Zafar, U., Urteaga, E., Valleriani, G., Muhindo, J., and Aziz, S. (2022) *Social Protection and Jobs Responses to COVID-19: A Real-Time Review of Country Measures* Version 16. World Bank.

Gentilini, U., Almenfi, M., Iyengar, H., Valleriani, G., Okamura, Y., Urteaga, E., Aziz, S., Noruzi, M., and Chu, M. (2023) "Tracking Global Social Protection Responses to Inflation—Living Paper v.5." Social Protection and Jobs Discussion Paper 2305. World Bank.

Gentilini, U., Grosh, M., Rigolini, J., and Yemtsov, R. (eds) (2020) *Exploring Universal Basic Income. A Guide to Navigating Concepts, Evidence, and Practices.* World Bank.

Gentilini, U., Khosla, S., and Almenfi, M. (2021) "Cash in the City: Emerging Lessons from Implementing Cash Transfers in Urban Africa." Social Protection and Jobs Discussion Paper 2101. World Bank and WFP.

Gentilini, U., Laughton, S., and O'Brien, C. (2018) *Human(itarian) Capital? Lessons on Better Connecting Humanitarian Assistance and Social Protection.* Social Protection and Jobs Discussion Paper 1802. World Bank and WFP.

Geremek, B. (1994) *Poverty: A History.* Blackwell.

Ghifari, N. (1989) *Social Security in Islam.* PhD Thesis, Punjab University.

Gilardi, F. (2016) "Four Ways We Can Improve Policy Diffusion Research." *State Politics and Policy Quarterly* 16(1): 8–21.

Gilbert, G. (2006) "Adam Smith on the Nature and Causes of Poverty." *Review of Social Economy* 55(3): 273–291.

Gilder, G. (1981) *Wealth and Poverty.* Basic Books.

Gilens, M. (1999) *Why Americans Hate Welfare: Race, Media, and the Politics of Antipoverty Policy.* University of Chicago Press.

Gill, I. (2017, February 6) "How to End Poverty? Give the Poor Cash and Access to Mobile Money and Text Them Reminders to Save and Take Their Meds – Not." *Brookings* Commentary [online]. https://www.brookings.edu/articles/how-to-end-poverty-give-the-poor-cash-and-access-to-mobile-money-and-text-them-reminders-to-save-and-take-their-meds-not/

Gilligan, D., Hoddinott, J., and Seyoum, A. (2009) "An Analysis of Ethiopia's Productive Safety Net Programme and its Linkages." *Journal of Development Studies* 45(10): 1684–1706.

Gingrich, N. (1996) *To Renew America.* Harper Collins.

Gittleson, B. (2021, May 7) "An Inside Look at How Donald Trump's Name Came to Appear on Stimulus Checks." *ABC News* [online]. https://abcnews.go.com/Politics/inside-donald-trumps-stimulus-checks/story?id=77534116

Gladden, W. (1892) "The Plain Path of Reform." *Charity Review* I: 251–256.

Glaessner, P., Lee, K., Sant'Anna, A. and de St. Antoine, J. (1994) *Poverty Alleviation and Social Investment Funds: The Latin American Experience.* World Bank.

Glenn, J. (1892) "Co-Operation Against Beggary." *Charity Review* I: 67–72.

GoA (Government of Afghanistan) (2008) *National Development Strategy 2008–2013: A Strategy for Security, Governance, Economic Growth and Poverty Reduction.* Government of Afghanistan.

GoB (Government of Brazil) (2022) *Manual Do Entrevistador. Cadastro Unico para Programas Sociais,* 5th edn. Government of Brazil.

GoC (Government of Cambodia), WFP, and World Bank (2009) *Cambodia Safety Net Review: Draft Policy Note.* Government of Cambodia.

GoE (Government of Ethiopia) (2009) *Food Security Programme 2010–2014.* Government of Ethiopia.

GoE (Government of Ethiopia) (2014) *Productive Safety Net Programme Public Works Operation and Maintenance Guideline: A Practical Guideline Manual for Development Agents in Ethiopia.* Government of Ethiopia.

Golan, J., Sicular, T., and Umapathi, N. (2015) "Unconditional Cash Transfers in China: An Analysis of the Rural Minimum Living Standard Guarantee Program." *Policy Research Working Paper* 7374. World Bank.

Golas, P. (1980) "Rural China in the Song." *Journal of Asian Studies* 39(2): 291–325.
Goldberg, C. (2007) *Citizens and Paupers: Relief, Rights, and Race from the Freedmen's Bureau to Workfare.* Chicago University Press.
GoM (Government of Malawi) (2007) *Social Protection Strategy: Draft.* Government of Malawi.
GoM (Government of Malawi) (2022) *Malawi Social Cash Transfer Programme: Strategic Plan 2022–2027.* Government of Malawi.
Gong, L., and Chen, J. (2023) "Disparities in Social Insurance Participation and Urban Identification Among In-Situ Urbanized Residents in China." *Applied Research in Quality of Life* 18: 1269–1289.
Gonnet, C., and Rodriguez, D. (2023) "Can I Borrow This? Policy Transfer from Chile to Paraguay in the Wave of Diffusion of Conditional Cash Transfer Programs in Latin America." *Latin American Policy* 14, 280–297.
GoP (Government of Pakistan) (2007) *A Social Protection Strategy to Reach the Poor and the Vulnerable.* Government of Pakistan.
GoP (Government of Pakistan) (2021) *Pakistan Economic Survey 2020–21—Chapter 15: Social Protection.* Government of Pakistan.
Gordon, M. (1964) *Assimilation in American Life: The Role of Race, Religion, and National Origin.* Oxford University Press.
Gorski, P. (2003) *The Disciplinary Revolution. Calvinism and the Rise of the State in Early Modern Europe.* University of Chicago Press.
Goubert, P. (1982) *The French Peasantry in the Seventeenth Century.* Cambridge University Press.
Gough, I. (1979) *The Political Economy of the Welfare State.* Macmillan.
GoUK (Government of the United Kingdom) (1880) *Indian Famine Commission Part I: Famine Relief.* HMSO.
GoUK (Government of the United Kingdom) (1884) *Poor Law Conferences: Reports of the Poor Laws District Conferences Held During the Year 1883.* Knight & Co.
GoUK (Government of the United Kingdom) (1909a) *Report of the Royal Commission on the Poor Laws and Relief of Distress.* HMSO.
GoUK (Government of the United Kingdom) (1909b) *The Minority Report of the Poor Law Commission Part I: The Break-up of the Poor Law, Part 1.* HMSO.
GoUK (Government of the United Kingdom) (1909c) *The Minority Report of the Poor Law Commission Part II: The Unemployed.* HMSO.
GoUK (Government of the United Kingdom) (1834a) *Report from His Majesty's Commissioners for Inquiring into the Administration and Practical Operation of the Poor Laws.* House of Commons Parliamentary Papers. HMSO.
GoUK (Government of the United Kingdom) (1834b) *Report from His Majesty's Commissioners for Inquiring into the Administration and Practical Operation of the Poor Laws Appendix (F): Foreign Communications.* House of Commons Parliamentary Papers. HMSO.
GoUS (1935, December 10) "*Charities-Paupers-Illinois Emergency Relief Commission Payment of Relief in Cash.*" Opinion 867. Illinois Office of the Attorney General.
GoUS (1966) *January 1966 Economic Report of the President: Hearings Before the Joint Economic Committee, Part 2 (February 3, 4 and 8).* US Government Printing Office.
GoUS (1983) *Final Report of the Seattle-Denver Income Maintenance Experiment.* US Government Printing Office.
GoUS (Government of the United States) (1942) *Security, Work and Relief Policies.* National Resources Planning Board. US Government Printing Office.
GoZ (Government of Zambia) and AU (2006) *Livingstone Call for Action: A Transformative Agenda for the 21st Century.* HelpAge International.

Graeber, D. (2011) *Debt: The First 5,000 Years.* Neville House Publishing.

Graham, C. (1994) *Safety Nets, Politics, and the Poor: Transitions to Market Economies.* Brookings Institution.

Graham, C. (1998) "From Safety Nets to Social Policy: Lessons for the Transition Economies from the Developing Countries." In Nelson, J., Tilly, C., and Walker, L. (eds) *Transforming Post-Communist Political Economies*, 385–399. National Academies Press.

Grant, K. (2005) *A Civilised Savagery: Britain and the New Slaveries in Africa, 1884–1926.* Routledge.

Grech, S. (2015) *Disability and Poverty in the Global South: Renegotiating Development in Guatemala.* Palgrave Macmillan.

Greeley, D. (2022) *Beyond Benevolence: The New York Charity Organization Society and the Transformation of American Social Welfare, 1882–1935.* Indiana University Press.

Green, D. (2008) *From Poverty to Power: How Active Citizens and Effective States Can Change the World.* Oxfam International.

Green, E. (2017) *This Business of Relief: Confronting Poverty in a Southern City, 1740–1940.* University of Georgia Press.

Greenbaum, S. (2015) Blaming the Poor: The Long Shadow of the Moynihan Report on Cruel Images about Poverty. Rutgers University Press.

Greenberg, M. (2002, July 2) "Bush's Blunder." *The American Prospect* [online]. http://www.prospect.org/print/V13/13/greenberg-m.htm

Greenberg, M., Levin-Epstein, J., Hutson, R., Ooms, T., Schumacher, R., Turetsky, V., and Engstrom, D. (2000) "Welfare Reauthorization: An Early Guide to the Issues." Paper prepared for the First Draft Working Session on The Impact of Welfare Reform on Children. Center for Law and Social Policy.

Greif, A., and Iyigun, M. (2013) "What Did the Old Poor Law Really Accomplish? A Redux." IZA Discussion Papers 7398. Institute of Labor Economics.

Grendi, E. (1982) "Ideologia della Carità e Società Indisciplinata: La Costruzione del Sistema Assistenziale Genovese (1470-1670)." In Politi, G., Rosa, M. and Della Peruta, F. (eds) *Timore e Carità: I Poveri nell'Italia Moderna*, 66. Biblioteca Statale e Libreria Civica di Cremona.

Grisewood, W., and Hanewinkel, A. (1898) *The Elberfeld System of Poor Law Relief.* Marples & Co.

Grisolia, F. (2024) "Can Cash Transfers Really Be Transformative? A Literature Review of the Sustainability of Their Impacts." Discussion Paper 2024.02. Institute of Development Policy.

Groebner, V. (2007) *Who Are You? Identification, Deception, and Surveillance in Early Modern Europe.* Zone Books.

Groeneveld, L. P., Brandon Tuma, N., and Hannan, M. T. (1980) "The Effects of Negative Income Tax Programs on Marital Dissolution." *Journal of Human Resources* 15(4): 654–674.

Grogger, J., Haider, S., and Klerman, J. (2003) "Why Did the Welfare Rolls Fall During the 1990s? The Importance of Entry." *American Economic Review* 93(2): 288–292.

Gronbach, L., Seekings, J., and Arthur, W. (2023) *Lessons Learned on Social Protection Responses to Covid-19 in Botswana.* University of Cape Town and World Bank.

Grosh, M., Leite, P., Wai-Poi, M., and Tesliuc, E. (eds) (2022) *Revisiting Targeting in Social Assistance: A New Look at Old Dilemmas.* World Bank.

Grzybek, D. (2024) "Classical Economists in the Face of the Old English Poor Law: Prejudice in Scholarly Clothes." *Krakow Review of Economics and Management* 2(1004): 5–19.

Guadagno, J. (1994) *The Color of Welfare: How Racism Undermined the War on Poverty.* Oxford University Press.

Guarducci, M. (1933) "Intorno alla Decima dei Cretesi." Rivista di Filologia e di Istruzione *Classica* 61: 488–491.

Guimaraes, N., Magno, L., de Paula, A., Silliman, M., Anderle, R., Rasella, D., Macinko, J., de Souza, L., and Dourado, I. (2023) "The Effects of Cash Transfer Programmes on HIV/AIDS Prevention and Care Outcomes: A Systematic Review and Meta-Analysis of Intervention Studies." *The Lancet HIV* 10(6): E394–403.

Guizzi F. (1999) "Sissizi a Creta in età imperiale? Forme di imposizione tradizionali e finanze cittadine a Lyttos." *Actes de la Xe Rencontre franco-italienne sur l'épigraphie du monde romain* (Rome, 27–29): 275–284.

Gumbo, P. (1998) "The Gender Dimension in Social Security: A Historical Perspective." In Kaseke, E. (ed) *Social Security Systems in Rural Zimbabwe*. Friedrich Ebert Stiftung.

Gunckel, L. B. (1897) "Outdoor Relief in Ohio." *Charities Review* 7 (September–February): 755–763.

Gupta, S., Verhoeven, M., Gillingham, R., Schiller, C., Mansoor, A., and Cordoba, J. (2000) *Equity and Efficiency in the Reform of Price Subsidies: A Guide for Policymakers*. IMF.

Gurteen, S. (1882) *A Handbook of Charity Organization*. The Courier Company.

https://research.cs.queensu.ca/home/cisc853/readings/papers/microsoftLonghorn.pdf

Gwenda M. and Rushton, P. (2013) *Banishment in the Early Atlantic World: Convicts, Rebels and Slaves*. Bloomsbury.

Gygax, D. (2016) *Benefaction and Rewards in the Ancient Greek City: The Origins of Euergetism*. Cambridge University Press.

Haang'andu, P., and Beland, D. (2020) "Transnational Actors and the Diffusion of Social Policies: An Ideational Approach." In Schmitt, C. (ed) *From Colonialism to International Aid: External Actors and Social Protection in the Global South*, 305–332. Palgrave MacMillan.

Hacker, J. (2008) *The Great Risk Shift: The New Economic Insecurity and the Decline of the American Dream*. Oxford University Press.

Hacking, I. (1990) *The Taming of Chance*. Cambridge University Press.

Hall, R. (1975) "Effects of the Experimental Negative Income Tax on Labor Supply." In Pechman, J., and Timpane, M. (eds) *Work Incentives and Income Guarantees: The New Jersey Negative Income Tax Experiment*, 115–156. Brookings Institution.

Hallaq, W. (2009) *Sharia: Theory, Practice, Transformations*. Cambridge University Press.

Hall-Matthews, D. (2008) "Inaccurate Conceptions: Disputed Measures of Nutritional Needs and Famine Deaths in Colonial India." *Modern Asian Studies* 42(6): 1189–1212.

Hamer, S. and Seekings, J. (2019) "Social Assistance, Electoral Competition, and Political Branding in Malawi." In Hickey, S., Lavers, T., Niño-Zarazúa, M., and Seekings, J. (eds) *The Politics of Social Protection in Eastern and Southern Africa*, 225–248. Oxford University Press.

Hamid, S. (2003) "An Islamic Alternative? Equality, Redistributive Justice, and the Welfare State in the Caliphate of Umar." *Renaissance* 13(8) [online]. http://www.monthly-renaissance.com/issue/content.aspx?id=355

Hammond, D. (2019) *Politics and Policy in China's Social Assistance Reform: Providing for the Poor?* Edinburgh University Press.

Hammad, M. (2022) "Overview of Zakat Practices Around the World". IPC-IG Research Report 69. Brasilia.

Hammond, J., and Hammond, B. (1911) *The Village Labourer, 1760–1832*. Longmans, Green, and Co.

Handa, S., Daidone, S. Peterman, A., Davis, B., Pereira, A., Palermo, T., and Yablonski, J. (2018) "Myth-Busting? Confronting Six Common Perceptions about Unconditional Cash Transfers as a Poverty Reduction Strategy in Africa." *World Bank Research Observer* 33(2): 259–298.

Handler, J. (1995) *The Poverty of Welfare Reform*. Yale University Press.

Hands, A. (1968) *Charities and Social Aid in Greece and Rome*. Cornell University Press.

Hanlon, J., Barrientos, A., and Hulme, D. (2010) *Just Give Money to the Poor: The Development Revolution from the Global South.* Kumarian Press.

Hannan, M., and Tuma, N. (1990) "A Reassessment of the Effect of Income Maintenance on Marital Dissolution in the Seattle–Denver Experiment." *American Journal of Sociology* 95(5): 1270–1298.

Hannan, M., Tuma, N., and Groeneveld, L. (1977) "Income and Marital Events: Evidence from an Income Maintenance Experiment." *American Journal of Sociology* 82(6): 1186–1211.

Hannon, J. (1984) "Poverty in the Antebellum Northeast: The View from New York State's Poor Relief Rolls." *Journal of Economic History* 44(4): 1007–1032.

Hannon, J. (1997) "Shutting Down Welfare: Two Cases from America's Past." *Quarterly Review of Economics and Finance* 37(2): 419–438.

Hansen, A. (1939) "Economic Progress and Declining Population Growth." *American Economic Review* 29: 1–15.

Hanusheck, E. (1986) "Non-Labor-Supply Response to the Income Maintenance Experiments." In Munnell, A. (ed) *Lessons from the Income Maintenance Experiments.* Federal Reserve Bank of Boston.

Hareven, T. (1969) "An Ambiguous Alliance: Some Aspects of American Influences on Canadian Social Welfare." *Social History* 2(3): 82–98.

Harris, J. (1977) *William Beveridge: A Biography.* Clarendon Press.

Harrison, M. (1988) *Crowds and History: Mass Phenomena in English Towns, 1790–1835.* Cambridge University Press.

Harvey, D. (2005) *A Brief History of Neoliberalism.* Oxford University Press.

Harvey, P. (1999) "Joblessness and the Law before the New Deal." *Georgetown Journal on Poverty Law and Policy* 6(1): 2–41.

Harvey, P. (2007) "U.S. Job Creation Programs in the 1930s." Background Paper for the Human Sciences Research Council Mid-Term Review of South Africa's Expanded Public Works Program. HSRC.

Harvey, P. (2010) *The Right to Work and Basic Income Guarantees: Competing or Complementary Goals?* Rutgers School of Law.

Hasan, M. (1997) *Hadrat Umar Farooq.* Kitab Bhavan.

Hasbach, W. (1894) *A History of the English Agricultural Labourer.* King & Son (translated edition of 1920).

Haskel, H. (2009) *The New Deal in Old Rome.* Argos Editions.

Haskins, R., Sawhill, I., and Weaver, R. K. (2001) "Welfare Reform Reauthorization: An Overview of Problems and Issues." *Policy Brief* 2. Brookings Institution.

Haveman, R., Blank, R., Moffitt, R., Smeeding, T., and Wallace, G. (2014) "The War on Poverty: Measurement, Trends, and Policy." *Journal of Policy Analysis and Management* 34(3): 593–638.

Hay, R. (1988) "Famine Incomes and Employment: Has Botswana Anything to Teach Africa?" *World Development* 16(9): 1113–1125.

Hayman, R. (2009) "Rwanda: Milking the Cow. Creating Policy Space in Spite of Aid Dependence." In Whitfield, L. (ed) *The Politics of Aid: African Strategies for Dealing with Donors,* 156–184. Oxford University Press.

Head, B. (1911) *Historia Numorum: A Manual of Greek Numismatics.* Oxford Clarendon Press.

Heath, C., and Heath, D. (2007) *Made to Stick: Why Some Ideas Survive and Others Die.* Random House.

Heidemarie, K. (1996) *So Says King Darius: Life in the Persian Empire.* Mainz-Rhein von Zabern.

Hemsteede, R. (2023) "Reshaping State-Citizen Relationships Through Donor-Designed Targeting Systems in Lesotho and Malawi." Social Policy and Administration 57(6): 961–975.
Henderson, C. (1894) "Public Relief and Private Charity." *Charities Review* III: 226–235.
Henderson, C. (1897) "Poor Laws of the United States." *Charities Review* VI: 476–492.
Hennock, E. (2007) *The Origin of the Welfare State in England and Germany, 1850–1914.* Cambridge University Press.
Henriques, U. (1979) *Before the Welfare State: Social Administration in Early Industrial Britain.* Longmans.
Herodotus (1890/c.430 BC) *The History of Herodotus.* G. Macaulay (trans.). Macmillan and Co.
Hickel, J. (2018) *The Divide: Global Inequality from Conquest to Free Markets.* Norton.
Hickey, S., Lavers, T., Seekings, J. and Niño-Zarazúa, M. (2019) "The Negotiated Politics of Social Protection Eastern and Southern Africa." In Hickey, S., Lavers, T., Niño-Zarazúa, M., and Seekings, J. (eds) *The Politics of Social Protection in Eastern and Southern Africa,* 1–41. Oxford University Press.
Higginbotham, P. (2012) *The Workhouse Encyclopedia.* The History Press.
Higginbotham, P. (2013) *A Grim Almanac of the Workhouse.* History Press.
Higgs, M. (2007) *Life in the Victorian and Edwardian Workhouse.* History Press.
Hill, C. (1952) "Puritans and the Poor." *Past & Present* 2(1): 32–50.
Hilton, B. (1988) *The Age of Atonement: The Influence of Evangelicalism on Social and Economic Thought, 1795–1865.* Clarendon Press.
Himmelfarb, G. (1984a) *The Idea of Poverty: England in the Early Industrial Age.* Knopf.
Himmelfarb, G. (1984b) "The Idea of Poverty." *History Today* 34(4): 22–30.
Himmelfarb, G. (1991) *Poverty and Compassion: The Moral Imagination of the Late Victorians.* Vintage Books.
Himmelfarb, G. (1995) *The De-Moralization of Society: From Victorian Virtues to Modern Values.* Knopf.
Hindle, S. (2004a) "Dependency, Shame and Belonging: Badging the Deserving Poor, c.1550–1750." *Cultural and Social History* 1(1): 6–35.
Hindle, S. (2004b) *On the Parish? The Micro-Politics of Poor Relief in Rural England 1550–1750.* Oxford University Press.
Hiogo News (1874, March 26) "A Japanese Workhouse." n.p.
Hirschman, A. (1991) *The Rhetoric of Reaction: Perversity, Futility, Jeopardy.* Harvard University Press
Hitchcock, T. (2017) "The Body in the Workhouse: Death, Burial, and Belonging in Early Eighteenth-Century St Giles in the Fields." In Braddick, M., and Innes, J. (eds.) *Suffering and Happiness in England 1550-1850: Narratives and Representations—A Collection to Honour Paul Slack,* 149–170. Oxford University Press.
HLR Notes (2021, March 10) "The Agreement and the Girmitiya." *Harvard Law Review* 134(5): 1826–1858. https://harvardlawreview.org/print/vol-134/the-agreement-and-the-girmitiya/
Hobsbawm, E., and Rude, G. (1968) *Captain Swing.* Pantheon.
Hoey, J. (1944) "The Significance of Money Payment in Public Assistance." *Bulletin* Sept: 3–5.
Holland, T. (2005) *Persian Fire: The First World Empire and the Battle for the West.* Abacus.
Holmes, R., and Jones, N. (2009) *Putting the Social Back into Social Protection: A Framework for Understanding the Linkages Between Economic and Social Risks for Poverty Reduction. Background Note.* ODI.
Homer, S., and Sylla, R. (2005) *A History of Interest Rates,* 4th edn. John Wiley and Sons, Inc.
Hook, B., and Twitchett (1991) *The Cambridge Encyclopedia of China.* Cambridge University Press.

Horn, S. (2019) *Damnation Island: Poor, Sick, Mad and Criminal in 19th-Century New York*. Algonquin Books.

Hort, S. (2011) "How Did Sweden Do it? The Development of the Swedish Welfare Model." In Nycander, G. (ed) *Cash in the Hand: Rights-Based Social Protection as a Method of Eradicating Poverty and Hunger—An Anthology*, 131–142. Nordic Africa Institute and Church of Sweden.

Hossain, N. (2022) "The Politics of Distributing Social Protection in Bangladesh: Insights from the Primary Education Stipends Project." In Lavers, T. (ed) *The Politics of Distributing Social Transfers*, 179–204. Oxford University Press.

Howell, J. (1999) "Deeds Registration in England: A Complete Failure?" *Cambridge Law Journal* 58(2): 366–398.

Hu, A. (2016) "Social Insurance Ideas in the People's Republic of China: A Transnational and Historical Analysis." *Transnational Social Review* 6(3): 297–312.

Hu, A. (2021) "The Early Rise of Social Security in China: Ideas and Reforms, 1911–1949." In Leisering, L. (ed) *One Hundred Years of Social Protection: The Changing Social Question in Brazil, India, China, and South Africa*, 55–90. Palgrave.

Hufton, O. (1983) "Social Conflict and the Grain Supply in Eighteenth-Century France." *Journal of Interdisciplinary History* 14(2): 303–331

Hughes-Johnson, S. (2017) "The Poveri Vergognosi: Fallen Nobility or an Ethical Abstraction Operating within the Boundaries Set by Poverty?" *Confraternitas* 28(1): 3–15.

Hulme, M., and Hulme, R. (2008) "The International Transfer of Global Social Policy." In Yeates, N. (ed) Understanding Global Social Policy, 49–72. Policy Press and The Social Policy Association.

Hum, D., and Simpson, W. (1993) "Economic Response to a Guaranteed Annual Income: Experience from Canada and the United States." *Journal of Labor Economics* 11(1): S263–S296.

Humphries, J. (2003) "English Apprenticeship: A Neglected Factor in the First Industrial Revolution." In David, P., and Thomas, M. (eds) *The Economic Future in Historical Perspective*, 72–102. Oxford University Press.

Humphreys, S. (1978) *Anthropology and the Greeks*. Routledge.

Hunter, B., Harrison, S., Portela, A., and Bick, D. (2017) "The Effects of Cash Transfers and Vouchers on the Use and Quality of Maternity Care Services: A Systematic Review." *PLoS One* 12(3): e0173068. doi.org/10.1371/journal.pone.0173068.

Huzel, J. (1989) "The Labourer and the Poor Law." In Mingay, G. E. (ed) *The Agrarian History of England and Wales*, 755–810. Cambridge University Press.

Hyslop, J. (1894) "Charity Organization and Labor Bureaus." *Charity Review* IV: 1–16.

Ibrahim, M. (2023) "From Policy to Politics? Exploring Feedback Effects of Social Protection on State-Citizen Relations in Ghana." *Social Policy & Administration* 57(6): 902–918.

IDS, ODI (Overseas Development Institute), UEA-DEV (School of International Development at the University of East Anglia) and RHVP (Regional Hunger and Vulnerability Programme) (2010) *Social Protection in Africa: Where Next?* Institute of Development Studies.

Iglikowski-Broad, V. (2021, July 29) "The Rebel Councillors: The 1921 Poplar Rates Rebellion." The National Archives [blog]. https://blog.nationalarchives.gov.uk/the-rebel-councillors-1921-poplar-rates-rebellion/

Iliffe, J. (1987) *The African Poor*. Cambridge University Press.

Iliffe, J. (1990) *Famine in Zimbabwe, 1890–1960*. Mambo.

ILO (1942) "Approaches to Social Security: An International Survey." *Studies and Reports Series* 18. ILO.

ILO (1994) *Declaration of Philadelphia concerning the aims and purposes of the International Labour Organisation*. ILO.

ILO (2012) *Social Protection Floors Recommendation*, No. 202. ILO.

ILO and UNICEF (2019) *Towards Universal Social Protection for Children: Achieving SDG 1.3*. ILO.

ILO and WHO (2009) *The Social Protection Floor: A joint Crisis Initiative of the UN Chief Executives Board for Co-ordination on the Social Protection Floor*. ILO.

Immervoll, H., and Knotz, C. (2018) *How Demanding Are Activation Requirements for Jobseekers*. Social, Employment and Migration Working Paper 215. OECD.

Ingold, T. (1983) "The Significance of Storage in Hunting Societies." *Man* 18(3): 553–571.

Innes, J. (1999) "The State and the Poor: Eighteenth-century England in Comparative Perspective." In Brewer, J., and Hellmuth, E. (eds) *Rethinking Leviathan: The Eighteenth-Century State in Britain and Germany*, 225–280. Oxford University Press.

Innes, J. (2002) "The Distinctiveness of the English Poor Laws, 1750–1850." In Winch, D., and O'Brien, P. (eds) *The Political Economy of British Historical Experience, 1688–1914*. Oxford University Press.

Innes, J. (2021) "The Regulation of Charity and the Rise of the State." In Hitchcock, D., and McClure, J. (eds) *The Routledge History of Poverty*, c.1450–1800. Routledge.

Islamic Development Bank Group. (2022) *Islamic Finance Development Report 2022: Embracing Change*. Refinitiv.

Iyengar, H., Almenfi, M., and Gentilini, U. (2023) *Estimating Global Coverage of Cash Transfers, 2000–2022*. World Bank. Mimeo.

Jacobs, J. (2009) *There Shall Be No Needy: Pursuing Social Justice Through Jewish Law and Tradition*. Jewish Light Publishing.

Jacobs, W., and Downey, L. (2022) "Impact of Conditional Cash Transfer Programmes on Antenatal Care Service Uptake in Low and Middle-Income Countries: A Systematic Review." *BMJ Open* 12(11): e064673.

Jager, A., and Zamora Vargas, D. (2023) *Welfare for Markets: A Global History of Basic Income*. University of Chicago Press.

Jansson, B. (2009) *The Reluctant Welfare State: Engaging History to Advance Social Work Practice in Contemporary Society*, 6th edn. Brooks/Cole.

Jaroszewicz, A., Jachimowicz, J., Hauser, O., and Jamison, J. (2022, July 5) "How Effective Is (More) Money? Randomizing Unconditional Cash Transfer Amounts in the US." SSRN Working Paper. https://ssrn.com/abstract=4154000

Jevons, F. (1896) "Some Ancient Greek Pay-Bills." *Economic Journal* 6(230): 470–475.

Jojima, M-P. (1997) "Spanish Attitudes to Poverty as Reflected in a Selection of Representative Literary Texts: c.1500–c.1635." PhD Thesis,University College London.

Jolliffe, D., Margitic, J., and Ravallion, M. (2019) *Food Stamps and America's Poorest*. NBER Working Paper 26025. National Bureau of Economic Research.

Jones, A. (1986) *The Later Roman Empire, 284–602: A Social, Economic, and Administrative Survey*. Volume I. Johns Hopkins Press

Jones, A., and Rutman, L. (1981) *In the Children's Aid: J. J. Kelso and Child Welfare in Ontario*. University of Toronto Press.

Jones, C. (1989) "Eastern Alimenta and an Inscription of Attaleia." *Journal of Hellenic Studies* 109: 189–191.

Jones, M. (2002) "Australia." In Dixon, J., and Scheurell, R. (eds) *The State of Social Welfare: The Twentieth Century in Cross National Review*, 1–42. Praeger.

Jones, P. (2007) "Swing, Speenhamland and Rural Social Relations: The 'Moral Economy' of the English Crowd in the Nineteenth Century." *Social History* 32(3): 271–290.

Jutte, R. (1994) *Poverty and Deviance in Early Modern Europe*. Cambridge University Press.

Jutte, R. (1996) "Poor Relief and Social Discipline in Sixteenth-Century Europe." *European History Quarterly* 11(1): 25–52.

Kaasch, A., and Martens, K. (eds) *Actors and Agency in Global Social Governance*. Oxford University Press.

Kahl, S. (2005) "The Religious Roots of Modern Poverty Policy: Catholic, Lutheran, and Reformed Protestant Traditions Compared." *European Journal of Sociology* 46(1): 91–126.

Kahl, S. (2009) "Religious Doctrines and Poor Relief: A Different Causal Pathway." In van Kersbergen, K., and Manow, P. (eds) *Religion, Class Coalitions, and Welfare States*, 267–296. Cambridge University Press.

Kahl, S. (2014) *Just Deserts: The Moral Economy of Welfare in Europe and the United States*. Yale University Press.

Kalita, N. (2016) "The Idea of Welfare State in the Arthaśāstra and Yājñavalkyasmṛti." *Prācyā* 8(1): 132–138.

Kanbur, R. (2011) "Why Might History Matter for Development Policy?." In Bayly, C., Rao, V.,Szreter, S., and Woolcock, M. (eds) *History, Historians, and Development Policy: A Necessary Dialogue*. Manchester University Press.

Kanbur, R., and Squire, L. (1999) "The Evolution of Thinking About Poverty: Exploring the Interactions." Working Paper 127697. Cornell University.

Kangas, O. (2012) "Testing Old Theories in New Surroundings: The Timing of First Social Security Laws in Africa." *International Social Security Review* 65(1), 73–97.

Kaniewski, D., and Marriner, N. (2020) "Conflicts and the Spread of Plagues in Pre-Industrial Europe." *Nature: Humanities and Social Sciences Communications* 7(1): 2–10.

Kaplan, B. (1978) "Reformers and Charity: The Abolition of Public Outdoor Relief in New York City, 1870–1898." *Social Service Review* 52(2): 202–214.

Kaplan, D. (2000) "The Darker Side of the Original Affluent Society." *Journal of Anthropological Research* 56(3): 301–324.

Kaseke, E. (1988) "Social Security in Zimbabwe." *Journal of Social Development in Africa* 3(1): 5–19.

Kaseke, E. (1994) *Rural Security Needs: The Case of Zimbabwe*. School of Social Work.

Kaseke, E. (2000) "The Implications for Structural Adjustment for the Family in Zimbabwe." In Jones F., and Kumssa (eds) *The Cost of Reform: The Social Aspect of Transitional Economy*. Nova Signs Publishers.

Kaseke, E. (2008) "Social Security Provisioning in Southern Africa: Developing a Framework for the Integration of Informal Social Security into the Formal Systems." *Zeitschrift für ausländisches und internationals Arbeits und Sozialrecht* 22: 64–73.

Kaseke, E. (2011) "The Poor Laws, Colonialism and Social Welfare: Social Assistance in Zimbabwe." In Midgley, J., and Piachaud, D. (eds) *Colonialism and Welfare. Social Policy and the British Imperial Legacy*, 119–130. Edward Elgar.

Katz, M. (1983) *Poverty and Policy in American History*. Academic Press.

Katz, M. (1986) *In the Shadow of the Poorhouse: A Social History of Welfare in America*. Basic Books.

Katz, M. (1989) *The Undeserving Poor: From the War on Poverty to the War on Welfare*. Pantheon.

Katz, M. (1995) *Improving Poor People: The Welfare State, the "Underclass," and Urban Schools as History*. Princeton University Press.

Katz, M. and Sachsse, C. (eds) (1996) *The Mixed Economy of Social Welfare: Public/Private Relations in England, Germany, and the United States, the 1870s to the 1930*. Nomos.

Kaus, M. (1992) *The End of Equality*. Basic Boooks

Kautilya (2013) *King, Governance, and Law in Ancient India: Kautilya's Arthasastra. A New Updated Translation by Patrick Olivelle*. Oxford University Press.

Kennedy, M. (2015) "Homelessness in Victorian London: Exhibition Charts Life on the Streets." *The Guardian* [online]. https://www.theguardian.com/artanddesign/2015/jan/02/homelessness-victorian-london-exhibition-geffrye-museum

Kenny, C. (2011) *Getting Better: Why Global Development Is Succeeding and How We Can Improve the World Even More*. Basic Books.

Kerr, D. (2011) *Derelict Paradise. Homelessness and Urban Development in Cleveland, Ohio*. University of Massachusetts Press.

Kerr, G., and Wood, G. (1911) *Dr. Chalmers and the Poor Laws: A Comparison of Scotch and English Pauperism and Evidence before the Committee of the House of Commons.* Edinburgh University Press.

Kerr, R., and Lockie, J. (1962) "Scottish Beggars' Badges." Proceedings of the Society of Antiquaries of Scotland 95: 291–299.

Kershaw, D. (1972) "A Negative-Income-Tax Experiment." *Scientific American* 227(4): 19025.

Khan, M., Hazra, A., Kant, A., and Ali, M. (2016) "Conditional and Unconditional Cash Transfers to Improve Use of Contraception in Low- and Middle-Income Countries: A Systematic Review." *Studies in Family Planning* 47(4): 371–383.

Khandker, S., Samad, H., Fuwa, N., and Hayashi, R. (2021) "The Female Secondary Stipend and Assistance Program in Bangladesh: What Did It Accomplish?." South Asia Working Paper Series 81. ADB.

Kidd, S., and Athias, D. (2020) "Hit and Miss: An Assessment of Targeting Effectiveness in Social Protection—Summary Version with Updated Analysis." Working Paper. Development Pathways.

Killick, T. (1978) *Development Economics in Action: A Study of Economic Policies in Ghana.* Heinemann Educational Books.

Kim, J. Y. (2018, November 1) "World Bank Group President Jim Yong Kim's Remarks at the International Forum on China's Reform and Opening Up and Poverty Reduction." Diaoyutai State Guest House.

Kinball, M. (1988) "Farmers' Cooperatives as Behavior Toward Risk." *American Economic Review* 78(1): 224–232.

King, M. L., Jr. (1968) *Where Do We Go from Here: Chaos or Community?* Beacon Press.

King, S. (2000) *Poverty and Welfare in England 1700–1850: A Regional Perspective.* Manchester University Press.

Kingdon, R. (1971) "Social Welfare in Calvin's Geneva." *American Historical Review* 76(1): 50–69.

Klebaner, B. (1954) "Public Poor Relief in Charleston, 1800–1860." *South Carolina Historical Magazine* 55(4): 210–220.

Klein, P. (2009) "Book Review: Paul Pierson, *Dismantling the Welfare State? Reagan, Thatcher and the Politics of Retrenchment.*" *Journal of Public Policy* 15(2): 199.

Knotz, C. (2020a) "A Rising Workfare State? Unemployment Benefit Conditionality in 21 OECD Countries, 1980–2012." *Journal of International and Comparative Social Policy* 34(2): 1–18.

Knotz, C. (2020b) "Does Demanding Activation Work? A Comparative Analysis of the Effects of Unemployment Benefit Conditionality on Employment in 21 Advanced Economies, 1980–2012." *European Sociological Review* 36(1): 121–135.

Knox-Vydmanov, C. (2014) "Why 'The Poor' Don't Exist (and What This Means for Social Protection Policy)."Pathways' Perspectives 16. https://www.developmentpathways.co.uk/wp-content/uploads/2014/02/16-PathwaysPerspective-Why-the-Poor-Dont-Exist-Charles-Knox-Vydmanov.pdf

Kohler, T., and Bhorat, H. (2021) "Can Cash Transfers Aid Labour Market Recovery? Evidence from South Africa's Special COVID-19 Grant." DPRU Working Paper 202108. University of Cape Town.

Kondylis, F., and Loeser, J. (2021) "Intervention Size and Persistence."Policy Research Working Paper 9769. World Bank.

Kott, S., and Droux, J. (eds) (2013) *Globalizing Social Rights: The Internationalization Labour Organization and Beyond.* Palgrave Macmillan.

Kpessa, M., Béland, D., and Lecours, A. (2011) "Nationalism, Development, and Social Policy: The Politics of Nation-Building in Sub-Saharan Africa." *Ethnic and Racial Studies* 34(12): 2115–2133.

Kreidler, C., Battas, S., Seyfert, K., and Saidi, M. (2022) *Linking Humanitarian Cash Assistance and National Social Protection Systems*. World Bank.
Kuhnle, S., and Sander, A. (2010) "The Emergence of the Western Welfare State." In Castles F. G., Leibfried, S., Lewis,J., and Obinger, H. (eds) *The Oxford Handbook of the Welfare State*, 61–80. Oxford University Press.
Kumar, B. (1985) *The Ethiopian Famine and Relief Measures: An Analysis and Evaluation*. UNICEF.
Kumar, B. (1991) "Ethiopian Famines 1973–85: A Case Study." In Dreze, J., and Sen, A. (eds) *The Political Economy of Hunger Volume 2: Famine Prevention*, 173–216. Oxford University Press.
Kunzler, D. (2016) "Health Care and Old Age Pensions in Latin America and Africa: Introduction to the Issue." *Sozialpolitik* 1: 1–17.
Kunzler, D. (2020) "The Influence of Colonialism and Donors on Social Policies in Kenya and Tanzania." In Schmitt, C. (ed) *From Colonialism to International Aid: External Actors and Social Protection in the Global South*, 79–108. Palgrave MacMillan.
Kuran, T. (2001) "The Provision of Public Goods under Islamic Law: Origins, Impact, and Limitations of the Waqf System." *Law & Society Review* 35(4): 841–898.
Kuss, M., and Gerstenberg, A. (2023) "The Role of Elected Politicians in Donor-Led Social Protection: Insights from Zambia." Social Policy and Administration 57(6): 919–931.
Lambrecht, T., and Winter, A. (2018) "An Old Poor Law on the Continent? Agrarian Capitalism, Poor Taxes, and Village Conflict in Eighteen-Century England." *Economic History Review* 71(4): 1173–1198.
Lampe, P. (2016) "Social Welfare in the Greco-Roman World as a Background for Early Christian Practice." *Acta Theologica* 23: 1–28.
Lange, M. (2004) "British Colonial Legacies and Political Development." *World Development* 32(6): 905–922.
Landa Jocano, F. (1980) *Social Work in the Philippines: A Historical Overview*. New Day.
Lang, M. (1990) "Ostraka." *The Athenian Agora* 25: 1–188.
Langnel, Z., and Tweneboah-Koduah, D. (2024) "The Politics of the Targeting and Expansion of Pro-Poor Programs in Ghana." *Development in Practice*: 1–14 https://www.tandfonline.com/doi/full/10.1080/09614524.2024.2344514
Larkin, P. (2014) "The New Puritanism: The Resurgence of Contractarian Citizenship in Common Law." *Journal of Law and Society* 41(2): 227–256.
Latte, K. (1947) "Kollektivbesitz und Staatsschatz in Griechenland." *Nachrichten von der Akademie der Wissenschaften in Gottingen* 1946–47: 64–75.
Lavers, T. (2019a) "Distributional Concerns, the 'Developmental State' and the Agrarian Origins of Social Assistance in Ethiopia." In Hickey, S., Lavers, T., Niño-Zarazúa, M., and Seekings, J. (eds) *The Politics of Social Protection in Eastern and Southern Africa*, 68–94. Oxford University Press.
Lavers, T. (2019b) "Understanding Elite Commitment to Social Protection: Rwanda's Vision 2020 Umurenge Programme." In Hickey, S., Lavers, T., Niño-Zarazúa, M., and Seekings, J. (eds) *The Politics of Social Protection in Eastern and Southern Africa*, 95–121. Oxford University Press.
Lavers, T. (2022) "The Politics of Distributing Social Transfers." In Lavers, T. (ed) *The Politics of Distributing Social Transfers: State Capacity and Political Contestation in Sub-Saharan Africa and South Asia*, 30–56. Oxford University Press.
Lavers, T., and Hickey, S. (2016) "Conceptualising the Politics of Social Protection Expansion in Low Income Countries: The Intersection of Transnational Ideas and Domestic Politics." *International Journal of Social Welfare* 25(4): 388–398.
Lavinas, L. (2021) "The Anatomy of the Social Question and the Evolution of the Brazilian Social Security System, 1919–2020." In Leisering, L. (ed) *One Hundred Years of Social Protection: The Changing Social Question in Brazil, India, China, and South Africa*, 303–341. Palgrave.

Lawson, C., Koudeka, M., Cárdenas Martínez, A., Encinas, L. and George, T. (2023) "Harnessing Artificial Intelligence to Deliver Shock-Responsive Social Protection." Social Protection and Jobs Discussion Paper 2306. World Bank.

Le Goff, J. (2012) *Money and the Middle Ages: An Essay in Historical Anthropology Money and the Middle Ages*. Cambridge University Press.

Lees, L. H. (1998) *The Solidarities of Strangers. The English Poor Laws and the People 1700–1948*. Cambridge University Press.

Legovini, A. (2023) "Reducing Poverty 2.0: Cash, Cows, and Beyond." In Legovini, A. (ed) *Driving Revolutionary Ideas into Practice*, 19–20. World Bank.

Leibenstein, H. (1957) "The Theory of Underemployment in Backward Economies." *Journal of Political Economy* 65 (2): 91–103.

Leight, J., Hirvonen, K. and Zafar, S. (2024) "The Effectiveness of Cash and Cash Plus Interventions on Livelihoods Outcomes: Evidence from a Systematic Review and Meta-analysis". IFPRI, Discussion Paper 2262. Washington, DC.

Leisering, L. (2018) *The Global Rise of Social Cash Transfers: How States and International Organizations Constructed a New Instrument for Combating Poverty*. Oxford University Press.

Leisering, L. (2021) "One Hundred Years of Social Protection: The Rise of the Social Question in Brazil, India, China, and South Africa, 1920–2020." In Leisering, L. (ed) *One Hundred Years of Social Protection: The Changing Social Question in Brazil, India, China, and South Africa*, 383–428. Palgrave.

Lekachman, R. (1966) *The Ages of Keynes*. McGraw-Hill.

Lennon, C. (1999) "Dives and Lazarus in Sixteenth-Century Ireland." In Hill, J., and Lennon, C. (eds) *Luxury and Austerity*, 56–57. University College Dublin University Press.

Lentz, E., Barrett, C., Gomez, M., and Maxwell, D. (2013) "On the Choice and Impacts of Innovative International Food Assistance Instruments." *World Development* 49: 1–8.

Lester, A., and Dussart, F. (2014) *Colonization and the Origins of Humanitarian Governance: Protecting Aborigines across the Nineteenth-Century British Empire*. Cambridge University Press

Levin, J. (2019) *The Queen: The Forgotten Life Behind an American Myth*. Little, Brown and Company.

Levine, D. (1988) *Poverty and Society: The Growth of the American Welfare State in International Comparison*. Rutgers University Press.

Levine, R. (1975) "How and Why the Experiments Came About." In Pechman, J., and Timpane, M. (eds) *Work Incentives and Income Guarantees: The New Jersey Negative Income Tax Experiment*. Brookings Institution.

Levine, R., Watts, H., Hollister, R., Williams, W., O'Connor, A., and Widerquist, K. (2005) "A Retrospective on the Negative Income Tax Experiments: Looking Back at the Most Innovative Field Studies in Social Policy." In Widerquist, K., Lewis, M. A., and Pressman, S. (eds) *The Ethics and Economics of the Basic Income Guarantee*, 95–106. Routledge.

LeVine, T. (1992) "Inka State Storage in Three Highland Regions: A Comparative Study." In LeVine, T. (ed) *Inka Storage Systems*, 107–150. University of Oklahoma Press.

Levy, S. (2007) *Progress Against Poverty: Sustaining Mexico's PROGRESA-Oportunidades Program*. Brookings Institution.

Levy, S., and Cruces, G. (2021) "Time for a New Course: An Essay on Social Protection and Growth in Latin America." LAC Working Paper 24. UNDP.

Lewis, O. (1966) "The Culture of Poverty." *Scientific American* 215(4): 19–25.

Li, M. (2007) *Fighting Famine in North China: State, Market, and Environmental Decline, 1690s–1990s*. Stanford University Press.

Li, W., and Yang, D. (2005) "The Great Leap Forward: Anatomy of a Central Planning Disaster." *Journal of Political Economy* 113(4): 840–877.

Li, Y. (2019) "The Economic Implications of Wang Anshi's Reform." Paper presented at the 2nd International Conference on Economic Management and Green Development (August 2–3). Oxford.

Liddell Hart, B. (2012) *Why Don't We Learn from History?* Sophron.

Lierse, H., Obinger, H., Schmitt, C., and Seelkopf, L. (2015) "The Global Emergence of Social Protection: Explaining Social Security Legislation 1820-2013" *Politics & Society*, 43(4), 503–524.

Lindemann, M. (1990) *Patriots and Paupers: Hamburg, 1712–1830*. Oxford University Press.

Lindenmeyr, A. (1996) *Poverty is Not a Vice: Charity, Society, and the State in Imperial Russia*. Princeton University Press.

Lindert, P. (1994) "The Rise in Social Spending, 1880–1930." *Explorations in Economic History* 31(1): 1–37.

Lindert, P. (1998) "Poor Relief before the Welfare State: Britain versus the Continent, 1780–1880." *European Review of Economic History* 2(2): 101–140.

Lindert, P. (2004) *Growing Public. Social Spending and Economic Growth since the Eighteenth Century Volume I: The Story*. Cambridge University Press.

Lindert, P. (2014) "Private Welfare and the Welfare State." In Neal, L., and Williamson, J. (eds) *The Cambridge History of Capitalism*, 464–500. Cambridge University Press.

Lindert, P. (2021) *Making Social Spending Work*. Cambridge University Press.

Lindert, K., Karippacheril, T. G., Rodriguez Caillava, I. and Nishikawa Chavez, K. (2020) *Sourcebook on the Foundations of Social Protection Delivery Systems*. World Bank.

Ling, Z., and Zhongyi, J. (1995) "'Yigong-Daizhen' in China: A New Experience with Labour-Intensive Public Works in Poor Areas." *Development Policy Review* 13(4): 349–370.

Linsley, C., and Linsley, C. (1993) "Booth, Rowntree, and Llewelyn Smith: A Reassessment of Interwar Poverty." *Economic History Review* 46(1): 88–104.

Lipkin, Z. (2005) "Modern Dilemmas: Dealing with Nanjing's Beggars, 1927–1937." *Journal of Urban History* 31(5): 583–609.

Lipset, S. (1963) *Political Man*. Doubleday.

Lis, C. (1986) *Social Change and the Labouring Poor: Antwerp, 1770–1860*. Yale University Press.

Lis, C., and Soly, H. (1979) *Poverty and Capitalism in Pre-Industrial Europe*. Harvester Press.

Little, M., Roelen, K., Lange, B., Steinert, J., Yakubovich, A., Cluver, L., and Humphreys, D. (2021) "Effectiveness of Cash-Plus Programmes on Early Childhood Outcomes Compared to Cash Transfers Alone: A Systematic Review and Meta-Analysis in Low- and Middle-Income Countries." *PLOS Medicine* [online]. doi.org/10.1371/journal.pmed.1003698

Liu, T., and Sun, L. (2016) "Pension Reform in China." *Journal of Aging and Social Policy* 28(1): 15–28.

Liu, W. (2015) "The Making of a Fiscal State in Song China, 960–1279." *Economic History Review* 68(1): 48–78.

Lo Cascio, E. (1998) "Registri dei Beneficiari e Modalità delle Distribuzioni nella Roma Tardoantica." In *La Mémoire Perdue. Recherches sur l'Administration Romaine*, 287–318. École française de Rome.

Loch, C. (1893) "Some Controverted Points in the Administration of Poor Relief, Part II." *Economic Journal* 3(12): 584–599.

Loch, C. (1895) "Manufacturing a New Pauperism." *Nineteenth Century* XXXVII (April): 698–699

Lockley, T. (2005) "Rural Poor Relief in Colonial South Carolina." *The Historical Journal* 48(4): 955–976.

Loeser, J., Ozler, B., and Premand, P. (2021, May 10) "What Have We Learned about Cash Transfers?" Development Impact [blog]. World Bank. https://blogs.worldbank.org/en/impactevaluations/what-have-we-learned-about-cash-transfers.

Looijesteijn, H., and van Leeuwen, M. (2012) "Establishing and Registering Identity in the Dutch Republic." In Breckenridge, K., and Szreter, S. (eds) *Recognition and Registration: Documenting the Person in History*, 211–252. Oxford University Press.

Loveday, A. (1914) *The History and Economics of Indian Famines*. Bell and Sons.

Lowell, C. (1890) "The Economic and Moral Effects of Public Outdoor Relief." Proceedings of the National Conference of Charities and Correction 1890, 81–91. Geo. H. Ellis.

Lowell, J. (1884) *Public Relief and Private Charity*. Putnam.

Lowrey, A. (2018) *Give People Money: How a Universal Basic Income Would End Poverty, Revolutionize Work, and Remake the World*. Crown.

Lubbock, G. (1895) *Some Poor Relief Questions. With the Arguments on both Sides, together with the Summary of the Report of the Royal Commission on the Aged Poor, and Extracts from the Evidence Taken Before that Commission: A Manual for Workers*. John Murray.

Lugo, M., Chiyu, N., and Yemtsov, R. (2021) "Rural Poverty Reduction and Economic Transformation in China: A Decomposition Approach." Policy Research Working Paper 9849. World Bank.

Lustig, N., Pabon, V., Neifhofer, G., and Tommasi, M. (2023) "Short and Long-Run Distributional Impacts of COVID-19 in Latin America." *Economía LACEA Journal* 22(1): 96–116.

Luther, M. (1520) "Open Letter to the Christian Nobility of the German Nation Concerning the Reform of the Christian Estate." Adapted from C. M. Jacobs (trans) (1915) *Works of Luther*. A. J. Holman Company. http://www.iclnet.org/pub/resources/text/wittenberg/luther/web/nblty-03.htm.

Lyu, W., Wehby, G., and Kaestner, R. (2024) *Effects of Income on Infant Health: Evidence from the Expanded Child Tax Credit and Pandemic Stimulus Checks*. NBER Working Paper 32310. National Bureau of Economic Research.

Ma, D., and von Glahn, R. (eds) (2022a) *The Cambridge Economic History of China. Volume 1: To 1800*. Cambridge University Press.

Ma, D., and von Glahn, R. (eds) (2022b) *The Cambridge Economic History of China. Volume 2: 1800 to the Present*. Cambridge University Press.

Ma, T. (2012) "A Chinese Beveridge Plan: The Discourse on Social Security and the Post-War Construction of China." *European Journal of East Asian Studies* 11(2): 329–349.

MacDonald, D. (1963, January 19) "Our Invisible Poor." *The New Yorker*, 82–132.

Machingura, F. (2012) *The Messianic Feeding of the Masses: An Analysis of John 6 in the Context of Messianic Leadership in Post-Colonial Zimbabwe*. University of Bamberg Press.

Mackay, T. (1893) "On the Co-Operation of Charitable Agencies with the Poor Law." *Charity Organization Review* 9(101): 237–248.

MacKay, T. (1894) "Plain Words on Out-Relief." *Charity Organisation Review* 10(109): 59–66.

MacKinnon, M. (1987) "English Poor Law Policy and the Crusade Against Outrelief." *Journal of Economic History* 47(3): 603–625.

MacLean L. (2002) "Constructing a Social Safety Net in Africa: An Institutionalist Analysis of Colonial Rule and State Social Policies in Ghana and Côte d'Ivoire." *Studies in Comparative International Development* 37: 64–90.

Maclean, L. (2011) "Exhaustion and Exclusion in the African Village: The Non-State Social Welfare of Informal Reciprocity in Rural Ghana and Cote d'Ivoire." *Studies in Comparative International Development* 46(1): 118–136.

MacLean, L. (2017) "Neoliberal Democratisation, Colonial Legacies and the Rise of the Non-State Provision of Social Welfare in West Africa." *Review of African Political Economy* 44(153): 358–380.

Madembo, R. (1998) "The Role of Savings and Credit Schemes in Meeting the Social Security Needs of Communal Farmers." In Kaseke, E. (ed), *Social Security Systems in Rural Zimbabwe*, n.p. Friedrich Ebert Stiftung.

Madison, B. (1962) "Reviewed Work: A Report on Social Security Programs in the Soviet Union." *Slavic Review* 21(1): 182–184.
Madison, B. (1963a) "Welfare Services for Children in the Soviet Union." *American Journal of Orthopsychiatry* 33(4): 743–746.
Madison, B. (1963b) "Welfare Services for Children in the Soviet Union, 1945–1963." *Child Welfare* 42(7): 319–330.
Madison, B. (1964) "Social Welfare: Soviet Model." *Social Service Review* 38(2): 191–205.
Madison, B. (1980) *The Meaning of Social Policy: The Comparative Dimension in Social Welfare*. Routledge.
Madison, J. (1788/2008) "Federalist #51." In Goldman, L. (ed) *The Federalist Papers*. Oxford University Press.
Mahoney, J. (2010) *Colonialism and Postcolonial Development: Spanish America in Comparative Perspective*. Cambridge University Press.
Mair, L. (1944) *Welfare in the British Colonies*. Royal Institute of International Affairs.
Maitino, M., Mariani, M., Patacchini, V., Ravagli, L., and Sciclone, N. (2022) "Employment Effects of Reddito di Cittadinanza, Before and During the Covid-19 Pandemic." Working Paper 6/2022. IRPET.
Majumdar, S. (2023) *Mahasthan Record Revisited: Querying the Empire from a Regional Perspective*. Routledge.
Maldini, D. (1978) "Pauperismo e Mendicità a Torino nel Periodo Napoleonico." *Studi Piemontesi* VIII(1): 50–54.
Maldini, D. (1982) "Il *Dépot de Mendicité* del Dipartimento di Po: Analisi di una Struttura Assistenziale nel Piemonte Napoleonico." In Politi, G., Rosa, M. and Della Peruta, F. (eds) *Timore e Carità: I Poveri nell'Italia Moderna*, 331–345. Biblioteca Statale e Libreria Civica di Cremona.
Mallaby. S. (2004) *The World's Banker: A Story of Failed States, Financial Crises, and the Wealth and Poverty of Nations*. Penguin Press.
Mallory, W. (1926) *China: Land of Famine*. American Geographic Society.
Malthus, T. (1798) *An Essay on the Principle of Population, as It Affects the Future Improvement of Society*. Johnson.
Malthus, T. (1800) *An Investigation of the Cause of the Present High Price of Provisions, Containing an Illustration of the Nature and Limits of Fair Price in Time of Scarcity and Its Application to the Particular Circumstances of this Country*. Johnson.
Mamdani, M. (1996) *Citizen and Subject: Contemporary Africa and the Legacy of Late Colonialism*. Princeton University Press.
Mandler, P. (1987) "The Making of the New Poor Law *Redivivus*." *Past and Present* 117: 131–157.
Mandler, P. (1990) "Tories and Paupers: Christian Political Economy and the Making of the New Poor Law." *Historical Journal* 33(1): 81–103.
Manhattan Institute for Policy Research (1985) "Losing Ground: Why the War on Poverty Failed." *Manhattan Report on Economic Policy* 5(1): 1–28.
Manley, J., Alderman, H., and Gentilini, U. (2022) "More Evidence on Cash Transfers and Child Nutritional Outcomes: A Systematic Review and Meta-Analysis." *BMJ Global Health* 7: e008233.
Mann, M. (1986) *The Sources of Social Power*. 4 Volumes. Cambridge University Press.
Manow, P. (2005) "Germany: Cooperative Federalism and the Overgrazing of the Fiscal Commons." In Obinger,H., Liebfried, S., and Castles, F. G. (eds) *Federalism and the Welfare State: New World and European Experiences*, 222–262. Cambridge University Press.
Manow, P. (2015) "Workers, Farmers and Catholicism: A History of Political Class Coalitions and the South-European Welfare State Regime." *Journal of European Social Policy* 25(1): 32–49.

Mararike, C. (2001) "Revival of Indigenous Food Security Strategies at the Village Level: The Human Factor Implication." *Zambezia* 28(1): 53–65.
Marinescu, I. (2018) *No Strings Attached: The Behavioral Effects of U.S. Unconditional Cash Transfer Programs.* NBER Working Paper 24337. National Bureau of Economic Research.
Marinescu, I., Skandalis, D., and Zhao, D. (2020, July 30) "Job Search, Job Posting and Unemployment Insurance During the COVID-19 Crisis." SSRN Working Paper. https://papers.ssrn.com/sol3/papers.cfm?abstract_id=3664265
Markoff, J. (1996) *Waves of Democracy: Social Movements and Political Change.* Pine Forge Press.
Marr, H. (1899) "The Brabazon Scheme in an Asylum; History of its Introduction, and Record of a Years Working." *Journal of Mental Science* 45(190): 534–536.
Marshall, J. (1985) *The Old Poor* Law, 1795–1834. Macmillan.
Marshall, T. (1950) *Citizenship and Social Class. And Other Essays.* Cambridge University Press.
Marshall, T. (1963) *Sociology at the Crossroads.* Heinemann.
Martens, K., and Kruse, J. (2015) "NGOs as Actors in Global Social Governance." In Kaasch, A., and Martens, K. (eds) *Actors and Agency in Global Social Governance,* 175–194. Oxford University Press.
Martin, C. (2021) "Adam Smith and the Poor: A Textual Analysis." *Journal of Economic Behavior & Organization* 184(C): 837–849.
Martinez Franzoni, J., and Voorend, K. (2011) "Actors and Ideas Behind CCTs in Chile, Costa Rica and El Salvador." *Global Social Policy* 11(2–3): 279–298.
Martz, L. (1983) *Poverty and Welfare in Habsburg Spain: The Example of Toledo.* Cambridge University Press.
Marx, K. (1867) *Capital. A Critique of Political Economy.* Volume I. E. P. Dutton.
Matsaganis, M. (2018) "The Contorted Politics of Guaranteed Minimum Income in Greece." DAStU Working Paper 2/2018. Politecnico di Milano.
Matthews, D. (2014, July 23) "A Guaranteed Income for Every American Would Eliminate Poverty—And It Wouldn't Destroy the Economy." *Vox* [online]. https://www.vox.com/2014/7/23/5925041/guaranteed-income-basic-poverty-gobry-labor-supply
Matthews, D. (2018) "The Working-Class Struggle for Welfare in Britain." *Monthly Review* 69(9): 33–45.
Matthews, D. (2021, February 5) "The Year that Congress Just Gave People Money." *Vox* [online]. https://www.vox.com/future-perfect/22213822/will-americans-get-another-stimulus-check
Matthews, D. (2022, August 31) "The Rise and Rise of GiveDirectly." *Vox* [online]. https://www.vox.com/future-perfect/2022/8/31/23329242/givedirectly-cash-transfers-rory-stewart
Maul, D. (2012) *Human Rights, Development and Decolonization: The International Labour Organization 1940–1970.* Palgrave Macmillan.
Maul, D. (2019) *The International Labour Organization: 100 Years of Global Social Policy.* De Gruyter.
Maupain, F. (2009) "New Foundation or New Facade? The ILO and the 2008 Declaration on Social Justice for a Fair Globalization." *European Journal of International Law* 20(3): 823–852.
Maxon, R. (1980) *John Ainsworth and the Making of Kenya.* University Press of America.
Maxwell-Stewart, H. (2018) "Transportation from Britain and Ireland, 1615–1875." In Anderson, C. (ed) *A Global History of Convicts and Penal Colonies,* 183–210. Bloomsbury Academic.
May, D. (1981) *From New Deal to New Economics: The Liberal Response to the Recession.* Garland Publishing.

Mayer, C. (2011) "Poverty, Education and Gender: Pedagogic Transformations in the Schools for the Poor (Armenschulwesen) in Hamburg, 1788-1871" *International Journal of the History of Education* 47(1-2): 91–107.
Mayhew, H. (1969) *London Labor and the London Poor. The Classical Study of the Culture of Poverty and the Criminal Classes in the 19th* Century. Dover Publications.
Maynard, R., and Murnane, R. (1979) "The Effects of a Negative Income Tax on School Performance: Results of an Experiment." *Journal of Human Resources* 14(4): 463–476.
Mazumdar, D. (1959) "The Marginal Productivity Theory of Wages and Disguised Unemployment." *Review of Economic Studies* 26(3): 190–197.
McArdle, M. (2020, April 29) "Republican Senators Warn of Rising Unemployment Rate as Benefits Outpace Wages for Many." *National Review* [online]. https://www.nationalreview.com/news/republican-senators-warn-of-rising-unemployment-rate-as-benefits-outpace-wages-for-many/
McCabe, C. (2018) *Begging, Charity and Religion in Pre-Famine Ireland.* Liverpool University Press.
McCarthy, J., Nooteboom, G., Hadi, S., Kutanegara, P., and Mulia, N. (2023) "The Politics of Knowledge and Social Cash Transfers: The Constitutive Effects of An Anti-Poverty Regime in Indonesia." *Journal of Contemporary Asia* 54(4): 549–572.
McChesney, K. (1990) "Family Homelessness: A Systemic Problem." *Journal of Social Issues* 46(4): 191–205.
McCloskey, D. (1972) "The Enclosure of Open Fields: Preface to a Study of Its Impact on the Efficiency of English Agriculture in the Eighteenth Century." *Journal of Economic History* 32(1): 15–35.
McCloskey, D. (1973) "New Perspectives on the Old Poor Law." *Explorations in Economic History* 10(4): 419–436.
McColloch, O. (1888) "The Tribe of Ishmael: A Study in Social Degradation." National Conference of Charities and Correction: 154–159.
McCook, J. (1895) "The Tramp Problem: What it is and What to Do With It." *National Conference of Charities and Correction*: 288–302.
McCord, A. (2012) *Public Works and Social Protection in Sub-Saharan Africa: Do Public Works Work for the Poor?* United Nations University Press.
McCulloch, J. (1828) "Poor Laws." *Edinburgh Review* 47(94): 303–330.
McCullough, M. (2020a) *The Kindness of Strangers: How a Selfish Ape Invented a New Moral Code.* Basic Books.
McCullough, M. (2020b, September 21) "The Earthquake that Catalyzed the Humanitarian Big Bang" *Behavioral Scientist*[blog]. https://behavioralscientist.org/the-earthquake-that-catalyzed-the-humanitarian-big-bang/
McDonnell, P. (2007) *Disability and Society: Ideological and Historical Dimensions.* Orpen Press.
McGonnigle, R. (1894) "The Winter in Pittsburg." *National Conference of Charities and Correction*: 36–42.
McGuire, J. (2021) *The Cost-Effectiveness of Cash Transfers at Increasing Subjective Wellbeing and Affective Mental Health.* Happier Lives Institute.
McIntosh, M. (2012) *Poor Relief in England 1350–1600.* Cambridge University Press.
McKinnon, R., Charlton, R., and Munro, H. (1997) "The National Provident Fund Model: An Analytical and Evaluative Reassessment." *International Social Security Review* 50(2): 43–61.
McLanahan, S., Cain, G., Olneck, M., Piliavin, I., Danziger, S., and Gottschalk, P. (eds) (1985) *Losing Ground: A Critique.* Special Report 38. Institute for Research on Poverty.

McMillan, R. (2019) "'The Healing Hand Laid on a Great Wound': The Elberfeld System and the Transformation of Poverty in Germany, Britain, and the United States." PhD Dissertation, University of Arkansas.
McStay Adams, T. (2011) "Universalism in One Country: *La Protection Sociale* over the *Longue Durée*." *French Historical Studies* 34(3): 433–471.
McStay Adams, T. (2023a) *Europe's Welfare Traditions Since 1500: Reform Without End Volume 1: 1500–1700*. Bloomsbury.
McStay Adams, T. (2023b) *Europe's Welfare Traditions Since 1500: Reform Without End Volume 2: 1700–2000*. Bloomsbury.
Mead, L. (1986) *Beyond Entitlement: The Social Obligations of Citizenship*. The Free Press.
Mead, L. (1994) "Poverty: How Little We Know." *Social Service Review* 68(3): 322–350.
Mead, L. (1996) "Welfare Reform at Work." *Society* 33(5): 37–40.
Mead, L. (1998) "Telling the Poor What to Do." *Public Interest* 132: 97–112.
Mead, L. (2001) "The Politics of Conservative Welfare Reform." In Blank, R., and Haskins, R. (eds) *The New World of Welfare*, 201–220. Brookings Institution.
Mehrkens, J. (2019, December 27) "Opinion: The Case for the Whacky Mackie Plan. Is the Permanent Fund a Rainy Day Account or Entitlement?" *Juneau Empire* [online]. https://www.juneauempire.com/opinion/opinion-the-case-for-the-whacky-mackie-plan/
Mencher, S. (1968) *Poor Law to Poverty Program: Economic Security Policy in Britain and the United States*. University of Pittsburgh Press.
Menger, K. (1892) "On the Origins of Money." *Economic Journal* 2(6): 239–255.
Mentzer, R. (1991) "Organizational Endeavour and Charitable Impulse in Sixteenth-Century France: The Care of Protestant Nîmes." *French History* 5(1): 1–29.
Mesa-Lago, C. (1978) *Social Security in Latin America. Pressure Groups, Stratification, and Inequality*. University of Pittsburgh. Pittsburg.
Mesa-Lago, C. (1991) "Social Security in Latin America and the Caribbean: A Comparative Assessment." In Ahmad, E., Dreze, J., Hills, J., and Sen, A. (eds) *Social Security in Developing Countries*, 356–394. Oxford University Press.
Mesa-Lago, C. (2007) *Reassembling Social Security. A Survey of Pensions and Healthcare Reforms in Latin America*. Oxford University Press.
Mettler, S. (2018) *The Government–Citizen Disconnect*. Russell Sage Foundation.
Mhone, G. (2004) "Historical Trajectories of Social Policies in Post-Colonial Africa: The Case of Zambia." In Mkandawire, T. (ed) *Social Policy in a Development Context*, 308–337. UNRISD.
Michalopoulos, S., and Papaioannou, E. (2013) "Pre-Colonial Ethnic Institutions and Contemporary African Development." *Econometrica* 81(1): 113–152.
Midgley, J. (1984a) "Diffusion and Development of Social Policy: Evidence from the Third World." *Journal of Social Policy* 13: 167–184.
Midgley, J. (1984b) "Poor Law Principles and Social Assistance in the Third World: A Study of the Perpetuation of Colonial Welfare." *International Social Work* 27: 19–29.
Midgley, J. (1984c) *Social Security, Inequality, and the Third World*. Wiley.
Midgley, J. (1994a) *Social Development: The Development Perspective in Social Welfare*. Sage Publications.
Midgley, J. (1994b) "Social Security Policy in Developing Countries: Integrating State and Traditional Systems." *Focaal* 22(34): 219–230.
Midgley, J. (2011) "Imperialism, Colonialism and Social Welfare." In Midgley, J., and Piachaud, D. (eds) *Colonialism and Welfare. Social Policy and the British Imperial Legacy*, 36–52. Edward Elgar.
Midgley, J., and Piachaud, D. (2011) "Introduction." In Midgley, J., and Piachaud, D. (eds) *Colonialism and Welfare. Social Policy and the British Imperial Legacy*, 1–16. Edward Elgar.

Milanovic, B. (2006) "An Estimate of Average Income and Inequality in Byzantium Around Year 1000." *Review of Income and Wealth* 52(3): 449–470.
Milanovic, B. (2017, March 16) "The Welfare State in the Age of Globalization." *Global Inequality* [blog]. https://glineq.blogspot.com/2017/03/the-welfare-state-in-age-of.html
Milanovic, B. (2019) "Income Level and Income Inequality in the Euro-Mediterranean Region, c. 14–700." *Review of Income and Wealth* 65(1): 1–20.
Milanovic, B. (2019) *Capitalism, Alone. The Future of the System that Rules the World.* Harvard University Press.
Milanovic, B., Lindert, P., and Williamson, J. (2007) *Measuring Ancient Inequality.* NBER Working Paper 13550. National Bureau of Economic Research.
Milanovic, B., Lindert, P., and Williamson, J. (2011) "Pre-Industrial Inequality." *Economic Journal* 121(55): 255–272.
Milicevic, N. (2002) "The Hospice Movement: History and Current Worldwide Situation." *Archive of Oncology* 10(1): 29–32.
Mill, J. S. (1848) *Principles of Political Economy with Some of Their Applications to Social Philosophy.* Appleton and Co.
Millett, P. (1989) "Patronage and Its Avoidance in Classical Athens." In Wallace-Hadrill, A. (ed) *Patronage in Ancient Society*, 15–47. Routledge.
Millikan, M., and Blackmer, D. (1961) *The Emerging Nations: Their Growth and United States Policy.* Little, Brown and Company.
Minkoff, J., and Turgeon, L. (1977) "Income Maintenance in the Soviet Union in Eastern and Western Perspective." In Horowitz, I. (ed) *Equity, Income and Policy: Comparative Studies in Three Worlds of Development*, 176–211. Praeger Publisher.
Mioni, M., and Petersen, K. (2020) "Cold War and Social Protection in Burma and Malaysia." In Schmitt, C. (ed) *From Colonialism to International Aid: External Actors and Social Protection in the Global South*, 45–77. Palgrave MacMillan.
Mishra, R. (2018) *A Business of State: Commerce, Politics, and the Birth of the East India Company.* Harvard University Press.
Mitchell, I. (1913) "What is Money?" *Banking Law Journal* 30(5): 377–408.
Mitchison, R. (1989) "North and South: The Development of the Gulf in Poor Law Practice." In Houston, R., and Whyte, I. (eds) *Scottish Society, 1500–1800.* Cambridge University Press.
Mkandawire, T. (2001) "Social Policy in a Development Context." Social Policy and Development Programme Paper 7. UNRISD.
Mkandawire, T. (2006) "Transformative Social Policy: Lessons from UNRISD Research." Research and Policy Brief 5. UNRISD.
Mkandawire, T. (2010) *On Tax Efforts and Colonial Heritage in Africa.* Institute for Future Studies.
Mkandawire, T. (2016) "Colonial Legacies and Social Welfare Regimes in Africa: An Empirical Exercise." *Working Paper* 2016-4. UNRISD.
Mkandawire, T., and Soludo, C. (1998) *Our Continent, Our Future: African Perspectives on Structural Adjustment.* Council for the Development of Social Science Research in Africa.
Moffitt, R. (1989) "Estimating the Value of an In-Kind Transfer: The Case of Food Stamps." *Econometrica* 57(2): 385–409.
Moffitt, R. (ed) (2003a). *Means-Tested Transfer Programs in the United States.* University of Chicago Press and National Bureau of Economic Research.
Moffitt, R. (2003b) "The Negative Income Tax and the Evolution of U.S. Welfare Policy." *Journal of Economic Perspectives* 17(3): 119–140.
Moffitt, R. (2003c) *The Role of Randomized Field Trials in Social Science Research: A Perspective from Evaluations of Reforms of Social Welfare Programs.* NBER Technical Working Paper 295. National Bureau of Economic Research.

Moffitt, R. (2015) "The Deserving Poor, the Family, and the US Welfare System." *Demography* 52(3): 29–749.

Moffitt, R., and Kehrer, K. (2012) "The Effect of Tax and Transfer Programs on Labor Supply: The Evidence from the Income Maintenance Experiments." In Polachek, S., and Tatsiramos, K. (eds) *35th Anniversary Retrospective*. Research in Labor Economics 35. Emerald Group.

Moffitt, R., and Ziliak, J. (2020) *Covid-19 and the U.S. Safety Net*. NBER Working Paper 27911. National Bureau of Economic Research.

Mokyr, J. (2016) *A Culture of Growth: The Origins of the Modern Economy*. Princeton University Press.

Mollat, M. (1986) *The Poor in the Middle Ages: An Essay in Social History*. Yale University Press.

Molyneux, M. (ed) (2018) *The Social and Political Potential of Cash Transfers*. Routledge.

Monbiot, G. (2015, June 23) "Skivers and Strivers: This 200-Year-Old Myth Won't Die." The Guardian [online]. https://www.theguardian.com/commentisfree/2015/jun/23/skivers-strivers-200-year-old-myth-wont-die

Montalvo, J., and Ravallion, M. (2010) "The Pattern of Growth and Poverty Reduction in China." *Journal of Comparative Economics* 38(1): 2–16.

Moore, M., Prichard, W., and Fjeldstad, O. (2018) *Taxing Africa: Coercion, Reform and Development*. Zed Books.

Mora, J., de Crombrugghe, D., and Gassmann, F. (2022) "Money Is Not Enough: Unintended Negative Effects of Cash Transfer Design." Working Papers 38. UNU-MERIT.

Moran, G. (2021, May 9) "End of Project 100% in County Marks New Era in Assisting Needy." *The San Diego Union Tribune* [online]. https://www.sandiegouniontribune.com/2021/05/09/end-of-project-100-in-county-marks-new-era-in-assisting-needy/

Morgan, M. (2019) *Charles Booth's London Poverty Maps: A Landmark Reassessment of Booth's Social Survey*. Thames and Hudson.

Morichini, C. (1842) *Degl'Istituti di Pubblica Carità ed Istruzione Primaria e delle Prigioni in Roma – Volume 1*. Tipografia Marini e Compagno.

Morley, N. (2006) "The Poor in the City of Rome." In Atkins, M., and Osborne, R. (eds) *Poverty in the Roman World*, 21–39. Cambridge University Press.

Morrisson, C., and Snyder, W. (2000) "The Income Inequality of France in Historical Perspective." *European Review of Economic History* 4(1): 59–83.

Moynihan, D. (1965) *The Negro Family: The Case for National Action*. Government of the United States, Department of Labor.

Moynihan, D. (1968) "The Professor and the Poor." In Moynihan, D. (ed) *On Understanding Poverty*, 3–35. Basic Books.

Moynihan, D. (1973) *The Politics of a Guaranteed Income: The Nixon Administration and the Family Assistance Plan*. Vintage.

Mpedi, L. (2018) "Towards the Africanisation of Social Protection in Southern Africa." *Journal of Social Development in Africa* 33(1): 81–106.

Muhammad, I. (2019) "Analysis of Zakat System in High-Income Islamic Countries." *Journal of Muamalat and Islamic Finance Research* 16(2): 1–11.

Mulligan, C., and Sala-i-Martin, X. (1999) *Gerontocracy, Retirement and Social Security*. NBER Working Paper 7117. National Bureau of Economic Research.

Mulligan, C., Gil, R., and Sala-i-Martin, X. (2002) *Social Security and Democracy*. NBER Working Paper 8958. National Bureau of Economic Research.

Mundell, R. (2002) "The Birth of Coinage." Department of Economics Discussion Paper Series 0102–08. Columbia University.

Munnell, A. H. (ed.) *Lessons from the Income Maintenance Experiments*. Federal Reserve Bank of Boston.

Munsterberg, E. (1904) "The Problem of Poverty." *American Journal of Sociology* 10(3): 335–353.

Mupedziswa, R. (1995) "Social Welfare Services." In Hall, N., and Mupedziswa, R. (eds) *Social Policy and Administration in Zimbabwe*, 81–105. School of Social Work.

Muralidharan, K., Niehaus, P., and Sukhtankar, S. (2011) *Assessing the Scope for Cash Transfers in lieu of the TPDS in Rural and Urban Bihar: Pre-Pilot Study Summary Report.* J-PAL.

Muralidharan, K., Niehaus, P., and Sukhtankar, S. (2017) *General Equilibrium Effects of (Improving) Public Employment Programs: Experimental Evidence from India.* NBER Working Paper 23838. National Bureau of Economic Research.

Muralidharan, K., Niehaus, P., and Sukhtankar, S. (2018, October 3) "We Need a Choice-Based Approach in the Public Distribution System." *Hindustan Times* [online].https://www.hindustantimes.com/columns/we-need-a-choice-based-approach-to-the-public-distribution-system/story-RY7jEYDmXfsxOMEsZguxmJ.html

Murphy, J. (2006) "The Other Welfare State: Non-Government Agencies and the Mixed Economy of Welfare in Australia." *History Australia* 3(2): 44.1–44.15.

Murphy, J. (2008) 'The Poverty of Liberalism: The First Old Age Pensions in Australia." *Thesis Eleven* 95(1): 33–47.

Murray, C. (1984) *Losing Ground: American Social Policy 1950–1980.* Basic Books.

Murray, C. (1994, December) "What to Do About Welfare." *Commentary* [online]. https://www.commentary.org/articles/charles-murray/what-to-do-about-welfare/

Murray, C. (2006) *In Our Hands: A Plan to Replace the Welfare State.* AEI Press.

Murton, B. (1984) "Spatial and Temporal Patterns of Famine in Southern India before the Gamine Codes." In Currey, B., and Hugo, G. (eds) *Famine as a Geographical Phenomenon*, 71–90. Reidel Publishing.

Muto, G. (1982) "Forme e Contenuti Economici dell'Assistenza nel Mezzogiorno Moderno: Il Caso di Napoli." In Politi, G., Rosa, M., and Della Peruta, F. (eds) *Timore e Carità: I Poveri nell'Italia Moderna*, 255–257. Biblioteca Statale e Libreria Civica di Cremona.

Myles, J. (1998) "How to Design a 'Liberal' Welfare State: A Comparison of Canada and the United States." *Social Policy and Administration* 32(4): 341–364.

Nadvi, M. (2012) "Social Security During the Reign of Caliph 'Umar Ibn al-Khattab." *Ma'arif Research Journal* 3(1): 33–40.

Nadvi, M. (2022) "Understanding the Historical Perspective of the "Social Security System of Islam" (A Case Study of 'Umar Ibn Al-Khattab)." *Asian Journal of Sociological Research* 6(4): 20–25.

Naismith, R. (2018) "Money and Society." In Naismith, R. (ed) *Money and Coinage in the Middle Ages*, 179–202. Brill.

NASA (2021) "Brief History of Rockets." *NASA* [online]. https://www.grc.nasa.gov/www/k-12/TRC/Rockets/history_of_rockets.html#:~:text=The%20date%20reporting%20the%20first,of%20a%20solid%2Dpropellant%20rocket

Nash, G. (1976) "Poverty and Poor Relief in Pre-Revolutionary Philadelphia." *The William and Mary Quarterly* 33(1): 3–30.

Navarrini, R., and Belfanti, C.M (1982) "Il Problema della Povertà nel Ducato di Mantova: Aspetti Istituzionali e Problemi Sociali (Secoli XIV–XVI)." In Politi, G., Rosa, M., and Della Peruta, F. (eds) *Timore e Carità: I Poveri nell'Italia Moderna*, 130–131. Biblioteca Statale e Libreria Civica di Cremona.

NCSW (National Conference on Social Welfare) (1888) *Official Proceedings of the Annual Meeting of the National Conference on Social Welfare.* University of Michigan Library.

Nelson, M. (1988) "Bitter Bread: The Famine in Norrbotten 1867–1868." PhD thesis, Uppsala University.

Neuman, M. (1969) "A Suggestion Regrading the Origins of the Speenhamland Plan." *English Historical Review* 84(331): 317–322.

Neves, C. (2023) *Reciprocity, Guaranteed Income and Gift: Evidence from a Guaranteed Income Experiment*. Mimeo.

Newman, L., Boegehold, A., Herlihy, D., Kates, R., and Raaflaub, K. (1990) "Agricultural Intensification, Urbanization, and Hierarchy." In Newman, L. (ed) *Hunger in History: Food Shortage, Poverty and Deprivation*, 101–125. Blackwell.

Nicholls, G. (1854) *History of the English Poor Law in Connexion with the Legislation and Other Circumstances Affecting the Condition of the People*. Volume II. University of Michigan Library.

Nill, J., M'Connicle, R., Henderson, C., Barbour, L., Holden, E., and Codman, J. (1891) "Arguments Against Public Outdoor Relief." National Conference on Charities and Corrections: 36–49.

Niskanen, W. (1996) "Welfare and the Culture of Poverty." *Cato Journal* 16(1): 1–15.

NLCHP (National Law Center on Homelessness and Poverty) (2019) *Housing Not Handcuffs: Ending the Criminalization of Homelessness in U.S. Cities*. NLCHP.

Nobili, G. (1621) *Il Vagabondo, Ouero Sferza de Bianti e Vagabondi*. Viterbo.

Noble, C. (1997) *Welfare as We Knew It: A Political History of the American Welfare State*. Oxford University Press.

North, D. (1981) *Structure and Change in Economic History*. Norton.

North, D. (1990) *Institutions, Institutional Change and Economic Performance*. Cambridge University Press.

North, D., and Weingast, B. (1989) "Constitutions and Commitment: The Evolution of Institutions Governing Public Choice in Seventeenth-Century England." *Journal of Economic History* 49(4): 803–832.

Nowak-Garmer, R. (2023) "Social Protection in Africa." In Patel, L., Plagerson, S., and Chinyoka, I. (eds) *Handbook on Social Protection and Social Development in the Global South*, 112–129. Elgar.

Ntseane, D., and Solo, K. (2007) *Social Security and Social Protection in Botswana*. Bay Publishing.

Nullmeier, F. and Kaufmann, F. (2010) "Post-War Welfare State Development." In Castels, F. G., Leibfried, S., Lewis, J., Obinger, H., and Pierson, C. (eds) *The Oxford Handbook of the Welfare State*, 81–102. Oxford University Press.

Nunn, N. (2009) *The Importance of History for Economic Development*. NBER Working Paper 14899. National Bureau of Economic Reseach.

Nunn, N. (2014) "Historical Development." In Aghion P., and Durlauf, S. (eds) *Handbook of Economic Growth*, 347–402. Elsevier.

Nunn, N. (2020a) "The Historical Roots of Economic Development." Science 367(1441): 1–7.

Nunn, N. (2020b) "History as Evolution." In Bisin, A., and Federico, G. (eds) *Handbook of Historical Economics*, 41–91. Academic Press.

Nunn, N., and Wantchekon, L. (2011) "The Slave Trade and the Origins of Mistrust in Africa." *American Economic Review* 101(7): 3221–3252.

Nussbaum, M. (2013) *Creating Capabilities: The Human Development Approach*. Harvard University Press.

Nyamweru, C., and Chidongo, T. (2018) "Elders in Modern Kenya: 'Dying Institutions' or 'Reinventing Themselves'?." *African Studies* 77(2): 240–256.

O'Brien, G. (2020) Trajan's Imperial Alimenta: An Analysis of the Values Attached to Children in Roman Society in the Alimenta of Trajan. Leiden University.

O'Connor Newell, M. (1912, August) "Four Counties that Prefer Mothers to Orphan Asylums." *The Delineator*, 85–86.

O'Connor, A. (2001) *Poverty Knowledge: Social Science, Social Policy, and the Poor in Twentieth-Century U.S. History*. Princeton University Press.

Obaidullah, M., and Shirazi, N. (2015) *Islamic Social Finance Report 2015*. IRTI.
Obama, B. (2020) *A Promised Land*. Crown.
Ober, J. (1989) *Mass and Elite in Democratic Athens: Rhetoric, Ideology, and the Power of the People*. Princeton University Press.
Obinger, H., and Schmitt, C. (2011) "Guns and Butter? Regime Competition and the Welfare State during the Cold War." *World Politics* 63(2): 246–270.
Obinger, H., Schmitt, C. and Starke, P. (2013) "Policy Diffusion and Policy Transfer in Comparative Welfare State Research." *Social Policy and Administration* 47(1): 111–129.
OECD (2009) *Making Economic Growth More Pro-Poor: The Role of Employment and Social Protection*. OECD.
OECD (2018) *The Future of Social Protection: What Works for Non-standard Workers?* OECD.
Olasky, M. (1992) *The Tragedy of American Compassion*. Crossway Books.
Ole, P. Cunningham, A., and Arrizabalaga, J. (1997) *Health Care and Poor Relief in Counter-Reformation Europe 1500–1770*. Routledge.
Ole, P., Cunningham, A., and Grell, R. (2002) *Health Care and Poor Relief in 18th-* and 19th-Century Northern Europe. Routledge.
Olie, L., Delpy, L. and Ballet, J. (2024) "From Colonialism to International Aid: Social Protection in Former French Colonies in Sub-Saharan Africa, 1890–2020". *Journal of International Development*: 1–18. In press (DOI:10.1002/jid.3924).
Oliphant, L. (2000, August 22) "Four Years of Welfare Reform: A Progress Report." Cato Institute, *Policy Analysis* 378 [online. http://www.cato.org/pubs/pas/pa378.pdf
Onwuchekwa, C., Verdonck, K., and Marchal, B. (2021, July 14) "Systematic Review on the Impact of Conditional Cash Transfers on Child Health Service Utilisation and Child Health in Sub-Saharan Africa." *Frontiers in Public Health* 9 [online]. https://doi.org/10.3389/fpubh.2021.643621
Orenstein, M. (2010) *Privatizing Pensions: The Transnational Campaign for Social Security Reform*. Princeton University Press.
Orloff, A. (1993) *The Politics of Pensions: A Comparative Analysis of Britain, Canada, and the United States, 1880-1940*. University of Wisconsin Press.
Orloff, A., and Skocpol, T. (1984) "Why Not Equal Protection? Explaining the Politics of Public Social Spending in Britain, 1900–1911, and the United States, 1880s–1920." *American Sociological Review* 49(6): 726–750.
Orr, C. (1966) "Trade Unionism in Colonial Africa." *Journal of Modern African Studies* 4: 65–81.
Ortiz, I., Behrendt, C., Acuña-Ulate, A., and Nguyen, Q. (2018) "Universal Basic Income Proposals in Light of ILO Standards: Key Issues and Global Costing." ESS Working Paper 62. ILO.
Ortiz, J., Dick, M., and Rankin, S. (2015) *The Wrong Side of History: A Comparison of Modern and Historical Criminalization Laws*. Seattle University School of Law.
Osborne, R. (2006) "Roman Poverty in Context." In Atkins, M., and Osborne, R. (eds) *Poverty in the Roman World*, 1–20. Cambridge University Press.
Osei, P. (2001) "Has Poor Relief Declined in Jamaica? A Preliminary Investigation." *Social and Economic Studies* 50(1): 229–262.
Osmani, S. (1991) "Social Security in South Asia." In Ahmad, E., Dreze, J., Hills, J., and Sen, A. (eds) *Social Security in Developing Countries*, 305–355. Oxford University Press.
Ottaway, S. (2017, March 31) "Workload and Labour Discipline in the Eighteenth-Century Workhouse." Paper presented at the Economic History Society Annual Meeting. Royal Holloway University of London.
Ouma, M., and Adesina, J. (2019) "Solutions, Exclusion and Influence: Exploring Power Relations in the Adoption of Social Protection Policies in Kenya." *Critical Social Policy* 39(3): 376–395.

Outhwaite, R. (1981) "Dearth and Government Intervention in English Grain Markets, 1590–1700." *Economic History Review* 34(3): 389–406.
Outhwaite, R. (1991) *Dearth, Public Policy and Social Disturbance in England, 1550–1800.* Macmillian.
Owusu-Addo, E., Renzaho, A., and Smith, B. (2018) "The Impact of Cash Transfers on Social Determinants of Health and Health Inequalities in Sub-Saharan Africa: A Systematic Review." *Health Policy and Planning* 33(5): 675–696.
Oxley, G. (1974) *Poor Relief in England and Wales, 1601–1834.* David and Charles.
Özler, B. (2018, March 26) "Dear Governments: Want to Help the Poor and Transform Your Economy? Hold On, Recalculating . . . ." *Development Impact* [blog]. https://blogs.worldbank.org/en/impactevaluations/dear-governments-want-help-poor-and-transform-your-economy-hold-recalculating
Packard, T., Gentilini, U., Grosh, M., O'Keefe, P., Palacios, R., Robalino, D. and Santos, I. (2019) *Protecting All: Risk Sharing for a Diverse and Diversifying World of Work.* World Bank.
Palier, B. (2010) "Ordering Change: Understanding the "Bismarckian" Welfare Reform Trajectory." In Palier, B. (ed) *A Long Goodbye to Bismarck? The Politics of Welfare Reform in Continental Europe*, 19–44. Amsterdam University Press.
Parker, J. (2023) *Analysing the History of British Social Welfare: Compassion, Coercion and Beyond.* Policy Press.
Parkin, A. (2006) "You Do Him No Service: An Exploration of Pagan Almsgiving." In Atkins, M., and Osborne, R. (eds) *Poverty in the Roman World*, 60–82. Cambridge University Press.
Parrott, A. (1968). "Problems Arising from the Transition from Provident Funds to Pension Schemes." *International Social Security Review* 21(4): 530–557.
Pasha, A., Urueña, V., Knoll, S., Wolf, K., De Swardt, C., Featherston-Lardeux, M., and Hörner, D. (2023) *Cash Transfers and Cash Plus Programs in Low-and Middle-Income Countries: Evidence Gap Map.* Center for Evaluation and Development and German Institute for Development Evaluation. Bonn.
Patel, L. (2005) *Social Welfare and Social Development in South Africa.* Oxford University Press.
Patel, L. (2009) *The Gendered Character of Care in the Non-Profit Sector in South Africa.* UNRISD.
Patel, L. and Midgley, J. (2023) "The Social Development Approach to Social Portection and Social Welfare." In Patel, L., Plagerson, S., and Chinyoka, I. (eds) *Handbook on Social Protection and Social Development in the Global South*, 12–27. Edward Elgar.
Patel, L., Kaseke, E., and Midgley, J. (2015) "Indigenous Welfare and Community-Based Social Development: Lessons from African Innovations." *Journal of Community Practice* 20(1): 12–31.
Paterson, A. (1976) "The Poor Law in Nineteenth-Century Scotland." In Fraser, D. (ed) *New Poor Law in the Nineteenth Century*, 171–193. Springer.
Patlagean, E. (1977) *Pauvreté Economique et Pauvreté Sociale à Byzance: 4e–7e Siècles.* De Gruyter.
Patterson, J. (1994) *America's Struggle Against Poverty 1900–1994.* Harvard University Press.
Paul, J. (1887) "On Beggars' Badges, with Notes on the Licensed Mendicants of Scotland." Proceedings of the Society of Antiquaries of Scotland 21: 169–179.
Pavlov, V. (2016) *The Indian Capitalist Class: A Historical Study.* Aakar Books.
Peattie, L. (1974) "The Concept of 'Marginality' as Applied to Sqautter Settlements." In Conrelius, W., and Trueblood, F. (eds) *Lation American Urban Research.* Sage.
Pedersen, S. (1993) *Family, Dependence, and the Origins of the Welfare State: Britan and France, 1914-1945.* Cambridge University Press.

Pega, F., Pabayo, R., Benny, C., Lee, E., Lhachimi, S., and Liu, S. (2022) "Unconditional Cash Transfers for Reducing Poverty and Vulnerabilities: Effect on Use of Health Services and Health Outcomes in Low- and Middle-Income Countries." *Cochrane Database of Systematic Reviews* 3 10.1002/14651858.CD011135.pub3

Pell, A. (1890) "Out-Relief." Paper presented at the Poor Law Conference (Arms Hotel, October 14, Crewe).

Pennestri, S. (1989) "Distribuzioni di Denaro e Viveri su Monete e Medaglioni di Età Imperiale: I Protagonisti, gli Scenari." *Mélanges de l'École française de Rome—Antiquité* 101(1): 289–315.

Peppiatt D., Mitchell J., and Holzmann, P. (2001) "Cash Transfers in Emergencies: Evaluating Benefits and Assessing Risks." Humanitarian Practice Network Paper 35. ODI.

Pescarini, J., Campbell, D., Amorim, L., Falcao, I., Ferreira, A., Allik, M., Shaw, R., Malta, D., Ali, M., Smeeth, L., Barreto, M., Leyland, A., Craig, P., Aquino, E., and Katikireddi, S. (2022) "Impact of Brazil's Bolsa Familia Programme on Cardiovascular and All-Cause Mortality: A Natural Experiment Study Using the 100 Million Brazilian Cohort." *International Journal of Epidemiology* 51(6): 1847–1861.

Peterman, A. (2021, June 30) "Do Child Grants Lead to Increased Pregnancies? An Evidence View from Asia and the Pacific." DAI Global UK Ltd. https://www.calpnetwork.org/publication/share-space-do-child-grants-lead-to-increased-pregnancies-an-evidence-view-from-asia-and-the-pacific/

Peterman, A. Wang, J., Kamto Sonke, K., and Steinert, J. (2024) "Social Safety Nets, Women's Economic Achievements and Agency: A Systematic Review and Meta-Analysis." *Working Paper* 684. Center for Global Development.

Pfister, C. (1990) "Food Supply in the Swiss Canton of Bern, 1850." In Newman, L. (ed) *Hunger in History: Food Shortage, Poverty and Deprivation*, 281–304. Blackwell.

Phillips, K. (1990) *The Politics of Rich and Poor: Wealth and the American Electorate in the Raegan Aftermath.* Random House.

Pierson, C. (1991) *Beyond the Welfare State? The New Political Economy of Welfare.* Penn State University Press.

Pierson, C., and Leimgruber, M. (2000) "Intellectual Roots." In Castles F. G., Leibfried, S., Lewis,J., and Obinger, H. (eds) *The Oxford Handbook of the Welfare State*, 32–44. Oxford University Press.

Pierson, P. (1994) *Dismantling the Welfare State? Reagan, Thatcher and the Politics of Retrenchment.* Cambridge University Press.

Piff, P., Kraus, M., Cote, S., Cheng, B., and Keltner, D. (2010) "Having Less, Giving More: The Influence of Social Class on Prosocial Behavior." *Journal of Personality and Social Psychology* 99(5): 771–784.

Piketty, T. (2016, December 14) "What Unequal Societies Need Is Not a 'Basic Income' But a Fair Wage." *The Wire* [online]. https://thewire.in/uncategorised/basic-income-fair-wage-piketty

Piketty, T. (2021) *A Brief History of Equality.* Harvard University Press.

Pimpare, S. (2002) "No Relief: The Politics of Welfare Retrenchment, 1873–1898 and 1973–2002." PhD Dissertation,City University of New York.

Pimpare, S. (2004) *The New Victorians: Poverty, Politics and Propaganda in Two Gilded Ages.* The New Press.

Pinstrup-Andersen, P., and Alderman, H. (1988) "The Effectiveness of Consumer-Oriented Food Subsidies in Reaching Rationing and Income Transfer Goals." In Pinstrup-Andersen, P. (ed) *Food Subsidies in Developing Countries Costs, Benefits, and Policy Options*, 21–35. Johns Hopkins University Press.

Piven, F., and Cloward, R. (1971) *Regulating the Poor: The Functions of Public Welfare.* Pantheon.

Piven, F., and Cloward, R. (1977) *Poor People's Movements: Why They Succeed, How They Fail.* Vintage Books.

Plange, N-K. (2023) "Colonial Political Economy, Social Policy and Poverty in Fiji: 1874-1970." *Pacific Dynamics* 76(1): 354–373.

Plange, N-K., and Alam, M. (2023) "Re-thinking Colonialism and Social Policy: With the Logic of Imperialism." *Social Sciences & Humanities Open* 8(1): 1–7.

Plant, R. (1994) *Labour Standards and Structural Adjustment.* ILO.

Plastow, C. (2020) *Homicide in the Attic Orators: Rhetoric, Ideology, and Context.* Routledge.

PNA (Palestinian National Authority) (2010) *Social Protection Sector Strategy,* First Draft. Palestinian National Authority.

Polanyi, K. (1944) *The Great Transformation: The Political and Economic Origins of Our Time.* Beacon Press.

Polanyi, K., Arensberg, C., and Pearson, H. (eds) (1957) *Trade and Market in the Early Empires. Economies in History and Theory.* Free Press.

Politi, M. (1982) "Padroni di Niente: Povertà e Assistenza a Como tra Medioevo ed Età Moderna." In Politi, G., Rosa, M., and Della Peruta, F. (eds) *Timore e Carità: I Poveri nell'Italia Moderna.* Biblioteca Statale e Libreria Civica di Cremona.

Porisky, A. (2022) "The Distributional Politics of Social Transfers in Kenya." In Lavers, T. (ed) *The Politics of Distributing Social Transfers: State Capacity and Political Contestation in Sub-Saharan Africa and South Asia,* 149–176. Oxford University Press.

Porisky, A., Shariff, T., and Muthui, P. (2023) "Kenya's 'Universal' Social Pension: The Politics of Registration in Marsabit County." *World Development* 164: 1–15.

Porter, A. (2001) "Trusteeship, Anti-Slavery, and Humanitarianism" In Porter, A. (ed) *The Oxford History of the British Empire Volume III: The Nineteenth Century,* 198–221. Oxford University Press.

Porter, B. (1975) *The Lion's Share. A Short History of British Capitalism 1850–1970.* Longman.

Porter, T. (1986) *The Rise of Statistical Thinking, 1820–1900.* Princeton University Press.

Portes, A., and Ferguson, F. (1977) "Comparative Ideologies of Poverty and Equity: Latin America and the United States." In Horowitz, I. (ed) *Equity, Income and Policy: Comparative Studies in Three Worlds of Development,* 70–105. Praeger Publisher.

Portes, A., and Walton, J. (1976) *Urban Latin America: The Political Condition from Above and Below.* Universtity of Texas Press.

Post, J. (1990) "Nutritional Status and Mortality in Eighteenth-Century Europe." In Newman, L. (ed) *Hunger in History: Food Shortage, Poverty and Deprivation,* 241–280. Blackwell.

Powell, M. (2020) "The Eureka Moment? The Creation of the British Welfare State." *Social Work and Social Sciences Review* 18(1): 15–30.

Poynter, J. (1969) *Society and Pauperism: English Ideas on Poor Relief, 1795–1834.* Routledge.

Prasad, M. (1995) "Social Justice in Ancient India: In *Arthaśāstra.*" In Irani, D., and Silver, M. (eds) *Social Justice in the Ancient World,* 91–98. Greenwood Press.

Pratt, M. (1970) "A Model for Social Welfare National Development." *International Social Work* 13(1): 2–11.

Pressman, S. (2005) "Income Guarantees and the Equity-Efficiency Tradeoff." LIS Working Papers 348. LIS.

Pritchett, L. (2006) "Who Is Not Poor? Dreaming of a World Truly Free of Poverty." *World Bank Research Observer* 21(1): 1–23.

Pritchett, L. (2017, March 28) "Getting Kinky with Chickens." *Center for Global Development* [blog]. https://www.cgdev.org/blog/getting-kinky-chickens

Pritchett, L., and Kenny, C. (2013) "Promoting Millennium Development Ideals: The Risks of Defining Development Down." Working Paper 265. Center for Global Development.

Pruce, K., and Hickey, S. (2019) "The Politics of Promoting Social Cash Transfers in Zambia." In Hickey, S., Lavers, T., Niño-Zarazúa, M., and Seekings, J. (eds) *The Politics of Social Protection in Eastern and Southern Africa*, 176–201. Oxford University Press.

Pugh, W. (1974) "Social Welfare and the Edict of Nantes: Lyon and Nimes." *French Historical Studies* 8(3): 349–376.

Pullan, B. (1964) "The Famine in Venice and the New Poor Law, 1527–1529." *Bollettino dell'Istituto di Storia della Società e dello Stato Veneziano* 5–6: 173–174.

Pullan, B. (1971) *Rich and Poor in Renaissance Venice. The Social Institutions of a Catholic State, to 1620*. Harvard University Press.

Pullan, B. (1994) *Poverty and Charity: Europe, Italy, Venice, 1400–1700*. Routledge.

Pullan, B. (2005) "Catholics, Protestants, and the Poor in Early Modern Europe." *Journal of Interdisciplinary History* 35(3): 441–456.

Purdy, F. (1860) "The Statistics of the English Poor Rate before and since the Passing of the Poor Law Amendment Act." *Journal of the Statistical Society of London* 23(3): 286–329.

Puri, R. (2022) "Improving In-Kind Food-Based Safety Nets: The Case of India's Public Distribution System." In Gentilini, U. (ed) *Social Protection, Food Security and Nutrition: An Update of Concepts, Evidence and Select Practices in South Asia and Beyond*, 77–92. World Bank.

Quigley, W. (1996a) *Five Hundred Years of English Poor Laws, 1349–1834: Regulating the Working and Nonworking Poor*. New Orleans College of Law Legal Studies.

Quigley, W. (1996b) "Work or Starve: Colonial American Poor Laws." *University of San Francisco Law Review* 31: 35–83.

Radelet, S. (2015) *The Great Surge: The Ascent of the Developing World*. Simon and Schuster.

Radford, M. (2009) "The Bang Beggars of Derry City: Borough Policing in Londonderry, c.1832–70." *Irish Studies Review* 17(3): 347–359.

Rainwater, L. (1967) "Neutralizing the Disinherited: Some Psychological Aspects of Understanding the Poor." Occasional Paper 30. US Department of Health, Education, and Welfare.

Rainwater, L. (1968) "The Problem of Lower-Class Culture and Poverty-War Strategy." In Moynihan, D. (ed) *On Understanding Poverty*, 229–259. Basic Books.

Ramsey, M. (2002) "Poor Relief and Medical Assistance in 18th and 19th Century Paris". In Ole, P. Cunningham, A., and Arrizabalaga, J. (eds) *Health Care and Poor Relief in 18th- and 19th-Century Northern Europe*, 280–308. Aldershot.

Rank, M. (2011) "Rethinking American Poverty." *Contexts* 10(2): 16–21.

Ranney, C., and Kushman, J. (1987) "Cash Equivalence, Welfare Stigma, and Food Stamps." *Southern Economic Journal* 53: 1011–1027.

Rathbone, D. (2006) "Poverty and Population in Roman Egypt." In Atkins, M., and Osborne, R. (eds) *Poverty in the Roman World*, 100–114. Cambridge University Press.

Ravallion, M. (1997) "Famines and Economics." *Journal of Economic Literature* 35(3): 1205–1242.

Ravallion, M. (2009) "Economic Growth and Poverty Reduction: Do Poor Countries Need to Worry About Inequality?" In von Braun, J., Vargas Hill, R., and Pandya-Lorch, R. (eds) *The Poorest and Hungry. Assessments, Analyses, and Action*, 179–186. IFPRI.

Ravallion, M. (2013) *The Idea of Antipoverty Policy*. NBER Working Paper 19210. National Bureau of Economic Research.

Ravallion, M. (2016) *The Economics of Poverty: History, Measurement and Policy*. Oxford University Press

Ravallion, M. (2018) "Guaranteed Employment or Guaranteed Income?" Working Paper 482. Center for Global Development.

Ravallion, M. (2020) *On the Origins of the Idea of Ending Poverty*. NBER Working Paper 27808. National Bureau of Economic Research.

Ravallion, M. (2021) *Poverty in China since 1950: A Counterfactual Perspective.* NBER Working Paper 28370. National Bureau of Economic Research.

Ravallion, M., and Chen, S. (2007) "China's (Uneven) Progress Against Poverty." *Journal of Development Economics* 82(1): 1–42.

Ravallion, M., and Chen, S. (2015) *Benefit Incidence with Incentive Effects, Measurement Errors and Latent Heterogeneity: A Case Study for China.* NBER Working Paper 21111. National Bureau of Economic Research.

Rector, R. (2000) "Welfare: Broadening the Reform." In Butler, S., and Holmes K. (eds) *Issues 2000: The Candidates' Briefing Book*, 287–325. Heritage Foundation.

Rein, L. (2020, April 14) "In Unprecedented Move, Treasury Orders Trump's Name Printed on Stimulus Checks." The Washington Post [online]. https://www.washingtonpost.com/politics/coming-to-your-1200-relief-check-donald-j-trumps-name/2020/04/14/071016c2-7e82-11ea-8013-1b6da0e4a2b7_story.html

Reinarz, J., and Schwarz, L. (eds) (2013) *Medicine and the Workhouse.* University of Rochester Press.

Reinhart, C., and Rogoff, K. (2011) *This Time Is Different: Eight Centuries of Financial Folly.* Princeton University Press.

Reinhart, E. (2024) "Money as Medicine—Clinicism, Cash Transfers, and the Political-Economic Determinants of Health." *The New England Journal of Medicine* 390(14): 1333–1338.

Reinhart, U. (2013) *On the Economics of Benefits In-Kind.* Princeton University Press.

Resta, G., and Catanzariti, M. (2014) *Karl Polanyi: For a New West: Essays, 1919–1958.* Polity Press.

Reynolds, D. (1993) *China, 1898–1912: The Xinzheng Revolution and Japan.* Brill.

Rezneck, S. (1950) "Distress, Relief, and Discontent in the United States During the Depression of 1873–1878." *Journal of Political Economy* 58(6): 494–512.

Ribe, H., and Carvalho, S. (1990) "World Bank Treatment of the Social Impact of Adjustment Programs." Working Paper 521. World Bank.

Ribe, H., Robalino D., and Walker, I. (2010) *From Rights to Reality: Achieving Effective Social Protection for All in Latin America and the Caribbean.* World Bank.

Ribton-Turner, C. (1887) *A History of Vagrants and Vagrancy, and Beggars and Begging.* Chapman and Hall.

Ricardo, D. (1821) *On the Principles of Political Economy of Taxation.* Cambridge University Press (1951 edition).

Ricci, L. (1787) *Riforma degli Istituti Pii della Città di Modena.* Soliani.

Rice, E. (1970) *The Foundations of Early Modern Europe, 1460–1559.* Norton & Company.

Richardson, G. (2005) "The Prudent Village: Risk Pooling Institutions in Medieval English Agriculture." *Journal of Economic History* 65(2): 386–413.

Richterman, A., Millien, C., Bair, E., Jerome, G., Suffrin, J., Behrman, J., and Thirumurthy, H. (2023) "The Effects of Cash Transfers on Adult and Child Mortality in Low- and Middle-Income Countries." *Nature* 618: 575–582.

Richterman, A., Steer-Massaro, J., Jarolimova, J., Nguyen, L., Werdenberg, J., and Ivers, L. (2018) "Cash Interventions to Improve Clinical Outcomes for Pulmonary Tuberculosis: Systematic Review and Meta-Analysis." *Bulletin of the World Health Organization* 96(7): 471–483.

Rickman, C. (1980) *The Corn Supply of Ancient Rome.* Oxford University Press.

Ridgeway, W. (1892) *The Origin of Coin and Weight Standards.* Cambridge University Press.

Riis, J. (1890) *How the Other Half Lives: Studies Among the Tenements of New York.* Hill and Wang.

Riis, T. (1979) "Poverty in the Middle Ages." *Scandinavian Economic History Review* 27(2): 174–176.

Riis, T. (1981) “Poverty and Urban Development in Early Modern Europe (15th–18th/19th Centuries): A General View.” In Riis, T. (ed) *Aspects of Poverty in Early Modern Europe*, 1–28. Sijthoff.

Rimlinger, G. (1971) *Welfare Policy and Industrialisation in Europe, America and Russia*. John Wiley and Sons.

Riskin, C. (1987) “Feeding China: The Experience Since 1949.” Working Paper 27. WIDER.

Rivlin, A. (1971) *Systematic Thinking for Social Action*. Brookings Institution.

Robins, P. (1985) “A Comparison of the Labor Supply Findings from the Four Negative Income Tax Experiments.” *Journal of Human Resources* 20(4): 567–582.

Rodney, W. (2018) *How Europe Underdeveloped Africa*. Verso.

Rodriguez Noboa, P. (1992) “New Directions and Trends in Social Compensation Programmes in the Region.” LC/L.717(Conf.82/7). CEPAL.

Rodrik, D. (2022, April 11) “Development Economics Goes North.” *Project Syndicate* [online]. https://www.project-syndicate.org/commentary/rich-countries-with-developing-country-problems-by-dani-rodrik-2022-04?barrier=accesspaylog

Roemer, J. (2000) *Equality of Opportunity*. Harvard University Press.

Rook J., Yama C., Schickedanz A., Feuerbach A., Lee S., and Wisk L. (2023) “Changes in Self-Reported Adult Health and Household Food Security with the 2021 Expanded Child Tax Credit Monthly Payments.” *JAMA Health Forum* 4(6): e231672.

Rose, E. (1971) *The English Poor Law 1780–1930*. David & Charles.

Rose, G. (1990) “Imagining Poplar in the 1920s: Contested Concepts of Community.” *Journal of Historical Geography* 16(4): 425–437.

Rose, G. (1988) “Locality, Politics, and Culture; Poplar in the 1920s.” *Environment and Planning D: Society and Space* 6(2): 151–168.

Rose, M. (1966a) “The Allowance System under the New Poor Law.” *Economic History Review* 19(3): 607–620.

Rose, M. (1966b) *The English Poor Law, 1780–1930*. Barnes and Noble.

Roselli, D. (2009) “Theorika in Fifth-Century Athens.” *Greek, Roman, and Byzantine Studies* 49: 5–30.

Rosinsky, K., Murray, D., Nagle, K., Boyd, S., Shaw, S., Supplee, L., and Putnam, M. (2022) “A Review of Human-Centered Design in Human Services.” OPRE Report 2022-78. US Office of Planning, Research, and Evaluation.

Rosivach, V. (1991) “Some Athenian Presuppositions about The Poor.” *Greece and Rome* 38(2): 189–198.

Rosling, H., Rosling, O., and Ronnlund, A. (2018) Factfulness*: Ten Reasons We're Wrong About the World—and Why Things Are Better Than You Think*. Hodder and Stoughton.

Rossel, C., Antía, F., and Manzi, P. (2023) “The Politics of Sanctioning the Poor Through Welfare Conditionality: Revealing Causal Mechanisms in Uruguay.” Social Policy and Administration 57(5): 789–803.

Rostovtzeff, M. (1957) *The Social and Economic History of the Roman Empire*. Volume I. Peter Marshall.

Rowe, W. (1993) “State and Market in Mid-Qing Economic Thought. The Case of Chen Hongmou (1696–1771).” *Études Chinoises* 12(1): 7–40.

Rowe, W. (2017) “Urban Agency in Early Modern and Modern China.” *Urban History* 44(1): 123–129.

Rowland, R. (1976) “The ‘Very Poor’ and the Grain Dole at Rome and Oxyrhynchus.” *Zeitschrift für Papyrologie und Epigraphik* 21: 69–73.

Roy, I. (2023) “How Welfare Wins: Discursive Institutionalism, the Politics of the Poor, and the Expansion of Social Welfare in India during the Early 21st Century.” *Policy and Society* 42: 506–525.

Roy, K. (1994) *The Emergence of Monarchy in North India, Eighth–Fourth Centuries B.C. as Reflected in the Brahmanical Tradition*. Oxford University Press.

Rudra, N. (2008) *Globalization and the Race to the Bottom in Developing Countries: Who Really Gets Hurt?* Cambridge University Press.

Rudra, N. (2015) "Social Protection in the Developing World: Challenges, Continuity, and Change." *Politics and Society* 43: 463–470.

Rudra, N., and Haggard, S. (2005) "Globalization, Democracy, and Effective Welfare Spending in the Developing World." *Comparative Political Studies* 38(9): 1015–1049.

Ruggles, T. (1793) *The History of the Poor: Their Rights, Duties, and the Laws Respecting Them Volume 1*. Deighton.

Rule, J. (1978) *Insight and Social Betterment: A Preface to Applied Social Science*. Oxford University Press.

Ruparanganda, L., Ruparanganda, B., and Mupfanochiya, A. (2017) "Traditional Social Security Systems in the Face of Urbanization: Lessons from a Rural Community in Buhera District of Zimbabwe." *International Journal of Humanities and Social Science* 7(2): 214–220.

Rushton, P., and Morgan, G. (2013) *Banishment in the Early Atlantic World: Convicts, Rebels and Slaves*. Bloomsbury.

Russell-Wood, A. (1969) *Fidalgos and the Philanthropists*. Macmillan.

Ruswick, B. (2012) *Almost Worthy: The Poor, Paupers, and the Science of Charity in America, 1877–1917*. Indiana University Press.

Ryan, W. (1971) *Blaming the Victim*. Vintage.

Sabates-Wheeler, R., and Haddad, L. (2005) "Reconciling Different Concepts of Risk and Vulnerability: A Review of Donor Documents." Paper prepared for the OECD-DAC Povnet. IDS.

Sachs, J. (2003) *Institutions Don't Rule: Direct Effects of Geography on Per Capita Income*. NBER Working Paper 9490. National Bureau of Economic Research.

SADC Parliamentary Forum and RHVP (2009) *Statement: Regional Workshop on Poverty and Social Transfers*. Maputo, 25–26 August 2009.

Sagarra, E. (1977) *A Social History of Germany, 1648–1914*. Routledge.

Sahlins, M. (1972/2017) *Stone Age Economics*. Routledge.

Salas, M. (1958) *Historia de la Asistencia Social en España en la Edad Moderna*. Instituto Balmes de Sociología.

Salkind, N., and Haskins, R. (1982) "Negative Income Tax: The Impact on Children from Low-Income Families." *Journal of Family Issues* 3(2): 165–180.

Salter, F. (1926) *Some Early Tracts on Poor Relief*. Methuen and Co.

Saminathen, M. (2019) "Policy Diffusion, Domestic Politics, and Social Assistance in Lesotho, 1998–2012." In Hickey, S., Lavers, T., Niño-Zarazúa, M., and Seekings, J. (eds) *The Politics of Social Protection in Eastern and Southern Africa*, 148–175. Oxford University Press.

Samons, L. (2000) *Empire of the Owl: Athenian Imperial Finance*. Franz Steiner Verlag.

Samuelson, P. (1968, June 10) "Negative Income Tax." *Newsweek* 71: 76.

Sanbu, M. (2020, October 11) "Dawn Breaks on a New Age of Economic Thinking." *Financial Times* [online]. https://www.ft.com/content/70e3fd73-6fb8-4363-8530-dee01665d978

Santens, S. (2018, April 13) "It's Time for Technology to Serve all Humankind with Unconditional Basic Income." *Medium* [online]. https://medium.com/basic-income/its-time-for-technology-to-serve-all-humankind-with-unconditional-basic-income-e46329764d28

Santens, S. (2021) *Let There Be Money: Understanding Modern Monetary Theory and Basic Income*. Independently published book.

Saunier, P-Y. (2010) "Borderline Work: ILO Explorations onto the Housing Scene until 1940." In Van Daele, J., Rodríguez García, M., Van Goethem, G., and van der Linden, M. (eds)

*ILO Histories: Essays on the International Labour Organization and its Impact on the World during the Twentieth Century*. Peter Lang.

Scheidel, W. (2017) *The Great Leveler: Violence and the History of Inequality from the Stone Age to the Twenty-First Century*. Princeton University Press.

Schiedel, W., and Friesen, S. (2009) "The Size of the Economy and the Distribution of Income in the Roman Empire." *Journal of Roman Studies* 99: 61–91.

Schmidt, V. (2002) "Does Discourse Matter in the Politics of Welfare State Adjustment?" *Comparative Political Studies* 35(2): 168–193.

Schmitt, C. (2015) "Social Security Development and the Colonial Legacy." *World Development* 70(C): 332–342.

Schmitt, C. (2020a) "External Actors and Social Protection in the Global South: An Overview." In Schmitt, C. (ed) *From Colonialism to International Aid: External Actors and Social Protection in the Global South*, 189–220. Palgrave MacMillan.

Schmitt, C. (2020b) "The Colonial Legacy and the Rise of Social Assistance in the Global South." In Schmitt, C. (ed) *From Colonialism to International Aid: External Actors and Social Protection in the Global South*, 137–160. Palgrave MacMillan.

Schreiber, K., and Topic, J. (1985) "Staple Finance, Wealth Finance, and Storage in the Inka Political Economy." *Current Anthropology* 26(2): 187–206.

Schubert, B. (2005) "The Pilot Social Cash Transfer Scheme in the Kalomo District, Zambia." Working Paper 52. CPRC.

Schubert, B., and Huijbregts, M. (2006) "The Malawi Social Cash Transfer Pilot Scheme: Preliminary Lessons Learned." In Minujin, A., and Delamonica, E. (eds) Social Protection Initiatives for Children, Women and Families: An Analysis of Recent Experiences. The New School/UNICEF.

Schuring, E., and Loewe, M. (eds) (2021) *Handbook on Social Protection Systems*. Edward Elgar.

Schwab, B., Margolies, A., and Hoddinott, J. (2013) *Impact Evaluation of Cash and Food Transfers for the Seasonal Emergency Safety Net in Hajjah and Ibb Governorates, Yemen – Endline Report*. IFPRI.

Schwartz, J. (2000) *Fighting Poverty with Virtue: Moral Reform and America's Urban Poor, 1825–2000*. Indiana University Press.

Schwarz, L. (2007) "Custom, Wages and Workload in England during Industrialization." *Past & Present* 197(1): 143–175.

Scogin, H. (1978) "Poor Relief in Northern Sung China." *Oriens Extremus* 25(1): 30–46.

Seaby, W. (1970) "Ulster Beggars' Badges." *Ulster Journal of Archaeology* 33: 95–106.

Seal, G. (2021) *Condemned: The Transported Men, Women and Children Who Built Britain's Empire*. Yale University Press.

Seekings, J. (2007a) "'Pa's Pension': The Origins of Non-Contributory Old-Age Pensions in Late Colonial Barbados." *Journal of Imperial and Commonwealth History* 35(4): 529–547.

Seekings, J. (2007b) "Not a Single White Person Should Be Allowed to Go Under: Swartgevaar and the Origins of South Africa's Welfare State, 1924–1929." *Journal of African History* 48(3): 375–394.

Seekings, J. (2008) "Welfare Regimes and Redistribution in the South." In Shapiro, I., Swenson, P., and Donno, D. (eds) *Divide and Deal: The Politics of Distribution in Democracies*, 19–42. New York University Press.

Seekings, J. (2013) "The Beveridge Report, the Colonial Office, and Welfare Reform in British Colonies." University of Cape Town.

Seekings, J. (2014) "Are African Welfare States Different? Welfare State-Building in (Anglophone) Africa in Comparative Perspective." Paper presented at the workshop *Social Policy and Regimes of Social Welfare in Africa*. UNRIDS.

Seekings, J. (2016a) "Drought Relief and the Origins of a Conservative Welfare State in Botswana, 1965–1980." Working Paper 378. CSSR.
Seekings, J. (2016b) "A Lean Cow Cannot Climb Out of the Mud, but a Good Cattleman Does Not Leave It to Perish: The Origins of a Conservative Welfare Doctrine in Botswana under Seretse Khama, 1966–1980." Working Paper 387. CSSR.
Seekings, J. (2017) "'Affordability' and the Political Economy of Social Protection in Contemporary Africa". Working Paper 2017/43. WIDER.
Seekings, J. (2019) "Building a Conservative Welfare State in Botswana." In Hickey, S., Lavers, T., Niño-Zarazúa, M., and Seekings, J. (eds) *The Politics of Social Protection in Eastern and Southern Africa*, 42–67. Oxford University Press.
Seekings, J. (2020) "The Effects of Colonialism on Social Protection in South Africa and Botswana." In Schmitt, C. (ed) *From Colonialism to International Aid: External Actors and Social Protection in the Global South*, 109–135. Palgrave MacMillan.
Seekings, J. (2024) "Conditional Inclusion and the Enduring Appeal of Colonial Poor Laws." In Carr, H., Kirton-Darling, E., Meers, J., and Salcedo Repolês, H. F. (eds) *Research Handbook on Social Welfare Law*. In press.
Seekings, J. and Nattrass, N. (2005) *Class, Race, and Inequality in South Africa*. Yale University Press.
Segura-Ubiergo, A. (2007) *The Political Economy of the Welfare State in Latin America: Globalization, Democracy, and Development*. Cambridge University Press.
Seleka, T., Siphambe, H., Ntseane, D., Mbere, N., Kerapeletswe, C., and Sharp, C. (2007) *Social Safety Nets in Botswana: Administration, Targeting and Sustainability*. Lightbooks.
Seligman, D. (2000, December 25) "The Welfare Surprise" *Forbes*: 94.
Seltman, C. (1924) *Athens, Its History and Coinage Before the Persian Invasion*. Cambridge University Press.
Semba, R., Manley, J., Rosman, L., Rahman, N., and Bloem, M. (2022) "Relationship of Cash Transfers with Risk of Overweight and Obesity in Children and Adults: A Systematic Review." *BMC Public Health* 22(1190) [online]. doi.org/10.1186/s12889-022-13533-x
Semple, J. (1993) *Bentham's Prison: A Study of the Panopticon Penitentiary*. Oxford University Press.
Sen, A. (1981) *Poverty and Famines. An Essay on Entitlement and Deprivation*. Oxford University Press.
Sen, A. (1988) "Africa and India: What Do We Have to Learn from Each Other?" In Arrow, K. (ed) *The Balance between Industry and Agriculture in Economic Development—Volume 1: Basic Issues*, 105–137. Palgrave Macmillan.
Sen, A. (1999) *Development as Freedom*. Anchor Books.
Sen, A. (2006) *Identity and Violence: The Illusion of Destiny*. Norton & Company.
Sen, A. (2021) *Home in the World: A Memoir*. Norton & Company.
Sen, J. (1910) "Shah Jehan." *The Indian Review* 11: 838–840.
Senauer, B., and Young, N. (1986) "The Impact of Food Stamps on Food Expenditures: Rejection of the Traditional Model." *American Journal of Agricultural Economics* 68: 37–43.
Senior, N. (1831) *A Letter to Lord Howick: On a Legal Provision for the Irish Poor, Commutation of Tithes, and a Provision for the Irish Roman Catholic Clergy*. John Murray.
Sequeira S., Nunn N., and Qian N. (2020) "Immigrants and the Making of America." *Review of Economic Studies* 87(1): 382–419.
Shaeublin, E. (2014) "Zakat Practice in the Islamic Tradition and Its Recent History in the Context of Palestine." In Davey, E., and Svoboda, E. (eds) *Histories of Humanitarian Action in the Middle East and North Africa*, 19–26. Overseas Development Institute.
Shapiro, G., and Markoff, J. (1998) *Revolutionary Demands: A Content Analysis of the Cahiers de Doléances of 1789*. Stanford University Press.
Sharma, R. (1989) *Origin of the State in India*. University of Bombay.

Sharma, R. (2007) *Material Culture and Social Formations in Ancient India.* Macmillan.

Sharpe, P. (1997) "The Bowels of Compassion: A Labouring Family and the Law, c.1790–1834." In Hitchcock, T., King, P., and Sharpe, P. (eds) *Chronicling Poverty: The Voices and Strategies of the English Poor, 1640–1840*, 87–108. Macmillan.

Shaw, J. (2001) *The UN World Food Programme and the Development of Food Aid.* Palgrave.

Shaw, J. (ed) (2019) *The Loes and Wilford Poor Law Incorporation, 1765–1826: A Prison with a Milder Name.* Boydell Press.

Shilliam, R. (2018) *Race and the Undeserving Poor: From Abolition to Brexit.* Agenda Publishing

Shipler, D. (2004) *The Working Poor Invisible in America.* Knopf.

Shriwise, A. (2020) "Advancing Transnational Approaches to Social Protection in the Global South." In Schmitt, C. (ed) *From Colonialism to International Aid: External Actors and Social Protection in the Global South*, 19–42. Palgrave MacMillan.

Siddiqi, A., Rajaram, A., and Miller, S. (2018) "Do Cash Transfer Programmes Yield Better Health in the First Year of Life? A Systematic Review Linking Low-Income/Middle-Income and High-Income Contexts." *Archives of Disease in Childhood* 103: 920–926.

Simoncelli, P. (1982) "Note sul Sistema Assistenziale a Roma nel XVI Secolo." In Politi, G., Rosa, M., and Della Peruta, F. (eds) *Timore e Carità: I Poveri nell'Italia Moderna*, 200–252. Biblioteca Statale e Libreria Civica di Cremona.

Sims, G. (1902) *Living London: Its Work and Its Play, Its Humour and Its Pathos, Its Sights and Its Scenes*, Volume II. Cassell and Co.

Singer, A. (2005) "Serving Up Charity: The Ottoman Public Kitchen." *Journal of Interdisciplinary History* 35(3): 481–500.

Singer, A. (2006) "Soup and Sadaqa: Charity in Islamic Societies." *Historical Research* 79(205): 306–324.

Singer, A. (2008) *Charity in Islamic Societies.* Cambridge University Press.

Singer, A. (2013) "Giving Practices in Islamic Societies" *Social Research* 80(2): 341–358.

Singer, A. (2018) "The Politics of Philanthropy." *Journal of Muslim Philanthropy and Civil Society* 2(1): 2–20.

Singh, U. (2008) *A History of Ancient and Early Medieval India: From the Stone Age to the 12th Century.* Pearson.

Sirks, B. (1991) *Food for Rome: The Legal Structure of the Transportation and Processing of Supplies for the Imperial Distributions in Rome and Constantinople.* Studi.

Siu, J., Sterck, O., and Rodgers, C. (2023) "The Freedom to Choose: Theory and Quasi-Experimental Evidence on Cash Transfer Restrictions." *Journal of Development Economics* 161: 103027.

Skocpol, T. (1985) "Bringing the State Back In: Strategies of Analysis in Current Research." In Evans, P., Rueschemeyer, D., and Skocpol, T. (eds) *Bringing the State Back In.* Cambridge University Press.

Skocpol, T. (1992) *Protecting Soldiers and Mothers: The Political Origins of Social Policy in the* United States. Harvard University Press.

Slack, P. (1988) *Poverty and Policy in Tudor and Stuart England.* Longman.

Slack, P. (1998) *From Reformation to Improvement: Public Welfare in Early Modern England.* Oxford University Press.

Slater, R. (2023) "Universal, Categorical and Targeted Social Protection: Issues, Debates and Solutions." In Patel, L., Plagerson, S., and Chinyoka, I. (eds) *Handbook on Social Protection and Social Development in the Global South*, 188–204. Elgar.

Smil, V. (1999) "China's Great Famine: 40 Years Later." *British Medical Journal* 319(7225): 1619–1621.

Smith, B. (1862) "Report on the Famine of 1860–61." Secretary of State for India.

Smith, P. (1993) "State Power and Economic Activism during the New Policies, 1068–1085: The Tea and Horse Trade and the 'Green Sprouts' Loan Policy." In Hymes, R., and Schirokauer, C. (eds) *Ordering the World: Approaches to State and Society in Sung Dynasty China*, 76–127. University of California Press.

Smith, R. (1986) "Transfer Incomes, Risk and Security: The Roles of the Family and the Collectivity in Recent Theories of Fertility Change." In Coleman, D., and Schofield, R. (eds) *The State of Population Theory: Forward from Malthus*, 188–211. Blackwell.

Smith, R. (1996) "Charity, Self-Interest and Welfare: Reflections from Demographic and Family History." In Daunton, M. (ed) *Charity, Self-Interest, and Welfare in the English Past*, 23–28. UCL Press.

Smith, R. (1998) "Ageing and Well-Being in Early Modern England: Pension Trends and Gender Preferences under the English Old Poor Law c.1650–1800." In Johnson, P., and Thane, P. (eds) *Old Age from Antiquity to PostModernity*, 64–95. Routledge.

Smith, R. (2011) "Social Security as a Development Institution? The Relative Efficacy of Poor relief Provisions Under the English Old Poor Law." In Bayly, C., Rao, V., Szreter, S., and Woolcock, M. (eds) *History, Historians and Development Policy: A Necessary Dialogue*, 75–102. Manchester University Press.

Smith, R. (2015) "Dearth and Local Political Responses: 1280–1325 and 1580–1596/7 Compared." In Kowaleski, M., Langdon, J., and Schofield, P. (eds) *Peasants and Lords in the Medieval English Economy: Essays in Honour of Bruce M. S. Campbell*, 387–391. Brepols.

Smith, R. (2017) "Contrasting Susceptibilities to Famine in Early Fourteenth- and Late Sixteenth-Century England: The Significance of Late Medieval Rural Social Structural and Village Governmental Changes." In Braddick, M., and Withington, P. (eds) *Popular Culture and Political Agency in Early Modern England and Ireland*, 35–54. Boydell Press.

Smith, R., and Satchell, M. (2018) "Malthus, Poverty and Population Change in Suffolk, 1780–1834." Proceedings of the Suffolk Institute of Archeology 44(2): 256–269.

Snell, K. (1985) *Annals of the Labouring Poor: Social Change and Agrarian England.* Cambridge University Press.

Snell, K. (1991) "Pauper Settlement and the Right to Poor Relief in England and Wales." *Continuity and Change* 6(3): 375–415.

Sojo, A. (1990) "Nature and Selectivity of Social Policy." *CEPAL Review* 41:175–190.

Sokoll, T. (1993) *Household and Family among the Poor. The Case of Two Essex Communities in the Late Eighteenth and Early Nineteenth Centuries.* Universitatsverlag Dr. N. Brockmeyer.

Solar, P. (1995) "Poor Relief and English Economic Development Before the Industrial Revolution." *Economic History Review* 48(1): 1–22.

Solar, P., and Smith, R. (2003) "An Old Poor Law for the New Europe? Reconciling Local Solidarity with Labour Mobility in Early Modern England." In David, P., and Thomas, M. (eds) *The Economic Future in Historical Perspective*, 472–473. Oxford University Press.

Solow, R. (1986) "An Economist's View of the Income Maintenance Experiments." In Munnell, A. H. (ed.) *Lessons from the Income Maintenance Experiments*, 218–222. Federal Reserve Bank of Boston.

Somers, M. (2020, September 14) "Even the Republican 'Skinny' Relief Bill Failed. How is Such Unnecessary Suffering Justified?" The Guardian. [online]. https://www.theguardian.com/commentisfree/2020/sep/14/republican-skinny-coronavirus-relief-mitch-mcconnell

Somers, M. (2022a) "Dedemocratizing Citizenship: How Neoliberalism Used Market Justice to Move from Welfare Queening to Authoritarianism in 25 Short Years." *Citizenship Studies* 26(4–5): 661–674.

Somers, M. (2022b) "Legal Predistribution, Market Justice, and Dedemocratization: Polanyi and Piketty on Law and Political Economy." *Journal of Law and Political Economy* 3(2): 225–279.

Soraci, C. (2006) "Dalle 'Frumentationes' alle Distribuzioni di Pane. Riflessioni su una Riforma di Aureliano." *Quaderni Catanesi di Studi Antichi e Medievali* IV–V: 345–437.

Southworth, H. (1945) "The Economics of Public Measures to Subsidize Food Consumption." *Journal of Farm Economics* 27(1): 28–36.

Spencer, H. (1864) *The Principles of Biology*, Volume 1. Williams and Norgate.

Spencer, T. (1843) *Reasons for a Poor Law Considered*. John Green.

Spender, J. (1892) *The State and Pensions in Old Age*. Swan Sonnenschein and Co.

Spicker. P. (ed) (2020) *The Origins of Modern Welfare*. Peter Lang.

Splane, R. (1965) *Social Welfare in Ontario 1791–1893: A Study of Public Welfare Administration*. University of Toronto Press.

Spufford, P. (1988) *Money and Its Use in Medieval Europe*. Cambridge University Press.

Stabel, P. (1995) "Demography and Hirarchy: The Small Towns and the Urban Network in Sixteenth-Century Flanders" In Clark, P. (ed) *Small Towns in Early Modern Europe*, 206–228. Cambridge University Press.

Standing, G. (2011) *The Precariat. The New Dangerous Class*. Bloomsbury.

Standing, G. (2012) "Why a Basic Income Is Necessary for a Right to Work." *Basic Income Studies* 7(2): 19–40.

Stapleton, K. (2000) *Civilizing Chengdu: Chinese Urban Reform, 1895–1937*. Harvard University Press.

Stedman Jones, G. (2004) *An End to Poverty? A Historical Debate*. Columbia University Press.

Steensland, B. (2006) "Cultural Categories and the American Welfare State: The Case of Guaranteed Income Policy." *American Journal of Sociology* 111(5): 1273–1326.

Steensland, B. (2008a) *The Failed Welfare Revolution: America's Struggle over Guaranteed Income Policy*. Princeton University Press.

Steensland, B. (2008b) "Why Do Policy Frames Change? Actor-Idea Coevolution in Debates over Welfare Reform." *Social Forces* 86(3): 1027–1054.

Stevenson, J. (1979) *Popular Disturbance in England, 1700–1870*. Routledge.

Stewart, C. (2019) "Fractional Arithmetic in the Tabula Alimentaria of Veleia." *Journal of Roman Studies* 109: 89–102.

Stewart, F. (1995) *Adjustment and Poverty. Options and Choices*. Routledge.

Stigler, G. (1946) "The Economics of Minimum Wage Legislation." *The American Economic Review* 36(3): 358–365.

Stirk, C. (2015) "An Act of Faith: Humanitarian Financing and Zakat". Development Initiatives. Bristol.

Stokes, P. (2001) "Bentham, Dickens, and the Uses of the Workhouse." *Studies in English Literature 1500–1900* 41(4): 711–727.

Stoner, M., Kilburn, K., Godfrey-Faussett, P., Ghys, P., and Pettifor, A. (2021, November 29) "Cash Transfers for HIV Prevention: A Systematic Review." *PLoS Medicine* 18(11). https://doi.org/10.1371/journal.pmed.1003866

Stubbs, P. 2003. "International Non-State Actors and Social Development Policy." *Global Social Policy* 3(3): 319–348.

Subbarao, K., del Ninno, C., Andrews, C., and Rodríguez-Alas, C. (2013) *Public Works as a Safety Net: Design, Evidence, and Implementation*. World Bank.

Sugita, Y. (2014) "The Beveridge Report and Japan." *Social Work in Public Health* 29(2): 148–161.

Sumner, W. (1880) "Socialism." In Bannister, R. (ed) *On Liberty, Society, and Politics: The Essential Essays of William Graham Sumner*. Liberty Fund.

Sumner, W. (1914) "The Challenge of Facts." In Keller, A. (ed) *On the Challenge of Facts and Other Essays*. Yale University Press.

Sun-Hong, Y. (1998) *Welfare, Modernity, and the Weimar State, 1919–1933*. Princeton University Press.

Suplicy, E. (2002) *Renda de Cidadania: a Saída é Pela Porta*. Cortez Editora.

Surender, R. (2013) "The Role of Historical Contexts in Shaping Social Policy in the Global South." In Surender, R., and Walker, E. (eds.) *Social Policy in a Developing World*, 14–36. Edward Elgar.

Suzman, J. (2020a, August 28) "The 300,000-Year Case for the 15-Hour Week." Financial Times [online]. https://www.ft.com/content/8dd71dc3-4566-48e0-a1d9-3e8bd2b3f60f

Suzman, J. (2020b) *Work: A History of How We Spend Our Time*. Bloomsbury.

Sweezy, P., Dobb, M., Hill, C., Lefebvre, G., Procacci, G., Takahashi, K., Merrington, J., and Hobsbawn, E. (1978) *The Transition from Feudalism to Capitalism*. Verso.

Szreter, S. (2007) "The Right of Registration: Development, Identity Registration, and Social Security: A Historical Perspective." *World Development* 35(1): 67–86.

Szreter, S. (2015) "What Can History Tell Us about Current Health Inequalities?." *Behaviour and Health Research Unit Annual Lecture* (Downing College, June 4). Cambridge University Press.

Szreter, S. (2020) "The Capacity to Surprise: On the Importance of History for Public Health Policy." *American Journal of Public Health* 110(3): 337–338.

Szreter, S. (2021) "The Epidemiologic Transition Turned Upside Down: Britain's Mortality History as an Imaginative Resource for Africa." In Vaughan, M., Adjaye-Gbewonyo, K., and Mika, M. (eds) *Epidemiological Change and Chronic Disease in Sub-Saharan Africa: Social and Historical Perspectives*. UCL Press

Szreter, S., and Breckenridge, K. (2012) "Editors' Introduction: Recognition and Registration: The Infrastructure of Personhood in World History." In Breckenridge, K., and Szreter, S. (eds) *Registration and Recognition: Documenting the Person in History*, 1–36. Oxford University Press.

Tang, K. (1997) "Noncontributory Pensions in Hong Kong: An Alternative to Social Security?" In Midgley, J., and Sherraden, M. (eds) *Alternatives to Social Security: An International Inquiry*, 61–74. Greenwood Press.

Tang, K. (2011) "Colonial Policy and Social Welfare: The Hong-Kong Experience." In Midgley, J., and Piachaud, D. (eds) *Colonialism and Welfare. Social Policy and the British Imperial Legacy*, 100–118. Edward Elgar.

Tawney, R. (1926) *Religion and the Rise of Capitalism. A Historical Study*. John Murray.

Taylor, J. (1972) "The Unreformed Workhouse, 1776–1834." In Martin, E. (ed) *Comparative Development in Social Welfare*, 57–84. Allen and Unwin.

Taylor, J. (1991) "A Different Kind of Speenhamland: Nonresident Relief in the Industrial Revolution." *Journal of British Studies* 30(2): 183–208.

Taylor-Gooby, P. (2002) "The Silver Age of the Welfare State: Perspectives on Resilience." *Journal of Social Policy* 31(4): 597–622.

Tcherneva P. (2012) "The Job Guarantee: Delivering the Benefits That Basic Income Only Promises—A Response to Guy Standing." *Basic Income Studies* 7(2): 66–87.

Teles, S. (1996) *Whose Welfare? AFDC and the Elite Politics*. University Press of Kansas.

Tengström, E. (1974) *Bread for the People. Studies of the Corn Supply of Rome During the Late Empire*. Svenska Institutet i Rom.

Tennant, M. (2007) *The Fabric of Welfare: Voluntary Organisations, Government and Welfare in New Zealand, 1840-2005*. Bridget Williams Books.

Testart, A. (1982) "The Significance of Food Storage Among Hunter-Gatherers: Residence Patterns, Population Densities, and Social Inequalities." *Current Anthropology* 23(5): 523–537.

Thapar, R. (1991) *From Lineage to State: Social Formations of the Mid-First Millennium* BC *in the Ganga Valley*. Oxford University Press.

Thomson, B. (1796) *Essays, Political, Economical, and Philosophical*. Cadell and Davies.

Thota, A., de Groot, R., and Mogo, E. (2023) *What Works to Improve Outcomes for Children? A Rapid Evidence Assessment of Cash Plus Programmes in Low- and Middle-Income Countries, Informed by Social and Behaviour Change (SBC) Strategies*. UNICEF Innocenti.

Tierney, B. (1959a) "The Decretists and the 'Deserving Poor.'" *Comparative Studies in Society and History* 1(4): 360–373.

Tierney, B. (1959b) *Medieval Poor Law: A Sketch of Canonical Theory and Its Application in England*. University of California Press.

Tilly, C. (1990) *Coercion, Capital, and European States, AD 990-1992*. Blackwell.

Timmer, P. (1969) "The Turnip, the New Husbandry, and the English Agricultural Revolution." *Quarterly Journal of Economics* 83(3): 375–395.

Timmer, P. (1986) "Private Decisions and Public Policy: The Price Dilemma in Food Systems of Developing Countries." International Development Paper 7. Michigan State University Press.

Titmuss, R. (1950) "Problems of Social Policy." HMSO.

Tobin, J. (1976) "Hansen and Public Policy." *Quarterly Journal of Economics* 90(1): 32–27.

Todd, M. (1987) *Christian Humanism and the Puritan Social Order*. Cambridge University Press.

Tomkins, A. (2021) "Poverty and the Workhouse." In Hitchcock, D., and McClure, J. (eds) *The Routledge History of Poverty, c.1450–1800*, 234–249. Routledge.

Torry, M. (2021) *Basic Income: A History Hardcover*. Elgar.

Townsend, J. (1786) *A Dissertation on the Poor Laws*. University of California Press (1971 edition).

Townsend, P. (1979) *Poverty in the United Kingdom*. Penguin.

Townsend, P. (2009) "Social Security and Human Rights." In Townsend, P. (ed.) *Building Decent Societies: Rethinking the Role of Social Security in State Building*, 29–59. Palgrave. London.

Trattner, W. (1974) *From Poor Law to Welfare Reform: A History of Social Welfare in America*, 6th edn. The Free Press.

Trisi, D. (2023) *Government's Pandemic Response Turned a Would-Be Poverty Surge Into a Record Poverty Decline*. Center on Budget and Policy Priorities.

Turchin, P. (2023) *End Times: Elites, Counter-Elites, and the Path of Political Disintegration*. Penguin Random House.

Twitchett, D. (1963) *Financial Administration under the T'ang Dynasty*. Cambridge University Press.

Ullman, H. (1981) "German Industry and Bismarck's Social Security System." In Mommsen, W. (ed) *The Emergence of the Welfare State in Britain and Germany, 1850–1950*, 133–149. Croom Helm.

Ulriksen M., and Katusiimeh M. (2014) "The History of Resource Mobilization and Social Spending in Uganda." Working Paper 2014–2016. UNRISD.

Ulriksen, M. (2019) "Pushing for Policy Innovation: The Framing of Social Protection Policies in Tanzania." In Hickey, S., Lavers, T., Niño-Zarazúa, M., and Seekings, J. (eds) *The Politics of Social Protection in Eastern and Southern Africa*, 122–147. Oxford University Press.

UN (2010) "Rights and Extreme Poverty." A/65/259. United Nations.

UN (2021) "Global Fund for Social Protection: International Solidarity in the Service of Poverty Eradication – Report of the Special Rapporteur on Extreme Poverty and Human Rights, Olivier De Schutter." A/HRC/47/36. United Nations.

UNCTAD (1993) "Recent Developments in Social Funds and Safety Nets." Background note by the UNCTAD Secretariat, GE.93-54356. United Nations.

UNDP (2019) "The State of Social Assistance in Africa Report." United Nations.

UNICEF (2008) "Social Protection in Eastern and Southern Africa: A Framework and Strategy for UNICEF." United Nations.
UNICEF (2012) "UNICEF Social Protection Strategic Framework: Integrated Social Protection Systems – Enhancing Equity for Children." United Nations.
UNICEF (2019) "UNICEF's Global Social Protection Programme Framework." United Nations.
USDA (1981) *Food Problems and Prospects in Sub-Saharan Africa: The Decade of the 1980s.* Economic Research Service.
Valentine, C. (1969) *Culture and Poverty: Critique and Counter Proposals.* University of Chicago Press.
Van Bavel, B., and Rijpma, A. (2016) "How Important Were Formalized Charity and Social Spending Before the Rise of the Welfare State? A Long-Run Analysis of Selected Western European Cases, 1400–1850." *Economic History Review* 69(1): 159–187.
Van Berchem, D. (1939) *Les Distributions de Blé et d'Argent à la Plèbe romaine sous l'Empire.* Georg et Cie.
Van der Hoeven, R. (1991) "Adjustment with a Human Face: Still Overtaken by Events?" *World Development* 19(12): 1835–1845.
Van Kersbergen, K., and Manow, P. (2009) "Religion and the Western Welfare State." In van Kersbergen, K., and Manow, P. (eds) *Religion, Class Coalitions, and Welfare States*, 1–38. Cambridge University Press.
Van Leeuwen, M. (1993) "Surviving with a Little Help: The Importance of Charity to the Poor of Amsterdam 1800–50, in a Comparative Perspective." *Social History* 18(3): 319–338.
Van Leeuwen, M. (1994) "Logic of Charity: Poor Relief in Preindustrial Europe." *Journal of Interdisciplinary History* 24(4): 589–613.
Van Leeuwen, M. (2000) *The Logic of Charity: Amsterdam, 1880–50.* MacMillan.
Van Leeuwen, M. (2012) "Guilds and Middle-Class Welfare, 1550–1800: Provisions for Burial, Sickness, Old Age, and Widowhood." *Economic History Review* 65(1): 61–90.
Van Leeuwen, M. (2016) *Mutual Insurance 1550–2015: From Guild Welfare and Friendly Societies to Contemporary Micro-Insurers.* Palgrave.
Van Parijs, P., and Vanderborght, Y. (2019) *Basic Income: A Radical Proposal for a Free Society and a Sane Economy.* Harvard University Press.
Van Ufford, P., Harland, C., Michelo, S., Tembo, G., Toole, K., and Wood, D. (2016) "The Role of Impact Evaluation in the Evolution of Zambia's Cash Transfer Program." In Davis, B., Handa, S., Hyper, N., Winder Rossi, N., Winters, P., and Yablonski (eds) *From Evidence to Action: The Story of Cash Transfers and Impact Evaluation in Sub-Saharan Africa*, 197–225. Oxford University Press.
Veyne, P. (1990) *Bread and Circuses: Historical Sociology and Political Pluralism.* Viking Penguin.
Vidican Auktor, G. and Loewe, M. (2021) "Subsidy Reforms in the Middle East and North Africa: Strategic Options and Their Consequences for the Social Contract". German Development Institute, Discussion Paper 12/2021. Bonn
Virgolino, A., Costa, J., Santos, O., Pereira, M.E., Antunes, R., Ambrosio, S., Heitor, M., and Carneiro, A. (2022) "Lost in Transition: A Systematic Review of the Association between Unemployment and Mental Health." *Journal of Mental Health* 31(3): 432–444.
Virlouvet, C. (1985) *Famines et Emeutes à Rome des Origines de la République à la Mort de Néron.* École française de Rome.
Virlouvet, C. (2014) "L'Approvvigionamento di Roma Imperiale: Una Sfida Quotidiana." In Lo Cascio, E. (ed) *Roma Imperiale: Una Metropoli Antica*, 3rd edn. Carocci.
Vives, J. L. (2020/1526) *On the Relief of the Poor.* In Spicker, P. (ed) *The Origins of Modern Welfare*: Volume 1, 35–43. Peter Lang.

Vivien, J. (1994) "Social Safety Nets and Adjustment in Developing Countries." Occasional Paper 1. UNRISD.

Von Glahn, R. (1996) *Fountain of Fortune. Money and Monetary Policy in China, 1000–1700.* University of California Press.

Von Glahn, R. (2012) "Household Registration, Property Rights, and Social Obligations in Imperial China: Principles and Practices." In Breckenridge, K., and Szreter, S. (eds) *Recognition and Registration: Documenting the Person in History*, 39–66. Oxford University Press.

Von Glahn, R. (2022) "State and Economy: Production, Extraction, and Distribution." In Ma, D., and von Glahn, R. (eds) *The Cambridge Economic History of China. Volume 1: To 1800*, 92–130. Cambridge University Press.

Von Voght, C. (1817) *Account of the Management of the Poor in Hamburgh, Between the Years 1788 and 1794: In a Letter to Some Friends of the Poor in Great Britain.* Davidson.

Vorspan, A., and Saperstein, D. (1998) *Jewish Dimensions of Social Justice: Tough Moral Choices of Our Time.* UAHC Press.

Wagner, M., Liptak, K., and Bohn, K (2020, April 20) "Here's What the Stimulus Checks with Trump's Name May Look Like." CNN [online]. https://www.cnn.com/2020/04/20/politics/trump-stimulus-check-prototype-trnd/index.html

Walker, R. and Yang, L. (2024) "The Politics of Poverty Alleviation in China." In Biswas, S. D., Sambo, C. G., and Pellissery, S. (eds) *Politics of Welfare in the Global South*, In Press. Oxford University Press.

Walker, R., Li, M., and Yang, L. (2023) "Social Assistance: A Defence Against Poverty." *Routledge Encyclopaedia of Chinese Studies.* In Press.

Wallace, E. (1950) "The Origins of the Social Welfare State in Canada, 1867-1900". *Canadian Journal of Economics and Political Science* 16(3): 383–393.

Wallace, J. (2014) *Cities and Stability: Urbanization, Redistribution, and Regime Survival in China.* Oxford University Press.

Wallich, H. (1968, August) "The Negative Income Tax." *Vogue*: 82.

Walter, J. (1989) "The Social Economy of Dearth in Early Modern England." In Walter, J., and Schofield, R. (eds) *Famine, Disease and the Social Order in Early Modern Society*, 75–128. Cambridge University Press.

Waltzing, J.P. (1896) *Étude Historique sur les Corporations Professionnelles Chez Les Romains Depuis Les Origines Jusqu'à la Chute de l'Empire d'Occident*, Tome II. Charles Peters.

Wandel, L. P. (1990) *Always Among Us: Images of the Poor in Zwingli's Zurich.* Cambridge University Press.

Warde, B. (2017) *Inequality in U.S. Social Policy: An Historical Analysis.* Routledge.

Waterman, A. (1991) *Revolution, Economics and Religion: Christian Political Economy, 1798–1833.* Cambridge University Press.

Watson, F. (1922) *The Charity Organization Movement in the United States: A Study in American Philanthropy.* MacMillan (1971 reprint Arno Press).

Weatherford, J. (1997) *The History of Money.* Three Rivers Press.

Weaver, R. K. (2000) "Ending Welfare as We Know It: Policy Making for Low-Income Families in the United States." Brookings Institution.

Webb, S., and Webb, B. (1913) *English Poor Law History.* Part I and II. Frank Cass.

Webb, S., and Webb, B. (1927) *English Local Government: English Poor Law History—The Old Poor Law.* Longmans.

Webb, S., and Webb, B. (1929) *English Local Government: English Poor Law History–The Last Hundred Years.* Longmans.

Webber, C., and Wildawsky, A. (1986) *History of Taxation and Expenditure in the Western World.* Simon and Schuster.

Weber, M. (1904) *The Protestant Ethic and the Spirit of Capitalism.* Routledge (1930 edition).

Weible, K., and Leisering, L. (2012) "South Africa's System of Social Cash Transfers: Assessing its Social Quality." In Burchardt, H. Tittor, A., and Weinmann, N. (eds) *Sozialpolitik in globaler Perspektive: Asien, Afrika und Lateinamerika*, 247–269. Campus Verlag.

Weir, M., and Skocpol, T. (1985) "State Structures and the Possibilities for 'Keynesian' Responses to the Great Depression in Sweden, Britain and the United States." In Evans, P., Rueschemeyer, D., and Skocpol, T. (eds) *Bringing the State Back In*, 107–164. Cambridge University Press.

Weisman, J. (2021, September 6) "From Cradle to Grave, Democrats Move to Expand Social Safety Net." New York Times [online]. https://www.nytimes.com/2021/09/06/us/politics/democrats-biden-social-safety-net.html?searchResultPosition=1

Weissman, D., Hatzenbuehler, M., Cikara, M., Barch, D., and McLaughlin, K. (2023) "State-Level Macro-Economic Factors Moderate the Association of Low Income with Brain Structure and Mental Health in U.S. Children." *Nature Communications* 14(2085): 1–13.

Wells, R. (1988) *Wretched Faces: Famine in Wartime England, 1793–1801*. St Martin Press.

WFP (2004) "WFP and Food-Based Safety Nets: Concepts, Experiences and Future Programming Opportunities." EB.3/2004/4–A. WFP.

WFP (2009) "United Nations World Food Programme in China 1979–2009: Celebrating 30 Years of Cooperation." WFP.

WFP (2012) "Update of WFP's Safety Net Policy." EB.A/2012/5–A. WFP.

WFP and ADB (1986) "Food Aid for Development in Sub-Saharan Africa." Report from a seminar by the World Food Programme and African Development Bank (September 8–11). WFP.

Wheeler, M. (2023) *The Year That Shaped the Victorian Age: Lives, Loves and Letters of 1845*. Cambridge University Press.

Whitfield, L., and Fraser, A. (2010) "Negotiating Aid: The Structural Conditions Shaping the Negotiating Strategies of African Governments." *International Negotiation* 15(3): 341–366.

Widerquist, K. (2005) "A Failure to Communicate: What (If Anything) Can We Learn from the Negative Income Tax Experiments?" *Journal of Socio-Economics* 34(1): 49–81.

Widlok, T. (2017) *Anthropology and the Economy of Sharing*. Routledge.

Will, P. E. (1990) *Bureaucracy and Famine in Eighteenth-Century China*. Stanford University Press.

Will, P. E., and Wong, R. B. (1991) *Nourish the People: The State Civilian Granary System in China, 1650–1850*. Michigan Monographs in Chinese Studies. University of Michigan Press.

Williams, E. (1944) *Capitalism and Slavery*. University of North Carolina Press.

Williams, K. (1981) *From Pauperism to Poverty*. Routledge.

Williams, S. (2011) *Poverty, Gender and Life-Cycle under the English Poor Law, 1760–1834*. Woodbridge.

Willis, J. (2016) "The Elberfeld System: Poor Relief and the Fluidity of German Identity in Mid-Nineteenth Century Germany." PhD Dissertation, Boise State University.

Wollburg, C., Steinert, J., Reeves, A., and Nye, E. (2023) "Do Cash Transfers Alleviate Common Mental Disorders in Low- and Middle-Income Countries? A Systematic Review and Meta-Analysis." *PLoS One* 18(2): e0281283.

Wong, C., and Yuan, R. (2020) "Managing Across Levels of Government: The Challenge of Pension Reform in China." In Kim, J., and Dougherty, S. (eds) *Ageing and Fiscal Challenges across Levels of Government, OECD Fiscal Federalism Studies*, 77–100. OECD Publishing.

Wong, R. B. (1997) *China Transformed: Historical Change and the Limits of European Experience*. Cornell University Press.

Woodroofe, K. (1977) "The Royal Commission on the Poor Laws, 1905-09." *International Review of Social History* 22(2): 137–164.

Woolcock, M., Szreter, S., and Rao, V. (2012) "How and Why History Matters for Development Policy." In Bayly, C., Rao, V., Szreter, S., and Woolcock, M. (eds) *History, Historians and Development Policy: A Necessary Dialogue*, 3–38. Manchester University Press.

Woolf, G. (1990) "Food, Poverty and Patronage: The Significance of the Epigraphy of the Roman Alimentary Schemes in Early Imperial Italy." *Papers of the British School at Rome* 58: 197–228.

Woolf, S. (1986) *The Poor in Western Europe in the Eighteenth and Nineteenth Centuries.* Routledge.

Wordie, J. (1983) "The Chronology of English Enclosure, 1500–1914." *Economic History Review* 36(4): 483–505.

World Bank (1994) *Adjustment in Africa: Reforms, Results and the Road Ahead.* World Bank.

World Bank (2001) "Social Protection Sector Strategy Paper: From Safety Net to Springboard." World Bank.

World Bank (2006) "Social Safety Nets in Bangladesh: An Assessment." Bangladesh Development Series Paper 9. World Bank.

World Bank (2007a) "Malawi Social Protection Status Report." Africa Region Report No.40027-MW. World Bank.

World Bank (2007b) "Social Protection in Pakistan: Managing Household Risks and Vulnerability." South Asia Region Report 35472–PK. World Bank.

World Bank (2009) From Poor Areas to Poor People: China's Evolving Poverty Reduction Agenda – An Assessment of Poverty and Inequality. World Bank.

World Bank (2012) *Resilience, Equity and Opportunity: The World Bank's Social Protection and Labor Strategy 2012–2022.* World Bank.

World Bank and DRC (Development Research Center of the State Council) (2022) *Four Decades if Poverty Reduction in China: Drivers, Insights for the World, and the Way Forward.* World Bank.

World Bank and DRC (Development Research Center of the State Council) (2013) *China 2030: Building a Modern, Harmonious, and Creative Society.* World Bank.

Wray, L. (2012) "Introduction to an Alternative History of Money." *Working Paper* 717. Levy Institute.

Wrigley, E. (1999) "Corn and Crisis: Malthus on the High Price of Provisions." *Population and Development Review* 25(1): 121–128.

Wrigley, E. and Smith, R. (2020) "Malthus and the Poor Law." *Historical Journal* 63(1): 33–62.

Yang, A. (2018) *The War on Normal People: The Truth About America's Disappearing Jobs and Why Universal Basic Income Is Our Future.* Hachette Books.

Yang, L. (1957) "Economic Justification for Spending—An Uncommon Idea in Traditional China." *Harvard Journal of Asiatic Studies* 20(1/2): 36–52.

Yavetz, Z. (1969) *Plebs and Princeps.* Oxford University Press.

Young, A. (1801) *An Inquiry into the Propriety of Applying Wastes to the Better Maintenance and Support of the Poor.* Rackham Hill.

Zelizer, V. (1997) *The Social Meaning of Money: Pin Money, Paychecks, Poor Relief, and other Currencies.* Princeton University Press.

Zemon Davis, N. (1968) "Poor Relief, Humanism and Heresy: The Case of Lyon." In Bowsky, W. (ed) *Studies in Medieval and Renaissance History – Volume V*, 217–275. University of Nebraska Press.

Zerbe, R., and Anderson, C. (2001) "Culture and Fairness in the Development of Institutions in the California Gold Fields." *Journal of Economic History* 61(1): 114–143.

Zhang, H., Yang, L., Walker, R., and Wang, Y. (2022) "How to Influence the Professional Discretion of Street-Level Bureaucrats: Transformational Leadership, Organizational Learning, and Professionalization Strategies in the Delivery of Social Assistance." *Public Management Review* 24(2): 208–232.

Zhao, X. and Drechsler, W. (2018) "Wang Anshi's Economic Reforms: Proto-Keynesian Economic Policy in Song Dynasty China." *Cambridge Journal of Economics* 42(5): 1239–1254.
Ziliak, S. (1997) "Kicking the Malthusian Vice: Lessons from the Abolition of 'Welfare' in the Late Nineteenth Century." *Quarterly Review of Economics and Finance* 37(2): 449–468.
Ziliak, S. (2004) "Self-Reliance Before the Welfare State: Evidence from the Charity Organization Movement in the United States." *Journal of Economic History* 64(2): 433–461.
Zimmerman, A., Garman, E., Avendano-Pabon, M., Arayal, R., Evans-Lacko, S., McDaid,D., Park, A., Hessel, P., Diaz, Y., Matijasevich, A., Ziebold, C., Bauer, A., Paula, C., and Lund, C. (2021) "The Impact of Cash Transfers on Mental Health in Children and Young People in Low-Income and Middle-Income Countries: A Systematic Review and Meta-Analysis." *BMJ Global Health* 6: e004661.
Zucco, C. (2013) "When Payouts Pay Off: Conditional Cash Transfers and Voting Behavior in Brazil 2002-10." *American Journal of Political Science* 54(13): 810–822.
Zuiderhoek, A. (2009) *The Politics of Munificence in the Roman Empire:Citizens, Elites and Benefactors in Asia Minor.* Cambridge University Press.

# Index

*For the benefit of digital users, indexed terms that span two pages (e.g., 52–53) may, on occasion, appear on only one of those pages.*